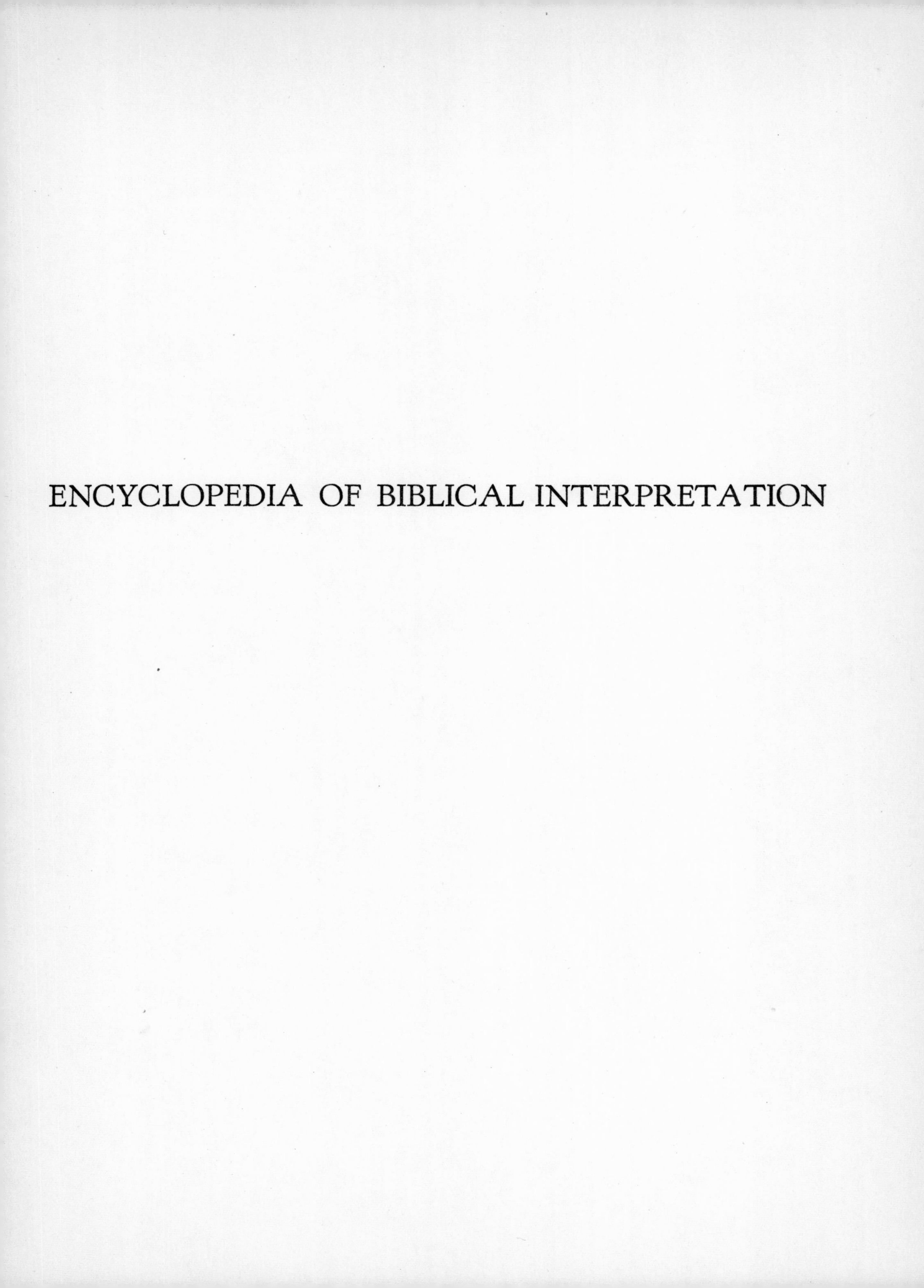

ENCYCLOPEDIA OF BIBLICAL INTERPRETATION

ENCYCLOPEDIA *of* BIBLICAL INTERPRETATION

תּוֹרָה שְׁלֵמָה

a millennial anthology

by MENAHEM M. KASHER

translated under the editorship of
RABBI DR. HARRY FREEDMAN, B.A., PH.D.

GENESIS: VOLUME I

AMERICAN BIBLICAL ENCYCLOPEDIA SOCIETY
New York

Printed in the United States of America by
SHULSINGER BROS. LINOTYPING & PUBLISHING CO.
23 EAST 4TH STREET, NEW YORK 3, N. Y.
253

THE PUBLICATION OF THIS VOLUME HAS BEEN MADE POSSIBLE
BY THE FRIENDS AND ADMIRERS OF

הרב ד״ר אברהם משה הירשמאן

RABBI DR. ABRAHAM M. HERSHMAN

RABBI, CONGREGATION SHAAREY ZEDEK, DETROIT, MICHIGAN

AS A TOKEN OF HONOR TO THIS SCHOLAR AND SAGE,
BELOVED TEACHER AND DEVOTED COMMUNITY LEADER,
WHOSE BENEFICENT INFLUENCE HAS INSPIRED AND ENNOBLED
A GENERATION OF MEN AND WOMEN,
IN GRATEFUL APPRECIATION OF HIS CONSECRATED
DEVOTION TO GOD AND TIRELESS SERVICE TO THE COMMUNITY.

Sponsors Committee of Detroit, Michigan

SPONSORS

OF DETROIT, MICHIGAN

GEORGE D. SEYBURN, *Chairman*

DAVID M. MIRO, *Co-Chairman*

Vice-Chairmen

LOUIS BERRY
ALLAN B. KRAMER
MAX HANDLER
PAUL ZUCKERMAN

Abel, Jack
Alpert, Ferdinand
Alper, Henry S.
Alper, Louis
Aronsson, Maurice
Berman, Julius
Blumberg, Irving
Borman, Tom
Borin, Jacob
Brody, Robert
Brody, Sam
Canvasser, Charles
Canvasser, Morris
Carnick, Robert
Clark, Harry
Cohen, Sam A.
Cohn, Irwin
Cooper, Abe
Davidson, Harry C.
Davidson, Israel
Deutsch, Alfred
Deutsch, Alfred L.
Deutsch, Adolph
DeWoskin, Morris R.
Dworman, Irving
Dunitz, Saul J.
Eisenberg, Sol
Ettenheimer, A. H.
Federal Pipe & Supply
Fenton, Ben
Fisher, Max M.
Fishman, Meyer
Fishman, Nathan
Fleishman, Arthur
Frenkel, Joseph
Freedland, Harry
Freedland, Nathan
Freedman, Louis
Friedman, Judge William
Galanty, Herman
Gendelman, Joe
Gershenson, Aaron
Gershenson, Charles
Gershenson, Sam
Gershenson, William
Gerson, Bernard
Goldberg, David
Goldberg, Sam
Golden, Irving
Goldin, Nate
Goldman, Harvey
Gottesman, Harry
Gottesman, Harvey
Green, Abe
Grosberg, Charles
Gurwin, A. J.
Hamburger, Charles
Hamburger, Louis
Hamburger, Sam
Hechtman, Samuel
Holtzman, Joseph
Isaacs, John
Israel, Morris
Jacobs, M. L.
Jacobson, Alex
Jaffa, Harry
Kalt, Saul
Kane, Samuel
Kaplan, Harold
Kasle, Abe
Kass, Herman
Katkin, Samuel
Klein, Maurice
Kukes, J. H.
Langer, Carl
Lanyi, Shephen
Lapides, Charles
Lapides, Lester
Lavin, Dan
LeBost, Paul
Levinson, Ben
Lichter, Adolph
Luckoff, Lou
Madden, Milton
Marks, Sam
Matler, Charles
Matler, Harry
Modell, Louis
Moss, Sam
Orley, George
Osnos, Max
Pariser, Henry
Radner, Herman
Radner, Joseph
Robinson, Eli
Robinson, Morris
Rose, Edward
Rose, Irving
Rosenfeld, Max
Rosenthal, C. M.
Ross, Norman
Rott, David
Rott, Harry
Rubin, Nathan
Safran, Hyman
Satovsky, A.
Schaver, Morris L.
Scholnick, Morris
Scholnick, Nathan
Schumer, C. J.
Schumer, Harry
Schuster, Sam
Schwartz, Joseph
Seyburn, Sam
Shaye, Max
Shaye, Nate
Shaye, Rubin
Shaye, Sol
Shiffman, Abe
Sidlow, Leonard
Sidney, S. D.
Silverman, Nathan
Simons, Leonard
Slatkin, Adolph
Slatkin, Joe
Sloan, Saul
Smith, Barney
Smokler, Bert
Snider, Norman
Sofferin, Sam
Solomon, Julius
Solomon, Sam
Srere, Abe
Sylvan, Jack
The Tann Foundation
Victor Paint Co.
Wilbur, Joseph J.
Wilke, Ben
Wilkus, David
Wisock, Robert
Wrigley Stores
Zack, M. W.
Zivian, Max J.

IN TRIBUTE

TO

The Honorable Harry S. Truman

32ND PRESIDENT OF THE UNITED STATES

BECAUSE HE REPRESENTS A NATION WHOSE LOFTY DEMOCRATIC AND HUMANITARIAN IDEALS ARE FOUNDED UPON THE HIGH MORAL AND ETHICAL TEACHINGS OF THE BIBLE; AND BECAUSE HIS PROFOUND GOOD WILL PROMPTED HIM TO EXTEND THE HAND OF ENCOURAGEMENT AND RECOGNITION TO THE INFANT STATE OF ISRAEL.

CONTENTS

FOREWORD

Torah literature is what Israel's noblest hearts and finest minds have felt, said and written down in interpretation of the Divine Torah or Direction. Its preceptive element (Halakhah) has been illustrated by meditation — maxim, parable and legend (Agadah) — through integration with the best thought of every age and the occasional naturalization of foreign words or methods. (Rabbinic writings abound in Persian, Greek and Roman terms, and the architectural scheme in Maimonides' great Code has definite Aristotelian features.) Torah literature mirrors, as it is mirrored by, our people's ethical passion, gnomic wisdom, intellectual curiosity, social awareness and, above all, its profound reverence for Our Father in heaven and the divine spirit in every human. But also this: The philosophy of Judaism, from Moses to Rabbi Akiba, to Maimonides, to Caro, to Elijah Gaon and the Baal-Shem-Tob, to Samson R. Hirsch and indeed down to our own days, has been buttressed by the solid realities of Jewish law and thus prevented from being lost in the sands of imitative, anemic enterprise.

This interaction of these two not always interdependent but often converging approaches to ultimate verities has stamped Torah with freshness and strength in the millennia of its existence. The progressive revelation of its message has been throughout encouraged by the traditional principle of Freedom of Interpretation, in equal challenge and promise to scholar, thinker and dreamer, thus rendering the quest for the knowledge of God's mind (*Death Elokim*) the primary impulse of Hebrew study. *Shiv'im Panim la-Torah* — Torah has seventy facets, say the Sages of the Talmud. There are text-meanings, and between-the-lines-meanings, obvious and esoteric ones — so insists the Holy Book of Splendor (the *Zohar*), in a celebrated passage. The judicious prose of the Codes and the Agadist's unconfined roaming have begotten many thousands of commentaries and super-commentaries on the Bible, an inexhaustible treasure house, with a golden message for every person, mood, time or place.

In the thirty-five volumes of his monumental TORAH SHELEMAH (Complete Torah), fourteen of which have been published by the American Biblical Encyclopedia Society, Dr. M. M. Kasher has essayed to organize, systematize, and clarify this enormous literary material — a feat of historical significance. Almost as heroic is the effort presented by this book, to translate into English the first volume of the grand undertaking, offering a tantalizing glimpse of the original's riches. Every excerpt invites reflective lingering, as one admires the author's thought and the anthologist's art.

The acknowledgment of appreciation given Rabbi Dr. Abraham M. Hershman for years of service to the Jewish community of Detroit, is an honor well deserved. The tribute paid the beloved thirty-second President of the United States, whom in crucial times Providence chose to perform vital service, crown the work with timeless significance.

LEO JUNG,
Honorary President
AMERICAN BIBLICAL ENCYCLOPEDIA SOCIETY

ב"ה

INTRODUCTION

This work, THE ENCYCLOPEDIA OF BIBLICAL INTERPRETATION, is based on my Hebrew Biblical Encyclopedia TORAH SHELEMAH, which literally translated means the *complete Torah*. What do we mean by the *complete Torah*?

WRITTEN AND ORAL LAW. Torah refers in the first place to the five Books of Moses, and then to the other Biblical books, which were *written* down from the very beginning. According to tradition a great body of exegesis and commentary was given with them. A fundamental system, too, was given of ways and means of elucidating and interpreting the Written Torah. This, however, was not written, but for many centuries transmitted from generation to generation by word of mouth only (written records being kept by none but a few great teachers and leaders). Thus there arose the conception of the Written Law (*Torah Shebik'thav*) and the Oral Law (*Torah Sheb'al Peh*) which together constitute Torah in its fuller sense.

This combined Written and Oral Law is the source of all the legal, moral, ethical and religious precepts which govern and guide the life of the Jewish people. It is a vast treasure-house of Jewish culture and learning, containing the accumulated wisdom of our Sages, their observations and legal decisions. It interprets, elaborates, and analyzes the precepts contained in the Written Law.

The result of this study first produced the Mishnah and a number of other works known collectively as the Tannaitic literature, the teachers in them being known as Tannaim.[1]

The Mishnah consists mainly of laws which define the precepts of the Written Law more clearly and in detail. This in turn, together with the other works mentioned, was elaborated and analyzed by the Amoraim, the name given to the teachers who followed the Tannaim. Their work is known as Gemara. Mishnah and Gemara together constitute the Talmud, of which there are two recensions, the Babylonian Talmud and the Jerusalem Talmud. (It is the former that is mostly studied.) It is not confined to law in its narrow sense.

It seeks to standardize and codify the vast body of Jewish custom and practice. It also contains moral reflections and apologues; maxims of worldly wisdom; metaphysical discussions; tales of Israel's past, both historical and legendary; visions of its future; and obiter dicta — often showing remarkable perception and powers of observation — on geometry, medicine, astronomy, physiology, botany, and other scientific subjects. Much of it is bound up with the Written Law, which is the axis on which rotates the Oral Law. It covers the lore of Israel from the time that the Torah was given at Sinai — according to tradition, the year 2448 (1312 B.C.E.) — until 4265 (about the beginning of the sixth century C.E.), when the Oral Law assumed its present written form.

The Oral Law consists of about three hundred works, large and small (listed in TORAH SHELEMAH, vol. 1, Introd.). Some are of later composition, but their material is drawn from the earlier period with which we are dealing. About another hundred works of later authors (the Geonim and Early Scholars) must also be listed (see TORAH SHELEMAH, v. 1, 3rd ed., Introd. and p. 21), for they include passages and quotations from the teachings of

[1] In addition to the Mishna, which was codified by R. Judah Ha-Nasi in 3983 (219 C.E.) we have Tosefta, B'raithoth, Mekilta, Sifra, Sifre and several other works.

the Sages for which we have no other sources. The whole of this vast complex, together with the Talmud, may be described as the TALMUDIC-MIDRASHIC LITERATURE (Midrashic from *darash,* to interpret). It covers the whole gamut of Jewish life — religious worship, family and sex relationships, health and diet, study, business, labor, recreation, social intercourse, and so forth. Every conceivable thought, emotion, attitude and relationship is governed and guided by these teachings. It is the repository of the collective genius of our greatest minds and most revered personalities.

If the vastness of the Talmud alone has earned for it the appellation *Yam Ha-Talmud,* the Sea of the Talmud, how much the more is that true of the whole Talmudic-Midrashic Literature! In relation to the Written Law, it is indeed an *uncharted* sea. To find the Rabbinic interpretations of a particular verse or phrase one might have to range over many, many volumes. Students and scholars, therefore, have long felt the need for an encyclopedia which would give for every verse of the Bible all the passages, comments and interpretations found in the great body of Talmudic-Midrashic Literature.

In my Introduction to the first volume a special chapter is devoted to an account of the numerous attempts made throughout the centuries in that direction.

"TORAH SHELEMAH" — COMPLETE TORAH. The TORAH SHELEMAH is a new attempt to compile such an encyclopedia — a complete compendium of this vast material on the Bible. In one comprehensive work, to consist of thirty-five volumes (fourteen of which have already appeared), it assembles and collates every known commentary, homily, parable, and exegetical interpretation on the Bible, from the very earliest to those of the Gaonic period. It covers Jewish traditions and interpretations of the Bible for a period of approximately 1800 years — from the Revelation at Sinai to the close of the Talmudic-Midrashic era, as described above.

To this is added a commentary on the Talmudic-Midrashic material, which is based in the main on the succeeding 900 years of Jewish literary creation — the work of the Geonim and the Earlier Scholars who succeeded them, i.e., up to about 5250 (1500 C.E.). The best of their comments has been selected and interwoven into a running commentary to elaborate on and enrich the above described textual material. In addition, the commentary gives variant readings of the Talmudic-Midrashic passages found in manuscript and other sources, in order to establish the correct text. Complete cross-references for every passage are also given. I have added glosses and notes of my own, to show how this vast material adds to our knowledge of every aspect of Torah. Many valuable comments of the scholars of the last four centuries are included as well.

OTHER INTERESTING FEATURES. In addition to the material gathered from every printed source extant, TORAH SHELEMAH includes thousands of passages on the Biblical verses gleaned from rare, little known, and hitherto unpublished manuscripts, collected from libraries the world over. Especially important is the material gathered from thirteen rare Yemenite Hebrew and Arabic manuscripts, as yet unedited and unpublished. (A list is given in TORAH SHELEMAH, v. 1, 3rd, ed., Introduction, and p. 23).

Thus, drawing on all available sources, printed and unprinted, TORAH SHELEMAH presents a *complete Torah* — an encyclopedia of the rich treasure-house of Jewish Interpretation of the Bible.

PREFACE

The first volume of the ENCYCLOPEDIA OF BIBLICAL INTERPRETATION represents my attempt to introduce to the English-speaking world a treasure-house that is old, and yet new — which for the most part has remained inaccessible to the reader of English until now.[2] In this book is gathered a rich selection of the thought and work of Sages and scholars which constitute the Oral Law referred to above.[3] I have tried, as it were, to lead the reader into a garden where men of great learning and erudition are discoursing on the problems that have ever beset the human mind — God and nature, man and fellow-man, life and death, ethics and justice, good and evil. The Bible with its interpretations is timeless. The teachings of these Sages are as valid and cogent for us today as they were when first uttered.

Needless to say, the *literal* meaning of the Bible, based on a knowledge of language, philology, grammar, history and tradition, retains at all times its own prime position of authority, as can be seen in the section marked *Commentary* in this volume.

This is a new feature in the English edition. It includes all significant commentaries of a strictly exegetical character, contained in the literature from earliest times to the present. As this material is found scattered throughout the voluminous glosses in the Hebrew TORAH SHELEMAH, I thought it advisable to collect it into a separate section with the addition of much that is new. The sources of the *Commentary* are numerically indexed. The explanations of each verse are marked alphabetically.

But, as we have already indicated, the Sages went beyond strict exegesis, and in their homiletical interpretations of the Bible, their methods may seem strange to the present-day reader. For here are adages and parables; profound ethical teachings; keen insights and perceptive observations on human nature; a broad knowledge of natural phenomena; tales and legends — all expressed in the form of interpretations of Biblical verses. The reader may well wonder why they chose this unique form of homiletical, allegorical and exegetical interpretations of the Bible.[4]

To understand this, we must bear in mind one basic fact. The Bible is the one written work which has occupied a central, dominant position in the life of the Jewish people. It was the sacred Book, the Divine Word received from God and recorded by Moses and the Prophets. As such, it was known and revered by all Israel. For rabbi and layman, scholar and unlettered, this one book of Scriptures was the corner-stone of religious and ethical growth. It was law and guide, teacher and mentor.

What then was more natural than that it should be studied, that its contents should be pored over with loving care? Every verse, every phrase — even every word — evoked a

[2] It is interesting to note that our Sages themselves possessed a tradition that Israel's sacred lore should be available to all in understandable form. Thus, in *Mishnah* Sotah 7, 5 and *Tanhuma* Deuteronomy it is stated that the Pentateuch was translated into all languages, that all who wished might study it. It is clear, then, that it is important, according to the Sages, that our sacred teachings be available for all to read and know. (See also Exodus Rabbah 28, 4.)

The tradition was continued with Oral Law when R. Joseph ibn Abitur, in the Middle Ages, made an Arabic translation of the Mishnah; soon after Maimonides wrote his commentary on Mishnah in Arabic, so that it could be read by the Jews of Islam.

[3] This edition is an abridgment of the Hebrew. Only those passages which lend themselves to translation, which retain their full impact and significance in another tongue, have been included. The reader who seeks a more complete edition, as well as full cross-references, will find them in the Hebrew version of TORAH SHELEMAH.

[4] It should be noted that the allegorical and homiletical methods of interpretation used by the Sages are of great antiquity. It is becoming increasingly clear in our own time that many of their interpretations parallel the writings of Philo, who lived in Alexandria at the time of the second Temple. It would seem that these interpretations already existed in Israel at the time of Philo, and they served as his source. See T.S., v. 14, Supplement, no. 10, and Isaac Heinemann, *Darke Ha-Aggadah,* Jerusalem, 1951.

host of ideas, insights, maxims and ethical precepts. Even the purely historical sections of the Bible were not to be regarded as a dead relic, as the bare record of a forgotten past. The words of the Scriptures were vital, pulsing with the message of God to mankind — His words of guidance to the actual living present.

It was the herculean task of the Sages to lead their people in religious and ethical growth. For inspiration, for keys to the deeper meanings and more sublime teachings of the precepts than might appear on the surface, they turned to Scripture. This was the God-given, the right way for them. They studied avidly every line of it. They sought to capture its every mood and spirit, every nuance and inflection of meaning. Thus the Bible became the source of all their teachings.

Because the Bible was so revered, once a teaching was definitely based on one of its verses, it would certainly be heeded and retained. Once associated with Scripture, a precept, adage or homily became for all time part of Israel's sacred lore. As a means of teaching, then, Bible interpretation was highly effective.

It is not surprising, therefore, to find that the single word *B'reshith* ("In the beginning" — Genesis 1:1) produced no fewer than 195 passages in the lore of the Sages, and as many again in later writings (see Hebrew edition, TORAH SHELEMAH). Or, to take another example from our volume on Genesis which is particularly instructive: In the dialogue between God and the guilt-laden Cain the Eternal says, "*If thou doest well, shall it not be lifted up? And if thou doest not well, sin coucheth at the door . . .*" (Genesis 4:7). This one last expression, *sin coucheth at the door,* — a rich, meaningful figure of speech — became a vehicle for many teachings and precepts.

One meaning given is that sin lies in wait at "the doorway of the heart," seeking to lure and entice man. Another explanation is that sin waits to be recalled on Judgment Day — either at the "door of the grave," or at the "doorway to the heavenly Court." Again, *the door* is made to mean the mouth — a doorway for man's thoughts, feelings and wishes. This verse is used to impress on us the evil that talk can cause. "Sin lies in wait" — to get through the doorway of the mouth. Another view regards the *eyes* of man as "the doorway of sin." The hungry, greedy eyes of Cain, his hostile, jealous glances, can be a "doorway to sin."

And yet another thought — "*sin coucheth at the door* of the House of Study"; sin can never be effective within the *Beth Hamidrash* — the place of sacred study; once across the threshold, man has left sin behind the *doorway* of the *Beth Hamidrash.* Here was an interpretation which gave dramatic expression to the importance and efficacy of sacred study.

For yet another Sage *the door* referred to the portals of the Temple, and *sin* meant the sin-offering, the animal sacrifice that an Israelite brought to atone for a transgression of law. This Sage taught: "The sin-offering — the Israelite's attempt to find forgiveness for his transgression — *lies at the door:* it does not rise to be accepted on high — unless it is accompanied by a change of heart and a mending of one's ways." Out of the verse then came the clear idea that this, and not the sin-offering, is the important factor in repentance and atonement.

Another Sage had a different inspiration. "*At the door* of one's own house — the threshold one crosses every morning to begin the day's activities — *sin coucheth:* one should beware, for the evil inclination lies in wait to mislead and trap." (This by far does not exhaust all the meanings and ideas given. See TORAH SHELEMAH *ad. loc.*)

Thus one tiny fragment of Scriptural text evoked ideas and thoughts far beyond its exact, literal meaning; for certainly the dialogue between God and Cain could not refer to many of the above interpretations; for example, the *Beth Hamidrash* (House of Study) and the Temple did not as yet exist. But the phrase was an excellent tool; it gave the Sages a uniquely effective means of transmitting ethical teachings of the highest value, and they did so in a masterly fashion.

And not merely basic principles and weighty ideas. Even for simple maxims and epigrams, wise observations and bits of folk-lore, the Sages had a remarkable gift of skillfully finding apt references and allusions in Scriptures. Thus, we find on Genesis 3:14, "A lie has no feet, as it is written, *upon thy belly shalt thou go*." The proverbial instability and impermanence of a lie ("a lie has no feet") is given a basis in the Bible: the serpent lost his *feet* because he *lied*.

Similarly: "Sweat is a good sign for the invalid, as it is written: *In the sweat of thy face shalt thou eat bread* (Genesis 3-19). The observation that an invalid who perspires is on his way to health is read into the Biblical verse: sweat is a sign that the individual will be able to eat bread, i.e., will be well.

With this vast apparatus of allegorical, homiletical, and exegetical interpretation, the Sages taught an ethical system of values and attitudes, a Jewish orientation to life. By their addition of tradition, legend and intuition, the words of the Bible became alive and meaningful. The heroes and villains of the Sacred Book became three-dimensional, full-blooded personalities — models for character training.

One purpose in particular they had. They sought to teach the laws and ethics of Judaism and the duties of the heart. It is to their everlasting glory that this great body of sacred Biblical interpretation teaches so well the sanctity and dignity of human life, and brings man closer to his God.

APPENDIX

This volume is supplemented by four essays, which deal more fully with matters raised in the body of the work.

1. The Concept of Time in Biblical and Post-Biblical Literature[5]

In a detailed discussion I cite all the philosophical views, from Plato to Einstein, on the nature and measurement of time. I have then gathered the opinions of the Sages and the Earlier Commentaries which are found in the ancient Jewish literature. In the course of the discussion I have shown how the very foundations of the Jewish belief in monotheism are rooted in our ideas about elusive, intangible time and space. Major concepts in Judaism, such as the Sabbath, Foreknowledge, Free Will, and Repentance, are shown to be integrally related to and founded upon our philosophic concept of time and space.

2. The Atom in Jewish Sources[6]

Without doubt the most important scientific discovery to date is atomic energy — the ability to convert matter into energy with devastating results. Strangely enough, the interpretations of the first verses of the Bible, as found in ancient Jewish literature, agree with present-day scientific atomic theory. In the second essay I show that whereas science speaks of the possibility of changing matter into energy, the Earlier (Jewish) Commentators speak of the creation of pure primal energy which was later transformed into matter-plus-energy (the atom, and from it, all matter). This suggests the possibility of re-converting matter to its previous state: pure (destructive) energy. The essay discusses the new insights which this concept gives us in our efforts to comprehend the subtle ideas of Immortality.

3. Creation and the Theory of Evolution[7]

The third essay begins with a full presentation of the doctrine of evolution, the arguments in its favor, and the arguments against it. This is followed by many passages from the teachings of the Sages and Earlier Scholars, drawn from the rich material in the Anthology, which cast a highly interesting light on both sides of the debate concerning evolution. The deeply meaningful quotations from the Talmudic-Midrashic lore reveal that all points

[5] Published originally in Hebrew in *Talpioth*, 5th year, v. 3-4, 1952.

[6] Published originally in *Talpioth*, 3rd year, v. 1, 1946. It should be noted that in a book published this year, there is a summary of this Hebrew article, printed without credit.

[7] Written originally in Hebrew for *Talpioth*, 6th year, v. 1.

raised by the evolutionists, which allegedly prove the doctrine of evolution, were known to the Sages. Their ideas and thoughts, however, tend to negate the theory of evolution. The essay finally arrives at this conclusion: Were the doctrine of evolution definitely proven and accepted by all scientists, it could be reconciled with the Biblical account of creation as elaborated and interpreted by the Sages. But the theory of evolution is constantly losing ground among scientists, and may very likely be discarded altogether at some future date. There is no reason, therefore, for deviating from the literal meaning of the Chapter on Creation.

4. Creation and Human Brotherhood

In the fourth essay I demonstrate how the Sages stressed and emphasized the one central idea of the Bible — the importance of man's love for his fellow-man. I show how the great Jewish teachers of old taught and inculcated this crucial lesson of the brotherhood of man through homiletical, exegetical and allegorical interpretation of the Bible. For the Sages well understood that with this idea mankind lives; without it, mankind is threatened with mutual destruction. This fundamental lesson, first enunciated about 3,200 years ago, and stressed, developed and reiterated by our Sages for many centuries, has never been more vitally needed by mankind than in our own day.

ACKNOWLEDGEMENTS

In conclusion, I am happy to express my gratitude to the Sponsors' Committee of Detroit, Michigan, and its chairman, George D. Seyburn, who in honoring their beloved teacher and leader, Rabbi Dr. Abraham M. Hershman, have made possible the publication of this volume. My earnest thanks as well to the president and officers of the American Biblical Encyclopedia Society, whose untiring support and encouragement have ever been given to this work. May Heaven reward them in full measure.

I am also deeply indebted to the group of scholars who by long, painstaking effort have accomplished the prodigious task of the translation of sections of this work: Rabbi Alter Abelson, Rabbi Abraham Burstein, Prof. Joshua Finkel, Mr. Abraham Friedman, and Rabbi Charles Wengrov.

I am grateful to Rabbi H. M. Brecher and to my son-in-law, Rabbi Dr. Aaron Greenbaum for their scholarly selection and arrangement of the material for the *Commentary*.

My especial thanks are due to Rabbi Dr. Harry Freedman, who has edited the whole of this work and given it its final language and structure. Rabbi Dr. Freedman is well-known for his fine commentaries on several of the Soncino Books of the Bible and his collaboration in the Soncino editions of the Talmud and Midrash Rabbah. To his present task he has brought a great fund of knowledge and experience, for which I am grateful.

I would also express my appreciation to Rabbi Dr. Leo Jung, whose advice and help proved invaluable. I remain in his debt for many important suggestions and corrections in the translation of *The Concept of Time*.

My thanks, as well, to Rabbi Morris H. Finer, for his excellent assistance and suggestions.

My deep gratitude to my good friend Mr. Jacob Finer, without whose untiring and unstinting labors in the numerous technical tasks demanded by such a work, this volume could never have appeared.

I am indebted to the Jewish Publication Society for its gracious permission for the use throughout this work of its English translation of the Bible, as well as excerpts from other of its scholarly publications.

Nor can I close without especial mention of the printers, Shulsinger Brothers, and Mr. Irving Hunger, whose craftsmanship and labors of love and skill have contributed so much to the beautiful production of this book.

M.M.K.

EDITOR'S PREFACE

This book, The Encyclopedia of Biblical Interpretation, is based on the monumental work by Rabbi Menahem M. Kasher, the TORAH SHELEMAH, a compilation comprising every saying and interpretation on the Bible by our Sages from the very earliest period down to the Geonic age (see Introduction). This work, of which to date 14 volumes have been published, has attracted world-wide attention, which in turn has awakened the desire for its understanding in those who, Jews and non-Jews alike, realize the immense contribution which the Bible and its commentators have made to the spiritual enrichment of human civilization. For the Bible is the cultural and spiritual heritage of all mankind, irrespective of their national, ethnic, religious or sociological affiliations. But to understand the original, couched as it is in the terse Hebrew or Aramaic and in the peculiar idiom of Rabbinic, Midrashic and Mystic Jewish Literature, requires many years of intensive study, without which even the best-versed Hebraist will find it a sealed book. And, of course, it is completely inaccessible to those who do not know Hebrew thoroughly. The insistent demand for an English translation led to the present work. It is offered to the public in the confident belief that it will prove valuable to scholar and layman alike.

It is shorter than the original. That, being an Encyclopedia, has literally omitted nothing, and includes as separate items many similar passages. It was felt, however, that a service would be rendered to those who would know the essential teachings of the Sages, but lack the time for the exhaustive approach which characterizes the original, if something shorter was available. Out of that vast mass of material therefore only the most interesting and significant has been chosen for inclusion.

The nature of this material requires some explanation. A modern exegete seeks the literal sense of a text, and then may comment on its significance, spirit, message, and so on. He avoids "reading into." Our Sages too were fully aware of this cardinal principle of interpretation, and they established that אין מקרא יוצא מידי פשוטו, a text can never lose its plain, literal meaning. But they also believed that over and above this literal meaning the earnest and devout student would find many deep thoughts. For after all, the Bible is not simply a book of narrative and precept: It is Torah, mistranslated Law, but in reality meaning Teaching, in the widest sense. Going out from that standpoint they declared that there are ע׳פנים לתורה seventy (the number simply means many) aspects or interpretations of the Torah. These interpretations fall into four categories, viz., *P'shat, Remez, D'rush* and *Sod;* i.e., Literal meaning, Allusion, Exegetic meaning, and the Hidden or Esoteric meaning: the third, *D'rush,* generally includes all but the Literal meaning. To achieve their end they analyzed literally every word, every letter of the Sacred Writ. Not a word or letter could be redundant or chosen at random. It was exactly this word that had to be used, and no other. The results of their method will occasionally appear strange; yet no matter how far-fetched some of these interpretations may seem, they generally stem from a really true understanding of the inner spirit of the Bible. How true this understanding was may be gauged by a comparison with the Allegorical School of interpretation which developed in Alexandria, of which Philo was the chief exponent. Their exegesis was perhaps no more far-fetched that many interpretations which are included here, yet the greater part of it fell into complete oblivion. The reason is not far to seek. The Bible is the product of the Jewish spirit and Jewish genius, and so are the dicta in this work; whereas the motivating factor of much in the Alexandrian allegorism was the desire to force the Bible into the mold of Hellenistic thought, in order to synthesize Hebraism and Hellenism. It did not spring from truly Jewish roots, and so was inevitably destined to wither away.

To return to the present work. It is evident that such an approach gave the widest possible scope for every shade of thought. The work is thus an encyclopedia not only from the Biblical angle, in that it contains every interpretation as categorized above, but is also an encyclopedia of Rabbinic thought, in the sense that it contains the fullest expositions of their beliefs and ideals, the things by which they lived. (The term "Rabbinic" generally means of the age of the Talmud. But it is used here in a much wider sense as embracing the Geonic age and even that of the Early Scholars, i.e., those who immediately succeeded the Geonic age.)

In addition to the Rabbinical dicta, this work is furnished with a Commentary. It too is encyclopedic in scope, and comprises the essence and most significant interpretations and observations of exegetes from the earliest times right down to our own day.

Since the authors of these comments are always given, direct quotations have not been put in inverted commas. In general, quotation marks have been used as sparingly as possible.

A word must be added on the English rendering of the Biblical texts employed in this work. Generally speaking, the version of the Jewish Publication Society has been used (referred to as AJV). However, where the Rabbinic saying clearly pre-supposes a different rendering, it is given straight in the text. Occasionally the Hebrew is given alongside the English, to show exactly the basis of the Rabbinical dictum. At times too a particular word or phrase is given only in Hebrew, where discussion centers on the precise meaning of that word.* The translation has endeavored to combine literal accuracy with the requirements of style and good English. However, where it was necessary to add words or phrases in order to make it intelligible, the addition, contrary to usual practice, has not been placed in parentheses except on rare occasions. The use of these breaks up the even flow of the text, is disturbing to the eye, and lessens the reader's enjoyment. For the same reasons redundancies and repetitions are occasionally omitted.

In the main the order of the original has been followed. Nevertheless, the reader will observe deviations here and there. In the original the passages are given in order of the chronology of their respective authors and sources. But for the wider public for which this is intended it was felt that the order should be determined rather by association of interest and subject-matter. This led inevitably to such deviations as will be found in this volume. For the same reason separate passages from different sources and ages have occasionally been combined.

This work is presented to the English-reading public in the earnest hope that it will help to make the treasures of Jewish thought mode widely accessible than hitherto, give a deeper understanding of the spirit and genius of an ancient people, their undying hopes and aspirations, and their unshakeable belief in humanity's future.

H. Freedman

* In transliterating the Hebrew into English the ordinary reader has been kept in mind. The ק for instance, appears as k rather than q, thus *makom* rather than *maqom*. In many words the doubling of the consonant which is effected by the *dagesh forte* has been omitted, particularly after the def. art.; hence *hashishi,* not *hashshishi.* For the same reason the ' and ' for א and ע respectively have been omitted, and both ה and ח appear as *h*.

GENESIS

In Rabbinic literature the first book of the Bible is called *B'reshith.*

"Why is it called *B'reshith* ('In the beginning')? Because it contains an account of the Creation of the world. It relates how God was the Beginning of everything, that all generations may know that He preceded the world, and created it in His wisdom, taking counsel with none; and He alone rules the world in His glory" (*Midrash Tadshe,* chap. 20). According to this the name *B'reshith* teaches that the world is not eternal; it was created by a Supreme Power. R. Isaac Abrabanel writes at the end of his commentary on Genesis: "*B'reshith* is called 'The Book of Creation' (*Sefer ha-B'riah*) or 'The Book of Formation' (*Sefer ha-Yetsirah*)." Nahmanides likewise writes in his Introduction: "*B'reshith,* which is the Book of *Yetsirah* (formation) teaches that the world is 'new' (i.e., not eternal)." Some call it "The Book of the Creation of the World." The popular designation, Genesis, denotes generation and coming into existence. (See T.S., Exodus, Supplement, 1.)

Midrash Habiur (T.S., v. 1, par. 283), states on the basis of Abodah Zarah 25a: "Why is *B'reshith* called 'The Book of *Yashar*' (the Righteous; based on Joshua 10:13, *Is not this written in the Book of* Yashar)? Because it contains the history of Abraham, Isaac and Jacob, who were called the Righteous, as it is written, *Let me die the death of the righteous*" (Num. 23:10). It is likewise called *Sefer ha-Y'sharim* (the Book of the Righteous) in the *Yalkutim* (midrashic anthologies)of Yemen (see T.S., vol. 8, p. 188-9). Thirty-nine chapters of this Book do deal, in fact, with the lives of the Patriachs. Some have therefore called it "The Book of the Patriarchs."

However, the name *B'reshith,* which the book has borne in Hebrew from the earliest days to our own, is indeed the most fitting, as an affirmation of the faith of the Jewish people in their Maker — the Creator and Ruler of the Universe.

SIDRAH B'RESHITH

(Genesis 1:1 — 6:8)

GENESIS

CHAPTER I

[1] In the beginning God created the heaven and the earth.

COMMENTARY

[1]In the beginning. Heb. *B'reshith.* This has the following meanings: **a.** "Prior to," i.e., before God brought all things He had already created to their final state of proportion and symmetry, chaos was rampant everywhere.[1] **b.** At the very inception of the creation of heaven and earth, etc., God said: "Let there be light." That is to say, Scripture does not intend to indicate that heaven and earth preceded all other things in creation, for if it did, it would not use the word "*b'reshith*" but *barishonah,* which means "first of all."[2] **c.** "Anterior to all existence," i.e., before anything was yet created.[3] **d.** "In the beginning of time," the word "time" being elided, time itself being one of the things created.[4] **e.** "At some remote period of time." This interpretation is based upon the fact that the Targum (the Aramaic translation of the Pentateuch) renders both *b'reshith* and *l'fanim* (I Sam. 9:9) by *bekad'min.* Since *l'fanim b'yisrael,* the phrase referred to, means "at some early period in the history of Israel," it follows by analogy that *b'reshith* means at some early period in the history of the cosmos. (See also Appendix 1.) **f.** Before the creation of heaven and earth, and before the earth was *tohu* and *bohu* (Heb. for "unformed and void" in v. 2, but here regarded as substances specially created by God for the raw material, as it were, out of which to fashion the Universe;

ANTHOLOGY

1. **In the beginning God created.**

A heretic asked R. Akiba: "Who created this world?" The sage answered, "God." "Give me clear proof," he demanded. Akiba rejoined, "Come tomorrow." When he came the next day, the sage asked him what he was wearing. "A garment." "And who made it?" Akiba persisted. "A weaver," was the answer. "I do not believe you; give me clear proof," the sage returned. "But do you not know that a garment is made by a weaver?" the infidel protested. "And do you not know that God is the creator of His world?" the sage retorted. When he took his leave, Akiba's disciples asked him, "What is the incontestable proof?" "My sons," the sage replied, "just as a house implies a builder; a dress, a weaver; a door, a carpenter; so the world proclaims God, Who created it."

Midrash T'mura. T.S. 1, p. 178. Add. 4.

2. IN THE BEGINNING GOD CREATED. The Roman Emperor Hadrian asked R. Joshua, "Has the world a master?" The sage replied, "Is then the world ownerless, anarchic?"[1] "And who created heaven and earth?" "God," was the reply, "as it says, *In the beginning God created,*" etc. "Then why," asked the emperor, "does He not reveal Himself twice a year, so that people might see Him and stand in awe of Him?" "The world could not endure His dazzling splendor," Hadrian was told, "as Scripture writes, *Man cannot see Me and live*" (Exod. 33:20).

Midrash Abakir. T.S. 1, 214.

3. IN THE BEGINNING GOD CREATED. This reads literally, In the beginning created God. The act of creation is mentioned first, because the created testifies to the existence of the Creator. Thus from the created, man recognizes the Creator (God), even as Job declared, "*Out of my own flesh will I discern God*" (Job 19:26), i.e., the very fact that I exist, a thing created, is proof of the existence of God the Creator.

Yalkut R. Samuel Masnuth. T.S. 1, p. 184.

4. IN THE BEGINNING (B'RESHITH) GOD CREATED. R. Phineas and Rab on the authority of R. Joshua b. R. Levi, quoting R. Levi, said: A builder requires six materials, viz.: water, earth, wood, stones, laths and iron. Even the rich, who does not use laths, still requires a measuring rod, as we read, *And in the man's hand there was a measuring-rod* (Ezek. 40:5). Therefore He first created six pre-requisites, as it says, *The Lord made me as the beginning of*

§ 2 [1] The original has a double meaning: ownerless, whence, completely unlicensed, anarchic.

COMMENTARY

see T.S. I, par. 99), God had said: "Let there be light."[6] **g.** *In the beginning.* Verse 1 is a majestic summary of the story of Creation: God is the beginning, nay, the Cause of all things. The remainder of the chapter gives details of the successive acts of creation. Ages untold may have elapsed between the calling of matter into being and the reduction of chaos to ordered arrangement.[7] **h.** Genesis consists of an account of the creation of the world, implying that the world is in harmony with the Law, and the Law with the world, and that the man who observes the law is constituted thereby a loyal citizen of the world, regulating his doings by the purpose and will of Nature, in accordance with which the entire world itself also is administered.[8] **created.** Heb. *bara,* which stands for *creatio ex nihilo* (commentators), producing something out of nothing. Its meaning may be extended to include any act transcending the ordinary.[9] **God.** Heb. *Elohim,* denotes "the most exalted being." אל means "power" in Hebrew, and a similar root means "fear" in Arabic. The plural form is indicative of the abundance of the divine faculties and the manysidedness of God's Sovereignty over all natural phenomena. However, the predicate verb of Elohim, which in this case is *bara* (created), is in the singular. Secondary meanings of Elohim are angels, kings or judges.[10]

ANTHOLOGY

His way, the first (1) *of His works of old;* (2) *I was set up from everlasting,* (3) from *the beginning,* (4) *or ever the earth was* (5-6) (Prov. 8:22-23).[1] Hence Scripture says B'reshith, which reads *bara shith,* He created six.

Midrash Hagadol B'reshith. T.S. 1, 48.

5. In the beginning God created. R. Judah b. Pazzi lectured: At first there was only a universe of water in water, as we read, *and the spirit of God hovered over the face of the waters.* He then converted this to snow, as it says, *He casteth forth His ice like crumbs* (Ps. 147:17). Then He transformed the snow into earth, Scripture stating, *For He saith to the snow, "Be thou earth"* (Job 37:6). The earth, again, stands on water: compare, *To Him that spread forth the earth upon the waters* (Ps. 136:6). The waters stand upon the mountains: compare, *the waters stood upon the mountains* (ibid. 104:6). The mountains stand upon wind, as we read, *For, lo, He that formeth the mountains, and createth the wind* (Amos 4:13). The wind is appended to the whirlwind, as it says, *Wind of whirlwind, fulfilling His word* (Ps. 148:8). This whirlwind God made like a talisman pendent from His arm, as it is written, *and underneath are the everlasting arms* (Deut. 34:27).

J. Hagigah 2:1. T.S. 1, 296.

6. In the beginning (B'reshith) God created. R. Judah said: By three things did the Holy One, blessed be He, create the world: by Number, Speech and Writ, which correspond to wisdom, understanding, and knowledge. Thus it is written, *The Lord by* wisdom *founded the earth; by* understanding *He established the heavens. By his* knowledge *the depths were broken up* (Prov. 3:19-20). R. Nehunia said: By wisdom alone were all the worlds created. Thus it is written, *By* reshith *God created, reshith* meaning wisdom. This coincides with the view that the world was created with the letter *he,* which comprises all three.[1]

Midrash Haneelam B'reshith, Zohar Hadash 3. T.S. 1, 63.

7. In the beginning God created. When the will of the King began to take effect, He engraved signs into the heavenly sphere that surrounded Him. Within the most hidden recess a dark flame issued from the mystery of *Eyn Sof,* the Infinite, like a fog forming in the unformed—enclosed in the ring of that sphere, neither white nor black, neither red nor green, of no color whatever. Only after this flame began to assume size and dimension, did it produce radiant colors. From the innermost center of the flame sprang forth a well out of which colors issued and spread upon everything be-

§ 4 [1] Each of these words or phrases is understood to refer to a preliminary act of creation, whereby the primal raw materials were created.

§ 6 [1] For the world being created by a *he* see Chapter II, par. 52. The rest of the passage is obscure.

ANTHOLOGY

neath, hidden in the mysterious hiddenness of *Eyn Sof*.

The well broke through and yet did not break through the ether (of the sphere). It could not be recognized at all until a hidden, supernal point shone forth under the impact of the final breaking through.[1]

Beyond this point nothing can be known. Therefore it is called *reshith*, beginning—the first word (out of the ten) by means of which the universe was created.

Zohar, p. 27. G. Scholem.

8. In the beginning God created. It is impossible to express the great creative power of God, and to unfold its working to mortals; therefore Scripture described it in general terms only. From this we derive the law not to expound the forbidden degrees of consanguinity before three, nor the cosmology before two, nor the Chariot mystery (as told in Ezek. 1) before one, unless he be a wise man and understand such matters himself.

Midrash Shne Ketubim. T.S. 1, 80.

9. In the beginning. R. Shimi stated: Not less than ten Scriptural verses should be read in the synagogue in the New Year's Service. These proclaim God's Kingship, treat of Remembrance, and deal with the Shofar, ten verses being assigned to each. What do these ten represent? R. Johanan said: The ten utterances with which the world was created. What are they? The expressions "*and* (God) *said*." But these are only nine? *In the beginning* is also a creative utterance, as it is written, *By the word of the Lord the heavens were made, and all the host of them by the breath of His mouth* (Ps. 33:6).

Rosh Hashanah 32a; Megilah 21a. T.S. 1, 40. 41.

10. In the beginning. A wealthy and pious old man of seventy, being childless, distributed his estates among scholars.[1] "Perhaps," said he, "this will help me to share your lot in the Hereafter." Straightway God, in His compassion, blessed him with a son in his seventieth year. When the child was five years old, his father took him to school,[2] riding on his shoulder. "With which Book will he commence?" asked he. The teacher answered, "The Book of Leviticus."[3] "Let him rather begin from Genesis," suggested his father, "because that contains a eulogy of God."[4] The teacher did so. (The narrative relates at length how the child was taken captive and brought to the royal palace. The Holy One, blessed be He, afflicted the king with sickness. The medical book was [miraculously] turned into the Book of Genesis.[5] But no one could read it, save this child whom his father[6] had taught. In return for this the king restored him to his parents and heaped great riches upon him.) Commenting on this the Sages observed: If he who learned only the Book of Genesis was so greatly rewarded, how much more so he who teaches his son Torah or Mishnah!

Midrash Asereth Hadibroth on the Fourth Commandment. T.S. 1, 274.

11. In the beginning. One who teaches his child the book of Genesis will have it accounted to him as if he engaged in the creation of the world.

Seder Arkim Bik'vod Chuppah. T.S. 1, 81.

§ 7 [1] This primordial point is identified by the Zohar with the wisdom of God (*hokhmah*), the ideal thought of Creation.

§ 10 [1] Lit., disciples of the wise. Except where otherwise stated it always refers to students of the Torah.

[2] Here as elsewhere the religious school is meant.

[3] This was the general practice in ancient days (Lev. R. 87). The reason given there is that as children are pure and sacrifices are pure, it is fitting that the pure should study the laws of the pure.

[4] Viz., that He is the Creator.

[5] The meaning is obscure. It is apparently that the book prescribing the treatment for this sickness was miraculously changed into Genesis, the reading of which was now prescribed as a cure (probably as a prophylactic).

[6] By proxy—since it is stated earlier that he took him to a teacher. There may, however, be variant readings in the sources.

ANTHOLOGY

12. In the beginning. Solomon said: *Wisdom is as unattainable to a fool as corals* (Prov. 24:7). A fool flees at the very gate of the school. For he asks: What will you give me to learn first? He is told: A Table. And after that?—A Scroll. And after that?—Genesis. And after that?—The Bible. And after that?—The Six Orders of the Mishnah. And after that?—The Priestly Law. And after that?—The Mechilta. And after that the Tosefta, which is followed by Talmud and Agada.[1] Whereupon he exclaims, Can I really master all that! But the sensible man observes, I will study two laws today, two tomorrow, until I learn them all.

Tanhuma Nitsabim; Deuteronomy. T.S. 1, 285.

13. In the beginning God created. For twenty-six generations the *aleph* complained to God, saying: "Sovereign of the Universe! Thou didst make me the first letter, and yet didst create the world with a '*beth*,' (i.e., *beth* is the first letter used in the Creation narrative) as it says, *B'reshith* (*In the beginning*) *God created the heaven and the earth*." God answered: "The world and the fulness thereof were created only in the merit of the Torah, as we read, The *Lord founded the earth* in the merit of Wisdom (which is the Torah) (Prov. 3:19). Tomorrow I will reveal Myself and give the Torah to Israel; then I will place you at the head of the Ten Commandments, commencing them with you; as it says, *Onochi*: *I am the Lord, your God* (Exod. 20:2).

Midrash on Song of Songs, 5. T.S. 1, p. 178. Addenda.

14. In the beginning. R. Abba, quoting R. Johanan, said: Before God created the world, He and His name were one. He contemplated creating our world, but created a thousand other worlds prior to this, as it says, *The thousand* (worlds) *are Thine, O Sh'lomo* (Song 5:12).[1] Then God created still other worlds, in order to teach that all is as naught in comparison with Him. This coincides with R. Hiyya's observation: Why is Aleph, which means a thousand, the first letter of the alphabet? Because He first created a thousand worlds, which preceded this world.[2] After the *alef* comes *beth*, which, suggesting, as it does, *binyan* (building), stands for the building of heaven and earth. R. Huna said: He first established His throne of glory, of which it is written, *Thousand thousands minister unto Him* (Dan. 7:10); *alef*—a thousand—is the first letter. After this He set up kings and made the earth, the former guaranteeing the permanence of the world.[3] Then comes *gimel*, standing for Gan Eden, the Garden of Eden (Paradise), which is the reward of the righteous. This is followed by *daleth*, the numerical value of which is four, to symbolize man, who is compounded of four elements.

Midrash Haneelam B'reshith in Zohar Hadash. T.S. 1, 29.

15. In the beginning (b'reshith). What distinguishes the letter *beth* more than any other of the 22 letters of the Hebrew alphabet, that God created the world with it, that is to say, employed the letter *beth* to commence the account of the Creation, as Genesis relates, *B'reshith—In the beginning—God created the heaven and the earth?* (*beth* is the first letter of *B'reshith.*) Surely it would have been more fitting to say, Elohim (God) created Heaven and Earth in the beginning (thus commencing with an *alef*, the first letter of the alphabet)? You may find an analogy for this in education, where one day we teach a child *aleph beth*, and the next day we reverse it, *beth aleph*. (So we see

§ 12 [1] Various Rabbinic works are enumerated. This passage is interesting as showing the order of studies. It is rather a surprising one.

§ 14 [1] Mystically the Sh'lomo (Solomon) in the Song of Songs was identified with God.

[2] The original has "the other worlds." But "this world" makes better sense.

[3] Lit., these being the house (*bayith—beth*) of the world. Therefore *beth* is the second letter. The passage apparently means that after these thousand worlds, which did not last, He made this earth and established a monarchic system. The kings, representing law and order, are "the house of the world," i.e., they are the stabilizing forces of human society which give this world permanence, in contrast to the other thousand worlds.

ANTHOLOGY

that the natural order may be disregarded). But whence do you learn that it was fitting that the order should be reversed in the present instance? From the blessing and curses recounted in Deuteronomy, where the blessings which commence with *beth,* precede the curses, of which the first letter is *alef*. For that reason the Torah commences with *beth beth alef alef*, these being the initial letters of the first four words, viz., *B'reshith Bara Elohim Eth*. An additional reason is that *beth* implies *b'rakah* (blessing), while *alef* suggests *arur* (a curse). But should you object, *bako tivkeh* (*she weepeth sore—Lam.* 1:2) commences with a *beth,* the answer is that that passage (of grief) does indeed commence with an *alef*, viz., *Ekah*! (*How doth the city sit solitary*), to which is added the meaning of curse in the word *arur*.

Seder Eliyahu Rabbah 31. T.S. 1, 21.

15A. In the beginning (b'reshith). Rabbah b. Bar Hana, citing R. Johanan, stated: The Pits[1] have existed since the six days of creation. The School of R. Ishmael taught: *B'reshith*: read not *b'reshith* but *bara shith* (i.e., He created the Pit).

Sukkah 49b. T.S. 1, 42.

16. In the beginning God created. The Torah begins and ends on a note of reticence. It begins on a note of reticence, for it simply says, *In the beginning God created*, without describing how, as in the case of the progeny of heaven and earth. For concerning the latter we are told, "*And God said,*" which teaches that they were created by His utterance. Whereas this is not stated here, though we are told in the Writings, *By the* utterance *of the Lord the heavens were made* (Ps. 33:6). Similarly, it ends on a note of reticence, by concealing the place of Moses' burial, as we read, *And no man knoweth of his sepulchre unto this day* (Deut. 34:6). Just then as these facts, viz., that heaven and earth were created by His utterance, and the place of Moses' sepulchre, are suppressed; so must we suppress our thoughts and refrain from seeking and exploring what is above and below, what is before and what is beyond. R. Johanan deduced this in R. Levi's name from the fact that the first letter of the Torah is a *beth,* shaped thus ב: this teaches that just as the *beth* is closed on all sides and open on one side only, so must you not enquire what is above or below (the Universe), what was before Creation and what will be after.

Midrash in Sefer Maaloth Hamidoth.
T.S.N.E., p. 183:6. Addenda.

17. In the beginning God created the heaven and the earth. R. Judah said: Why did the Almighty mention the creation of heaven and earth first, when in fact the angels and the Throne of Glory were created first? So that man should not meditate on things which are hidden from the eye and which were not revealed from the beginning. Rabbi said: In order to show a man that he does not possess the wisdom to qualify him to receive the secrets of the Torah. For R. Isaac said: The secrets of the Torah are revealed only to the wise, who has studied the Bible and the Mishnah, has succeeded in his studies, is God-fearing and conversant with all other knowledge. But if a man who has not reached this stage asks concerning the celestial secrets and mysteries, answer him: Why do you ask? Lift up your eyes and see how Scripture writes, *In the beginning God created the heaven and the earth,* but reveals nothing more. Now, should you think that there are no esoteric teachings in the Torah, know that upon every word there are countless mysteries, laws and interpretations. Thus Scripture writes, His locks (k'vutsothaw, here derived from *kots,* a tittle) *are curled* (taltalim) (Song of Songs 5:11): upon every jot and tittle there are mountains (*tel,* connected with *taltalim* in the proof-text) upon mountains of teachings.

Midrash Haneelam B'reshith Zohar
Hadash 6. T.S. 1, 264.

§ 15A [1] Deep shafts under the Altar.

ANTHOLOGY

18. IN THE BEGINNING (B'RESHITH). R. Jonah said in R. Levi's name: The world was created with a beth, shaped thus ב. (That is, *beth* is the first letter employed in the Creation story). When the *beth* is asked, Who created thee?,[1] it answers by pointing to its upward stroke, indicating, He who is above all. When asked, What is His name?, it answers by indicating its backward projection which points back to the *alef*, thus intimating: His name is Adonai (Lord); His name is Adon (Sovereign)—both of which commence with an *alef*.[2]

J. Hag. 2:5. T.S. 1, 6.

19. IN THE BEGINNING (B'RESHITH). The Bible begins with the Hebrew word "*B'reshith*," *in the beginning*, of which the first letter *beth* is the *second* letter of the alphabet. Various *midrashim* explain why the second letter and not the first was thus honored. The *beth* has two strokes on top,[1] alluding to the two Courts of Judgment, the human and the divine, both of which are equal on the Day of Judgment.[2] Another interpretation: They correspond to the two worlds, this world and the Hereafter. The numerical value of the *beth*[3] indicates that man possesses two inclinations, the Good and the Evil. Further: God said, I will create the world to consist of two chambers, Heaven and Earth, the former My domain, the latter Man's. Again: Everything which God created He created in pairs. The Torah: the Written and the Oral. Precepts: positive and negative. The Liberators of Israel: Moses and Aaron. The Mishnah: compiled by Rabbi (i.e. R. Judah the prince) and R. Nathan. The Baraitha: compiled by R. Hiyya and R. Hoshaya. The Talmud: edited by Rabina and R. Ashi. The World: Heaven and Earth. The luminaries: Sun and moon. Man: man and female. Recompense: the Garden of Eden and Gehinom. Man's limbs are mostly dual: two eyes, two ears, two nostrils, a mouth and tongue, two feet, ribs on each side. Thus you are taught that everything has its mate, save He who is One in His kingdom.

Midrashim. T.S. 1, 3.15.17. 36. 279. p. 183.

20. IN THE BEGINNING (B'RESHITH). When God was about to create the world by His word, the twenty-two letters of the alphabet descended from the terrible and august crown of God whereon they were engraved with a pen of flaming fire. They stood round about God, and one after the other spake and entreated, "Create the world through me!" The first to step forward was the letter Taw. It said: "O Lord of the world! May it be Thy will to create Thy world through me, seeing that it is through me that Thou wilt give the Torah to Israel by the hands of Moses, as it is written, 'Moses commanded us the Torah.'" The Holy One, blessed be He, made reply, and said "No!" Taw asked, "Why not?" and God answered: "Because in days to come I shall place thee as a sign of death upon the foreheads of men." As soon as Taw heard these words issue from the mouth of the Holy One, blessed be He, it retired from His presence disappointed.

The Shin then stepped forward, and pleaded: "O Lord of the world, create Thy world through me, seeing that Thine own name Shaddai begins with me." Unfortunately, it is also the first letter of Shaw, lie, and of Sheker, falsehood, and that incapacitated it. Resh had no better luck. It was pointed out that it was the initial letter of Ra', wicked, and Rasha', evil, and after that the distinction it enjoys of being the first letter in the Name of God, Rahum, the Merciful, counted for naught. The Kof was rejected, because Kelalah, curse, outweighs the advantage of being the first in Kadosh, the

§ 18 [1] I.e., who created the world, the story of which commences with thee—*b'reshith* (in the beginning).
[2] J. Hag. a.l. reads: י״י is His name, Adon (אדון) is His name. Thus the backward projection points back to *alef*, standing for אדון. But Yalkut reads: the Lord is One (אחד) is His name; i.e., it points back to א, which is numerically one.

§ 19 [1] In the traditional writing of the Torah certain letters are embellished with strokes or "crowns."
[2] Neither the text nor the exact meaning is certain.
[3] All Hebrew letters are also numbers.

ANTHOLOGY

Holy One. In vain did Zadde call attention to Zaddik, the Righteous One; there was Zarot, the misfortunes of Israel, to testify against it. Pe had Podeh, redeemer, to its credit, but Pesha', transgression, reflected dishonor upon it. 'Ain was declared unfit, because, though it begins 'Anawah, humility, it performs the same service for 'Erwah, immorality. Samek said: "O Lord, may it be Thy will to begin the creation with me, for Thou are called Somek, after me, the Upholder of all that fall." But God said: "Thou art needed in the place in which thou art; thou must continue to uphold all that fall." Nun introduces Ner, "the lamp of the Lord," which is "the spirit of man," but it also introduces Ner, "the lamp of the wicked," which will be put out by God. Mem starts Melek, king, one of the titles of God. As it is the first letter of Mehumah, confusion, as well, it had no chance of accomplishing its desire. The claim of Lamed bore its refutation within itself. It advanced the argument that it was the first letter of Luhot, the celestial tables for the Ten Commandments; it forgot that the tables were shivered in pieces by Moses. Kaf was sure of victory. Kisseh, the throne of God, Kabod, His honor, and Keter, His crown, all begin with it. God had to remind it that He would smite together His hands, Kaf, in despair over the misfortunes of Israel. Yod at first sight seemed the appropriate letter for the beginning of creation, on account of its association with Yah, God, if only Yetser ha-Ra, the evil inclination, had not happened to begin with it, too. Tet is identified with Tob, the good. However, the truly good is not in this world; it belongs to the world to come. Het is the first letter of Hanun, the Gracious One; but this advantage is offset by its place in the word sin, Hattat. Zain suggests Zakor, remembrance, but it is itself the word for weapon, the doer of mischief. Waw and He compose the Ineffable Name of God; they are therefore too exalted to be pressed into the service of the mundane world. If Dalet had stood only for Dabar, the Divine Word, it would have been used, but it stands also for Din, justice, and under the rule of law without love the world would have fallen to ruin. Finally, in spite of reminding one of Gadol, great, Gimel would not do, because Gemul, retribution, starts with it.

After the claims of all these letters had been disposed of, Bet stepped before the Holy One, blessed be He, and pleaded before Him: "O Lord of the world! May it be Thy will to create Thy world through me, seeing that all the dwellers in the world give praise daily unto Thee through me, as it is said, 'Blessed be the Lord forever. Amen, and Amen.'" The Holy One, blessed be He, at once granted the petition of Bet. He said, "Blessed be he that cometh in the name of the Lord."[1] And He created His world through Bet, as it is said, "Bereshit God created the heaven and the earth."

The only letter that had refrained from urging its claim was the modest Alef, and God rewarded it later for its humility by giving it the first place in the Decalogue.

Alphabet 2 of Rabbi Akiba, 50-55.
Ginzberg Legends, pp. 5-8.

21. IN THE BEGINNING (B'RESHITH). Abraham spake before the Holy One, blessed be He: "Sovereign of the Universe! Why hast Thou exiled my children and delivered them into the hands of heathen nations who murdered them with all kinds of unnatural deaths; and why hast Thou destroyed the Temple, the place where I offered my son Isaac as a burnt-offering before Thee?" The Holy One, blessed be He, replied to Abraham, "Thy children sinned and transgressed the whole of the Torah and the twenty-two letters in which it is composed"; and so it is stated, *Yea, all Israel have transgressed Thy law* (Dan. 9:11). Abraham spake before the Holy One, blessed be He: "Sovereign of the Universe, who testifies against Israel that they transgressed Thy law?" "Let the twenty-

§ 20 [1] The point of this utterance by the *beth* is that its plea succeeded because it was made "*in the name of the Lord*" and to His glory. (Ed.)

ANTHOLOGY

two letters come and testify against Israel," said the Almighty . . . The *beth* came to testify against Israel, but Abraham reproached it, saying: "My daughter, thou comest to testify against my children who are zealous about the Pentateuch of which thou are the first letter, as it is written, *B'reshith* (*in the beginning*) *God created*!" The *beth* immediately stood aside and gave no testimony against them.

Proem to Lam. R. 24. T.S. 1, 10.

21A. In the beginning (b'reshith). R. Johanan opened his discourse: *A house is to be built with wisdom* (Prov. 24:3). The proper order of things is for one first to build a house to live in, then plant a vineyard for his livelihood, and after that marry, raise and support a family. This we learn from God. First He built a house, and then provided food and the means of maintenance before man arrived. Thus He first created the world, man's home; then He prepared sustenance—cattle, fowl, fish, and vegetation. Only then did He create man and his mate, so that children were born and society established. Therefore Scripture writes *B'reshith*, which can be read *Bayith rosh* (the house is first).

Midrash Haneelam B'reshith. T.S. 1, 64.

22. In the beginning (b'reshith). Wherefore is the letter *beth* closed on all sides save in the front? To indicate that He (God) is the home (*bayith*) of the world, that is to say, He is the place of the world, but the world is not His place.[1] Therefore, do not call the letter *beth*, but *bayith*, a house. Thus Scripture writes, *Through wisdom doth God, the Home of the world, build the universe* (Prov. 24:3).[2]

Sefer Habahir 11. T.S. 1, 23.

23. In the beginning (b'reshith). The Torah commences with a *beth* and ends with a *lamed*, its last words being, *in the sight of all Israel*. These two letters combined form the word *bal* (nought); reversed, they read *leb* (heart). Thus said God to Israel: If ye will serve Me in this twofold manner, viz., with a sense of your own nothingness and with your heart (i.e., with humility and devotion), I will account it to you as if you fulfilled the entire Torah from the *beth* to the *lamed*.

Alphabet of Rabbi Akiba. T.S. 1, 19.

24. In the beginning God created. When it entered His mind to create the world, He drew the plan of a world, but it would not stand until He created repentance. Seven things were created prior to the creation of the world, viz.: the Law, repentance, the throne of glory, the Garden of Eden, Gehinom, the site of the temple, and the name of the Messiah.

Ten things were paramount in the thought of God at the creation, viz.: Jerusalem, the spirits of the patriarchs, the ways of the righteous, Gehinom, the flood, the double tables of stone, the Sabbath, the temple, the ark, and the light of the future world.

Chronicles of Jerahmeel.
Gaster, pp. 5,6 1:1; 1:4.

25. In the beginning (b'reshith) God created. R. Oshaya commenced his exposition thus: *Then I was by Him, as an amon* (AJV: nursling) (Prov. 8:30). *Amon* is a workman (*uman*). The Torah declares: "I was the working tool of the Holy One, blessed be He." Now, when a king builds a palace, he employs an architect. The architect does not build it out of his head, but uses plans and diagrams for the correct placing of the chambers and doors. Similarly, God consulted the Torah and created the world. Hence the Torah states, *By means of the* Beginning *God created*, "*beginning*" meaning the Torah, as in the verse, *The Lord made me* (*the Torah*) *as* the beginning *of His way* (Prov. 8:22).

Gen. R. 1. T.S. 1, 45.

§ 22 [1] The world is contained in Him, but He is not contained in it.
[2] AJV: *Through wisdom a house is builded.* The present rendering is required by the context, as otherwise it is irrelevant. It involves reading *yivneh* (*kal*, active) instead of *yibaneh* (*nifal*, passive) in the Hebrew. The letters are the same.

ANTHOLOGY

26. IN THE BEGINNING (B'RESHITH) GOD CREATED. R. Banait said: The world in its fulness was created only for the sake of the Torah, as it says, *The Lord founded the earth for the sake of wisdom* (i.e., the Torah) (Prov. 3:19). R. Berekiah said: For the sake of Moses, as it says, *And He* (Moses) *saw that the Beginning* (i.e., the creation) *was for his own sake* (Deut. 33:21).

R. Huna said in R. Mattenah's name: The world was created for the sake of three things: The first-dough (one of the priestly dues), tithes, and first-fruits. What is the proof? For the *sake of* Reshith *God created. Reshith* means the first dough, for it is written, *Of the first* (*reshith*) *of your dough* (Num. 15:20); it also means tithes, for it is written, *The first-fruits* (*reshith*) *of thy corn* (Deut. 18:4); and finally it connotes first-fruits, for it is written, The *first-fruits* (reshith) *of the ripening produce of thy land,* etc. (Exod. 23:19).

Another interpretation: The world was created for the sake of the three things which are called *reshith,* viz., the Torah, Israel, and the fear of God. Torah: *The Lord made me* (the Torah) *as the beginning of* (reshith) *His way* (Prov. 8:22). Israel: *Israel is the Lord's hallowed portion, His first-fruits* (reshith) *of the increase* (Jer. 2:3). The fear of God: *The fear of the Lord is the beginning of* (reshith) *wisdom* (Prov. 3:10).

Gen. R. 1; Alphabet of Rabbi Akiba. T.S. 1, 47. 53.

27. IN THE BEGINNING GOD CREATED. The whole world naturally was created for the pious, the God-fearing man, whom Israel produces with the helpful guidance of the law of God revealed to him. It was Israel therefore who was taken into special consideration at the time man was made. All other creatures were instructed to change their nature, if Israel should ever need their help in the course of his history. The sea was ordered to divide before Moses, and the heavens to give ear to the words of the leader; the sun and the moon were bidden to stand still before Joshua, the ravens to feed Elijah, the fire to spare the three youths in the furnace, the lion to do no harm to Daniel, the fish to spew forth Jonah, and the heavens to open before Ezekiel.

Gen. R. 1: 4; 5:5. Ginzberg Legends, p. 50.

28. IN THE BEGINNING (B'RESHITH) GOD CREATED. R. Abba expounded: *In that day the Lord made a covenant with Abraham* (15:18). Covenants were subsequently made in respect of five objects, namely — Circumcision, the Rainbow, Salt (as an essential of sacrifices), Suffering, and the Priesthood. Before then there was only the covenant of fire made with Abraham, as it says . . . *behold a smoking furnace and a torch of fire that passed between these pieces. In that day the Lord made a covenant with Abram* (15:17-18); thus in the beginning there was only a covenant of fire. This is implied in the word *B'reshith*: by removing *esh* from the middle you are left with *b'rith*: thus *B'reshith-b'rith esh* (a covenant of fire).

Midrash Haneelam B'reshith Zohar Hadash 4. T.S. 1, 65.

29. IN THE BEGINNING (B'RESHITH). R. Nehemiah, brother of R. Shalemia, observed: The letters of *B'reshith,* when transposed, read *Yare Shabbath,* a Sabbath observer. This intimates that Sabbath observance is an acknowledgment that the world was newly created, and not eternal. This in turn is a confession of Him who so created it. In like manner, all fundamental articles of faith are interwoven, and all ultimately find expression in Sabbath observance.[1]

Midrash Me Hashiloach. T.S. 1, 84.

30. IN THE BEGINNING (B'RESHITH). The Hebrew words *Reshith* and *Rishon* are always spelled out in full, to indicate that God is the

§ 29 [1] Every principle of Faith presupposes the existence of God, the Creator, to the belief in Whom Sabbath observance testifies.

ANTHOLOGY

head of all, and created the world alone, without anyone else participating.

Midrash Haseroth Viy'theroth. T.S. 1, 55.

31. IN THE BEGINNING GOD CREATED. R. Judah said, quoting Akilas:[1] Him it is fitting to designate God. An earthly king is praised by his subjects even before he has built them public or private baths. Thus he first mentions his name and only afterwards his achievements. But God first wrought, and then was praised. Simeon b. 'Azzai quoted: *And Thy modesty hath made me great* (2 Sam. 22:36). A human being states his name first and then his title, thus: So-and-so the Prefect, So-and-so of whatever title it may be. But the Holy one, blessed be He, is not so, for He recorded His name only after creating the requirements of His universe: *In the beginning created,* and then *God.*

Gen. R. 1. T.S. 1, 200.

32. IN THE BEGINNING GOD CREATED. A man should practice worldly pursuits, yet set aside a time for the study of the Torah too, laboring in both, for this will keep him from sin. Should one say, "I come from aristocratic forebears, of noble lineage; it is not proper for me to degrade myself by work," then say to him, "Fool, long ago your Maker preceded you as a worker, as we read, *In the beginning God created the heaven and the earth.* He did work before you came into the world, as it says, *And He rested from all His work which God in creating had made.* Thus He called His act of creation work. It is also so designated in the verse, *and He rested on the seventh day from all His work which He had made.* In like vein R. Johanan observed: Do you know why God formed man last of all His creations? In order to teach you that He worked every day and created the world and all the hosts thereof, and on the sixth day, which was the last working day, He created man, saying to him, "Up to now *I* worked diligently, from now on it behooves you to do the same." This motive is implied in the passage, *In the beginning God created*: before Man came upon the scene, so that His working should be an example to him.

Midrash Haneelam B'reshith in Zohar Hadash 5. T.S. 1, 263.

33. GOD CREATED (BARA ELOHIM). Heretics asked Rabbi Simlai: "How many gods created the world?" He answered, "Why ask me? Go to Adam, and ask him, as it says, *For ask now of the days past, since the day that God created Adam upon the earth* (Deut. 4:32), where 'created' (*bara*) is in the singular, and not in the plural (*bar'u*)." They retorted: "But the Bible says, *In the beginning elohim* (plural) *created!*" He rejoined: "But *bara* (singular) is used, and not *bar'u* (plural)."

J. Berachot 9:1. T.S. 1, 196.

34. IN THE BEGINNING GOD CREATED. R. Isaac commenced with, *The beginning of Thy word is truth; and all Thy righteous ordinance endureth for ever* (Ps. 119:160). Said R. Isaac: From the very commencement of the world's creation, *The beginning of Thy word is truth. In the beginning God created* corroborates the statement, for "God" means truth, as it says, *But the Lord God is the true God* (Jer. 10:10). In consequence, *All Thy righteous ordinance endureth for ever* (Ps. loc. cit.). For in every single decree which Thou dost order concerning Thy creatures, they affirm the righteousness of Thy judgment and accept it with faith. And no person can affirm that two powers gave the Torah or two powers created the world. For "*And* the gods *spake*" is not written here, but, *And* God *spake all these words* (Exod. 20:1).[1]

§ 31 [1] The famous proselyte who translated the Bible into Greek, and who was said to be a relation by marriage to Hadrian; v. J.E. s.v. Aquila.

§ 34 [1] This is the verse which introduces Revelation.

ANTHOLOGY

Not *In the beginning the gods created,* but *In the beginning God created.*[2]

Gen. R. 1. T.S. 1, 199.

35. IN THE BEGINNING GOD CREATED. Ordinarily a human king is honored in his realm and the great of the realm are honored with him. Wherefore? Because they bear the burden of State with him. The Holy One, blessed be He, however, is not so, but He alone created His world, and He alone is glorified in His universe. R. Tanhuma quoted, *For Thou art great and doest wondrous things* (Ps. 86:10). Wherefore? *Because Thou God art alone* (ibid.). Thou alone didst create the world. Hence, *In the beginning God created.*

Gen. R. 1. T.S. 1, 198.

36. GOD CREATED. Scripture teaches that the world was created from naught; therefore the term Creation is used.[1]

Midrash Hagadol. T.S. 1, 224.

37. IN THE BEGINNING GOD CREATED. It is related of King Ptolemy that he brought together seventy-two Elders and placed them in seventy-two rooms, without telling them why he had brought them together. Then he visited each separately and said to him, "Translate for me the Torah of Moses your teacher." God prompted each of them, and they all conceived the same idea and wrote for him, *God created in the beginning.*[1]

Megillah 9a. T.S. 1, 197.

38. IN THE BEGINNING (ELOHIM) GOD CREATED. R. Judah said: May the name of God, King of kings, the Holy One, be blessed and exalted, for He is the first and the last, and beside Him there is no God. He created the world with the mystery of three great and good powers: Knowledge, Wisdom and Intelligence. At the head of all created things He created the form of the holy angels, who were the first of all created beings, emanating from the light of His lustrous glory. Ten names they bear in their mystery, one of these names being Elohim. Thus Scripture teaches, *In the beginning He* (God) *created* (the form of the angels, who are called) *Elohim.* They were the foundation of all the subsequent creation. From this foundation heaven was subsequently created by the mystery of Intelligence.

Midrash Haneelam B'reshith in Zohar Hadash 4. T.S. 1, 218.

39. IN THE BEGINNING ELOHIM (GOD) CREATED. Scripture says, *They exist today according to Thy judgments* (Ps. 119:91).[1] God first created the world on the basis of absolute justice, as it says, *In the beginning Elohim* (the God of Justice) created. But He did not rest content until He tempered justice with mercy as a principle of Divine government, even as we read, *on the day that Adonai Elohim* (the God of mercy and justice) *made earth and heaven* (2:4). For that reason Elohim is always spelled defectively in the Bible (without the letter *waw* which is used in many words for the vowel ō). Now, consider the first time it occurs, viz., *In the beginning Elohim created*: why is it spelled defectively there? Because God does not exact full justice from His creatures; for if He did, the world could not exist even a single hour. Rain too did not descend until it was blended with the spirit of mercy, as is written, *For Adonoi Elohim withheld rain from the earth* (Ibid. 2:5). Adam, the first man, did not come into existence until He compounded him with the quality of mercy, as it says, Adonai Elohim *formed man* (Ibid. 2:7).

Midrash Jelamdenu; Midrash Haser V'yatir. T.S. 1, 209. 213.

[2] The point is that though *Elohim* (God) is plural in form, the accompanying verb is always in the singular. This is a polemic against the Gnostics; v. Graetz, *History of the Jews* (Eng. trans.), vol. II, pp. 377 *seq.*

§ 36 [1] That is the meaning of *bara*, created.

§ 37 [1] Instead of: In the beginning God created. Several explanations of the change of order have been suggested. The most likely is that the usual order might mean: In the beginning one created God.

§ 39 [1] This Midrash rests on the Rabbinic interpretations of *Elohim* and *Adonai* as the God of justice and mercy respectively.

ANTHOLOGY

40. IN THE BEGINNING GOD (ELOHIM) CREATED. It is written, *The king by justice establisheth the land* (Prov. 29:4); this refers to the Holy One, blessed be He, who created the world with Justice, as it says, *In the beginning God (Elohim) created.* It does not say, The Lord (Adonai) created, but *Elohim;* likewise, not, and the Lord (Adonai) said: Let there be a *firmament,* but *God* (Elohim) *said,* etc.; and similarly the rest.[1] Thus too said David: *For God* (Elohim) *is judge* (Ps. 75:8)—to teach you that the world was created with Justice. *But the man of separation* (terumoth) *overthroweth it* (Prov. 29 4)—this refers to Adam.[2]

Gen. R. 14; Exod. R. 30. T.S. 1, 201.

41. IN THE BEGINNING ELOHIM (GOD) CREATED. R. Levi commented on, *In the beginning Elohim* (the God of justice) *created*: this teaches that the Attribute of Justice stipulated with the works of Creation to be subservient to it when necessary, and change their nature and function.[1]

Midrash Me Hashiloah. T.S. 1, 221.

42. IN THE BEGINNING GOD CREATED. R. Simeon b. Yohai said: Woe to the blasphemers, who take God's name needlessly. For one must not declare, "I vow this to the Lord as a sacrifice," . . . "to the Lord as a burnt-offering" . . . "to the Lord as a peace-offering"; but as it says, *When any man of you bringeth an offering unto the Lord* (Lev. 1:2), "*offering*" preceding "*the Lord*"; so must one declare, "I vow a sin-offering," or "a burnt-offering," or "a meal offering, to the Lord." You may learn this from the verse, *In the beginning created,* after which comes "*God*" (this being the order in Hebrew): only after describing His work does it mention His name.

Tanhuma Yashan B'reshith 1:6. T.S. 1, 206.

43. **The heaven (shamayim).**

Shamayim is equivalent to *Shamim* (they weigh), indicating that they (the heavens) weigh men's deeds: if one is worthy, *The heavens declare his righteousness* (Ps. 97:6); but if not, *the heavens shall reveal his iniquity* (Job 20:27).

Gen. R. 4. T.S. 1, 232.

44. THE HEAVEN (SHAMAYIM). *Shamayim* is so called because men wonder (*mishtommemim*) at it, saying: "Of what is it composed? Of fire? Of water? 'Tis a mystery!" R. Phinehas said in R. Levi's name: Scripture explains it: *Who layest the beams of Thine upper chambers in the waters* (Ps. 104:3): this shows that it is of water.

Gen. R. a. l. T.S. 1, 233.

45. THE HEAVEN (SHAMAYIM). What does *shamayim* mean? R. Jose b. Hanina said: It means, In that place is water (*sham mayim*). In a Baraitha it was taught: Fire and water (*Esh mayim*): this teaches that the Holy One, blessed be He, fused these elements and made from them the firmament.

Hagigah 12b. T.S. 1, 225.

46. THE HEAVEN (SHAMAYIM). What does the word *Shamayim* connote? That God kneaded fire and water and fused them, and made them the subject of His first utterance, as it is written *Thy first utterance is true* (Ps. 119:160). That is the meaning of *Shamayim,* which can be read both as *Sham Mayim,* water is found there, and *Esh Mayim,* fire and water; and they were charged: Thus far and no further (each element being forbidden to encroach upon the other). Thus may God, Who makes

§ 40 [1] "*Adonai*" stresses God's attribute of Mercy, and "*Elohim*" that of strict Justice; cf. Gen. R. 14:1.
[2] I.e., Adam, by separating himself from God's command and disobeying it, overthrew the concept of Justice as the *sole* basis of Divine Judgment, since now Mercy had to be added. AJV: *But he that exacteth gifts.*

§ 41 [1] From the very beginning of the Creation it was ordained that Nature abandon its laws when the dictates of Justice demand it. This explains that the violation of the laws of Nature which miracles necessitate is only apparent, because it was inherent in Nature from the very beginning.

ANTHOLOGY

peace above,[1] make us dwell in peace and mutual love.

Sefer Habahir 29. T.S. 1, 268.

47. THE HEAVEN AND THE EARTH. There are three basic elements in the world, viz., air, water, and fire. First Heaven was created from fire; then the Earth from water, and finally the air from wind, to preserve the balance.[1]

Sefer Yetsira 3:3. T.S. 1, 254.

48. THE HEAVEN (SHAMAYIM). R. Isaac said: *Shamayim* means *sa mayim,* be laden with water. Compare this to milk in a bowl: before a drop of rennet falls into it, it quivers; but as soon as a drop of rennet falls into it, it curdles and becomes firm. Similarly, on the first day *The pillars of heaven quiver* (*Job* 26:11); after that (on the second day) the solidifying substance was infused into them, whereupon, *And there was evening and there was morning, a second day.*

Gen. R. 4. T.S. 1, 235.

49. THE HEAVEN (SHAMAYIM). Whence was the Heaven created?—From the light of God's garment. From that He took light and spread it like a garment, and it went on extending until God said, "Enough!" God is called *Shaddai,* because He said to Heaven, "Dai!" (Enough), whereupon Heaven stood still. Whence do we learn that Heaven was created from the light of God's garment? From the verse, *Who coverest Thyself with light as with a garment, Who stretchest out the heavens like a curtain* (Ps. 104:2).

Pirke di-Rabbi Eliezer Chap. 3. T.S. 1, 249.

50. AND THE EARTH (HA-ARETZ). It is so called because all speed (*ratz*) to it, as it says, *all are derived from the earth and all return thereto* (Ecc. 3:20).

P'sikta Zutrathi B'reshith. T.S. 1, 275.

51. THE HEAVEN AND THE EARTH. The School of Shammai holds that heaven was created first, and then the earth. The School of Hillel maintains that the earth was created first, and heaven came later. Both offer reasons for their views. The former quoted, *In the beginning God created the heaven and the earth,* heaven being mentioned first. It is just as a king makes a throne and then constructs a footstool for it; so we read, *The heaven is My throne, and the earth is My footstool* (Isa. 66:1). The latter cited, *In the day that the Lord God made earth and heaven* (2:4), earth coming first. Just as a king who builds a palace constructs the lower stories first and then the upper ones. So also it says, *Yea, My hand hath laid the foundation of the* earth, *and My right hand hath spread out the* heavens (Isa. 48:13). R. Judah b. Pazzi said: This text supports the School of Hillel: *Of old Thou didst lay the foundations of the earth, and the heavens are the work of Thy hands* (Ps. 102:26). R. Hanina observed: From the very passage the Shammaites quote, the Hillelites refute them: Thus the proof of the former is the verse: *In the beginning God created the heaven and the earth*: but this is immediately followed by the words: *And the earth was,* etc., which means that the earth had already been in existence before the heaven was formed.[1] R. Johanan taught in the name of the Sages: Heaven was *created* first, but the earth was *perfected* first. Thus, *In the beginning God created the heaven and the earth;* whereas the second text reads, *in the day that the Lord God made* (i.e., perfected) *earth and heaven.* R. Simeon b. Yohai commented: I am astonished that these great teachers debated the matter at all; surely both heaven and the earth were forged simultaneously like a pot with its lid (which are made simultaneously in the same mould), as the Bible expresses it: *Yea, My hand hath laid the foundations of the earth, and My right hand hath*

§ 46 [1] By reconciling even such elements which by nature are at war, for water extinguishes fire, whilst fire makes water evaporate.

§ 47 [1] Air is regarded as partaking of both heaven and earth. This third element thus preserves the balance in Nature between the celestial and the terrestrial, that neither may claim predominance.

§ 51 [1] The Hebrew is really pluperfect: And the earth had been.

ANTHOLOGY

spread out the heavens. R. Eleazar b. R. Simeon commented: My father's opinion explains why Scripture sometimes gives precedence to the earth over the heaven, and at others the reverse, which teaches that they are equals.

J. Hagigah 2:1. T.S. 1, 230.

52. THE HEAVEN AND THE EARTH. Alexander of Macedon put ten questions to the elders of the South,[1] of which one was, Was heaven or earth created first? They replied: Heaven, as it says: *In the beginning God created* heaven *and* earth.

Tamid 32. T.S. 1, 228.

53. THE HEAVEN AND THE EARTH. When a human king wishes to build a palace, he first builds the nether stories and then the upper ones; but with God it is not so, for only after He had built the topmost stories did He build the lower ones, for it says, *In the beginning God created the heaven and* then *the earth*.

Exod. R. 25. T.S. 1, 243.

54. THE HEAVEN AND THE EARTH. Our Rabbis said: Mortal man builds an edifice, and if he succeeds in his plan he can widen it as the building rises;[1] otherwise he must broaden it below and narrow it above. The Holy One, blessed be He, is not so, however; *He created the heaven*, i.e., the heaven which he originally contemplated, and *the earth*, the earth which he originally contemplated.[2] R. Huna said, quoting R. Eliezer b. R. Jose the Galilean: Even those whereof it is written, *For, behold, I create new heavens* (Isa. 65:17), have been created long ago, since the six days of Creation, as it is written, *For as the new heavens and the new earth* . . . (ibid. 22): not "new" is written here, but "*the new*."[3]

Gen. R. 1. T.S. 1, 238.

55. **God created (eth) the heaven and (eth) the earth.**

R. Ishmael asked R. Akiba when they were travelling together: You who have studied twenty-two years under Nahum of Gimzo, who expounded every particle "*eth*" in the Torah, tell me how he explained the *eth* in (eth)[1] the *heaven and* (eth) *the earth*? Said R. Akiba to him: If it said, heaven and earth, without *eth* before each noun, I might have said that Heaven and Earth were names of the Holy One, blessed be He.[2] But now that *eth* stands before each, actual heaven and earth are meant. But why do we need *eth* before "*the earth*?"—To show that heaven was created before earth.[3]

Hagigah 12b. T.S. 1, 227.

56. GOD CREATED (ETH) THE HEAVEN AND (ETH) THE EARTH. R. Ishmael asked R. Akiba: Since you studied twenty-two years under Nahum of Gimzo, who formulated the principle that *ak* (save that) and *rak* (except) are limitations, while *eth* (the sign of the accusative) and *gam* (also) are extensions,[1] tell me what of the *eth* written here? Said he to him: If *eth* were omitted, we might have thought that heaven and earth too are divine powers.[2] Thereupon he cited the text *For it is no empty thing*

§ 52 [1] The Negev, the southern portion of Israel.

§ 54 [1] Only if it turns out as strong as he planned it can the upper portions be broader than the lower.

[2] He had no need to modify His original designs. Hence the definite article; for otherwise, since these were new creations, Scripture should have written, God created heaven and earth.

[3] The definite article implies the specific new heavens, viz., those created aforetime. 'E. J.: It intimates therefore that the new heavens were already created, but only potentially, i.e., in God's thought. Mah. explains it differently.

§ 55 [1] *Eth* is the sign of the accusative. But in Nahum of Gimzo's system of exegesis it was assumed to have a meaning over and above its grammatical function.

[2] I.e., these words might have been intepreted as standing in apposition to God: In the beginning, God (who is called) "heaven" and "earth," created.

[3] This is not clear. The point of the question is apparently that since the *eth* before "heaven" indicates that actual heaven is meant, this could then be taken for granted in the case of the earth.

§ 56 [1] Which extend and add to the verse.

[2] Rendering: In the beginning God, heaven, and earth created.

[2]**Now the earth was unformed and void, and darkness was upon the**

COMMENTARY

[2]**Now the earth.** Scripture's main interest is the earth, where man has his being. The earth, therefore, is its first subject of comment.[11] **unformed and void.** Heb. *tohu* and *bohu.* The following are the various interpretations: **a.** Desolation and emptiness.[12] **b.** Emptiness and chaos.[13] **c.** According to modern as well as some ancient commentators the earth, when first created, was an unformed and rarefied entity. Nowadays scientists call it "energy", and this is the *tohu* of Scripture. Subsequently this entity was condensed into "first matter," whose composition is commonly known today as "atomic"; this state of matter Scripture calls *bohu.*[14] (See also Appendix 2.) **darkness.** Heb. *hoshek,* may signify: **a.** Lack of light.[15] **b.** A positive entity.[16] **c.** The overcast air.[17] **upon the face of the deep.** Above the water

ANTHOLOGY

(Deut. 32:47), and if it is empty, that emptiness comes *from you* (ibid.), because you are unable to interpret it properly. *No*: *eth* preceding *the heavens* is to include the sun and moon, the stars and planets; *eth* preceding *the earth* is to include trees, herbage, and the Garden of Eden.

Gen. R. 1. T.S. 1, 236.

57. **Now the earth was unformed and void.**

Consider: Scripture commenced with Heaven: why then does it first treat of the earth? The School of R. Ishmael taught: It is like a king who said to his servants: Come early to my door. He rose early and found there men and women. Whom does he praise? Those who are not accustomed to but yet did rise early.[1]

Hagigah 12b. T.S. 1, 291.

58. NOW THE EARTH WAS UNFORMED (TOHU) AND VOID (BOHU). R. Judah said: The Holy One, blessed be He, treated the earth like a woman who first becomes pregnant and then brings forth the child. So did the earth become pregnant from the elements which entered in her, and then produced all her offspring. On the very day that she was created she was impregnated with everything which she subsequently begot, as it is written, *In the beginning God created the heaven and the earth.* In that very instant the earth conceived *tohu* and *bohu, darkness* and *wind;* these comprised the four elements: fire, water, wind, and darkness. These two generated all her offspring; from these all natural phenomena were produced, and all their issue were engendered by these powers.

Midrash Haneelam B'reshith Zohar Hadash 13. T.S. 1, 266.

59. NOW THE EARTH WAS UNFORMED AND VOID. This may be likened to a king who had two ministers; one sang whilst the other wept. "Why do you weep," the king asked; "have I not made you both equal?" "Sire," replied he, "my colleague abides with you and boards at your table; it is natural for him to sing. Me, you alienated and sent away far from you, and made my livelihood dependent on others; hence I weep." So it is with God. Heaven and Earth are to Him alike, as we read, *I call unto them* (Heaven and Earth): *they stand up together* (Isa. 48:13). Heaven sings, as it says, *The heavens declare the glory of God* (Ps. 19:2). But Earth weeps. She supplicates Heaven, saying, "O, Master of the Universe, Heaven and all that is therein enjoy the radiance of the Shekinah, and the Angel of Death has no dominion over them; hence they sing. But as for me, Thou has made me dependent on others for a livelihood, and the Angel of Death has dominion over all that is upon me; I therefore weep." God comforted the Earth, "Fear not, you too

§ 57 [1] In the same way it was quite natural for heaven to spring into existence immediately at God's fiat; earth however, might have been expected to show greater tardiness. Since she did not, but came into existence at His command simultaneously with heaven, she is praised by receiving this priority.

will sing one day"; as it says, *The Lord reigneth; let the earth rejoice* (ibid. 97:1); it is also written, *From the uttermost part of the earth have we heard songs* (Isa. 24:16).

Midrash Abakir, quoted in Yalkut Shimoni B'reshith. T.S. 1, 253.

60. AND THE EARTH WAS UNFORMED (TOHU) AND VOID (BOHU). R. Abbahu said: This may be compared to a king who bought two slaves on the same bill of sale and at the same price. One he ordered to be supported at the public expense, but the other he ordered to toil for his bread. The latter sat bewildered and astonished:[1] "Both of us were bought at the same price," exclaimed he, "yet he is supported from the treasury, whilst I have to gain my bread by my toil!" Thus the earth sat bewildered and astonished, saying, "The upper and the lower were created at the same time: yet the former are fed by the radiance of the *Shekinah,* whereas the latter if they do not toil, do not eat." R. Judah b. R. Simon said: Compare this to a king who bought two bondmaids, both on the same bill of sale and at the same price. One he commanded not to stir out of the palace, whereas the other he banished. The latter sat bewildered and astonished. "Both of us were bought on the same bill of sale, and at the same price," she exclaimed, "yet she does not stir from the palace, while me he has banished!" Thus the earth sat bewildered and astonished, lamenting, "The upper and the lower were created at the same time: why do the former live eternally, whereas the latter are mortal?" Therefore, *and the earth was tohu and bohu* (*bewildered and astonished*).

Gen. R. 2. T.S. 1, 300.

61. AND THE EARTH WAS UNFORMED (TOHU) AND VOID (BOHU). R. Tanhuma said: This may be compared to a royal infant sleeping in his cot, while his nurse sat by anxious and troubled. Why? Because she knew that she was fated to receive punishment at his hand. Thus the earth foresaw that she was destined to meet her doom at the hand of man, as it is written, *Cursed is the ground for thy sake* (3:17). Therefore *the earth was tohu and bohu* (*desolate and anxious*).

Gen. R. 2. T.S. 1, 301.

62. NOW THE EARTH WAS TOHU AND BOHU. When an earthly monarch builds a palace on a site of sewers, dunghills, and garbage, and one draws attention to the fact, does he not discredit it? Thus, whoever declares that this world was created out of *tohu* and *bohu*[1] and darkness, does he not indeed impugn God's creative activity! R. Huna said in Bar Kappara's name: If the matter were not written, it would be impossible to say it, viz., *God created heaven and earth;* out of what? Out of the materials mentioned in the verse, *Now the earth was tohu and bohu.*[2]

Gen. R. 2. T.S. 1, 239.

63. NOW THE EARTH WAS UNFORMED AND VOID. R. Berekiah quoted: *Even a child is known by his doings* (Prov. 20:11). While the earth was as yet in her infancy she produced thorns; and so the prophet was one day destined to prophesy of her, *I beheld the earth, and, lo, it was waste and void* (Jer. 4:23).[1]

Gen. R. 2. T.S. 1, 299.

64. AND THE EARTH WAS UNFORMED (TOHU). God formed from the void (tohu) a substance and made the nothing into a something, and quarried mighty pillars out of the insubstantial air. (Its mark of recognition is both revealing and concealing. The Maker of everything, and of all creatures, bears the stamp of the one

§ 60 [1] The words are connected with *tohu* and *bohu.*

§ 62 [1] Regarded as eternal, uncreated substances (matter).

[2] God first created *tohu* and *bohu,* these being very fine substances, and out of these He created the world. But this is not to be taught publicly (Y. T.).

§ 63 [1] This renders the text: In the beginning God created heaven and earth, and immediately after earth was created she was waste and void, producing nothing but spiritual thorns.

ANTHOLOGY

name—God, its sign-manual being, 22 elements compounded into one frame).[1]

Sefer Yetsira 2:6. T.S. 1, 318.

65. And the earth was unformed (tohu) and void (bohu), etc. A philosopher asked R. Gamaliel: "Your God was indeed a great artist, but surely He found good materials which assisted Him, viz., *tohu, bohu,* darkness, water, wind (*ruah*), and the deep?" "Confusion take you!" he exclaimed. "Creation" is written of all of them. *Tohu* and *bohu*: *I make peace and create evil* (Isa. 45:7);[1] darkness: *I form the light, and create darkness* (ib.); water: *Praise Him, ye heavens of heavens, and ye waters that are above the heavens* (Ps. 148:4) —wherefore?—*For He commanded, and they were created* (ib. 5); wind: *For, lo, He that formeth the mountains, and createth the wind* (Amos 4:13); the depths: *When there were no depths, I was brought forth* (Prov. 8:24).[2]

Gen. R. 1. T.S. 1, 298.

66. And the earth was tohu and bohu. The third mystic creative category consists of water distilled from spirit, out of which He hewed tohu and bohu.[1] The mire and refuse He graved into earthbed-like forms, hewed them into a wall-like shape, pressed them into loam, poured snow over them, and they became earth, as it says, *For He saith to the snow, Be thou earth* (Job 37:6). *Tohu* is the green line encompassing the whole world, out of which issued darkness, as it says, *He made* darkness *His hiding place round about Him* (Ps. 18:12). *Bohu* is the smooth stones sunk into the deep from between which issues the water.

Sefer Yetsira 1:11; Hagigah 12b. T.S. 1, 292. 316.

67. Now the earth was tohu and bohu. R. Berekiah said: When Scripture writes, *Now the earth was tohu and bohu,* "was" (Heb. ḥay'tha) implies that it had formerly been thus (tohu and bohu).[1] *Tohu* means a substance beyond human comprehension;[2] *bohu* is in a more developed state,[3] as it really should read *bo hu* (as two separate words), meaning, something substantial.

Sefer Habahir. T.S. 1, 325.

68. Now the earth was tohu and bohu. Now, what is meant by, *God also set one over against the other?* (Ecc. 7:14) He created *bohu,* and placed it in Peace; He created *tohu,* and set its place in Evil.[1] He placed bohu in Peace: This we learn from the text, *He maketh peace in His high places* (Job 25:2). Now Michael, the Prince at God's right hand, is Water and Hail, whilst Gabriel, the Prince at His left, is Fire. Thus they are mutually destructive, yet the Prince of Peace preserves a balance between them. Hence, the expression *He maketh peace in His high places.* And whence do we know

§ 64 [1] The "22 elements" is probably a reference to the letter mysticism, there being 22 letters in the Hebrew alphabet.

§ 65 [1] By *tohu* and *bohu* the philosopher meant primeval matter, without form. Thereupon R. Gamaliel quoted: I make *shalom* (that which is whole, i.e., what contains both matter and form) and evil, i.e., that which is defective, consisting of matter only without form. Thus that too was created. Perhaps, too, this is an allusion to the view that matter is a source of evil.

[2] Since at one time there were no depths, God must have created them.

§ 66 [1] *And the earth was tohu and bohu* is rendered by AJV *unformed and void.* But here they are understood to designate primal substances.

§ 67 [1] The meaning is doubtful. Several alternatives have been suggested.

a. The earth, i.e., the place which subsequently became the earth, had originally been tohu and bohu.
b. When the earth was already in existence it was still tohu and bohu.
c. The earth already existed before heaven was created. Most probably the first or second is meant here; the present rendering assumes the first interpretation.

[2] Tohu is here connected with *mat'he.* The substance is matter so fine, that the human mind cannot conceive it.

[3] Possibly tohu is formless matter whilst bohu is matter plus form. The rendering of the whole passage is only conjectural.

§ 68 [1] *Tohu* and *bohu* are regarded as elements created by God; whilst Peace and Evil are hypostatized as spiritual entities.

face of the deep; and the spirit of God hovered over the face of the

COMMENTARY

which covered the earth.[18] *the deep.* The primeval ocean that enveloped the whole globe.[19] **the spirit of God. a.** A wind sent by God that was blowing, etc.[20] **b.** The substratum of the atmosphere.[21] **c.** A raging tempest.[22] **d.** A spirit of grace and loving kindness emanating from God and hovering over the waters, as much as to say that the Shekinah (the Divine Presence) in Divine tranquility was engaged in bringing order into the chaos.[23] **the spirit of God hovered.** The Throne of Glory was suspended in the air and hovered over the waters like a dove hovering over a nest, sustained by the breath of God. It is called *the spirit of God,* because it was His servant to realize His will, that the waters be dried up and the land appear.[24]

ANTHOLOGY

that tohu is set in Evil? Because it is written, *I make peace, and create evil* (Isa. 45:7); now since *bohu* is associated with Peace, *tohu* must be associated with Evil.[2]

Sefer Habahir 1:9. T.S. 1, 326.

69. **And darkness was upon the face of the deep.**

Lo and behold, on the very first day of creation, God created the angel of death. Whence do we know this? R. Berekiah said: From the verse, *And darkness was upon the face of the deep,* which is an allusion to the angel of death who darkens the face of men.

Tanhuma Vayesheb. T.S. 1, 309.

70. AND DARKNESS WAS UPON THE FACE OF THE DEEP. R. Judah b. R. Ilai said: This may be likened to a king who desired to build a palace, but found the site dark. He therefore had to kindle a light before building his house. So did God. The world was dark, as we read, *Darkness was upon the face of the deep.* So He wrapped Himself with light and then created the world.

Midrash Tanhuma Vayakhel. T.S. 1, 310.

71. **And the spirit (ruah) of God, etc.**

You may raise the cartilage by means of a bandage on the Sabbath. Which cartilage do you mean? Said Rabbi Abba: The cartilage in front of the heart. What is the remedy for the nausea which its pressure causes? Take cumin, carraway, mint, wormwood, saturera and hyssop mixed in wine; catchwords: wine *maketh glad the* heart of *man* (Ps. 104:15). For defective breathing take this mixture in water. Catchwords: *the* breath (ruah) *of God hovered over the face of the* water.

Avodah Zorah 29a. T.S. 1, 295.

72. AND THE RUAH OF GOD HOVERED OVER THE FACE OF THE WATERS. *Tohu* is a colorless, nondescript place; *bohu* is one that has shape and form. *Hoshek*—darkness—is black fire of deepest hue, deep red fire, bright green fire, and white fire, which comprises all the other hues. *Hoshek*—darkness—is the most powerful of all fires, which overwhelmed and transformed *tohu. Hoshek* is a fire which ceased to be pure black when it overwhelmed *tohu. Ruah* —wind—is a sound which hovers over *bohu* and seizes and leads it wherever it is required. That is the esoteric meaning of the verses, *The voice of the Lord is upon the waters* (Ps. 29:3); and similarly, *And the* ruah *of God hovered over the face of the waters.*

Zohar 1:16. T.S. 1, 327.

73. AND THE EARTH WAS UNFORMED (TOHU) AND VOID (BOHU); AND DARKNESS WAS UPON THE FACE OF THE DEEP. *And the earth* alludes to the upper earth which has no light in herself. *Was* indicates that the world *had been* in its proper form, but was now *unformed and void. And darkness was*: Scripture says *was* precisely, which means, after it shrank

[2] Since tohu and bohu are coupled in Genesis, whilst Peace (which another verse has linked with bohu) and Evil are coupled in this verse, symmetry demands that tohu shall be linked with Evil.

COMMENTARY

hovered. The Heb. word occurs again only in Deut. 32:11, where it is descriptive of the eagle hovering over its young to care for and protect them. Matter in itself is lifeless. The Spirit of God quickens and transforms it into material for a living world. The Jerusalem Targum translates this verse: "And the earth was vacancy and desolation, solitary of the sons of men and void of every animal, and darkness was upon the face of the abyss; and the Spirit of Mercy from before the *Lord* breathed upon the face of the waters."[25]
over the face of the waters. That is, above the dark chaos and desolation hovered God, Source of Order,

ANTHOLOGY

and its light was diminished (only then did darkness cover the deep). *Tohu* (formlessness), *Bohu* (void),[1] *Darkness and Ruah* (Spirit)[2] are the four elements out of which the world was created. Another interpretation: The text *magnifies* the inferior (sublunar) earth, which consists of many compartments, unlike the superior (supra-lunar) earth, which has but one. This then is the meaning of the text, viz., *And the earth* (which was originally greater) *had become Tohu, Bohu, Darkness, and Ruah.*[3] The following are the different compartments of the Earth: Earth, Ground, Valley, Oblivion (N'shiyah), Desert (Tsiyah), dryland (Arka), and *tebel* (the populated earth); the greatest of all is *tebel,* as it is written, *And He will judge the tebel in righteousness* (Ps. 9:10). R. Jose asked: What is the meaning of Tsiyah? He was answered: The place of Gehinom, as Scripture says, *a land of tsiyah* (AJV: *drought*) *and the shadow of death* (Jer. 2:6). This mystery indeed is implied in the text, *And darkness was upon the face of the deep,* the esoteric teaching of which is, this is the place of Gehinom, this is Tsiyah, the place of the Angel of Death who darkens the faces of all creatures; the same is the place of upper darkness. *Tohu* is identical with N'shiyah, where nothing is seen and where one is forgotten by all, hence it is called N'shiyah (oblivion). *Bohu* is identical with Arka, the place where there is not oblivion. R. Hiyya said: It is rather to be identified with *Gey* (valley). *And the spirit of God hovered*: This corresponds to *Tebel,* which is nourished by the spirit of God. In like manner all this is contained in the superior (supra-lunar) world, where, however, it is all fused into one.

Zohar 8:39. T.S. 1, 329.

74. AND THE SPIRIT OF GOD HOVERED OVER THE FACE OF THE WATERS. Of two elements we are not told that they were created, viz., spirit and water, of which we read: *And the spirit of God hovered over the face of the water.* Creation is mentioned in the Creation story in reference to the universe and all therein, with the exception of water, spirit, and darkness, for it says, *And darkness was upon the face of the deep; and the spirit of God hovered over the face of the water.* This omission was made good by Isaiah, who declared, *I (God) form the light, and create darkness* (Isa. 45:7).

Midrash T'mura. T.S. 1, 320.

75. AND THE RUAH (SPIRIT) OF GOD, etc. R. Ishmael said: The numeral *one* has no exchange, nor a second.[1] So God too has no *second.* No man knows where God's habitation is. The celestial beings do not know this, not

§ 73 [1] Kasher in T.S. 1, 325, quotes two opposite views on tohu and bohu, according to which they are Formless Matter (Potentiality) and Form (Actuality) respectively, or the reverse.
[2] See p. 20, note 2 on par. 75.
[3] This rendering is only conjectural. Another possible (though rather improbable) meaning is this: And these many compartments are Tohu, etc., regarding Tohu, Bohu, Darkness (envisaged not as merely the absence of light but as a positive element in itself) and Ruach. In that case what follows is *another* classification of Earth's compartments.

§ 75 [1] This apparently means that whilst the word "first" is relative and automatically implies a second, "one" is absolute. The allusion is to the fact that whereas the days of Creation from the second onwards are described as "a second day," "a third day," etc., the first is not called "a first day" but "one day." This implies absoluteness, a day which stands quite apart, self-contained, as it were, and it is taken as providing an analogy for God, that He too is absolute.

ANTHOLOGY

even the angels who hymn His glory, as it says, *Blessed be the glory of the Lord from His place* (Ezek. 3:12), not stating where that place may be. Neither do heaven and earth sing His praises from the place where He abides, not knowing His place. Thus, the members of the Great Sanhedrin of the Chamber of Hewn Stones in the Temple called God the place of the world, but not the world His place. The *ruah*[2] has no existence but as an appanage of the Almighty, as we read, *And the ruah hovered; The ruah* (AJV *spirit*) *of God hath made me* (Job 33:4); *By the ruah* (AJV *breath*) *of God ice is given* (ibid. 37:10); *And now the Lord God hath sent me and His ruah* (AJV *spirit*) (Isa. 48:16); *The ruah of the Lord spoke by me* (2 Sam. 23:2); *Thou sendest forth Thy ruah and they are created* (Ps. 104:30). One has but to add, *Give instruction to a wise man and he will be wiser yet* (Prov. 9:9).[3]

Midrash T'mura 2. T.S. 1, 321.

76. AND THE SPIRIT (RUAH) OF GOD, etc. Four winds were created in the world, viz., the winds coming from the east, south, north, and west. From the eastern corner the light of the world goeth forth; from the south, the dews of blessing descend upon the world; from the west emanate the stores of snow, hail, cold and heat, and rains for the benefit of the world; the north corner of the world He created, but did not complete, for He said: Whoever declares himself to be God, let him come and finish this corner which I have left, and then shall all know that he is God.[1]

Chronicles of Jerahmeel. Gaster, p. 6. (1:7).

77. AND THE SPIRIT OF GOD HOVERED OVER THE FACE OF THE WATERS. A royal personage asked Rabbi Akiba on what the world is based. The Sage answered that it stands on wind.[1] "Prove it to me," he demanded. "Bring me camels laden with salt," said R. Akiba. When they were brought before him he led them all around the house and asked them what they saw. "Camels laden with salt," they answered. Akiba then called for a rope. It was brought, whereupon he wound them about their necks, gave the ends to two men and told each to pull his end, until they strangled the camels. Now, said he, make them stand up. "What!" the questioner rejoined, "You who are the Sage of the Jews ask me to make them stand up after you strangled them!" "But the camels lost only their breath," R. Akiba retorted. This proves that the world exists only through the spirit, which is indeed precious and wonderful and already existed at the very beginning, as it says, *And the spirit of God hovered over the face of the waters.*

Midrash T'mura. T.S. 1, 319.

78. AND THE SPIRIT OF GOD HOVERED OVER THE FACE OF THE WATERS. Our Rabbis taught: R. Joshua b. Hanina was standing on a step on the Temple Mount, and Ben Zoma saw him and did not stand up before him. So (R. Joshua) said to him: "Whence and whither, Ben Zoma?" He replied: "I was meditating upon the upper and the lower waters, and concluded that there is only a bare three fingers' breadth between them, for it says, *And the spirit of God hovered over the face of the waters,* like a dove which hovers over her young without touching them." Thereupon R. Joshua said to his disciples: "Ben Zoma is still out of his mind. See now, when was it that *the spirit of God hovered over the face of the waters?* On the first day (of Creation); whereas the division took place on the second day, for it is written: *And let it divide the waters from the waters* (1:6). And how great (is the interval?)" R. Aha b. Jacobs said:

[2] *Ruah* is variously rendered spirit, wind and breath. In the present instance it may simply connote air. (So also Maimonides.)

[3] In all these verses "*ruah*" is coupled with "God," which is taken as proving that it has no independent existence. The last verse suggests that all these verses are a hint from which the wise man can learn yet deeper mysteries.

§ 76 [1] In this passage the text "And the ruach of God" is rendered "*And the* wind *of God*."

§ 77 [1] Heb. *ruach,* which variously means wind, breath, and spirit.

ANTHOLOGY

As a hair's breadth; whilst the Rabbis said: As between the boards of a landing bridge. Mar Zutra, or according to others R. Assi, said: As between two cloaks spread one over the other; others say: As two cups tilted one over the other.

Hagigah 15a. T.S. 1, 293.

79. NOW THE EARTH WAS TOHU (UNFORMED), etc. R. Simeon b. Lakish applied our text to the countries of exile. *Now the earth was tohu (unformed)* symbolizes Babylonia: *I beheld the earth, and lo, it was tohu (waste)* (Jer. 4:23);[1] *And bohu (void)* symbolizes Media: *They hastened* (wa-yabhillu) *to bring Haman* (Est. 6:14).[2] *And darkness* symbolizes Greece, which darkened the eyes of Israel with its decrees, ordering, "Write on the horn of an ox that ye have no portion in the God of Israel."[3] *Upon the face of the deep* alludes to this evil Empire (Rome), whose wickedness is as unfathomable as the great deep. *And the spirit of God hovered*: this alludes to the spirit of Messiah, who has existed from the very beginning of Creation, as you read, *And the spirit of the Lord shall rest upon him* (Isa. 11:2). In whose merit will this spirit eventually come? Scripture writes, *Hovered over the face of the waters,* i.e., the Messiah hovers and waits for repentance which is likened to water, as it is written, *Pour out thy heart like water* (Lam. 2:19).

Gen. R. 2; P'sikta Rabbathi 33.
T.S. 1, 303. 312.

80. AND THE SPIRIT OF GOD HOVERED. R. Johanan commenced his discourse: *Thou hast formed me late and early,* etc. (Ps. 139:5). R. Simeon b. Lakish interpreted: He was the latest in the work of the last day and the earliest in the work of the first day. That is consistent with another teaching of his, viz.: *And the spirit of God hovered* refers to the soul of the King, the Messiah, as you read, *And the spirit of the Lord shall rest upon him* (Isa. 11:12). If a man deserves it, he is told, You were created before the angels. If not, he is told, Flies preceded you; gnats preceded you; worms preceded you.

Gen. R. 2. T.S. 1, 306.

81. AND THE SPIRIT OF GOD HOVERED OVER THE FACE OF THE WATERS. The care which God exercised in fashioning every detail of the body of man is as naught in comparison with His solicitude for the human soul. The soul of man was created on the first day, for it is the spirit of God moving upon the face of the waters. Thus, instead of being the last, man is really the first work of creation.

This spirit, or, to call it by its usual name, the soul of man, possesses five different powers. By means of one of them she escapes from the body every night, rises up to heaven, and fetches new life thence for man.

With the soul of Adam the souls of all the generations of men were created. They are stored up in a promptuary, in the seventh of the heavens, whence they are drawn as they are needed for human body after human body.

Gen. R. 8:1; 14.9; Tanhuma Pekude 3.
Ginzberg Legends, pp. 55-56.

82. AND THE SPIRIT OF GOD, etc. The following are the ten Sefiroth:[1] (1) Belimah; (2) the spirit of the living God; (3) Spirit from Spirit; (4) water from spirit; (5) fire from water; (6) the supra-lunar heights and the sublunar; (7) East, (8) West, (9) North, and (10) South.

Sefer Yetsira 1:11. T.S. 1, 317.

§ 79 [1] Jeremiah refers to the desolation wrought by the conquering might of Babylonia. *Tohu* and *bohu* are applied to Babylonia and Media (Persia) respectively in the sense that they caused chaos and destruction.
[2] This happened in Media. By a play on words *wa-yabhillu* is given the same derivation as *bohu*.
[3] The reference is to Antiochus who endeavored to annihilate Judaism by replacing it by Hellenism (hence "Greece"). "Write on the horn of an ox" probably implies a public disavowal of Judaism.

§ 82 [1] A term used in Kabbalah (a mystic Jewish lore) to denote the successive emanations from the Almighty which culminated in the Creation of the world.

waters. [3]And God said: 'Let there be light.' And there was light. [4]And

COMMENTARY

light and life.[26] [3]**And God said.** "Said" may mean: **a.** He willed.[27] **b.** He decreed in His wisdom.[28] **c.** An expression suggesting putting a plan into execution.[29] **d.** It may be taken in its ordinary sense, the Torah using here a human metaphor (anthropomorphism), as if God were a monarch issuing decrees at his pleasure, which are promptly complied with; that is to say, it did not require exhausting labor.[30] **Let there be light.** The following are the various opinions of the nature of the light that was created before the luminaries came into being: **a.** This light that pervaded the whole globe did not originate from the luminaries.[31] **b.** Some forces must have activated it to pass from potential to actual existence. Its luminescence was similar to that of the Aurora Borealis and Aurora Australis today, whose precise and immediate factors are likewise unknown, except for a vague feeling that some electromagnetic waves are responsible for their appearance.[32] As for the

ANTHOLOGY

83. **Let there be light.**

That light blazed forth and illumined the universe from end to end, and the world was created therewith. God saw it and, meditating on the wicked who would one day people the earth, He hid it away from them. Yet it still exists, preserving the world. This is the meaning of the text, *But the righteous is the foundation of the world* (Prov. 10:25). So too will he who is worthy resolve the mysteries of the Torah, as it says, *The Torah is a light* (*ibid.* 6:23), and, *God saw the light—eth haor,* the numerical value of which is 613, the number of the commandments which constitute the Torah; and that is the hidden light.

Midrash Ruth Zohar Hadash 85. T.S. 1, 403.

84. LET THERE BE LIGHT. This light emerged from the darkness which was hewed out by the strokes of the Most Secret; and likewise, from the light which was hidden away, through some secret path, there was hewed out the darkness of the lower world in which inheres light. This lower darkness is called "night" in the verse, *and the darkness He called night.*

Zohar, p. 30. G. Scholem.

85. LET THERE BE LIGHT. But was the light created on the first day? Surely it is written, *And God set them in the firmament of the heaven;* and in this same connection it is further written, *And there was evening and there was morning, a fourth day!* This is to be explained as R. Eleazar said: By the light which the Holy One, blessed be He, created on the first day one could see from one end of the world to the other; but when He beheld the generation of the Flood and the generation of the Division of races (Gen. 10:25; 11:1-9) and their corruptness, He arose and hid it from them, as it says, *But from the wicked their light is withholden* (Job 38:15). Now, for whom did He reserve it? For the righteous in the time to come, for it is said: *And God saw the light that it was good;* "good" refers to none but the righteous, as it says; *Say ye of the* righteous, *that he is* good (Isa. 3:10). As soon as the light saw that He had reserved it for the righteous, it rejoiced, for it is said, *The light of the righteous rejoiced* (Prov. 13:9). Scholars differ on the point. For we learned: By the light which the Holy One, blessed be He, created on the first day, one could see from one end of the world to the other; this is the view of R. Jacob. But the Sages say: It is identical with the luminaries, which were created on the first day, but not hung up in the firmament until the fourth day.

Hagigah 12b. T.S. 1, 386.

86. LET THERE BE LIGHT. Moses wrote many things in the Torah without explaining them; it was left to David to clarify them. Thus we find in the Creation story that *after* He had created the heavens and the earth He created the light, for it says: *In the beginning God created the heaven and the earth* and after that *And God said: Let there be light.* But David explained that it was in the reverse order, for

COMMENTARY

manner in which this light shed its luster upon the earth, opinions also vary: **c.** It shone twelve hours on one hemisphere, while darkness at the same time reigned over the other, the reverse taking place in the next twelve hours.[33] **d.** Twelve hours of light and twelve hours of darkness lingered alternately on the entire globe.[34] **e.** A moment of light and a moment of darkness alternately.[35] **f.** The light was ubiquitous and unintermittent for the first three days of creation.[36] But whatever the initial disposition of the light, God concealed it to become effulgent again in the end of days.[37] **g.** This light was really the light of the luminaries that broke through the misty and turbid air, the atmosphere clearing only on the fourth day to allow the luminaries to manifest their full radiance.[38] **h.** *Light* here is a designation for the upper transparent air.[39] **i.** *Let there be light.* A sublimely simple phrase to express a sublime fact . . . The old question, Whence did the light issue before the sun was made, is answered by nebular theory! The great astronomer Halley, wrote: "These nebulae

ANTHOLOGY

it says: *Who coverest Thyself with light as with a garment* (Ps. 104:2), which is followed by *Who stretchest out the heavens like a curtain*—a proof that the heavens were created after He had created light.[1] Three elements preceded the creation of the world: water,[2] ruah[3] and fire.[4] The waters conceived and gave birth to thick darkness; the fire conceived and gave birth to light; the wind conceived and gave birth to wisdom, and by these six the world is maintained: ruah, wisdom, fire, light, darkness, and water. For this reason did David say: *Bless the Lord, O my soul, O Lord my God, Thou art very great* (ib. 1).

Gen. R. 15. T.S. 1, 242.

87. Let there be light. Great is Peace, for the Holy One, blessed be He, commenced His creation with nought else but the equivalent of peace, viz., light, as it says: *And God said: "Let there be light."* Whence do we know that Light is Peace? From the verse, I *form* the light, *and create* darkness; I *make* peace, and *create* evil (Isa. 45:7).[1] Hence our Rabbis of blessed memory said: If a man can afford for the Sabbath only either a lamp for the home or wine for Sanctification, the former is preferable, for the sake of peace in the home.

Midrash Gadol U'Gedulah. T.S. 1, 382.

88. Let there be light. Alexander of Macedon put ten questions to the elders of the South. One was: Was light created first or darkness? They replied: This question can not be solved. Why did they not reply that darkness was created first, since it is written, *Now the earth was unformed and void, and* (there was) *darkness*, and after that, *And God said: "Let there be light." And there was light*? They thought to themselves: Perhaps he will go on to ask what is above and what is below, what is before and what is beyond.[1]

Tamid 32a. T.S. 1, 292.

89. And God said: Let there be light. R. Isaac took as his text: *The opening of Thy words giveth light; it giveth understanding unto the simple* (Ps. 119:130). R. Judah maintained: Light was created first. This is like a king who, wishing to build a palace, and finding that the site was a dark one, lit lamps and lanterns, to know where to lay the foundations; similarly, light was created first. R. Nehemiah said: The world was created first, just like a king who

§ 86 [1] This is not a contradiction, but rather shows that in the light of David's statement Gen. 1:1f. must be translated: In the beginning of God's creating the heaven and the earth, God said: "Let there be light." (Cf. Rashi's commentary on the Pentateuch ad loc.)

[2] I.e., these were created by God before the world; but they are not to be regarded as eternal uncreated matter which formed God's raw material, as it were.

[3] This means both wind and spirit; the context makes the latter necessary here, although the original does not differentiate between these two meanings.

[4] For all six are mentioned in this Psalm (Y. M.).

§ 87 [1] By the rule of parallelism light and darkness correspond to peace and evil respectively.

§ 88 [1] See par. 16.

ANTHOLOGY

built a palace and then adorned it with lights. Thus did R. Judan expound. But R. Phinehas and R. Judah b. R. Simon came, and R. Hanin in the name of R. Samuel B. R. Isaac, and preached: *The opening of Thy words giveth light*: The opening of Thy mouth was light to us: *And God said*: "*Let there be light.*"[1]

Gen. R. 3. T.S. 1, 344.

90. LET THERE BE LIGHT. *In front of the candlestick*, etc. (Num. 8:2). A human being lights a lamp from a burning lamp; can he, however, light a lamp from the darkness? Yet of God it says, *And darkness was on the face of the deep*, which is followed by, *And God said*: "*Let there be light.*" Out of the darkness I brought light; do I then need your light? I told you to kindle lamps only in order to elevate you. Thus Scripture writes, *To elevate* (you) *for all time through the lamp* (Exod. 27:20).[1]

Num. R. 15. T.S. 1, 308.

91. AND GOD SAID: LET THERE BE LIGHT. Said the Holy One, blessed be He: "How long shall the world remain in darkness: Let the light come!" So, *And God said*: "*Let there be light.*" This alludes to Abraham, as it is written, *Who hath raised up* (heir) *one from the east, whom He calleth in righteousness to His foot* (Isa. 41:2)? Read not *heir* with an *ayin* (meaning raised up) but *heir* with an *alef*, which means illumined.[1]

Gen. R. 2. T.S. 1, 343.

92. LET THERE BE LIGHT. R. Simeon b. Yohai opened his discourse with the text, *A man hath joy in the utterance of his mouth, and a word in due season, how good is it*! (Prov. 15:23). A man *hath joy* refers to God, as it says, *The Lord is* a man *of war, the Lord is His name* (Exod. 15:3). *The utterance of his mouth*, viz., *And God said*: "*Let there be light.*" *And a word in due season, how good is it!* even as Scripture continues, *And God saw the light, that it was good.*

Gen. R. 3. T.S. 1, 346.

93. AND THERE WAS LIGHT. R. Berekiah expounded, citing R. Judah b. R. Simon: *By the word of the Lord were the heavens made, and all the host of them by the breath of His mouth* (Ps. 33:6): not by labor or toil but only *by the word of the Lord*—and lo! *the heavens were* already *made*. So here too, Scripture does not say, and light came (later), but *And there was light*—simultaneously with God's fiat.

Gen. R. 3. T.S. 1, 345.

94. AND THERE WAS LIGHT. R. Simeon b. R. Jehozadak asked R. Samuel B. Nahman: "As I have heard that you are a master of *aggadah*, tell me whence the light was created?" He replied: "The Holy One, blessed be He, wrapped Himself therein as in a robe and irradiated with the luster of His majesty the whole world from one end to the other." Now he had answered him in a whisper, whereupon he observed, "This is explicitly stated in Scripture, *Who coverest Thyself with light as with a garment* (Ps. 104:2), yet you say it in a whisper!" "Just as I heard it in a whisper, so have I told it to you in a whisper," he rejoined. R. Berekiah remarked: Had not R. Isaac taught it publicly, we could not have said it.[1] Before this, what did they say on the matter?—R. Berekiah said in R. Isaac's name: The light was created from the place of the Temple, as it is said, *And, behold, the glory of the God of Israel came from the east; and His voice was like the sound of many waters; and the earth did shine with His glory* (Ezek. 43:2). "*His glory*" is nought else but the Temple, as you read: *Thou throne of glory, on high from the beginning, Thou place of our sanctuary* (Jer. 17:12).

Gen. R. 3. T.S. 1, 347.

§ 89 [1] I.e., God's *first* creative act was to decree light, which thus preceded darkness (regarded as an entity). But this is learned directly from the verse quoted, and not merely by analogy.
§ 90 [1] The "lamp" is probably understood as the lamp of the Torah. AJV: *to cause a lamp to burn continually.*
§ 91 [1] Rendering the text: Who illumined from the east, proclaiming God's justice in his wake?—(Abraham).
§ 94 [1] It would be treated as esoteric lore, notwithstanding the explicit Scriptural text.

ANTHOLOGY

95. AND GOD SAID: "LET THERE BE LIGHT." Even though light dwelt with Him before He created this light. And thus sang David: O *Lord my God, Thou art very great . . . Thou coverest Thyself with light as with a garment, and stretchest out the heaven like a curtain* (Ps. 104:1). Our text teaches that the Shekinah is all light, and from the radiance of the Shekinah, on the very first day of creation, did He create the light which illumines the world for humanity, even as it is written, *And God said: "Let there be light."* Some maintain that this light issued from the water, for the sentence, *The spirit of God hovered over the face of the water,* is immediately followed by the line *And God said: "Let there be light."* In many places in Scripture water is designated light. E.g., *His light reaches to the ends of the earth* (Job 37:3); *He spreadeth abroad the cloud of His light* (*ibid.* 11); *He covereth His hands with light* (*ibid.* 36:32).[1] Similarly, the light of the eyes is the water of the eyes, and so it says, *Mine eyes fail with tears* (Lam. 2:11).[2]

P'sikta Zutrathi Chap. 1. T.S. 1, 384.

96. LET THERE BE LIGHT. God created the world with ten utterances and not with eleven, to correspond to the Ten Commandments with which the Torah was given to Israel. How so? On the first day *God said: "Let there be light,"* to correspond to the first commandment, *"I am the Lord Thy God,"* (Exodus 20:2), for it is written, *But the Lord shall be unto thee an everlasting light* (Isa. 60:19), thus identifying God with light.

P'sikta. T.S. 1, 351.

97. LET THERE BE LIGHT. R. Simeon b. Lakish lectured: In the Creation narrative Scripture alludes to seven Dedications which are symbolized by light. The first Dedication of the Creation is intimated in *Let there be light;* here you have one lamp of dedication. On the second day we read, *And there was evening and there was morning.* Now, this may be compared to an architect who sought where to lay the foundations, so he took a lamp to light up the site. In the same way God lit up the second day by the Torah, as we read, *For the precept is a lamp, and the Torah is light* (Prov. 6:13). On the third day trees were created, including the olive tree whose oil gives light. On the fourth the luminaries and David's Throne, of which it is written, *And his throne shall be as the sun before me* (Ps. 84:37); also, *There have I ordered a* lamp *for Mine anointed* (ibid. 132:17). On the fifth lightning was created, as we read, *The voice of Thy thunder was in the whirlwind, the* lightnings *lighted up the world* (ibid. 77:19). On the sixth day man was created, of whom it says, *The spirit of man is the* lamp *of the Lord* (Prov. 20:27).[1]

Midrash Y'lamdenu. T.S. 1, 352.

98. LET THERE BE LIGHT. R. Simon said: "Light" is written five times in the Creation story, which corresponds to the five Books of the Torah (the Pentateuch). *And God said, "Let there be light"* corresponds to the Book of Genesis, in which the Almighty created the world. *And there was light,* to Exodus, in which the Israelites went forth from darkness into light. *And God saw the light, that it was good,* to Leviticus, which is filled with numerous laws. *And God divided the light from the darkness,* to Numbers, which makes a distinction between the emigrees from Egypt (the Israelites) and the next generation.[1] *And God called the light day* corresponds to Deuteronomy,

§ 95 [1] In all these passages "light" is understood to mean water.
[2] I.e., my tears wash away the other water of the eyes, so that their light ceases.

§ 97 [1] Thus every day saw something which symbolized dedication. Only six are actually enumerated; see T.S. 1, 432, where it is stated that the seventh is reserved for the Messianic era.

§ 98 [1] The sense and rendering are doubtful. On the present rendering this would allude to the dooming of the generation that left Egypt to die in the wilderness, whilst only the next generation would enter the promised land. But it is doubtful whether "the next generation" is correct; the original Heb. is generally a term for mankind. In that case the distinction is between Israel and the rest of mankind, in that God frequently had the former numbered (hence the name "Numbers"), but not the latter.

which is filled with numerous laws. R. Simon's colleagues objected: But Leviticus too is filled with numerous laws! He answered: Yet this verse contains a repetition, viz., *And God called the light day*: now, are not light and day identical? 'Tis indeed amazing.[2]

Num. R. 3. T.S. 1, 348.

99. **And God said, "Let there be light," and there was light.**

From this point we can begin to discover hidden things relating to the creation of the world in detail. For up to this point the Creation has been described in general; further on we have again a general description: so that we have a sequence of general - particular - general. Up to this point the whole was suspended in void by the mystery of the Limitless. When, however, energy had been extended through the supernal palace which is the mystery of God, the term "saying" is used in connection with it, in the words *And God said*. For prior to that there is no specific "saying," for although the word *b'reshith* is a creative utterance (*maamar*), the actual words "and said" are not used in connection with it. This expression "and said" (*vayomer*) opens the door to inquiry and understanding. We define this "saying" as an energy that was culled, as it were, in silence from the mystic Limitless through the mystic power of thought.

Zohar Hadash 1:16. T.S. 1, 361.

100. LET THERE BE LIGHT, AND THERE WAS LIGHT. Rabbi Hezekiah related: I was in Arab,[1] where I saw men living secluded in a mountain cave, who returned to their homes every Friday for the Sabbath. On asking them what they were doing there, they informed me: "We are hermits, and daily occupy ourselves in the study of the Torah." I then said to them, "My children, I adjure you, what new interpretation did you light upon today?" They replied: "*We* studied the verse, *And God said: Let there be light, and there was light*, regarding which Rabbi Kruspedai taught: The repetition of the word *light* indicates that it was unique, viz., the great light of Intelligence which emanated from the light of His lustrous splendor; it is the identical luster which shines behind the curtain of the innermost Presence."

Zohar Hadash 8. T.S. 1, 380.

101. AND GOD SAID, "LET THERE BE LIGHT," AND THERE WAS LIGHT. (The words "God said" implies that He addressed others, saying to them, "Let there be light for this world, and let there be light for the Hereafter.")

This is the primal light which God created on the First Day; it is the light of the eye, the light which God showed Adam, by which he could see the world from one end to the other. It is the same light which God showed David, whereupon he burst into praise, "*Oh how abundant is Thy goodness, which Thou hast laid up for them who fear Thee!*" (Ps. 31:20). This is also the light which God revealed to Moses and by which Moses saw the Land of Israel from Gilead unto Dan. When God perceived that three corrupt generations would arise, namely the generation of Enosh, the generations of the Flood and that of the Dissensions (Gen. 11:1-9), He hid the light, that they should not be able to use it. He gave it to Moses, which Moses used for the three months left him from the day when he was conceived,[1] as we read, *and she hid him three months* (Exod. 2:2). After the three months, when he entered Pharaoh's palace, God took that light from him until he would stand on Mount Sinai to receive the Torah, when He returned it to him; Moses made use of it every day; therefore the chil-

[2] Hence it corresponds more closely to Deuteronomy than to Leviticus, for the former, as its name implies, contains repetitions of many laws already stated in the earlier Books.

§ 100 [1] A town near Sepphoris in Upper Galilee.

§ 101 [1] According to tradition Moses was born three months prematurely; for that reason his mother could hide him for three months, because Pharaoh's officers did not expect him to be born yet. Thus he had, as it were, three months owing to him when his soul should have been in the celestial sphere.

God saw the light, that it was good;

COMMENTARY

reply fully to the difficulty which has been raised against the Mosaic description of creation, in asserting that light could not be generated without the sun."[40] [4]**Good.** Equal to its purpose.[41]

ANTHOLOGY

dren of Israel could not approach him until he put a veil over his face, as we read, *And they were afraid to come nigh him . . . and he put a veil on his face* (Exod. 34:30,33). He wrapped himself with the light as with a praying shawl; as it says, *enwrapping Himself with light as with a garment* (Ps. 104:2). As to the verse, *Let there be light; and there was (vay'hi) light,* whenever the word *vay'hi* is employed, it means in this world and in the Hereafter.

Zohar 1:31. T.S. 1, 363.

102. AND GOD SAID: "LET THERE BE LIGHT," AND THERE WAS LIGHT. R. Jose said: That light was hidden and kept in store for the righteous in the world to come, as it is written, *A light is sown for the righteous* (Ps. 97:11). R. Isaac observed: Then will the worlds be in harmony, and all will be united into one. Thus that light functioned in the world only on the first day of Creation, after which it was hidden away. Said R. Judah: Had it been hidden away altogether, the world could not have existed for a single moment. But it was only hidden, like a seed which generates other seeds and fruits, and the world is sustained by it. There is not a day that something does not emanate from the light to sustain all things, for it is with this that the Holy One, blessed be He, nourishes the world. Moreover, whenever the Torah is studied by night, a little thread of this hidden light steals down and plays upon them that are absorbed in its study, wherefore it is written: *The Lord commandeth His lovingkindness in the daytime, and in the night His song is with me* (Ps. 42:9).

Zohar 2:148. T.S. 1, 369.

103. AND GOD SAID: "LET THERE BE LIGHT," AND THERE WAS LIGHT. R. Hiyya commenced his lecture with the text, *Light is sown for the righteous, and gladness for the upright in heart* (Ps. 97:11). God foresaw that the world could not stand without a foundation. And what is the true foundation on which the world stands? The righteous man, as it is written, *The righteous is the foundation of the world.* He was the first foundation which God created in His world, and *he* (the righteous) is called "light," as it says, *Light is sown for the righteous.* This interpretation is corroborated by the text, *And God saw the light, that it was good* (1:4). Now, Scripture says here, *that it was good;* whilst elsewhere we read, *Say ye of the* righteous, *that he is* good (Isa. 3:10). The latter text proves, by the verbal identity, that the righteous is meant in the former. Rabbi said: This light of our text is the light of the angels, which was created before anything else in the world. Should you object that we can see from the Bible that heaven and earth were created first, the answer is that the statement *And there was light* means that this was the first thing created (for the text should be rendered, And there had been light). R. Judah said: This light is verily the light of God's Throne of Glory, and out of it were fashioned all the other creations. Heaven was shaped therefrom; but the Throne of God was fashioned first, as it says, *Thou throne of glory, on high from the beginning* (Jer. 17:12).

Zohar Hadash 8. T.S. 1, 378.

104. **And God saw the light, that it was good.**

What does *In Thy light do we see light* (Ps. 36:10) mean? This refers to the light which God created on the first day, and which served the world for three days, before the creation of the luminaries on the fourth day. Then, no sooner were the luminaries created on the fourth day, as it says, *And God made the two great luminaries,* than God immediately hid that original light. Now why did He do that? Because He knew that some day the heathen who deny

ANTHOLOGY

the Torah would anger Him. Therefore God declared: These evil-doers shall not merit the privilege of this light. Let the light of the sun and moon, which will one day cease, serve their needs. But this light, which will endure to all eternity, is reserved for the righteous who will inherit the Hereafter, as it says, *And God saw the light, that it was good, and He set it apart,* etc. The original light then said to God: "Master of the Universe! Although I was denied serving the worthy Israelites in this world, and am to be their light in the Hereafter, still, I yearn only for the light of Thyself, which Thou wilt radiate on them."

Tana debe Eliyahu Zuta 21. T.S. 1, 644.

105. AND GOD SAW THE LIGHT, THAT IT WAS GOOD. R. Abbahu said: From the very beginning of the world's creation the Holy One, blessed be He, foresaw the deeds of the righteous and the deeds of the wicked. Thus it is written, *For the Lord knoweth the way of the righteous* (Ps. 1:6). Thus, *The earth was formless and void* alludes to the deeds of the wicked; *And God said: "Let there be light,"* to the deeds of the righteous. I still might not know in which of these He delights, the former or the latter.[1] But when Scripture writes, *And God saw the light, that it was good,* it follows that He desires the deeds of the righteous, and not the deeds of the wicked.

Gen. R. 2. T.S. 1, 305.

106. AND GOD SAW THE LIGHT, THAT IT WAS GOOD. R. Eleazar said: Even for the sake of a single righteous man would this world have been created, for it says, *And God saw the light, that it was* (for one who is) *good,* "good" meaning none but the righteous, as it says, *Say ye of the righteous, that he is* good (Isa. 3:10).

Yoma 38b. T.S. 1, 385.

107. AND GOD SAW THE LIGHT, THAT IT WAS GOOD. King David, inspired by the Holy Spirit, declared: *For with Thee is the fountain of life; in Thy light do we see light* (Ps. 36:10). He expressed this as the protagonist of the Congregation of Israel, which said to the Almighty: "Sovereign of the Universe! Because of the Torah which Thou hast given us, which is the fountain of life, we are destined to delight in Thy radiance in the Messianic era." *In Thy light do we see light*: the light which the Congregation of Israel is expectantly awaiting is none other than the light of the Messiah, as it says, *And God saw the light, that it was good,* the exegesis of which is that God saw the Messiah and his achievements before the world was created, and reserved him for his own proper generation under His Throne of Glory.

P'sikta Rabbathi 36. T.S. 1, 392.

108. AND GOD SAW THE LIGHT, THAT IT WAS GOOD. (KI TOB). R. Levi said: Somewhere South there was an innkeeper who would rise in the night, dress himself, and order his guests to rise, saying, "Start on your journey, and I will accompany you." No sooner were they on their way when robbers who had been lying in wait for them, fell on them, robbed them of their possessions, and divided the loot with the innkeeper. One day R. Meir happened to lodge there. As was his wont, the innkeeper dressed, woke the rabbi, and said that he would accompany him a little distance on the way. R. Meir answered: "I must wait here for my brother." "Where is your brother?" the innkeeper asked. "In the synagogue," he was told. "Tell me his name and I will go there and fetch him," the innkeeper proposed. On being told that the name was Ki Tob, the landlord went there and repeatedly summoned Ki Tob, but none answered. In the morning R. Meir arose and prepared his donkey for the journey. The innkeeper asked, "Where is this brother of yours?" The sage replied: "Behold, he has arrived; the light is my brother." He then quoted the biblical verse, *And God saw the light, that it was good—Ki Tob.* (The story bears out the rabbi-

§ 105 [1] This is best understood as rhetorical, to lead to the homiletic interpretation which follows.

and God divided the light from the darkness. [5]And God called the light

COMMENTARY

and God divided the light from the darkness. Either: **a.** He appointed for each its time and place;[42] or **b.** God interposed the twilight between day and night so that one come not upon the other with sudden impact.[43] **[5]And God called the light Day.** Five things were named by God, there being yet no man to name them, viz.: light, darkness, heaven, earth and sea; to which man (Adam) must also be added.[44] In

ANTHOLOGY

nic counsel that one should enter and leave a place during daylight.)

Gen. R. 92. T.S. 1, 390.

109. AND GOD SAW THE LIGHT, THAT IT WAS GOOD. R. Eliezer b. R. Simeon visited R. Jose b. Simeon b. Lakunya, his father-in-law. Both rose in the dawning light for his departure. His father-in-law accompanied him about half a mile and bestowed on him a blessing, saying, "This is the hour when the blessing of the righteous is fulfilled. We deduce it from the verse, *And God saw the light, that it was good;* while elsewhere it is written, *It was* good *in the eyes of the Lord to bless Israel* (Num. 24:1), indicating that when light dawns it is 'good'—i.e., efficacious—to utter a blessing." R. Eliezer rejoined: "Any man's blessing at that hour will be fulfilled, for heaven, the stars, and the angels then break out in song."

Midrash Haneelam Zohar Hadash 8. T.S. 1, 402.

110. AND GOD SAW THE LIGHT, THAT IT WAS GOOD. You must not recite a blessing over a lamp unless you can enjoy its light. R. Zeira son of R. Abbahu inferred this from the text which first says, *And God saw the light, that it was good*, and only after that, *and God pronounced a division,* on which R. Berekiah commented: Two outstanding scholars interpreted this as meaning the actual Habdalah benediction.[1] R. Judah b. R. Simon said: He (God) set it apart for Himself.[2] Our Rabbis said: He set it apart for the righteous in the Messianic era. Imagine a king who had two officers, each of whom claimed command by day. Thereupon the king summoned the first and said to him, "So-and-So, the day shall be your province"; summoning the second he addressed him, "So-and-So, night shall be your province." Thus, *God called the light* (for service by) *Day,* saying to it, "The day shall be thy province"; *And the darkness called He* (for service at) *Night,* saying to it, "Night shall be thy province." R. Johanan observed: That is what the Holy One, blessed be He, said to Job: *Hast thou commanded the morning, and caused the dayspring to know its place*? (Job 38:12) hast thou really made it known which is its place (i.e., time) to function in? R. Tanhuma said: I can cite the grounds for this statement, viz., *I form the light, and create darkness, I make peace* (Isa. 45:7): having created them, He makes peace between them.

J. Berakoth 8:6. T.S. 1, 389.

111. **That it was good (tob).**

R. Joshua said: If one sees the letter *teth* in a dream, it is a good omen for him. Why so? Because Scripture used this letter to express something good for the first time. For from the beginning of Genesis up to the verse "*And God saw the light,*" no *teth* occurs (which is then used for the first time in the word "good").

Baba Kama 55a. T.S. 1, 388.

112. **And God divided the light from the darkness.**

R. Eleazar the Great declared: The light of the angels was first created, for it is written,

§ 110 [1] This is a ceremony marking the termination of Sabbaths and Festivals, in which God is thanked for making a distinction between holy and profane. Part of it consists of a benediction over light. The verse is thus interpreted as meaning that God Himself performed this ceremony and recited this benediction, but only after He actually saw and enjoyed the light, as it were.

[2] This first light which He created.

Day, and the darkness He called Night. And there was evening and

COMMENTARY

calling the light Day, God defines the significance of light in human life. In the Bible account of creation, everything centers round man and is viewed from his angle.[45] **called.** Figuratively, as a King would call his servant to assign to him his schedule of service.[46] **and there was evening.** The day, according to the Scriptural reckoning of time, begins with the preceding evening. Thus, the observance of the Day of Atonement is to be "*from even unto even*" (Lev. 23:32); and similarly of the Sabbath and festivals.[47] **evening** (*ereb*) . . . **morning** (*boker*). *Ereb* (from *arab,* to mingle) denotes that part of the day when day and night are comingled, being neither quite day nor night. *Boker* (from *bakker,* "to search," "examine") is the reverse of *ereb,* i.e., when one can distinguish the exact quality which characterizes it, viz., daylight.[48]

ANTHOLOGY

And God saw the light, that it was good. And God divided the light from the darkness: that is to say, He distinguished that light from the darkness, which is the world. It is the heavens that divide our world from the light of the angels; they likewise separate, being in the middle, the light from the darkness.[1] R. Johanan b. Zaccai said: God gave the angels dominion over heaven, and heaven over earth; but all subserve His throne, to manifest "*that One higher than the high watcheth*" (Ecc. 5:7).

Zohar Hadash 7. T.S. 1, 400.

113. **And God called the light Day.**

But are not light and day identical? It was taught: The primeval light[1] cannot shine by day, because it would eclipse the light of the sun, nor by night, because it was created only to illumine by day. Then where is it? It is reserved for the righteous in the Messianic future, as it says, *Moreover the light of the moon shall be as the light of the sun, and the light of the sun shall be sevenfold, as the light of the seven days* (Isa. 30:26). Seven days! surely there were only three, since the luminaries were created on the fourth day![2] It is like a man who says, "I am providing so much for the seven days of my wedding feast."[3] R. Nehemiah said: It refers to the seven days of mourning for Methuselah, when the Holy One, blessed be He, lavished light upon them.

Gen. R. 3. T.S. 1, 420.

114. AND GOD CALLED THE LIGHT DAY. R. Eleazar remarked: God never associates His name with evil, but only with good. Thus, it does not say, And *God* called the light Day, and *God* called the darkness Night, but rather, *And the darkness He called Night.*

Gen. R. 3. T.S. 1, 421.

115. AND GOD CALLED THE LIGHT DAY. The light symbolizes the day of Messianic redemption, as it says, *Behold, a day of the Lord cometh* (Zech. 14:1), to which this verse alludes.

Midrash Haneelam Zohar Hadash 8. T.S. 1, 442.

116. **And there was (vay'hi) evening, etc.**

R. Simeon b. R. Abba said in R. Johanan's name: Wherever *vay'hi* (and it came to pass) is employed, it connotes trouble. They objected: But it is written, *And there was* (vay'hi) *evening and there was* (vay'hi) *morning.* That was not an occasion of complete joy, replied he, for everything created on the first day is destined to wear out, as it is written, *For the heavens shall vanish away like smoke, and the earth shall*

§ 112 [1] Or, the angels separate, etc.

§ 113 [1] I.e., the light which came into existence at God's command, not that shed by the sun. It is the former which God specifically called day, for that is not identical with day.

[2] *The light of the seven days* is the special light created by God's fiat: "Let there be light." But this served for three days only, not seven, since the sun was created on the fourth day, which rendered the first light superfluous.

[3] Though he does not intend it to suffice for the whole period. Similarly we speak of the light of the seven days, though it did not serve for so long.

there was morning, one day. [6]And

COMMENTARY

one day. Not, "the first day"; because: **a.** There is no "first" without a "second," which had not yet eventuated.[49] **b.** It is idiomatic to say "one" for "first" in enumerating time.[50] **c.** As for the six days of creation, some commentators surmise that they stand for millennia, as it is said, *For a thousand years in Thy sight are but as yesterday* (Ps. 90:4).[51] Earthly and human measurement of time, by a clock of human manufacture, cannot apply to the first three days, as the sun was not then in existence. The beginning of each period of creation is called "morning"; its close, "evening" (Delitzsch); in the same way, we speak of the

ANTHOLOGY

wax old like a garment (Isa. 51:6). They objected: But it is written, *And there was* (vay'hi) *evening and there was* (vay'hi) *morning, a second day* (1:8) . . . *a third day* (ib. 13) . . . *a fourth day* (ib. 19), etc.? These still do not connote absolute joy, he answered, for whatever was created in the six days of Creation needs preparation, e.g., mustard must be sweetened, wheat must be ground, lupines must be sweetened.

Gen. R. 42. T.S. 1, 427.

117. AND THERE WAS EVENING. R. Judah b. R. Simon said: It does not say, "Let there be evening," but, *And there was evening*: from this you learn that a time-order existed before this.[1]

T.S. 1, 422.

118. AND THERE WAS EVENING, etc. Every judge who judges with complete fairness even for a single hour, the Writ gives him credit as though he had become a partner of the Holy One, blessed be He, in the Creation. Here it is written, *And the people stood about Moses from the morning unto the evening* (Exod. 18:13); whilst elsewhere we read, *And there was morning and there was evening, one day.*[1]

Shabbath 10a. T.S. 1, 410.

119. AND THERE WAS EVENING, etc. R. Johanan said: The reunion of the Exiles is as important as the day when heaven and earth were created, for it is said, *And the children of Judah and the children of Israel shall be gathered together, and they shall appoint themselves one head, and shall go up out of the land; for great shall be the* day *of Jezreel* (Hosea 2:2); and it is written: *And there was evening, and there was morning, one* day.

Pes. 88a. T.S. 1, 412.

120. **And there was morning.**

Morning (*Boker*) is defectively spelled, the letter *waw* being omitted, to indicate that there will not be a perfect morning in the present world until the advent of the future world,[1] as we read, *The watchman said: The morning cometh, and also the night* (Isa. 21:12).

Another interpretation: The defective spelling teaches that before the very first night was over Adam sinned, as we read, *Man did not pass the night in honor, but he became like the beasts that perish* (Ps. 49:13).

Another interpretation: It teaches that all, like the very cattle (*bakar*), need a goad to guide them in the right path.

Midrash Habiur. T.S. 1, 446.

121. AND THERE WAS EVENING AND THERE WAS MORNING, ONE DAY. *Evening* issued from the spring of darkness, whilst *morning* emerged out of the well of light;[1] and because they both combine in one, the Bible calls them *one day*. R.

§ 117 [1] By rendering: And evening (already) was—ere now.

§ 118 [1] Moses, judging in equity *"from the morning unto the evening,"* was continuing the work of Creation, when *"there was morning and there was evening."*

§ 120 [1] This may mean either that there will not be perfect morning until the messianic era (in which case *olam haba*, here rendered the future world, means this world in a future era); or that perfect morning will be found only in the Hereafter.

§ 121 [1] Lit., the "side" of darkness . . . the "side" of light. The mystics hypostasized light and darkness, frequently identifying them with good and evil respectively, the two constituting the two "sides" of existence, like the face of a coin and its obverse.

ANTHOLOGY

Judah declared that the repetition of "there was evening and there was morning" for each day is intended to convey that there is no day without night and no night without day, and they refuse to separate.

R. Jose observed: That day on which the primal light appeared extended itself into all succeeding days, hence the word *Day* is mentioned in connection with all the days of creation. R. Eleazar said: This follows from the daily repetition of "*there was morning,*" morning issuing only from the spring of primal light. R. Simeon observed too: The Primal Day accompanied all the succeeding days, and they in turn are all embraced in it, which shows there is no schism amongst them, and they are all one.[2]

Zohar 1, 46. T.S. 1, 436.

122. AND THERE WAS EVENING, AND THERE WAS MORNING, ONE DAY. The scholars propounded a problem: If a man erred and did not say the afternoon Prayer (*minhah*), should he say it twice in the evening? Should you argue from the fact that if he erred in the evening he prays twice in the morning, I may reply that the reason for that is because it is all one day, as it is written, *And there was evening and there was morning, one day;* but in this case, prayer being in place of sacrifice, since the day has passed the sacrifice lapses. Or should we rather say that since prayer is a supplication for mercy, a man may pray whenever he likes? Come and hear: If a man erred and did not say the afternoon Prayer, he says it twice in the evening, and we do not apply here the principle that if the day has passed the offering lapses.

Berakoth 26a. T.S. 1, 409.

123. AND THERE WAS EVENING AND THERE WAS MORNING. The Mishnah teaches: From what time may the Shema[1] be read in the evening, etc.? On this the Gemara asks: What authority has the Tanna for the reading of the Shema at all, that he raises the question: "From what time?" Further, why does he first deal with the evening Shema; let him first deal with the morning Shema? He learns from the account of Creation; for it is written; *There was evening and there was morning, one day* (thus evening precedes.)

Berakoth 2a. T.S. 1, 408.

124. AND THERE WAS EVENING AND THERE WAS MORNING, ONE DAY. R. Johanan b. Zaccai observed: We find that the day and the night together are called "day," as it is written, *And there was evening and there was morning, one day.*

P'sikta Rabbathi 17. T.S. 1, 433.

125. AND THERE WAS EVENING AND THERE WAS MORNING, ONE DAY. I.e., a thousand years, which are but one day in God's time, as it says, *For a thousand years in Thy sight are as yesterday when it is past* (Ps. 90:4).

B'reshith Rabbathi of R. Moshe Hadarshon. T.S. 1, 448.

126. AND THERE WAS EVENING AND THERE WAS MORNING, ONE DAY. "One" (and not first) is employed, because Israel was destined to proclaim God's unity with that word, as we read, *Hear O Israel, the Lord our God the Lord is* One (Deut. 6:2). For that reason the first day is called one day, because whoever asserts the unity (oneness) of His Name acknowledges that He is the Creator of His world, blessed be He and blessed be His Name.

P'sikta Zutrathi. T.S. 1, 449.

127. AND THERE WAS EVENING AND THERE WAS MORNING, ONE DAY. Mishna: The "one day," in which an animal and its young may not both be killed (Lev. 22:28), means the day and the night preceding it. Thus taught R. Simeon b. Zoma: "One day" is stated in the Creation narrative (1:5), and also in the aforementioned law, viz., *And whether it be cow or ewe, ye*

[2] The thought is probably that all Creation displays harmony and unity.

§ 123 [1] The passage commencing "*Hear*" (Shema) *O Israel, the Lord our God, the Lord is One* (Deut. 6:4).

God said: 'Let there be a firmament in the midst of the waters, and let it

COMMENTARY

morning and evening of life.[52] **[6]Let there be a firmament.** "Firmament" is the stratum of air dividing the waters of the earth below from the waters of the clouds above. It is called *rakia* (literally, "beaten into a sheet"), because it extends in space like metal beaten into a plate.[53] **Made. a.** He

ANTHOLOGY

shall not kill it with its young both in one day (ibid.): just as in the case of the "one day" of the Creation, day follows night to make the one day, so too the "one day" in the latter instance means the day and the night preceding it.

Hulin 83a. T.S. 1, 416.

128. **One day.**

R. Tanhum said: It was the day on which unique things were created, viz., heaven, earth, and light. R. Judah said: The day in which God was alone (i.e., one) in His universe. This agrees with R. Johanan but not with R. Hanina. For R. Johanan said: The angels were created on the second day.

Gen. R. 3. T.S. 1, 425.

129. ONE DAY. Rab Judah said in the name of Rab: Ten things were created the first day, viz.: Heaven and earth, *tohu, bohu,* light and darkness, wind and water, day and night. Heaven and earth, for it is written: *In the beginning God created heaven and earth. Tohu* and *bohu*: *And the earth was tohu and bohu.* Light and darkness: *And darkness was upon the face of the deep*; also, *And God said; "Let there be light."* Wind and water: *And the* wind *of God hovered over the face of the* waters. Day and night: *And there was* evening *and there was* morning, one day.[1]

Hagigah 12b. T.S. 1, 226.

130. **Let there be a firmament in the midst of the water.**

Our Rabbis said: When the Holy One, blessed be He, ordered, *Let there be a firmament in the midst of the waters,* the middle layers of water solidified, and the nether heavens and the uppermost heavens were formed. Rab said: The heaven was still liquid on the first day, and on the second day it congealed; thus, *Let there be a firmament* means, Let the firmament be made strong and lasting, let it congeal and extend. R. Judah b. Pazzi explained it: Let it become like a plate. This interpretation is supported by the verse, *And they did beat* (*va'yrak'u,* same root as *rakia*) *the gold into thin plates* (Exod. 39:3). It was taught in R. Joshua's name: The thickness is about the breadth of two fingers. R. Hanina disagrees with this, for Rabbi, quoting him, said: In the verse, *Canst thou with Him spread out* (tarkia) *the sky, which is strong as a molten mirror* (Job 37:18)? the word *tarkia* teaches that the sky is like a thin beaten plate, much less than two fingerbreadths in thickness.

J. Berakoth Ch. 1; Gen. R. 4.
T.S. 1, 451, 454.

131. LET THERE BE A FIRMAMENT. One method of exegesis is this: When one subject is to illumine another, it may itself be illumined thereby. E.g.: We are not told in the Creation narrative that fire burnished the sky's surface. Now, when Scripture says, *Oh that Thou wouldst rend the heavens as when Thou didst descend* (to reveal Thy Torah) *and the mountains quaked at Thy presence, for this* (Revelation) *was as when the* (primeval) *fire blazed o'er the dividing* (heavens) (Isa. 63:19; 64:1), it clearly implies, even as Thou didst at the Creation, so didst Thou at Revelation; thus Creation is to illumine Revelation. For when

§ 129 [1] This is a polemic against the view that *tohu, bohu,* and darkness constituted primeval and eternal uncreated matter, out of which God created the world. Hence he says that these too were created.—*Ruach* means both wind and spirit (AJV: *And the spirit of God hovered,* etc.).

ANTHOLOGY

God said on the second day, *"Let there be a firmament,"* which had actually been already created on the first day, He could only have meant, Let a fire come forth from above and burnish the as yet unpolished heavens. Thus the Creation story comes to shed light on the Revelation, but itself is illumined thereby.

Baraitha of 32 Middoth of R. Eliezer b. R. Jose. T.S. 1, 463.

132. LET THERE BE A FIRMAMENT. On the second day He created the firmament, the angels, the heat of the living bodies, and the heat of Gehinom. But were not the heavens created on the first day, as it is said, *In the beginning God created the heavens?* What, then, is this heaven which was created on the second day? R. Eliezer said: That firmament which is above the heads of the four holy creatures, as it is said, *In the likeness of a firmament above the holy creatures* (Ezek. 1:22). It appears like unto hoar-frost, consisting of precious stones and pearls; it lights up the whole heavens as the light which lights up the house, and as the sun which lights up the world at noon, as it is said, *And light dwells with Him* (Dan. 2:22). Similarly the righteous are destined in the future to enlighten the world, as it is said, *And the wise will shine as the brightness of the firmament* (ibid. 13:3).

Chronicles of Jerahmeel. Gaster, p. 7 (1:8).

133. AND GOD SAID: "LET THERE BE A FIRMAMENT," etc. R. Judah said: When God created the world, He created seven skies above and seven continents below, seven seas, seven streams; (and divided time into periods of) seven days, seven weeks, seven years, seven times seven years, and the seven thousand years that the world of the Almighty is destined to exist, the seventh thousand being the festival Sabbatical.[1] He created seven skies above, in each one of which there are countless myriads of stars and heavenly constellations and ministering angels serving in every heaven. In all of these are Heavenly Chariots, all thronging to submit to the Kingly yoke of their Master. Yea, in every sky bands of ministering servants, each different from the other, press forward to His service, some with six wings, others with four; some with four faces, others with two, some having but one. Some are flaming fire, others water or wind (*ruah*), as we read, *who makest* winds *Thine angels, the* flaming fire *Thy ministers* (Ps. 104:4). All the heavens are one above the other like layers of onions, some below and others above, and every sky moves and quakes in awe of its Sovereign, for by His command they may vanish, and by His decree do they exist. Above them all is God, blessed be He, Who bears and maintains all with His power and might. In like manner are the seven landmasses below, all habitations for men, some above and some below. The Land of Israel is above all, and Jerusalem is above all habitable places.[2]

Zohar 3:9. T.S. 1, 467.

134. LET THERE BE A FIRMAMENT IN THE MIDST OF THE WATERS. It is written, *Who roofs Thine upper chambers with water* (Ps. 104:3); when an earthly monarch builds a palace, he roofs it over with stones, timber, and earth; but the Holy One, blessed be He, roofed over His world with nought but water, as it is said, *Who roofs Thine upper chambers with water.*

Gen. R. 4. T.S. 1, 453.

135. LET THERE BE A FIRMAMENT. R. Johanan said: The Holy One, blessed be He, took all the primeval water and poured half into the firmament and half into the ocean; thus it is written, *God's division fills the waters* (Ps. 65:10). This half in the firmament is like a lake, and above the lake is a vault, and through the heat of the lake the vault sweats heavy drops

§ 133 [1] Just as the seventh day of the week is the Sabbath.
[2] The rendering of much of this is conjectural.

ANTHOLOGY

of water, which descend into the salt water yet do not combine with it.

Gen. R. 4. T.S. 1, 455.

136. LET THERE BE A FIRMAMENT, etc. On the second day He divided the water, assigning part thereof to the upper sphere, and part as a base for the seven abysses.[1] He spread the firmament between the upper and the lower waters. Now, why did He separate them? Because the upper water is male, whilst the nether water is female, and when they desired to unite, they threatened to destroy the world. The water roared up mountains and hurtled down hills, the male in hot pursuit of the female, until the Holy One, blessed be He, rebuked them, as it says, *At Thy rebuke they fled* (Ps. 104:7). Whence do we know that He set a separate boundary for each? From the text, *Thou didst set a bound which they should not pass over* (ibid. 9). Between the upper and the nether waters there are but three fingerbreadths, and the vault of the firmament interposes between them in order to keep them apart.

Seder Rabbath B'reshith. T.S. 1, 500.

137. LET THERE BE A FIRMAMENT. On the second day He said: *Let there be a firmament in the midst of the waters,* charging the waters to divide, one half to rise above and the other half to stay below. But wilfully they all rose above. Said God to them, "I bade only half of you to ascend, but you have all ascended." Defying their Creator they answered, "We will not descend." Hence they are called "*rebellious waters*" (Isa. 43:16). Putting forth His little finger, He instantly tore them in two and forcibly placed half of them below. That is what Scripture writes, *And God said*: "*Let there be a Rakia* (*firmament*)": read not *Rakia* but *k'riah* (a rent: Let there be a rent in the waters of heaven). It was His intention to burn them up, but they pleaded with Him. Said He to them: Know that I will desire to lead My children through you dryshod. Should I seek to make you sea or dry land, thus must it be. There and then He made this stipulation with them, as it says, *And the sea returned l'ethano* (AJV: *to its strength*) (Exod. 14:27), which means, in accordance with the *t'nai* (stipulation) which He had made with it at the Creation. He also stipulated that the sea should rage, so as not to permit Jonah to flee to Tarshish. He also stipulated with them to distinguish between clean and unclean, so that they be a means of purification.[1] And thus it was. After parting the waters He created Erelim, Angels, Ophanim and Hashmalim (angels of different degree and function). He also blew up the fire and heated the seven spheres (pyres?) of Gehinom.

Midrash Jonah; Midrash Konen.
T.S. 1, 462. 465.

138. The separation of the waters into upper and lower waters was the only act of the sort done by God in connection with the work of creation. All other acts were unifying.

Gen. R. 4. Ginzberg Legends, p. 14.

139. LET THERE BE A FIRMAMENT IN THE MIDST OF THE WATERS. R. Phinehas said in R. Oshaya's name: As much space as there is between the earth and the firmament, so is there between the firmament and the upper waters; as it is written, *Let there be a firmament in the midst of the waters,* meaning, midway between them. R. Tanhuma said: I will state the proof. If it said, *And God made the firmament, and He divided between the waters . . . which are upon the firmament,* I would say that the water lies directly on the firmament itself. Since, however, it is stated, *And between the waters which are above the firmament,* it follows that the upper waters are suspended by the word of God. R. Aha said: It is like the flame of a lamp,[1] and their fruits are the rain.[2]

§ 136 [1] A mystic Cabbalistic idea.
§ 137 [1] Through immersion a person ritually unclean becomes clean.
§ 139 [1] Which seems to be suspended in the air.
[2] The upper waters drip through the heat of the firmament, the dripping being the rain we enjoy.

divide the waters from the waters.' [7]And God made the firmament, and divided the waters which were under

COMMENTARY

set it in position.[54] **b.** He perfected it to be adequate for its purpose.[55] [7]**divided the waters.** The mystics observed that the waters wept when they were thus forcibly separated, and still weep to this very day.

ANTHOLOGY

A Samaritan asked R. Meir: "Can upper water really be suspended by God's word?" "Yes," he answered. "Bring me a water-clock,"[3] he added. When he brought it, he placed a gold plate upon it, but the water did not stand still; then a silver plate, but the water did not stand still. But as soon as he placed his finger upon the aperture, the water stood still. "But you have put your finger there," he objected.—"If my finger stays the water, though I am but flesh and blood, how much more so the finger of the Holy One, blessed be He! Hence the upper waters are suspended by God's word."

Gen. R. 4. T.S. 1, 483.

140. LET THERE BE A FIRMAMENT. *Thy word standeth fast in heaven* (Ps. 119:89). Which word then stands fast in heaven? But the meaning is this: God said, Whereupon does heaven stand? Surely on the strength of My fiat, *Let there be a firmament*, etc. Scripture also writes, *He Hath also established them for ever and ever; He hath made a decree which shall not be transgressed* (Ps. 148:6). What was the decree? *Let there be a firmament*, etc.: from that selfsame day it remained stationary and never stirred. Thus it is written, *For He spoke, and it was* (Ps. 33:9) — that which He said, He accomplished. Therefore Scripture continues, *He commanded, and it stood*: by God's word were the heavens formed, and with the same word with which He created them, by that very word they endure forever. That is the significance of our text.

Midrash Psalms 119, 148. T.S. 1, 458. 459.

141. AND GOD MADE THE FIRMAMENT. This is one of the verses which the son of Zoma vociferously questioned: He *made* — how remarkable! surely God's *word* sufficed, as it is written, *By the* word *of the Lord were the heavens made, and all the host of them by the breath of His mouth* (Ps. 33:6).

Gen. R. 4. T.S. 1, 482.

142. **And let it divide the waters from the waters.**

The thickness of the firmament equals that of the earth: compare, *It is He that sitteth above the circle* (hug) *of the earth* (Isa. 40:22) with, *And He walketh in the circuit* (hug) *of the heaven* (Job 22:14): the use of "*hug*" in both verses teaches that they are alike. R. Aha said in R. Hanina's name: It is only as thick as a metal plate. R. Joshua b. R. Nehemiah said: It is about two or three fingers in thickness. R. Simeon b. Pazzi said: The upper waters exceed the lower ones by about thirty *xestes*,[1] *for it is written, And let it divide the waters from the waters* (*la-mayim*): *lamed* is thirty.[2] Our Rabbis said: They are half and half (i.e., equal).

Gen. R. 4. T.S. 1, 456.

143. AND LET IT DIVIDE THE WATERS FROM THE WATERS. I.e., the upper from the nether water, the former being male, the latter, female. The upper distills the grateful, blessed and generous dew, the lower expands the rivers. As there can be no world without male and female, so there can be none without rain. Since He partitioned the waters, He set the firmament between them and separated one from the other, as it says, *God said*: "*Let there be a firmament*," etc.

Midrash Hagadol B'reshith 6. T.S. 1, 480.

[3] Or, a syringe or squirt (Levi, Wörterbuch).

§ 142 [1] A dry and liquid measure, nearly a pint.

[2] Hebrew letters have numerical values. He interprets the verse thus: and let there be firmament between the upper and nether waters of thirty (measures of) water.

the firmament from the waters which were above the firmament; and it was so. [8]And God called the firmament Heaven. And there was eve-

COMMENTARY

How deeply attuned these mystics, the so-called dry legalistic Pharisees, must have been to Nature, and how great their love![56] **and it was so. a.** Its capacity to hold the waters aloft so that they do not mingle with the waters below was established for ever.[57] **b.** This is to be connected with the next verse: When it was so, then *God called the firmament Heaven.* It was immediately accomplished.[58]

[8]**And God called the firmament Heaven.** He assigned it definite tasks with respect to rain, hail, etc.[59] **heaven. a.** Heb. *shamayim* is a compound of *shem mayim,* "the designation of water" — i.e., Heaven is a particular formation of water. This interpretation, based on the Talmud (see par. 45) is usually pointed *sham mayim,* water is there.[60] **b.** In the Bible, Heaven is represented as the habitation of God, in the figurative sense in which the Temple is similarly described: "*Behold heaven and the heaven of heavens cannot contain Thee; how much less this house which I have builded!*" (1 Kings 8:27)[61] **and there was evening.** On

ANTHOLOGY

144. **And it was so.**

Why is "And it was so" not stated in connection with the first day? The Sages remarked that the phrase, "And it was so," is left out with references to three creations, viz.: Heaven,[1] the great Sea-monsters, and Man. Why so? Because the act of creation is mentioned in connection with these;[1] hence there was no need to say "And it was so."

Midrash Habiur. T.S. 1, 447.

145. AND IT WAS SO. *The lips of the wise disseminate knowledge* (Prov. 15:7): this refers to Israel that avows daily, evening and morning, God's Sovereignty and Unity. *But the heart of fools is not so* (ibid.): this applies to the wicked, God saying to them, "I created the world affirmatively, with the word *so,* whereas you say negatively, *not so*; I therefore vow, *Because of that so, the wicked shall not stand in the judgment*" (Ps. 1:4). But surely it is to their advantage not to stand to judgment and not to give an account of themselves? It is in the sense of the colloquial phrase, So-and-So stood to judgment, but had no leg to stand on.

Midrash Psalms 1. T.S. 1, 484.

146. **And God called the firmament heaven, etc.**

R. Huna said in the name of Rab: At the creation of the world God named three things: heaven, earth and water. Heaven: *God called the firmament heaven.* Earth: *And God called the dry land earth.* Water: *And the gathering together of the waters called he seas.* Now, why did He name these? So that He might perform all His work with them.[1] What issued from these He left for man to name.

Gen. R. 5. T.S. 1, 546. 150.

147. "For it was good" is not stated in respect of the second day, because of the schism of that day. When the nether waters were parted from the upper, they broke out into bitter weeping that they should be consigned to a place of uncleanness. The Almighty sought to pacify them: "Still your tears, and I will order Water Libations on the altar as a recompense." But they were not appeased, because that takes place only once a year (on the Feast of Tabernacles). Thereupon He made a covenant with them that sacrifices should always require salt (and water), as it says, *And every meal-offering of thine shalt thou season with*

§ 144 [1] The others were ordered to appear, hence the Bible tells that "it was so," God's decree being obeyed. But where the Bible explicitly says that He created, "It was so" would be superfluous. By "Heaven" is meant the creation of the first day (*In the beginning God created the heaven and the earth*), and not the sky (*rakia*) of the second day, where "and it was so" is indeed said. Cf. par. 130, which states that the actual creation took place on the first day, but that it solidified in the second.

§ 146 [1] By Personally naming them He made them especially subservient, as it were, to His purposes.

ning and there was morning, a second day. [9]And God said: 'Let the waters under the heaven be gathered together unto one place, and let the

COMMENTARY

the second day the usual formula, "And God saw that it was good," is omitted. The work begun on that day did not terminate until the middle of the third day. Hence, an uncompleted piece of work could not properly be pronounced "good."[62] [9]**And God said.** Better, "now God had said," which is connected with the earlier verse: *And God called the firmament Heaven . . .* for God had said, *"Let the waters under the heaven,"* etc. Accordingly, heaven and dry land were created on the same day, as it is written, *In the day that the Lord God made heaven and earth* (2:4), and the phrase *and God saw that it was*

ANTHOLOGY

salt; neither shalt thou suffer the salt of the covenant of thy God (which He made with the nether waters) *to be lacking* (Lev. 2:13). So, because this day saw schism, "for it was good" is not stated thereon. For thus we read, *As they went out before the army they were to exclaim: "Give thanks unto the Lord, for His mercy endureth for ever"* (2 Chron. 20:21), but not, for He is good (as, e.g., in Ps. 118:1 *et passim*), because it deals with war. R. Tabyomi commented: If *for it was good* cannot be said even of a schism necessary for the greater stability and orderliness of the world, how much the more is this true of one which leads to its confusion! R. Banaah b. R. Ulla said: "It was good" is omitted because on this day the fire of Gehinom was created.

Gen. R. 4; Pesahim 54a; Midrash. T.S. 1, 501.

148. R. Levi said in the name of R. Tanhum b. Hanilai: It is written, *Declaring the end from the beginning* (Isa. 46:10); from the very beginning of the world's creation God foresaw Moses who was called *good,*[1] and that he was destined to be punished on account of water;[2] therefore *"for it was good"* is not written in connection therewith.

R. Simon said in the name of R. Joshua b. Levi: This is similar to a king who had a very cruel legion. "Since this legion is so cruel," said he, "let it not bear my name." Thus the Holy One, blessed be He, said: Since the generation of Enosh, the generation of the Flood, and the generation of the separation of races were punished by means of water, let *"for it was good"* not be written in connection therewith.

Gen. R. 4. T.S. 1, 496.

149. **A second day.**

It is written: *And he* (Solomon) *began to build* (the Temple) *in the second* (day) *of the second month, in the fourth year of his reign,* etc. (2 Chron. 3:2). But perhaps "second" refers to the day of the *week*? We do not find the days of the week thus designated. But surely it is written, *And there was evening and there was morning, a second day*?[1] No inference can be made from the story of the Creation.[2]

J. Rosh Hashanah 1:5. T.S. 1, 493.

150. A SECOND DAY. Eight things were also created on the second day: The well (of Miriam), manna, the rod (of Moses), the rainbow, the letters and the writing, the clothes (of Adam and Eve), and demons (mazikim).

Chronicles of Jerahmeel. Gaster, p. 6 (1:3).

151. **Let the waters under the heavens be gathered together.**

Rabbi commenced his discourse with the text, *Above the voice of many waters, the mighty*

§ 148 [1] In Sot. 12a R. Meir explained the verse, *And when she saw that he was good* (Exod. 2:2), as meaning that his name was "Tob" (good).
[2] Through his sin at the waters of Meribah (Num. 20:12f).

§ 149 [1] There it certainly means the second day of the week.
[2] Because there it could not mean anything else.

COMMENTARY

good in verse 10 applies to the second day, the account of the third day's creation commencing in verse 11.[63] **let the waters . . . be gathered.** They were scattered over the surface of the earth, and He gathered them into one place, viz., the ocean.[64] **unto one place.** Let them be assembled in a special area.[65]

ANTHOLOGY

breakers of the sea, the Lord on high is mighty (Ps. 93:4). *Above the voices of many waters*: When the Almighty bade the waters gather unto one place, they rushed about hither and thither, swelling up high against the sky. Said R. Isaac: At that time the waters, which had been gathered within the earth, overwhelmed and spread over it, whereupon God rebuked them: Not thus, but *Be gathered together into one place and let the dry land appear*. Now, since Scripture writes *the dry land*, and not simply *dry land*, it implies that dry land, devoid of moisture, but enwrapped in waters, had already existed. The waters continued to mount and fall, mount and fall, their roar reaching to the ends of heaven, until God rebuked them and gathered them into the *t'hom* (deep); there indeed is the gathering of waters, and even now their voices are not still. God calls them Seas. When they rise and rage and exhaust their strength, they soon must fall back to their shores and press no further in awe of their Almighty Master. Hence the words of the psalmist, *mightier than the mighty sea, the Lord on high is mighty*.

Midrash Haneelam Zohar Hadash 12.
T.S. 1, 541.

152. Let the waters be gathered together. The waters became very mighty and they came up even to the Throne of the Glory of God, and the spirit of God hovered over them. And God said, "*Let the waters be gathered together!*" When the earth heard this utterance of the Lord it brought forth mountains and hills and there were numerous valleys, and the waters ran down into them and filled them, and then the waters again became very powerful and boasted about themselves, saying, "There is nothing so mighty in all creation; come, let us cover the whole earth, for this place is too narrow for us." Then the Lord rebuked them, saying, "Boast not because of your might. For I shall send the sand, and I will set it as a boundary for you, beyond which you cannot pass." But when the waters saw the grains of sand, and how exceedingly small and frail they were, they despised them, and said, "What hurt can these do to us? If but the smallest of our waves passes over them they will be swept away and overwhelmed." When the largest grain of sand saw how terrified the others were, he called to them and said, "Fear not. It is true that we are very small and frail, and each of us singly is as nothing. If the slightest wind blows upon him he is scattered to the uttermost ends of the earth. But let us all join together and become united and be at peace with each other, and let us not be separated for ever, and these proud waters will see our strength and our power and will no longer despise us." When the grains of sand heard these words, they flew from the uttermost ends of the earth and became united and encamped in heaps and mounds upon the edge of the waters and were a boundary against them. Then the waters beheld how very great and mighty was the sand and they trembled and retreated. Then the Prince of the sea said to the waters, "Ponder well upon this action of the sand, and you will understand that even those with very little power can become mighty if they but band themselves together and are united."

Midrash on Psalms; Legend of Israel, p. 25. J. B. Levner.

153. Let the waters be gathered together (Yikkawu) unto one place, etc. It is

written, *At Thy rebuke they fled, at the voice of Thy thunder they hasted away* (Ps. 104:7). R. Berekiah explained it in the name of R. Abba b. Yoma: Let there be a measure set for the water, as you read, *And a line* (kaw) *shall be stretched forth over Jerusalem* (Zech. 1:16);[1] likewise, *And I* (God) *said: Thus far shalt thou come, but no further* (Job 38:11). Let the waters be gathered together for My purpose, for what I will one day do by means of them. Compare this to a king who built a palace and tenanted it with dumb people, who used to rise early and pay their respects to the king with gestures, with their fingers and with their handkerchiefs.[2] Said the king, "How much more would they do homage if they possessed all their faculties!" Thereupon the king tenanted it with men gifted with speech. They, however, arose and seized the palace, asserting, "This is not the king's palace: it is ours!" "Then let the palace return to its original state!" the king ordered. Similarly, at the very beginning of the world's creation the praise of the Almighty ascended from nought but the water, as it is written, *From the voices of many waters* (Ps. 93:4); and what did they proclaim? "*The Lord on high is mighty*" (ib.). Said the Holy One, blessed be He: "If these which have neither mouth nor speech praise Me, how much more will I be praised when man is created!" But the generation of Enosh arose and rebelled against Him; the generation of the Flood arose and rebelled against Him; the generation of the Separation of Tongues arose and rebelled against Him. Thereupon the Holy One, blessed be He, ordered: "Let these be removed and the former arise and take their place." Hence it is written, *And the rain was upon the earth forty days and forty nights* (Gen. 7:12).

Gen. R. 5; Midrash Haneelam Zohar Hadash 12a. T.S. 1, 512. 540.

154. LET THE WATERS BE GATHERED. Moses said to the sea: "Did you not assert that you will not divide? Yet now I see you flee: *What ails you, O sea, that you flee?*" (Ps. 114:5). The sea replied: It is not from you that I fly, nor is it fitting that I should divide before you. I was created on the third day, as it is written: *God said, "Let the waters be gathered" . . . And there was evening and morning, a third day.* Whereas you were created only on the sixth day, as it says, *And God said: "Let us make man" . . . and there was evening and there was morning, the sixth day.* Therefore it is not from you that I flee, but *at the presence of the Lord who conceived the earth* (ibid.), yea, before the Sovereign who created the world.

Midrash Psalms 114. T.S. 1, 524.

155. LET THE WATERS BE GATHERED TOGETHER. Jerusalem was called by seventy names. One of these is "Sea," as it says, *and all the nations shall be* gathered *unto it, to the name of the Lord, to Jerusalem* (Jer. 3:17), which compares with our text, *Let the waters under the heaven be* gathered *together unto one place.* Just as the Sea received all the primeval waters, so will Jerusalem one day receive all her children.[1]

Midrash Zuta on Song of Songs. T.S. 1, 521.

156. LET THE WATERS BE GATHERED TOGETHER. On Tuesdays they (the men of the Watch) used to fast on behalf of wayfarers, because on that day God said, *Let the waters under the heaven be gathered together.*[1]

J. Taanith 4:3. T.S. 1, 511.

§ 153 [1] "*Yikkawu*" is thus derived from a *kaw*, a measuring line, and the verse is translated: let the waters be confined to a definite measure or quantity.
[2] Or, spears.

§ 155 [1] The use of the same word "gather" in both places leads to the interpretation in the former that Jerusalem herself is a Sea into which the waters (here, her children) will pour.

§ 156 [1] This suggests rain. They therefore fasted that the rain should be in moderation and not sweep them away.

dry land appear.' And it was so. [10]And God called the dry land Earth, and the gathering together of the waters called He Seas; and God saw that it was good. [11]And God said: 'Let the earth put forth grass, herb

COMMENTARY

[10]**Earth.** Here it signifies that part of the terrestrial surface which was to be the abode of man and the scene of his activity.[66] **that it was good.** I.e., a fitting stage for the drama of human history.[67] [11]**Let the earth put forth.** **a.** Let it possess the power for all time to produce vegetation.[68] **b.** The Heb. *tadshe,* fr. *deshe,* grass, which grows in close profusion, implies that it should grow close-pressed.[69] **c.** Let it be clothed with a mantle of verdure.[70]

ANTHOLOGY

157. **And God called the dry land eretz—Earth.**

Why *eretz?* Because she conformed (*razethah*) to His will (*razon*). R. Nathan commented in R. Aha's name, and R. Berekiah in R. Isaac's name: *I am* El Shaddai *God Almighty* (17:1): It was I who said to heaven and earth, "*Dai!*" (enough). For had I not done so, they would have continued to extend to this very day.

Gen. R. 5. T.S. 1, 546.

158. **Called He Seas.**

R. Jose Ha-M'shulam said: Whence do we know that just as He provides delectable things on the land, so too does He provide them in the sea? From the verse, *And the gathering together of the waters called He Seas.* But surely there is only *one sea,* as it is written, *Let the waters under the heaven be gathered together unto* one *place!* Wherefore then the passage, *And the gathering together of the waters called He Seas?* This teaches that the savour of the fish of Acco differs from the taste of the fish of Tyre; and the fish of Tyre has a different flavor from that of Aspamia.

Sifri Ereb Chap. 39. T.S. 1, 545.

159. And the gathering together of the waters called He Seas. "Seas" comprises the following: the Sea of Sodom, the Sea of Solith, the Sea of Jarmukh, the Salt Sea, the Sea of Arabah, the Sea of Tiberias, and the Great Sea. Though these are arms of the Ocean,[1] they are still called Seas, as it says, *And the gathering together of the waters called He Seas.*

Midrash Konen. T.S. 1, 548.

160. And the gathering of the waters called He Seas. All seas may serve as a *mikveh* (ritual bath), for it is said, *And the gathering of* (*mikveh*) *the waters called He Seas.* This is R. Meir's view. R. Judah said: The Great Sea alone may serve as a *mikveh,* the word "seas" being employed only because it contains many kinds of water.[1] R. Jose maintained: All seas, including the Great Sea, purify when running, but are unfit for *zabim* (sufferers of gonorrhea), lepers, and for the water of lustration.[2]

Mikwaoth 5:3. Para 8:8; Shabbath 109a. T.S. 1, 452.

161. **And God said: "Let the earth put forth grass."**

It is written, *And God said: "Let the earth put forth grass,"* etc. R. Phineas b. Jair observed: Why did God issue His fiat to the earth to produce herbs, grass, and fruit-trees on the third day of Creation, and create light only on the

§ 159 [1] Not all of these can be identified. The Sea of Sodom is generally identified with the Salt Sea. Here, however, it is counted separately. The Great Sea and the Ocean both usually mean the Mediterranean; since they are distinct here, the "Ocean" is probably a more comprehensive term, embracing its furthest reaches, whilst the "Great Sea" would be the nearer waters with which they were more familiar. The "Sea" of Tiberias, also called the Sea of Galilee, is now known as Lake Kinnereth. The Sea of Jarmukh is actually a river, a tributary of the Jordan, which it joins below Lake Tiberias. The Sea of Arabah is not mentioned elsewhere; neither is the Sea of Solith. See T.S. 1, 548, and commentary a.l.

§ 160 [1] But only the Great Sea is meant in the text.
[2] See the whole ritual in Num. 19.

COMMENTARY

grass, herb yielding seed. The Heb. for grass and herb are *deshe* and *eseb* **respectively, which are** variously interpreted: **a.** *Deshe* is a generic term including all plants, while each particular species is called *eseb* or *etz.*[71] **b.** *Deshe* is vegetation for animals, while *eseb* is fit for human consumption.[72] **c.** *Deshe* and *eseb* are young plants and plants which have reached maturity respectively.[73] **d.** *Deshe* is non-edible; *eseb* is edible plants.[74] **e.** *Deshe* is vegetation whose stalk and leaves are eaten, while *eseb* is grain or legumes of which only the kernel is eaten. Because *deshe* is mentioned first, its cognate verb *tadshe* is used.[75] **f.** *Deshe-eseb* are

ANTHOLOGY

fourth? In order to display His power in making the earth yield even without light.

Midrash Tadshe 1. T.S. 1, 569.

162. And the earth put forth grass. By this the self fertilizers, needing no seed, are meant. *Herb yielding seed*: viz., vegetables and plants that require seed. *And fruit-tree bearing fruit*: i.e., trees in general. This verse teaches that all issued forthwith complete and perfect. (Not as now that when a man plants the slip of a fig tree, he waits three years or more before it bears fruits, the same being typical of all trees and plants.)[1] *Wherein is the seed thereof, upon the earth*: of those which have seed, the seed was created first; but of those that bear no seed, their fruit being their seed, the fruit was created first.

Midrash Hagadol B'reshith. T.S. 1, 581.

163. Let the earth put forth grass, etc. *And the land shall yield her produce* (Lev. 26:4). Not as at present, but as in the days of Adam. And how do we know that the earth will in the future be sown and bear fruit in one and the same day? Because we are taught, *He hath made a memorial for His wonderful works* (Ps. 111:4).[1] Likewise it says, *Let the earth put forth grass and herbs,* which also indicates that on the very day the earth was sown, she bore fruit.

Torath Kohanim Behukothai. T.S. 1, 561.

164. And God said: "Let the earth put forth grass." It has been taught: R. Eliezer says: Whence do we know that the world was created in Tishri? Because it says, *And God said*: *"Let the earth put forth grass, herb yielding seed, and fruit-tree."* Now, in which month does the earth put forth grass and the trees are full of fruit? You must say that this is Tishri. It was then the season of rain, and the rain came down and the plants sprouted, as it says, *And a mist went up from the earth* (2:6). R. Joshua said: How do we know that the world was created in Nisan? Because it says, *And the earth brought forth grass, herb yielding seed after its kind, and tree bearing fruit*: now, in which month is the earth full of grass and trees (begin to) yield fruit? None other than Nisan. That is the season when cattle, beasts, and fowls mate, as it says, *The rams have mounted the sheep*, etc. (Ps. 65:14). Then how does the other (R. Eliezer) explain the text, *tree bearing fruit*? That was a blessing for future generations.[1] Then what does the other (R. Joshua) make of the words, *"fruit tree?"*[2] This is to be explained in accordance with the dictum of R. Joshua b. Levi, who said: All creatures were created in their full stature, like trees in Nisan, when they are laden with fruit, and not as they are in Tishri. And why did the Creator so create them? So that Adam might find his food ready at hand; for such is the normal practice: one first prepares the banquet and then receives his guests.

Rosh Hashanah 11a, b; P'sikta Zutrathi. T.S. 1, 582. 592.

§ 162 [1] This is in parenthesis as a probable later addition—Kasher.
§ 163 [1] I.e., the future will recall the marvelous days of Creation in sowing and yielding on the same day.
§ 164 [1] But does not mean that the trees actually yielded fruit at that time.
[2] Which implies fruit-bearing trees, but not trees that actually yielded fruit at that time.

yielding seed, and fruit-tree bearing fruit after its kind, wherein is the

COMMENTARY

synonyms in construct relationship, analogous to *admath-afar* ("dust of the earth") (Dan. 12, 2).[76] **yielding seed.** Which produce seed that have the power to perpetuate their species.[77] **bearing fruit after its kind.** That the fruit and its tree should be of the same kind.[78] **tree . . . wherein is the seed thereof,**

ANTHOLOGY

165. AND GOD SAID: "LET THE EARTH PUT FORTH GRASS," etc. It was taught in R. Nathan's name: *Three* entered for judgment, yet *four* came out guilty. Adam and Eve and the serpent entered for judgment, whereas the earth was cursed with them, as it is written, *Cursed is the ground for thy sake* (3:17), which means that it will produce accursed things for you (Adam), such as gnats, insects, and fleas. R. Isaac of Magdala observed: Yet there is benefit in them too.[1] Now why was the earth cursed? R. Judah b. Shalom said: Because she disobeyed God's command. For the Holy One, blessed be He, said thus: *Let the earth put forth grass, herb yielding seed, and fruit-tree bearing fruit*: just as the fruit is eaten, so should the tree be edible. She, however, did not do thus, but, *And the earth brought forth grass, herb yielding seed after its kind, and tree bearing fruit*: the fruit was edible, but not the tree. R. Phinehas said: She *exceeded* His command, thinking to do the will of her Creator: thus, *and tree bearing fruit* implies that even non-fruit-bearing trees yielded fruit. Now no difficulty arises on R. Judah's view. But on R. Phinehas's view, why was she cursed? It is as one might say: "Cursed be the breast that suckled such a one as this." Whence do we learn that in the future the tree itself will be edible? From the phrase, *fruit-tree*. Now, if the epithet "fruit" is to convey that a tree *bearing* fruit is meant, that is already implied in the expression *"yielding fruit."* Why then does Scripture say, *"fruit-tree?"* To teach that just as the fruit can be eaten, so will the tree itself be edible.

Gen. R. 5; Torath Kohanim Behukothai. T.S. 1, 563. 564.

166. LET THE EARTH BRING FORTH GRASS. *His riding seat is purple* (argaman) (Song 3:10). This refers to the Holy One, blessed be He, of whom it is written, *He rideth upon the heaven* (Deut. 33:26). And He weaves (*oreg*, connected with *argaman*) the world in such manner that all created beings come forth after their kind, no species becoming commingled with another, even as we read, *Let the earth bring forth grass*, etc.

Num. R. 12. T.S. 1, 565.

167. **After its kind.**

R. Hanina b. Papa expounded: *May the glory of the Lord endure forever; let the Lord rejoice in His work!* (Ps. 104:31). This verse was said by the Prince of the Universe (an angel). For when the Holy One, blessed be He, ordered the earth to put forth the fruit tree *"after its kind,"* the grasses argued: If He desired confusion, why did He enjoin *"after its kind"* upon the trees? Moreover, they reasoned, if trees, which by nature do not grow in jumbled species, were commanded by the Holy One, blessed be He, to come forth each *"after its kind,"* how much more so does it apply to us! Immediately each herb came forth after its kind. Thereupon the Prince of the Universe broke into song, *May the glory of the Lord endure forever; let the Lord rejoice in His works.*

Hulin 60a. T.S. 1, 559.

168. AFTER THEIR OWN KIND. It was taught in the name of R. Eleazar: A heathen may wear garments of linen and wool mixture, and sow his fields with diverse seeds; but may not cross

§ 165 [1] On the present reading R. Isaac held that even gnats, etc., have their uses. But there is a variant reading, as follows: Then let the earth produce (pests as large as) a camel. Said R. Isaac of Magdala: In that there would be benefit too—(though a pest, it could be used).

seed thereof, upon the earth.' And it was so. [12]And the earth brought forth grass, herb yielding seed after

COMMENTARY

upon the earth. a. when the seed of the fruit tree falls to the earth, it should produce a tree like itself.[79] **b.** Let the tree possess everything necessary to perpetuate its kind upon the earth.[80] **[12]that it was**

ANTHOLOGY

diverse animal species, nor graft trees of different species. Why so? Because in the case of the latter Scripture specifies, *after their own kind.* But the same is used of grasses too? It is not stated as a command, but only that they did come forth thus. If so, why was the earth cursed? Said R. Judah b. Shalom: For transgressing God's fiat, which ran, *Let the earth put forth grass, herb yielding seed.* Disobeying, *the earth brought forth grass, herb yielding seed after its kind.*[1] R. Phineas said: The earth rejoiced in her command and added non fruit-bearing trees of her own accord.

J. Kelayim 1:7. T.S. 1, 560.

169. After its kind. Rabina propounded the question: If a man grafts two grasses of different species, what is the law according to R. Hanina b. Papa?[1] Since *after its kind* is not expressly stated with regard to these, he is not liable; or seeing that the Lord approved of their action, it is as if "*after its kind*" were expressly stated (and he is liable)? The question remains undecided.

Hulin 60a, b. T.S. 1, 583.

170. **Wherein is the seed thereof, upon the earth.**

He opened an entrance to the Garden of Eden and took out plants, which He planted upon the face of all the earth, all kinds of trees yielding fruit according to their kind, and all kinds of herbs and grass in which resided their seed, as it is said, *Wherein is the seed thereof* (he planted) *upon the earth.*

Pirke d' Rabbi Nathan Chap. 5. T.S. 1, 566.

171. **And the earth brought forth grass.**

He fainteth not, nor toileth (Isa. 40:28). God knows not of toil; with a mere word He created the present world, and with a word He will renew it in the world to come. Thus it is written, *And God said: "Let the earth put forth grass,"* and forthwith *the earth brought forth grass.* So in the Messianic era He will but utter a word and everything will be accomplished immediately.

Aggadah B'reshith 23. T.S. 1, 568.

172. And the earth brought forth grass. R. Assi pointed out a contradiction. One verse says, *And the earth brought forth grass,* referring to the third day; whereas another verse when speaking of the *sixth* day says, *No shrub of the field was yet on the earth* (2:5)?—This teaches us that the plants commenced to grow but stopped just as they were about to break through the soil, until Adam came and prayed for rain on their behalf; and when rain fell they sprouted forth. This teaches you that the Holy One, blessed be He, longs for the prayers

§ 168 [1] The point is not clear. T.S. a.l. explains: God's command was that the tree itself should be edible, whereas the earth brought forth trees of which only the fruit was edible. In that case the proof-texts are abbreviated, since the deduction is made from the unquoted portions of the verses. In the texts actually quoted the only differences between command and fulfillment are: (i) The command was *tadshe,* etc., let the earth *clothe* itself with grass; whilst the fulfillment was *wa-totse,* etc., and the earth *brought forth* grass; (ii) The command did not specify "*after its kind*" for grass and herbs, yet they were brought forth after their kind. It is not likely (though not impossible) that the latter was the transgression, since the grasses are elsewhere praised for this (par. 167). Perhaps (assuming the texts complete) *tadshe,* clothe itself, suggests greater abundance than *wa-totse,* brought forth, in which case the earth was cursed for niggardliness in its obedience. R. Phineas' statement which follows is in that case a separate observation, unconnected with the preceding.

§ 169 [1] He maintained that herbage was not expressly ordered to grow after their own kind. See last par.

its kind, and tree bearing fruit, wherein is the seed thereof, after its kind; and God saw that it was good. [13]And there was evening and there

COMMENTARY

good. As food for man and beast (cf. v. 29f).[81] **and God saw that it was good.** This is said twice in connection with the third day, in reference to the completion of the gathering of the waters and the creation of plant life respectively.[82] A separate day was not assigned to the latter, because it was

ANTHOLOGY

of the righteous. R. Dostai said: They appeared then, but it was not yet in their power to engender fruit. Why? Because God had not yet sent rain upon the earth, not even a mist to rise upward. Though all that grew had the potential power to generate and multiply, in the absence of rain they lacked the actual powers of propagation.

Hulin 60b; Midrash Haneelam 13b. T.S. 1, 584. 590.

173. **And tree bearing fruit.**

In life a Jew is ritually clean, but when dead he is unclean, for then his soul ascends to heaven, and only the animal soul[1] is left in the body. The heathen is clean when he dies. This may be likened to two trees, one holy and one unclean; so are Israel and the heathen nations. The first has a spirit of holiness and the other of uncleanness, though each is planted in the same earth and each is akin to it in body. The one which is well watered and bears fruit is Israel, which has a holy Torah that has been likened to water, as it says, *Ho, everyone that thirsteth, come ye for water* (Isa. 55:1), "*water*" meaning naught else but the Torah. It is in reference to Israel that Scripture says, *and tree bearing fruit, wherein is the seed thereof.*

Zohar Hadash Ruth 71. T.S. 1, 591.

174. **And God saw that it was good.**

While travelling in the desert R. Isaac said to R. Eleazar, "I would ask you a question, if you will not think it improper." R. Eleazar answered, "You may ask anything you wish regarding a Scriptural matter." R. Isaac rejoined: "Scripture says, *And God saw that it was good.* Now, if this were stated *prior* to the actual creation, it were well. But it was uttered *after* creation, and therefore implies that God did not perceive before creation the world's perfection. Only when creation was completed did God survey it as it stood before Him and then exclaim, 'It is good!' For the text says first, *And He saw,* and then, *that it was good.*" R. Eleazar replied: "Your query is a very proper one. Indeed, you were in duty bound to ask it. Our text is meant as a warning to man. For R. Judah said: When one studies the cosmogony, with its daily creations, he should not ask questions about matters which are none of his business, such as why one thing was made in this form and another in a different form. You must answer him: Scripture declares, *And God saw that it was good* to create it thus or thus. It is also a warning to man and a guide to right conduct. Just as God did not say that it was good, despite His foreknowledge how it would turn out, until He completed His creation; so is it unmeet for a man to praise anything before its completion, lest it be found faulty and he be revealed as a boaster and a liar."

Midrash Haneelam Zohar Hadash 12b. T.S. 1, 556.

175. AND GOD SAW THAT IT WAS GOOD. This teaches that the Garden of Eden was created for the righteous, as it says, *Oh how abundant is Thy goodness, which Thou hast laid up for them that fear Thee* (Ps. 31:20).

P'sikta Zutrathi. T.S. 1, 593.

§ 173 [1] Man was conceived of as having a superior, spiritual soul, and an inferior, animal soul.

was morning, a third day. [14]And God said: 'Let there be lights in the firmament of the heaven to divide the day from the night; and let them be for signs, and for seasons, and for days

COMMENTARY

not a separate act of creation, since the earth is the same whether fruitful or not.[83] **[14]lights. a.** Resplendent lanterns, luminous bodies.[84] **b.** The Heb. word signifies sources of light: hence "luminaries" would be a better translation. Other ancient peoples ascribed to the sun, moon and stars a beneficent or malevolent potency over the lives of men and nations. Here, however, all idolatry and superstition are swept away. These lights are works of one Almighty God, and are created for His appointed purposes; see Jer. 10:2.[85] **in the firmament of**

ANTHOLOGY

176. **A third day.**

On the third day He created various trees in the Garden of Eden, and all sorts of trees in this world, both fruit-bearing (edible) and sterile (non-edible), as well as the plants of Paradise. When the cedar in Lebanon and the oak of Bashan and all lofty trees saw themselves among the first on the scene, they waxed proud and haughty. Then said God: "I hate pride and haughtiness, for none is exalted save Myself." Forthwith He created the mountain of iron. When the trees saw the mountain, they wept, and for this reason trees are called the weepers, in the verse, *over against the weepers* (2 Sam. 5:23—AJV: *mulberry-trees*). To God's query why they wept they gave answer: "Because Thou hast created the iron mountain to uproot us. Once we believed none in the world as high as we; now a destroyer has been created to hurl us down." Said the Almighty: "From yourselves shall come the handle for the iron axe to fell you. Without your assistance the iron will be powerless against you. But I will so contrive that you shall have dominion over each other, you over the iron and the iron over you." Thus God made peace between them.

Midrash Konen 25. T.S. 1, 595.

177. A THIRD DAY (SH'LISHI). *Sh'lishi* is an allusion to the fact that on this day might[1] was created, as we read, *warriors* (shalishim) *and councillors, all of them riding upon horses* (Ezek. 23:23).

Gen. R. 5. T.S. 1, 594.

178. A THIRD DAY. The letter *gimel* is adorned with three strokes on top, to symbolize the three days during which the world enjoyed the light specially created by God.[1] Again, it is because three things took place on the third day, viz.: (i) The dry land was created and named Earth; (ii) It was carpeted with verdure; and (iii) All the waters of the world returned to their proper place, and seas and rivers were created.

Midrash Akiba b. Joseph. T.S. 1, 549.

179. **And God said: Let there be lights.**

R. Johanan began his lecture thus: *Who appointest the moon for seasons* (Ps. 104:19). He commented: The orb of the sun alone was created to give light. If so, why was the moon created? *For seasons*: in order to sanctify new moons and years by them.[1] R. Shila of K'far Temarta[2] said in R. Johanan's name: Yet even so, *The sun knoweth its coming* (ib.): from the sun one knows the coming of the month,

§ 177 [1] "Might" (lit., mighty men) was created in that iron, with which men wage war, was created on this day.

§ 178 [1] *Gimel* is the third letter of the Hebrew alphabet. In the Torah Scroll it is traditionally written with three strokes or daggers on top (Cf. par. 19, n. 1). The luminaries (sun, moon and stars) were created on the fourth day. Therefore for the first three days the world had only the light which He had called into existence on the first day.

§ 179 [1] The Jewish year is lunar, and the actual fixing of the months and the years depends on the moon, though a month is intercalated in leap years in order to harmonize the lunar with the solar years.

[2] The townlet of Temarta in Judea; Hul. 62a.

and years; [15]and let them be for lights in the firmament of the heaven to give light upon the earth.' And it

COMMENTARY

the heaven. In the vault of the firmament which is called heaven.[86] **for signs. a.** They serve as signs, because when they are eclipsed it is an evil omen for the world.[87] **b.** To help man locate his position when moving over the surface of the earth: they were primitive man's compass.[88] **c.** "Signs" stands for the Sabbath, as in Exod. 31:16-17: *Wherefore the children of Israel shall keep* the Sabbath . . . *It is a* sign, etc.[89] **for seasons. a.** "Seasons" was an anticipation of the future: the festivals (also called "seasons")

ANTHOLOGY

for we count the beginning of the month only from sunset.

Gen. R. 6. T.S. 1, 598.

180. **And let them be for lights.**

R. Azariah said in R. Hanina's name: The orb of the sun alone was created to give light; yet if so, why was the moon created? Because the Holy One, blessed be He, foresaw that the peoples of the world would treat them as divinities. Said the Lord: "If they are two, opposed to each other,[1] and yet the peoples of the world treat them as divinities, how much more would they do so if there were but one!" R. Berekiah said in R. Simon's name: Both were created in order to give light, as it says, *And let them be for lights,* etc.

Gen. R. 6. T.S. 1, 599.

181. **To divide the day from the night.**

"This day, the beginning of Thy work." That means, New Year[1] was at the beginning of Thy work. For He created the world on the 25th of Elul, this first day of the first year of Creation falling within the 2,000 years by which the Creation of the Torah preceded that of the world.[2] Now, the luminaries were created on the world's first day, but not suspended in the heavens until the fourth; hence the light which He called forth on the first day (which was other than that of the luminaries) functioned three days, which is 36 hours. For Scripture states, *And God said: "Let there be lights in the firmament of the heaven."* Wherefore? *"To divide the day from the night."* Thus we see that only now were they suspended, but prior thereto there was no night to separate day from day, so that the light shone for three days without interruption. It was likewise so on the Sabbath day, which was New Year. For two days were still wanting to complete the thirty days of Elul; these were made up by one day of Elul and the sixth day.[3] The following day, which was the Sabbath, was New Year. That day too lasted 36 hours, it having no night.[4] Thus the light of this Sabbath New Year's day was as the light of the first day, each lasting 36 hours. That is what we mean when we say in our liturgy, "This (New Year's) day at the beginning of Thy work (i.e., at the Creation) was a memorial of the first day."

P'sikta Rabbathi 46. T.S. 1, 611.

182. **And let them be for signs.**

This refers to the Sabbaths;[1] *And for seasons*: to the three pilgrimage festivals; *And for days*: to the New Moons; *And years* means the sanctification of the years.[2]

Gen. R. 6. T.S. 1, 600.

§ 180 [1] The reference is possibly to the eclipse of the sun and the moon (commentaries).

§ 181 [1] Which is on the first of Tishri. The preceding month is Elul.
[2] See T.S. 1, 67.
[3] I.e., after these three days and the fourth on which the luminaries were suspended, there were still two days to go in Elul, and they were made up by the fifth and the sixth days of that week.
[4] See Chapter II, par. 3 (T.S. 2, 39).

§ 182 [1] Cf. Exod. 31:17, where the Sabbath is called a sign.
[2] I.e., the proclamation of the New Year by the proper authorities.

COMMENTARY

were fixed by lunar calculation.[90] **b.** To regulate the calendar. The "seasons" are spring, summer, autumn, and winter; also seed-time and harvest. The Heb. word for "seasons" later acquired the meaning of "festivals," since these were fixed by the year's seasons.[91] **c.** "Signs" means minutes and "seasons" hours.[92] [15]**let them be for lights.** To illuminate the earth would be an additional function.[93] **light upon the earth.** Without

ANTHOLOGY

183. AND LET THEM BE FOR SIGNS, etc. He who beholds the sun commencing its (28-year) cycle, the moon commencing its cycle, or the sky in all its brightness, must recite the benediction "Blessed be He who performed the work of the Creation." When one beholds the moon as it is renewed, one must recite the benediction "Blessed be He who renews the month," inserting this in the principal Prayer.[1] According to R. Jose b. Nehorai the benediction is: "Blessed be He who sanctifies Israel and renews the months." R. Hiyya b. R. Ashi gave this version: "Blessed be He who sanctifies Israel and the beginning of the months." Samuel said: "One must recite, 'Bestow upon us Thy blessings.' "[2] Rab said: "One must mention the festive season."[3] R. Hoshea quoted: "*And let them be for signs, and for seasons, and for days and years.*"[4]

J. Berakoth 9:2. T.S. 1, 596.

184. AND LET THEM BE FOR SIGNS, etc. R. Levi said, quoting R. Jose b. Ilai: It is but natural that the great should count by the great, and the small by the small. Esau[1] counts by the sun, which is large: just as the sun rules by day but not by night, so does Esau enjoy this world, but has nought in the World to Come. Jacob counts by the moon, which is small: just as the moon rules by day and by night, so has Jacob a portion in this world and in the World to Come. Thus also it is written, *Who is she* (sc. the Community of Israel) *that looketh forth as the dawn, fair as the moon, clear as the sun* (Song of Songs 6:10)?[2] Here too Israel is compared to the sun and the moon. R. Nahman made another observation: As long as the light of the greater luminary functions, the light of the smaller one is not noticeable; but when the former sets, the latter becomes noticeable. Even so, as long as the light of Esau prevails, the light of Jacob cannot be distinguished; but when the light of Esau will set, that of Jacob shall be distinguished, as it is written, *Arise, Shine, . . . For, behold, darkness shall cover the earth, and gross darkness the peoples, but upon thee the Lord will arise, and His glory shall be seen upon thee* (Isa. 60:1f).

Gen. R. 6. Exod R. 6. T.S. 1, 630. 675.

185. **And let them be for lights in the firmament of the heaven.**

The stars radiate a mystic influence on everything, as is taught in the Book of Celestial Wisdom of the Ancients. The same is intimated in the Book of Solomon regarding the knowledge of the properties of precious stones. If the stones want the lustre or the glow of the stars, they cannot be an influence for good in the life of the world. God created all for the benefit of the world, as Scripture says, *To give light upon the earth,* which means to be beneficent

§ 183 [1] The Eighteen Benedictions known collectively as Tefilah, the Prayer *par excellence.*
[2] A prayer recited on festivals, commencing with these words. Samuel maintains that it is also recited on New Moon.
[3] This likewise is part of the festival prayers, which Rab would include on New Moon too.
[4] The point of the quotation is not clear. Probably: Since both luminaries, the sun and the moon, are to serve the same purpose, it follows that New Moon, which is dependent solely on the moon, requires rubrics similar to those of festivals, which are determined by both the sun and the moon.

§ 184 [1] The other nations.
[2] The Rabbis interpreted the Song of Songs allegorically as a dialogue between God and Israel, the Lover being God and Israel His beloved.

was so. [16]And God made the two great lights: the greater light to rule

COMMENTARY

which life and growth are impossible.[94] [16]**great.** I.e., that appear to the human eye greater than any of

ANTHOLOGY

agencies for the betterment of everything on earth.

Zohar 2:172. T.S. 1, 625.

186. LET THERE BE LIGHTS IN THE FIRMAMENT OF THE HEAVEN. An example of a general statement followed by an action which is a detailed account of the former, is the following: *And God said: "Let there be light." And there was light.* Then He repeated, *"Let there be lights in the firmament of the heaven."* One might mistake this for another creation, whereas it is merely a detailed account of the first. We find support for this view in a Baraitha which states: The lights mentioned on the fourth day of creation are really those which were created on the first day, but He did not suspend them in the firmament until the fourth day.

The 32 Middoth of R. Eliezer, son of R. Jose T.S. 1, p. 178 Addenda 9.

187. **And God made the two great lights.**

To Thee the day, to Thee also the night (Ps. 74:16): to Thee the day gives praise, to Thee the night gives praise. To Thee it is fitting to utter song by day and by night. Wherefore? Because *Thou hast established luminary and sun* (Ps. loc. cit.), and Thou hast made the two great lights, as it says, *And God made the two great lights.*

Gen. R. 6. T.S. 1, 628.

188. THE TWO GREAT LIGHTS, etc. All the stars and constellations and the two luminaries were created at the beginning of the night of the fourth day, none preceding the other by more than two-thirds of an hour. Every motion of the sun is done with deliberation, whilst every motion of the moon is done quickly, because the distance covered by the sun in a year is covered by the moon in thirty days.

Pirke d'R. Eliezer Chap. 7. T.S. 1, 638.

189. AND GOD MADE THE TWO GREAT LIGHTS. On the fourth day God took fire, sealed and orbed it, and named it Sun, to serve by day, and that is His gift to the world. The very same day He took light, sealed and orbed it, and named it Yareach (Moon), because it runs its course—*orach* (as in Ps. 19:6). It is also called *sahar,* because it ministers at night, lighting the world when it is darkened like a dungeon (*sohar*). Both the sun and moon then were equal peers, as we read, *God made the two great lights.* Both were equally great, until the moon challenged God's way, saying, "Why didst Thou create the world with the letter *beth?*"[1] *God* answered: "In order to make it known that, as the numerical value of the letter *beth,* which is two, suggests, there are two worlds and two witnesses."[2] "Which then is greater, this world or the future?" the moon queried. "The future is greater than this world," came the reply. But the moon pertinaciously continued: "Why didst Thou create these two worlds one larger and one smaller? Again, Thou didst create heaven and earth, the former larger than the latter. Thou hast created fire and water; water quenches fire. Similarly, since Thou hast created sun and moon, one should be greater than the other." God retorted: "It is obvious that you want Me to magnify you and diminish the sun. Go; be diminished to a sixtieth part of the sun." Thereupon the moon remonstrated: "O Master of the universe, so harsh a sentence for a single utterance?" God's word of comfort followed: "One day you will be restored to your original state and shine like the sun," as it says, *Moreover the*

§ 189 [1] See par. 19.
[2] The point of "two witnesses" is doubtful. Perhaps it means that these two worlds testify to His creative activity. Possibly, again, it refers to the sun and moon, with the same meaning.

ANTHOLOGY

light of the moon shall be as the light of the sun (Isa. 30:26). "O Master of the Universe, pray, what will be then the light of the sun?" the moon insinuated. "You still expostulate!" exclaimed He. "By My life, the sun's light will grow sevenfold!" Thus the prophecy continues, *And the light of the sun shall be seven-fold, as the light of the seven days* (ibid.).

Midrash Konen. T.S. 1, 645.

190. AND GOD MADE THE TWO GREAT LIGHTS. R. Simeon b. Pazzi pointed out a contradiction between verses. One verse says, *And God made the two great lights*; but immediately the verse continues, *The* greater *light . . . and the lesser light*?—The moon said unto the Holy One, blessed be He: "Sovereign of the Universe! Is it possible for two kings to wear one crown?" He answered, "Go then, and make thyself smaller." "Sovereign of the Universe!" cried the moon, "because I have suggested that which is proper, must I then make myself smaller?" He replied, "Go, and thou wilt rule by day and night." "But what is the value of this?" cried the moon, "of what use is a lamp in broad daylight?" He replied: "Go, Israel shall reckon by thee the days and the years." "But it is impossible," said the moon, "to do without the sun for the reckoning of the seasons," as it is written, *And let* them *be for signs, and for seasons, and for days and for years* (1:14). "Go!" He rejoined, "My righteous shall be named after thee," as we find, Jacob the younger, Samuel the small, David the youngest (1 Sam. 17:14).[1] Seeing that it would not be consoled, the Holy One, blessed be He, said: "Bring an atonement for Me for making the moon smaller." This is what was meant by R. Simeon b. Lakish when he declared: Why is it that the he-goat offered on the new moon is distinguished in that there is written concerning it *Unto the Lord* (Num. 28:15)?—Because the Holy One, blessed be He, said: "Let this he-goat be an atonement for Me for making the moon smaller."

Hulin 60b. T.S. 1, 627.

191. AND GOD MADE THE TWO GREAT LIGHTS. Scripture exclaims, *Arise, Shine!* (Isa. 60:1); and again, *Therefore glorify the Lord with lights, and the name of the Lord, the God of Israel, in the isles of the seas* (ibid. 24:15). Now, how do we glorify Him? Said R. Abbahu b. Kahana: By the torches which we light in the synagogue. R. Abbahu said: Through the two lights which are referred to in the verse, *And God made the two great lights*: viz., by reciting blessings over the sun and moon respectively when each shines.

P'sikta 21. T.S. 1, 636.

192. THE TWO GREAT LIGHTS. Three letters of the Ineffable Name of God are written upon the heart of the sun, and angels lead it. Those that lead it by day do not lead it at night, and those that lead it at night do not lead it by day. The sun rises in a chariot, and rides forth crowned as a bridegroom, as it is said, *And he goeth forth from his canopy as a bridegroom* (Ps. 19:6). The horns (the rays) and the fiery face of the sun look upon the earth in the summer, and would consume it with fire if the ice above would not temper the heat, as it is said, *Nothing is hidden from his heat* (ibid. 7). In the winter-time the sun turns his icy face to the earth, and were it not for the fire which warms the cold, the world would not be able to endure it, as it is said, *Who can stand before his cold* (Ps. 147:17)? The sun rises in the east and sets opposite in the west. The Shekinah always resides in the west, and the sun enters in its presence, and, bowing down before the King of kings, says: "O Lord of the universe, I have fulfilled all Thy commands." These are some of the ways of the sun.

Chronicles of Jerahmeel, p. 11 (3:5).

§ 190 [1] Both Jacob and David, the *younger* sons, were chosen by God (in Heb. the same word means small and young: the moon would be the small luminary, and even so the "small" i.e., younger sons, were chosen for pre-eminence); Samuel too heard God's call when a small lad (1 Sam. 3:1-4).

the day, and the lesser light to rule the night; and the stars. [17]And God

COMMENTARY

the stars.[95] **to rule.** To sustain with their light and warmth both plant and animal life.[96] **and the**

ANTHOLOGY

193. **The greater light, etc.**

On the fourth day He created the two luminaries, of which one was not greater in size than the other. They were equal in height, form, and light, as it says, *And God made the two great lights*. Rivalry ensued between them, each saying to the other, "I am bigger than thou." What did the Holy One, blessed be He, do? He increased the one and diminished the other, as it is said, *The greater light to rule the day, and the lesser light to rule the night*.

Pirke d' Rabbi Eliezer Chap. 15. T.S. 1, 637.

194. **The greater light to rule the day, etc.**

On the fourth day I (God) created the sun and the moon, the sun to light by day and the moon to light by night. In the same manner, I will one day ordain for the Israelites two pillars for their guidance: one, a pillar of fire to give light by night; the other, a pillar of cloud to give light by day.

Pirke d' Rabbi Eliezer. T.S. 1, 641.

195. **The two great lights . . . and the stars.**

In what order are they placed in heaven? They are distributed there as sun and moon and the five planets. The firmament is divided into seven degrees, one above the other. There are seven distinct places for these seven planets; and this is their order: The first degree is near the earth, and this lowest degree is the habitation of the moon, in which the moon makes a circuit round the firmament. The second degree is the habitation of Mercury, in which it describes its circuit in the firmament. The third degree is the habitation of Venus, in which it also describes its circuit in the firmament. The fourth degree is the middle of them, viz., the habitation of the sun, which completes its circuit of the heaven in twelve months. The fifth degree is the habitation of Mars, which makes its circuit in the firmament.[1] The seventh degree is the highest of all, viz., the habitation of Saturn, which completes its circuit in three years.

Chronicles of Jerahmeel, p. 12 (4:3-4).

196. AND THE STARS. This is the order of their work: Saturn is appointed over the poor and needy women, over faintness and sickness, diseases of the body, and over death. His appearance is like that of an old man with a sickle in his hand. Mars is appointed over war (bloodshed) and the sword, over the wicked, over slander, over strife, battle, hatred, jealousy, quarrels, over warriors, wounds, injuries, bruises, over fire, water, and destruction. His appearance is like that of an armed warrior with a sword in his right hand, and he appears like a man of wrath and a stirrer up of strife. Wherever he turns wickedness ensues; he looks terrible in his coat of mail, and with the spear which he bears in his left hand. Jupiter is appointed over life, peace and good, over prosperity, tranquillity, joy, pleasant conversation, rejoicing, riches, greatness, sovereignty and majesty. His appearance is like that of a valiant and noble-looking man, and his head is that of a ram. Venus is appointed over kindness, favor, love, lust, passion, desire, marriage, the birth of man and animals, the fruits of the earth and the fruits of the tree. Its form is that of a young girl beautifully adorned, and swaying a branch of a tree in her hand. Mercury is appointed over wisdom, discretion, understanding, knowledge, and the active intellect enabling one to unravel mysteries, to devise plans in every branch of work, and in the writings of any language. Its form is that of an old man with thin lips; he possesses wings, and the lower part of the body is like a dragon. The sun is appointed over light, to separate light from

§ 195 [1] The sixth degree is missing in the MS.

set them in the firmament of the heaven to give light upon the earth, [18]and to rule over the day and over the night, and to divide the light

COMMENTARY

stars. They are mentioned last and without explanation, because they play a subordinate part in the life of man, as compared with the sun and moon.[97] [18]**over the day and over the night. a.** By day and by night.[98] **b.** Over those creatures that are chiefly active by day and over

ANTHOLOGY

darkness, and through it to enable us to calculate the days, months and years, and to do every kind of work, to make any cunning work, to walk any distance, and to migrate from city to city and from town to town. The moon holds the key of heaven and earth, and is appointed over morning and evening. She is set over all creatures, to lead them in the right or wrong way, although she has no power in herself either to do good or evil. But everything is done by order and command.

Chronicles of Jerahmeel, pp. 12-13 (4:5-9).

197. AND THE STARS. The following seven planets God created and placed in order in the firmament for the benefit of the world; for by means of them people calculate the signs, seasons, and astronomical computations; the time of summer, the number of the hours, days and months, periods and festivals (appointed times), as it is said, *They shall be for signs, for seasons, for days and for years.* The seven days of the week are called after the seven planets, the Sun, Venus, Mercury, the Moon, Saturn, Jupiter, and Mars. On the first day Sol, i.e., the sun, rules and this day is called Zondakh. On the second day the moon serves; it is called Luna, therefore the second day is called Lunedi, i.e., Mondakh. On the third day Mars serves; it is called Mars, hence Marsdi, i.e., Diensdakh. On the fourth day Mercury, or Marcurios, serves, therefore it is called Markusdi, i.e., Godansdakh. On the fifth day Jupiter serves; it is called Iovis, hence Iovisdi, i.e., Donnersdakh. On the sixth day Venus, i.e., Veneri, serves, therefore the day is called Vindredi, that is Vredakh. On the seventh day Saturnus serves, therefore the day is called Sabbatdi, i.e., Satuldakh.

Chronicles of Jerahmeel, pp. 11-12 (4:1-2).

198. AND THE STARS. R. Aha said: Imagine a king who had two governors, one ruling in the city and the other in a province. Said the king: "Since the former has humbled himself to rule in the city only, I decree that whenever he goes out, all the people shall go out with him, and whenever he enters, the Senate and the people shall enter with him." Thus did the Holy One, blessed be He, say: "Since the moon humbled itself to rule by night, I decree that when she comes forth, the stars shall accompany her, and when she retires, the stars shall retire with her."

Gen. R. 6. T.S. 1, 631.

199. AND THE STARS (KOKABIM). When God rebuked the moon and she fell from her high estate, sparks fell from her over the whole sky and extinguished the lights. These were called *Kokabim* (stars), because they put out (*kabu*) the light of the moon.

Midrash. T.S. 1, 647.

200. **And God set them in a firmament of the heaven.**

R. Jonathan said: Three things were made a gift to the world, viz., the Torah, the luminaries, and rain. Whence do we know it of the luminaries?—*And God gave them in the firmament of the heaven.*

Gen. R. 6. T.S. 1, 658.

201. AND GOD SET THEM IN THE RAKIA (FIRMAMENT) OF THE HEAVEN. R. Judah said: There are two firmaments. Resh Lakish said: There are seven, namely: Wilon (curtain), Rakia (firmament), etc. *Rakia* is that in which sun and moon, stars and constellations are set, for it is said, *And God set them in the Rakia (firmament) of the heaven.*

Hagigah 12b. T.S. 1, 657.

from the darkness; and God saw that it was good. [19]And there was evening and there was morning, a fourth day. [20]And God said: 'Let the waters swarm with swarms of living creatures, and let fowl fly above the earth in the open firmament of heaven.'

COMMENTARY

those that are chiefly active at night.[99] **[20]let the waters swarm. a.** Or, "teem." Heb. *sharatz.* Movement as well as fecundity is implied. It is used in connection with fishes and aquatic animals, rodents and insects.[100] **b.** Let the waters be agitated by the movements of the creatures generated in it.[101] **swarms** (*sheretz*). **a.** *Sheretz* is any creature that is low upon the earth, e.g., flies, ants, worms and rodents.[102] **b.** Creatures which are characterized by continual motion.[103] **c.** The whole phrase means: Let the waters *swarm a*

ANTHOLOGY

202. AND GOD SET THEM IN THE FIRMAMENT OF THE HEAVEN. God acted with abundant grace in not setting the sun in the sky visible to us. R. Yannai and R. Hanina said: He placed the luminaries in the second heaven, as it says: *And God set them in the firmament of the heaven:* not in the heaven, but *in the firmament of the heaven,* which implies in the firmament which is above the visible heaven. R. Abbahu observed: Scripture states explicitly that He placed it only in the upper firmament, for it is written, *Thou art the Lord, even Thou alone; Thou hast made the heaven, the heaven of heavens, with all their host* (Neh. 9:6). It does not say, the heaven with all their host, but, *the heaven, the heaven of heavens, with all their host:* hence, where are the Lord's hosts (the luminaries) set? Surely in the *heaven of heavens.* This teaches that God did not set them in the first heaven. Why so? Were the sun set in the visible heaven, its heat, as it goes forth in its circuit, would burn up all creatures. Therefore He placed the sun in the second heaven.

P'sikta d'Rabbi Kahana 29. T.S. 1, 662.

203. **To give light.**

Israel said: O *send out Thy light and Thy truth; let them lead me* (Ps. 43:3). Great is the light of the Holy One, blessed be He! The sun and the moon illumine the world; but whence do they derive *their* radiance? They catch a few sparks of the celestial light; as it says, *The sun and the moon . . . at the light of Thine arrows as they go, at the shining of Thy glittering spear* (Hab. 3:11). Great is the celestial light, for only a hundredth part of it was given to all mankind, as it says, *He knoweth what* (mah)[1] *is in the darkness* (Dan. 2:22). "Therefore," says God, "did I make the sun and the moon, that they might give you light"; as it says, *And God set them in the firmament of the heaven to give light.*

Num. R. 15. T.S. 1, 660.

204. **And God said: "Let the waters swarm." etc.**

Scripture writes, *There is none like unto Thee among the gods, O Lord* (Ps. 86:8). A human king can mould a figure out of earth; but God, blessed be He, can create a form also in water, as it says, *And God said: "Let the waters swarm with swarms of living creatures."*

Gen. R. 7. T.S. 1, 680.

205. **And let fowl fly, etc.**

He spoke also of (*al*) *the beasts, and of the fowl* (1 Ki. 5:13). But can a man speak to beasts and fowl?[1] No; what it means is that Solomon argued: Why is a beast permitted as food only through the cutting of both organs of the throat,[2] while fowl requires one only? Be-

§ 203 [1] *Mah* is read *meah,* a hundred, and the verse is rendered: He bestoweth a hundredth (of the heavenly light) to illumine the darkness.

§ 205 [1] The Midrash apparently renders the Heb. *al,* "to"; hence the difficulty. So *infra* in connection with fish.

[2] The windpipe and the gullet.

COMMENTARY

swarming of living creatures, *sheretz* being the cognate accusative of the Heb. *yishr'tzu.*[104] **creatures** (*nefesh*). **a.** Usually *nefesh* means "soul," but here it means creatures. The construct *nefesh* serves *hayyah* as well as *of* (fowl), as much as to say: marine creatures and winged creatures.[105] **fowl.** This is a collective noun, meaning winged things.[106] **and let fowl fly. a.** I.e., and let the waters generate fowl that will fly.[107] (This makes "fowl" a second object of *yishr'tzu,* thus: let the waters swarm with swarms of living creatures and fowl.) **b. and let fowl fly . . in the open firmament.** Let fowl come into existence and fill the sky in their flight.[108] **in the open firmament of heaven. a.** Over against the blue vault that forms the upper part of the firmament.[109] **b.** In the lower part of upper air (i.e., in mid-air), which from the point

ANTHOLOGY

cause the beast was created out of dry land; whereas one text says that fowl was created from the ground, as it is written, *And out of the ground the Lord God formed every beast of the field, and every fowl of the air* (2:19); whilst another text says, *Let the waters swarm with swarms of living creatures and let fowl fly.*[3] Bar Kappara said: They were created from the alluvial mud in the sea. R. Abin in the name of R. Samuel observed: Nevertheless a cock's feet resemble the scale-covered skin of the fish. The text continues, *and fishes* (ib.). But can such a thing be said? It means that he reasoned: Why do cattle, beast, and fowl require ritual slaughter, while fishes do not require it? Because of the following text: *If flocks and herds be* slain *for them, will they suffice them? Or if all the fish of the sea be* gathered *together for them,* etc.[4] (Num. 11:22)?

Num. R. 19. T.S. 1, 683.

206. AND LET FOWL FLY. A Roman Governor asked R. Johanan b. Zakkai: One verse says, *And God said: "Let the waters swarm with swarms of living creatures, and let fowl fly,"* which shows that birds were created from the water; but another verse says, *And out of the ground the Lord God formed every beast of the field, and every fowl of the air* (2:19), which proves that they were created from the earth? He replied, They were created out of the alluvial mud.[1] He thereupon noticed his disciples looking at each other. "You are no doubt displeased," said he, "that I brushed aside my opponent with a straw. The truth is that they were created out of the water, but they were brought before Adam only that he might name them."[2] Others say that he gave the latter answer to the Governor, and the former to his disciples, since "*and every fowl of the air*" is written in connection with the expression, *And he formed out of the ground.*[3]

Hulin 27b. T.S. 1, 679.

207. LET THE WATERS SWARM. On the fifth day of the week the Men of the Watch[1] fasted and prayed that pregnant women should not bear still-born children and that nursing mothers should not lose their infants. They deemed the day propitious for such prayers because God said then, "*Let the waters swarm with swarms of living creatures.*"[2]

J. Taan. 26. T.S. 1, 678.

208. AND LET THE FOWL FLY ABOVE THE EARTH. A human king builds a palace and tenants the upper and the lower stories; but can he tenant the space between? Surely not! But the Holy One, blessed be He, tenanted the space

[3] Therefore one makes a compromise: they do not require *both* organs, as cattle; nor are they permitted without *any* ritual slaughter, as fish; hence one organ suffices.
[4] Thus whereas the flocks and herds must be "slain," fish need only to be "gathered."

§ 206 [1] Which is both water and earth.
[2] As the second verse continues. It is naming and not the origin that this verse describes.
[3] Hence he could not tell his disciples that they were created from the water.—The rendering, which adds to the original, is somewhat conjectural.

§ 207 [1] The priests were divided into 24 Watches, each serving one week in succession in the Temple.
[2] Thus that day is suggestive of the abundance of life.

[21]**And God created the great sea-monsters, and every living creature that creepeth, wherewith the waters swarmed, after its kind, and every winged fowl after its kind; and God saw that it was good.** [22]**And God blessed them, saying: 'Be fruitful, and multiply, and fill the waters in**

COMMENTARY

of view of the observer on earth is the "face" of the sky.[110] [21]**sea-monsters. a.** Large creatures of the sea.[111] **b.** Whales—Septuagint. Pagan mythologies envisaged the huge sea-monsters as antagonists of the Creator, fighting to hinder creation and succeeding at least in delaying it. The Biblical writer, therefore, makes exceptional mention of them (they are the only species stated by name) to emphasize that they had no independent existence, but were themselves created just like all other creatures, even insects and creeping things.[112] **that creepeth. a.** The Heb. *ha-romeseth,* spelled with a *sin,* is identical in meaning with the same word spelled with a *samekh,* meaning to "tread." Hence the word is descriptive of quadrupeds or multipedes.[113] **b.** It applies to marine creatures that can tread upon the dry land, i.e., the amphibians.[114] **creature.** lit. "soul." In Hebrew *soul* is used more widely than in English,

ANTHOLOGY

between, as it says, *And let fowl fly above the earth.*

Gen. R. 7. T.S. 1, 682.

209. **And God created the great sea-monsters.**

Here (in Babylonia) they explained: The sea-gazelles. R. Johanan said: This refers to Leviathan the slant serpent, and to Leviathan the tortuous serpent, for it is written: *In that day the Lord with His sore and great and strong sword will punish leviathan the slant serpent, and leviathan the tortuous serpent* (Isa. 27:1).

Baba Bathra 74b. T.S. 1, 695.

210. And God created the great sea-monsters. R. Phinehas said in R. Idi's name: The noun is in the singular, and refers to Behemoth and Leviathan,[1] which have no mates. Resh Lakish said: Behemoth has a mate, but it has no desire, for it is said, *The sinews of his thighs are knit together* (Job 40:17).[2]

Gen. R. 7. T.S. 1, 697.

211. **And God blessed them.**

Why did God not bless the beasts as He blessed the fish and fowl, seeing that man eats of the former as he does of the latter? Moreover, beasts feed on each other?[1] God knew full well that the serpent, who is also in the category of the beasts of the earth, would one day beguile Adam and Eve and cause them to sin; through it death would come into the world, for which He would curse it. For this reason God did not bestow a blessing on the beasts of the earth. Had He done so the serpent too would have been included in that blessing, and once he had been blessed, God could not any more curse him. It is of this serpent that it says, *One sinner destroyeth much good* (Ecc. 9:18): on account of the serpent all cattle, beasts, and the creeping things of the earth were deprived of God's blessings.

Midrash Aggadah B'reshith. T.S. 1, 733.

212. **And let fowl multiply in the earth.**

R. Meir said: Those creatures which were created from the earth increase and multiply on the earth, and those which were brought forth from the water increase and multiply in the water, except all kinds of winged birds, whose creation was from the water, yet increase and multiply on the earth, as it is said, *And let the fowl multiply in the earth.* Those which were brought forth from the water increase and

§ 210 [1] Legendary sea-animals reserved for the righteous in the Messianic future.
[2] Perhaps he interprets this in the sense of confined, their desires suppressed.
§ 211 [1] Which is an additional reason why they should have been blessed, to make up for their depletions.

the seas, and let fowl multiply in the earth.' [23]And there was evening and there was morning, a fifth day. [24]And God said: 'Let the earth bring forth the living creature after its kind,

COMMENTARY

often denoting, as here, merely a living being.[115] **[22]And God blessed them. a.** He bestowed His bounty upon them.[116] **b.** They needed a special blessing, because so many of them are caught and destroyed.[117] **let fowl multiply in the earth.** Although created from the water, they would nevertheless multiply on the *earth,* all birds laying their eggs on land and not in water. **c.** No blessing was bestowed upon the vegetation, as its growth is dependent upon sun and rain, and not upon its own volition.[118] **saying.** As if addressing them.[119] **Be fruitful and multiply.** Reproduce your kind and increase in number.[120] **and fill the waters in the seas.** Live in every part of the sea.[121] **and let fowl multiply in the earth.** Let them lay their eggs on the dry land.[122] **[24]Let the earth bring forth.** All these had already been created on the first day, but they were in *the earth,* which brought them forth on the fifth day.[123] **the living creature after its kind. a.** Living creatures of various species.[124] **b.** "Living creature" is the general term, which is followed by a detailed enumeration.[125]

ANTHOLOGY

multiply by the eggs; and such as were created from the earth increase and multiply by foetus (i.e., living offspring).

Pirke d'Rabbi Eliezer Chap. 9. T.S. 1, 706.

213. **The fifth day.**

On the fifth day He made the waters swarm with all kinds of fowl, fish, and locusts, reptiles and creeping things, male and female, clean and unclean; He also created the Leviathan on that day. On the fifth day of the week all the waters in Egypt turned to blood; our ancestors departed from Egypt; and the waters of the Jordan stood still before the Ark of the Lord. On that same day Hezekiah stopped up the springs of Jerusalem to deny their use to the beleaguering army, as it says, *This same Hezekiah also stopped the upper spring of the waters of Gihon* (2 Chron. 32:30). On the fifth day He made the waters spawn the Leviathan and the Flying Serpent, etc. And on the fifth day Jonah fled from God.

Pirke d'Rabbi Eliezer 9, 10; Seder Rabbah B'reshith. T.S. 1, 709. 711.

214. **Let the earth bring forth the living creature.**

This is a general statement; *cattle and creeping thing and beast of the earth* are particulars. Specifically, *cattle* comprehends the ox, ass, mule, horse, camel, and similar animals. *Creeping things* are the reptiles that crawl on their bellies. *Beast of the earth* embraces the hart, gazelle, the roebuck and those like them, together with the predatory wild beasts, such as the lion, bear, leopard and hyena. *And it was so*: in this manner did each generation produce its offspring.

Midrash Lekah Tob B'reshith. T.S. 1, 726.

215. LET THE EARTH BRING FORTH THE LIVING CREATURE. R. Simeon b. Lakish said: God created three things each day. On the first day He created heaven, earth, and light; on the second, sky, angels and Gehinom; on the third, grass, herbs and trees; on the fourth, the sun, moon and stars; on the fifth, reptiles, fish and fowl. On the sixth He purposed to create six, for the sixth and the seventh days, for thus Scripture expresses it: *Let the earth bring forth the living creature, after its kind,* which numbers one; *cattle, creeping thing, and beast of the earth,* give you four; Adam and Eve make six. Yet we find that Scripture enumerates only five creations, viz., *And God made* (1) *the beast of the earth after its kind, and* (2) *the cattle after their kind,* (3) *and every thing that creepeth upon the ground,* plus (4) Adam and (5) Eve: where then was *the living creature* (which was a separate creation)? The answer is that God first created their souls, and then their bodies. When He had formed five bodies, there yet remained *the living creature after its kind,* when twilight fell and the Sab-

cattle, and creeping thing, and beast of the earth after its kind.' And it was so. [25]And God made the beast of the earth after its kind, and the cattle after their kind, and every thing that creepeth upon the ground after its

COMMENTARY

cattle. Domestic animals.[126] **creeping thing.** Creatures that slither on their bellies or move on short legs.[127] **beast of the earth. a.** Wild animals.[128] **b.** "Cattle" and "beast" designate herbivorous and carnivorous animals respectively.[129] **after its kind.** I.e., each genus subdivided into different species.[130] [25]**God made.** He formed them in shape, color, height, etc.[131] **after its kind.** He endowed each species with the senses and faculties

ANTHOLOGY

bath commenced. So He did not create bodies for this last category, and these unbodied souls are the demons. It is regarding this left-over category that Scripture states, *And on the seventh day . . . God rested from all His work which He had created and had yet to complete* (2:3).

Midrash Yelamdenu. T.S. 1, 712.

216. THE LIVING CREATURE. On the sixth day God created cattle that graze on a thousand hills, and all other kinds of animals, and all other living creatures, creeping things, and reptiles; as it says: *Let the earth bring forth the living creature after its kind*, etc. Finally He created man who was to have dominion over all. Psalms and paeans He implanted in his mouth, and songs and hymns in his throat. He —God—uttered His word and set their hosts in array, assigning the duties of each, and appointing one head over all of them.

Seder Rabba B'reshith. T.S. 1, 716.

217. THE LIVING CREATURE. On the sixth day He brought forth from the earth all kinds of abominations and creeping things, all of which are unclean. Those which were created from the earth, their life (or soul) and body are from the earth, and when they die they return to the place whence they were created. Thus it is said, *Thou takest away their breath, they die, and return to their dust* (Ps. 104:29); and it is written, *And the spirit of the beast goeth to the earth* (Ecc. 3:21).[1]

On the sixth day He brought forth from the earth a beast (Behemoth) which lies stretched out on a thousand hills and every day has its pasture on a thousand hills.

Pirke d'Rabbi Eliezer Chap. 11. T.S. 1, 731.

218. THE LIVING CREATURE (NEFESH). *Let the earth bring forth the living creature* (nefesh): this refers to the creation of the soul (*nefesh*), whereas the text, *and God made the beast of the earth after its kind, and cattle,* etc. refers to bodies. R. Eleazar said: *The living soul* means the spirit of Adam.

Midrash quoted by R. Bachya; Gen. R. 7. T.S. 1, 713, 732.

219. **The beast of the earth after its kind.**

Whence do we learn that from the very day of creation, cattle, beasts, birds and reptiles were all charged not to mate with any but their own kind? From the verse, *And God made the beast of the earth after its kind,* etc. He bade them: "Let every species mate only with its own kind, but other than its own is forbidden."

Tanhuma 58. T.S. 1, 729.

220. THE BEAST OF THE EARTH. R. Hoshaya the Elder said: This means the serpent.

Gen. R. 7. T.S. 1, 727.

221. THE BEAST OF THE EARTH. On the sixth day He brought forth from the earth all kinds of animals, male and female, clean and unclean. On the sixth day (God) brought forth from

§ 217 [1] The distinction implied here between man and beast is in the origin of the spirit: that of man is heavenly, whereas that of the beast is of the earth.

kind; and God saw that it was good. [26]And God said: 'Let us make man in our image, after our likeness; and

COMMENTARY

it needed.[132] [26]**And God said.** A special "saying" is attributed to the making of man on account of his importance.[133] **Let us make. a.** God took counsel with the angels,[134] like a king taking counsel with his ministers.[135] **b.** The plural is employed as if God were addressing the elements,[136] or the earth and all that fills it.[137] **c.** It is a plural of Majesty, such as is employed by kings in their edicts and proclamations.[138] **d.** An individual speaks in the plural when making a solemn resolution. This is usually the case in Aramaic.[139] **e.** Mankind is described as

ANTHOLOGY

the earth seven clean beasts, viz.: the hart, gazelle, roebuck, wild-goat, pygarg, antelope and chamois. Their slaughter and consumption are similar to that of birds;[1] and all the rest of the beasts of the field are entirely unclean.

Pirke d'Rabbi Eliezer Chap. 11. T.S. 1, 730.

222. **And it was good.**

R. Judah and R. Nehemiah disagree. The former maintains that the world was created in six days, since Scripture concludes every day's creative acts with the words, *And it was so.* The latter holds that the whole world was created on the first day. Why then, R. Judah asks, does every act of creation conclude with the refrain, *And it was so?* R. Berekiah, agreeing with the view of R. Nehemiah, commented: *God said, "Let the earth bring forth"*: "bring forth" is applicable only to something that was there from the very beginning, as it says, *In the beginning,* etc.

Tanhuma Yashan B'reshith 1:1. T.S. 1, 205.

223. **And God said: "Let us make man," etc.**

With whom did He take counsel? R. Joshua b. Levi said: He took counsel with the works of heaven and earth, etc. R. Samuel b. Nahman said: He took counsel with the works of each day, etc. R. Ammi said: He took counsel with His own heart.

R. Berekiah said: When the Holy One, blessed be He, came to create Adam, He saw righteous and wicked descending from him. Said He: "If I create him, wicked men will spring from him; if I do not create him, how are the righteous to spring from him?" What then did the Lord do? He deliberately disregarded the wicked, and, taking Mercy as His associate, He created him. . . . R. Hanina said otherwise: When He came to create Adam He took counsel with the ministering angels and proposed to them, *"Let us make man in our image, after our likeness."* "What shall his character be?" asked they. "Righteous men shall spring from him," He answered, as it is written, *For the Lord knoweth the way of the righteous,* (Ps. 1:6), which means that the Lord made known the way of the righteous to the ministering angels; *but the way of the wicked shall perish* (ib.): He destroyed (hid) it from them. He revealed to them that the righteous would spring from him, but not the wicked, for had He done that, the Principle of Justice would not have permitted him to be created.

Gen. R. 8. T.S. 1, 739.

224. AND GOD SAID: "LET US MAKE MAN IN OUR IMAGE, AFTER OUR LIKENESS." Rab Judah said in Rab's name: When the Holy One, blessed be He, wished to create man, He first created a band of ministering angels and asked them, "Is it your desire that we make man in our image?" They answered: "Sovereign of the Universe, what will be his deeds?" "Such and such will be his deeds," He replied. Thereupon they exclaimed: "Sovereign of the Universe! *What is man that Thou are mindful of him, and the son of man that Thou thinkest of him?*" (Ps. 8:5).

§ 221 [1] This presumably means that when they are slaughtered their blood must be covered (see Lev. 17:13), which a domestic animal does not require. As for consumption, the similarity may be that in neither is any of the fat forbidden, whereas certain parts of the fat of a domestic animal, called *heleb,* are forbidden.

COMMENTARY

in a special sense created by God Himself. To enhance the dignity of this last work and to mark the fact that man differs in kind from the animals, Scripture represents God as deliberating over the making of the human species (Abarbanel). It is not "let man be created"[140] or "let man be made," but "let us make man." **man.** Heb. "Adam." The word is used here, as frequently in the Bible, in the sense of "human being." It is derived from *adamah,* "earth," to signify that man is earth-born.[141] **in our image. a.** In our type,[142] which the later commentary, *Sifthe Chachamim,* defined as: in the mould which We have prepared for his creation. **b.** Who will rank as Our image, i.e., Man shall be regarded as Our image on earth.[143] **c.** Man's upright posture and heavenward look are the visible indications of his divinely-bestowed superiority over all other living creatures.[144] **d.** "Image" is a metaphor for similarity, for Man is in certain respects similar to his Creator, Who is the Source of all wisdom and power[145] (of which his own wisdom and power are a reflection). **after our likeness. a.** With discernment and understanding,[146] and enjoying freewill.[147] **b.** "Image" and "likeness" refer to the qualities of man's soul wherein it is similar to God, viz., that it is immortal and fills man's body entirely, just as God fills the universe.[148] **c.** Man has a similarity to both his origins, viz., bodily he is like the earth whence he was taken, and his spirit is immortal like God Who breathed it into him.[149] **d.** The plural is an allusion to the angels, i.e., let us create man, who shall be similar

ANTHOLOGY

Thereupon He stretched out His little finger among them and consumed them with fire. The same thing happened with a second band. The third said to Him: "Sovereign of the Universe! what did the former avail? The whole world is Thine; and whatsoever that Thou wishest to do therein, do it." When He came to the generations of the Flood and the Division (of Tongues), whose deeds were corrupt, they said to Him: "Lord of the Universe, did not the former band speak aright?" *"Even to old age I am the same, and even to hoar hairs will I be patient"* (Isa. 46:4), He retorted.

Sanhedrin 38b. T.S. 1, 734.

225. AND GOD SAID: "LET US MAKE MAN IN OUR IMAGE, AFTER OUR LIKENESS." R. Berekiah said, quoting R. Eleazar: When God created Adam, He first made him a lifeless shape, extending from one end of the world to the other. R. Eleazar said: He filled the whole world. R. Simlai said: Just as man's paean to God follows that of all animals, as we read, *Praise ye the Lord from the heavens . . . ye beasts and all cattle, creeping things and winged fowl; kings of the earth and all people* (Ps. 148, 1-10); so too was his creation: after the creation of the cattle and fowl, only then was man formed. We learn this from the verses: *And God said: "Let the water swarm with swarms of living creatures . . . let the earth bring forth the living creature after its kind, cattle and creeping thing"* . . . which are followed by, *"Let us make man in our image."*

Gen. R. 8. T.S. 1, 738.

226. LET US MAKE MAN IN OUR IMAGE, AFTER OUR LIKENESS. I.e., partaking of six directions, compounded of all, after the supernal pattern, with limbs arranged so as to suggest the esoteric Wisdom, altogether an exceptional creature. *Let us make man*: the word *adam* (man) implies male and female, created wholly through the supernal and holy Wisdom. *In our image, after our likeness*: the two being combined, so that man should be unique in the world and ruler over all.

Zohar Hadash 1:47. T.S. 1, 750.

227. LET US MAKE MAN. R. Aha said: When the Holy One, blessed be He, came to create Adam, He took counsel with the ministering angels, proposing, *"Let us make man"* (1:26). "What will be the nature of this man?" they inquired. "His wisdom will exceed yours," He answered. After Adam was created, what did the Lord do? He brought the animals, beasts, and birds before the angels and asked them, "What should be the name of each?" but they did not know. Then He paraded them before Adam, and asked him, "What is the name of this?"—"An ox." "And of this?"—"A camel." "And of this?"—"An ass." "And of this?"—"A horse." "And what is thy name?" "It is fitting

COMMENTARY

to the angels in understanding, but unlike them and like God in the possession of free will, which the angels lack.[150] (All these interpretations seek to remove the anthropomorphic implications of the verse.) **e.** Man is made in the "image" and "likeness" of God: his character is potentially Divine. "God created man to be immortal, and made him to be an image of His own eternity" (Wisdom of Solomon 11, 23). Man alone among living creatures is gifted, like his Creator, with moral freedom and will. He is capable of knowing and loving God, and of holding spiritual communion with Him; and man alone can guide his actions in accordance with Reason. "On this account he is said to have been made in the form and likeness of the Almighty" (Maimonides). Because man is endowed with Reason, he can subdue his impulses in the service of moral and religious ideals, and is born to bear rule over Nature. Psalm 8 says of man, *O Lord . . . Thou hast made him but little lower than the angels, and hast crowned him with glory and honor. Thou hast made him to have dominion over the works of Thy hands.*[151] **f.** Moses tells us that man was created after the image of God and after His likeness (Gen. 1:26). Right well does he say this, for nothing earth-born is more like God than man. Let no one represent the likeness as one to a bodily form; for neither is God in human form, nor is the human body God-like. No, it is in respect of the Mind, the sovereign element of the soul, that the word "image" is used; for after the pattern of a single Mind, even the Mind of the Universe as

ANTHOLOGY

that I be called Adam, because I was created from the ground (*adamah*)," he replied. "And what is My name?"—"It is fitting for Thee to be called Adonai (Lord), since Thou art Lord over all Thy creatures," was the answer. R. Aha said: *I am the Lord, that is My name* (Isa. 42:8), means, That is My name by which Adam called Me.

Gen. R. 17. T.S. 1, 742.

228. Let us make man. The Holy One, blessed be He, spake to the Torah: "*Let us make man in our image, after our likeness.*" The Torah replied: "Sovereign of all worlds! The man whom Thou wouldst create will be but short-lived and full of anger; and he will come into the power of sin. Unless Thou wilt be long-suffering with him, it were better for him not to have come into the world." The Holy One, blessed be He, rejoined: And is it for nought that I am called "*long-suffering and abounding in love*" (Exod. 34:6)?

Pirke d'R. Eliezer Ch. 11. T.S. 1, 743.

229. Let us make man. R. Huna the Elder of Sepphoris said: While the ministering angels were arguing, the Holy One, blessed be He, created him. Said He to them: "What can ye avail? Man has already been made!"[1]

R. Joshua of Siknin said, quoting R. Simeon: He took counsel with the souls of the righteous, etc.

R. Samuel b. Nahman said in R. Jonathan's name: When Moses was writing the Torah, he recorded what God created each day. When he came to the verse, *And God said: "Let us make man in our image, after our likeness,"* etc., he expostulated: "Sovereign of the Universe! Why provide heretics with an argument for the plurality of gods?" "Write," replied He; "whoever wishes to err may err." "Moses," said the Lord to him, "this man that I have created, do I not cause men both great and small to spring from him? Now, should a great man have to obtain permission for aught from a lesser, he may object, Why should I ask permission from my inferior! Then they will answer him, 'Learn from your Creator, who created the upper and the lower, yet when He came to create man He took counsel with the ministering angels.' " R. Levi said: There is no taking counsel here. You may compare it to a king who was strolling in front of his palace, when he saw the ruins of a bath-house. Said he, "What shall we do with it?" Some answered: "Build public baths on it"; others proposed private baths. "I will make a reception hall," declared the king. Who then can hinder him?

Gen. R. 8. T.S. 1, 740.

§ 229 [1] In this interpretation *ne'esah* (is made) is read instead of *na'aseh* (we will make).

ANTHOLOGY

230. LET US MAKE MAN. We may regard the words, *Let us make man,* as conveying this: To the lower beings who derived from the side of the upper world God disclosed the secret of how to form the divine name Adam, in which is encompassed the upper and the lower, in the force of its three letters *alef, dalet,* and *mem* final. When the three letters had come down below, there was perceived in their form, complete, the name Adam, to comprehend male and female.

Zohar, p. 31. G. Scholem.

231. LET US MAKE MAN. R. Simlai said: Wherever heretics found a text which apparently supported their heresy, their refutation is found in the very same place. Then the heretics asked him, What is meant by, *Let us make man* in our *image, after* our *likeness*? Said he to them: It does not say, *And the gods* created *man in* their *image,* but, *And* God created *man in* His *own image.* After the heretics departed his disciples observed: Them you gave a flimsy rebuttal, but how will you explain the plural form to us? He replied: God said thus: In the past Adam was created from the dust and Eve from Adam. But from Adam on, men and women shall be created by our image and after our likeness, neither man without woman nor woman without man (shall engender), nor both together without the assistance of the Shekinah.

J. Berakoth 9:1. T.S. 1, 737.

232. LET US MAKE MAN, etc. The plural may be explained by an analogy with a king who, having dominion over all, desires to indicate that all are comprehended in him and he is all. Therefore he adopts the royal "we." So too God, wishing to show that the whole world is His, comprehended the whole in His hand and spoke in the plural, thus teaching that He is all.

Midrash Haneelam Zohar Hadash 16. T.S. 1, 759.

233. LET US MAKE MAN. God made three artisans, Heaven, Earth, and Water, to create the world in co-operation with them. Each served one day. When these three artisans completed their labors, God said to them: "I have yet one more piece of work, viz., Man. Do you unite, and with Me as your partner *Let us make man,* you providing the body. And as now, so later too, I will continue the partnership": the father performs the work of the heaven and the water; the mother performs the service of the earth; and God cooperates with both. Regarding this mystery the Psalmist declared: *Let Israel rejoice in his Maker* (Ps. 149:2). Hence the expression, *Let* us *make*—jointly.

Midrash Haneelam Zohar Hadash 3:219. T.S. 1, 756. 760.

234. LET US MAKE MAN. R. Eleazar b. Simeon said: The earth appropriated the powers of the three for herself[1] until she was constituted of four elements.[2] Two she absorbed from the Heaven, and one she drew from Water, whilst the fourth was inherent. Thus she fashioned man's mould and God breathed into him a soul, as we read, *Then the Lord God formed man of the dust of the ground, and breathed into his nostrils the breath of life* (2:7). These are the two parts of man, whom the Earth and God cooperated to make. For that reason Scripture says *Let* us *make man,* that is to say, God charged the earth, saying, You produce the body and I will provide the soul.

Midrash Haneelam Zohar Hadash 16. T.S. 1, 758.

235. LET US MAKE MAN. God said, "I will give man a soul"; for it is written, *in our image,* which means, with a soul; similarly it says, *Only by virtue of his bearing God's image does man walk* (Ps. 39:7). "You shall give him breath and life, and the earth will bestow on him the four elements; thus will he possess the qualities of the superior and the inferior. And

§ 234 [1] This refers to a statement in Zohar Hadash, 3:219 that God proposed to the Heaven, Earth and Sea to make man jointly.
[2] Either: Hot, Cold, Moist and Dry; or Earth, Air, Fire and Water, the primal elements according to the ancient mystics and philosophers.

let them have dominion over the fish of the sea, and over the fowl of the air, and over the cattle, and over all the earth, and over every creeping thing that creepeth upon the earth.'

COMMENTARY

an archetype, the mind in each of those who successively came into being is founded.[152] **let them have dominion.** I.e., with the qualities which will enable him to rule over the lower creatures, even as I rule over the heavenly beings.[153] **and over the cattle.** Heb. *b'hemah,* which usually means domestic animals, but in the present instance it includes wild beasts too.[154] **and over all the earth.** Over the actual earth, exploiting its wealth by mining and agricultural operations.[155] **and over every creeping thing.** Though they live in the soil,

ANTHOLOGY

as for My will that he shall bear dominion over you, you must recognize My justice therein, and it will redound to your welfare; for I have made My name rest upon him, and My seal, which is the seal of the covenant, is in his hand."

Tikune Zohar 137. T.S. 1, 763.

236. LET US MAKE MAN. The Holy One, blessed be He, prompted each one of them (the seventy Elders) and they conceived the same idea and wrote for him (King Ptolemy), *I shall make man in My image and likeness.*[1]

Megillah 9a. T.S. 1, 736.

237. IN OUR IMAGE, AFTER OUR LIKENESS. That is to say, in his very body he will manifestly be like you, the angels. For even as the *soul* which came from Me holds aloof from mundane matters, so will he in body yearn and aspire to the lofty and holy.

Midrash Haneelam Zohar Hadash 16. T.S. 1, 761.

238. IN OUR IMAGE, AFTER OUR LIKENESS. The body, which will be taken from you, will not enjoy eternal life, since it too is of dust like all other creatures. Only the sacred soul which I place in your bodies will endure forever in an incorporeal realm, and that soul will be like unto Me and as immortal as Myself.

Midrash Haneelam Zohar Hadash 16. T.S. 1, 757.

239. **And have dominion (r'du) over the fish of the sea.**

R. Hanina said: If he merits it, God says "ur'du" (have dominion); otherwise, God says "*yerdu*" (let them descend).[1] R. Jacob of K'far Hanan said: Of him who is in our image and likeness I say "*ur'du*"; but of him who is not in our image and likeness I say "*yerdu.*"[2] Further: Let him who is in our image and likeness rule over that which is not in our image and likeness, said God.

Gen. R. 8. T.S. 1, 741.

240. AND LET THEM HAVE DOMINION, etc. Not only do all creatures serve man, and contribute to his comfort, but also God "teacheth us through the beasts of the earth, and maketh us wise through the fowls of heaven." He endowed many animals with admirable moral qualities as a pattern for man. If the Torah had not been revealed to us, we might have learnt regard for the decencies of life from the cat, who covers her excrement with earth; regard for the property of others from the ants, who never encroach upon one another's stores; and regard for decorous conduct from the cock, who, when he desires to unite with the hen, promises to buy her a cloak long enough to reach to the ground, and when the hen reminds him of his promise, he shakes his comb and says, "May I be deprived of my comb, if I do not buy it when I have the means." The

§ 236 [1] Cf. par. 37.
§ 239 [1] Or, let others (the beasts) rule over him. I.e., ירדו instead of ורדו; וירדו is the word in v. 26.
[2] Man is entitled to pre-eminence only as long as he cultivates his God-like qualities; when he voluntarily abandons them he is even lower than the brute creation.

[27]**And God created man in His own image, in the image of God created**

COMMENTARY

they will be unable to hinder man from working it to his advantage.[156] [27]**in His own image.** In the mould made for him, for whereas everything else was created by God's word, man was created by His hand, as it is written, *And* (Thou hast) *laid Thy hand upon me* (Ps. 139:5).[157] **in the image of God created He him. a.** That mould was a reflection of his Creator.[158] **b.** Man's likeness to God is repeated

ANTHOLOGY

grasshopper also has a lesson to teach to man. All the summer through it sings, until its belly bursts, and death claims it. Though it knows the fate that awaits it, yet it sings on. So man should do his duty towards God, no matter what the consequences. The stork should be taken as a model in two respects. He guards the purity of his family life zealously, and toward his fellows he is compassionate and merciful. Even the frog can be the teacher of man. By the side of the water there lives a species of animals which subsist off aquatic creatures alone. When the frog notices that one of them is hungry, he goes to it of his own accord, and offers himself as food, thus fulfilling the injunction, "If thine enemy be hungry, give him bread to eat; and if he be thirsty, give him water to drink."

Shebet Musar 22, 70b, 73c; Erubin 100b. Ginzberg Legends p. 43.

241. **And God created man in His own image.**

This means that he was to live and endure forever, like Himself. But man went astray and voided God's plan, by eating from the forbidden tree. Then God told him: "*Dust thou art and to dust shalt thou return*" (3:19).

Num. R. 16. T.S. 1, 772.

242. AND GOD CREATED MAN IN HIS OWN IMAGE. Everything in the world was originally created before Adam, who was created last, on the sixth day, on the eve of Sabbath, lest people might say that God had a helper in the work of the creation.

Chronicles of Jerahmeel, p. 14 (6:2).

243. AND GOD CREATED MAN IN HIS OWN IMAGE. For this reason was man created alone, to teach thee that whosoever destroys a single soul of Israel, Scripture imputes guilt to him as though he had destroyed a complete world; and whosoever preserves a single soul of Israel, Scripture ascribes merit to him as though he had preserved a complete world. Furthermore, it was for the sake of peace among men, that one might not say to his fellows, "My father was greater than thine." Another reason: lest heretics say that there are many ruling powers in Heaven. Again, to proclaim the greatness of the Holy One, blessed be He; for if a man strikes many coins from the one mould, they all resemble one another; but the supreme King of kings, the Holy One, blessed be He, fashioned every man in the stamp of the first man, and yet not one of them resembles his fellows. Therefore every single person is obliged to say: The world was created for my sake.

Sanhedrin 37a. T.S. 1, 764.

244. AND GOD CREATED MAN IN HIS OWN IMAGE. Rab Judah pointed out a contradiction: It is written, *And God created man in His own image;* but it is also written, *male and female created He them* (5:2)? How then is this to be understood? At first it was God's intention to create two human beings, but finally only one was created.

Ketuboth 8a. T.S. 1, 766.

245. AND GOD CREATED MAN. On the day when the first man was created God said to the ministering angels, "Come, let us descend and show kindness to man and his helper, for upon kindness the world rests." He further said, "Kindness is much more acceptable to Me than the sacrifices of burnt-offerings, which the Israelites are destined in the future to offer to

ANTHOLOGY

Me upon the altar," as it is said, *For I desire kindness, and not sacrifice* (Hos. 6:6).

Chronicles of Jerahmeel, p. 18 (6:2).

246. AND GOD CREATED MAN. A non-believer said to Rabban Gamaliel: "He who created the mountains did not create the wind, for it is written, *For lo, there is a* former of mountains *and a* creator of wind (Amos 4:13).[1] "If so," rejoined he, "when we find it written of Adam, *And He* created (1:27) *and He* formed (2:7), would you also say that the creator in the one verse is different from that in the other? Now, there is a part of the human body just a handbreadth square, which contains two holes (the eye and the ear): because it is written, *He that* planted the ear, *shall He not hear? He that* formed the eye, *shall He not see?* you would maintain there too that He who created the one did not create the other?" "Even so," he answered. "Then in the hour of death both are brought to agree!"[2]

Sanhedrin 39a. T.S. 1, 767.

247. AND GOD CREATED MAN. God created only one man at first. Why? Lest the righteous boast that they are the descendants of a righteous first man, whilst the wicked plead that their first progenitor was evil. Another reason: So that families should not quarrel with each other. For if now, when man was created alone (and all have one common ancestor), there is strife, how much more so had two men been created! A further reason: On account of robbers and men of violence. If such exist even now that man was created alone (and they really rob their own kith and kin), how much more so if two had been created! Yet another explanation is this: Man was created alone to demonstrate God's greatness, that with a single die He created the entire world, and from that single die such an infinite number of dies resulted, as it says, *The die is changed as clay* (Job 38:10). Why are human physiognomies different one from the other? To safeguard against cheats, lest men take possession of their neighbors' fields or violate their wives through impersonation; as it says, *but from the wicked their light is withholden* (ibid. 15).[1] Rabbi Meir said: God differentiated men by appearance, temper, and voice. Appearance and temper, on account of robbers and men of violence; voice, to prevent immorality.

Tosefta Sanhedrin 8. T.S. 1, 765.

248. IN HIS OWN IMAGE. It is concerning the soul that the Bible states, *And God created man in His own image,* which means in the likeness of the Shekinah. Moreover, it is with reference to man's soul that we read, *Only because of that image doth man walk* (Ps. 39:7), for when the soul departs from man, he can move no more.

Tikkune Zohar, p. 94. T.S. 1, 788.

249. IN HIS OWN IMAGE. R. Joshua b. R. Nehemiah, quoting R. Hanina b. R. Isaac, and our Rabbis, quoting R. Eleazar, said: He created him with four attributes of the higher beings (viz., the angels). He stands upright, speaks, understands, and sees, all like the ministering angels. Yet does not a dumb animal see! Yes, but man can see from the side.[1] He has four attributes of the lower beings: he eats and drinks, procreates, excretes, and dies, all like dumb animals. R. Tifdai said in R. Aha's name: The celestial beings were created in the image and likeness of God but do not procreate,[2] while the terrestrial creatures (dumb animals) procreate but were not created in (His) image and likeness. Said the Holy One, blessed be He: "Behold, I will create him (man) in My image and likeness, like the celestial beings, while he

§ 246 [1] He based his contention on the different attributes, "former" and "creator," which in his opinion pointed to different subjects.
[2] Both creators would have to agree to the man's death simultaneously, since the eye and the ear die at the very same moment. But such a supposition is absurd!

§ 247 [1] I.e., their opportunity to sin.

§ 249 [1] He can direct his gaze at an object sideways, without turning his head, which an animal cannot do.
[2] Like God Himself.

ANTHOLOGY

will procreate, like the lower creatures." R. Tifdai said in R. Aha's name: The Holy One, blessed be He, said: "If I create him of the celestial elements he will live for ever and not die, and if I create him of the lower elements he will die and not live (in a future life). Therefore I will create him of the upper and of the lower elements:[3] if he sins, he will die; if he does not sin, he will live.

Gen. R. 8. T.S. 1, 771.

250. IN HIS OWN IMAGE. The perfections of Adam's soul showed themselves as soon as he received her, indeed, while he was still without life. In the hour that intervened between breathing a soul into the first man and his becoming alive, God revealed the whole history of mankind to him. He showed him each generation and its leaders; each generation and its prophets; each generation and its teachers; each generation and its scholars; each generation and its statesmen; each generation and its judges; each generation and its pious members; each generation and its average, ordinary members; and each generation and its impious members. The tale of their years, the number of their days, the reckoning of their hours, and the measure of their steps, all were made known unto him.

Of his own free will Adam relinquished seventy of his allotted years. His appointed span was to be a thousand years, one of the Lord's days. But he saw that only a single minute of life was apportioned to the great soul of David, and he made a gift of seventy years to her, and reduced his own years to nine hundred and thirty.

Midrash on Psalms 95, 408.
Ginzberg Legends, p. 60-61.

251. IN HIS OWN IMAGE. His spiritual qualities kept pace with his personal charm, for God had fashioned his soul with particular care. She is the image of God, and as God fills the world, so the soul fills the human body; as God sees all things, and is seen by none, so the soul sees, but cannot be seen; as God guides the world, so the soul guides the body; as God in His holiness is pure, so is the soul; and as God dwells in secret, so doth the soul.

Berakoth 10a; Tanhuma Hayye Sarah 3.
Ginzberg Legends, p. 60.

252. IN HIS OWN IMAGE. R. Johanan said: Why was man created in the image of God? It may be likened to a king who built castles and made other improvements in his land, the while all the citizens were his willing subjects. One day the king assembled the people of the city and appointed one of his princes, saying, "Until now *I* administered the affairs of state here, building fortresses and towers; from now on, this prince will minister to your needs." Addressing the new governor, he bade him: "Even as I ruled here and built it up, so must you now continue with its building and all its other requirements, for henceforth everything is in your hands, and everyone here must acknowledge your sovereignty, and all are to reverence you as they reverenced me." So was man appointed over all creatures, as we read, *And the fear of you and the dread of you shall be upon every beast of the earth* (9:2). For that reason, *in the image of God created He him*; yea, *God created man in His own image*, to promote the well-being of the world and care for its needs, even as *He* had done hitherto.

Zohar Hadash 5. T.S. 1, 787.

253. IN HIS OWN IMAGE. *He is terrible and dreadful* (Hab. 1:7). This verse alludes to Adam. How so? R. Kahana said: When God created Adam, He created him in His own image, as we read, *And God created man in His own image*. He extended him from one end of the world to the other, as it says, *For ask now of the days past, which were before thee, since the day that God created Adam upon the earth, and* (he reached) *from one end of the heaven unto the other* (Deut. 32). Adam ruled over

[3] His body of the earth and his soul of heaven.

He him; male and female created He them. [28]And God blessed them; and

COMMENTARY

in order to emphasize his overwhelming superiority over the dumb animals.[159] **male and female. a.** A general statement; man and woman, both alike, are in their spiritual nature akin to God.[160] **b.** Both sexes, in equal dignity, can solve the common task of Adam only in harmonious unity.[161] [28]**and God blessed them.** Here the words, "And God said unto them," are added, indicating a more intimate relationship between

COMMENTARY

the whole world, as we are told, *And have dominion over the fish of the sea;* also, *And the fear of you and the dread of you shall be upon every beast of the earth* (9:1). Hence Scripture says, *He is terrible and dreadful,* referring to Adam.

Tanhuma Yashan Tazria. T.S. 1, 775.

254. IN HIS OWN IMAGE. Like all creatures formed in the six days of creation, Adam came from the hands of the Creator fully and completely developed. He was not like a child, but like a man of twenty years of age. The dimensions of his body were gigantic, reaching from heaven to earth, or, what amounts to the same, from east to west. Among later generations of men, there were but few who in a measure resembled Adam in his extraordinary size and physical perfections. Samson possessed his strength, Saul his neck, Absalom his hair, Asahel his fleetness of foot, Uzziah his forehead, Josiah his nostrils, Zedekiah his eyes, and Zerubbabel his voice. History shows that these physical excellencies were no blessings to many of their possessors; they invited the ruin of almost all. Samson's extraordinary strength caused his death; Saul killed himself by cutting his neck with his own sword; while speeding swiftly, Asahel was pierced by Abner's spear; Absalom was caught up by his hair in an oak, and thus suspended met his death; Uzziah was smitten with leprosy upon his forehead; the darts that killed Josiah entered through his nostrils, and Zedekiah's eyes were blinded.

Hulin 60a; Hagigah 12a; Zohar 1, 123b; Gen. R. 14:7; Gen. R. 8:1. Ginzberg Legends, p. 59.

255. IN HIS OWN IMAGE. A general cosmological statement may be followed by another recorded act which is only a detailed account of the first. For example, *And God created man in His image,* is a general statement. Then comes a detailed account, viz., *Then the Lord God formed man of the dust of the ground . . . and He caused a deep sleep to fall upon the man . . . and He built the rib . . . into a woman* (2:7,21,22). One might mistakenly think that we have here a different act, whereas it is only a detailed account of the former.

The 32 Middoth. T.S. 1, 777.

256. IN HIS OWN IMAGE. Adam too[1] was born circumcised, as it says, *And God created man in His own image.*[2]

Aboth d'Rabbi Nathan Chap. 20. T.S. 1, 769.

257. IN HIS OWN IMAGE, IN HIS LIKENESS. One of the changes in the translation of the Hebrew Bible into Greek, made by the seventy-two Hebrew scholars for King Ptolemy, was the following: They wrote, And God created man after an image, after a pattern, instead of the original text which reads, *And the Lord God created man in* His *image, in* His *likeness.*

Tanhuma Yashan Sh'moth 6. T.S. 1, 774.

258. **Male (zakar) and female (n'kebah).**

R. Isaac citing R. Ammi stated: As soon as a male (*zakar*) comes into the world, peace

§ 256 [1] The passage enumerates twelve who were born circumcised.
[2] This can only mean that he was perfect in form and not in need of any further improvement, such as circumcision.

COMMENTARY

comes into the world, for it is said, *Send ye a gift* (kar) *for the ruler of the land* (Isa. 16:1); now *zakar* (male) reads *zeh kar*, this is a gift.[1] Again, when a male comes into the world his provision comes with him, *zakar* suggesting *zeh kar*, which means, he has his provisions with him, as in the text, *and he prepared a great provision* (*kirah*, same root as *kar*) *for them* (2 Kings 10:23). A female (*n'kebah*) brings nothing with her, *n'kebah* suggesting *nkiyah baah*, she comes with nothing. Until she demands her food nothing is given to her, for it is written, *demand* (nakebah) *from me thy wages, and I will give it* (Gen. 30:28).

Niddah 31b. T.S. 1, 768.

259. MALE AND FEMALE (N'KEBAH) CREATED HE THEM. This is one of the things which they altered for King Ptolemy:[1] "Male with his apertures (*n'kubaw*) created He them."[2]

Gen. R. 8. T.S. 1, 770.

260. **And God blessed them.**

God bestowed on Adam, the first man, ten blessings corresponding to the ten utterances with which He created the world. They are the following: (1) *Be fruitful,* (2) *and multiply,* (3) *and replenish the earth,* (4) *and subdue it;* (5) *and have dominion over the fish of the sea,* (6) *and over the fowl of the air,* (7) *and over every living thing that creepeth upon the earth. And God said:* (8) *"Behold, I have given you every herb yielding seed . . .* (9) *and every tree . . .* (10) *to you it shall be for food."* In like manner Abraham was tested with ten trials; ten covenants were stated in connection with the precept of circumcision; with ten blessings did Isaac bless Jacob, viz., *So God give thee of the dew of heaven . . . let peoples serve thee,* etc. (27:28); with ten plagues were the Egyptians smitten. Corresponding to all these are the Ten Commandments, which teaches that the world was created only for the sake of the Torah (of which the Ten Commandments are the kernel).

Midrash Tadshe 5. T.S. 1, 805.

261. AND GOD BLESSED THEM. R. Abbahu said: The Almighty took a Cup of blessing[1] and blessed them, just as a precentor stands and blesses a bride. R. Judah b. R. Simon said: The angels Michael and Gabriel acted as groomsmen for Adam. R. Simlai said: We find that God blesses bridegrooms. Where? In the verse, *And God blessed them.*[2]

Pirke d'Rabbi Eliezer Chap. 12; Gen. R. 8. T.S. 1, 797. 804.

262. AND GOD BLESSED THEM. The Sages observed: A man without a wife lives without blessing, without life, without joy, without a helpmate, in want of all that is good, and without peace. Without a blessing, for it says, *God blessed* them—only when they are a pair.

Midrash Psalms 59. T.S. 1, 802.

263. AND GOD BLESSED THEM. R. Eleazar b. Pedath said in the name of R. Judah: God's name is mentioned only in connection with good, but not with evil. This is attested by the fact that when He created Adam and Eve, He linked His name with them, as it says, *And* God *blessed them,* etc. But when He cursed them, God's name did not appear. Scripture merely remarks then, He *said to the woman* (3:16).

Tanhuma Tazria. T.S. 1, 801.

§ 258 [1] Gifts bring peace.
§ 259 [1] See par. 36.
[2] This change is to explain the plural "them" (v. *supra,* 1); or (since he was created in God's image), to avoid the implication that God is male and female.
§ 261 [1] The goblet of wine over which a benediction is recited at any solemn occasion, such as the Sanctification of the Sabbath and festivals, or the solemnization of a marriage, as here.
[2] Adam and Eve being bridegroom and bride.

God said unto them: 'Be fruitful, and multiply, and replenish the earth, and subdue it; and have dominion over the fish of the sea, and over the fowl of the air, and over every living thing that creepeth upon the earth.' [29]And God said: 'Behold, I have given you every herb yielding seed, which is upon the face of all

COMMENTARY

Him and human beings.[162] **and God said unto them.** He made His will clear to them, that they might strive to fulfill it.[163] **Be fruitful and multiply.** This is the first precept (*mitzvah*) given to man. The duty of building a home and rearing a family figures in the rabbinic Codes as the first of the 613 *Mitzvoth* (commandments) of the Torah.[164] **and subdue it. a.** Overcome all difficulties in making its wastes fruitful.[165] **b.** "The secret of all modern science is in the first chapter of Genesis. Belief in the dominion of spirit over matter, of mind over nature, of man over the physical and the animal creation, was essential to the possession of that dominion" (Lyman Abbott). "What we call the will or volition of Man . . . has

ANTHOLOGY

264. **And God said unto them: "Be fruitful and multiply."**

R. Huna b. Kattina said: There was a case of a woman who was half slave and half free, whose master they compelled to liberate her. Whose authority did they follow? Was it that of R. Johanan b. Beroka, who said: In reference to both of them (man and woman) the verse says, *And God blessed them and God said unto them*: "*Be fruitful and multiply*," etc.?[1] Said R. Nahman b. Isaac: This is not so; the reason was that they used her for immoral purposes.

Gittin 43b. T.S. 1, 792.

265. And God said unto them: "Be fruitful, and multiply." Mishnah: A man is commanded to propagate his kind, but not a woman. R. Johanan b. Beroka said: Concerning both of them it is said, *And God blessed them; and God said unto them*: "*Be fruitful and multiply*." Gemara: Whence is this deduced? R. Ilea replied in the name of R. Eleazar b. R. Simeon: Scripture states, *And replenish the earth and conquer it*: It is the nature of man but not of woman to conquer. On the contrary! *And conquer it,* with the verb read as a plural, implies two! R. Nahman b. Isaac replied: The verb is written in the singular.[1]

Yebamoth 65b. T.S. 1, 793.

266. "Be fruitful, and multiply." Studiously scanning men, and realizing that they would one day anger the Almighty, Noah exclaimed, Why then should I procreate! And so he did not beget children until he was 500 years old. But then he mused, Am I then to die childless, whereas the Almighty commanded man to beget children, as we read, *And God blessed them, saying*: "*Be fruitful, and multiply*." So, after 500 years he determined to bear children!

Tanhuma Yashan B'reshith. T.S. 1, 799.

267. **And God said: "Behold, I have given," etc.**

Rab Judah said in Rab's name: Adam was not permitted to eat flesh, for it is written, *Behold, I have given you all the herbs . . . To you it shall be for food and to all the beasts of the earth:* this implies, but the beasts of the earth shall not be for you. But with the advent of the sons of Noah it was permitted, for it is said, *Every moving thing that liveth shall be meat for you; even as the green herb have I given you all things* (9:3). Now one might think that the prohibition of flesh cut from the living animal does not apply to them (sc. the Noachides); therefore the Writ teacheth, *only flesh with the life thereof, which is the blood*

§ 264 [1] As a half-slave half-free she could marry neither a slave nor a free man, and so could not fulfill her duty.
§ 265 [1] Although the traditional reading (called *k'ri*) is plural, the actual written form (called *k'thib*) is singular.

the earth, and every tree, in which is the fruit of a tree yielding seed— to you it shall be for food; [30]and to every beast of the earth, and to every fowl of the air, and to every thing that creepeth upon the earth, wherein there is a living soul, [I have given] every green herb for food.' And it was so. [31]And God saw every

COMMENTARY

become a power in nature, an imperium in imperio, which has profoundly modified not only Man's own history, but that of the whole living world, and the face of the planet on which he lives" (Ray Lankester).[166] **have dominion.** Make them work for you, or expel or destroy them when they are harmful to you.[167] **[29]to you it shall be for food; [30]and to every beast of the earth. a.** Thus man and beast were permitted the same diet at the Creation, man being forbidden to kill animals for food. This was permitted to him only after the Flood.[168] **b.** Yet even at the Creation a distinction was drawn: man was allowed every form of plant life, as is enumerated in verse 29, whereas beasts were confined to *every green herb*.[169] **c.** In the primitive ideal age (as also in the Messianic future, see Isaiah 11:7), the animals were not to prey on one another.[170] **green herb.** I.e., the green leaves of the herbs.[171] **and it was so.** This sufficed for them, and they did not prey on one another.[172]

ANTHOLOGY

thereof, shall ye not eat (9:4). One might think that this prohibition applies even to reptiles; therefore it says, "*but.*" How is this implied? R. Huna said: The text, *only flesh with the life thereof, which is the blood thereof,* shows that the prohibition applies only to those creatures whose flesh is distinct from their blood in its prohibition; excluding reptiles, whose flesh is not distinct from their blood. An objection is raised: *And rule over the fish of the sea*: surely that means that they should serve as food? No: it refers to toil, etc. Come and hear: *and over the fowl of the heaven*: surely this is in respect of food? No: it refers to toil, etc. Come and hear: *And over every living creature that moveth upon the earth*? That refers to the serpent.

Sanhedrin 59b. T.S. 1, 808.

268. **Every herb.**

Thou shalt not steal (Exod. 20:15): this is in reference to the text, *And God said*: "*Behold, I have given you every herb yielding seed,*" etc. Said the Holy One, blessed be He: Let no man steal or appropriate another's wealth; take only what is ownerless, as are herbs (which generally grow wild). R. Hiyya taught: Whatever is watched over in a vegetable garden is forbidden as robbery; what is not thus watched over is not subject to the prohibition of robbery.

P'sikta Rabbathi 21. T.S. 1, 809.

269. **And it was so.**

For none can obstruct the decree of the King of kings. Thus too we read, *Our God is in the heavens; whatsoever pleased Him He hath done* (Ps. 115:3).

Midrash Hagadol. T.S. 1, 811.

270. Our Rabbis taught: It would take one five hundred years to travel the habitable part of the world. Of the whole world one third is sea, a third desert, and the remainder inhabited country. (Here follows a calculation based on the numerical value of certain Biblical texts in the Creation story.)

Midrash Konen. T.S. 1, 531.

271. **And God saw every thing that He had made, and, behold, it was very good.**

R. Johanan said: When a human king builds a palace, he can only survey the upper stories and the lower stories separately, but the Holy One, blessed be He, casts but a single look at the upper and the lower portions simultaneously.[1] R. Simeon b. Lakish said: *Behold, it was*

§ 271 [1] Interpreting: *And God saw everything that He had made* — in a single look.

thing that He had made, and, behold, it was very good. And there

COMMENTARY

[31]**very good. a.** Each created thing is "good" in itself; but when combined and united, the totality is proclaimed "very good." Everything in the universe was as the Creator willed it — nothing superfluous, nothing lacking — a harmony. "This harmony bears witness to the unity of God who planned this unity of Nature."[173] **b.** The adverb *very* is added to denote that the perfection of the total creation exceeded that of its separate parts.[174] **c.** The often repeated "And God saw that it was good" (1:4) is

ANTHOLOGY

very good refers to this world; *And, behold,* to the next: The Holy One, blessed be He, cast but one look at this world and at the future world together.[2]

Gen. R. 9. T.S. 1, 816.

272. AND GOD SAW EVERY THING THAT HE HAD MADE, AND, BEHOLD, IT WAS VERY GOOD. The Creator, exalted, ascended to His loftiest heights, whence He surveyed His works and saw that they were good, even as it says, *And God saw every thing that He had made, and, behold, it was very good.* By *good* God is meant, as we read, *The* Lord is good *to all; and His tender mercies are over all His works* (Ps. 145:9). Another exposition: *Good* alludes to the Torah, as it is written, *For I give you* good *doctrine; forsake not My* Torah (Prov. 4:2). Another interpretation: *Good* alludes to Moses, as it says, *And she* (Jochebed) *saw that He* (Moses) *was* good (Exod. 2:2).

Midrash on Alphabets. T.S. 1, 836.

273. AND GOD SAW EVERY THING THAT HE HAD MADE, AND, BEHOLD, IT WAS VERY GOOD. R. Hiyya said: This means that He saw that it would be very good that they should continue in the state they were formed, remaining so, unchanged forever.

Midrash Haneelam Zohar Hadash 13a. T.S. 1, 840.

274. AND GOD SAW EVERY THING THAT HE HAD MADE, AND, BEHOLD, IT WAS VERY GOOD. Our Rabbis explained the words, *But the profit* (*yithron*) *of a land every way is* (Ecc. 5:8), thus: Even those creatures you deem redundant in this world, like flies, bugs, and gnats, nevertheless have their allotted task in the scheme of creation,[1] as it says: *And God saw every thing that He had made, and, behold, it was very good* (1:31).

Exod. R. 10. T.S. 1, 826.

275. AND GOD SAW EVERY THING THAT HE HAD MADE, AND, BEHOLD, IT WAS VERY GOOD. "Whatever God created has value." Even the animals and the insects that seem useless and noxious at first sight have a vocation to fulfill. The snail trailing a moist streak after it as it crawls, and so using up its vitality, serves as a remedy for boils. The sting of a hornet is healed by the house-fly crushed and applied to the wound. The gnat, feeble creature, taking in food but never *secreting* it, is a specific against the poison of a viper, and this venomous reptile itself cures eruptions, while the lizard is the antidote to the scorpion.

Sabbath 77b. Ginzberg Legends, p. 42.

276. AND GOD SAW EVERY THING THAT HE HAD MADE, AND, BEHOLD, IT WAS VERY GOOD. God did not procrastinate in His rejoicing. No sooner was His creation completed than He ecstatically rejoiced in it, as we read, *The Lord rejoiceth in His works* (Ps. 104:31); also, *And God saw everything that He had made, and,*

[2] The idea underlying these two teachings is that heaven and earth, this world and the next, are all interlinked and have one purpose (Y.T.).

§ 274 [1] Translating *yithron,* superfluity. The Rabbis explain that their existence is ever a comfort to sinners who console themselves with the thought that if God keeps alive creatures which serve no useful purpose, He will certainly not destroy men who have a purpose to fulfill.

COMMENTARY

significant: not only is God the Creator, but the future existence of each creation depends on His will; it exists because it is "good," i.e., it corresponds with the Divine intentions. But at the close of the report on the Creation it says: "And God saw everything that He had made, and behold, it was very good" (1:31) — and "behold," the unexpected: it was not only good, but it was very good. Rabbi Meir comments that this refers to death and suffering. Man claims to be able to evaluate evil and good. Yet how often must he realize that many facts that appeared to be evil and disadvantageous turned out to be good and useful; and *vice versa.* Man is not able to judge, because his judgment extends to the individual and momentary fact alone. If he, as God, could perceive the detail in its combination with the entity, view his temporary life in its connection with eternity — he would speak with God; it is not only good, but very good![175] **d.** This report

ANTHOLOGY

behold, it was very good, thus demonstrating that God gloried and took pride in His creations.

Tanhuma Yashan Shemini. T.S. 1, 828.

277. AND GOD SAW EVERY THING THAT HE HAD MADE, AND, BEHOLD, IT WAS VERY GOOD. R. Levi commenced his address thus: *It is the glory of God to conceal a thing, but the glory of kings is to search out a matter* (Prov. 25:2). Said R. Levi in the name of R. Hama b. Hanina: From the beginning of the Book of Genesis up to this point, *It is the glory of God to conceal a thing.* But from here onward, *The glory of kings is to search out a matter,* it is the glory of the words of the Torah, which are likened to kings, as it is said, *By Me kings reign* (ib. 8:15), *to search out a matter.*[1]

Gen. R. 9. T.S. 1, 815.

278. EVERY THING THAT HE HAD MADE. R. Yannai said: The Torah need not have been expounded save from the verse, *This month shall be unto you the beginning of months* (Exod. 12:2).[1] Why then did God reveal to Israel the activity of each day up to the sixth? As a reward for their faith in exclaiming, *All that the Lord hath spoken we will do, and hearken* (Exod. 24:7).[2] R. Berekiah said: It is written *And He declared unto you His covenant* (b'ritho) (Deut. 4:13): this means, *He declared unto you* the Book of Genesis, which narrates the creation (*b'riatho*) of the world.

Shir Hashirim R. 1:4. T.S. 1, 51.

279. AND, BEHOLD, IT WAS VERY GOOD. R. Simon said: When the Holy One, blessed be He, came to create Adam, the ministering angels formed themselves into groups and parties, some of them saying, "Let him be created," whilst others urged, "Let him not be created." Thus it is written, *Love and Truth fought together, Righteousness and Peace took arms against each other* (Ps. 85:11):[1] Love said, "Let him be created, because he will act with love." Truth said, "Let him not be created, because he is compounded of falsehood." Righteousness said, "Let him be created, because he will perform righteous deeds." Peace said, "Let him not be created, because he is full of strife." What did the Lord do? He took Truth and cast it to the ground. Thus it is written, *and He cast down truth to the ground* (Dan. 8:11). Said the ministering angels before the Holy One, blessed be He, "Sovereign of the Universe! Why dost Thou despise Thine own panoply?[2] Let Truth

§ 277 [1] The meaning of the passage is that everything—until and including the creation of man—must be left in mystic obscurity, and one must study the Torah only from the creation of man (Y.T.).

§ 278 [1] This introduces the Passover Sacrifice, which was the first precept given to Israel as a people. Hence only from there on is a detailed exposition of historical events and precepts necessary. A few bold strokes would have sufficed for the earlier portions of the Bible, without e.g. the detailed narrative of the Creation, which enumerates each day's activity.

[2] Thus they undertook to "do" even before they would "hearken" and know what obedience would involve.

§ 279 [1] AJV: *Mercy and truth are met together; righteousness and peace have kissed each other.* The Midrash interprets *met* in the sense of fought, and derives *nashaku* (kissed) from *neshek,* arms.

[2] Truth is God's panoply, setting off His glory.

COMMENTARY

of the creation makes us realize God as אלהים. We find Elohim contains the root *eleh*, "these," as a demonstrative pronoun (plural) indicating a multiplicity which has some common characteristics and thus is combined into a unit . . . I.e., this multiplicity in the world, the infinite multitude of laws which are at work — which lead to the heathen's belief in idols — they are governed by God as the whole Elohim whose Divine will has given the law to the smallest and greatest in His creation. Justly the Sages define Elohim as God the Law-Giver, God, the Creator.[176] **e.** God's Torah need not teach us that there is God: *The heavens relate the glory of God. And the expanse tells of the works of His hands* (Ps. 19:2). The overwhelming regularity governing the orbit of the firmament's immense multitude, the never-changing course of day and

ANTHOLOGY

arise from the earth!" Hence it is written, *Let Truth spring up from the earth* (ib. 12). Our Rabbis interpreted thus: The word M'OD (very) is a permutation of *Adam*.[3] Hence the verse, *And God saw everything that He had made, and, behold, it was very* (m'od) *good*, means, *and behold* Adam (man) *was good.*

Gen. R. 8. T.S. 1, 814.

280. AND, BEHOLD, IT WAS VERY GOOD. Before the creation of woman it is written, *It is not good for man to be alone* (2:18). But when she was created, what do we read? *And God saw everything that He had made, and, behold, it was very good!* Thus, as Solomon said, *he who finds a woman finds what is good.*

Midrash Psalms 59. T.S. 1, 831.

281. AND, BEHOLD, IT WAS VERY GOOD. R. Simeon b. Eleazar said: *And, behold, it was very good* means, and, behold, sleep was good. Can then sleep be very good? I wonder! Did we not learn thus: Wine and sleep when enjoyed by the *wicked* are beneficial to them and beneficial to the world! But R. Simeon meant this: A man sometimes sleeps a little and arises and toils much in the study of the Torah.[1]

Gen. R. 9. T.S. 1, 818.

282. AND, BEHOLD, IT WAS VERY GOOD. R. Nahman said in R. Samuel's name: *Behold, it was very good* refers to the Good Desire; *And, behold, it was very good,* to the Evil Desire. Can then the Evil Desire be very good? How extraordinary!—But for the Evil Desire no man would build a house, marry, and beget children; and thus said Solomon: *Again, I considered all labor and all excelling in work, that it is a man's rivalry with his neighbor* (Eccl. 4:4).[1]

Gen. R. 9. T.S. 1, 819.

283. AND, BEHOLD IT WAS VERY GOOD. R. Simeon b. Abba said: *Behold, it was very good* alludes to God's bounty; *And, behold, it was very good,* to the principle of punishment in the scheme of Creation. Is then the latter very good? It means that He considered well how to inflict it.[1]

R. Simon said in R. Simeon b. Abba's name: All measures have ceased,[2] yet the rule of measure for measure[3] has not ceased. R. Huna said in R. Joseph's name: From the very beginning of the world's creation the Holy One, blessed be He, foresaw that man will receive measure for measure; therefore the Sages said, *And, behold, it was very good* means this (measure for measure) is an excellent rule.

Gen. R. 9. T.S. 1, 823.

[3] The letters are the same in Hebrew but in different order.

§ 281 [1] Such sleep is very good.

§ 282 [1] It is the Evil Desire which in the first place inspires this rivalry which leads to great efforts. One may triumph over his human failings by turning even them to noble purposes.

§ 283 [1] So as to cause a minimum of suffering. Or, so clearly a punishment for wrongdoing that it would lead to repentance. Others: He caused the Temple to be destroyed two years before its time (translating: He hastened to bring the punishment), for had He waited longer, Israel's sins would have condemned them to complete destruction. V. Lam. R. 1 (par. 42); Sanh. 38a.

[2] The phrase is somewhat obscure. In Sot. 8b a very similar phrase is explained as referring to the four modes of execution. Perhaps it simply means that every recognized principle of God's rule has ceased.

[3] I.e., punishment befitting the crime. V. Sot. ad. loc.

ANTHOLOGY

284. AND, BEHOLD, IT WAS VERY GOOD. R. Huna said: *Behold, it was very good* refers to happiness; *And, behold, it was very good,* to suffering. Can then suffering actually be very good? It is in fact so because through its instrumentality men attain to the life of the Hereafter;[1] and so said Solomon: *And reproofs of chastisement are the way of life* (Prov. 6:23). Say now, go forth and see which road leads man to the life of the Hereafter? Surely it is suffering.

Gen. R. 9. T.S. 1, 820.

285. AND, BEHOLD, IT WAS VERY GOOD. R. Samuel b. R. Isaac said: *Behold, it was very good* alludes to the angel of life; *And, behold, it was very good,* to the angel of death. In the copy of R. Meir's Torah (Pentateuch) it was found written, *And, behold, it was very* (*m'od*) *good*: and, behold, death (*maweth*) *was good*.[1] Is then the angel of death very good? This may be compared to a king who made a feast, invited guests, and set a dish filled with all good things before them: "Whoever will eat and bless the king," said he, "let him eat and enjoy it; but he who would eat and not bless the king, let him be decapitated with a sword." Similarly, for him who lays up precepts and good deeds, lo! there is the angel of life; while for him who does not lay up precepts and good deeds, lo! there is the angel of death.[2]

Gen. R. 9. T.S. 1, 817. 822.

286. AND, BEHOLD, IT WAS VERY GOOD. R. Ze'ira said: *Behold, it was very good* refers to Paradise; *And, behold, it was very good,* to Gehinom. Is then Gehinom very good? What an amazing statement! This may be compared to a king who had an orchard, into which he brought workers. He built a treasure house by its entrance and said: "Whoever will labor conscientiously in the work of the orchard may enter the treasure house, but he who will not show himself deserving may not enter therein." Thus for him who treasures up religious acts and good deeds there is Paradise; while for him who does not lay up religious acts and good deeds there is Gehinom.

Gen. R. 9. T.S. 1, 821.

287. AND, BEHOLD, IT WAS VERY GOOD. R. Simeon b. Lakish said: *Behold, it was very good* alludes to the kingdom of heaven; *And, behold, it was very good,* to the earthly kingdom. Is then the earthly kingdom very good? How amazing! It earns that title because it exacts justice for men; hence it is written, *I, even I, have made the earth, and created man* (adam)[1] *upon it* (Isa. 45:12).

Gen. R. 9. T.S. 1, 824.

288. AND, BEHOLD, IT WAS VERY GOOD. R. Tanhuma said: It was created in the proper time; unfit to have been created earlier, but at that very hour, as we read, *He has made everything well in its time* (Ecc. 3:11). R. Abbahu observed: We deduce therefrom that God created previous worlds and destroyed them, until He built the present one, declaring, "This pleases me, the others did not." R. Eliezer commented: This door (of creation) is open to the very deep, as it says, *And God saw everything that He had made, and, behold, it was very good.*[1]

Ecc. R. 3:11. T.S. 1, 827.

289. AND, BEHOLD, IT WAS VERY GOOD. While the Sages were in session, they observed R. Abba coming towards them. He told them that he came from the Masters of the Mishnah, whereupon they put the same question to him. Said he, This is how our Masters explained it:

§ 284 [1] Suffering chastens and purifies.

§ 285 [1] This may mean either that the Ms read מות instead of מאד, or that this was inserted as a marginal comment.
[2] Hence death is good because it urges one to repent.

§ 287 [1] Theodor: Instead of *Adam* he reads *Edom*, a synonym in Talmudic and Midrashic literature for Rome, to which "the earthly kingdom" alludes, this being also the reading in the Vilna edition.

§ 288 [1] The meaning is doubtful. Probably: The all-embracing comprehensiveness of the text implies that everything in nature, down to the very deep, was created in perfection.

was evening and there was morning, the sixth day.

COMMENTARY

night, the mysterious laws of nature which tie earth with heaven, light and rain, life and growth — all, the smallest and the largest, reveal an Almighty Creator; for there is no "law" without a "Law-Giver."[177] **the sixth.** Not as hitherto *a* but *the*. Scripture thus indicates that *the* sixth was at the same time the last of the six days of work.[178]

ANTHOLOGY

All that God created He did by charging a mediating agency[1] to perform. He bade the earth, "Do thus," and it did as it was told, and altered not. He charged the waters, "Do thus," and they did as they were bidden, without any changes. He assigned a commission to the sky and it obeyed punctiliously. When they fulfilled their tasks as commanded, God, seeing it, praised their work. Hence it is written, *And God saw that it was good,* which means that He saw that they had done their work well, as they had been bidden, whereupon He exclaimed, *It is good!* That indeed is the meaning of our text.

Midrash Haneelam Zohar Hadash 13a. T.S. 1, 557.

290. **And there was evening, and there was morning, the sixth day — ha-shishi.**

R. Judan said: This intimates the extra hour which we add from the profane to the sacred, and in it the work of creating the world was finished. Hence *the sixth* day is written.[1] *Ha-Shishi*: R. Simon said: (There came a weakening [*metash*] of the Creation):[2] hitherto world time was counted,[3] but henceforth we count it by a different reckoning.[4]

Gen. R. 9. T.S. 1, 825.

291. AND THERE WAS EVENING, AND THERE WAS MORNING, THE SIXTH DAY. R. Isaac gave the following reason for commencing the Torah with a detailed account of the Creation. Its purpose is to acquaint men with His power and might, as it says, *He hath declared to His people the power of His works, that He might give them the heritage of nations* (Ps. 111:6).[1]

Tanhuma Yashan B'reshith; Shir Hashirim R. 1:14. T.S. 1, 51. 52.

292. **The sixth day.**

Hezekiah said: What is meant by, *Thou didst cause sentence to be heard from Heaven; the earth feared and was tranquil* (Ps. 76:9)? If it feared, why was it tranquil, and if it was tranquil, why did it fear? At first it feared, but subsequently it was tranquil. And why did it fear? Even in accordance with the dictum of Resh Lakish, who taught: Why does Scripture say, *And there was evening and there was morning, the sixth day,* adding "*the*" to "*sixth day*"? It teaches that the Holy One, blessed be He, stipulated with the Works of Creation and said to them: "If Israel accepts the Torah (which will be given on the sixth day of Sivan), ye shall exist; but if not, I will turn you back into emptiness and formlessness."

Shabbath 88a. T.S. 1, 813.

§ 289 [1] From the whole passage it appears that he does not refer to such agencies as the sefirot or demiurges which are part of the Cabbalistic mysticism. The heaven, earth and sea are themselves the mediating agencies, each bringing forth its "hosts": heaven, its luminaries; the earth, plant and animal life; and the sea, aquatic life.

§ 290 [1] He interprets the additional def. art. *he* (ה) of הששי (in the case of other days we have *a* second, third, day, etc., without the def. art.) as intimating that the Sabbath must be commenced before actual nightfall, thus adding to the sacred period.

[2] Presumably *ha-shishi* is connected here with *tashash,* to weaken. The bracketed addition is according to Theodor.

[3] I.e., the second day, third day, etc., of the world's creation.

[4] I.e., first, second, third day of the week (Y.T., M.K.).

§ 291 [1] As Creator of the world He has the right to dispose of it.

ANTHOLOGY

293. THE SIXTH DAY. In the six days of creation God created twenty-two entities in the universe.

On the first day, seven, viz.: heaven, earth, water, darkness, breath,[1] the deeps, and light.

On the second day, only one: the firmament.

On the third day, four: He gathered the water into one place; drew sweet water from the earth; herbs; and trees.

On the fourth day, three: sun, moon and stars.

On the fifth day, three: reptiles, fowl and fish.

On the sixth day, four: beasts, cattle, reptiles and man.

These correspond to the twenty-two letters of the Hebrew alphabet, and the twenty-two generations from Adam to Jacob.

Midrash Tadshe. T.S. 1, 835.

§ 293 [1] Heb. *ruah,* which is variously rendered as breath, wind, spirit.

GENESIS

CHAPTER II

[1]**And the heaven and the earth were finished, and all the host of them.**

COMMENTARY

The Torah was not originally divided into chapters. Such division originated in the Middle Ages; and, because of its convenience, found its way into the *printed* Hebrew text. Sometimes, as here, the division is misleading. Thus, the next three verses belong to the preceding chapter, and form its worthy and incomparable conclusion. [1]**were finished.** With these six days of creation everything was completed and perfected.[2] **all the host of them. a.** The *host* of earth is man, animal and plant life; that of heaven is the luminaries. It also hints at the creation of the angels and the soul of man, both of which are the *host* of heaven.[3] **b. Host.** lit. "army"; the totality of the universe conceived as an organized whole, a cosmos.[4] "*And completed were heaven and earth and all their host*" — or better, what God wanted to achieve with their creation. Because God is Creator, everything has its (*tachlith*) goal. This entitles also men to speak

ANTHOLOGY

1. **And the heaven and the earth were finished.**

Raba—others state, R. Joshua b. Levi—said: Even when an individual prays on the eve of the Sabbath, he must recite, *And the heaven and the earth were finished* (etc.), for R. Hamnuna said: When one recites "*And the heaven and the earth were finished*" on the Sabbath eve, the Writ regards him a partner with the Almighty in the Creation, for it is said, *Way'kullu* (*and they were finished*): read not *wa-y'kullu* but *wa-y'kallu* (and they finished), "*they*" referring to God and to the one who acknowledges Him as the Creator. Again, when one recites this on the Sabbath eve, two ministering angels lay their hands on his head and say to him, *Thine iniquity is taken away and thy sin is expiated* (Isa. 6:7). This should be recited three times on Sabbath eve, once in the evening prayer, again after the evening prayer, and finally over a cup of wine, in the *kiddush*.[1] The threefold recital corresponds to the three verses comprising this passage.

Shabbath 119b; Midrash Way'kullu; Jerushalmi. T.S. 2, 1. 3. 4.

2. AND THE HEAVEN AND THE EARTH WERE FINISHED. R. Judah, b. R. Baba, whose sleep, from 18 till the age of 80, was as brief as the sleep of a horse, was led forth to execution on the eve of the Sabbath, after the ninth hour of the day (i.e., after three in the afternoon). The sage besought them to delay the execution until he performed one of God's commandments. Said the emperor to him: "Do you still have faith in God?" "Yes," he answered. He continued his plea, saying, "Oh emperor, by your life, pray, wait until I perform one commandment, the Sanctification of the Sabbath, which gives one a taste of the Future World." On the emperor granting his request, the sage then proceeded, reciting it calmly in a loud and pleasant voice, with the Sanctification prayer, *And the heaven and the earth were finished*, etc. All present were amazed. When he reached the words "*which God created to do,*" they stopped him and refused to let him finish, and the tyrant ordered his immediate execution. They slew him, and his soul departed with the utterance of the word "*Elohim—God.*" Then a voice from heaven proclaimed: "Blessed art thou, R. Judah, who wast like an angel and whose soul departed with the word 'Elohim—God.' " The tyrant ordered him to be cut to pieces, limb by limb, and thrown to the dogs. And none was permitted to deliver a dirge over him, nor was he interred.

Midrash Eleh Ezk'rah (a martyrology). T.S. 2, 20.

§ 1 [1] The Sanctification, the prayer recited at the beginning of Sabbaths and festivals.

ANTHOLOGY

3. AND THE HEAVEN AND EARTH WERE FINISHED. Scripture says, *I have seen an end to every purpose* (Ps. 119:96). This refers to the Creation of heaven and earth, as it says, *And the heaven and the earth were finished.*[1]

Gen. R. 10. T.S. 2, 6.

4. AND THE HEAVEN AND THE EARTH WERE FINISHED. R. Hama b. R. Hanina commenced his homily with the text, *Take away the dross from the silver*, etc. (Prov. XXV, 4). As long as *tohu* and *bohu*[1] existed, heaven and earth could not be seen; but as soon as these were eradicated, heaven and earth appeared. Thus the text continues, *And there cometh forth a vessel* (keli) *for the refiner* (ib.), i.e., they (heaven and earth) became finished articles (*kelim*): hence, *And the heaven and the earth were made into completed vessels.*[2]

Gen. R. 10. T.S. 2, 7.

5. WERE FINISHED (WAY'KULLU). R. Hoshaya said: R. Efes preached in Antioch:[1] The word *way'kullu* connotes nought but smiting and destruction (*kelayah*).[2]

Gen. R. 10. T.S. 2, 8.

6. WERE FINISHED (WAY'KULLU). R. Joshua b. Levi said: The heaven was adorned with the sun, moon, and planets; the earth[1] with trees, herbs, and the garden of Eden.

Gen. R. 10. T.S. 2, 9.

7. WERE FINISHED. R. Simon said in the name of R. Joshua b. Levi: The works of Creation, i.e., heaven and earth, were completed, but went on expanding.[1]

Gen. R. 10. T.S. 2, 10.

8. AND THE HEAVENS AND THE EARTH WERE FINISHED. But indeed, were the heavens and the earth completed so as not to require God's providence for their continued existence and maintenance? Has it not been written, *Do I not fill heaven and earth? Saith the Lord* (Jer. 23:24)?—But it means that the work of their creation and God's fiats which had brought them into existence, were now at an end.

Pirke d'R. Eliezer Chap. 18. T.S. 2, 12.

9. WERE FINISHED (WAY'KULLU). Seven dedications are mentioned in Scripture. The first dedication took place at the creation of the world, as the Bible relates, *And the heavens were finished* (way'kullu). This implies dedication, as it says in connection with the dedication of the Tabernacle, *And the work was completed* (*watekal*-same root) (Exod. 39:32).

P'sikta Rabbathi Chap. 2. T.S. 2, 13.

10. AND THE HEAVEN AND THE EARTH WERE FINISHED. God created the heaven and the earth, and all that is therein, and He completed them. He smoothed, solidified, moulded, shrunk, extended, ordered and compacted them. He perfected and smoothed them, as we read, *And the heaven and the earth were finished, and all the host of them.*

Seder Eliyahu Rabbah Chap. 31. T.S. 2, 14.

11. WERE FINISHED. R. Nahman said: This indicates that both the work and the planning were complete, and God established the Sabbath as a model for the Hereafter. For God will

§ 3 [1] The point is apparently that Heaven and Earth are finite.
§ 4 [1] See Chapter I, pars. 65 and 67.
[2] Deriving *way'kullu* from *keli.*
§ 5 [1] The capital of Syria founded by Seleucus Nicator, situated on the Orontes (Jast.).
[2] Rendering: And the heaven and the earth were smitten—as a result of Adam's sin. The punishment was that their orbit was prolonged, and they now travel through it slowly and laboriously, whereas previously their passage was swift and with ease (Midrash).
§ 6 [1] He derives *way'kullu* from *kelil*, a crown, and renders: The heaven and the earth were crowned (adorned).
§ 7 [1] Until the sixth day, when their boundaries were finally determined. He renders: And the heaven and the earth *had been finished* — already on the first day.

[2]And on the seventh day God finished

COMMENTARY

of tachlith, the aim of their lives.[5] **[2]on the seventh day God finished His work. a.** In the very moment which marked the completion of the sixth day, so that as He finished the seventh began.[6] **b.** Or: the world still lacked rest; by making the seventh day a day of rest He completed its creation, and thus in

ANTHOLOGY

again rest on the seventh, that is to say, in the Seven *Thousandth* year.[1]

Midrash Haneelam 16b. T.S. 2, 15.

12. WERE FINISHED. I.e., the works of the celestial and the terrestrial spheres, *Heaven and Earth* being the upper and the lower spheres respectively. R. Simeon said: Metaphorically they symbolize the artistically wrought Written Law and Oral Law respectively, whilst *All their hosts* alludes to the details of the Torah and its different interpretations. For there are seventy aspects to the Torah. Again, *were finished* expresses the complete integration of the Oral into the Written Law, *Heaven and Earth* symbolizes the particular and the general, whilst *All their hosts* alludes to the secrets of the Torah and its purifying powers.

Zohar Hadash 43. T.S. 2, 22.

13. **And all the host.**

R. Joshua b. Levi said: All the works of the creation were created in their full-grown stature, with their consent, and in the shape of their own choice, for it is written, *And the heaven and the earth were finished, and all the host of them*; read not *ts'baam* (the host of them) but *tsibyonam* (which suggests all three).

Hulin 60a. Rosh Hashanah 11a.

14. AND ALL THE HOST (TS'BAAM) OF THEM. R. Eleazar said: There is a fixed period for heaven and earth,[1] as it says: *And the heaven and the earth were finished, and all their fixed periods.* Nahman, the son of Samuel b. Nahman, said: When a man deserves it, the host (*ts'ba*) of divine powers acts on his behalf; when he does not, the host is against him.

Gen. R. 10. T.S. 2, 17.

15. AND ALL THE HOST OF THEM (TS'BAAM). The son of Sira said: God made chemicals grow out of the earth; with them the physician heals wounds and the apothecary compounds his preparations.[1]

Gen. R. 10. T.S. 2, 18.

16. **And on the seventh day God finished.**

Rabbi asked R. Ishmael b. R. Jose: "Have you heard from your father the actual meaning of this passage?"[1] Said he to him: "It is like a man striking the hammer on the anvil, raising it by day and bringing it down after nightfall."[2] R. Simeon b. Yohai said: Mortal man, who does not know his minutes, his exact times or his hours, must add from the profane to the sacred;[3] but the Holy One, blessed be He, who knows His moments, His times, and His hours, can enter it by a hair's breadth. Genibah and the Rabbis discussed this. Genibah said: This may be compared to a king who made a bridal chamber, which he plastered, painted, and adorned; now what did the bridal chamber lack?—A bride. Similarly, what did the

§ 11 [1] In ancient thought the world was created for six thousand years, to be followed by a Universal Sabbath of a thousand years. This is hinted at in the Six Days of Creation and the Seventh of rest, God's Day being a thousand years.

§ 14 [1] The rendering is conjectural, and follows Theodor and Yefath Toar, with the meaning that heaven and earth were created for a definitely fixed period.

§ 15 [1] Cf. Ecc. 38:4, 7, 8. He renders *ts'baam* "their desires," i.e., everything in creation serves a purpose (Mah.).

§ 16 [1] For surely God finished His work on the *sixth*, not on the seventh day.

[2] In the second between his raising it and his bringing it down night has commenced. Similarly, God finished His work right at the end of the sixth day, so that in that very moment the Sabbath commenced.

[3] And therefore must stop work on Friday before the day actually terminates.

His work which He had made; and

COMMENTARY

very truth He finished His work *on the seventh day*.[7] **c.** "Finishing" work is not the same as doing work, but is the equivalent of doing nought: hence Scripture states that He did no work on the seventh day but rested thereon. In accordance with this last interpretation "finished" is better rendered "had finished."[8]

ANTHOLOGY

world still lack?—The Sabbath. The Rabbis said: Imagine a king who made a ring: what did it lack?—A signet. Similarly, what did the world lack?—The Sabbath.[4] And this is one of the texts which they emended for king Ptolemy, making it read: "And He finished on the sixth day[5] and rested on the seventh."

Megillah 9a; Gen. R. 10. T.S. 2, 24.

17. AND ON THE SEVENTH DAY, etc. Among the questions submitted to our Holy Teacher[1] was the following: The Bible declares, *And on the seventh day God finished His work*. Did He then work on the seventh day? Heaven forfend! What then does *finished* mean?—On the eve of the Sabbath God was engaged all day in the creation of man. In the first hour He contemplated creating him, etc. . . . In the tenth hour Adam sinned. And so God grieved, if we might use such an expression, over the world, that sin had been committed therein, until the Sabbath arrived and received a pardon, the Almighty declaring, "Whatever I have made, the Sabbath has perfected." Hence Scripture states, *And God declared His work perfect on the seventh day*.

P'sikta Rabbathi Ch. 46. T.S. 2, 25.

18. AND ON THE SEVENTH DAY GOD FINISHED HIS WORK. But surely He did *not* finish on the *seventh* day, seeing that everything was created in six days? This then must refer to the ten things which were created at twilight, viz.: The mouth of the earth (Num. 16:32); the mouth of Miriam's well (ibid. 21:16); the mouth of Balaam's ass (ibid. 22:28); the rainbow; the manna; Moses' staff (Exod. 14:17); the *Shamir*;[1] the form of the letters; the art of writing; and the two Tables of Testimony.[2] The decision to create these was taken at twilight, between the sixth and the seventh days.[3] Hence our Sages are in doubt as to whether twilight belongs to the preceding day or the following night; consequently the stricter ruling is adopted in all cases of doubt.[4]

Midrash Hagadol B'reshith. T.S. 2, 35.

19. AND ON THE SEVENTH DAY, etc. The House of Israel is obliged to rest on the Sabbath, because God created the world in six days and

[4] Thus by giving the Sabbath as a day of rest He actually completed the work of Creation.

[5] To avoid the implication that He worked on the seventh day.

§ 17 [1] A frequent epithet for R. Judah the Prince, compiler of the Mishnah.

§ 18 [1] A worm which was said to split the hardest stone on which it was placed. It was therefore used by Solomon in fashioning the stones of the Temple, since the use of iron was forbidden (Exod. 20:25; Gittin 68a; Sotah 48b).

[2] On which were engraved the Ten Commandments.

[3] This decision, too, is regarded as an act of creation, and since twilight is on the borderline and it cannot be precisely ascertained whether it belongs to the previous or the next day, it can be said literally that from the human point of view God finished His work on the seventh day. Of the things enumerated, some, e.g., the rainbow, manna, Moses' staff, the Shamir, may be regarded as created, potentially or actually, at twilight; with respect to others, e.g., the opening of the earth to swallow up Korah and his confederates, or the opening of the mouth of Balaam's ass to speak, it probably means that these phenomena were willed at twilight.

[4] Work is forbidden at twilight, since it may be the Sabbath. On the other hand, a child born at twilight may not be circumcised a week later on the Sabbath, as would have been the case if it were born after nightfall, since it may have been day (circumcision is performed on the Sabbath only when it is definitely the eighth day); nor can it be circumcised on Friday, since twilight may rank as evening, in which case Friday would only be the seventh day. Hence it must be postponed to Sunday.

He rested on the seventh day from all His work which He had made.

COMMENTARY

rested. Heb. "desisted," from creating. In the fourth commandment (Exod. 20:11) God is said to have "rested" (*vayanah*) on the seventh day. This ascribing of human actions to God is called *anthropomorphism*, and is employed in the Bible to make intelligible to the finite, human mind that which relates to the Infinite. The Talmudic saying, דברה תורה בלשון בני אדם, "The Torah speaks the ordinary language of men," became a leading principle in later Jewish interpretation of Scripture.[9] **from all His work.** The Sages comment that God called to His work "enough": so far and no further, ever since this day there

ANTHOLOGY

rested on the seventh day, and hallowed and blessed it, just as a man who builds a house celebrates it with festivities, which people call "the dedication of the house." Thus it is written, *And God dedicated the seventh day*, saying to man, "Rest on the Sabbath day, as I rested thereon," as we read, *And He rested on the seventh day, wherefore God blessed the Sabbath day and sanctified it* (Exod. 20:11).[1]

Tanhuma B'reshith Par. 2. T.S. 2, 27.

20. **His work.**

Did not R. Berekiah say in the name of R. Judah b. R. Simon: Without labor or toil the Holy One, blessed be He, created the world, yet you say, *From all His work*! But it is so described in order to punish the wicked who destroy the world which was created with labor, and reward the righteous well, for preserving the world which was created with toil. And what was created therein after he rested?[1]—Tranquillity, ease, peace, and quiet. R. Levi said in the name of R. Jose b. Nehorai: As long as the hands of their Master were working on them they went on expanding; but when the hands of their Master rested, rest was afforded to them, and thus *He gave rest* to His world *on the seventh day* (Ex. 20:11).[2] R. Abba observed: When a human king orders rest for his troops, he stops their pay; conversely, when he orders them to be paid, he does not grant them leave. But the Almighty ordered rest and at the same time paid for it! Thus we read, *And He rested* (and ordered man to rest too), *and* yet *He blessed the seventh day!*

21. AND ON THE SEVENTH DAY GOD FINISHED HIS WORK. Great is the Sabbath, that He forbade work, which He loves so much, thereon. How precious work is in His sight is seen in the fact that though His creation of the world was effortless, yea, with a mere word, yet He called it work, as it says, *And on the seventh day God finished His* work; and again *because that in it He rested from all His* work (2:3).

Midrash Tannaim Debarim 5. 15. T.S. 2, 32.

22. AND ON THE SEVENTH DAY GOD FINISHED HIS WORK. No work is stated on the seventh day,[1] nor "and it was evening and it was morning," because it is reserved for future generations,[2] as it is said, *And there shall be one day which shall be known as the Lord's, not day, and not night* (Zech. 14:7). To what is this matter to be compared?—To a man who had a precious jewel, which he desired to bequeath to his son who served him. Likewise with the Holy One, blessed be He: The Sabbath day of rest and holiness which was before Him He desired to bequeath to Israel. Another reason is this: The Holy One, blessed be He, created seven entities which call for dedication; six He

§ 19 [1] The point of this passage is that the Sabbath is in the nature of the dedication festivities attendant upon the completion of a house. The text is rendered: And the heaven and earth were dedicated.

§ 20 [1] On the Sabbath, for the verse, *Because that in it He rested from all His work which God created to make* (lit. translation) implies that this resting itself was in order to make (i.e., create) something.

[2] Chapter II, par. 7.

§ 22 [1] No creative activity took place on that day.

[2] Presumably this means, the full glory of the Sabbath is reserved for the future.

[3]And God blessed the seventh day, and hallowed it; because that in it

COMMENTARY

is "Sabbath" in the creation and no new creation comes into existence.[10] **[3]blessed . . . hallowed. a.** He *blessed* it in respect of the manna, a double portion of which fell on the sixth day in preparation for the Sabbath, and *hallowed* it in respect of the manna which did not fall on the Sabbath at all (Exod. 16: 22f.). The verse is accordingly written in anticipation of the future.[11] **b.** The *blessing* is that the Sabbath gives man added physical and spiritual strength, and it was *hallowed* by having no work done on that day. This blessing is conferred only on those who believe in the sanctity of the Sabbath.[12] **c.** He appointed it for all future time as a day on which its observers should be blessed and sanctified.[13] **d.** He decreed that men should be cognizant of its superiority over all other days and abstain from work on it.[14] **e.** *hallowed* is lit. "set apart" from profane usage. The Sabbath demands more than stoppage of work. It is specifically marked

ANTHOLOGY

dedicated, but one is reserved for the future. He created the first day and dedicated it and completed all its work, as we read, *And there was evening and there was morning, one day.* And so it was with all the working days.[3] He created the seventh day too, but no work is stated thereon, nor the refrain *And there was evening and there was morning,* because its dedication is reserved for the future, as it says, *And there shall be one day which shall be known as the Lord's, not day, and not night* (Zech. 14:7).

Pirke d'Rabbi Eliezer Chap. 18.
T.S. 1, 432; 2, 33.

23. **He rested.**

This means that He rested from speech. For every day He would say, "Let it be thus," and it was so; but on the Sabbath His creative acts were concluded, and His speech ceased. How do we know that cessation of speech is called resting?—From the verse, *So these three men rested from answering Job* (Job 32:1).

Midrash Hagadol B'reshith. 2, 36.

24. AND HE RESTED ON THE SEVENTH DAY. God's day is a thousand years, as in Psalm 90:4: *For a thousand years in Thy sight are but as yesterday.* Just as we observe every seventh year as a sabbatical year, even so will God observe a Sabbatical year which will consist of a thousand years. Thus we read, *And there shall be one day which shall be known as the Lord's, not day, and not night; but it shall come to pass, that at evening time there shall be light* (Zech. 14:7). The future world and the resurrection of the dead are referred to here, and the light which the Almighty hid away for the righteous from the beginning,[1] as it is written, *And God saw the light, that it was good* (1:4); furthermore, *Light is sown for the righteous* (Ps. 97:11); also, *For with Thee is the fountain of life; in Thy light shall we see light* (ibid. 36:10). Again, we read, *And it shall come to pass that from one new moon to another, and from one Sabbath to another, shall all flesh come to worship before Me* (Isa. 66:23): this refers to the world (the Hereafter) which is all Sabbath.

Midrash on Psalms Ms. T.S.
1, Addenda 7, p. 178.

25. **And God blessed the seventh day.**

(By making it a day of universal joy.)

On the Sabbath, when all creation rested, the beings on earth and in heaven, all together, broke into song and adoration when God ascended His throne and sate upon it. It was the Throne of Joy upon which He sate, and He had all the angels pass before Him. . . . They all appeared before God with great joy, laved in a stream of joy, and they rejoiced and danced and sang, and extolled the Lord with many praises and many instruments. The ministering angels began, "Let the glory of the Lord endure forever!" And the rest of the angels took up

[3] He created each of the six days in which He labored, completed the work thereof, and dedicated it.

§ 24 [1] Zechariah means God's Sabbatical year, which will be followed by Resurrection, when the light hidden for the righteous from the Days of Creation will shine once more.

the song with the words, "Let the Lord rejoice in His works!" 'Arabot, the seventh heaven, was filled with joy and glory, splendor and strength, power and might and pride and magnificence and grandeur, praise and jubilation, song and gladness, steadfastness and righteousness, honor and adoration.

Then God bade the Angel of the Sabbath seat himself upon a throne of glory, and He brought before him the chiefs of the angels of all the heavens and all the abysses, and bade them dance and rejoice, saying, "Sabbath it is unto the Lord!" and the exalted princes of the heavens responded, "Unto the Lord it is Sabbath!" Even Adam was permitted to ascend to the highest heaven, to take part in the rejoicing over the Sabbath.

Zohar Hadash 2:4. Ginzberg Legends, pp. 83-4.

26. AND GOD BLESSED THE SEVENTH DAY. Thrice did God bless His world: The first blessing He bestowed on the fishes; the second, on man; the third, on the Sabbath. Corresponding to these the priests bless Israel with a threefold benediction, namely: *May the Lord bless thee; may the Lord cause His countenance to shine upon thee; may the Lord lift up His countenance upon thee* (Num. 6:24-26). It was taught: All these were fulfilled only through the blessing of the Sabbath.

Midrash Hagadol B'reshith. T.S. 2, 50.

27. AND GOD BLESSED THE SEVENTH DAY. Let our master instruct us:[1] When one builds a new house, what blessing must he recite? Thus did our Rabbis of blessed memory teach: He who builds a new house should recite the "Shehecheyanu" blessing,[2] in order to gratify his Maker. Hence the custom to recite a blessing when a new home is erected or when a new article is bought, in imitation of God who pronounced a blessing when He created the world, as we read, *and God blessed the seventh day* (2:3). Likewise when He created the beast and fowl, as it says, *And God blessed them* (1:22). It was the same in the case of man: *And He blessed them, and called their name Adam* (5:2). So too in the case of reptiles and in the matter of food.

Tanhuma B'reshith. T.S. 1, 705.

28. AND GOD BLESSED THE SEVENTH DAY, AND HALLOWED IT. R. Ishmael said: He blessed it with manna and hallowed it with manna, for every day of the week there fell one *omer* per person, but on the Sabbath eve two *omers*. And He hallowed it through manna, which did not fall on the Sabbath at all. R. Nathan said: He blessed it with manna and hallowed it with a blessing. R. Isaac said: He blessed it with manna and hallowed it through the man who gathered sticks.[1] He blessed it through the change of garments on the Sabbath. R. Eleazar said: He blessed it with the Sabbath lights . . . He blessed it with the luster of man's countenance, and sanctified it in the same way. For the luster of man's countenance during the week is quite unlike his radiance on the Sabbath.

Gen. R. 11. T.S. 2, 38.

29. AND GOD BLESSED THE SEVENTH DAY. He blessed it in respect of the luminaries. R. Simeon b. Judah said: Though the luminaries were doomed[1] on the eve of the Sabbath, they were not smitten until the termination of the Sabbath. When the sun set on the night of the Sabbath, the Holy One, blessed be He, desired to hide the light, but showed honor to the Sabbath; hence it is written, *And God blessed the seventh day*: wherewith did He bless it? With light. When the sun set on the night of the Sabbath, and the (primeval) light still continued to function, all Creation burst into song of praise, as it is written, *Under the whole heaven they sing praises to Him* (Job

§ 27 [1] This is a characteristic opening in the Midrash Tanhuma.
[2] Blessed art Thou, O Lord our God, King of the Universe, who hast kept us alive (shehecheyanu), preserved us, and enabled us to reach this season.
§ 28 [1] V. Num. 15:32 seqq. The sanctity of the Sabbath was thereby emphasized.
§ 29 [1] Through Adam's sin it was decreed that the primeval light should be hidden. *Var. Lec.*: cursed.

ANTHOLOGY

37:3): wherefore?—because *His light reaches unto the ends of the earth* (ib.).[2] Thus Scripture writes: *A psalm, a song, for the Sabbath day* (Ps. 92:1). R. Levi b. Zoma said: That means, for the day which was completely devoid of darkness. Every day of Creation, save the Sabbath day, closes with the phrase, *And there was evening, and there was morning;* but on the Sabbath "there was evening" is omitted.

Gen. R. 11; Midrash on Psalms Chap. 92. T.S. 1, 430; 2, 39.

30. AND GOD BLESSED THE SEVENTH DAY. He blessed it in respect of the additional expenditure which the Sabbath involves. R. Levi said in the name of R. Jose b. R. Hanina: A blessing is written in connection with every day in which there is a decrease, and so it suffers no loss at all. E.g.: on the fifth day birds and fish were created: now people kill birds and eat them, and catch fish and eat them; yet since a blessing is written in connection with it, the stock does not in any way decrease. On the sixth day man and cattle were created. Men slaughter cattle and eat them, and men die; yet since a blessing is written in connection with this day, they do not decrease. Then what can you say of the seventh day?[1]—Said R. Levi in the name of R. Hama b. R. Hanina: It is written on account of the additional expenditure.[2]

Gen. R. 11. T.S. 2, 40.

31. AND GOD BLESSED THE SEVENTH DAY. R. Eleazar said, quoting R. Jose: The blessing was for people with delicate digestions.[1] He blessed it with tasty dishes. Our Teacher (R. Judah the Prince) prepared a Sabbath meal for Antoninus.[2] Cold dishes were set before him, which he ate and found delicious. On another occasion he made a meal during the week, when hot dishes were set before him. Said he to him: "Those others I enjoyed more." "These lack a certain condiment," he replied. "Does then the royal pantry lack anything?" he exclaimed. "They lack the Sabbath," he retorted; "do you indeed possess the Sabbath?" Why did He bless it? R. Dostai said: Because it has no mate. Thus the first day of the week can be paired with the second, the third with the fourth, the fifth with the sixth; but the Sabbath cannot be paired. R. Simeon b. Gamaliel said: The blessing given to the Sabbath is that it is never postponed. The festivals and the Day of Atonement can be postponed,[3] but not the Sabbath.

Gen. R. 11. T.S. 2, 41.

32. AND GOD BLESSED THE SEVENTH DAY. Go out and see the difference between Israel and the heathen. The heathen works day and night without rest or pleasure; whereas the poorest Israelite, when Friday eve arrives, takes his rest and finds pleasure therein. That is why it is called blessed.

Midrash in a Ms. in the Schechter Cairo Genizah 3a. T.S. 2, 42.

33. AND GOD BLESSED THE SEVENTH DAY. How so?—By giving it as a sign to Israel. For when refugees from countries overseas where there are no Jews come to lands populated by both Jews and Gentiles, and see the marts and shops and commerce carried on by non-Jews open, whilst the shops and marts of Jews are closed, they naturally ask, "Why are these stores closed?" On being told that they belong to Jews, they enquire what kind of people are those Jews, whereupon they are further told how God created the world in six days and rested on the seventh, wherefore the Jews make this day a Sabbath of joy and banqueting. Then

[2] On this night.

§ 30 [1] When nothing was created.
[2] Incurred, without one's wealth being thereby diminished; cf. Betsah 16a.

§ 31 [1] To enable them to enjoy the rich Sabbath fare without suffering the consequences.
[2] On the identity of Antoninus see Sanh. (Sonc. ed.) p. 610, n. 7.
[3] Since they are dependent on the day which the Jewish Court proclaims as New Moon, if this is proclaimed one day later, they are observed one day later likewise.

ANTHOLOGY

they exclaim, "Blessed be their God who sanctified Israel, and bestowed on them such gifts as the Sabbath and its delight!"

Midrash *ibid.* 4a. T.S. 2, 43.

34. AND GOD BLESSED THE SEVENTH DAY. By bestowing Sabbath joy upon all beings, not excepting Adam, thus did the Lord dedicate His creation. Seeing the majesty of the Sabbath, its honor and greatness, and the joy it conferred upon all, being the fount of all joy, Adam intoned a song of praise for the Sabbath day. Then God said to him, "Thou singest a song of praise to the Sabbath day, and singest none to Me, the God of the Sabbath?" Thereupon the Sabbath rose from his seat, and prostrated himself before God, saying, "It is a good thing to give thanks unto the Lord," and the whole of creation added, "And to sing praises unto Thy name, **O Most High!"**

This was the first Sabbath, and this its celebration in heaven by God and the angels. The angels were informed at the same time that in days to come Israel would hallow the day in similar manner. God told them: "I will set aside for Myself a people from among all the peoples. This people will observe the Sabbath, and I will sanctify it to be My people, and I will be God unto it. From all that I have seen, I have chosen the seed of Israel wholly, and I have inscribed him as My first-born son, and I sanctified him unto Myself unto all eternity, him and the Sabbath, that he keep the Sabbath and hallow it from all work."

Seder Rabbah B'reshith 7-8; Jub. 2:17-20.
Ginzberg Legends, Vol. 1, p. 85.

35. AND GOD BLESSED THE SEVENTH DAY. *She hath hewn out her seven pillars* (Prov. 9:1): this refers to the seven days of Creation, as it is said, *For in six days the Lord made heaven and earth . . . and rested on the seventh day* (Exod. 20:11), hence, *And God blessed the seventh day.*

Lev. R. 11. T.S. 2, 45.

36. AND GOD BLESSED THE SEVENTH DAY, AND HALLOWED IT. The Holy One, blessed be He, blessed and hallowed the Sabbath day, and Israel is bound only to *keep* and to hallow the Sabbath day.[1] Hence they said: Whosoever says the benediction and sanctification over the wine on the eves of the Sabbath, his day will be increased in this world, and in the world to come.

Pirke d'Rabbi Eliezer Chap. 18. T.S. 2, 47.

37. AND GOD BLESSED THE SEVENTH DAY. At the seventh hour of the Sabbath eve (Friday) Adam entered the Garden of Eden; at twilight of the same day he was expelled. Came the Sabbath and pleaded for Adam, speaking thus: "Sovereign of all worlds! No man has been slain in the world during the six days of creation, and wilt Thou commence to do this with me? Is this its sanctity, and is this its blessing?" Hence it says: *And God blessed the seventh day, and hallowed it*: for the sake of the Sabbath day Adam was saved from the judgment of Gehinom. When Adam perceived the power of the Sabbath, he exclaimed: "Not for nought did the Holy One, blessed be He, bless and hallow the Sabbath day!"

Pirke d'R. Eliezer Chap. 19. T.S. 2, 48.

38. AND GOD BLESSED THE SEVENTH DAY. *I stood between the Lord and you* (Deut. 5:5): like a man who holds the marriage cup in his hand, whilst the Sabbath solemnizes the marriage, as it is written, *And God blessed the seventh day and hallowed it,* it consecrated Him, which teaches that the Sabbath is holy to the Almighty.[1] Thus we read, *A psalm, a song, for the Sabbath day. It is a good thing to give thanks unto the Lord and to sing praises unto*

§ 36 [1] If this reading is correct, the meaning is that Israel need only *keep* and hallow the Sabbath, whereas God blessed it too. However, the text may be incorrect and should read: "Israel is bound to keep" etc., omitting "only."

§ 38 [1] This rendering is based in the present text. It is, however, rather trite to say that the Sabbath is holy to the Lord. Moreover, it is than irrelevant. By reading קידש instead of קודש, which involves a very slight

He rested from all His work which God in creating had made. [4]These

COMMENTARY

off as a day consecrated to God and the life of the spirit.[15] **which God in creating had made. a.** The literal translation is "which God created to do" or "make." The work which there was still "to do" on the seventh day was done on the sixth day.[16] **b.** The work which God had created with the power to reproduce ("to make") itself.[17] **c.** *Bara,* "created," always refers to *creatio ex nihilo,* and *asah,* "made," to the shaping of existing matter. Accordingly, we render: "He rested from all His work (i.e., matter) which God had created (*ex nihilo*) to make" (from it the things which were made in the six days).[18] (This accords with the view that everything was potentially created on the first day. — Ed.) **d.** Lit., "which God created to make," i.e., to continue acting (Ibn Ezra; Abarbanel) throughout time by the unceasing operation of Divine laws. This thought is contained in the Prayer Book: "In His goodness He reneweth the creation every day continually." Or, as the Rabbis say, the work of creation continues, and the world is still in the process of creation, as long as the conflict between good and evil remains undecided. Ethically the world is thus still "unfinished," and it is man's glorious privilege to help finish it. He can by his life hasten the

ANTHOLOGY

Thy name, O Most High (Ps. 92:1-2). On the Sabbath the *Shekinah* is like a bridegroom adorned in his finery, and the Congregation of Israel like a bride; the Torah like a marriage certificate, with angels and seraphim encircling them both like the people at the gate when the bridal canopy is set up, and the Elders of the Congregation are as witnesses.

Midrash Hashkem Ms. T.S. 2, 49.

39. AND GOD BLESSED THE SEVENTH DAY AND HALLOWED IT. God received the Sabbath as a bridegroom receives a bride, with words of blessing and sanctification. *Blessed* refers to marriage blessing; *hallowed* is the marriage solemnization. The ancients used to go out to meet both: the Sabbath bride, saluting her with the greeting, "Come, O bride, come, O bride!" and the bridegroom, thus rejoicing in "*the voice of the bridegroom and the voice of the bride*" (Jer. 16:9).

Tikune Zohar 69. T.S. 2, 55.

40. AND GOD BLESSED THE SEVENTH DAY. R. Isaac observed: Concerning the manna it is said, *Six days ye shall gather it, but on the seventh day is the Sabbath, in it there shall be none* (Exod. 16:26): since no food is found on that day, what blessing is there in it?—The meaning is this: All the blessings of heaven and earth are due to the Sabbath. Because of this, the Sabbath is more prized than all other seasons and festivals, for the Sabbath comprehends all other days, which the seasons and festivals do not. R. Hiyya said: Because it comprehends all, the seventh day is mentioned three times in the story of creation, for it is written, *And on* the seventh day *God finished His work . . . and He rested on* the seventh day . . . *and God blessed* the seventh day.

Zohar 2:8. T.S. 2, 54.

41. **He rested from all His work.**

R. Phinehas said in R. Oshaya's name: He did indeed rest from the work of Creation, but not from the work of punishing the wicked and rewarding the righteous, for He works with the former and with the latter, revealing to them something of the retribution and reward that is in store for each respectively.

Gen. R. 11. T.S. 2, 56.

42. **Which God had created to do.**

Scripture writes: *Thus all the work of the Temple was completed* (1 Kings 7:51). Not simply *the work* but *all the work* is written,

change, we obtain the reading: This teaches that the Sabbath consecrated, i.e., betrothed the Almighty to Israel. This thought arises from the fact that *way'kaddesh* — hallowed — also means betrothed, the Hebrew for betrothal, *kiddushin,* really meaning hallowing or consecration. Hence the fancy that the Sabbath solemnized a betrothal between God and Israel, i.e.. it is the sacred link which unites them. The verse would then read: And God blessed the seventh day, and it consecrated Him (to Israel).

are the generations of the heaven and of the earth when they were

COMMENTARY

triumph of the forces of good in the universe.[19] Chapter II is *not* another account of Creation. No mention is made in it of the formation of the dry land, the sea, the sun, moon or stars. It is nothing but the sequel of the preceding chapter. In Chapter I man is considered as part of the general scheme of created things. Chapter II *supplements* the brief mention of the creation of man in verse 27 of the last chapter, by describing the formation of man and woman and their first dwelling place, as preliminary to the Temptation, and the consequent expulsion from the Garden of Eden in Chap. III. Only such details as are indispensable for the understanding of that event are given.[20] [4]**generations,** etc. **a.** All the created things mentioned in the previous chapter were the offspring

ANTHOLOGY

which means, the work of Creation. Similarly, Scripture states, *He rested from all His work which God had created to do.* Not "created and did" is written, but *created to do,* for there was still some work to do. When Solomon appeared and built the Temple, God said, "Now the work of heaven and earth is concluded, and all the labor of Creation is completed." For this reason he is called Solomon, which means complete, because through him and his work God completed the work of the six days of Creation.

P'sikta Rabbathi Chap. 6. T.S. 2, 59.

43. WHICH GOD HAD CREATED TO MAKE. R. Isaac said: When all His works were concluded, God surveyed and blessed them, established them firmly, and charged each not to change its nature from the purpose for which it was formed, but to produce the offspring befitting it henceforth and forever. That is the meaning of the text, *Which God had created to make, "to make"* signifying that everything in creation was *"to make,"* i.e., bear and bring forth offspring like itself.

Zohar Hadash 17. T.S. 2, 62.

44. **These are the generations of the heaven and of the earth.**

This would be a fit beginning for the Torah. *This month* (Nisan) *is the beginning of the months* (Exod. 12:2) would be a proper start for the book of Exodus; whilst the verse, *The enemy said: "I will pursue"* (ibid. 15:9), would be suitable for the opening of the Song of Victory. Why then did God abandon this order in the Torah? On account of the arrogant, to prevent a priest from reading in the section *B'reshith* and then boasting, "I started the Torah."[1]

Midrash Abakir. T.S. 2, 64.

45. THESE ARE THE GENERATIONS (TOL'-DOTH) OF THE HEAVENS (HASHAMAYIM) AND OF THE EARTH (W'HAARETS). The first letters of the last three words form the word *Tohu* (chaos). Now, we have laid it down that the expression *"these are"* denotes that those worlds which came before are of no account, those being the offspring of *tohu,* hinted at in the second verse, *and the earth was tohu and bohu* (1:2). These it is of which we have learnt that God creates worlds and destroys them. On account of this the earth was dazed (*tohah*) and bewildered (*bohah*), as if to say, "How could God create worlds to destroy them? It were better not to create them." But in fact we have here a deep mystery. For what does "destroys them" mean? Not that He really destroys the works of His hands. The explanation is this: The Torah is the salvation of the world, and the Gentiles who did not accept it were left dry and parched. It is in this sense that God creates worlds and destroys them, viz., those who do not keep the precepts of

§ 44 [1] Since *B'reshith* (in the beginning, etc.) is not the most suitable opening of the Torah in any case. It is not clear why the verses enumerated are regarded as the most fitting beginnings; various explanations have been offered.

COMMENTARY

of the heaven and the earth, being included in the latter's creation.[21] **b.** The former were created by means of the latter.[22] **c.** The preceding chapter contains an account of the primordial formation of heaven and earth, the initial creation being called generation.[23] **d.** What *follows* is what befell heaven and earth, the latter being dealt with first.[24] **e.** The verse explains how these things were brought forth, viz., by a mist ascending from the earth, etc.[25] **in the day. a.** Heb. idiom for "when."[26] **b.** The inference is that they were all created on the first day.[27] **c.** *In the day,* etc., means, when He ordered their eternal laws of existence, which was after the six days of Creation. Only then could He be called "*the* Lord *God*" (*Lord* denoting Him under the aspect of eternity).[28] **the Lord God** (Heb. Adonai Elohim). **a.** God (Elohim) whose Proper Name is Adonai.[29] **b.** This name is indicative of Divine Providence; in the present chapter and the next in relation to Adam, and in Scripture as a whole in relation to humanity in general.[30] **c.** This sacred binomial is employed

ANTHOLOGY

the Law; not that He destroys His own works, as people think.

Zohar 1:24. T.S. 1, 328.

46. THESE ARE THE GENERATIONS OF THE HEAVEN AND OF THE EARTH. Wherever Scripture writes "and these," it indicates an addition to objects previously mentioned; but "these" implies the disqualification of the preceding. For example?—*These are the generations of the heaven and of the earth when they were created.* What was disqualified there?—God created a heaven and earth, but when He looked at them they were not pleasing in His sight, so He changed them back into waste and void; but when He looked at this heaven and earth, it pleased Him, and He exclaimed, "These shall have generations!" Hence, *These are the generations of the heaven and of the earth*; but the former did not have any generations. Indeed, God created many worlds before the present one, but destroyed them. Thus we read: *Thou hast swept them away as with a flood; they are as a sleep* (Ps. 90:5). The reference is to the nine hundred and seventy-four generations prior to the creation of the world which were swept away in the twinkling of an eye because they were evil.

Exod. R. 30; Midrash Psalms (ed. Buber) 90. T.S. 2, 65.

47. THESE ARE THE GENERATIONS OF THE HEAVEN AND OF THE EARTH. It was taught: R. Eliezer the Great said: The generations of heaven[1] were created from the heaven, and the generations of the earth were created from the earth. But the Sages said: Both were created from Zion, as it is said, *Out of Zion, the perfection of beauty, God hath shined forth* (Ps. 50:2): this means that from it the beauty of the world was perfected.

Yoma 54b. T.S. 2, 68.

48. GENERATIONS (TOL'DOTH). *Tol'doth* is always spelled defectively in Scripture,[1] except twice, viz., *These are the* tol'doth (*generations*) *of Perez* (Ruth 4:18), and the present instance. And why are they defective? R. Judan said in R. Abun's name: The six which they lack corresponds to the six things which were taken away from Adam, viz., his luster, immortality, height, the fruit of the earth, the fruit of trees, and the luminaries.[2] They will not again return to their perfection until the son of Perez (the Messiah) comes. Hence *tol'doth* is spelled fully, with a *waw*, in the verse, *These are the* tol'doth (generations) *of Perez,* as an indication of the six things which will return.

Gen. R. 12. T.S. 2, 69.

49. THESE ARE THE GENERATIONS . . . WHEN THEY WERE CREATED. R. Judah said: *And the*

§ 47 [1] All things of heaven, viz., the stars, sun and moon. Similarly, "the generations of the earth" means plant and animal life, fish, fowl and reptiles.

§ 48 [1] Lacking a *waw*, i.e., תלדות instead of תולדות. Hebrew letters are also numerals: *waw* is six.

[2] These were reduced, the earth and trees having originally produced fruit in one day, and the light of the luminaries being far greater than it is now. The same applies to his height, etc., whilst he ceased to be immortal.

COMMENTARY

in the Adam story throughout up to his expulsion from the Garden of Eden, in order to convey the idea of His divine Essence. Y H W H (the Tetragrammaton, the letters which compose it), is the holiest name of the Deity, and it is forbidden to pronounce it as written Therefore its exact consonantal stem and vocalization are unknown to us.[31] **d.** Its stem is H W H (H Y H, "to be") meaning "the Ever Existing," "the Everlasting." This meaning, of course, gave rise to the connotation: Faithful in His covenant and steadfast in His promise.[32] **e.** This Divine Name is spoken of as the Tetragrammaton, which is a Greek word meaning "the Name of four letters." The High Priest of old pronounced it as *written,* on the Day of Atonement during the Temple Service; whereupon all the people fell on their faces and exclaimed, "Blessed be His Name whose glorious Kingdom is for ever and ever." The other and more general Divine Name is *Elohim.* Whereas *Adonai* is used whenever the Divine is spoken of in close relationship with men or nations, *Elohim* denotes

ANTHOLOGY

heaven and the earth were finished at their proper time, *and all their host* at their proper time.[1] Said R. Nehemiah to him: But it is written, *These are the generations of the heaven and of the earth when they were created,* which teaches that on the very day they were created they brought forth their generations.[2] R. Judah countered: Yet surely it is written, *And there was evening and there was morning, one day . . . a second day . . . a third day . . . a fourth day . . . a fifth day . . . the sixth day?*[3]—Said R. Nehemiah: It was like fig-gathering, when each appears in its own time.[4] R. Berekiah observed in support of R. Nehemiah: *And the earth brought forth,* etc. (1:12), implies something which was already stored within it.

Gen. R. 12. T.S. 2, 79.

50. THESE ARE THE GENERATIONS . . . WHEN THEY WERE CREATED. R. Judah b. Shalom said: On the very day heaven and earth were created, they all produced offspring lacking nothing.[1] This is implied in the verse, *These are the generations* (offspring) *of the heaven and of the earth.* Now, when were these offspring created?—*In the day that the Lord God made earth and heaven.* This emphasizes that on that very day all the world's necessities came into existence. Subsequently they were revealed, and their purposes declared, on the day they appeared. R. Eleazar said: All the offspring were created in the very same moment, the same hour, and the identical day; for it is written, *These are the generations of the heaven and of the earth when they were created, in the day that the Lord God made earth and heaven*; i.e., literally in the same day, the same hour, and the same moment.

Zohar Hadash 2. T.S. 2, 88.

51. WHEN THEY WERE CREATED (B'HIBARAM). *For all these things hath My hand made* (Isa. 66:2). R. Berekiah, quoting R. Judah b. R. Simon, objected: Without labor or toil the Holy One, blessed be He, created His world, yet you say, *For all these things hath My hand made!*[1] R. Judan said: It means that God created the world for the sake of the Torah which is referred to as "these" in the verse, These *are the statutes and ordinances and laws*—toroth (Lev. 26:46).[2] R. Joshua b. R. Nehemiah said: For the sake of the tribes, as it is written, *Now* these *are the names of the sons of Israel* (Exod. 1:1).

Gen. R. 12. T.S. 2, 67.

§ 49 [1] I.e., heaven and earth were first created and then the hosts of heaven and earth (M.K.).
[2] I.e., the heaven and earth were created simultaneously with their generations.
[3] On each of these days a generation of heaven or earth was created, whereas heaven and earth were themselves created on the first day.
[4] In a crop of figs all take shape about the same time, but they do not all ripen at the same time. Similarly the hosts (*"generations"*) were created simultaneously on the first day, but did not appear until later.

§ 50 [1] The offspring (AJV: generations) of heaven are the sun, moon, and stars; of earth, all forms of life.

§ 51 [1] This implies physical labor, where God's command was sufficient. The difficulty arises out of the interpretation of *b'hibaram* as indicating a completely effortless Creation; see Chap. II, par. 52.
[2] Pl. of Torah. He renders: And for the sake of all these things (sc. the Torah) hath My hand made, etc.

created, in the day that the Lord God made earth and heaven. [5]No shrub

COMMENTARY

God as the Creator and Moral Governor of the Universe.[33] **earth and heaven.** Since the center of interest now turns to man, earth is mentioned before heaven.[34] **[5]No shrub of the field was yet *(Heb. terem)* in the earth. a.** This verse is linked with the previous one, thus: *These are the generations . . . in the day that the Lord God made earth and heaven* (verse 5) and in the day that He made *all the shrubs of the earth* sprout forth instantaneously, without being sown (as was the case on the third day,

ANTHOLOGY

52. WHEN THEY WERE CREATED (B'HIBARAM). R. Eleazar, quoting R. Johanan, said: Read, *B'he baram,* He created heaven and earth with the letter *he.* Now, what business has the letter *he* here?—All other letters are uttered through the mouth by closing the mouth,[1] but the letter *he* can be articulated without closing the mouth.[2] It was in such an effortless manner that God created the world, as it says, *The Lord, the Creator of the ends of the earth, fainteth not, neither is He weary* (Isa. 40:28). R. Berekiah, citing R. Judah b. R. Simon, quoted: *By the word of the Lord,* and *the heavens were* already *made* (Ps. 33:5.). Further, it may be compared to a king who rebuked his servant and froze him in fearful amazement; even so, *The pillars of heaven tremble and are astonished at His rebuke* (Job 26:11).[3]

Gen. R. 12; Tanhuma Yashan B'reshith. T.S. 2, 74. 78.

53. WHEN THEY WERE CREATED (B'HIBARAM). R. Tahalifa said: The letters of *B'hibaram* when transposed read *B'Abraham,* meaning, all was created because of the merit of Abraham.

Tanhuma Yashan B'reshith. T.S. 2, 75.

54. **In the day that the Lord God made earth and heaven.**

The School of Shammai maintain: They were conceived at night and actually created by day; whereas the School of Hillel say: They were conceived at night and created by day; Yohai observed: I am astonished! How could the fathers of the world, these great schools, differ over the creation of heaven and earth! In truth they were conceived by both day and night, while they were actually created at sunset, when the sun is hushed.

Gen. R. 12. T.S. 2, 81.

55. THE LORD GOD (ADONAI ELOHIM). From the beginning of the Creation story until here Elohim is used, thus: *Elohim said, Elohim created, Elohim blessed.* You might think that Elohim designates angels. Therefore Scripture says, *In the day when the Lord God (Adonai Elohim) made earth and heaven,* thus teaching that none but God created them all.

Midrash Hagadol B'reshith. T.S. 2, 83.

56. IN THE DAY THAT THE LORD GOD (ADONAI ELOHIM) MADE EARTH AND HEAVEN. The sages asked R. Hiyya: Why is God's Unique Name (Adonai) not mentioned in the Creation story?[1] He answered them: It is not fitting for the King of Glory to attach His name to mortality, to things that perish, lest it be said that His name (i.e., His essence) is as perishable as His creatures. Hence He did not mention His Unique Name until after He had created everything mortal and perishable; only then did He mention it in connection with the things that endure forever, as it is written,

§ 52 [1] Either the lips, as the labials, e.g., b, m, p, or the dentals, as t, d, sh, s, or gutturals like ch. Some part of the mouth is closed or stopped up as these letters are articulated.
[2] It is a mere aspirate or breathing.
[3] Yet it required but the briefest of rebukes, like uttering the letter *he,* which is a mere breathing, to achieve this.

§ 56 [1] In the first chapter only Elohim, which is a generic name for the Deity, is used; whereas Adonai is the Unique Name, never used for any other but Him.

of the field was yet in the earth, and no herb of the field had yet sprung

COMMENTARY

when He commanded, "*Let the earth put forth grass,*" etc. — 1:11), before the shrubs grew naturally, and in the day that He made *all the herb of the field spring into existence by His* fiat, before it could grow naturally. On this interpretation *terem* means "before," i.e., before vegetation sprouted in its usual manner.[35] **b.** This was the position after the six days. Although they were brought forth on the *third* day (cf. 1:11 f.), they were still on the surface of the earth and needed the watering of the mist to make them grow.[36] **c.** On the third day they were indeed created with their form and stature; but they could not be further planted or sown or grow anew until the mist ascended.[37] **d.** With *terem* meaning "not yet" the verse may also convey the following sense: With the exception of the few plants that had been created

ANTHOLOGY

In the day that the Lord God (Adonai Elohim) *made earth and heaven.* Of all His other creations only those are mentioned here which endure forever. Thus, it does not enumerate man, beasts, cattle and fowl, which are perishable, but only earth and heaven, which are everlasting.

Midrash Haneelam Zohar Hadash 9. T.S. 2, 84.

57. EARTH AND HEAVEN. This may be compared to a legion which was the first to proclaim the king.[1] Said the king: "Since this legion was the first to act thus, I will give it a preferment which shall never be taken from it." "Thus," said the Holy One, blessed be He, "because the earth was the first to observe My wish, I will confer an honor upon her which will never be removed." Hence it is written, *Who didst establish the earth upon its foundations, that it should not be moved for ever and ever* (Ps. 104:5).[2]

Gen. R. 12. T.S. 2, 85.

58. IN THE DAY THAT THE LORD GOD MADE EARTH AND HEAVEN. R. Azariah said: This teaches that these two, heaven and earth, constitute the principal elements of creation; they then waited three days, and their work was completed on the fourth day.[1]

Gen. R. 12. T.S. 2, 86.

59. **No tree of the field was yet in the earth.**

Here you say that *No tree of the field* existed as yet, whereas further on you read, *And the Lord God had* (already) *made to grow out of the ground every tree,* etc. (ib. 9)?—Said R. Hanina: The latter verse refers to the Garden of Eden,[1] whereas our text speaks of the inhabited world. R. Hiyya taught: In both nothing grew until rain fell.[2]

Gen. R. 13. T.S. 2, 89.

60. NO TREE OF THE FIELD WAS YET IN THE EARTH. R. Simeon went on to say: The allusion is to the magnificent trees which grew later, but as yet were minute. Adam and Eve, as we have said, were created side by side. Why not face to face? For the reason that heaven and earth were not yet in complete harmony, *the Lord God had not caused it to rain upon the earth.* When the lower union was rendered perfect, and Adam and Eve turned face to face, then was the upper union perfected.

Zohar, p. 32. G. Scholem.

61. NO SIAH (TREE) OF THE FIELD, etc. All the trees, as it were, conversed (*masihim*) with

§ 57 [1] Before the other legions. This frequently happened in Rome under the Emperors.
[2] This is to explain why earth is mentioned here before heaven.

§ 58 [1] By the fourth day they had produced their offspring ("generations"), viz., plant life and the luminaries.

§ 59 [1] As appears from the rest of this verse and the following one.
[2] He reconciles the verses thus: The earth was endowed with plant-life on the third day, but the trees and herbs only reached the surface of the ground, until rain descended (in answer to Adam's prayer) and made them grow.

up; for the Lord God had not caused it to rain upon the earth, and there was not a man to till the ground;

COMMENTARY

at first, there was no abundant flora on earth, because there was none to promote its growth in a natural way.[38] **e.** There were not as yet non-fruit-bearing trees and inedible herbs.[39] **the earth . . . the** ground. The former term applies to the entire surface of the globe; the latter to its cultivable portion.[40] **not a man.** The edible fruits of the earth require not only God's gift of rain, but also man's cultivation. Man must be a co-worker with God in making this

ANTHOLOGY

each other;[1] all the trees, as it were, conversed with mankind; all the trees were created for man's benefit. A man once vintaged his grapes and spent the night in the vineyard; then the wind blew and injured him.[2] All the conversation of men is about the earth: "Has it produced, or has it not produced?" And all mankind's prayers center on the earth: "Lord! may the earth yield fruit"; or "Lord, may the earth be fertile!" All the prayers of Israel, however, are for the Temple: "Lord, may the Temple be rebuilt!" "Lord, when will the Temple be rebuilt?"[3]

Gen. R. 13. T.S. 2, 90.

62. **For the Lord God had not caused it to rain upon the earth.**

The complete Name of God is used only in conjunction with the complete world; it is likewise employed in connection with rain.[1] R. Simeon b. Yohai said: Three things are of equal importance, viz., earth, man, and rain. R. Levi b. Hiyya said: These three each consist of three letters,[2] to teach that without earth there would be no rain and without rain earth could not endure; while without both man could not exist.

Gen. R. 13. T.S. 2, 92.

63. **There was not a man.**

But for man there would have been no covenant with the earth that rain should fall upon it, as it says, *To cause it to rain on a land where no man is, on the wilderness, wherein is no man* (Job 38, 26).[1]

Gen. R. 13. T.S. 2, 93.

64. **And there was not a man to till the ground.**

There was no man to bring men to the service of God like Elijah and Honi *ha-m'agel.*[1]

§ 61 [1] The passage is based on the use of *siah* for tree instead of the more usual *etz;* hence the Midrash connects it with the verb *siah* to speak, converse. A secondary meaning of the verb is to meditate and pray, which explains the further comment which follows. This passage suggests that the tree is called *siah* because it is the object of man's conversation and prayers. The sighing of the wind in the trees is poetically conceived as their speech.

[2] Mah. and 'E.J.: the fruit on the trees protects man from the wind that blows through them; hence, when this man had gathered the grapes, leaving the vines bare, they no longer afforded him protection.

[3] Here *siah* is connected with prayer; cf. *And poureth out his petition* (siho) *before the Lord* (Ps. 102:1), while *field* is made to refer to the Temple.

§ 62 [1] God's complete name, "Lord God," is used for the first time in 2:4, after the world has been completed; similarly it is mentioned here.

[2] In Hebrew ארץ, אדם, גשם. Another reading is: All these are mentioned in the same verse, viz., *For the Lord God had not caused it to* rain *upon the* earth, *and there was not a* man to *till the* ground.

§ 63 [1] The proof-text is difficult, since it implies the reverse, viz., that even *without* man rain falls. Theodor reads: *Although there was not a man,* a covenant had been made with the earth, i.e., rain is independent of the presence of man. This does fit in with the proof-text. On the other hand, the comment is inappropriate when based on *There was not a man* (Th. justifies his reading only by referring to the *following* verse, which however is not quoted, so that the chief text is lacking). Perhaps our text may be retained, but with a different rendering of the proof-text, viz., *To cause it to rain on a land*: *is it not man?* etc. Of course, this rendering is at variance with the whole context, but in Midrashic exegesis a verse is very frequently taken out of its context.

§ 64 [1] A very pious Rabbi whose example inspired others to serve God. *Ha-ma'gel* may mean "circle-drawer" or "compass-maker."

[6]**but there went up a mist from the earth, and watered the whole face of**

COMMENTARY

earth a garden.[41] [6]**mist. a.** Heb. *ed* means mist or moisture.[42] **b.** In Assyrian the word means the "overflow of a river," and it may here have the same significance.[43] **there went up a mist. a.** Although there was as yet no rain, a mist went up to moisten the earth and keep the plants alive until the rain would fall.[44] **c.** And then a mist went up (which formed rain).[45] **d.** On the day that He ordered their eternal existence a mist ascended from which there came rains and dew, the necessary prerequisites of their continuity.[46] **e.** There used to go up. The Heb. verb expresses repeated action.[47] **f.** The negative particle *ayin* (not) of the previous verse may govern this verse too, in which case it reads: (and there was not a man to till the ground) nor was there a mist to go up from the earth.[48] **watered.** The vegetation did not therefore decay,

ANTHOLOGY

—Man was created for nought but toil: If he merits it, he toils in the Torah; if not, he tills the soil. Happy the man who toils in the Torah![2]

Gen. R. 13. T.S. 2, 94.

65. For there was not a man. Inasmuch as all above was not yet perfectly ordered, Adam and Eve were not created face to face. This is borne out by the order of the verses in the Scripture; first it is written, *For the Lord God had not caused it to rain upon the earth,* and following, *there was not a man to till the ground* (*ibid.*), and it signifies that man was yet imperfect, for only when Eve was made perfect, was he then made perfect too.

Zohar, p. 32. G. Scholem.

66. **But there went up a mist from the earth.**

R. Eliezer said: The whole world drinks from the waters of the ocean, as it is said, *But there went up a mist from the earth and watered the whole face of the ground.*[1] Said R. Joshua to him: But are not the waters of the ocean salty? He replied: They are sweetened by the clouds. R. Joshua maintained: The whole world drinks from the upper waters, as it is said, *And drinketh water as the rain of heaven cometh down* (Deut. 11:11). If so, how do I explain the phrase, *But there went up a mist from the earth*?—This teaches that the clouds grow in strength as they rise towards the firmament, and then open their mouths as a flask and catch the rain water.

Taanith 9b. T.S. 2, 99.

67. But there went up a mist from the earth, and watered the whole face of the ground. How did the earth drink?—R. Judah said: Like the River Nile which repeatedly waters the ground. R. Nahman said: Like the overflow of the river Kebaria. Our Rabbis explain it: As from an overflowing river (*tuvyah*). There is in fact a river in Babylonia called Tuvay, which is so named because it inundates the surrounding country every forty years. Thus did the earth drink at first (the water coming from below), for it is written, *There went* up *a mist,* etc. But the Holy One, blessed be He, reversed it, ordaining that the earth should drink only the waters that came from above. He decreed thus on account of four things: 1. On account of lawless men;[1] 2. In order that the descending rain may wash away noxious vapours; 3. That fields on a higher level may drink just as those on a lower level. And finally, 4. that all may lift their eyes heavenwards. Thus it is written, *That the lowly may turn their gaze upwards* (Job 5:11).

Gen. R. 13. T.S. 2, 100.

68. There went up a mist, etc. R. Hoshaya said: The Pentateuch, the Prophets and

[2] The verse is rendered thus: And when there is no man to make (men) serve (God), they serve the ground (Th.).

§ 66 [1] This mist is vapor which forms from the ocean.

§ 67 [1] Who could forcibly withhold it from their neighbors if it came from below.

the ground. [7]Then the Lord God formed man of the dust of the

COMMENTARY

though there was insufficient moisture for growth.[49] [7]**formed. a.** God fashioned the lifeless form of man out of a lump of earth.[50] **b.** Heb. *vayyitzer,* spelt with a double *yod*; this denotes a double "forming," once for this world and once for the resurrection.[51] (The meaning is that man was endowed with the potentiality of resurrection after death — Ed.) **c.** The Heb. וייצר, is from the same root, *yatzar,* as is used

ANTHOLOGY

the Writings corroborate the view that rain is as important as the Creation. The Pentateuch: *These are the generations of the heaven and the earth*; after which comes, *There went up a mist from the earth and watered the whole face of the ground.*[1]

Midrash Hagadol B'reshith. T.S. 2, 102.

69. **And watered the whole face of the earth.**

R. Eliezer b. R. Simeon said: The earth drinks up water in proportion to its porousness, as it is written: *And watered the whole face of the earth.*[1] With the residue of water available one waters the roots of trees every thirty days. For carob and sycamore trees, which are not reached by rain, God raises the water of the abyss once in seventy years, as it is written, *I, the Lord do guard it, I water it every moment* (Isa. 27:3).[2]

Midrash Hagadol B'reshith. T.S. 2, 109.

70. THERE WENT UP A MIST FROM THE EARTH AND WATERED THE WHOLE FACE OF THE GROUND. R. Simeon b. Levi commented: When the repentance of a contrite heart ascends from below, rain instantly descends.[1]

J. Taanith 2:1. T.S. 2, 97.

71. THERE WENT UP A MIST FROM THE EARTH. To make up for the lack of rain, *by watering the whole face of the ground,* and the mist rising is the yearning of the female for the male. Yet another interpretation says that we take the word "*not*" from the first verse to use in the second with "*mist,*" and this means that God failed to send rain because a mist had not gone up, for from below must come the impulse to move the power above.

Zohar, p. 33. G. Scholem.

72. **Then the Lord God formed man.**

That was after He first provided for his needs by creating plant life. Thus the Torah teaches common sense, that a man should not invite another to a feast before making all the necessary preparations for his proper entertainment.

Midrash Ms. in Introduction to Tanhuma Yashan. T.S. 2, 125.

73. THEN THE LORD GOD FORMED (VAYYITSER) MAN. Scripture describes God as *The Rock* (ha-tsur) *whose work is perfect* (Deut. 32:4). *Ha-tsur* means the artist (*tsayar*), who first artistically formed the world and then artistically moulded man in it. Thus our text really means, *The Lord God artistically shaped man.*

Sifre D'barim 32,3. T.S. 2, 111.

74. THEN THE LORD GOD FORMED (VAYYITSER) MAN. How do we know that there are two natal periods?—From the double *yod* in *vayyitzer* (*and He formed*), which implies a

§ 68 [1] Thus "*the generations of the heaven and the earth,*" i.e., the Creation, were dependent for their very existence on rain.

§ 69 [1] The reference to "*face*" implies that the earth is like a face with a mouth drinking the water. The more "open" the mouth, i.e., the more porous it is, the more it drinks. An alternate rendering is: According to its solidity or hardness.

[2] I.e., as required. Other readings have thirty days instead of seventy years, which seems more likely.

§ 70 [1] *Ed* (mist) also means calamity, destruction, whence by transference, the heart broken in contrition.

COMMENTARY

of the potter moulding clay into a vessel, possibly to remind us that man is "as clay in the hands of the potter."[52] **d.** "From which part of the earth's great surface did He gather the dust?" ask the Rabbis. Rabbi Meir answered, "From every part of the habitable earth was the dust taken for the formation of Adam." In a word, men of all lands and climes are brothers. Other Rabbis held that the dust was taken from the site on which the Holy Temple, with the Altar of Atonement, was in later ages to be built. That means, though man comes from dust, sin is not a permanent part of his nature. Man can overcome sin, and through

ANTHOLOGY

seven-months' and a nine-months' pregnancy.[1] The child conceived to be born after a seven months' pregnancy, but which is born in the eighth, is viable, and certainly so if born in the ninth. But the child conceived for a nine months' period but born after seven months cannot live. For consider: if an eight months' child is not viable, how much less so a seven months' child.

J. Yebamoth 4:2. T.S. 2, 112.

75. THEN THE LORD GOD FORMED (VAYYITSER) MAN. R. Jeremiah b. Eleazar said: God created two countenances in Adam, and out of one of them Eve was made, as it says, *Behind and before hast Thou formed me* (Ps. 139:5). Hence Scripture writes *vayyitser* with the letter *yod* repeated, to denote a double creation.

Berakoth 61a. T.S. 2, 113.

76. FORMED (VAYYITSER). R. Nahman b. R. Hisda expounded the double *yod* in *vayyitser* as teaching that God created two inclinations in man, the good and the evil. R. Nahman b. Isaac demurred: Then animals, of which *vayyitser* with a double *yod* is not written, should have no evil inclination, yet we see that they injure and bite and kick? Rather, the two *yods* are to be explained in accordance with R. Simeon b. Pazzi's dictum: Woe is me because of my Creator—*yotsri*—if I follow my evil inclination; woe is me because of my evil inclination—*yitsri*—if I combat it and suffer the pangs of unfulfilled desire.

Berakoth 61a. T.S. 2, 115.

77. FORMED (VAYYITSER). The double *yod* implies that man was formed for two lives, viz., life in this world and in the Hereafter. The School of Shammai maintain: His formation in the next world will differ from that of this world. In the latter, skin and flesh come first, sinews and bones last; but in the former, he will commence with sinews and bones and finish with the skin and flesh. The School of Hillel aver: Just as he is formed in this world, so will he be formed in the next.

Gen. R. 14. T.S. 1, 117.

78. HE FORMED (VAYYITSER). This is written with a double *yod*, because of all His creatures only Adam did God endow with superior excellencies and penetrating intelligence. Upon him He bestowed the power possessed by the superior (celestial) beings, the discernment to differentiate between good and evil; and He adorned him with glory and majesty. With all this exaltation, when man recalls that he is dust and will return to dust, everything becomes empty to him and he cries out *Vay* (Woe)! R. Johanan said: Divide the word, and then the verse reads, Vay (woe) that the Lord God formed man! for he must return to the dust that he was before.

Midrash Haneelam B'reshith 17. T.S. 2, 126.

79. HE FORMED (VAYYITSER). Another explanation of the double *yod* is that God created demons as a counterpart to man, who are like him in that they eat and drink, are born and die. Again, this double *yod* teaches that He created both Paradise and Gehinom for man.

Midrash Hagadol B'reshith. T.S. 2, 119.

§ 74 [1] I.e., some are conceived to be born after seven months', others after nine months' pregnancy. The reference is to human beings.

ANTHOLOGY

79A From the beginning of all things prevailed Divine goodness, without which nothing could have continued to exist. If not for it, the myriads of evil spirits had soon put an end to the generations of men. But the goodness of God has ordained, that in every Nisan, at the time of the spring equinox, the seraphim shall approach the world of spirits, and intimidate them so that they fear to do harm to men. Again, if God in His goodness had not given protection to the weak, the tame animals would have been extirpated long ago by the wild animals. In Tammuz, at the time of the summer solstice, when the strength of behemot is at its height, he roars so loud that all the animals hear it, and for a whole year they are affrighted and timid, and their acts become less ferocious than their nature is. Again, in Tishri, at the time of the autumnal equinox, the great bird ziz flaps his wings and utters his cry, so that the birds of prey, the eagles and the vultures, blench, and they fear to swoop down upon the others and annihilate them in their greed. And, again, were it not for the goodness of God, the vast number of big fish had quickly put an end to the little ones. But at the time of the winter solstice, in the month of Tebet, the sea grows restless, for then leviathan spouts up water, and the big fish become uneasy. They restrain their appetite, and the little ones escape their rapacity.

Finally, the goodness of God manifests itself in the preservation of His people Israel. It could not have survived the enmity of the Gentiles, if God had not appointed protectors for it, the archangels Michael and Gabriel. Whenever Israel disobeys God, and is accused of misdemeanors by the angels of the other nations, he is defended by his designated guardians, with such good result that the other angels conceive fear of them. Once the angels of the other nations are terrified, the nations themselves venture not to carry out their wicked designs against Israel.

That the goodness of God may rule on earth as in heaven, the Angels of Destruction are assigned a place at the far end of the heavens, from which they may never stir, while the Angels of Mercy encircle the Throne of God, at His behest.

Midrash Konen 37-38; Midrash Behokmah 63-66; P'sikta Hadat 48-49. Ginzberg Legends, Vol. 1, pp. 4-5.

80. THEN THE LORD GOD FORMED MAN. R. Joshua of Siknin said in the name of R. Simeon: God took counsel with the souls of the righteous in creating the world, as we read, *These were the formers* (Chron. 4:23), which has reference to our text, *Then the Lord God formed man. And they who dwelt among plantations* (ibid.) is likewise connected with our text, *Then the Lord God planted man of the dust of the ground.*[1]

Gen. R. 8. T.S. 2, 121.

81. THEN THE LORD GOD FORMED ADAM. Four men are described as God's formations. The first is Adam, as it says, *Then the Lord God formed Adam.* The others are Jacob, Isaiah and Jeremiah.

P'sikta Rabathi Chap. 26. T.S. 2, 124.

82. THEN THE LORD GOD FORMED MAN. R. Abba said: Why does "the Lord" (the Tetragrammaton) always precede "God" (Elohim)? —Because "the Lord," which is His actual name, denoting His eternity,[1] is the counterpart of the soul, which is the eternal part of man. Whereas "God" (Elohim), which is an associate Name, corresponds to the body, in which there is a partnership.[2]

Midrash Haneelam Zohar Hadash. T.S. 2, 128.

§ 80 [1] There is no such text. Perhaps the end of the verse, *of the dust of the ground,* suggests the idea that He formed man as a plant growing out of the earth.

§ 82 [1] The Tetragrammaton is a combination of the past, present and future tenses of the verb "to be," denoting that He was, is, and will be; hence it means The Eternal.

[2] The passage is obscure. Two meanings are possible: (i) "Elohim" is not fundamental, but an added designation, denoting the omnipotence (a secondary quality) of the Eternal, which is His primary characteristic;

ANTHOLOGY

83. **Then the Lord God formed man of the dust of the ground.**

Ecclesiastes describes life as vanity seven times, corresponding to the seven days of creation. What was created on the sixth day?—Man, as it says, *Then the Lord God formed man.* And what is man's end?—*For dust thou art, and unto dust shalt thou return* (3:19). (Thus life indeed is vanity.)

Midrash on Psalms 92. T.S. 2, 135.

84. THEN THE LORD GOD FORMED MAN OF THE DUST OF THE GROUND. Why was he called Adam? R. Judah said: Because of the earth—*adamah*—from which he was taken. R. Eliezer explained: "Adam" is an acrostic, reading Efer (ashes), Dam (blood) and Marah (gall). R. Joshua b. Karha said: Because he is flesh and blood.[1]

Midrash Hagadol B'reshith. T.S. 2, 129.

85. THEN THE LORD GOD FORMED THE MAN. For the sake of Abraham. R. Levi said: It is written, *The greatest man among the Anakim* (Josh. 14:15): "*man*" means Abraham, who is called the greatest man because he deserved to be created before Adam, but that the Holy On, blessed be He, reasoned: "He may sin and there will be none to set it right. Hence I will create Adam first, so that if he sins, Abraham will come and set things right."

Gen. R. 14. T.S. 2, 130.

86. OF THE DUST OF THE GROUND. God then called Gabriel, and said unto him: "Go and bring Me dust from the four corners of the earth, and I will create man out of it." Gabriel then went to gather dust from the earth, but the earth drove him away and would not allow him to take dust from it. Gabriel thereupon said: "Why, O earth, dost thou not hearken to the voice of thy Lord, who founded thee upon the waters without pillars?" The earth replied, and said: "I am destined to become a curse, and to be cursed through man, and if God Himself does not take the dust from me, no one else shall ever do so." When God saw this He stretched forth His hand, took of the dust, and created therewith the first man on the sixth day.

Gaster, Chronicles of Jerahmeel p. 15 (VI:6-7).

87. AFAR (OF THE DUST). R. Judah b. R. Simon said: Read this *ofer* (a young man): he was created as a young man in his fullness. R. Johanan said: Adam and Eve were created as at the age of twenty. R. Huna said: *Afar* (dust) is masculine, while *adamah* (ground) is feminine: a potter takes male dust (coarse earth) and female earth (soft clay)[1] in order that his vessels may be sound.

Gen. R. 14. T.S. 2, 131.

88. OF THE GROUND. R. Judah b. Pazzi observed: The Holy One, blessed be He, took a handful of dust from the place where the altar was subsequently to stand and created Adam from it, exclaiming, "O that he may be created from the place of the altar, that he may endure!" Thus Scripture writes, *Then the Lord God formed man of the dust of the ground (adamah)*; whilst elsewhere it is written, *an altar of earth* (adamah) *shalt thou make unto Me* (Exod. 20:21): just as *adamah* in the latter verse refers to the altar, so in our text too.

J. Nazir 7:2. T.S. 1, 132.

89. DUST OF THE GROUND, etc. R. Simeon b. Halafta said: Great is Peace, for when the Holy One, blessed be He, created His universe, He made peace between the superior and the inferior. On the first day He created both celestial and terrestrial, as it says, *In the begin-*

so also the body is but secondary to the soul. (ii) Whilst "the Lord" as a name is unique and applied only to God, the name Elohim is not peculiar to Him, since it is shared by others (e.g., judges; cf. Exod. 22:7, 8); the mating of man's body too cannot be ascribed to a single agent, since it is shared by the father and mother (cf. Chap. IV, par. 7). On both interpretations "the Lord" takes precedence because of its greater importance.

§ 84 [1] It is not clear how "flesh" is suggested by "Adam." Perhaps because it is red (*adom*) —Kasher.

§ 87 [1] The ancients believed that everything, including lifeless inorganic matter, consisted of male and female.

ground, and breathed into his nostrils the breath of life; and man be-

COMMENTARY

repentance attain to at-one-ment with his Maker.[53] **and breathed into his nostrils. a.** Heb. *b'apav*, which means into his nostrils (commentators); or "in his face," which includes both mouth and nostrils.[54] **b.** God's breathing is an allusion to the Divine inspiration of the human soul which gives it its superiority.[55] **c.** He infused vitality into him, i.e., excited in him a desire to breathe and live.[56] **d.** He breathed

ANTHOLOGY

ning God created the heavens and the earth (1:1). On the second day, celestial, as it is written, *And God said: "Let there be a firmament"* (ib. 6). On the third day, terrestrial, viz., *"Let the earth put forth grass,"* etc. On the fourth day, celestial: *"Let there be lights"* (ib. 14). On the fifth day, terrestrial, viz., *And God said: "Let the waters swarm with swarms of living creatures"* (ib. 20). On the sixth day, when He came to create man, He declared: "I will create him partly of the superior and partly of the inferior elements (viz., dust of the ground and the breath of God), for the sake of peace between the celestial and the terrestrial."

Gen. R. 12. T.S. 1, 244.

90. DUST OF THE GROUND. R. Abbahu exclaimed: How can man endure in this world, when the Torah itself testifies that he is but dust of the earth! R. Isaac observed: If man were of clay instead of dust, he would be more enduring, just as a building of clay is lasting, whereas one of dust (mud) has no permanence. Hence Scripture says, *For dust* (not clay) *thou art, and unto dust shalt thou return* (3:19).

Midrash Haneelam B'reshith. T.S. 2, 137.

91. **And He breathed into his nostrils the breath[1] of life.**

Why state the breath of life, and not simply life?—To teach that for every breath that man draws he owes praises to God, as it says, *Let every breath praise God* (Ps. 150:6).

Midrash Tanhuma Ms. T.S. 2, 140.

92. AND HE BREATHED INTO HIS NOSTRILS THE SOUL OF LIFE. R. Simeon b. Halafta said: Great is peace, for when the Holy One, blessed be He, created His universe, He made peace between the upper and the lower elements in Creation. On the first day He created part of the upper and part of the lower, as it says, *In the beginning God created the heavens and the earth* (1:1). On the second day, He created of the upper, as it is written, *And God said: "Let there be a firmament"* (ib. 6). On the third day He created of the lower, as it is written, *Let the waters under the heaven be gathered together . . . Let the earth put forth grass*, etc. (ib. 9ff.). On the fourth day again of the upper, as it is said, *Let there be lights in the firmament of the heavens* (ib. 14). On the fifth day of the lower, as it is said, *And God said: "Let the waters swarm with swarms of living creatures"* (ib. 20). On the sixth day, when He came to create man, He reasoned: "If I create man of the upper elements, they will outnumber the lower by one created object; if I create him of the lower, these will outnumber the upper by one." What then did He do? He created man of the upper as well as of the lower. Thus we read, *Then the Lord God formed man of the dust of the ground*, i.e., out of the lower elements; *and He breathed into his nostrils the soul of life*—out of the upper spheres.

Lev. R. 9. T.S. 2, 141.

93. AND HE BREATHED INTO HIS NOSTRILS THE SOUL OF LIFE. How was man formed? R. Judah b. Pedayah said: The day consists of twelve hours. In the first hour God conceived

§ 91 [1] The Heb. *n'shamah* means both breath and soul, and is understood in one or other of these meanings in this and the following passage.

ANTHOLOGY

the plan to create Adam. In the second He conferred with the angels; in the third hour, He gathered together the dust; in the fourth, He kneaded it; in the fifth, He moulded him; in the sixth, He stood him up as a lifeless mass; in the seventh hour He breathed into him a soul, as is narrated, *And He breathed into his nostrils the soul of life.*

Tanhuma Yashan Sh'mini 13. T.S. 2, 142.

94. THE SOUL OF LIFE. When man sins, it may be likened to two men, a villager and a courtier, who offended a king. The king pardoned the former, saying: "I forgive him, because he does not know one's obligations to royalty." But as to the latter he declared: "Since he is daily in my company and knows the requirements of court, judgment must be meted out to him." Man's body is the villager, as Scripture says, *The Lord God formed man of the dust of the ground;* but the soul is the courtier reared in the celestial palace, as we read, *And He breathed into his nostrils a living soul.* Therefore Scripture exclaims in amazement, *How strange that a soul should sin*! (Lev. 5:1).

Tanhuma Yashan Vayikra Par. 12. T.S. 2, 143.

95. AND HE BREATHED INTO HIS NOSTRILS THE SOUL OF LIFE. Scripture writes, *Let him kiss me with the kisses of his mouth* (Song of Songs 1:2). Two kisses are meant, the kiss in this world, and that in the Hereafter.[1] The kiss in this world, as we read, *And He breathed in his nostrils the soul of life.* The kiss in the Hereafter, as it says, *I will put My spirit in you, and ye shall live* (Ezek. 37:14).

Shir Hashirim Zuta Chap. 1. T.S. 2, 144.

96. HE BREATHED INTO HIS NOSTRILS THE BREATH OF LIFE. If a glass vessel, which is made by blowing with man's breath, can be mended when broken; how much more so man, made by the breath of God, as it is written: *He breathed into his nostrils the breath of life.*[1]

Midrash on Psalms 2:16. T.S. 2, 145.

97. AND HE BREATHED INTO HIS NOSTRILS THE SOUL OF LIFE. Man is like one married to a king's daughter. Daily when he rises early to greet the king, the sovereign gives him an account of his conduct at home. Amazed, the man asks the palace courtiers, "How does he know? Who has informed the king about all my daily doings?" Their answer is, "Fool, you are married to the king's daughter, and yet you ask how he knows!" So is it with man: he does whatever he pleases, and his soul relates all to God, who judges man as He recounts his deeds, the while he stands and wonders, "Who informed Him about all this?" He gets that very same answer: "Fool, you are married to His daughter, and His spirit is in you, as it says, *And He breathed into his nostrils the soul of life,* yet you wonder how He knows what you design in your heart! Your soul tells Him all."

P'sikta Rabathi Chap. 8. T.S. 2, 147.

98. AND HE BREATHED INTO HIS NOSTRILS THE SOUL OF LIFE. When God created Adam, he lay before Him a lifeless body, and God mused: Into which limb should I breathe a soul: the mouth? but he will use that for evil gossip; the eyes? with them he will leer at sin; the ears? with them he will listen to blasphemy and revilings. Hence I will choose his nostrils as the most fit: Just as the nostrils expel the noxious and inhale the fragrant, so will the righteous flee from malodorous sin and cleave to the words of the Torah, which are fragrant and sweet.

Midrash Hagadol. T.S. 2, 148.

99. AND GOD BREATHED INTO HIM THE SOUL OF LIFE. What charity does God do daily in His world?—He daily endows man with spirit, soul, knowledge and understanding. That He endows man with soul and spirit we learn from the verses, *And God breathed into him the soul of life; And the dust returneth unto*

§ 95 [1] The Song of Songs was allegorically interpreted as a dialogue between God and Israel. The speaker then in this verse is Israel, who longs for God's kisses.

§ 96 [1] This is to prove the fact of resurrection.

came a living soul. [8]And the Lord God planted a garden eastward, in

COMMENTARY

into him a vivifying soul ready to receive the image of God.[57] **a living soul. a.** A living entity.[58] **b.** The Heb. *nefesh hayyah* (which means literally: "soul—animal") may express the synthesis of the two contradictory tendencies of human nature, the phrase suggesting that though man, in his primitive impulses, more or less resembles the baser creatures, he is yet capable of lifting himself to great heights of spiritual perfection.[59] **c.** The same phrase was used of animals and beasts (1:30); it is specially mentioned

ANTHOLOGY

God as it was, and the spirit returneth unto God who gave it (Ecc. 12:7).[1]

Alphabet of R. Akiba. T.S. 2, 151.

100. **And man became a living soul.**

We learnt: In time of drought an individual may mortify himself by fasting.[1] R. Jose said: An individual may not afflict himself by fasting, lest one day he need the help of his fellow men and they have no mercy upon him.[2] Rab Judah said in the name of Rab: R. Jose's reason is because it is written, *And man became a living soul*: Scripture thereby implies that God says: "Keep alive the soul which I gave you."

Taanith 22b. T.S. 2, 154.

101. AND MAN BECAME A LIVING SOUL. R. Isaac, others say R. Eleazar, said: The Torah arraigns man, saying: The Holy One, blessed be He, created man and endowed him with a holy soul to make him worthy of a future life. But he turns himself, to his own hurt, into that animal soul which was hewn from the earth for beasts and cattle. R. Judah said: Scripture states, *And man became the soul of beast:* it does not say, and He made him *the soul of beast*, but, *And he became*—vay'hi—*the soul of beast*: this teaches that man caused himself to revert to that animal soul which was hewn from the earth.[1]

Midrash Haneelam Zohar Hadash 10. T.S. 2, 160.

102. *And man became as the soul of an animal.* R. Huna said: He became as a servant responsible to himself: If he does not toil he does not eat.[1]

Lam. R. 1. T.S. 2, 156.

103. **And the Lord God planted a garden.**

The School of Yannai said: Why does Scripture employ God's full Name in reference to the planting of the Garden?—Because from the very beginning of its creation it requires careful deliberation: before a tree develops out of its seed one must determine its exact location. Thus it is written, *The trees of the Lord have their fill, the cedars of Lebanon, which He hath planted* (Ps. 104:16). R. Hanina said: They were but as the antennae of locusts, when the Almighty uprooted and planted them in the Garden of Eden. This is the meaning of *The trees of the Lord have their fill.*[1]

Gen. R. 15. T.S. 2, 163.

104. **A garden in Eden mikedem (AJV: eastward).**

R. Judah b. R. Simon began his discourse with the text, *After the Lord your God*

§ 99 [1] Thus these verses show that God gave man soul and spirit. The passage probably desires to convey that He *renews* these daily. Later philosophers discussed the different meanings of soul (*n'shamah*) and spirit (*ruah*).

§ 100 [1] The Mishnah there states that for droughts lasting for certain times scholars prayed and fasted, and adds that ordinary individuals may do so likewise.

[2] Since he had no mercy on himself.

§ 101 [1] This passage assumes the rendering, *and man became the soul of the beast* (*hayyah* is so translated in 1:24), instead of our rendering, *and man became a living soul.* It contrasts man's soul, which came from the Divine soul, with that of the beast, which was created from the earth and is merely a life-force.

§ 102 [1] Just as an animal must work before its master gives it food.

§ 103 [1] The passage apparently means that He first planted these trees separately, because of the careful thought this involves, and then replanted them in the Garden of Eden.

COMMENTARY

here because man was made more *living* than they, in that he possesses knowledge and the power of speech.[60] **d.** Man at that stage was *only a living soul,* i.e., the same as the animals and beasts, until he was created in the image and likeness of God.[61] [8]**planted.** I.e., He *had* planted (before the creation of man).[62] **garden.** The ancient Versions translate it by the Persian word "Paradise," lit., enclosure or park.[63] **Eden.** The Heb. word means "delight"; but it is probably the name of a country, *Edinu* (signifying "plain," "steppe"), and may denote the extensive plain watered by the rivers Tigris and Euphrates. The phrase "Garden of Eden" became in course of time descriptive of any place possessing beauty and fertility. In later Jewish literature it signifies the Heavenly Paradise where the souls of the righteous repose in felicity.[64] **eastward.** Heb.

ANTHOLOGY

shall ye walk (Deut. 13:5). But can mortal man walk after the Holy One, blessed be He, of Whom it is written, *Thy way was in the sea, and Thy path in the great waters, and Thy footsteps were not known* (Ps. 77:20)? Again, Scripture adds, *And unto Him shall ye cleave* (Deut. loc. cit.). But can flesh and blood cleave to the Shekinah, of Whom it is written, *For the Lord thy God is a devouring fire* (ib. 4:24)? But it means this: The Holy One, blessed be He, from the very beginning of the Creation was before all else occupied with planting, as it says, *And the Lord God planted a Garden of Eden at the very first* (mikedem).[1] So when you enter into the Land, do you also engage first in nought else but planting; hence it is written, *And when ye shall come into the land, then ye shall plant* (Lev. 19:23).

Lev. R. 25. T.S. 2, 164.

105. AND THE LORD GOD PLANTED A GARDEN MIKEDEM (AJV: EASTWARD) IN EDEN. It was taught: Seven things were created before the world, viz.: The Torah, Repentance, the Garden of Eden, Gehinom, the Throne of Glory, the Temple, and the name of the Messiah. The Garden of Eden, as it is written, *And the Lord God planted a Garden in Eden from aforetime* (mikedem).[1]

Nedarim 39b; Pesahim 54a. T.S. 2, 162.

106. A GARDEN IN EDEN. R. Judah said: The Garden is larger than Eden, for it is written, *So that all the trees of* Eden, *that is* in the garden of *God, envied it* (Ezek. 31:9); and it is also said, *Thou wast in the Eden* of *the garden of God* (ib. 28:13).[1] R. Jose said: Eden is larger than the Garden, for it says, *Then the Lord God planted a Garden in Eden.* But surely it is written, *And a river went out of Eden to water the garden* (2:10)?—On R. Jose's view, the drainings of a *beth kor* will water a *tarkab*;[2] while on R. Judah's view, it is like a spring in the garden which waters the whole garden.[3] But R. Judah has two verses to support his contention, whereas R. Jose has but one?—Said R. Hanan of Sepphoris: The Holy One, blessed be He, opened R. Jose's eyes and he found a text to prove his view, viz.: *And He hath made her wilderness* (midbar) *like* Eden, *and her desert* ('arabah) *like the* Garden *of the Lord* (Isa. 51:3).[4]

Gen. R. 15. T.S. 2, 165.

107. A GARDEN IN EDEN . . . AND HE MADE TO GROW EVERY TREE. A text which is not fully explained in its own place is illuminated by another text. For instance, Scripture states, *And the Lord God planted a Garden in Eden . . . And He made to grow every tree,* etc. Thus we know that God planted in the Garden of Eden every kind of tree and choice fruit for

§ 104 [1] This is a possible meaning of *mikedem;* it may also mean "from aforetime," as in the next par.
§ 105 [1] See note on preceding passage.
§ 106 [1] Lit. translation; "*of*" implies that Eden was only *part* of the Garden.
[2] *Beth kor* is an area sixty times as large as *tarkab.* R. Jose explains that the text means that the excess water which could be drained off from Eden after it was watered sufficed to water the Garden; hence it was sixty times as large.
[3] So also Eden, though smaller, watered the Garden, which was larger.
[4] *Midbar* is larger than *Arabah.*

Eden; and there He put the man whom He had formed. [9]And out of the ground made the Lord God to grow every tree that is pleasant to the sight, and good for food; the

COMMENTARY

mi-kedem. This means either: **a.** East of Eden.[65] Or **b.** Aforetime, before man was created.[66] **[9]the ground.** I.e., of the garden of Eden.[67] **made . . . to grow. a.** When He made the trees to grow from the ground throughout the world, He did so likewise in the garden, but there He added two trees not found elsewhere.[68] **b.** He caused man's food to grow without the need of labor.[69] **pleasant to the sight.** Gladdening the heart and making it receptive of intelligence.[70] **tree of life.** The fruit of which prolongs life, or renders immortal. The phrase also occurs in a purely figurative sense, e.g., Prov. 3:18.[71] **in the midst** means here exactly in the middle.[72] The various

ANTHOLOGY

man. But we have no intimation here that God created for Adam and Eve canopies of gold and gems and all kinds of precious stones. Whence do we know this?—When it was said to Hiram king of Tyre, *Wast thou in Eden, the garden of God, with every precious stone for Thy covering* (Ezek. 28:13)? the speaker meant: Are you Adam, for whom I created such grandeur?

The 32 Middoth by R. Eliezer b. R. Jose. T.S. 2, 166.

108. And the Lord God planted a garden eastward in Eden. Eden is a unique place, segregated from the world, none knowing its exact location. At the advent of the Messiah God will reveal the place to Israel. He planted therein a garden with all kinds of choice fruits and all the delights which had been created during the six days of Creation. In it God also made canopies of precious stones for Adam, as we read, *Thou wast in Eden the garden of God; every precious stone was thy covering* (Ezek. 28:13). Since then, every good place has been compared to it. E.g., Egypt: *Like the* garden *of the Lord, like the land of* Egypt (Gen. 13:10). Jerusalem: *For the Lord hath comforted* Zion, *He hath comforted all her waste places, and hath made her wilderness like* Eden, *and her desert like the* garden *of the Lord* (Isa. 51:3). It is of him (Adam) that Scripture says, *The king brought me into his chambers* (Song of Songs 1:4), these chambers being those of the Garden of Eden that correspond to the chambers of heaven: this teaches that heaven and the Garden of Eden were created with one and the same utterance. Just as heaven comprises rows upon rows of stars, so does the Garden of Eden contain rows upon rows of the righteous, and they shine there like the stars. Thus it is said, *And out of the ground made the Lord God to grow every tree that is pleasant to the sight.* From this we infer that God stored there all kinds of plants, beautiful to see and delightful to the palate.

Midrash Hagadol B'reshith. T.S. 2, 171.

109. And the Lord God planted a garden in Eden. R. Isaac observed: The Garden of Eden of our text is the one which God planted on earth together with all the other plants which He planted.[1] Thus we read, *And the Lord God planted a Garden eastward, in Eden,* using His full name (the Lord God) in planting it. All forms and pictures of this world are portrayed therein, and that is the abode of the holy spirits.

Zohar Hadash 2:150. T.S. 2, 175.

110. **And there He set the man.**

R. Judah said: He exalted him, *set* having the same meaning as in the verse, *Thou shalt in any wise* set *him king over thee* (Deut. 17:15). R. Nehemiah said: He persuaded him to enter and eat thereof, like a king who prepared a banquet and then invited guests.

Gen. R. 15. T.S. 2, 172.

§ 109 [1] There is a celestial as well as a terrestrial Paradise; hence this observation that our text refers to the latter.

tree of life also in the midst of the garden, and the tree of the knowledge of good and evil. [10]And a river went out of Eden to water the garden; and from thence it was parted, and became four heads. [11]The name of the first is Pishon; that is it which compasseth the whole land of Ha-

COMMENTARY

views on the location of the trees in the garden of Eden: **a.** Both trees stood close to one another in the middle of the garden of Eden.[73] **b.** Only the tree of life stood in the middle of the garden.[74] **c.** Or, taking *etz* ("tree") to be a collective noun, the trees of knowledge, situated in the middle of the garden, encircled the tree of life, so that the latter formed an inner center within an outer center. This renders the verse: And the tree of life in the midst of the garden and in the midst of the tree of knowledge.[75] **the tree of the knowledge of good and evil. a.** *Knowledge* means desire: the partaking thereof would implant a desire for good or evil in the heart of man, whereas otherwise man would be naturally good.[76] **b.** *Good and evil* refers to man's power to choose the sweet even when it is harmful and reject the bitter even when beneficial.[77] **c.** The Targum paraphrase is, "the tree, the eaters of whose fruits know to distinguish between good and evil." The expression "good and evil" denotes the

ANTHOLOGY

111. **The tree of life also in the midst of the garden.**

It was taught: It was a tree which spread over all living things. R. Judah b. R. Ila'i said: The tree of life was a five hundred years' journey, and all the primeval waters branched out in streams under it. R. Judan said in the name of R. Judah b. R. Ila'i: Not only its boughs but even its trunk was a five hundred years' journey.

Gen. R. 15. T.S. 2, 176.

112. **The tree of knowledge of good and evil.**

That means that in its knowledge there was good and evil. What was the tree? R. Meir said: It was wheat: for of an ignoramus the popular saying is, "This man is as wise as one who has never eaten wheat in his life!" R. Zeira objected: The Bible calls it a *tree*; yet you say that it was wheat!—It sent up shafts as lofty as the cedars of Lebanon,[1] and they cast their seed on the ground. R. Judah b. R. Eliezer maintained that they were grapes. R. Eleazar of Acco said: It was a citron-tree (*ethrog*). R. Jose said: It was a fig-tree.

Midrash Hagadol B'reshith. T.S. 2, 182.

113. **And a river went out of Eden to water the garden.**

To what does *Eye hath not seen* (Isa. 64:3) refer?—R. Joshua b. Levi said: To the wine which has been preserved in its grapes for the righteous since the six days of creation. R. Samuel b. Nahmani said: To Eden, which no eye has ever beheld. Should you ask, Where then was Adam? He was in the Garden. Perhaps you would say, The garden and Eden are identical? Not so! For the text says, *And a river went out of Eden to water the garden*: thus the garden is one thing, and Eden is another.

Berakoth 34b. T.S. 2, 185.

114. **The name of the first was Pishon.**

It was so called because it makes flax (*pishton*) grow, and it flows with tranquillity (*be-shufi*). Gen. R. 16. T.S. 2, 193.

115. **That is it which compasseth the whole land of Havilah.**

Havilah was not yet in existence, yet you say, *That is it which compasseth the whole land of Havilah!* But, *He declareth the end from the beginning* (Isa. 46:10).[1]

Gen. R. 16. T.S. 2, 195.

§ 112 [1] For that reason it is called a tree.
§ 115 [1] Cf. pars. 121, 123.

vilah, where there is gold; [12]and the gold of that land is good; there is bdellium and the onyx stone. [13]And the name of the second river is Gihon; the same is it that compasseth the whole land of Cush. [14]And the

COMMENTARY

knowledge which infancy lacks and experience acquires ("Your children which this day have no knowledge of good or evil," Deut. 1:39). "Knowledge of good and evil" may also mean, knowledge of all things, i.e., omniscience.[78] [10]**a river went out of Eden.** Without the need of rain or man's toil.[79] [11]**Pishon.** I.e., the Nile.[80] **Havilah.** Cf. 10:29. N. E. of Arabia, on the Persian Gulf. Arabia was famed in antiquity for its gold.[81] **where there is gold.** The addition of *where*, etc., is to indicate that the Havilah of Egypt (mentioned in 25:18) is not intended here.[82] **bdellium.** This may signify "a tree secretion" or "pearls."[83] [13]**Gihon.** Its waters roar onward with great force, the word being derived from *nagah* "to gore," indicating the roar

ANTHOLOGY

116. **Where there is gold.**

Gold in its literal sense.[1]

Gen. R. 16. T.S. 2, 198.

117. **And the gold of that land is good.**

There are seven varieties of gold: good gold, pure gold, solid gold, refined gold, super-refined gold, beaten gold and gold of Parvaim.[1] "Good gold" is as the words literally suggest. Thus, commenting on the text, *And the gold of that land is good,* R. Isaac observed: It is good for use at home, and good when it accompanies you on your journeys.

J. Yoma 4:1. T.S. 2, 200.

118. AND THE GOLD OF THAT LAND IS GOOD. R. Abbahu said: The Holy One, blessed be He, conferred a great boon upon the world, for a man changes one gold piece and uses it for many purposes. R. Simeon b. Lakish said: The world did not deserve to have the use of gold. Why then was gold created? For the sake of the Temple, as it is written, *And the gold of that land is good,* which bears the same connotation as in the verse, *That* good hill, *and the Lebanon* (Deut. 3.25).[1]

Gen. R. 16. T.S. 2, 201.

119. THE WHOLE LAND OF HAVILAH, WHERE THERE IS THE GOLD. This is an allusion to the Torah, whose words are described as *more to be desired than gold, yea, than much fine gold* (Ps. 19:11). Thus it says, *And the gold of that land is good* (2:12).[1] R. Johanan remarked: This demonstrates that there is no Torah like the Torah of the Land of Israel, and no wisdom like the wisdom of the Land of Israel.[2]

Gen. R. 16. T.S. 2, 199. 202.

120. **There is bdellium and the onyx stone.**

This is an allusion to spiritual treasures, Scripture and Mishnah, Talmud, Tosefta and Aggadah.

Gen. R. 16. T.S. 2, 205.

121. **The whole land of Cush.**

Cush was not yet in existence, yet you say, *The whole land of Cush!* But, *He declareth the end from the beginning* (Isa. 46:10).

Gen. R. 16. T.S. 2, 206.

§ 116 [1] The point is that in addition to its allegorical interpretation as meaning the Torah (see par. 119), first it is to be understood literally.

§ 117 [1] The renderings are conjectural.

§ 118 [1] "Hill" is understood to mean the hills of Jerusalem. Lebanon (root: *laban,* white) was allegorically interpreted to mean the Temple, because it "whitened," i.e., made atonement for, the sins of Israel.

§ 119 [1] "Good" being understood to mean the Torah, as we read, *For I give you* good *doctrine; forsake ye not My* Torah.

[2] Havilah is apparently identified with the Land of Israel; cf. preceding par.

name of the third river is Tigris; that is it which goeth toward the east of Asshur. And the fourth river is the

COMMENTARY

and headlong rush of a bull as it hurls itself forward to attack.[84] Like the Pishon, the identity of this river is a matter of conjecture.[85] **Cush. a.** The name is written in anticipation of the future, as the land was not yet inhabited and named; similarly with *Asshur* in the next verse.[86] **b.** Usually rendered Ethiopia; but it may also denote some territory in Asia.[87] [14]**Tigris** (Hiddekel). So named because its waters are "sharp" (*had*) i.e., probably "fresh," and "clear" (*kal*).[88] **the east of Asshur. a.** Toward the East of a city called Asshur or Seleucia.[89] **b.** At the East of Greater Assyria, which includes Babylonia.[90] **c.** In front of Asshur, i.e., to the *west* of Asshur.[91] (This

ANTHOLOGY

122. **And the name of the third river is Hiddekel (Tigris).**

What does Hiddekel denote? Said R. Ashi: That its waters are swift (*had*) and light (*kal*).[1]

Berakoth 59b. T.S. 2, 209.

123. **That is it which goeth towards the east of Asshur.**

Does Scripture assume the future? Yes, for R. Joseph taught: Asshur is Seleucia. But was Seleucia already then in existence? It is, however, mentioned because it was to exist in the future.

Kethuboth 10b. T.S. 2, 213.

124. **And the fourth river is the Euphrates.**

The chief source of all waters is the Euphrates. For R. Judah taught in the name of Rab: If one vows not to benefit from the waters of the Euphrates, all the waters in the world are forbidden to him. How did he vow? "I will not drink from the waters which issue from the Euphrates." For R. Judah said in the name of Rab: All other rivers in the world are lower than the three other rivers of our text, which in turn are lower than the Euphrates.[1] But there are springs higher than the Euphrates? Said R. Mesharshia: Those are the sources of the Euphrates. But it is written, *And the fourth river is the Euphrates?*[2] Said R. Nahman b. Isaac (others say, R. Aha b. Jacob): That is the original Euphrates.[3]

Bekoroth 55a and b. T.S. 2, 215.

125. AND THE FOURTH RIVER IS THE EUPHRATES. R. Meir taught: Its name is Yubal (River), because Scripture says, *For he shall be as a tree planted by the waters, and that spreadeth out its roots by the river* (yubal) (Jer. 17:8).[1] And why is it called Perath? Because its waters are fruitful (*parin,* same root as Perath) and increase.[2] This supports Samuel. For Samuel said: The river grows from the waters coming down its banks.[3] In this he differs from Rab, in whose name R. Ammi said: The rise of the Euphrates is weighty testimony that it has rained in Palestine.

Bekoroth 55b. T.S. 2, 216.

126. AND THE FOURTH RIVER IS THE EUPHRATES. Rab said: The Euphrates is the greatest of all rivers. R. Hanina b. Igud and R. Joshua of Siknin in the name of R. Levi said:

§ 122 [1] The meaning is somewhat doubtful. "Swift" may mean either swift-running or readily saleable. "Light" probably means palatable and healthy.

§ 124 [1] Presumably because all other rivers branch off from these three, which in turn branch off from the Euphrates.
[2] Thus it is only one of the rivers, and not their source.
[3] Referred to in v. 10: *And a river went out of Eden.* The main stream as it flows on its straight course is the Euphrates of our text.

§ 125 [1] This tree is understood to be the Tree of Life in the Garden of Eden, which the Euphrates watered.
[2] Welling up spontaneously without the help of rain.
[3] *Aliter*: from its bed. Not from rain. And though Samuel does not distinctly mention the Euphrates, yet since all rivers draw from it, if ordinary rivers are fruitful, this is due to the waters of Euphrates being fruitful and increasing.

Euphrates. [15]And the Lord God took the man, and put him into the garden of Eden to dress it and to keep

COMMENTARY

would be from the viewpoint of one living in Palestine, which is the natural viewpoint of the Bible.—Ed.) **the Euphrates. a.** The most important of the four rivers on account of the Land of Israel, of which it was to be the ideal boundary (15:18). It was given its name, because its waters are ever "increasing" (*parin*) and give health to man.[92] **b.** No further description is given, because it was universally known as "the great River" (Deut. 1:7) and "*the* River" (Exod. 23:31; Isa. 7:20).[93] [15]**to dress it and to keep it. a.** To tend it by watering

ANTHOLOGY

The Ubal[1] is the greatest of all rivers. But it is written, *As I was by the side of the* great river, *which* is Hiddekel—Tigris (Dan. 10:4)? That is because Daniel had two dreams, one by Ubal and the other by the Tigris, and as the Tigris is larger than Ubal, he calls it the great river.[2] But at the creation of the world this (river Tigris) is not designated great; why then is it designated great elsewhere? Because it flows on its way and encompasses Eretz Israel, of which it is written, *For what* great *nation is there, that hath God so nigh unto them* (Deut. 4:7)? Hence the popular saying: "The king's servant is a king; cleave to someone who feels hot and you will feel warm."

Gen. R. 16. T.S. 2, 217.

127. **And the Lord God took the man.**

R. Judah said: "Took" means that He elevated him by placing him in the Garden of Eden, as in the verse, *And the peoples shall* take *them, and bring them to their place* (Isa. 14:2). R. Nehemiah said: He persuaded him to enter, as you read, Take *with you words, and return unto the Lord* (Hos. 14:3).

Gen. R. 16. T.S. 2, 220.

128. AND THE LORD TOOK THE MAN. Whence did He take him? He took him from the place of the Temple[1] and brought him into His palace, as it says: *And the Lord God took the man and put him into the garden of Eden.*

Pirke d'Rabbi Eliezer Ch. 12. T.S. 3, 223.

129. **And put him into the Garden of Eden.**

R. Judan said: He did actually give him repose, protect and delight him with all the trees of the Garden of Eden. R. Berekiah said: He put him there *in order* to give him repose, protect and delight him with all the trees of the Garden of Eden. (But this intention was never fulfilled, because of Adam's sin.)

Gen. R. 16. T.S. 2, 224.

130. AND PUT HIM INTO THE GARDEN OF EDEN. This means that He gave him the Sabbath, as you read, *And rested* (wayyanah) *on the seventh day* (Ex. 20:11).[1] *To work it*: as you read, *Six days shalt thou* work (ib. 9); *and to keep it:* as Scripture says, Keep *the* Sabbath *day, to hallow it* (Deut. 5:12).

Gen. R. 16. T.S. 2, 225.

131. **To dress it.**

R. Simeon b. Eleazar said: Adam too did not eat a thing before he labored, as Scripture states: *And He put him into the garden of Eden to dress it and to keep it:* only *after* thus tilling it was he told, *Of every tree of the garden thou mayest freely eat* (2:17).

Aboth d'Rabbi Nathan Chap. 11. T.S. 2, 226.

§ 126 [1] See Dan. 8:2: *And I was by Ubal Ulai* (AJV: *the stream Ulai.* But on the present reading Ubal is treated as a proper noun, this being the name of the stream.) But it has been objected that this Ubal is quite a small river. Hence an alternative reading, Yubal, has been suggested. This name occurs in Sifre Ekeb, chap. 35. See also preceding par., where Yubal is identified with the Euphrates, the primeval river whence all other rivers issue.

[2] This leaves the difficulty unanswered on the latter view, unless we read there Yubal.

§ 128 [1] Cf. par. 88.

§ 130 [1] He renders: And He made him rest.

it. [16]And the Lord God commanded the man, saying: 'Of every tree of the garden thou mayest freely eat;

COMMENTARY

and guard (*keep*) it from the wild beasts.[94] **b.** This refers to man's *breath of life,* which he was to tend and guard in Eden.[95] **c.** I.e., to till it and guard it from running wild. Not indolence but congenial work is man's Divinely allotted portion.[96]

[16]**commanded the man.** The text is literally "commanded upon the man," and when the verb is followed by "upon" it always denotes a prohibition: the command was that he was *not* to eat of the tree of knowledge.[97]

ANTHOLOGY

132. **And to serve it.**

This refers to study. But perhaps it means service literally? Consider: Scripture says, *To serve it and to keep it*: But what work was there in the Garden of Eden? To prune vineyards and plough the fields? Or to reap and bind? But did not all the trees grow up of their own accord? Or perhaps, to water the garden? But did not a river issue from Eden and water the garden, as it says, *And a river went out of Eden to water the garden* (3:10)? What then does *to serve it and to keep it* mean? To engage in the study of the Torah and "*keep the way to the tree of life*" (3:24), which is none other than the Torah, as it says, *It is a tree of life to them that lay hold upon it* (Prov. 3:18). Again, *To serve it* is an allusion to sacrifice, as is written, *Ye shall* serve *God upon this mountain* (Exod. 3:12); whilst *and to keep it* likewise has the same meaning, as Scripture says, *Ye shall keep* (it in mind) *to offer unto Me* (Num. 28:2). Thus both the service on the Altar and the study of the Torah are called service.

Gen. R. 16; Sifre Debarim Ekeb par. 41; Pirke d'Rabbi Eliezer Chap. 12. T.S. 2, 227. 228.

133. **And the Lord God commanded Adam, saying.**

One day when R. Abbahu was travelling in the company of heathens, they asked him: It is written in the Torah, *And the Lord God commanded Adam*: thus Adam was commanded not to sin, but not Eve: why then was she punished? Said he to them: What does Scripture say? *Commanded Adam, saying*: "saying" extends the command to all the limbs of Adam, and Eve was created from one of his ribs.

Yelamdenu. T.S. 3, 77.

134. AND THE LORD GOD COMMANDED ADAM, SAYING. Our Rabbis taught: Seven precepts[1] were the sons of Noah[2] commanded: 1) Social justice.[3] 2) To refrain from blasphemy. 3) Idolatry. 4) Adultery. 5) Murder. 6) Robbery. 7) Not to eat a limb cut from a living animal. Whence do we know this? Said R. Johanan: From the text, *And the Lord God commanded the man, saying: "Of every tree of the garden thou mayest freely eat." And He commanded* refers to the observance of social justice, and thus it is written, *For I know him, that he will command his children and his household after him, and they shall keep the way of the Lord, to do* justice *and* judgment

§ 134 [1] These commandments may be regarded as the foundation of all human and moral progress. Judaism has both a national and a universal outlook. In the former sense it is particularistic, setting up a people distinct and separate from any other by its peculiar religious institutions. But in the latter, it recognizes that moral progress and its concomitant Divine love and approval are the privilege and obligation of all mankind. And hence the Talmud lays down the seven Noachian precepts, by the observance of which all mankind may attain spiritual perfection, and without which moral death must inevitably ensue. That perhaps is the idea underlying the assertion (*passim*) that a heathen is liable to death for the neglect of any of these. The last mentioned is particularly instructive as showing the great importance attached to the humane treatment of animals; so much so, that it is declared to be fundamental to human righteousness.

[2] A technical expression for all peoples other than Jews. It applies also to Abraham and his descendants before Revelation.

[3] So Nahmanides on Gen. 34:13. Or perhaps: to establish Courts of Justice. Hast. Dict. (s.v. Noachican Precepts) renders: obedience to authority.

ANTHOLOGY

(18:19). *The Lord* interdicts blasphemy, as we read, *And he that* blasphemeth *the name of* the Lord, *he shall surely be put to death* (Lev. 24:16). *God* prohibits idolatry, as it is written, *Thou shalt have no other gods before Me* (Exod. 20:3). *The man* alludes to murder, and thus it is written, *Whoso sheddeth man's blood, by man shall his blood be shed* (9:6). *Saying* indicates adultery, and thus it is written, *They* say, *if a man put away his wife, and she go from him, and became another man's* (Jer. 3:1). *Of every tree of the garden*—but not of robbery.[4] *Thou mayest freely eat*—but not flesh cut from a living animal.[5] When R. Isaac came he taught a reversed interpretation: *And He commanded* refers to idolatry; *Elohim* (*God*), to social justice. Now *Elohim* may rightly refer to social justice, as it is written, *And the master shall be brought unto Elohim* (i.e., the judges) (Exod. 22:7).[6] But how can *and He commanded* connote a prohibition of idolatry? One scholar quoted: *They have turned quickly aside out of the way which I* commanded *them; they have made them a* molten calf (Exod. 32:8). Another cited: *Ephraim is oppressed and broken in judgment, because he willingly walked after the* commandment (Hos. 5:11).[7]

Sanhedrin 56b. T.S. 2, 230.

135. AND THE LORD GOD COMMANDED ADAM, SAYING. A Tanna of the School of Manasseh taught: The sons of Noah were given seven precepts, viz.: Prohibition of Idolatry, Adultery, Murder, Robbery, a limb cut from a living animal, emasculation, and forbidden mixture.[1] R. Judah said: Adam was prohibited idolatry only, for it is written, *And the Lord God commanded Adam.*[2] R. Judah b. Bathyra maintained: He was forbidden blasphemy too. Some add social laws. With whom does the following statement of R. Judah in the name of Rab agree, viz., God said to Adam: "I am God, do not curse Me; I am God, do not exchange Me for another; I am God, let My fear be upon you?"[3] This agrees with the last named, who adds social laws to the list. Now what is the standpoint of the Tanna of the School of Manasseh: If he interprets the verse, *And the Lord God commanded*, etc., as interpreted above, he should include these two (social laws and blasphemy) also; and if not, whence does he derive the prohibition of the rest? In truth, he rejects that interpretation, but maintains that each of these which he includes is separately stated. R. Joseph said: The Scholars stated: A heathen is executed for the violation of three precepts—adultery, murder and blasphemy. R. Shesheth taught: A heathen is also executed for idolatry.

Sanhedrin 56b. T.S. 2, 231.

136. AND THE LORD GOD COMMANDED ADAM, SAYING. R. Levi said: He gave him six precepts (viz., to refrain from idolatry, blasphemy, reviling duly constituted authority, murder, incest and theft).[1] The Rabbis interpreted the whole passage thus: *And the Lord God commanded*. He said to him: "I am merciful, yet am I a Judge to exact retribution.

[4] Since Adam needed express permission to eat of these, it is clear that without such permission, i.e., when they belong to another, they are forbidden.

[5] By interpreting thus: Thou mayest eat what is now ready for eating, but not when the animal is alive. It is perhaps remarkable that a verse, the literal meaning of which is obviously permission to enjoy, should be interpreted as a series of prohibitions. Yet it is quite in keeping with the character of the Talmud: freedom to enjoy must be limited by moral and social considerations, and indeed only attains its highest value when so limited. Cf. Aboth 6:2: No man is free but he who labors in the Torah.

[6] The root idea of *Elohim* is power, majesty.

[7] This refers to idolatry.

§ 135 [1] Heb. *kilayim.* This refers to the heterogeneous sowing of the diverse species together, the hybridization of different animals, and the wearing of a garment of wool and linen woven together; See Lev. 19:19; Deut. 22:9-11.

[2] Which means that He commanded him to recognize His Godhead, and not to reject Him for another deity.

[3] "Let My fear be upon you" is an exhortation to dispense justice fairly without fear of any man.

§ 136 [1] See par. 134 for the proof-texts; *seven* are stated there.

[17]but of the tree of the knowledge of good and evil, thou shalt not eat of

COMMENTARY

[17]thou shalt not eat. a. Man did indeed possess great knowledge without eating of this tree; he merely lacked *the knowledge of good and evil* in one respect (viz., sexual passion).[98] **b.** Man's most sacred privilege is freedom of will, the ability to obey or to disobey his Maker. This sharp limitation of self-gratification, this "dietary law," was to test the use he would make of his freedom; and it thus begins the moral discipline of man. Unlike the beast, man has also a spiritual life, which demands the subordination of his desires to the law of God. The will of God revealed in His Law is the one eternal and unfailing guide as to what constitutes good and evil — and not

ANTHOLOGY

Again, I am God: then treat Me as such and do not curse Me," as it is written, *Thou shalt not curse God* (Exod. 22:27).[2] *Thou mayest freely eat.* R. Jacob of K'far Hanin interpreted thus: When is it fit to be eaten? When it is ritually slaughtered. Thus He intimated an injunction against eating of a limb torn from a living animal.[3]

Gen. R. 16. T.S. 2, 232.

137. AND THE LORD GOD COMMANDED ADAM, SAYING. The Bible declares: *Wisdom hath builded her house . . . she calleth . . . "Whoso is thoughtless, let him turn in hither"* (Prov. 9:1-4). God prepared for man the Garden of Eden and Gehinom, and He warned Adam and his issue not to stray from His path, as it says: *And the Lord God commanded the man.* He enjoined them: "If you will keep My way of life, I will secure your welfare in this life and in the future world. If you do not keep My commandments, Gehinom stands ready for your retribution." Hence Scripture says, *Wisdom hath builded her house.*[1]

Midrash Ms. in the Schechter Genizah, 1, 82.

138. **Thou shalt not eat of it.**

R. Judah b. Pazzi exclaimed: "O Adam! would that one removed the dust from your eyes so that you could see your descendants' steadfastness! You could not stand constant in your trial even a single hour, whereas your descendants loyally observe all they were bidden!" Adam was enjoined, This you may eat, this you may not, as it says, *Of every tree of the garden thou mayest freely eat: but of the tree of the knowledge of good and evil, thou shalt not eat of it.* He did not remain obedient even one hour, but, as we read, *she gave also unto her husband with her, and he did eat* (3:6). But to his descendants many things were interdicted: they were told, *These may ye eat, these ye shall not eat* (Lev. 11:9,4), and they still practice them.

Tanhuma Yashan Sh'mini 13. T.S. 2, 235.

139. THOU SHALT NOT EAT OF IT. R. Joshua of Siknin said in the name of R. Levi: The serpent maligned his Creator. He asked Eve: "Why do you not eat of this tree?" Eve answered: "God commanded me not to eat thereof nor touch it!" Thereupon the serpent thrust Eve upon the tree, yet she did not die. Actually God had said only, *Thou shalt not eat of it;* it was Eve who added "nor touch it."

Midrash on Psalms 1,5. T.S. 2, 238.

140. THOU SHALT NOT EAT OF IT. They (the unborn generations) asked Adam: "Who was the cause of your death?" He answered: "I brought it on myself. Had I obeyed the Lord, I would not die." But they pursued the question further: "Did not the Lord bring about your death?" "No," he replied, "I am myself responsible for it." For it says, *Of every tree*

[2] This comment is based on the Rabbinic interpretation of *Adonai* (Lord) and *Elohim* (God) as meaning the God of Mercy and the God of Justice respectively.

[3] The Heb. for *thou mayest freely eat* is *akol tokal.* By a slight change of vocalization this may read *okel tokal,* thou mayest eat it when it is food, i.e., when it has been properly prepared for food.

§ 137 [1] Wisdom, i.e., the Torah, identified with God, has built a house—Paradise—and calls upon the thoughtless who are on the path to Gehinom to change their course.

it: for in the day that thou eatest thereof thou shalt surely die.' [18]And the Lord God said: 'It is not good that the man should be alone; I will

COMMENTARY

man's instincts, or even his Reason, which in the hour of temptation often calls light darkness and darkness light.[99] **thou shalt surely die. a.** This is meant literally. Had he not eaten thereof, he would have lived for ever.[100] **b.** Man will become mortal, not that he would die on that day.[101] **c.** Thou

ANTHOLOGY

of the garden thou shalt indeed eat[1] because it is good for thee, *but of the tree of the knowledge of good and evil, thou shalt not eat of it,* because it imperils thee to the very death. "I disobeyed and ate, and thus encompassed my own ruin." Thus he admitted that *the word of the Lord is upright* (Ps. 33:4).

Midrash on Psalms, Ps. 92. T.S. 2, 239.

141. **For in the day, etc.**

Remember, O Lord, Thy compassions and Thy mercies (Ps. 25:6). R. Joshua b. Levi interpreted: Show Thy mercies which Thou didst show to Adam, for thus saidst Thou to him, *For in the day that thou eatest thereof thou shalt surely die.* Now, hadst Thou not given him one day of Thine, which is a thousand years, how could he have applied himself to begetting posterity? That indeed is the meaning of the second half of the verse, *for they have been of old* (ibid.), i.e., from the days of Adam. Thus, in judging him God tempered justice with mercy, fusing both qualities. The quality of justice is demonstrated in the decree that on the day that he ate thereof he would die, and the sentence was actually pronounced on that very day. The quality of mercy lay in His not disclosing whether the day referred to was to be measured by a mortal's time or by God's standard where a day spells a thousand years.

Midrash on Psalms 25; P'sikta Rabbathi 40. T.S. 2, 242. 246.

142. FOR IN THE DAY, etc. *Come and see the works of God: He is terrible in His pretexts against* (AJV: doing toward) *the children of man* (Ps. 66:5). R. Joshua b. Karha commented: The terrors which Thou bringest upon us are brought with a pretext. Behold, on the very first day God created the angel of death, whereas Adam was created only on the sixth day, yet he is charged with bringing death to all mankind, as it says, *For in the day that thou eatest thereof thou shalt surely die.* Even thus does Adam challenge the Almighty: "O Master of the universe, 2000 years ere Thou didst create the world the Torah was as a nursling with Thee,[1] and therein it is written, *This is the law: when a man* dieth *in the tent* (Num. 19:14): hadst Thou not ordained death from aforetime, wouldst Thou have written thus? Surely it is but a pretext against me!

Tanhuma on Vayesheb par. 4. T.S. 2, 243.

143. **Thou shalt surely die (moth tamuth).**

The repetition of the verb intimated death for Adam, death for Eve, and death for his descendants. Another interpretation: Thou shalt die in this world and in the next. God purposed to try man with the one prohibition, whether he would overcome the momentary temptation or not. He failed in the trial on that very day, and on the very same day his doom was pronounced.

Gen. R. 16; Midrash Hagadol B'reshith. T.S. 2, 240. 241.

144. **It is not good that the man should be alone.**

The Mishnah states: A man may not abstain from procreation unless he already has children.

§ 140 [1] From the full context it appears that this is interpreted as mandatory and not merely permissive (as AJV: thou *mayest* freely eat). So we have here a twofold injunction: To enjoy what is permitted, and refrain from what is forbidden.

§ 142 [1] Cf. Chap. I, par. 25, where Prov. 8:30 (q. v.) is referred to the Torah.

COMMENTARY

shalt live in sorrow and privation.[102] [18]**it is not good.** From this verse the Rabbis deduce that marriage is a Divine institution, a holy estate in which alone man lives his true and complete life. Celibacy is contrary to nature.[103] **alone. a.** Lest it be said that there are two Powers in the universe, God being unique in the celestial sphere in having no companion, and man in the terrestrial sphere likewise having no counterpart.[104] **b.** It was never intended that man should not be able to propagate his species, because all life was created with that power; he was, however, first created endowed with both the male and female characteristics, so that he could as a single being have engendered and given birth. God then declared that this was *not good*.[105] **a help.** A wife is not a man's shadow or subordinate, but his other self, his "helper," in a sense which no other creature on earth can be.[106] **meet for him.** To match him. The Heb. term *k'negdo* may mean either "at his side," i.e., fit to associate with; or, "as over against him," i.e., corresponding to him.[107] **a help meet for him. a.** Lit., "a help against him," i.e., if he is worthy, she will be a help; if not, she will be against

ANTHOLOGY

This implies that if he has children, he may abstain from further procreation, but not from marriage. This supports a statement made by R. Nahman in the name of Samuel, viz.: Even if a man has many children, he must not remain without a wife, for it says, *It is not good that the man should be alone*. Others maintain: If he has no children he must marry a woman capable of childbirth; if he has children, he may marry one who is incapable of childbirth. What is the practical difference?[1] In respect of selling a Scroll of the Law for the sake of children.[2]

Yebamoth 61b. T.S. 2, 247.

145. IT IS NOT GOOD THAT THE MAN SHOULD BE ALONE. R. Tanhum stated in the name of R. Hanilai: A Jew who has no wife lives without joy, without blessing, and without goodness, etc. Without goodness, for it is written, *It is not good that the man should be alone*. In the West (i.e., Palestine) they said: He lives without Torah and without a (protecting) wall, etc. Raba b. Ulla said: Without peace.

Yebamoth 62b. T.S. 2, 248.

146. IT IS NOT GOOD THAT THE MAN SHOULD BE ALONE. When the earth heard the word "helpmeet" it shook and trembled, and said to its Creator: "O Lord of the world, I am not able to provide for the whole of mankind." To which God replied: "I will feed the whole of mankind." And God made a compact with the earth, and God created the sleep of life, so that when man lies down and goes to sleep, he is fed, strengthened and refreshed, and this is the healing and the feeding which God provides, as it is said, *Then I slept, then I felt refreshed*. God moreover assists the earth and waters it, so that it yields its fruits as food for all the creatures; but, in spite of all this, man obtains his food in toil and trouble.

Chronicles of Jerahmeel, p. 18 (6:14).

147. IT IS NOT GOOD THAT THE MAN SHOULD BE ALONE. We learnt: By ten commands was the world created, and these are they: (1) *In the beginning God created*[1] (1:1); (2) *And the spirit of God hovered* (ib. 2);[2] (3) And God said: "*Let there be light*" (ib. 3); (4) And God said: "*Let there be a firmament*" (ib. 6); (5) And God said: "*Let the waters be gathered together*" (ib. 9); (6) And God said: "*Let the earth put forth grass*" (ib. 11); (7) And God said: "*Let there be lights*" (ib. 14); (8) And God said: "*Let the waters

§ 144 [1] As regards the duty of marriage. In either case one must not remain single.
[2] Only a man who has no children must sell even such a precious object in order to marry a woman capable of procreation. If he has children such a sale is forbidden, and he must contract a less expensive marriage with an old or barren woman. Others explain: Even if he has children he must still rather marry a woman capable of childbearing, but is not obliged to sell a Scroll of the Law for that purpose.

§ 147 [1] This was regarded as a creative utterance. See Chap. I, par. 9.
[2] The Midrash a.l. states that a separate command was devoted to the wind (*ruah*), hence this verse is quoted as a separate utterance.

make him a help meet for him.' [19]And out of the ground the Lord God formed every beast of the field, and every fowl of the air; and brought

COMMENTARY

him.[108] **b.** "Opposite to," distinct from him (this follows Nahmanides' comment on *"alone"*).[109] **[19]The Lord God formed, etc.** Better, *The* Lord God, *having formed out of the ground every beast of the field, and every fowl of heaven, brought them unto the man* (S. R. Hirsch, Delitzch, and W. H. Green). See 1:21, 25. The fishes are not alluded to because they are precluded from becoming man's companions.[110] **formed . . . of the air.** *Formed* is identical in meaning with *made* in 1:25, and so the verse is apparently superfluous. It implies that birds (which are

ANTHOLOGY

swarm" (ib. 20); (9) And God said: *"Let the earth bring forth"* (ib. 24); (10) And God said: *"Let us make man"* (ib. 26). Menahem b. R. Jose omitted *And the spirit of God hovered over the face of the waters,* and put in its stead, *And the Lord God said: "It is not good that the man should be alone."*

Gen. R. 17. T.S. 2, 249.

148. IT IS NOT GOOD THAT THE MAN SHOULD BE ALONE. R. Aha commenced his discourse with the question: Was he then alone? Surely it is written, *Male* and female *created He* them (1:27)? Moreover, we learned that man was created *two-faced* with a dual sex, an hermaphrodite? The answer is that man had no access to his female parts, because they were at his side, so that in the rear he looked like a single being; hence he could be considered alone. The text continues: *I will make him a help k'negdo (meet for him)*. What is meant by *k'negdo?* Facing him, face shining to face. To effect this, God sawed Adam in two and removed his female part, as Scripture says, *He took one of his sides* (sic). As long as his female part was in the side of his body he was alone; when that was removed they became two, and they rose contented like one.

Zohar 3:44. T.S. 2, 257.

149. **I will make him a help meet for him.**

Scripture writes: *If there be among you a needy man . . . thou shalt surely lend him what is needed for him* (Deut. 15:7-8). *For him* means a wife, as it says, *I will make him a help meet for him.*

Tos. Pech 4. T.S. 2, 253.

150. I WILL MAKE HIM A HELP AGAINST HIM.[1] R. Eleazar said: What does this mean?[2] If he is fortunate, she is a help to him; if not, she is against him. Others say: R. Eleazar pointed out a contradiction: It is written K'negdo, but we read, *Kanigado* (his whipper)! If he is fortunate, she is *meet for him:*[3] if not, she chastises him. R. Joseph met Elijah and asked him:[4] It is written, *I will make him a help:* how then does a woman help a man? He replied: If a man brings wheat, does he chew the wheat? If flax, does he put on the flax? Does she not then bring light to his eyes and put him on his feet by grinding the wheat and spinning the flax?

Yebamoth 63a. T.S. 2, 254.

151. **And out of the ground the Lord God formed *(wayyitzer)* every beast of the field.**

R. Johanan b. Zakkai was asked: Since it is already written, *Let the earth bring forth the living creature* (1: 24), why does Scripture repeat, *And out of the ground the Lord God formed every beast of the field?* He replied: The earlier verse refers to their creation, whereas this treats of their subjection to man, *wayyitzer* being interpreted as in the verse, *When*

§ 150 [1] This is the literal translation.
[2] It is apparently self-contradictory.
[3] Rendering as AJV.
[4] The Rabbis were often said to meet and converse with Elijah.

them unto the man to see what he would call them; and whatsoever the man would call every living creature, that was to be the name thereof.

COMMENTARY

here said to have been formed *out of the ground,* whereas 1:20 states that they were formed from the water) were created from alluvial mud which partakes of both earth and water.[111] **to see.** So that Adam see them, i.e., observe them.[112] **what he would call them. a.** What name he would give each species, the underlying thought being that Adam was to ascertain their nature, so that he would know how to manage them to best advantage.[113] **b.** Man alone has language, and can give birth to languages. In giving names to earth's creatures, he would establish his dominion over them (1:26, 28). The name would also reflect the impression produced on his mind by each creature, and indicate whether he regarded it as a fit companion for himself.[114] **living creature. a.** This is in apposition to "whatsoever" (*kol*), the entire phrase meaning: and to whatever living creature Adam would give a name.[115] **b.** *living creature* refers to Adam, or to primal man before he developed: the whole phrase then reads: and whatsoever the man, the *living creature,* would call it.[116] **that was to be the name.** He named each animal and its mate, indicating by name which species naturally belonged to which. This interpretation makes clear the connection in the next verse between his naming of the animals

ANTHOLOGY

thou shalt besiege (tatsur) *a city a long time* (in order to reduce it to subjection) (Deut. 20:19).

Gen. R. 17. T.S. 2, 258.

152. **And whatsoever Adam would call every living creature, etc.**

When Moses urged his unfitness to speak to Pharaoh, God answered: "Moses! Moses! *Who gave Adam a mouth* (Exod. 4:10)? It was I who gave him a mouth and a tongue for speech. I gave him charge of all the world's creatures, to summon each by name and to give each a name," as it says, *And whatsoever Adam would call every living creature, that was to be the name thereof.*

Alphabet of Rabbi Akiba. T.S. 2, 259.

153. AND WHATSOEVER ADAM WOULD CALL EVERY LIVING CREATURE, etc. God made cattle, beasts and fowl pass before Adam, and Adam named them by species, viz., cattle, beast, fowl, etc. After that he named the different animals, etc., within the various species. The ministering angels he named generically *Meof'fim* (the winged and soaring ones), and then named them individually. It is said by some that Adam also conceived the name of God, as it says, *And whatsoever Adam would call every living creature, that was its name* (hu sh'mo). He (Adam) called him "Lord," and thus it is written, *The Lord is a man of war, "the Lord" is His name—hu sh'mo,* which means, "the Lord" is the name given to him by Adam.[1]

Aboth d'Rabbi Nathan Ms. T.S. 2, 260.

154. AND WHATSOEVER THE MAN WOULD CALL EVERY LIVING CREATURE, etc. Everything which God created Adam fittingly named, for it is written, *Whatsoever Adam called every living creature, that was the name thereof,* which means, that was its body and essence.[1] How do we know that the name is the bodily essence of its possessor? From the verse, *The memory of the righteous shall be for a blessing; but the name of the wicked shall rot* (Prov. 10:7). Can then the *name* rot? Surely it means his body. So here, too, the names given by Adam were the very essence of what he named.

Sefer Habahir 8. T.S. 2, 261.

155. AND WHATSOEVER ADAM CALLED, etc. R. Jacob b. Idi said: Adam was indeed a wise man. He recognized and knew who had but

§ 153 [1] Cf. Chap. I, par. 227.
§ 154 [1] To the ancients the name of a person or thing was not merely a means of identification, but regarded as partaking of its very essence.

[20]And the man gave names to all cattle, and to the fowl of the air, and to every beast of the field; but for Adam there was not found a help meet for him. [21]And the Lord God caused a deep sleep to fall upon the

COMMENTARY

and the lack of a mate for Adam.[117] **[20]but for Adam.** I.e., for himself, as a human being, Adam could not find a help meet for him.[118] **b.** The dignity of human nature could not, in few words, be more beautifully expressed.[119] **a help meet for him.** **[21]And the Lord God caused a deep sleep,** etc. God brought them in pairs, male and female, whereupon Adam complained, "They all have a companion, but I have none." Straightway *God*

ANTHOLOGY

the soul[1] of a beast, and who had a true soul. Hence Scripture states: *Whatsoever Adam called the soul of a beast,* etc., which means that he knew who would devote himself to the service of his Creator and who would not. The same is true today. One who does not know the Creator nor recognizes the duty of serving Him, or who does not occupy himself with the study of the Torah, has the soul of a beast, but not a true soul.[2]

Midrash Haneelam Zohar Hadash 16. T.S. 2, 262.

156. **And the man gave names.**

When Moses said to God, *"I am not a man of words"* (Exod. 4:10), and, *"I am of uncircumcized lips"* (ibid. 6:12), God answered him: "Behold Adam; he had no teachers, how then did he know all the seventy languages?" For the Bible does not say that he gave a *name* to all the cattle, but, *And the man gave names to all cattle.* Thus said He, *Who gave Adam a mouth* (ibid. 4:11) that he could name all cattle, each in the seventy languages? ("I taught him, and I can also teach you.")

Tanhuma Yashan D'barim. T.S. 2, 264.

157. AND THE MAN GAVE NAMES. Adam named not only cattle and beasts, but also all countries and wildernesses; and whatever he designated as habitable stays habitable, and what he called desert remains desert.

Midrash Aggadah. T.S. 2, 267.

158. **But for Adam there was not found, etc.**

In the ancient books I have seen it said that here the word "one" means "one woman," that is, the original Lilith, who lay with him and from him conceived. But up to that time she was no help to him, as it is said, *"But for Adam there was not found a help meet for him"* (Gen. 2:20). Adam, then, was the very last, for it was right that he should find the world complete when he made his appearance.

Zohar, p. 32. G. Scholem.

159. **And the Lord God caused a deep sleep to fall upon the man, etc.**

The Emperor[1] once remarked to Rabban Gamaliel:[2] Your God is a thief, for it is written, *And the Lord God caused a deep sleep to fall upon the man* (Adam), *and he slept; and He took one of his ribs,* etc. Thereupon his (the Emperor's) daughter said to him: "Let me answer him." Turning to the Emperor she requested, "Give me an officer." "What for?" he asked. "Thieves visited us last night and robbed us of a silver pitcher, leaving a golden one in its place." "Would that such visited us every day," he exclaimed. "Ah!" she re-

§ 155 [1] Heb. *nefesh,* which is understood as the lower, brute soul, while *n'shamah* (soul) is the superior soul, a spark of the Divine.

[2] Cf. *supra* par. 101 and Commentary on verse 7, *a living soul,* b.

§ 159 [1] So Ms. M. Cur. edd. כופר, an unbeliever.

[2] Gamaliel II, also known as Gamaliel of Jabneh. He visited Rome twice—once during the reign of Domitian and again during that of Nerva, his successor. This debate may have taken place on one of these occasions, probably the latter; v. Graetz, MGWJ I, 192ff.

man, and he slept; and He took one of his ribs, and closed up the place with flesh instead thereof. [22]And the

COMMENTARY

caused a deep sleep, etc.[120] **a deep sleep.** As in 15:12, the word implies that something mysterious and awe-inspiring was about to take place.[121] **ribs.** Others render "sides," quoting Exod. 26:20, where the Hebrew word is rendered *side.* This is in conformity with the view that man was originally created male and female in one. God now separated the one (female) side.[122] **one of his ribs.** We have here a wonderfully conceived allegory designed to set forth the moral and social relation of the sexes to each other, the dependence of woman upon

ANTHOLOGY

torted, "was it not to Adam's gain that he was deprived of a rib and given a wife[3] instead to serve him?" He replied: "This is what I mean: He should have taken the rib from him openly, when awake." Said she to him: "Let me have a piece of raw meat." When it was brought she placed it under her armpit, then took it out and offered it to him. "It makes my stomach turn," he objected.[4] "Even so would Eve have been repulsive to Adam had she been taken from him openly," she retorted.[5]

Sanhedrin 39a. T.S. 2, 270.

160. **And he slept, and He took one of his ribs.**

R. Simeon b. Lakish was asked: Why do dreams fatigue men so?[1] He answered: Because woman's creation was in a dream, as we read, *And he slept, and He took one of his ribs:* He took her from him in a dream, and in a dream he enjoyed her intimacy. Otherwise he would never have known how to love. Therefore a dream has reality.

Midrash Abakir from a Ms. in Debir Part 1. T.S. 2, 273.

161. AND HE TOOK ONE OF HIS RIBS. Pharaoh told the midwives: "*If it be a son, then ye shall kill him*" (Exod. 1:16). (His order was to slay the child before it was actually born, whereupon they asked him: "But before it is born how are we to know if it be male or female?") R. Hanina said: He gave them a clear sign: "If its face be turned downward, know ye that it is a male, because he is looking through his mother at the earth from which he was created; but if its face is turned upward, then it is a female, because it is looking at the source of its creation—the rib; as it is said, *And He took one of his ribs.*

Exod. R. 1. T.S. 2, 277.

162. HE TOOK ONE OF HIS SIDES. R. Isaac said in the name of Rab: Man was created together with his mate as a single entity, as it says, *Male and female created He them* (5:2). He took her from his side and brought her to him, as it is written, *He took one of his sides.* R. Joshua said: It was the first Eve who was taken from Adam, and she is the harmful demon. And for that reason Scripture adds, *And He closed the flesh in her stead,* which means that He created a second Eve to take the place of the first. Raba said: This second Eve was formed of flesh; not so the first. What then was *she?* Said R. Isaac: A creature of the dregs and lees of the earth.[1]

Midrash Haneelam Zohar Hadash 16. T.S. 2, 278.

163. ONE OF HIS SIDES. The female was fastened to the side of the male, and God cast the male into a deep slumber, and he lay on the site of the Temple. God then cut the female from him and decked her as a bride and led her to him, as it is written, *And He took one of his sides, and closed up the place with flesh.*

Zohar, p. 32. G. Scholem.

[3] Lit., a handmaid.
[4] Because it had come in contact with her body.
[5] Had he actually seen her taken from his body.
§ 160 [1] It is clear that this refers to a dream of sexual intercourse, which causes an actual emission.
§ 162 [1] For the whole passage see pars. 148, 165.

rib, which the Lord God had taken from the man, made He a woman,

COMMENTARY

man, her close relationship to him, and the foundation existing in nature for the attachment springing up between them. The woman is formed out of the man's side; hence it is the wife's natural duty to be at hand, ready at all times to be a "help" to her husband; it is the husband's natural duty ever to cherish and defend his wife, as part of his own self.[123] [22]**a woman.** Hebrew *ishah,* i.e., a creature having the

ANTHOLOGY

164. AND HE TOOK ONE OF HIS RIBS (TSAL'OTHAW). R. Samuel b. Nahmani said: He took one of his sides, as you read, *And for the second side* (tsela') *of the tabernacle, on the north side* (Ex. 26:20). But Samuel maintained: He took one rib from between two ribs, for it is not written, *And He closed with flesh in* its *place,* but *And He closed with flesh in* their places.

Gen. R. 17. T.S. 2, 275.

165. **And the tsela (AJV rib) which the Lord God had taken from man, He built into a woman.**

Rab and Samuel explained this differently. One maintained that this *tsela* was a face; the other, that it was a tail. On the former view we understand the verse, *Behind and before hast thou formed me* (Ps. 139:5).[1] But how explain that verse on the latter view? In accordance with R. Ammi, who said: *Behind* (i.e., last) in the work of creation, and *before* (i.e., first) for punishment. The former interpretation harmonizes with the verse, *He closed up the place with flesh instead thereof.*[2] But how explain it if it was but a tail? It applies to the place of the cut. The view that it was a tail agrees with the words, *He built.* But if it was a face, why say *He built?*[3] As explained by R. Simeon b. Manasseh.[4] If it was a face, which of the two faces went in front? Said R. Nahman b. Isaac: Presumably the man's, since it was taught: A man should not walk behind a woman, even his own wife, on the road.[5] If one happens to be in front of him on a bridge, he should pass her on the side.

Berakoth 61a. T.S. 2, 281.

166. AND HE CLOSED (VAYISGOR). In the word *vayisgor* (and He closed) there occurs for the first time in this passage the letter *samekh,* which signifies "support," as much as to say that as male and female they now supported the one the other. In like wise, do the lower world and the upper sustain each other. Not until the lower world was made perfect was the other world also made perfect. When the lower world was made to support the upper, by being turned face to face with it, the world was then finished, for previously *the Lord God had not caused it to rain upon the earth.*

Zohar, p. 33. G. Scholem.

167. HE BUILT. R. Hisda said (some say, it was taught in a Baraitha): This teaches that He built Eve after the fashion of a storehouse. Just as a storehouse is narrow at the top and broad at the bottom, so as to hold the produce safely, so a woman is narrower above and broader below, so as to hold the embryo.

Berakoth 61a. T.S. 2, 282.

168. MADE HE (WA-YIBEN) A WOMAN. R. Joshua of Siknin said in R. Levi's name: *Wa-yiben* is written, signifying that He considered well (*hithbonen*) from what part to create her. Said He: "I will not create her from (Adam's) head, lest she be swelled-headed; nor from the eye, lest she be a coquette; nor from

§ 165 [1] I.e., one face in front and one behind.
[2] Since a whole half was taken from him, the place had to be closed up.
[3] The face needed no "building," since it was already there.
[4] See par. 169.
[5] To avoid unchaste thoughts.

and brought her unto the man. [23]And the man said: 'This is now bone of my bones, and flesh of my flesh; she

COMMENTARY

same general appearance and qualities as *ish* (man), differing from him only in sex.[124] **[23]This is now. a.** At long last I have found a suitable mate, because she is bone of my bones.[125] **b.** Lit., "this time it is bone." Only this time is she literally bone of my bone, etc.; henceforth, however, woman will be formed separately from man.[126] **bone of my bones.** The phrase passed into popular speech (29:14).[127] **she,** etc. Lit., "this one": a creature like this one shall be called in the future "woman."[128] **woman.** The Heb. is *ishah;* that for man is *ish.* The similarity

ANTHOLOGY

the ear, lest she be an eavesdropper; nor from the mouth, lest she be a gossip; nor from the heart, lest she be prone to jealousy; nor from the hand, lest she be light-fingered; nor from the foot, lest she be a gadabout; but from the modest part of man, for even when he stands naked, that part is covered." And as He created each limb He ordered her, "Be a modest woman."

Gen. R. 18. T.S. 2, 285.

169. BUILDED THE RIB. A woman who plaits and rouges on the Sabbath is culpable on the score of building. Does this then constitute building? Yes; as R. Simeon b. Menassia expounded: *And the Lord God builded the rib into a woman*: This teaches that the Holy One, blessed be He, plaited Eve's (hair) and brought her to Adam, for in the sea-towns plaiting is called "building."

Shabbath 95a. T.S. 2, 283.

170. BUILT (WA-YIBEN). *Mishnah:* The vows of a girl eleven years and one day old must be examined;[1] the vows of one who is twelve years and one day are binding. Our Rabbis taught: This is the ruling of Rabbi. R. Hisda explained: What is Rabbi's reason?[2] Because it is written, *And the Lord God built* (*wa-yiben*), which means that the Holy One, blessed be He, gave woman more understanding (*binah*) than man, (rendering, And the Lord God made the tsela —rib—into an understanding woman).

Niddah 45b; Gen. R. 18. T.S. 2, 284.

171. **And He brought her unto the man.**

Scripture writes: *All the ways of the Lord are love and truth* (Ps. 25:10). The very beginning of the Torah is love—the love that God showed to brides and grooms. He manifested His love for Adam and Eve, as it says, *And the Lord God built out of man's rib a woman.* R. Abbahu said: In Arabia they call dressing the hair building: God, blessed be He, decked out Eve and brought her to Adam. Do you think He brought her to him under an olive or fig tree? No; He made a canopy for her of the most precious stones. He adorned Eve with 24 ornaments. He did more. He took her by the hand and led her to Adam. R. Abin the Levite B'Rabbi[1] exclaimed: Happy the man who is privileged to see his mate taken by the hand of the King and led to his home, as it says, *And He brought her unto the man.*

Tanhuma Yashan Vayera 64. T.S. 2, 287.

172. AND HE BROUGHT HER TO ADAM. R. Judah b. Eleazar said: This teaches that the Almighty acted as best man for Adam. Thus the Torah teaches that the greater should act as best man for the lesser.

Tanhuma Haye Chap. 2. T.S. 2, 286.

173. **And Adam said: "This once it is bone of my bones and flesh of my flesh."**

Only once was Eve taken from man. But henceforth a man must betroth the daughter of another. Once God acted as best man for

§ 170 [1] If she understands their nature, they are valid; but we do not automatically assume that she does, as when she is twelve years old.
[2] For setting an earlier age for a girl than for a boy (as stated a.l.). A boy's vows are not automatically binding until the age of thirteen.

§ 171 [1] A scholar's title.

shall be called Woman, because she was taken out of Man. [24]**Therefore**

COMMENTARY

in sound emphasizes the spiritual identity of man and woman.[129] [24]**therefore.** Because of Adam's and Eve's common origin and affinity for each other.[130] **shall a man leave,** etc. **a.** There is an innate tendency in man to leave his parents and beget children with a woman of his choice.[131] **b.** Or, "therefore doth a man leave his father and his mother, and doth cleave . . . and they become one flesh." Rashi says: "These words are by the Holy Spirit (רוח הקודש)"; i.e., this verse is not spoken by Adam, but is

ANTHOLOGY

man; henceforth man must provide himself with a best man.

Aboth d'Rabbi Nathan Chap. 4. T.S. 2, 289.

174. BONE OF MY BONES, AND FLESH OF MY FLESH. Why is it more difficult to appease a woman than a man? Because she was created from bone, whereas man was created from the dust. Soak a bone in water ever so long, it does not dissolve: so too is woman. But pour a drop of water upon dust and it immediately dissolves: so is man. Again, why does woman adorn herself, but not man? Because she was created from man, and man was created from the dust: just as meat without spices putrefies, so a woman, if she does not adorn herself, loses her savour. But dust does not putrefy: so is man. Why is a woman's voice piercing, whilst a man's is not? It may be compared to a pot full of meat the contents of which no one knows. Throw a bone into it and it at once resounds and betrays its contents; so too is a woman's voice, piercing and strident. Why does the man do the wooing and not the woman? Because the man seeks what he lost, but what is lost (woman) does not seek him.

Aboth d'Rabbi Nathan Chap. 9. T.S. 2, 290.

175. BONE OF MY BONES, AND FLESH OF MY FLESH. R. Tanhum said: When a man marries one of his relations, of him it is said, *Bone of my bones, and flesh of my flesh.*

Gen. R. 18. T.S. 2, 292.

176. BONE OF MY BONES. The Holy One, blessed be He, had compassion upon him (Adam), and, in order that he should not feel any pain, He cast upon him a deep slumber, whilst He took one of his bones from his side and flesh from his heart, made them into a helpmate, and placed her opposite him. When he awoke and saw her standing there, he embraced and kissed her, exclaiming, "Blessed art thou of the Lord; thy bone is of my bones, and thee it is fitting to call *ishah!*" Thus it says, *Bone of my bones and flesh of my flesh.* As long as he was alone he was called Adam (man). R. Joshua b. Karhah said: He was called Adam as a being of flesh and blood (*dam*). But when He built him a woman as a help-mate, he was called *ish* (man) and she was called *ishah* (woman).[1]

Pirke d'Rabbi Eliezer Chap. 12. T.S. 2, 293.

177. **She shall be called Ishah (Woman).**

While he was yet alone, he was called Adam. R. Joshua b. Karha said that his name was Adam on account of the flesh and blood (of which he was composed). God said to him, "Thou art Adam." But when a helpmeet was made for him he was called Living Being, i.e., Fiery Being (Heb. אש). God then added two letters of His name to it and made the name of man to be איש, and the name of woman אשה, saying, "If they walk in My ways and observe My commandments, behold My name will abide with them and deliver them from all trouble; but if not, behold I will take away My name from them, so that their names will become again אש ואש, i.e., fire consuming fire.

Chronicles of Jerahmeel, p. 18 (6:16).

178. SHE SHALL BE CALLED ISHAH (WOMAN), BECAUSE SHE WAS TAKEN OUT OF ISH (MAN). This proves that the Torah was given in the Hebrew language. R. Papa and R. Hanina in

§ 176 [1] See next par.

shall a man leave his father and his mother, and shall cleave unto his wife, and they shall be one flesh. [25]And they were both naked, the man and his wife, and were not ashamed.

COMMENTARY

the inspired comment of Moses in order to inculcate the Jewish ideal of marriage as a unique tie which binds a man to his wife even closer than to his parents. The Biblical ideal is the monogamic marriage; a man shall cleave "to his *wife*," not to his wives. The sacredness of marriage relations, according to Scripture, thus goes back to the very birth of human society; nay, it is part of the scheme of Creation. The Rabbinic term for marriage is קידושין, lit., "The sanctities," sanctification; the purpose of marriage being to preserve and sanctify that which had been made in the image of God.[132] **and they shall be one flesh. a.** They will join in complete partnership as if they were one flesh.[133] **b.** A man should seek to marry a woman harmoniously suited to him, so that together they form *one flesh,* a perfect whole.[134] [25]**and were not ashamed. a.** Of each other.[135] **b.** Because before eating of the forbidden fruit they knew nought of passion.[136] **c.** So far all their acts were in the service of their Maker, and not for the satisfaction of desire; consequently the act of cohabitation was as innocent as eating and drinking.[137] **d.** Before eating of the forbidden fruit they were like children in the Orient, who in the innocence and ignorance of childhood run about unclothed.[138]

ANTHOLOGY

the name of R. Simon averred that not only was the Torah given in the Hebrew language, but that the world too was created with the Hebrew language. Have you ever heard one speak of *gini* and *ginya, anthripi* and *anthripia, gavra* and *g'vartha*? But one does speak of *ish* and *ishah,* because the latter is the natural feminine form of the former.[1]

Gen. R. 18. T.S. 2, 294.

179. SHE SHALL BE CALLED WOMAN. She was destined to lead him astray, and he would have to stand at the bar of Judgment on her account. Hence he exclaimed, "On her account I will be called to judgment!" as we read, *And the Lord God called Adam* (to judgment) (3:9). Thus our text is to be rendered: On account of this woman would he (Adam) be summoned. And just as Adam clave to Eve though he knew what would befall, so all men are destined to surrender essentials of life and cleave unto the woman.

Midrash Abakir from a Ms. T.S. 2, 295.

180. **Therefore shall a man leave his father and mother, etc.**

R. Eliezer said: *His father means* his father's sister; *his mother,* his mother's sister.[1] R. Akiba said: *His father* means his father's wife; *his mother* is literally meant. *And he shall cleave,* but not to a male;[2] *to his wife,* but not to his neighbor's wife; *and they shall be as one flesh:* this applies to those that can become one flesh, thus excluding cattle and beasts which cannot become one flesh with man.

Sanhedrin 58a. T.S. 2, 297.

181. **And shall cleave unto his wife.**

R. Jose said: Isaac observed three years' mourning for his mother. After three years he married Rebecca and ceased to mourn for his mother. Hence you learn that until a man marries, his love centers in his parents. When he marries, his love is bestowed upon his wife, as it is said, *Therefore shall a man leave his father and his mother, and shall cleave unto his wife.* Does a man then repudiate the honor due to his father and mother? Surely not! But it means that the love of his soul cleaves unto his wife, as it says, *And shall cleave unto his wife.*

Pirke d'Rabbi Eliezer Chap. 32. T.S. 2, 303.

182. HE SHALL CLEAVE TO HIS WIFE. But not to his betrothed, with whom co-habitation is forbidden.

P'sikta Zutrathi B'reshith. T.S. 2, 302.

§ 178 [1] The point is that in Greek and Aramaic the word for woman is not simply the feminine form of man, as it is in the Hebrew. Thus only the Hebrew expresses the direct relationship of the two as told in the Bible.

§ 180 [1] I.e., that union with these relations are forbidden.

[2] I.e., a prohibition of pederasty, for it is natural only for opposite sexes to cleave to each other.

GENESIS

CHAPTER III

[1]**Now the serpent was more subtle than any beast of the field which the Lord God had made. And he said unto the woman: 'Yea, hath God said: Ye shall not eat of any tree of the garden?' [2]And the woman said unto the serpent: 'Of the fruit of the trees of the garden we may eat; [3]but**

COMMENTARY

[1]**the serpent. a.** The sequel to the last verse, stating that they were naked, should have been verse 21, *and the Lord God made for Adam and for his wife garments of skin* (on the assumption that these were made as a protection against the cold, before the sense of shame was awakened in the human complex). The story of the serpent, however, is introduced here because its seductive counsel was due to its desire for Eve, which was aroused when it saw them naked and cohabiting without concealment.[1] **b.** The serpent is a symbol of the tempter (Satan).[2] **c.** This passage is meant literally and is not to be understood symbolically only.[3] **subtle.** The same Heb. root signifies both "naked" and "subtle," "clever," "mischievous." Seeming simplicity is often the most dangerous weapon of cunning. The gliding stealthy movement of the serpent is a fitting symbol of the insidious progress of temptation.[4] **and he said. a.** Literally: the serpent had

ANTHOLOGY

1. **Now the serpent was subtle.**

"Was" (*hayah*) always implies destiny. Thus, *Now the serpent* was *subtle* indicates that it was destined to suffer retribution.

Exod. R. 2. T.S. 3, 3.

2. NOW THE SERPENT WAS SUBTLE. Wherein lay his subtlety? In his knowledge that because his eyeball resembled man's, he could tempt him, for man can be enticed only by one who is like himself.

Midrash Hagadol. T.S. 3, 4.

3. NOW THE SERPENT WAS MORE SUBTLE THAN ANY BEAST OF THE FIELD. It was taught in R. Meir's name: According to the greatness of the serpent so was his downfall: because he was *more subtle than all,* he was more cursed than all (3:14). R. Hoshaya the Elder said: He stood erect like a reed, and had feet. R. Jeremiah b. Eleazar said: He was an unbeliever. R. Simeon b. Eleazar said: He was like a camel. He deprived the world of much good, for had this not happened, one could have sent one's merchandise through him, and he would have gone and returned.

Gen. R. 19. T.S. 3, 5.

4. WAS SUBTLE. In what language did the serpent converse with Eve? In Hebrew; for Scripture records that the serpent was subtle, walked erect, and understood human speech.[1]

P'sikta Zutrathi B'reshith. T.S. 3, 9.

5. AND THE SERPENT. R. Isaac said: This is the Evil Tempter. R. Judah said: It means literally a serpent. They consulted R. Simeon, who told them: Both these views are identical. It was Samael, who appeared as a serpent, for in this form the serpent is indeed Satan. Thus *And the serpent was subtle* alludes to the Evil Tempter and the Angel of Death. It is because the serpent is the Angel of Death that it brought death to the world.

Zohar Hadash 1, 35b. T.S. 3, 10.

6. **And he said unto the woman.**

He reasoned thus: If I essay to beguile the man, I know he will resist me. I will go and

§ 4 [1] Which was Hebrew when the world was created; see Chap. II, par. 178.

of the fruit of the tree which is in the midst of the garden, God hath said: Ye shall not eat of it, neither shall ye touch it, lest ye die.' [4]And the serpent said unto the woman: 'Ye shall not surely die; [5]for God doth know that in the day ye eat thereof, then your eyes shall be opened, and

COMMENTARY

actually the power of speech.[5] **b.** An angel spoke for the serpent.[6] **c.** The serpent did not speak, but the woman, seeing him eat repeatedly of the fruit of the tree with impunity, regarded this as an insinuation, as though he had indeed spoken these very words.[7] **yea, hath God said. a.** Is it really possible that God has spoken thus?[8] **b.** Even though God has said, etc., ye shall nevertheless not die (v. 4), the woman interrupting the serpent's speech with words of her own (vv. 2-3).[9] **c.** The serpent's speech is given incompletely, the whole being something like this: God indeed hates you. That is certain in any case: but how much more so now that God hath said, etc.[10] **d.** The Heb. *af ki* means alas! Alas that God hath said![11] **e.** The serpent's language has remained, for all time to come, the language of temptation. The description places us in the middle of the dialogue between the serpent and the woman: " . . . and even though God has ordered you not to eat from all the trees in the garden" — everything is denied you, nothing — no enjoyment is permitted! This is a lie — but it has always been the method of temptation.[12] **[3]neither shall ye touch it. a.** With these words Eve enlarged upon the Divine command (2:17) and therefore came to transgress it.[13] **b.** Do not even try it by the touch of the tongue.[14] **[5]for God doth know.** That, and not because it may cause your death, is why He forbade it to you.[15] **your eyes shall be opened. a.** You shall attain clear insight.[16] **b.** To new sources of knowledge,

ANTHOLOGY

tempt the woman, knowing that she will hearken, for women are more easy to beguile. Thus he approached Eve, saying, "*Yea, hath God said,* etc. Is it possible that God forbade you to eat all the trees? Why has He created them, if they are not to be enjoyed?" R. Isaac said: The speech of the serpent was one tissue of falsehoods. His first remark, *Yea, God hath said: "Ye shall not eat of any tree of the garden,"* was a lie, because God had said, "*Of every tree of the garden thou mayest freely eat*" (2:16).

Midrash Hagadol; Zohar Hadash 1, 36a. T.S. 3, 8. 11.

7. **Neither shall ye touch it.**

What fence did Adam make in his speech? Scripture merely says, *But in the day that thou eatest thereof thou shalt surely die* (2:17). But Adam did not repeat to Eve these words of the Almighty. He made it stricter than had God by telling her that death would ensue at the very touch of the tree, thinking thus to insure Eve as well as himself from temptation. The serpent, knowing this, and sure that he could not tempt man, came to the woman, beguiled the time with her in speech, and then said to her: "If you say that God has forbidden us to touch it, see, I touch it, and do not die. So may you too touch it, and you will not die either." Hezekiah said: How do we know that when one adds he subtracts? From the above verse. *Add thou not unto His words, lest He reprove thee, and thou be found a liar* (Prov. 30:6): That means, Do not make the fence more than the principal, lest it fall and destroy the plants.[1] Thus, the Holy One, blessed be He, had said, *For in the day that thou* eatest *thereof thou shalt surely die* (2:17); whereas she did not say thus, but, *God hath said*: "*Ye shall not eat of it, neither shall ye touch it*"; when he (the serpent) saw her passing in front of the tree he thrust her against it. "Have you then died?" he said to her; "just as you did not die through touching it, so will you not die when you eat it."

Aboth d'Rabbi Nathan 1; Sanhedrin 29a; Gen. R. 19. T.S. 3, 13-15.

§ 7 [1] The "fence" is the additional prohibition, intended to safeguard the thing that is really forbidden (the "principal"). But if the former is disproportionately heavy, it may have the reverse effect.

ye shall be as God, knowing good and evil.' [6]And when the woman saw that the tree was good for food, and that it was a delight to the eyes, and that the tree was to be desired to

COMMENTARY

hidden from ordinary sight — a strong appeal to the curiosity of the woman.[17] **as God. a.** Either literally; or, as judges.[18] **b.** Like the angels.[19] **ye shall be as God. a.** Able to create worlds like Him.[20] **b.** You will become omniscient, just like God. Then you will be able to repudiate His authority.[21] **good and evil.** A Heb. idiom for "all things" (Cheyne, Ehrlich); cf. 2 Sam. 14:17. The same Heb. idiom occurs in a negative form in 24:50 and 31:29, where it means "nothing at all." The ordinary explanation of the phrase "good and evil" in the literal sense, assumes that God would for any reason withhold from man the ability to discern between what

ANTHOLOGY

8. **Ye shall be as God.**

R. Joshua of Siknin said in R. Levi's name: He (the serpent) began speaking slander of his Creator, saying, "Of this tree did He eat and then create the world; hence He orders you not to eat thereof, lest you create other worlds, for every person hates his fellow craftsman."

Gen. R. 19. T.S. 3, 18.

9. YE SHALL BE AS ELOHIM (AJV: GOD). All non-sacred nouns spelled with the letters of the name of God may be erased. An example of this is the verse, *For God doth know that in the day ye eat thereof, then your eyes shall be opened, and ye shall be as elohim* (the great).[1]

Soferim Chap. 4. T.S. 3, 19.

10. YOU WILL BE LIKE ELOHIM. The silver basin weighing 70 shekels, which the Prince of each Tribe contributed to the Tabernacle in the Wilderness at its dedication (Num. 6:13 *et passim*), corresponded to the seventy times that the Sacred Name of God is mentioned from the beginning of Genesis until the serpent narrative, inclusive. Should you object that God's name is mentioned 71 times, the answer is that *elohim* in the line *You will be like elohim* is not considered holy.

Num. R. 10. T.S. 3, 20.

11. **And the woman saw that it was good.**

R. Judah b. R. Simon said: The serpent argued: Whatever was created after its companion dominates and makes it serve it. Thus: heaven was created on the first day and the firmament on the second: does it not bear its weight? The firmament was created on the second and herbage on the third; must it not supply it with water? Plant life was created on the third day and the luminaries on the fourth: do they not ripen its fruits? The luminaries were created on the fourth and the birds on the fifth: now, the *ziz* is a clean bird, and when it flies it obscures the orb of the sun.[1] Now, you were created after everything in order to rule over everything; make haste and eat before He creates other worlds which will dominate you. Hence it is written, *And the woman saw that it was good*: she saw how plausible were the words of the serpent.

Gen. R. 19. T.S. 3, 23.

12. **The tree was good for food.**

R. Abba of Acco said: It was the *ethrog* (citron), as it is written, *And when the woman saw that the tree was good for food.* Consider: what tree is it whose stem can be eaten just like its fruit? you find none but the *ethrog*.[1]

Gen. R. 15. T.S. 3, 25.

§ 9 [1] Elohim is the name of God. If an error occurs in its writing in the Sefer Torah (the Sacred Scroll), it may not be erased, but must be cut out from the parchment and buried. Occasionally, however, the same word does not stand for the Diety but simply means great men, judges, or leaders. In that case it may be erased. In this passage *Elohim* is so regarded, the verse reading: Ye shall be as the great, knowing good and evil. This *Elohim,* therefore, is not sacred but profane, and may be erased. But see par. 8, where it is regarded as God's name.

§ 11 [1] And thus dominates it, as it were.

§ 12 [1] The deduction is that "the tree" itself, i.e., its stem, was edible.

make one wise, she took of the fruit thereof, and did eat; and she gave also unto her husband with her, and he did eat. [7]And the eyes of them both were opened, and they knew that they were naked; and they sewed

COMMENTARY

is morally right and wrong — a view which contradicts the spirit of Scripture. Moreover, Adam would not have been made "in the image of God" if he did not from the first possess the faculty of distinguishing between good and evil. And if he lacked such faculty, his obedience or disobedience to any command whatsoever, could have no moral significance. None of these objections holds good in regard to the temporary withholding of ordinary knowledge from Adam, pending his decision to work with or against God.[22] [6]**saw. a.** I.e., understood, the serpent having convinced her.[23] **b.** The general appearance and situation of the tree convinced her that it was not in fact deadly, as she had feared.[24] **c.** Though the tempter did not tell the woman to eat the fruit, he had woven the spell. The woman looked upon the tree with a new longing — it was good to eat, a delight to the eyes, and it would give wisdom. She turns her back upon the impulses of gratitude, love, and duty to God. The story mirrors human experience.[25] **was good.** To make one as God.[26] **a delight to the eyes. a.** As the serpent had told her, "and your eyes shall be opened."[27] This may be rendered: "a desire to the eyes" — she saw that it would awaken desire.[28] **she gave also unto her husband.** So that she should not die and he be left to take another wife.[29] **with her. a.** Who was with her.[30] **b.** To eat with her.[31] **c.** This picture of woman as man's necessary counterpart and then as his temptress, and so the stronger character of the two — over against her Adam is just a compliant gentlemen — introduces us to the theme and depiction of woman throughout the Bible . . . There may exist

ANTHOLOGY

13. SAW THAT THE TREE WAS GOOD, etc. It behooves all to observe the many accursed things caused by wine. It destroyed the firstborn of the world, viz., Adam. For R. Abin said: Eve first tendered Adam a draught of wine, and he drank. For Scripture says here, *And when the woman saw that the tree was good for food;* now, "*saw*" refers to wine, for it says, *see not the* wine *when it is red* (Prov. 23:31). Thus, through his drinking he brought death upon himself and all his descendants.

Yelamdenu. T.S. 3, 26.

14. **She gave also unto her husband.**

The woman went and touched the tree. Seeing the Angel of Death coming towards her, she exclaimed: "Woe is me! I shall now die, and the Holy One, blessed be He, will make another woman and give her to Adam. I will therefore make him eat with me; if we die, we shall both die, and if we live, we shall both live." So she took of the fruit of the tree and ate, and also gave thereof to her husband to eat with her, as it says, *She took of the fruit thereof, and did eat; and she gave also unto her husband.*

Pirke d'Rabbi Eliezer Ch. 13. T.S. 3, 30.

15. SHE GAVE ALSO UNTO HER HUSBAND. *Also* is an extension: she gave the cattle, beasts, and birds to eat of it. All obeyed her, except a certain bird named *hol* (phoenix), as it is written, *Then I said: . . . I shall multiply my days as the hol* (phoenix) (Job 29:18). The School of R. Jannai maintained: It lives a thousand years, at the end of which a fire issues from its nest and burns it up, yet as much as an egg is left, and it grows new limbs and lives. R. Judan b. R. Simeon said: It lives a thousand years, at the end of which its body is consumed and its wings drop off; yet as much as an egg is left, and then it grows new limbs.

Gen. R. 19. T.S. 3, 33.

16. **And the eyes of them both were opened.**

Were they then blind? He showed them how many generations they had destroyed.

Gen. R. 19. T.S. 3, 35.

17. **And they knew that they were naked.**

Even of the one precept which they had possessed they had stripped themselves.

Gen. R. 19. T.S. 3, 36.

fig-leaves together, and made themselves girdles. [8]And they heard the voice of the Lord God walking in the garden toward the cool of the day;

COMMENTARY

today, especially in the feminine mind, accustomed within only a generation or two to the legal equality of the sexes, the tendency to look askance upon the woman of the ancient world, and in particular of the Orient down to our own day. But all that history reveals is the high part that woman has taken as man's partner, and this by virtue of her own genius, in spite of the restraints of law and the ancient claims of the superiority of the male . . . Also in the Biblical history and story, which later exhibits actual life better than the theories of law and religion, women are depicted with wonderful objective *finesse,* and as often with more character than the men their partners.[32]

ANTHOLOGY

18. **And they sewed fig-leaves together.**

R. Nehemiah said: The forbidden tree was the fig-tree, for by the very thing by which they were disgraced they were restored, as it is said, *And they sewed fig-leaves together.* R. Jose said: They were figs. He learns the obscure from the explicit, and the meaning of a statement from its context, thus: This may be compared to a royal prince who sinned with a slave girl, and the king on learning of it expelled him from court. He went from door to door of the slaves, but they would not receive him; but she who had sinned with him opened her door and received him. So when Adam ate of that tree, He expelled him and cast him out of the Garden of Eden; and he appealed to all the trees, but they would not receive him. What did they say to him? Said R. Berekiah: "Behold, a deceiver who deceived his Creator, who deceived his Master!" But the fig-tree, whose fruit he had eaten, opened its doors and received him; hence it is written, *And they sewed fig-leaves together,* etc. Of what species was that fig-tree? R. Abin said: It was the "*berath sheva,*" so called because it brought seven (*shiv'a*) days of mourning into the world. R. Joshua of Siknin said in R. Levi's name: It was the *berath ali,* because it brought lamentation (*alitha*) into the world.

Gen. R. 15; Berakoth 40a; Sanhedrin 70a. T.S. 3, 37. 38.

19. **And made themselves girdles.**

R. Abba b. Kahana observed: Scripture writes *girdles,* not girdle: they made many kinds of girdles, embroidered girdles, wide girdles, and fine linen girdles. Further, just as the man's needs were[1] thus supplied, so too were the woman's, such as wraps, bonnets, and turbans.

Midrash Abakir. T.S. 3, 41.

20. **And they heard the voice.**

Do not seek to look upon a man in his disgrace. You may learn this from Adam, who ate of the tree and was disgraced. The Almighty did not appear to them immediately, but waited until they had sewn the fig-leaves together, and only after that *They heard the voice of the Lord God.* It also teaches that none should enter another's home suddenly and unannounced. God gave man an example of good manners. He stood at the door of the garden of Eden and summoned Adam before entering, as it says, *And the Lord God called unto Adam, and said unto him: "Where art thou?"*

Yelamdenu; Derek Eretz Rabbah Ch. 5. T.S. 3, 42. 51.

21. **And they heard the voice of the Lord God travelling (mith-hallek) in the garden.**

R. Halapun said: We know from here that a voice may travel; we also know that fire can

§ 19 [1] This seems to be the meaning. The text, however, reads: Just as we supply a man's needs, so must we provide for a woman's. If this be correct, R. Abba may have been deducing a practical moral: Adam and Eve made themselves various kinds of girdles, as they found necessary. So must we too supply those who need it, whether men or women, with the garments demanded by their station in life.

and the man and his wife hid themselves from the presence of the Lord God amongst the trees of the garden.

COMMENTARY

[7]**opened. a.** With wisdom, and the phrase is not to be understood literally.[33] **b.** They now thought of and desired every pleasure, though it was harmful.[34] **c.** The knowledge attained is neither of happiness, wisdom, or power, but of consciousness of sin and its conflict with the will of God (Ryle). Next come shame, fear, and the attempt to hide.[35] **that they were naked. a.** They realized that shame attaches to nakedness.[36] **b.** Even a blind person knows when he is naked! It means, however, that they realized that they were now bereft (*naked*) of the only precept which God had given them.[37] **c.** They understood that their bodies should be covered, since henceforth their main purpose would be the satisfaction of a degrading desire.[38] **d.** They lost Eden and they gained a conscience.[39] **fig-leaves. a.** The Heb. is in the sing. (*aleh-leaf*), but it is to be understood as a collective noun; hence the plural rendering.[40] **b.** The fig was the tree whereof they had eaten; as the Talmud asserts, "Wherewith they had sinned they also made amendment."[41] [8]**voice.** Or, "sound."[42] **walking. a.** The verb refers to the *voice*, not to God, and means "sounding": they heard the voice of God resounding.[43] **b.** Another rendering: "As he (Adam) was walking." The general sense is that the Divine Presence manifested itself.[44] **toward the cool of the day. a.** The Heb. *l'ruah*, etc., means "to the side of" (cf. Ezek. 42:20), i.e., in the direction where the sun shone brightest, so as to make them more selfconscious of their state of nudity.[45]

ANTHOLOGY

travel, from the verse, *And the fire travelled down upon the earth* (Ex. 9:23).[1] R. Abba b. Kahana said: Not *mehallek* but *mith-hallek* is written here, which means that it repeatedly leaped and ascended. The real home of the Shekinah was in the nether sphere; when Adam sinned, it departed to the first *rakia* (firmament). (He goes on to explain how with every successive generation of sinners it departed still higher; but was brought back to earth by the righteous in successive generations.)

Gen. R. 19. T.S. 3, 43.

22. AND THEY HEARD THE VOICE OF THE LORD GOD WALKING (MITH-HALLEK) IN THE GARDEN IN THE RUAH (AJV: COOL) OF THE DAY. Read not, *vayishm'u* (they heard) but *vayashmiu* (and they caused to hear): they heard the voice of the trees declaiming, "Behold the deceiver who deceived his Creator!"[1] Another interpretation: They heard the voice of the angels saying: "The Lord God goes to those in the garden to punish them."[2] R. Levi said: The angels were exclaiming, "He of the garden is dead and gone (*meth halak*)!" They exclaimed: "Does the dead still go about! Incredible!"[3] Said the Holy One, blessed be He, to them: "The answer lies *in the ruah*[4] of the day. I will make the day live for him. I said to him thus, *In the* day *that thou eatest thereof thou shalt surely die*" (2:17). Now, you do not know whether this means My day or your day of 24 hours. I will give him one day of Mine, which is a thousand years. He will live 930 years, and leave 70 years to his descendants." Hence it is written, *The days of our years are threescore years and ten* (Ps. 90:10).

Gen. R. 19. T.S. 3, 44.

23. **And the man and his wife hid themselves.**

It was taught: Before a man sins he is invested with awe and dread, and creatures fear him. But after he sins he is filled with awe and

§ 21 [1] The point is not clear. The first half shows that he links "travelling" with "voice," not with God—probably to avoid the implied anthropomorphism. But this does not seem to be his main purpose. Perhaps it is simply a comment on linguistic usage.

§ 22 [1] Through their sin they made the angels to be heard as they thus declaimed.
[2] Rendering: *They heard the voice* (of the angels): *"The Lord goeth,"* etc.
[3] Both these interpretations are a play on words. The second reflects the angels' wonder that Adam still walked, when God had said that he would die in the day that he ate of the forbidden tree.
[4] *Ruah* (AJV: cool) variously means breath, wind, spirit. Giving it the last meaning, it is identified with life: God made the day live for them, by interpreting "day" as a day of His—1000 years.

[9]And the Lord God called unto the man, and said unto him: 'Where art

COMMENTARY

b. Or as our rendering, i.e., toward evening.[46] **c.** In that quarter (*ruah*) where the sun sinks, viz., the west.[47] **d.** "In the wind (*ruah*) of the day," the manifestation of the Divine Presence being signalized by a strong wind (cf. 1 Kings 19:11).[48] **e.** In accordance with the needs of the day, i.e., to perform the particular action that God has planned for that day.[49] **f.** The whole passage has been rendered thus: they heard the voice of God withdrawing in the garden in the direction of the Day (West). This was, according to the Sages, the first sad withdrawal of the Shekinah (Divine Presence) in the history of man: The Glory of God withdrew.[50] **hid themselves. a.** They realized that it was not fitting that God should look upon their nakedness (cf. Deut. 23:15).[51] **b.** Conscience made cowards of them.[52] **amongst the trees of the garden.** Or: within a hollow tree.[53] **[9]Where art thou? a.** God

ANTHOLOGY

dread, and he fears others. In proof of this Rabbi observed: Before Adam had sinned, he stood dignifiedly erect when he heard God's voice, and had no fear. But after he sinned, he hid himself in fear on hearing the voice of God, as we read, *I heard Thy voice in the garden, and I was afraid.* R. Abin declared: Before Adam sinned God's voice sounded soft and intimate; after his sin, it sounded harsh and stern.

Num. R. 11; Song R. 3. T.S. 3, 48. 59.

23A AND ADAM AND HIS WIFE HID THEMSELVES. Before Adam sinned, he stood dignifiedly erect when he heard God's voice and could endure it. But after he sinned, he hid himself when he heard the voice of God, as it says, *Adam and his wife hid themselves.* R. Abin said: Before Adam sinned, God's voice was gently intimate; after his sin, he heard God's voice angrily harsh.

Num. R. 11; Midrash R. 11. T.S. 3, 48.

24. **The Lord God called.**

One cannot find in Scripture the two names of God mentioned together in connection with any of the curses against the enemies of Israel,[1] save in the curse against Adam, as it says, *And the* Lord God *called unto Adam.*[2]

Midrash Tadshe ch. 20. T.S. 3, 56.

25. THE LORD GOD CALLED. When the Sabbath arrived and freed God from His work of creation, He began to converse with Adam, hoping that he would repent. For it says, *And the Lord God* (Adonai Elohim) *called to Adam, and said unto him: "Where art thou?"*—where do you stand in the matter of repentance? For "Lord" (Adonai) means the God of mercy, as we read, *The Lord, the Lord* (Adonai) *God, merciful and gracious* (Exod. 34:6). Thus He showed His quality of mercy to Adam before His quality of justice, in order that he might repent.[1] For that reason too He said to him: *"Where art thou?"* Did He then not know where he was? But He asked this in order to open the way for him, that he might repent.

Tanhuma Tazria 1:9; Midrash Aggadah. T.S. 3, 55. 57.

26. **"Where art thou (ayekah)?"**

This teaches that the Holy One, blessed be He, admonished him: "How lowly art thou become! Yesterday thou wast ruled by My will, and now by the will of the serpent; yesterday thou didst extend from one end of the world to the other, whereas now thou must hide *amongst the trees of the garden.*" It also teaches that He pronounced a dirge over him: "*Ekah* (How art thou fallen)!"[1]

Gen. R. 19; Midrash Haseroth Viy'theroth. T.S. 3, 52. 53.

§ 24 [1] A euphemism for Israel itself.
[2] Though this introduces God's curses of Adam and Eve and the serpent, it yet bears this double name.

§ 25 [1] This is based on the well-known Rabbinic interpretation of *Adonai* (Lord) and *Elohim* (God) as meaning the God of mercy and the God of justice respectively.

§ 26 [1] By a change in vocalization *ayekah* reads *ekah,* the formal commencement of a dirge; cf Lam. 1:1: *How* (ekah) *doth the city sit solitary!*

thou?' [10]And he said: 'I heard Thy voice in the garden, and I was afraid, because I was naked; and I hid myself.' [11]And He said: 'Who told thee that thou wast naked? Hast thou eaten of the tree, whereof I com-

COMMENTARY

knew where he was, but the question was merely a means of opening the conversation with him, so that he might not be too terrified by an abrupt pronouncement of judgment without any introduction. For other instances, cf. 4:9; Num. 22:9.[54] **b.** The Heb. *ayyekkah* does not express a simple question, but rather the surprise to find Adam where he should not have been found.[55] **c.** "*Where art thou?*" is the call which, after every sin, resounds in the ears of the man who seeks to deceive himself and others concerning his sin.[56] **[10]because I was naked.** The Rabbis maintain that "one sin leads to another sin." Adam commits a further offence by attempting to conceal the truth by means of this excuse.[57] **[11]Who told thee that thou wast naked?** How do you know that nakedness is shameful?[58]

ANTHOLOGY

27. AND THE LORD GOD CALLED UNTO ADAM, AND SAID UNTO HIM: "WHERE ART THOU?" Rab Judah said in Rab's name; Adam was a heretic, for it is written: *And the Lord God called unto Adam, and said unto him: "Where art thou?"* that is, whither has thy heart turned?

Sanhedrin 38b. T.S. 3, 50.

28. "WHERE ART THOU?" From this we learn that a man must be judged only by his actions at the particular moment when he is being judged.[1]

Midrash Habiur. T.S. 3, 58.

29. **I heard Thy voice in the garden, and I was afraid.**

God, the righteous and true Judge, sat down to render a true judgment. Summoning Adam, He demanded: "Why didst thou flee before Me?" He answered Him: "I heard Thy voice and my bones trembled," as it says, *I heard Thy voice in the garden, and I was afraid, because I was naked; and I hid myself:—I hid myself* from my Maker[1] and *I was afraid* on account of my deeds; *because I was naked*—stripped bare of my one commandment.[2]

Pirke d'Rabbi Eliezer Ch. 14. T.S. 3, 60.

30. **And He said: "Who told thee that thou wast naked?"**

What was the dress of the first man? A skin of nail,[1] and a cloud of glory covered him. When he ate of the fruits of the tree, the nail-skin was stripped off him, and the cloud of glory departed from him, and he saw himself naked; as it says, *And He said: "Who told thee that thou wast naked? Hast thou eaten of the tree, whereof I commanded thee,* etc.?"

Pirke d'Rabbi Eliezer Ch. 14.
Friedlander. T.S. 3, 62.

31. **Hast thou eaten of the tree (hamin haetz)?**

God started this conversation in the hope that Adam would acknowledge his sin and be pardoned. But Adam did not confess his sin; on the contrary, he hurled the very kindness

§ 28 [1] See par. 25. Thus God was ready to take Adam's present frame of mind into account if he had repented.

§ 29 [1] Or: because of my action.
[2] Cf. par. 17.

§ 30 [1] The dress of Adam and Eve was, according to the Pal. Targum, Gen. 3:7, "onyx-coloured"; cf. Gen. R. 20:12. The legend of an original skin of nail is preserved in the custom which still obtains among orthodox Jews, who gaze at their nails with the Habdalah light at the termination of the Sabbath. Dr. S. Daiches considers this custom as a relic of nail magic (see Jews' College Publications, V, p. 31f, n. 1). According to the Church Father Ephraim, Adam and Eve lost their angelic endowments immediately after their sin, their sight and power of discerning became limited only to matters corporeal and sensible; see the Book of Adam and Eve (ed. Malan), p. 215, for this reference. See also Odes of Solomon, pp. 66ff and 69, notes 1, 2.

manded thee that thou shouldest not eat?' [12]And the man said: 'The woman whom Thou gavest to be with me, she gave me of the tree, and I did eat.' [13]And the Lord God said unto the woman: 'What is this thou hast done?' And the woman said: 'The serpent beguiled me, and I did eat.'

COMMENTARY

[12]**whom Thou gavest to be with me. a.** He thus displayed his ingratitude.[59] **b.** Adam pleaded that since she was given to be his helpmate, he was justified in assuming that her counsel was good.[60] **c.** Since it was Thou Who gavest her to me, it is Thou Who has caused me to sin.[61] [13]**What is this thou hast done? a.** God said this to urge her to repent.[62] **b.** Instead of a question, the words may be taken as an exclamation, "What is this thou hast done!"[63] **beguiled me.** By allaying my fear of punishment.[64] [14]**the serpent.** As the tempter and instigator of the offense, sentence is passed upon it first; and as the tempter, the serpent is

ANTHOLOGY

which God had shown him, viz., the gift of Eve, against God, saying, "*The woman whom Thou gavest,*" etc., that is to say, Thou didst cause me to sin, by giving me a woman who *gave me of the tree, and I ate.*"

Midrash Aggadah. T.S. 3, 65.

32. HAST THOU EATEN OF THE TREE (HAMIN HAETZ)? God said: "You sinned through the tree, and therefore deserve to die on it; but instead let it be reserved for Haman to be hung upon it." Thus do not read *hamin haetz,* but Haman *haetz,* the tree is for Haman.[1] Where do we find an allusion to Haman in the Torah? In this verse, which we read as stated.[2]

Midrash; Hulin 139b. T.S. 3, 63. 64.

33. **The woman whom Thou gavest to be with me, etc.**

Adam said before the Holy One, blessed be He: "Sovereign of all worlds! When I was alone, did I sin against Thee? But the woman whom Thou hast brought to me enticed me away from Thy bidding," as it says, *The woman whom Thou gavest to be with me, she gave me of the tree, and I did eat.*

Pirke d'Rabbi Eliezer Ch. 14. T.S. 3, 69.

34. **And the Lord God said unto the woman: "What is this thou hast done?"**

Seeing that Adam had not expressed regret, God started questioning Eve, "*What is this thou hast done*?" in the hope that she would confess, "I have sinned," so that He could forgive both. But she did not do thus. Instead, she saddled the sin on the serpent, as it says, *And the woman said*: "*The serpent beguiled me, and I did eat.*"

Midrash Aggadah. T.S. 3, 73.

35. **The serpent beguiled me, and I did eat.**

This provides an opportunity for comparing Adam with Moses. They may be compared to two great physicians: one, bitten by a snake, did not know an antidote to the poison, and died. The other physician healed everyone bitten by the snake. Who then was the greater physician? Surely he who healed all. Even so, Adam was like the former; he declared, *The serpent beguiled me, and I did eat,* and he died through the serpent's enticement. Moses, on the other hand, fashioned a brass serpent and all who were bitten by the serpent had but to look at this brass serpent to be healed, as we read, *And it came to pass, that if a serpent had bitten any man, when he looked upon the serpent of brass,*

§ 33 [1] The idea is that the gallows (Heb. *etz,* tree, also means gallows) is preordained for all who, like Haman, seek to destroy the Jewish people.

[2] Two passages from different sources are combined here. The second, "where do we find," etc. probably has the same idea as the first, viz.: Where do we find an allusion to Haman's preordained doom?

[14]And the Lord God said unto the serpent: 'Because thou hast done this, cursed art thou from among all cattle, and from among all beasts of the

COMMENTARY

cursed, and not its dupes and victims.[65] **Because thou hast done this.** Hence we learn that we do not seek to justify or excuse one who incites to sin; because the serpent might have pleaded that it was not responsible, since Eve should not have listened to its suggestion rather than to God's command.[66] **cursed art thou.** I.e., singled out for evil.[67] **upon thy belly shalt thou go. a.** It originally had feet which were now cut off.[68] **b.** Better, *upon thy belly thou goest and dust thou eatest.* Till the eighteenth century is was the general belief that the serpent had been walking upright and was now reduced to crawling. This is quite un-Biblical. The meaning is: Continue

ANTHOLOGY

he lived (Num. 21:9). Thus we see that Moses was greater than Adam.

Midrash on The Death of Moses our Teacher. T.S. 3, 78.

36. **And the Lord God said unto the serpent: "Because thou hast done this."**

Rabbi declared: In bestowing honors we start with the greatest; but when meting out punishment we begin with the least. Whence do we learn this? From the passage: *And the Lord God said unto the serpent*: "*Because thou hast done this,*" etc. . . . "*And I will put enmity between thee and the woman,*" etc. . . . *Unto the woman He said . . . And unto Adam He said.* First the serpent was cursed, then Eve, and finally Adam.

Torath Kohanim Sh'mini. T.S. 3, 79.

37. AND THE LORD GOD SAID UNTO THE SERPENT. When this sin was committed the Holy One, blessed be He, said: "If I do not judge the serpent, I will indeed have destroyed the world. For," said He, "he whom I made ruler of the world, how he has been corrupted to have eaten of the forbidden tree!" Therefore He immediately pronounced judgment against him and cursed him, as it is written, *And the Lord God said unto the serpent.*[1]

Aboth d'Rabbi Nathan Ch. 1. T.S. 3, 81.

38. **Cursed be thou.**

Six—some say, seven—curses, irremediable, were pronounced by the just Judge against the serpent, because through his evil speech the whole world was punished. Thus we read, *Cursed be thou above all the cattle,* etc. Why so? Because he brought on man painful toil, hardship and humiliation, as it says, *In the sweat of thy face shalt thou eat bread.* For enticing the woman to eat from the forbidden tree, he was condemned to eat the dust of the ground.

Midrash Tadshe Chap. 7. T.S. 3, 92.

39. CURSED ART THOU ABOVE ALL CATTLE. Being covetous of Eve, the serpent plotted to slay Adam and marry Eve. Said the Almighty to him: "I designed thee to be king of the beasts and cattle, but now, *cursed art thou above all cattle and all beasts.* I intended thee to walk upright, but now, *upon thy belly shalt thou go.* I intended thee to eat dainty viands, like man, but now, *dust shalt thou eat.* Thou didst scheme to kill Adam and take Eve, but now, *I will put enmity between thee and the woman.* Thus what he sought he did not obtain, whilst that which he had was taken from him.

Tosefta Sotah Chap. 4. T.S. 3, 80.

40. MORE CURSED ART THOU, etc. A certain philosopher wished to know after what period of time a serpent bears. When he saw them copulating, he took and placed them in a barrel and fed them until they bore. When the Sages visited Rome, they were asked how long it takes a serpent to bear. R. Gamaliel turned pale with shame and could not answer

§ 37 [1] The sense of the whole passage is not quite clear. The probable meaning is this: If God let the serpent go unpunished after his corrupting man, the ruler of Creation, He would destroy the moral foundation of the world.

field; upon thy belly shalt thou go,

COMMENTARY

to crawl on thy belly and eat dust. Henceforth it will be regarded as a curse, recalling to men thy attempt to drag them to the dust.[69] **c.** (Though) *upon thy belly thou goest and dust thou eatest,* so there is really no occasion for conflict between thee and man, yet *I will put enmity,* etc. (verse 12).[70] **d.** The

ANTHOLOGY

him. R. Joshua, meeting him, asked him, "Why is your face wan?" "I was asked a question," replied he, "and could not answer it." "And what is it?" "After how long does a serpent bear?" "After seven years," he told him. "How do you know that?" he inquired. "Because the dog, which is an unclean beast, bears at fifty days, whilst an unclean animal calves at twelve months. Now, it is written, *More cursed art thou than all cattle, and than all beasts of the field*: hence just as the cattle are seven times more accursed than the beast, so is the serpent seven times more accursed than the cattle."[1] At eventide R. Gamaliel went and told it to the philosopher, who beat his head against the wall in grief, crying out, "All that for which I toiled seven years, this man has come and offered to me on the end of a cane!"[2]

Gen. R. 20. T.S. 3, 88.

41. **Upon thy belly thou shalt go.**

When the Holy One, blessed be He, said to him, *Upon thy belly shalt thou go,* ministering angels descended and cut off his hands and feet, and his cries resounded from one end of the world to the other. Thus the serpent comes to throw light upon the downfall of Egypt, and is itself illumined thereby, viz., *The cry thereof shall go like the serpent's* (Jer. 46:22).[1] Rab Judah and R. Huna commented: The Almighty said to the serpent: "Thou hast caused people to follow their dead prostrate with grief,[2] therefore thou too, *upon thy belly shalt thou go.*" R. Eliezer observed: Even in God's curse there is a blessing: had He not sentenced him, *upon thy belly shalt thou go,* how could he have fled to a hole in a wall and escape his pursuers?

Gen. R. 20. T.S. 3, 89.

42. UPON THY BELLY SHALT THOU GO. That means, upon thine intestines thou shalt scrape along.

Targum Jerushalmi. T.S. 3, 95.

43. UPON THY BELLY SHALT THOU GO. The current proverb, "A lie has no feet to stand on," is based on the serpent's mendacity against God, for which he was punished by losing his feet, when he was sentenced, *Upon thy belly shalt thou go.*

Tikkune Zohar 22:60. T.S. 3, 96.

44. UPON THY BELLY SHALT THOU GO. The serpent, too, is other than it was at first. Before the fall of man it was the cleverest of all animals created, and in form it resembled man closely. It stood upright, and was of extraordinary size. Afterward, it lost the mental advantages it had possessed as compared with other animals, and it degenerated physically, too; it was deprived of its feet, so that it could not pursue other animals and kill them.

Ginzberg Legends, p. 40. Gen. R. 19:1.

45. UPON THY BELLY SHALT THOU GO. Then the Holy One, blessed be He, summoned the serpent and said to him, "*Because thou hast done this . . . upon thy belly shalt thou go.*" Upon hearing his doom the serpent answered:

§ 40 [1] "Beast" and "animal" (Heb. *hayah* and *behemah* respectively—the latter term is also rendered cattle) are undomesticated and domesticated animals respectively. The dog in eastern countries is semi-savage; hence it belongs to the former category.
[2] An idiom: without the least effort.

§ 41 [1] Egypt's cry at her downfall is likened to the serpent's: since the former's cry resounded throughout the world, it follows that the serpent's did likewise.
[2] By bringing death into the world. "Prostrate with grief" is literally "going on their bellies."

and dust shalt thou eat all the days of thy life. [15]And I will put enmity between thee and the woman, and between thy seed and her seed; they

COMMENTARY

whole verse means that the serpent will derive less pleasure from life, and procure its food with more difficulty than all animals and beasts.[71] **all the days of thy life.** As long as thy species lasts.[72] [15]**enmity.** The sight of the serpent will create loathing in man, and fear of its deadly sting will call forth an instinctive desire to destroy it.[73] **enmity between thee and the woman. a.** The serpent sinned because of its desire for the woman (see on verse 1); the consequence will be the reverse of what it hoped.[74] **b.** Those who unite against God, God brings hatred, envy, and contention between them until they separate. Such was the case of the serpent and Eve, of the men who built the city and tower, of Balak and Balaam, of Abimelech and the men of Shechem, of Ahitophel and Absalom, of Abner and Ish-Bosheth, of Haman and Ahasuerus, and that of all wicked

ANTHOLOGY

"Sovereign of the universe! if so be Thy will, then let me be like the fish in the sea which have no feet." Now, when He added, *and dust shalt thou eat,* the serpent rejoined: "Sovereign of the Universe! If the fish eat dust, then must I too eat dust." Thereupon God seized him and slithered his tongue in two and addressed him thus: "Miserable wretch! the first to display an evil tongue; therefore I make it known to all that it was thine own tongue which brought this evil upon thee."[1]

Alphabet of Rabbi Akiba. T.S. 3, 91.

46. **And dust shall thou eat.**

At the dedication of the Tabernacle the Prince of each Tribe brought as an offering a silver basin weighing seventy shekels. Now, the question arises, Why just seventy, and not sixty or eighty? Because from the beginning of the Book of Genesis until the verse, *and dust shalt thou eat,* there are seventy verses.[1] Similarly, from the beginning of Genesis to the sentence, *upon thy belly shalt thou go,* the name of God is mentioned seventy times. Two enemies, the serpent and the wicked Haman, were cursed only after seventy verses.[2] As for the serpent, from "*In the beginning*" until "*cursed art thou*" there are seventy verses.

Midrash Tadshe Chapter 10. T.S. 3, 93.

47. **And I will put enmity, etc.**

Ten sentences were pronounced against Adam, ten against Eve, ten against the serpent, and ten against the earth. These are the ten against the serpent: (1) His mouth is closed.[1] (2) His hands and feet were cut off. (3) He must eat dust. (4) He sloughs his skin with the pain of a woman in travail, and though his cries of pain travel from one end of the earth to the other, yet none hears them. (5) *And I will put enmity.* (6) R. Halfa said, quoting R. Eleazar: Let him eat the choicest viands and drink the sweetest drinks, everything turns to dust in his mouth, as it says, *dust is the food of the serpent* (Gen. 3:14). (7) He bears only after seven years of pregnancy. (8) A man may see a beast or fowl and not mind it, but when he sees a serpent he always resents and curses it. (9) All other creatures will be blessed in the Messianic future, but he alone will remain cursed. (10) To it R. Meir, on the strength of a tradition, ap-

§ 45 1 That is why its tongue is forked.

§ 46 1 Counting "Lord" and "God" separately, and not including the phrase "Lord God" in this very verse now under discussion. This also assumes that the second *elohim* in 3:5 does not mean God, but only the great (see par. 9). The idea is that this basin of seventy shekels was to make atonement for the profanation of the name of God, mentioned seventy times, of which the serpent was guilty by inciting man to disobedience.

2 Haman is first mentioned in Esther 3:1; his execution is related in 7:10; from the former to the latter there are seventy verses, thus: Ch. 3, 15 verses; ch. 4, 17 verses; ch. 5, 14 verses; ch. 6, 14 verses; ch. 7, 10 verses: 15+17+14+14+10=70.

§ 47 1 By having his tongue slit (see par. 45) he was made mute.

shall bruise thy head, and thou shalt bruise their heel.' [16]Unto the woman He said: 'I will greatly multiply thy

COMMENTARY

men.[75] **they shall bruise thy head.** And the utmost pleasure which it will be able to expect from life is the negative one of not being hurt.[76] **thou shalt bruise their heel. a.** Fear and the desire to avoid being hurt arouse the instinct to hurt others.[77] **b.** Since the serpent is low, it will only be able to bruise man in the heel.[78] **c.** The Heb. rendered "bruise," viz., *y'shufka,* may be derived from *shaaf,* to pant after, and so the verse may mean: they shall pant after thy head, and thou shalt pant after their heel — in each case, to hurt and destroy.[79] [16]**greatly multiply . . . over thee.** Better, *Much, much will I make thy pain and thy travail; in pain wilt thou bring forth children, and thy desire is unto thy husband and he ruleth over thee.* This is no sentence upon the woman. It does not contain the term "cursed." Moreover, God Himself pronounced the fruitfulness of

ANTHOLOGY

plied the verse, *And I will cause evil beasts to cease out of the land* (Lev. 26:6).[2]

Perek Adam ha-Rishon. T.S. 3, 97.

48. AND I WILL PUT ENMITY. Between Eve and thee, because thou didst mar the love, peace, tranquillity, and the pleasant relationship between God and His creatures. *And between thy seed and her seed.* Why so? Because he was the cause of the pain which the bearing and rearing of children entail, as it says, *I will greatly multiply thy pain and thy travail.*

Midrash Tadshe Chap. 7. T.S. 3, 99.

49. I WILL PUT ENMITY, etc. Come and see! When men unite against God, He divides them by stirring up animosity, hatred, envy, strife, and rivalry among them. Thus, Eve and the serpent joined to entice Adam to sin. With what result? *"I will put enmity between thee and the woman."*

Midrash Hagadol B'reshith. T.S. 3, 105.

50. AND I WILL PUT ENMITY, etc. Scripture writes: *When a man's ways please the Lord, He maketh even his enemies to be at peace with him* (Prov. 16:7). R. Samuel b. Nahmani said: This applies to the serpent. Although it was said of him, *and I will put enmity,* etc., yet when God is pleased with man's ways He has even the serpent make peace with him.

Tanhuma Yashan B'shallah 3. T.S. 3, 102.

51. **It shall bruise thy head.**

R. Levi in the name of R. B'zira observed: The light which was created on the first day functioned 36 hours.[1] When the Sabbath departed, darkness started creeping on. Adam was terrified, exclaiming, "It was of this that God said, '*It shall bruise thy head, and thou shalt bruise its heel.*'[2] The serpent may now attempt to bite me." Thus Scripture writes, *And I* (Adam) *said: "Surely the darkness shall bruise me"* (Ps. 139:11). Said R. Levi further: God immediately provided Adam with two flints, which he struck one against the other and so produced light. Hence Scripture continues, *Yet even the night is light about me* (ibid.). Over that light Adam recited, "Blessed be the Creator of the light of the fire."

J. Berakoth 8:5. T.S. 3, 101.

52. HE WILL BRUISE THY HEAD, AND THOU SHALT BRUISE HIS HEEL. A man was once walking in a field, holding in his hand a pitcher of milk, when he lighted on a snake, who was crying with thirst. Being asked why he cried, the snake answered, "I am thirsty. What have you in your hand?" "Milk," was the answer. "Let me have the milk, and I will reveal to you a treasure which will enrich you," he pleaded. The traveler gave him the milk, and after he had slaked his thirst he demanded to be shown the treasure. "Follow me," said the snake. The man followed; when they came to

[2] It will one day be entirely extinct.

§ 51 [1] On Friday (12 hours) and the whole 24 hours of the Sabbath (see Chap. II, par. 29).

[2] In the dark the serpent will find its opportunity.

pain and thy travail; in pain thou shalt bring forth children; and thy desire shall be to thy husband, and he shall rule over thee.' [17]And unto Adam He said: 'Because thou hast hearkened unto the voice of thy wife,

COMMENTARY

man a blessing (1:28), and therewith woman's pain and travail are inextricably bound up, being part of woman's physical being. The words addressed to the woman are therefore parenthetical, and signify in effect: "Thee I need not punish. A sufficiency of woe and suffering is thine because of thy physical being."[80] **pain. a.** Of rearing children.[81] **b.** This refers to the loss of virginity.[82] **c.** Menstruation is meant.[83] **travail.** Of pregnancy.[84]

ANTHOLOGY

a huge rock the serpent told him that heaps of money were under it. When the stone was raised, the man found the treasure, but as he was about to carry it off, the serpent coiled himself around the traveler's neck. To the man's protests, the snake said, "I am going to kill you for taking all my money." "Then come with me to Solomon's Court of Law," he proposed. They went, and the serpent, still coiled about the man's neck, presented his case: "I wish to slay him, since it is written, *And thou shalt bruise his heel.*" "Get off his neck," the king ordered, " 'tis not fitting that you should have a stronger hold on him than I, seeing that you are both in a Court of Law." When he had slid down from his neck to the ground, the king said to him, "You may now plead your case." He commenced his plea thus: "I wish to slay him, as the Holy One, blessed be He, bade me, '*thou shalt bruise his heel.*' Said the king to the man: But thee the Almighty bade, '*he shall bruise thy head.*' " He immediately stamped on him and crushed his brains. Hence, said our Sages, runs the proverb: "The best of serpents, crush his brains."

Ms. in Introduction to Tanhuma Yashan 78. T.S. 3, 107.

53. HE SHALL BRUISE THY HEAD, etc. R. Jose asked: On the view that the serpent is man's Evil Inclination, how can one explain this verse? R. Jose answered: It teaches that the only way to destroy the serpent is to crush him with the head; and who is the head? The head of the Academy of Torah, that is, only with Torah can the serpent (the Evil Inclination) be crushed. Conversely, the serpent can slay a man only through the heel, that is to say, when one transgresses and tramples God's commandments under his heel. That is the meaning of, *And thou shalt bruise him in the heel*—through the sin of that trampling the Evil Inclination slays man.

Midrash Haneelam Zohar B'reshith 19. T.S. 3, 108.

54. **In pain (*b'etseb*) shalt thou bring forth children.**

R. Johanan said: The struggle for food is twice as fierce as labor in childbirth, for the latter is described in the word *b'etseb* (in pain), whereas of the former Scripture writes *b'itsabon* (in toil—a much stronger word) *shalt thou eat* (3:17).

Pesahim 118a. T.S. 3, 113.

55. **And he shall rule over thee.**

R. Jose Ha-Galilee said: You might think that man's rule over woman is unlimited; therefore Scripture writes, *No man shall take the mill or the upper millstone to pledge* (Deut. 24:6).[1]

Gen. R. 20. T.S. 3, 119.

56. **And unto Adam He said.**

On that very day a triple penalty was decreed against him, as it says, *And unto Adam He said*: "*Because thou hast hearkened unto*

§ 55 [1] "*Mill*" is understood as a figurative allusion to a woman, and the sentence is allegorically interpreted to mean that a pledge must not be taken from a women. The idea is that her very weakness must inspire the man to be even more careful of her rights, and so his "rule" over her is in fact her protection.

and hast eaten of the tree, of which I commanded thee, saying: Thou shalt not eat of it; cursed is the ground for thy sake; in toil shalt thou eat of it all the days of thy life.

COMMENTARY

thy desire. a. Of cohabitation.[85] **b.** Or: "Thine obedience."[86] **c.** In spite of the pangs of travail, the longing for motherhood remains the most powerful instinct in woman.[87] [17]**unto the voice of thy wife.** When she imputed to God falsehood and jealousy.[88] **cursed is the ground. a.** It shall bring forth accursed things, such as flies and insects.[89] **b.** It will yield its produce but scantily.[90] **c.** It was Adam's duty from the beginning to till the ground (11:15); but the work would now become much more laborious. The soil would henceforth yield its produce only as the result of hard and unceasing toil.[91] **shalt thou eat of it.** Of its produce.[92]

ANTHOLOGY

the voice of thy wife . . . cursed is the ground for thy sake; in toil shalt thou eat of it all the days of thy life. Thorns also and thistles shall it bring forth to thee; and thou shalt eat the herb of the field."

Aboth d'Rabbi Nathan Chapter 1. T.S. 3, 122.

57. AND UNTO ADAM HE SAID: "BECAUSE THOU HAST HEARKENED UNTO THE VOICE OF THY WIFE." R. Simlai said: Eve came to persuade Adam with ready arguments. "What do you think," she demanded, "that I will die and another Eve will be created for you? *There is nothing new under the sun* (Ecc. 1:9). Or do you think that I will die and you will remain idle? *He created it not a waste, He formed it to be inhabited*" (Isa. 45:18). Our Rabbis said: She began weeping over him with loud voice. Hence it is written, *And unto Adam He said: "Because thou hast hearkened unto the voice of thy wife"*: it is not written, "To the *words* of thy wife," but *To the* voice *of thy wife.*

Gen. R. 20. T.S. 3, 123.

58. BECAUSE THOU HAST HEARKENED, etc. There are various forms of uncleanness, but the gravest is that of a man in death. That is because death was decreed against him on account of sin, as it says, *And unto Adam He said: "Because thou hast hearkened unto the voice of thy wife, and hast eaten of the tree . . . unto dust shalt thou return."*

Midrash Tadshe Chap. 15. T.S. 3, 126.

59. **Cursed is the ground.**

We find that when the Almighty judges a man, He penalizes him first in his lesser possessions, and then in his weightier ones. Thus, God told Adam, *In the day that thou eatest thereof thou shalt surely die* (2:17). And yet when he sinned and did eat thereof, He did not punish him so, but cursed his wealth, as it is written, *And to Adam He said: "Cursed is the* ground *for thy sake."* After that He decreed death for *him,* as it says, *For dust thou art and unto dust shalt thou return.*[1]

Midrash Tadshe Chap. 17. T.S. 3, 141.

60. CURSED IS THE GROUND FOR THY SAKE. Had man not sinned fig-trees, vines, and the pomegranate would have borne fruit on the very day they were planted as it was when the world was created,[1] as stated in Scripture: *Fruit-trees* immediately *bearing fruit after its kind* (1:11). Had man deserved this boon, it would still be so. Men would plant trees and they would immediately bear fruit. But when man sinned, the ground was cursed, as it says, *Cursed is the ground for thy sake.*

Tanhuma Yashan K'doshim 38. T.S. 3, 135.

§ 59 [1] Thus He first punished his lesser possessions—the ground—and then his more important—his very life.

§ 60 [1] An alternative rendering could be: Before man sinned every one planted a fig-tree, etc., and they bore fruit on the same day. The end of this passage rather suggests that that indeed is the correct version, as on the rendering given here the second half of this passage is mere repetition. Nevertheless it has been adopted in preference, since before Adam sinned no other people yet existed.

[18]Thorns also and thistles shall it bring forth to thee; and thou shalt eat the herb of the field. [19]In the sweat of thy face shalt thou eat

COMMENTARY

[18]thou shalt eat the herb of the field. a. When you plant species of vegetables, it will bring forth thorns and thistles and other weeds, and you will have no choice but to eat them.[93] **b.** Render, *"whereas thou eatest the herb of the field."* The spontaneous growth of the soil will be weeds, which

ANTHOLOGY

61. CURSED IS THE GROUND FOR THY SAKE. The Psalmist says, *The earth feared and was tranquil* (Ps. 76:9). Now if she feared, why was she tranquil; whilst if she was tranquil, why did she fear? The earth soliloquized thus: "One precept was given to Adam and he violated it, and because of him I was cursed, as it is written, *Cursed is the ground for thy sake.* Now, when the Torah is given, with 248 positive and 365 negative commandments, how much worse will be my plight." But God reassured her, as it says, *O earth, earth, earth, hear the word of the Lord* (Jer. 22:29). "You heard Me say, '*Cursed is the ground for thy sake; in toil shalt thou eat of it.*' But you did not hear My other pronouncement, '*I will not again curse the ground any more for man's sake*'" (8:21). Hearing this last, she forthwith became tranquil.

P'sikta Rabbathi Ch. 21. T.S. 3, 139.

62. CURSED IS THE GROUND FOR THY SAKE. If Adam sinned, what was the sin of the earth, that she should be cursed? Because she did not reveal the evil deed, therefore she was cursed. When men commit the graver sins, God sends a plague upon them personally. But when they commit lesser sins, He smites the fruits of the earth for their transgressions, as it says, *Cursed is the ground for thy sake.*

Pirke d'Rabbi Eliezer Ch. 14. T.S. 3, 140.

63. CURSED IS THE GROUND FOR THY SAKE. Why was the ground cursed? Because she too was implicated. When the Almighty ordered, *Let the earth put forth* . . . fruit-tree *bearing fruit* (1:11), the command was that the tree should taste like its fruit. When Adam was bidden not to eat of the fruit, he would have obeyed and eaten of the tree but not the fruit. But because the earth did not do thus, but brought forth *tree* bearing *fruit,* the tree itself not being as the fruit, Adam disobeyed His edict and ate of the fruit; therefore was the earth cursed.

Midrash Aggadah B'reshith. T.S. 3, 142.

64. **Thorns also and thistles shall it bring forth unto thee.**

R. Joshua b. Levi said: When the Holy One, blessed be He, said to Adam, "*Thorns also and thistles shall it bring forth unto thee,*" he wept bitterly and pleaded: "Sovereign of the Universe! Shall I and my ass eat out of the same crib!" But when He added, "*In the sweat of thy face shalt thou eat* bread" (3:19), his mind was set at rest. R. Simeon b. Lakish said: Happy were we had we remained with the first![1] Nor have we yet escaped it, for we do eat wild herbs.

Pesahim 11a. T.S. 3, 146.

65. **And thou shalt eat the herb of the field.**

R. Judah commented: Had you been worthy, it would have yielded all the trees of the Garden of Eden for you; now that you have proved unworthy, *Thorns also and thistles shall it bring forth to thee.* R. Nehemiah said: Had you merited it, you would have taken herbs from the Garden of Eden and tasted in them every conceivable delight; now that you did not, *Thou shalt eat the herb* of the field.[1]

Gen. R. 20. T.S. 3, 149.

§ 64 [1] We are even worse off now.
§ 65 [1] Only, but not of the Garden of Eden.

bread, till thou return unto the ground; for out of it wast thou taken; for dust thou art, and unto dust shalt thou return.' [20]And the

COMMENTARY

are unsuitable for human consumption. Man's food is the herb, which he can only acquire by toil.[94] **[19]In the sweat of thy face. a.** With hard labor that makes the face sweat.[95] **b.** The necessity of labor has proved man's greatest blessing, and has been the cause of all progress and improvement.[96]

ANTHOLOGY

66. **In the sweat of thy face, etc.**

Six things are good signs for a sick person. They are: sneezing, sweating, free bowel motion, semen, sleep and dreams. Sweating: for the Bible states, *In the sweat of thy face thou shalt eat bread,* i.e., if one sweats he will live to eat bread.

Berakoth 57b. T.S. 3, 153.

67. **For dust thou art and unto dust shalt thou return.**

When God came to create Adam, He gathered dust from the four corners of the earth. For that reason whithersoever a man goes, and his end approaches, thence is the dust of his body and thither it returns to the dust, and that dust will mourn for him, as it is said, *For dust thou art, and unto dust shalt thou return.*

Pirke d'Rabbi Eliezer Ch. 11. T.S. 3, 161.

68. FOR DUST THOU ART, AND UNTO DUST SHALT THOU RETURN. The ball of Adam's heel eclipsed the orb of the sun; how much more so the brightness of his face! R. Levi said in the name of R. Hama b. Hanina: The Holy One, blessed be He, erected thirteen canopies for him in the Garden of Eden. Yet after all this glory he is told: "*For dust thou art, and unto dust shalt thou return.*"

Lev. R. 20. T.S. 3, 159.

69. FOR DUST (AFAR) THOU ART. After his disobedience Adam was told that he was dust and would return to dust, and so become food for the serpent. Hence, God said to the serpent, *And dust* (afar) *shalt thou eat all the days of thy life* (3:14), i.e., the dust of man; hence Scripture writes *afar,* not *adamah* (earth) or *homer* (clay).

Zohar 2:168. T.S. 3, 168.

70. FOR DUST THOU ART, AND UNTO DUST SHALT THOU RETURN. R. Simeon b. Yohai said: Here we have a Scriptural hint of resurrection, for it does not say, *For dust thou art, and unto dust shalt thou* go, but *shalt thou* return.[1]

Gen. R. 20. T.S. 3, 158.

71. FOR DUST THOU ART, AND UNTO DUST SHALT THOU RETURN. Rabbah said: Why did the Torah order dust in the trial of an alleged adulteress?[1] To indicate that if innocent, she would be blessed with a son like Abraham, who declared, "*I am but dust and ashes*" (18:27). But if not, she would return to her original dust, as it says, *For dust thou art and unto dust shalt thou return.*

Sotah 17a. T.S. 3, 157.

72. DUST THOU ART AND UNTO DUST SHALT THOU RETURN. When God created Adam, the ministering angels mistook him for the Deity and wished to proclaim him as the Holy One. God forestalled this by putting Adam to sleep, that they might know that he was but a man, and apostrophized him, "*Dust thou art and unto dust shalt thou return.*"

Eccl. R. 6. 1:10. T.S. 3, 160.

73. FOR DUST THOU ART, AND UNTO DUST SHALT THOU RETURN. Solomon said: I should have learned a lesson from Adam. Everything that was created was put into his hand, and he was endowed with might and power like the

§ 70 [1] The implication being, though you will indeed go to dust, yet you will return.
§ 71 [1] See Num. 5:11 seq. and verse 17.

man called his wife's name Eve; because she was the mother of all

COMMENTARY

[20]**And the man called.** This resumes the narrative of giving names to all creatures, which was interrupted by the episode of the serpent.[97] **Eve** (Havvah). Derived from *hayah*, "living." He did not call her "Hayah," because that is the word for beast.[98] **of all living. a.** Better, of all humankind, since it obviously does not include animal life.[99] **b.** The Heb. חי , here rendered "living," is the primitive Semitic for "clan"; Eve was the mother of every

ANTHOLOGY

heroes in heaven, and he married only one woman, and yet through her, he and his progeny and the endless generations were doomed to death, as it says, *For dust thou art, and unto dust shalt thou return.* How do we know that this doom applied to all his progeny? From the verse, *And the dust returneth to the earth as it was* (Ecc. 12:7).

Midrash on the Alphabet. T.S. 3, 165.

74. AND UNTO DUST SHALT THOU RETURN. Rabbi Jose says, "If thou desirest to know the reward of the righteous in the world to come, come hither and learn it from what has befallen Adam. He was commanded to perform an easy precept, and because he transgressed it, God punished him and all subsequent generations with many kinds of death. Therefore the sages have said that, on the contrary, whoever studies and observes the law and performs good deeds shall be delivered from the punishment of Gehinom and the sorrows of the grave."

Chronicles of Jerahmeel, Gaster, pp. 27-28 (11:4).

75. FOR DUST THOU ART, etc. God said to Moses: "Do thou tell Aaron he is about to die; I feel ashamed to inform him of this." R. Huna said in the name of R. Tanhum Bar Chiya: Moses rose very early in the morning and came to Aaron. Both opened the Book of Genesis and read it section by section, and on each portion he commented: "God did well and created well." When they came to the creation of man, Moses observed, "What can I say of Adam who brought death into the world?" Aaron replied: "O brother Moses, say not that this is a thing we cannot subscribe to, since it too is God's decree." He then proceeded to discuss how Adam and Eve were created; how 13 canopies were erected for them, as we read, *Thou wast in Eden the garden of God; every precious stone was thy covering*, etc. (Ezek. 28:13); how he ate of the tree and received his sentence, *for dust thou art, and unto dust shalt thou return.* "Yes," said Aaron, "after enjoying such honor they came to this!" Then Moses interposed: "What about you and me? I who conquered the angels in heaven, and you who arrested death when the great plague broke out, is not our destiny the same as that of Adam? How many years can we yet expect?" And so he continued until he broke to him the news of his impending death.

Yelamdenu. T.S. 3, 166.

76. FOR DUST THOU ART, AND UNTO DUST SHALT THOU RETURN. Moses implored the earth to intercede in his behalf, saying: "O earth, earth, beseech God to be merciful to me, peradventure He will be gracious to me and let me live." At this utterance, a voice from heaven was heard: "Is it not written, *Now the earth was unformed and void* (1:2); also, *and the earth shall wax old like a garment, and they that dwell therein shall die in like manner* (Isa. 51:6)? Instead of invoking God's pity for you, she should beseech it for herself, for there is but one destiny for both of you, as Scripture states: *Dust thou art and unto dust shalt thou return.*"

Midrash on the Death of Moses. T.S. 3, 167.

77. **Because she was the mother of all living.**

R. Simon said: That means, The artificer of all living creatures (including the demons). Throughout the entire one hundred and thirty years that Adam shunned Eve, male demons were made ardent by her and she bore, while

living. [21]And the Lord God made for Adam and for his wife garments of skins, and clothed them. [22]And the

COMMENTARY

clan, i.e., of the entire human race.[100] **[21]And the Lord God made. a.** I.e., He put in into their minds to make.[101] **b.** Despite their sin, God had not withdrawn His care from them. Divine punishment is at once followed by Divine pity.[102] **garments of skins. a.** The skins of animals.[103] or **b.** He hardened their own skin.[104] **c.** Man himself had covered his nakedness, for he was ashamed of his body; now, according to the Divine will, his clothes should not only be a protection against the forces of nature, but should serve as a permanent warning not to

ANTHOLOGY

female demons were inflamed by Adam and they bore.

Gen. R. 20. T.S. 3, 172.

78. **And the Lord God made for Adam and his wife garments of skin.**

R. Hama b. Hanina said: What means the text, *After the Lord your God shall ye walk* (Deut. 13:5): is it then possible for a human being to walk after the Shekinah? But the meaning is to walk after (emulate) His virtues. Just as He clothes the naked, for it is written, *And the Lord God made for Adam and his wife garments of skin, and clothed them,* so do thou also clothe the naked.

Sotah 14a. T.S. 3, 174.

79. AND THE LORD GOD MADE FOR ADAM AND FOR HIS WIFE GARMENTS OF SKIN. R. Simlai expounded: The Torah begins and ends with the love of mankind. It begins with the love of mankind, for it is written, *And the Lord God made for Adam and for his wife garments of skin, and clothed them.* And it ends with the love of mankind, for it is written, *And He buried him* (Moses) *in the valley* (Deut. 34:6).

Sotah 14a. T.S. 3, 175.

80. GARMENTS OF SKIN (OR). In R. Meir's Torah was found written, "Garments of light (or)":[1] this refers to Adam's garments, which were like a torch (shedding radiance), broad at the bottom and narrow at the top. Isaac the Elder said: They were as smooth as a fingernail and as beautiful as a jewel.

Gen. R. 20. T.S. 3, 178.

81. GARMENTS OF SKIN. R. Levi said: The Torah teaches you here a rule of practical behavior: Spend according to your means on food, as it is written, *Of every tree of the garden thou mayest freely eat* (2:16). Less than you can afford on clothing, for *the Lord God made for Adam and for his wife garments of skin* (only).[1] More than you can afford on a home: for lo! they were but two, yet they dwelt in the whole world.

Gen. R. 20. T.S. 3, 180.

82. GARMENTS OF SKIN. One should honor the Sabbath by donning festive apparel on that day, as Scripture enjoins, *Thou shalt call the Sabbath a delight* (Isa. 58:13). And how do Israelites honor the Sabbath? With special viands, with festive drinks, and with fresh garments. For so did God himself at the creation of the world, as the Bible relates: *The Lord God make for Adam and his wife garments of skin, and clothed them.*[1] And what were those garments? The vestments of the High Priesthood, with which the Almighty clothed them because Adam was the world's first-born.[2]

Tanhuma Yashan Tol'doth Par. 12.
T.S. 3, 182.

§ 80 [1] I.e., אור instead of עור. Cf. Chap. I, par. 285.
§ 81 [1] But no finery or costly raiment.
§ 82 [1] As this occurred in the closing hours of Friday (see *infra* par. 100), these garments are assumed to be in honor of the Sabbath.
[2] The priestly service was originally performed by the first-born. The text reads בכבודו: for Adam was the glory of the world; but is probably an error for בכורו the first-born.

Lord God said: 'Behold, the man is become as one of us, to know good

COMMENTARY

let himself be dominated by the sensuality of his body: — the clothes admonish man always to remember his dignity and destination.[105] [22]**is become as one of us, to know good and evil. a.** "As I am unique among the celestial beings," said God, "so is he now unique among the terrestrial in that he knows good and evil."[106] **b.** As one of the angels, able to do whatever he desires.[107] **c.** "Us" may be a plural of Majesty (cf. 1:26), meaning, man is become as God — omniscient. Man, having through disobedience secured the faculty of unlimited knowledge, there was real danger that his knowledge would outstrip his sense of obedience to Divine Law. In our own day, we see that deep insight into Nature's secrets, if unrestrained by considerations of humanity, may threaten

ANTHOLOGY

83. GARMENTS OF SKIN. Adam was the first-born of the world, and when he offered his sacrifices, as it says, *And it shall please the Lord better than a bullock that hath horns and hoofs* (Ps. 69:32),[1] he donned the vestments of a High Priest, as it is written, *And the Lord God made for Adam and for his wife garments of skin, and clothed them.* They were festive Sabbath garments, which the first-born in each generation wore.[2] When Adam was about to die, he gave them to Seth, who in turn delivered them to Methuselah. At his death he handed them over to Noah. Eventually they came down to Isaac, who transmitted them to Jacob.

Num. R. 4. T.S. 3, 181.

84. GARMENTS OF SKIN. They were embroidered with all the birds of the world. Adam bequeathed them to Cain, and when Cain was slain, Nimrod obtained them, for which reason he is described as *a mighty hunter* (10:9).[1] When Esau slew Nimrod, Esau appropriated them. This is what Scripture means when it speaks of "*the coveted garments of Esau*" (27:15), i.e., coveted from Nimrod.

Midrash quoted in Tol'doth Yitzhak by R. Joseph Caro. T.S. 3, 184.

85. GARMENTS OF SKIN. R. Eliezer said: From the skin which the serpent sloughed off, the Holy One, blessed be He, made coats of glory for Adam and his helpmate, as it is said, *And the Lord God made for Adam and for his wife garments of skin, and clothed them.*

Pirke d'Rabbi Eliezer Ch. 20. T.S. 3, 183.

86. GARMENTS OF SKIN. These were skin to cover their flesh, which they did not yet have.

Quoted by Kimchi as a Midrash. T.S. 3, 186.

87. **And the Lord God said.**

From the beginning of Genesis up to this verse God's name occurs seventy-one times:[1] this teaches that Adam was sentenced by a full Court of Law (Sanhedrin).

P'sikta Zutrathi. T.S. 3, 205.

88. **Behold, the man was as one of us.**

Thus Scripture writes, *Behold, this only I have found, that God made man upright* (Ecc. 7:29). That is, God, Who is called righteous and upright, did not create man in His own image for any other reason than that he should be righteous and upright like Himself. Yet, though God did make man upright, the Evil Inclination rose and degraded him. Therefore the Psalmist cries out, *I said: Ye shall be godlike beings, and all of you sons of the Most High. Nevertheless ye shall die like men* (Ps. 82:6-7).

Tanhuma B'reshith 7. T.S. 3, 197.

89. BEHOLD, THE MAN, etc. Let our master teach us: What is the punishment of a slanderer?

§ 83 [1] The Rabbis interpreted this: better than the bullock offered by Adam.
[2] Originally first-born and not priests officiated at the sacrificial service. Hence these vestments, worn by the first-born, are understood to refer to the priestly (i.e., sacrificial) robes.

§ 84 [1] Having won such a "mighty" prize.

§ 87 [1] This is not correct. T.S. a.l. discusses how the number is made up.

ANTHOLOGY

Our Sages taught thus: A slanderer is worse than one who commits a crime, for our forefathers in the wilderness were doomed to die in the desert only because of slander.[1] Our Rabbis said: Slander is indeed heinous, in that it brought death upon Adam. The serpent slandered God, saying to Adam and Eve, *For God doth know that in the day ye eat thereof . . . ye shall be as God* (3:5). Adam and Eve gave ear to his words, and thus brought death upon themselves and their descendants to the end of time. This is inferred from the Scriptural expression, *Behold, man*, etc., "*behold*" signifying death, as it says, *Behold, thy days approach that thou must die* (Deut. 31:14).

Tanhuma B'reshith par. 8. T.S. 3, 199.

90. BEHOLD, THE MAN IS BECOME AS ONE OF US. Moses pleaded: "Sovereign of the Universe! thirty-six transgressions punishable by extinction are enumerated in the Torah, for any one of which a man earns death. Have I then transgressed any one of them? Why dost Thou decree death upon me?" God replied: "You must die because of the sin of Adam, who brought death into the world." Thus Scripture says, *Behold thy days approach that thou must die* (Deut. 31:14). What does "behold" imply here? For the sin of him concerning whom Scripture writes "Behold," viz., Behold, *the man is become as one of us.*

Deut. R. 9. T.S. 3, 196.

91. BEHOLD, THE MAN WAS AS ONE OF US. *Was* implies that he was doomed to die.[1] R. Berekiah said: When God willed to create the world, He began it with the creation of man's body. When, however, He was about to breathe a soul into him, He meditated, "If I give him life now, it may be said that he collaborated with Me in the creation of the world. I will therefore leave him a lifeless mass until I have created everything else." When He finished all other things, His ministering angels said to Him, "Hast Thou resolved not to make man, as Thou didst originally intend?" God answered, "I have already formed him. All he wants now is a soul." He thereupon gave man life and with him completed the creation of the world. Thus with man He began and with man He concluded, as it is written, *Thou hast formed me last and first* (Ps. 139:5). Hence the Almighty said: "*Behold, the man was as one of us.*"[2]

Midrash Abakir. T.S. 3, 200.

92. AS ONE OF US. R. Pappos expounded: This means, like one of the ministering angels. Said R. Akiba to him: "Enough, Pappos!" Pappos retorted: "How then do you explain it?" It means that God set two paths before him, life and death, but alas, he chose the path of death. R. Judah b. Simon interpreted: Like the Unique One of the universe, as it is written, *Hear, O Israel; the Lord our God, the Lord is one* (Deut. 6:4). Our Rabbis said: Like Gabriel, of whom Scripture writes, *And one man in the midst of them clothed in linen* (Ezek. 40:2). Resh Lakish said: It means like Jonah, of whom is written, *But as* one *was felling a beam*, etc. (2 Kings 6:5): just as the latter fled from God's command, so did the former; just as Jonah's glory did not stay the night with him, so Adam's glory too did not stay one night with him. R. Berekiah said in R. Hanina's name: Like Elijah: just as he did not experience the taste of death, so Adam too was not meant to experience death.

Gen. R. 21; M'kilta B'Shallah.
T.S. 3, 189. 190.

93. AS ONE OF US. When Israel exclaimed, "*All that the Lord hath spoken will we do, and obey*" (Exod. 24:7), the Holy One, blessed be He, said: "I gave but one commandment to Adam to fulfill, and I made him equal to the ministering angels, for it says, *Behold, the man was as one of us* — how much more should

§ 89 [1] For listening to and accepting the evil report of the spies; see Num. Chapters 13-14.
§ 91 [1] Cf. par. 1.
[2] The point is not clear. Probably: like one of us, he already was before everything else.

and evil; and now, lest he put forth his hand, and take also of the tree of life, and eat, and live for ever.' [23]Therefore the Lord God sent him forth from the garden of Eden, to till the ground from whence he was

COMMENTARY

the very existence of mankind! e.g., through chemical warfare.[108] **and live for ever. a.** This would enable him to deceive other creatures into thinking that he is a god.[109] **b.** And thus nullify My warning that on the day he ate thereof he should die.[110] **c.** Adam already knows good and evil, since he is formed in the Divine image. Should he also be immortal, he would spend all his time in pursuit of earthly pleasures and care nought about things spiritual or good deeds, and thus fail to attain to that spiritual bliss which God intended for him in making him in His likeness.[111] **d.** This was spoken in ironic reference to the serpent's blasphemy (*"then your eyes shall be opened, and ye shall be as God"*)—now we must indeed show how false were these words! But actually Adam's expulsion was the punishment for

ANTHOLOGY

these, who practice and fulfill all the six hundred and thirteen commandments, their general principles, details, and minutiae, enjoy eternal life?" As soon, however, as they declared, *"This is thy god, O Israel"* (Ex. 32:4), God said: "You have followed the course of Adam who did not withstand temptation for more than three hours, and at nine hours[1] death was decreed upon him. *I said: Ye are godlike beings;* but since you have followed the footsteps of Adam, *nevertheless ye shall die like men"* (Ps. 82:6). What is the meaning of, *and fall like one of the princes* (ibid.)? R. Judah said: Like Adam or Eve.

Exod. R. 32. T.S. 3, 194.

94. **Perhaps he will put forth his hand.**

Scripture writes, *I went by the field of the slothful* (Prov. 24:30): *"slothful"* alludes to Adam of whom God said, *Perhaps he will put forth his hand,* to accept Mine stretched out to him in an invitation to repent. But he was *slothful,* neglecting this opportunity to repent, with the result that *lo, it was all grown over with thistles*: his sentence was decreed, whereupon God lamented his fate.[1]

Midrash. T.S. 3, 203.

95. **Therefore the Lord God (Adonai Elohim) sent him forth.**

Why are both names, *Adonai Elohim,* employed? The answer is that God charged the angels with the task of sending him forth *from the Garden of Eden to till the ground from whence he was taken.*[1] Altogether, Adam lodged only one night in the Garden of Eden, and so it says, *Man* (Adam) *passeth not the night in his glory* (Ps. 49:13).

Midrash Aggadah. T.S. 3, 213.

96. SENT HIM FORTH FROM THE GARDEN OF EDEN. Behold what misfortune sin caused! Adam committed one sin: through that his stature diminished, his glory dwindled, his food deteriorated and he became a fugitive and vagabond over all the earth. And he and his generations, to the end of time, were all doomed to die!

Midrash Hagadol B'reshith. T.S. 3, 211.

97. **To serve the ground from whence he was taken.**

He expelled him from the Garden of Eden and placed him on Mount Moriah, the site of the Temple, to which the gate of the Garden of Eden is nigh, there to serve God until the day of his death, as it says, *to serve the ground*

§ 93 [1] I.e., about 3 in the afternoon, the day being counted from dawn to nightfall.

§ 94 [1] He lamented that man's stubborness had sealed his doom, death—a harvest of thistles instead of the harvest of good fruit—eternal life—which would have been his had he repented.

§ 95 [1] He renders: Therefore the Lord (instructed) Elohim (i.e., the angels; cf. Chap. VI, par. 8) (and they) sent him forth.

taken. [24]**So He drove out the man;**

COMMENTARY

his sin.[112] [24]**So He drove out the man. a.** That neither he nor his descendants should ever return there.[113] **b.** Better, *so having driven out the man* (as stated in V. 23), He placed, etc.[114] **c.** Yet another rendering is: So He drove out the man after having placed (before his expulsion) at the east, etc.[115] **d.** Sin drives man from God's presence; and when man banishes God from his world, he dwells in a wilderness instead of a Garden of Eden.[116] **at the east.** Either because man dwelt to the east of the Garden, or because the entrance was on that side.[117] **cherubim. a.** Destroying angels.[118] **b.** Terrifying apparitions.[119] **c.** The first

ANTHOLOGY

from whence he was taken.[1] For it was from that place that the dust of which he was formed was taken, and thither he was now returned. Never again did he or his descendants return to the Garden of Eden; but in the Messianic era they will indeed return.

Midrash Hagadol B'reshith; Pirke d'Rabbi Eliezer Ch. 25. T.S. 3, 212. 225.

98. **So He drove out the man.**

R. Johanan said: Like the daughter[1] of a priest who has been divorced and cannot return to her husband. R. Simeon b. Lakish said: Like the daughter[1] of an Israelite (i.e., a non-priest) who has been divorced and can return. In R. Johanan's view He was severe towards him; in the view of R. Simeon b. Lakish He was lenient toward him.

Gen. R. 21. T.S. 3, 217.

99. HE DROVE OUT THE MAN. Our Rabbis aver: At the conclusion of the Sabbath the luster of Adam's countenance was taken from him and he was expelled from the Garden of Eden. Thus we read, *He drove out the man;* whilst it is also written, *Thou changest his countenance* (by depriving it of its luster), *and sendest him away* (Job 14:20).

Gen. R. 12. T.S. 3, 215.

100. SO HE DROVE OUT THE MAN. R. Judah said: At the first hour of the sixth day God conceived the idea of creating man; in the second hour He took counsel with His ministering angels; in the third hour He gathered the dust; in the fourth He kneaded it; fashioned it in the fifth, and formed it into a body in the sixth. In the seventh hour He breathed into it the breath of life; in the eighth He led him into the Garden of Eden; in the ninth He commanded him not to eat of the forbidden tree. In the tenth hour, Adam sinned; in the eleventh he was judged, and in the twelfth he was expelled; as it is written *So He drove out the man.* These strong words, *He drove out,* imply that he was painfully expelled. A variant interpretation is that he was the cause of the destruction of the Temple, when Israel was driven out of his land.

Targum Jonathan on Genesis 1.25 par. 25. T.S. 3, 223.

101. SO HE DROVE OUT THE MAN. R. Eliezer said: The Book and the Sword came down from Heaven bound together. God said to man: "If you will follow the Torah written in this Book, you will be spared the Sword; if not, you will be smitten by it." This exhortation is implied in our text, *So He drove out the man; and He placed at the east of the garden of Eden the cherubim, and the flaming sword which turned every way, to keep the way of the tree of life.*[1]

Sifre Ekeb Ch. 40. T.S. 3, 214.

§ 97 [1] The idea is that the opportunity for service is man's Garden of Eden on earth. On the whole passage cf. Chap. II, par. 88.

§ 98 [1] I.e., wife. An Israelite (a non-priest) may remarry his divorced wife, but not a priest. "Daughter" is used here for "wife," because a priest's daughter generally married a priest, and an Israelite's daughter generally married an Israelite (T.S.).

§ 101 [1] Rendering: *He placed . . . the flaming sword* before man to spur him *to keep the way of* (AJV: *to*) *the tree of life,* which is the Torah.

and He placed at the east of the garden of Eden the cherubim, and the

COMMENTARY

man was forbidden to enter the Garden again, and the slightest attempt on his part to do so would bring down upon him instant destruction. In the Bible generally the cherubim are symbols of God's presence (Exod. 25:18).[120] **the cherubim, and the flaming sword. a.** These appeared to them in a vision, so as to frighten them from daring to attempt to re-enter the garden of Eden.[121] **b.** While God is indeed one, His highest and chiefest powers are two, goodness and sovereignty. Through His goodness He begat all that is, through His sovereignty He rules what He has

ANTHOLOGY

102. So He drove out the man. King David said: "Master of the Universe! But for Thy mercy, which anticipated the creation of Adam, he could not have endured. For how didst Thou deal with him? Thou didst expel him from the Garden of Eden, as it says, *So He drove out the man*. Why was he driven out? For bringing death on the future generations. Now, he deserved to die immediately; but that Thou didst show compassion on him and drive him out instead, like an unintentional homicide who is exiled from his home town and confined in the city of refuge." Hence Scripture says, *Remember, O Lord, Thy compassions and Thy mercies, for they have been from of old* (Ps. 25:6).

Tanhuma Massei Ch. 11. T.S. 3, 224.

103. So He drove out the man. After Adam's expulsion from Paradise, he prayed to God in these words: "O God, Lord of the World! Thou didst create the whole world unto the honor and glory of the Mighty One, and Thou didst as pleasing unto thee. Thy kingdom is unto all eternity, and Thy reign unto all generations. Naught is hidden from Thee, and naught is concealed from Thine eyes. Thou didst create me as Thy handiwork, and didst make me the ruler over Thy creatures, that I might be the chief of Thy works. But the cunning, accursed serpent seduced me with the tree of desire and lusts, yea, he seduced the wife of my bosom. But Thou didst not make known unto me what shall befall my children and the generations after me. I know well that no human being can be righteous in Thine eyes, and what is my strength that I should step before Thee with an impudent face? I have no mouth wherewith to speak and no eye wherewith to see, for I did sin and commit a trespass, and, by reason of my sins, I was driven forth from Paradise. I must plough the earth whence I was taken, and the other inhabitants of the earth, the beasts, no longer, as once, stand in awe and fear of me. From the time I ate of the tree of knowledge of good and evil, wisdom departed from me, and I am a fool that knoweth naught, an ignorant man that understandeth not. Now, O merciful and gracious God, I pray to Thee to turn again Thy compassion to the head of Thy works, to the spirit which Thou didst instill into him, and the soul Thou didst breathe into him. Meet me with Thy grace, for Thou art gracious, slow to anger, and full of love. O that my prayer would reach unto the throne of Thy glory, and my supplication unto the throne of Thy mercy, and Thou wouldst incline to me with loving-kindness. May the words of my mouth be acceptable, that Thou turn not away from my petition. Thou wert from everlasting, and Thou wilt be unto everlasting; Thou wert king, and Thou wilt ever be king. Now, have Thou mercy upon the work of Thy hands. Grant me knowledge and understanding, that I may know what shall befall me, and my posterity, and all the generations that come after me, and what shall befall me on every day and in every month, and mayest Thou not withhold from me the help of Thy servants and of Thy angels."

Safer Raziel. Ginzberg Legends, pp. 90-91.

104. **At the east (mi-kedem) of the garden of Eden, etc.**

Mi-kedem teaches that the angels were created before (*kodem*) the Garden of Eden, as it is

flaming sword which turned every way, to keep the way to the tree of life.

COMMENTARY

begotten. And in the midst between the two there is a third which unites them, Reason (the Logos), for it is through Reason that God is both Ruler and good. Of these two potencies, sovereignty and goodness, the Cherubim are symbols, as the fiery sword is the symbol of the Logos.[122] **to keep the way to the tree of life.** The purpose (of these cherubim) was to "preserve" for man the road to the tree of life, so that he might find it again. That is why God stationed the "Cherubim and the flame of the burning sword" on the road to Gan-Eden . . . These Cherubim point out the way (obedience to God's Commandments) which leads back to Gan-Eden. "The flame of the burning sword," however, shows admonishingly the ways by which Gan-Eden will never be achieved. They are the

ANTHOLOGY

written, *This is the living creature that I saw under the God of Israel by the river Chebar; and I knew that they were cherubim* (Ezek. 10:20). The text therefore means this: He placed there the cherubim, who were created before the Garden of Eden, *and the flaming sword,* by which angels are meant, so called in accordance with the verse, *His ministers are as flaming fire* (Ps. 104:4). *Which turns every way*: They (the angels) change (turn about): sometimes they appear as men, sometimes as women, sometimes as spirits, sometimes as angels.

Gen. R. 21. T.S. 3, 230.

105. **To keep the way to the tree of life.**

The first time Adam witnessed the sinking of the sun he was also seized with anxious fears. It happened at the conclusion of the Sabbath, and Adam said, "Woe is me! For my sake, because I sinned, the world is darkened, and it will again become void and without form. Thus will be executed the punishment of death which God has pronounced against me!" All the night he spent in tears, and Eve, too, wept as she sat opposite to him. When day began to dawn, he understood that what he had deplored was but the course of nature, and he brought an offering unto God, a unicorn whose horn was created before his hoofs, and he sacrificed it on the spot on which later the altar was to stand in Jerusalem.

Avodah Zorah 8a. Ginzberg Legends, Vol. 1, p. 89.

106. TO KEEP THE WAY TO THE TREE OF LIFE. Adam noticed that the days were growing shorter, and he feared the world might be darkened on account of his sin, and go under soon. To avert the doom, he spent eight days in prayer and fasting. But after the winter solstice, when he saw that the days grew longer again, he spent eight days in rejoicing, and in the following year he celebrated both periods, the one before and the one after the solstice. This is why the heathen celebrate the calends and the saturnalia in honor of their gods, though Adam had consecrated those days to the honor of God.

Ginzberg, *loc. cit.*

107. TO KEEP THE WAY TO THE TREE OF LIFE. (The Midrash relates how after that Adam repented, whereupon God absolved him, giving him the Torah as a substitute for the Garden of Eden which he had lost; thus did he indeed receive a tree of life and was absolved. The Midrash then continues:) This eventful day was the first of the month of Tishri. Therefore God spoke to Adam: "Thou shalt be the prototype of thy children. As thou hast been judged by Me on this day and absolved, so thy children Israel shall be judged by Me on this New Year's Day, and they shall be absolved."

Aboth d'R. Nathan 1, 5, 6, 8. Ginzberg, *loc. cit.,* p. 82.

108. TO KEEP THE WAY OF THE TREE OF LIFE. God concealed the tree which conferred eternal life upon all who ate thereof and gave us instead His Torah, which is the tree of life, as it says, *She is a tree of life to those who hold fast to it* (Prov. 3:18). Man peruses it and contemplates God's wisdom, learns His just, wise and

COMMENTARY

consuming flames of the ever-returning suffering, brought about by force and the hunger for power which fills the history of mankind.[123] According to S. D. Luzzatto, this story is meant as a rebuke (and at the same time a comfort) to those who complain that man suffers more and is subject to more misfortunes than all other living creatures. For the cause of this is man's haughty pride in his God-given faculties; it is this from which stem his endless sorrows and grief. Though it may appear to be a Divine punishment, in truth it is the result of His infinite goodness (presumably, in endowing him with Free Will) which should make man rejoice in his lot and give thanks to the Almighty. Similarly, the curse of the serpent is merely a graphic description of its natural characteristics, for the serpent of this narrative, subtle, upright in stature, and possessing the power of speech, existed only as a special and temporary creation in the Garden of Eden.

ANTHOLOGY

equitable laws, and makes a noble resolution and occupies himself with the study thereof and thereby acquires this world and the Hereafter, as we read, *And the Lord commanded us to do all these statutes,* to *fear the Lord our God, for our good always, that He might preserve us alive, as it is this day* (Deut. 6:24).

Midrash Hagadol B'reshith. T.S. 3, 243.

109. And God saw into the heart of Adam and Eve and knew that they had repented of the evil they had done and He had pity upon them and said, "Unhappy children! I judged you and gave you the punishment you earned, and I drove you from that most desirable place —the Garden of Eden—where you dwelt amidst the greatest pleasures, and now you have come to a place of evil and great trouble, such as you have never known till this day. Yet, know for a surety, that notwithstanding all this, My lovingkindness towards you will never cease, and My love for you will be unending. I know, however, that many trials and tribulations await you, and they will be heavy upon you and will embitter your lives. Therefore I will bring out for you from my treasure-house this pearl—the Tear—and when danger threatens you and your lot is very bitter, and you are full of sorrow and depressed—then the tears will run down from your eyes, and the burden will become lighter upon you and you will have relief." And while God was still speaking, the eyes of Adam and Eve ran with tears and they rolled down their cheeks and fell upon the ground, and those were the first tears that moistened the earth. And the more Adam and Eve shed tears the greater was their relief and comfort, and their hope revived; and the tears were an inheritance for their children and their children's children throughout their generations. No creature in the world weeps and sheds tears like man. The source of the tear which is concealed within the eye of man is always ready to ease the sorrows of his broken heart. But should man's sorrow be too great and the source of his tears becomes dry and withered, then the eye has no motion and not one tear will fall. Then there is nothing on earth, and no manner of comfort that will lighten the affliction of one so unhappy.

Bibel und Talmud Schatz. (J. B. Levner. The Legends of Israel, Par. 13.)

GENESIS

CHAPTER IV

[1]**And the man knew Eve his wife; and she conceived and bore Cain, and**

COMMENTARY

[1]**knew.** Had known before he was expelled from Eden, "knew" being a delicate expression for intimacy.[1] **gotten.** The derivation is based on the resemblance of sound between Cain and the Heb. root *kanah* — to acquire.[2] **I have gotten a man. a.** I have brought another man into the world.[3] **b.** I have gained the lasting love of my man (through the birth of

ANTHOLOGY

1. **And Adam knew Eve his wife.**

When he saw that his descendants were doomed to descend into Gehinom, he refrained from his marital duties. But when he saw that after twenty-six generations Israel would accept the Torah, he decided to perpetuate the race; hence, *And Adam knew Eve his wife.*

Gen. R. 21. T.S. 4, 1.

2. AND ADAM KNEW EVE HIS WIFE. Cain was born as the result. Her pregnancy was painless; and her delivery was likewise without pain.

Midrash Aggadah. T.S. 4, 11.

3. AND ADAM KNEW EVE HIS WIFE. Samael, riding on the serpent, came to her, and she conceived Abel, as it says, *And Adam knew Eve his wife*. What is the meaning of "*knew?*" He knew that she had conceived. As she gazed upon his likeness and saw that her offspring was not of earthly but of heavenly beings, she declared: "*I have gotten a man by* (an angel of) *the Lord.*" R. Ishmael said: From Seth were descended all the generations of the righteous, and from Cain were descended all the generations of the wicked who sinned and rebelled against the Almighty.[1]

Pirke d'Rabbi Eliezer Chap. 21. T.S. 4, 7.

4. **And bore Cain.**

R. Jose said: His name denotes that he was the source[1] of the evildoers who came into the world from the impure side.[2]

Zohar Hadash 1, 54. T.S. 4, 13.

5. AND BORE CAIN. He was thus named in anticipation of his fate, which was to become as nought (*ke-ayin*).

Midrash Hagadol. T.S. 4, 12.

6. AND BORE CAIN. R. Miasha said: Cain was born together with a twin sister; and likewise Abel. R. Simeon objected: But surely Scripture says, *And if a man shall take his sister . . . it is a shameful thing* (Lev. 20:17)? From these words, he replied, you must know that there were no other women whom they could marry, hence these were permitted to them. R. Joseph said: Cain and Abel were twins, as it is said, *And she conceived, and bore Cain;* and in that very hour she bore again, as Scripture immediately continues, *and* again *she bore his brother Abel* (ibid. 2).

Pirke d'Rabbi Eliezer Ch. 21. T.S. 4, 8.

7. **And bore Cain, and said: "I have gotten a man from the Lord."**

Why was he named Cain (which means acquisition)? Because he was formed through

§ 3 [1] R. Ishmael apparently renders: *I have gotten a man* (who will rebel) *against the Lord*. Thus she predicted the wickedness of Cain and his descendants.

§ 4 [1] Heb. *kina,* lit., nest.

[2] In cabbalistic thought evil came into the world from the "other" or "impure" side, i.e., a power seeking to frustrate God's designs for universal righteousness.

said: 'I have gotten a man with the help of the Lord.' [2]And again she bore his brother Abel. And Abel was

COMMENTARY

Cain).[4] **with the help of the Lord. a.** He alone created us, but in the creation of this child the three of us were partners.[5] **b.** This child shall be the possession of the Lord, that when we die he may serve Him.[6] **c.** Or the Heb. may simply mean "before the Lord."[7] [2]**Abel** (Hebel). **a.** She called her two sons Cain and Abel to imply that man's hold on this earth (deriving *Cain* from *kinyan* "possession") is but vanity (*hebel*). She did not desire to make

ANTHOLOGY

Adam, Eve, and God, acquiring three things from each of the three partners. Thus: breath, life, and soul[1] from God; bone, tendons, and mind from Adam; skin, flesh, and blood from Eve. For this Scripture decreed that when a man becomes unclean through a corpse he must undergo ritual purification with the waters of lustration on the third day.[2]

Midrash Tadshe Ch. 7. T.S. 4, 9.

8. I HAVE GOTTEN A MAN, etc. How do we know that the sons of Cain are called the sons of God? From Eve's remark, "*I have gotten a man from God.*"[1]

Midrash. T.S. 4, 10.

9. I HAVE GOTTEN A MAN WITH THE HELP OF GOD. R. Joshua b. Levi said: There is much to meditate upon in this chapter, and particularly in this verse, where Eve said: "*I have gotten a man with the help of God.*"[1] R. Isaac said, I understand it in its plain meaning. For we learnt: Rab Judah said, quoting Rab: When a son is born, he must be taught some Biblical verses as soon as he begins to speak, to train him in the fear of God.[2] Thus when he grows up he will remember these verses, which were indeed written for the very purpose of inculcating the fear of God.

Midrash Haneelam Zohar Hadash 19. T.S. 4, 16.

10. I HAVE GOTTEN A MAN WITH THE HELP OF GOD. It is written, *I said that this also is vanity* (Eccl. 8:14). The Rabbis referred this to Jethro, Moses' father-in-law, who was called the Kenite because he was descended from Cain. Then arose the Holy Lamp[1] and said: For this reason it says, *I have gotten a man with the help of God:* Eve saw by the holy spirit that his (Jethro's) descendants would one day sit in the Chamber of Hewn Stones.[2]

Zohar Hadash 3:216. T.S. 4, 15.

11. **And again she bore his brother Abel.**

It was taught: On the very day of their creation Adam and Eve retired to rest, two people only; but when they left their couch, they were four. R. Judah b. Baba said: When they left their couch, they were six, having given birth to Cain and his sister Knunto, and Abel and his sister Lubdao.

Midrash Hagadol. T.S. 4, 25.

§ 7 [1] The exact meaning of the three Hebrew words is doubtful. *Ruah* is variously translated as breath, spirit, and wind; *nefesh* means life or soul; and *n'shamah* is generally rendered soul, though it may also mean breath.
[2] See Num. 19:11-12, 17-19.

§ 8 [1] Referring to Cain. Hence he and his children are "*from God,*" i.e., His children.

§ 9 [1] Apparently he found it strange that the birth of Cain, who was fated to be a murderer, should be announced in such terms. Or perhaps: This verse shows that Cain's destiny was indeed solely to serve God (rendering: I have gotten a man to serve God), but he proved faithless to his destiny.
[2] This text itself is such a verse, for it teaches that one owes one's very existence to the Almighty.

§ 10 [1] R. Simeon b. Yohai, who is generally thus designated in the Zohar.
[2] This was the chamber in the Temple where sat the highest Sanhedrin (Supreme Court). The idea is that even from the most unpromising ancestors there may be noble descendants. Cain was a murderer, yet Jethro (himself regarded as a proselyte) was descended from him, and his descendants in turn occupied the loftiest positions in Israel—truly this breathes the spirit of universalism! The text is apparently rendered: I have gotten a man who will be with God—if not himself, then in his descendants.

a keeper of sheep, but Cain was a tiller of the ground. [3]And in process of time it came to pass, that Cain

COMMENTARY

this pessimism explicit, so Scripture does not give the interpretation of Abel as it does of Cain.[8] **b.** In Assyrian, *ablu* means "son." The Heb. word signifies "a breath," like his life, so tragically brief. As the younger brother, Abel is given the lighter task of caring for the flocks; while Cain assists his father in the cultivation of the soil.[9] **[3]in the process of time. a.** After a certain time.[10] **b.** A year after he began to cultivate the soil.[11] **offering. a.** The Heb. *minhah* denotes a propitiatory offering to a ruler. Cain thus sought to win God's favor to make the soil productive.[12] **b.** This is the first mention of worship in Scripture. The religious instinct is part of man's nature, and sacrifice

ANTHOLOGY

12. **And Abel was a keeper of sheep.**

Because he feared the curse which God had pronounced against the ground, as it says, *In toil shalt thou eat of it* (3:17). He therefore preferred being a shepherd, caring for flocks and herds. Cain, on the other hand, being stiff-necked, defiant, and not fearing God, said: "I choose to be a husbandman," and he persisted in tilling the soil, defying the decree, declaring that the curse applied only to Adam, who had sinned, and not to any other.

Midrash Aggadah. T.S. 4, 23.

13. AND ABEL WAS A KEEPER OF SHEEP, etc. Abel loved to be a herdsman, whilst Cain preferred husbandry, tilling the earth and sowing. They would exchange with each other the products of their respective pursuits for their maintenance.

Pirke d'Rabbi Eliezer Ch. 21. T.S. 4, 22.

14. **But Cain was a tiller of the ground.**

Whence do we learn that abstinence from wine prolongs life? From the fact that four men who had a passion for (the vine of) the earth proved to be unworthy, viz.: Cain, Noah, Lot, and Uzziah. Cain: *But Cain was a tiller of the ground.*[1] Noah: *And Noah the husbandman began, and planted a* vineyard (9:20). Lot: *And Lot lifted up his eyes, and beheld all the plain of the Jordan, that it was rich in drink* (13:10).[2] Uzziah: *For he loved the ground* (2 Chron. 26:10).[1]

Mekilta of R. Simeon b. Yohai, Jethro 18, 27. T.S. 4, 20.

15. **And it came to pass at the end of some time, etc.**

Three were smitten with leprosy: Cain, Job, and Uzziah, because they had a passion for property and not for the Torah. Now, Scripture relates: *Cain was a tiller of the soil.* He ate his fill and was satiated, and brought as an offering only what was left over, as the narrative continues, *And it came to pass at the* end *of some time* (but not at the beginning), for he did not study the Torah, which says, *The choicest* first-fruits *of thy land thou shalt bring into the house of the Lord your God* (Exod. 23:19). He was banished from the haunts of men (like a leper), as Scripture says, *A fugitive and a wanderer shalt thou be in the earth* (4:12). He was smitten with leprosy, as it says, *And the Lord set a* sign *for Cain* (ibid. 15). Now, we know that this sign was leprosy, because in the case of Hezekiah it is written, *What is the* sign (Isa. 38:22)? whilst earlier it says, *and lay it for a plaster on the* leprous *boil* (ibid. 21).[1]

Yelamdenu. T.S. 4, 26.

16. AND IT CAME TO PASS AT THE END OF SOME TIME (LIT., DAYS). Sometimes *"at the end"* means after a year, sometimes after two

§ 14 [1] In both cases it is assumed (possibly on the strength of an ancient tradition) that they engaged in viniculture.
[2] AJV: That it was well-watered (Heb. *mashkeh*) everywhere. The Heb. can mean any liquid, and it is here understood to refer to wine.

§ 15 [1] Thus *"sign"* is used of leprosy.

brought of the fruit of the ground an offering unto the Lord. [4]And Abel, he also brought of the firstlings

COMMENTARY

is the earliest outward expression of that worship. Its purpose was to express acknowledgment of His bounty to the Giver of all.[13] [4]**firstlings.** The most highly-prized among the flocks.[14] **of the fat thereof. a.** Of the fattest of them.[15] **b.** Literally, of their fat pieces.[16] On the latter interpretation the sacrifice was a peace-offering, of which the fat only was burned on the altar.[17] **c.** Of the first milk of ewes delivered of their firstlings.[18] **had respect unto.** I.e., accepted. God signified His preference for Abel by a fire that descended from heaven and consumed his

ANTHOLOGY

years. Again "*days*" is used literally as an indefinite period, yet it may also mean forty years.[1] Our Sages of blessed memory said: Cain and Abel were forty years old when they brought their offerings.

Tanhuma B'reshith Par. 9. T.S. 4, 28.

17. AND IN THE PROCESS OF TIME IT CAME TO PASS. It was the time of Passover; Adam then said to his sons: "One day all the people of Israel will at this season bring their paschal sacrifices, and they will be favorably accepted by God. This is therefore a propitious time for you too to bring your sacrifices to God, and God will be pleased with you."

Midrash Aggadah B'reshith. T.S. 4, 29.

18. **And Cain brought of the fruit of the earth an offering unto the Lord.**

It was of the leavings, like a bad steward who ate the first fruit himself, and honored the king with the shrivelled late fruits. Our Rabbis say: It consisted of flax-seed. Now, Scripture continues: *And Abel, he also brought of the firstlings of his flock and of the fat thereof*, i.e., its wool. For this reason the blending of flax and wool was forbidden, as we read, *Thou shalt not wear a mingled stuff, linen and wool together* (Deut. 22:11). Said the Almighty: "It is not proper to mingle the offering of a sinner with the offering of the righteous."

Midrash Aggadah B'reshith; Tanhuma B'reshith Par. 9. T.S. 4, 30. 31.

19. **And Abel, he also brought, etc.**

Sacrifice brings Israel nigh the Shekinah. Thus Noah came closer to God when he brought an offering, as it says, *And Noah builded an altar unto the Lord* (8:20). It is also written, *And he* (Abraham) *builded there an altar unto the Lord* (12:7); *And* (Isaac) *builded an altar there, and called upon the Name of the Lord* (26:25); *And* (Israel) *offered sacrifices unto the God of his father Isaac* (46:1). Similarly Abel, of whom Scripture says, *And Abel, he also brought*, etc.

Midrash Haseroth Viy'theroth. T.S. 4, 33.

20. AND ABEL, HE ALSO BROUGHT, etc. His sacrifice was of the fattest of his flock. Fire descended from heaven and devoured Abel's offering, but left Cain's untouched. Another indication of God's acceptance and rejection of their respective offerings was that Abel's affairs prospered, whilst Cain's languished. For this reason Scripture states, *And the Lord had respect unto Abel and to his offerings*. Because Abel brought his offering in a spirit of gladness and eagerness, it was indeed pleasing to God. Of him Scripture writes, *Then shall the offering of Judah and Jerusalem* be pleasant *unto the Lord, as in the days of old, and as in ancient years* (Mal. 3:4). Rabbi said: *As in the days of old* means as in the days of Noah, as it says, *For this is as the waters of Noah unto Me* (Isa. 54:9); while *as in ancient years* means as in the days of Abel, when idolatry was unknown. R. Judah said: Cain's offering was

§ 16 [1] This may be based on the fact that the forty years which the Israelites wandered in the wilderness are described as "*many days*" (cf. Deut. 2:1, which was said at the end of their wanderings).

of his flock and of the fat thereof. And the Lord had respect unto Abel and to his offering; [5]but unto Cain and to his offering He had not respect. And Cain was very wroth, and his countenance fell. [6]And the Lord said unto Cain: 'Why art thou wroth? and why is thy countenance fallen? [7]If thou doest well, shall it

COMMENTARY

sacrifice;[19] or, Cain inferred that from Abel's subsequent prosperity.[20] **[5]He had not respect. a.** No fire descended upon it.[21] **b.** The sacrifice was not followed by an increase in the produce of the soil.[22] **c.** Each of the brothers brings a sacrifice to God. These sacrifices are as old as mankind itself. They are the natural expression of human emotions and thoughts. They represent the personality of their sponsors, and their acceptance depends on the sponsor and the thoughts which accompany his sacrifice. Significantly it does not say, "God turned to the sacrifice of Abel," but, "God turned to Abel and his sacrifices, but to Cain and his sacrifices He did not turn."[23] **wroth.** through jealousy of Abel.[24] **his countenance fell. a.** His head drooped in

ANTHOLOGY

in a spirit of arrogance, while Abel's was in a spirit of humility; and Scripture writes, *The sacrifices of God are a broken spirit* (Ps. 51:19). Cain felt disgraced that his offering had been rejected, and so *he was very wroth, and his countenance fell.*

Midrash Hagadol; Midrash Aggadah and P'sikta Zuta on B'reshith; Midrash Haneelam Zohar Hadash 19. T.S. 4, 39. 40. 44. 45. 46.

21. **Of the firstlings of his flock and of the fat thereof.**

That means, of sheep which were unshorn and unused in labor, and not employed in the commission of any sin.

Midrash Hagadol B'reshith. T.S. 4, 34.

22. **And the Lord had respect unto Abel and to his offering.**

Scripture writes, *And God seeketh that which is pursued* (Eccl. 3:15). R. Judah b. R. Simon said: The Holy One, blessed be He, always demands the blood of the pursued from their pursuers. The proof of this is that Abel was pursued by Cain, and the Almighty chose Abel, as it says, *And the Lord had respect unto Abel and to his offering.*

Lev. R. 27. T.S. 4, 36.

23. AND THE LORD HAD RESPECT, etc. Sacrifices are a test proving the distinction between the righteous and the wicked. The story of Cain and Abel attests this, as it says, *And the Lord had respect unto Abel and to his offering; but unto Cain and to his offering He had not respect.*

Midrash Tadshe Ch. 13. T.S. 4, 38.

24. AND THE LORD HAD RESPECT UNTO ABEL AND TO HIS OFFERING. The Psalmist sings: *For the Lord taketh pleasure in His people* (Ps. 149:4). R. Joshua of Siknin in the name of R. Levi interpreted this: The Holy One, blessed be He, taketh pleasure in the sacrifices of Israel. *He adorneth the humble with salvation* (ibid.) means that He is glorified by the sacrifices of the humble and poor, for "*salvation*" (Heb. *y'shuah*) implies sacrifice, as it is written, *And the Lord had respect* (*va-yisha*, same root as *y'shuah*) *unto Abel and to his offering.*

P'sikta Rabbathi. T.S. 4, 37.

25. **If thou doest well, wilt thou not receive?**

Scripture writes: *Behold, I set before you this day a blessing and a curse: the blessing, if ye shall hearken unto the commandments of the Lord your God . . . and the curse, if ye shall not hearken* (Deut. 11:26-27). Similarly our text states: *If thou doest well, wilt thou not receive?* — a blessing; *and if thou doest not well, wilt thou not receive?* — a curse.

Sifre R'eh 54. T.S. 4, 48.

not be lifted up? and if thou doest not well, sin coucheth at the door;

COMMENTARY

shame.[25] **b.** He lost his wonted cheerfulness.[26] **6Why art thou wroth?** Why are you jealous, as though My acceptance of Abel's offering was arbitrary?[27] **and why is thy countenance fallen?** You need not grieve so much for the wrong you committed, seeing that you can readily make atonement.[28] **7If thou doest well.** By ceasing to harbor rancor and jealousy.[29] **lifted up. a.** Your countenance, which has fallen.[30] **b.** You shall be exalted above your brother in dignity (for this meaning of the Heb. *s'eth* cf. 49:3), for you are the firstborn.[31] **c.** You

ANTHOLOGY

26. IF THOU DOEST WELL, SHALL IT NOT BE LIFTED UP? *If thou doest well,* I will forgive thee thine iniquities; but if not, thy sin overflows the brim. R. Berekiah quoted in R. Simeon b. Ammi's name: *Happy is he who is uplifted over transgression, whose sin is pardoned* (Ps. 32:1): this means, happy is he who is master over his transgressions, but his transgressions are not master over him.

Gen. R. 22. T.S. 4, 52.

27. IF THOU DOEST WELL, etc. God thus said to Israel: "My children, I created the Evil Inclination, but I also created its antidote. As long as you occupy yourself with the study of the Torah, the Evil Inclination will have no dominion over you." For it is written, *If thou doest well, wilt thou not be accepted?* The power of the Enticer ends at the door of the House of Study. He cannot enter within, though he be one's companion all the way. Thus Scripture says, *Sin coucheth at the door* (but can go no further). The Evil Inclination cannot have dominion over him who occupies himself with the Torah. "But if you do not concern yourself with the Torah, you will fall to its lure"; as it says, *and if thou doest not well, sin coucheth at the door.* "Moreover, it will seek complete control over you," as it says, *and unto thee is its desire.* "However, if you really wish it, you can master it," as Scripture concludes, *but thou mayest rule over it.*

Sifre Ekeb Par. 45; Midrash on Psalms 119. T.S. 4, 49. 60.

28. IF THOU DOEST WELL, etc. R. Judah said: What does this verse mean? If thy conduct is proper, thou wilt enjoy the dignity (*s'eth* — AJV: it will be lifted up) due to thee as firstborn, for *s'eth* has the same meaning here as in the verse, *Reuben, thou art my firstborn . . .* (to thee pertaineth) *the excellence of dignity* (s'eth) (49:3). Such, indeed, is the permanent privilege of the firstborn in all things, provided he properly demeans himself. Our text continues: *And if thou doest not well, sin coucheth at the door.* By *"door"* is meant the door of the Heavenly Court, whence issue decrees against the evildoers of the earth. At that very door coucheth sin, *"sin"* being none other than the Angel of Death, ready to exact retribution.

Zohar Hadash 1, 33. T.S. 4, 66.

29. IF THOU DOEST WELL, WILT THOU NOT BE ACCEPTED (S'ETH). God said to Cain: "If from now on you change your way for the better, the past will be forgiven," *s'eth* meaning forgiveness, as in the verse, *Thou hast forgiven* (*nasatha,* same root as *s'eth*) *the iniquity of Thy people* (Ps. 85:3). "But if not, *sin coucheth at the door:* you surrender to the Tempter that lies in wait at your door."

Midrash Hagadol B'reshith. T.S. 4, 64.

30. **Sin coucheth at the door.**

Although *hattath,* the Heb. for sin, is a feminine noun, yet the verb in this phrase is in the masculine: at first sin is weak, like a woman, but then it grows strong, like a man. R. Akiba said: Though no more than a spider's thread at first, eventually it is like a ship's rope, as it is written, *Woe to them that draw iniquity with the flimsiest of cords, and sin as it were with a cart rope* (Isa. 5:18). R. Isaac said: At first it is like a passing visitor, then like

COMMENTARY

can reach the heights of exaltation.[32] **d.** You shall earn forgiveness.[33] **and if thou doest not well.** If you do not relinquish your grudge and malice, **sin coucheth at the door. a.** You will be ready to lapse into greater sin — sin as painfully real as if it were lying in wait for you at your door-step to encompass your

ANTHOLOGY

a guest who stays longer, and finally like the master of the house. Thus it is written, *And there came a* traveller *unto the rich man* (2 Sam. 12:4): (this pictures the Tempter) as a traveller who passes on; *and he spared to take of his own flock and of his own herd, to dress for the* guest *that was come unto him* (ibid.): now he is a guest; *and he dressed it for the* man *that was come to him* (ibid.): he is now the master. R. Hanina b. Papa said: If the Tempter comes to beguile you, repulse him with the words of the Torah. Yet should you think that you cannot control him, Scripture writes, *When the Tempter layeth siege, thou wilt* master him *completely, for he is in thy control* (Isa. 26:3).[1] Moreover, I have already written in the Torah, says God, *And unto thee is its desire, but thou mayest rule over it.*

Gen. R. 22. T.S. 4, 54.

31. Sin coucheth at the door. Rab said: The evil impulse is like a fly and dwells between the two entrances of the heart, as it is said, *Dead flies make the ointment of the perfumer fetid and putrid* (Ecc. 10:1). Samuel said: It is like a grain of wheat (*hittah*), as it is said, *Sin* (hattath) *coucheth at the door.*[1]

Berakoth 61a. T.S. 4, 55.

32. Sin coucheth at the door. Antoninus asked Rabbi: "From what time does the Evil Tempter hold sway over man: from when the embryo is formed, or from when he issues forth into the world?" "From the formation," he replied. "If so," he objected, "it would rebel in its mother's womb and go forth. Hence it must be from when he is born." Rabbi observed: This thing Antoninus taught me, and Scripture supports him, for it says, *Sin coucheth at the door* (of man's entrance into the world).

Sanhedrin 91b. T.S. 4, 57.

33. Sin coucheth at the door. R. Simlai lectured: The embryo in its mother's womb is taught the Torah from beginning to end. But as it is about to come into the world an angel comes and strikes it on its mouth, which makes it forget the whole Torah, as it says, *Sin coucheth at the door.*[1]

Niddah 30b. T.S. 4, 58.

34. Sin coucheth at the door. R. Reuben b. Eztrubli said: How can one flee from the evil impulse within him, seeing that the first approach of man toward woman is the result of passion? Moreover, this evil impulse lurks at the very door of the heart, as it says, *Sin coucheth at the door.*

Aboth d'Rabbi Nathan Chap. 16. T.S. 4, 59.

35. Sin coucheth at the door. He who dwells without a wife, though his drawn sword be in his hand, yet will the Evil Inclination conquer him. It will follow him into the market-place, watching for every opportunity to make him perish from the earth altogether, as it says, *Sin coucheth at the door.* Satan will drive him to drink from a cup that does not belong to him and so destroy himself, as it says, *He that committeth adultery with a woman . . . would destroy his own soul* (Prov. 6:32).

Midrash. T.S. 4, 65.

§ 30 [1] This apparently is the Midrashic rendering of the verse: AJV: *The mind stayed on Thee Thou keepest in perfect peace, because it trusteth in Thee.*

§ 31 [1] Probably both mean that the evil impulse at the beginning is but a light thing, which if opposed there and then can easily be vanquished.

§ 33 [1] At the entrance to life, because the Torah is forgotten.

and unto thee is its desire, but thou mayest rule over it.' [8]And Cain spoke unto Abel his brother. And it came

COMMENTARY

ruin.[34] **b.** It coucheth at the door of the grave, i.e., punishment awaits you there.[35] **unto thee is its desire. a.** The tempter ever seeks to entice thee.[36] **b.** Sin is willing to submit to you, if only you desire it.[37] **c.** The phrase harks back to verse 7: If you do well, your brother will obey you and you will rule over him, as befits the first-born.[38] **but thou mayest rule over it. a.** You can conquer it, if you wish.[39] **b.** Repentance and forgiveness are always open to you.[40] [8]**spoke. a.** He engaged him in conversation in order to draw him into a quarrel.[41] **b.** He related to Abel what God had said to him;[42] this put Abel off his guard.[43] **c.** Many old codices have a *piska*

ANTHOLOGY

36. **And unto thee is its desire.**

The Evil Inclination seeks mastery only over Cain and his ilk, as it says, *And unto thee* (Cain) *is its desire.* Another interpretation: All the passion and desire of the Evil Inclination will be bent solely on thee; yet if thou wilt, thou canst rule him.

Song R. 7:16; P'sikta Zuta B'reshith. T.S. 4, 61. 67.

37. AND UNTO THEE IS ITS DESIRE. Scripture says, *And Satan came also among them* (Job 2:1). He was permitted to enter within. So too it is stated in the case of Cain, *Sin coucheth at the door:* it all depends on thee. If so be thy wish, then *unto thee is its desire,* and it will take possession of thy very body. But if thou desirest, thou canst overawe it, and it will flee. In the same way, God said, the Tempter lurks over every generation. If he attains mastery over a man, sin will have dominion over him. But if a man masters his Evil Impulse, it will flee from him, while the man's good angel will commend his good deeds to his Creator.

Midrash Job 2. T.S. 4, 62.

38. **But thou mayest rule over it.**

R. Judah said: That day was New Year, the day when all souls pass before Him for judgment. Said the Almighty to Cain: Why be wroth? . . . *If thou doest well, shalt thou not be forgiven,* that is to say, If you make amends, you shall be forgiven. *And if thou doest not well, sin coucheth at the door,* which means, At the door of the Garden of Eden through which the souls pass, there your sins lie in wait for you, and there you will receive your punishment. *And unto thee is its desire:* If you amend your deed, though sin longs for you to transgress, *thou mayest rule over it,* and it cannot become your accuser.

Midrash Haneelam 19. T.S. 4, 68.

39. **And Cain spoke unto Abel his brother.**

Cain thought he had been wronged, and a dispute followed between him and Abel. "I believed," he said, "that the world was created through goodness, but I see that good deeds bear no fruit. God rules the world with arbitrary power, else why had He respect unto thy offering, and not unto mine also?" Abel opposed him; he maintained that God rewards good deeds, without having respect unto persons. If his sacrifice was accepted graciously by God and Cain's not, it was because his deeds were good, and his brother's wicked.

Yerushalmi Targumim a.l. Ginzberg Legends, 1, 108.

40. AND CAIN SPOKE UNTO ABEL HIS BROTHER, etc. What did they quarrel about? Cain and Abel divided the world between them, one taking all the land, and the other taking everything movable. Said one to the other, "The ground you stand on is mine," to which he rejoined, "The garment you wear is mine." "Put off your dress!" cried one; "Fly into the air!" cried the other. While thus quarreling, Cain arose and slew his brother Abel. R. Joshua of Siknin said, citing Resh Lakish: Both took land and moveables. About what then

to pass, when they were in the field, that Cain rose up against Abel his brother, and slew him. [9]And the

COMMENTARY

(a vertical line, denoting a break in the sentence) after "brother," this suggesting that "let us go into the field" is to be supplied after it.[44] **when they were in the field.** Away from their parents'

ANTHOLOGY

did they quarrel? Each demanded that the Temple be built on *his* territory, as Scripture records: *And it came to pass, when they were in the* field: "*field*" alludes to the Holy Temple, as we read, *Zion* (i.e., the Temple) *shall be plowed like a* field (Micah 3:12). In the heat of the quarrel *Cain rose up against Abel his brother, and slew him.*

Gen. R. 22. T.S. 4, 69.

41. AND CAIN SPOKE UNTO ABEL HIS BROTHER. What did he say to him? "Come, let us divide the world between us. I being the first-born will take a double portion." "Agreed," said Abel, "but that being so, I will then take in addition to my portion the place where my sacrifice was favorably received by God." But Cain refused, whereupon strife broke out between them, as it says, *And it came to pass, when they were in the field;* while elsewhere it is written, *Zion* (i.e., the Temple) *shall be plowed like a field* (Micah 3:12).[1]

Tanhuma B'reshith Par. 9. T.S. 4, 70.

42. **And it came to pass, when they were in the field.**

Cain proposed to Abel: "Since you maintain that there is a future world, let us divide. I will take this present world for my portion, and you take the other world as yours." When Cain discovered Abel pasturing his flocks in the field, he remonstrated, "Have we not already divided the world between us, this world falling to me? Why then do you pasture your flocks in my portion?" Abel replied: "It was never my intention, when agreeing to your proposal, to leave my flocks without pasture, since they must have pasture ground." This exchange of angry words led to a quarrel, and Cain killed Abel.

Midrash Aggadah B'reshith. T.S. 4, 74.

43. **And Cain rose up against his brother Abel, etc.**

R. Johanan said: Abel was stronger than Cain, for the expression *rose up* can only imply that he (Cain) lay beneath him. He (Cain) said to him, "We two only are in the world: what will you tell our father if you kill me?" At this he was filled with compassion and released him, whereupon Cain rose up and slew him. Out of that incident was born the proverb, "Do not good to the evil, and evil will not befall you."

Gen. R. 22. T.S. 4, 76.

44. CAIN ROSE UP AGAINST ABEL HIS BROTHER, AND SLEW HIM. Three meditated evil, and God exposed their wicked designs to all mankind. They were Cain, Esau, and Absalom. Cain said in his heart, "I will slay my brother and inherit the whole world," as it says, *Cain rose up against Abel his brother, and slew him.* God revealed his evil design to all, as it says, *And now cursed art thou from the ground that opened her mouth . . . when thou tillest the ground, it shall not henceforth yield unto thee her strength.*[1]

Aboth d'Rabbi Nathan Ch. 45.
T.S. 4, 77.

45. CAIN ROSE UP AGAINST ABEL HIS BROTHER, AND SLEW HIM. In the Song of Songs the Shulammite exclaims: *Oh that thou wert as my*

§ 41 [1] As "*field*" in the proof-text refers to sacrifices, so is it interpreted in our text as bearing upon the sacrifices which they had offered. The translation follows the emendations suggested in T.S. a.l.

§ 44 [1] By not yielding her strength the ground would expose his evil designs. Possibly too he renders it: *Cursed art thou* on account of the ground, i.e., because you coveted the *whole* earth.

Lord said unto Cain: 'Where is Abel thy brother?' And he said: 'I know

COMMENTARY

presence.[45] **[9]Where is Abel thy brother?** God knew well, but asked him to give him an opportunity

ANTHOLOGY

brother! (8:1). But the question arises, as which brother? From the beginning of creation to the present day, history's record of brothers is that they hate each other. Cain hated and killed his brother, as it says, *And Cain rose up against Abel his brother, and slew him.* (The Midrash concludes: She meant a brother like Joseph and Benjamin, and Moses and Aaron.)

Targum Jonathan on Exodus 1:24. T.S. 4, 79.

46. AND CAIN ROSE UP, etc. It is written, *Whoso diggeth a pit shall fall therein; and he that rolleth a stone, it shall return upon him* (Prov. 26:27). Cain killed his brother with a stone. How did he kill him? He took a stone and smote him on every limb, wounding him again and again. How do we know this? Because Lamech said to his wives, *"For I have slain a man by wounding him* (4:23) until he died."[1] Cain too was killed with a stone, as it is written, *And Cain went out from the presence of the Lord,* etc. (verse 16). There a stone fell on him and he died, thus exemplifying the truth of the verse, *And he that rolleth a stone,* etc.

Aggadath B'reshith Chap. 26. T.S. 4, 81.

47. **Where is *(ey)* Abel thy brother?**

God said to him: "Alas *(way)* for Abel your brother, who was merciful and did not kill you when you fell before him; yet you attacked and killed him!" To God's question, *"Where is thy brother Abel?"* he answered, "I know not; am I my brother's guardian? Thou, God, art the Guardian of all, and Thou demandest him of me!" This may be likened to a thief who stole in the night, without being caught. But in the morning the watchman seized him and demanded, "Why did you rob the houses?" "I stole," replied he, "and did not neglect my profession. But you, the watchman, neglected your duty, and now you rebuke me!" So too, Cain challenged God. "I slew Abel, for Thou didst create an evil impulse within me. But Thou art the Guardian of all, yet Thou didst permit me to slay him! Thou, who art proclaimed as 'I,'[1] hast slain him, for hadst Thou accepted my sacrifice as Thou didst his, I would not have envied and slain him." R. Simeon b. Yohai said: It is difficult to say this thing, and the mouth cannot utter it. This may be compared to two athletes wrestling before the king; had the king wished, he could have separated them. But he did not so desire, and one defeated the other and killed him, the latter crying out before he died, "Who will plead my cause against the king!" "Even so," God declared, *"The voice of thy brother's blood crieth out against Me."*[2]

Tanhuma B'reshith Par. 9; Gen. R. 22. T.S. 4, 84, 90.

48. WHERE IS ABEL THY BROTHER? R. Johanan said: Cain, now knowing that all secrets are revealed before the Omnipresent, took his brother's corpse and hid it in the ground. The Holy One, blessed be He, said to him: "Where is Abel thy brother?" He replied: "Sovereign of the world! A keeper of vine-

§ 46 [1] See *infra ad loc.*, where "the man" is referred to Cain, whom he killed by wounding. It is assumed therefore that Cain killed Abel in like manner. But the manner of death is there differently described.

§ 47 [1] In Exod. 20:2: *I am the Lord thy God.* He renders it: Thou, the "I," art my brother's Guardian—as Thou art the Guardian of all Thy creatures. The philosophic idea of this bold passage is apparently a challenge to the belief in free will, on the grounds of one's innate propensity to evil, whereby God is made responsible for man's crimes. However, it is much more likely that its purpose is precisely the opposite, to *uphold* free will by a *reductio ad absurdum*, by showing that the inevitable corollary of denying free will is to make God responsible for all evil.

[2] This reads עָלַי (against Me) instead of אֵלַי (unto Me).

not; am I my brother's keeper?' [10]And He said: 'What hast thou done? the voice of thy brother's blood crieth unto Me from the

COMMENTARY

to confess and repent.[46] **am I my brother's keeper? a.** I alone?[47] **b.** Cain's answer is both false and insolent. Only a murderer altogether renounces the obligations of brotherhood.[48] **[10]What hast thou done?** The note of interrogation should be replaced by a note of exclamation. The meaning is: What a deed of horror hast thou wrought! This is further indicated by the fact that the word "brother" is used no less than six times in verses 8-11.[49] **the voice.** This can not mean "the voice of thy brother's blood crieth unto me," for the subject (*kol*, "voice") is in the singular, whereas "crieth " (*tzoakim*) is in the plural. Hence "crieth" (better, cry) must refer to "blood," which appears here also in the plural (*d'mei*). Hence it must be rendered: The voice of thy brother is heard; his blood crieth, etc.[50] **b.** Or *kol*="hark!" — Hark! the blood of thy brother, etc.[51] **thy brother's blood.** The Hebrew for *blood* is plural, i.e., the blood of thy brother and of his (potential) descendants, all of whom thou hast slain. Alternatively, Cain wounded him in many places, from all of which blood gushed forth, because he did not know where it would be fatal.[52] **crieth unto Me.** For vengeance. See Job 16:18: O, *earth, cover not thou my blood, and let my cry have no resting-place.*[53]

ANTHOLOGY

yard and field hast Thou made me. A keeper of my brother Thou hast not made me"; as it says, *Am I my brother's keeper? "Hast thou killed, and also taken possession?"* (1 Kings 21:19), came the Divine accusation, "*The voice of thy brother's blood crieth unto me from the ground.*" On thus hearing the Divine speech Cain was stricken with terror. Another version: "Dost Thou suffer talebearers in Thy presence?" he exclaimed. "My father and mother are on earth, yet they do not know that I have slain him; whereas Thou art in heaven — whence then dost Thou know?" "Fool," He replied, "I bear the whole world; yet thou canst imagine that I do not know what thou hast done!"

Pirke d'Rabbi Eliezer Ch. 21; Yelamdenu. T.S. 4, 86, 91.

49. WHERE IS ABEL THY BROTHER? Whoever confesses his errors, God delivers and admits him into the life of the Hereafter. But him who does not confess He curses. Thus, when Cain murdered Abel, God asked him, "*Where is Abel thy brother?*" Cain answered: "O Master of the universe, Abel and I brought offerings unto Thee; his Thou didst accept, whilst me Thou didst turn away sick at heart. Dost Thou demand him of me! Nay, Thou alone art accountable for him, for Thou art the Keeper of all!" "I will indeed show thee where Abel is," God replied, and immediately cursed him, as it says, *And now cursed art thou from the ground.*

Shitah Hadashah Birkath Jacob. T.S. 4, 88.

50. **Am I my brother's keeper?**

This is like the case of a man who entered a garden, and gathered mulberries and ate them. The owner of the garden pursued him, demanding, "What are you holding?" "Nothing," replied he. "But surely your hands are stained with juice!" Similarly, when Cain defiantly answered, *Am I my brother's keeper?*, God hurled at him the accusation, "Wretch! *The voice of thy brother's blood crieth unto Me from the ground.*"

Gen. R. 22. T.S. 4, 82.

51. **The voice of thy brother's blood cries unto me.**

The Mishnah states: How do we impress witnesses in capital cases with the grave consequences of their testimony?[1] We say to them: Know well that capital cases are quite different from civil cases. In the latter, a false witness can make monetary restitution and thus find atonement. But in capital cases a false witness is guilty of the blood of his victim and that

§ 51 [1] Witnesses were not sworn, but impressed with the gravity of false testimony.

ground. [11]And now cursed art thou from the ground, which hath opened her mouth to receive thy brother's blood from thy hand. [12]When thou tillest the ground, it shall not henceforth yield unto thee her strength; a fugitive and a wanderer shalt thou

COMMENTARY

[11]**from. a.** Better, "more than": cursed art thou, more than the ground which was cursed on account of Adam (cf. 3:17).[54] **b.** From the ground shall come your curse.[55] **c.** Cursed art thou from dwelling upon the ground, etc., i.e., He informed him that his punishment would be exile from the land of his birth.[56] **d.** Viz., that it shall not henceforth yield unto you her strength.[57] **to receive.** You made the ground hide your crime; as a punishment the ground will not yield you her produce.[58] [12]**When thou tillest.** Wherever he lives, the curse will follow him

ANTHOLOGY

of his children and his children's children till the end of time. For thus we find that when Cain killed Abel, he was accused, *The voice of thy brother's bloods cries unto Me from the ground.* It does not say, thy brother's blood, but, *thy brother's bloods* (lit. translation), which means, his blood and the blood of his descendants who might have been born. Another interpretation of the plural is that his blood was scattered in many places, upon trees and stones.

Mishnah Sanhedrin 37a. T.S. 4, 89.

52. **And now cursed art thou from the ground.**

When the Egyptians were drowned in the Red Sea, the sea cast them up on the dry land; but the land refused to harbor them and threw them back again into the sea, protesting: "For receiving the blood of Abel, who was but a single person, I was told, *Cursed art thou;*[1] how then shall I receive the blood of this vast multitude!" She (the sea) persisted in her refusal until God swore to her that He would not bring her to judgment.

Mekilta B'shallah 9:15, 12. T.S. 4, 92.

53. **It shall not henceforth yield unto thee her strength.**

Her strength it shall not yield unto thee, but it shall yield the fruit of *thy* strength; it shall not yield *all* her strength, yet it shall yield part of her strength.[1]

Gen. R. 22. T.S. 4, 96.

54. **A fugitive and a wanderer shalt thou be.**

Great is the efficacy of prayer before God. R. Eleazar said: If you would know the power of prayer, see: if it does not achieve its whole purpose, it yet achieves half. Thus Cain murdered his brother, for which he was sentenced, *A fugitive and a wanderer shalt thou be in the earth.* But he immediately confessed his crime and pleaded, "*Is my iniquity too great to be pardoned?*" (verse 13). "Sovereign of the Universe!" cried he, "canst Thou not bear my sin? It is written, *Who is a God like unto Thee, that pardoneth iniquity?* (Micah 7:18). Then pardon my crime, great though it be." Straightway he found grace in God's eyes, and half of his sentence, that he become a fugitive, was remitted. For thus it is written, *And Cain . . . dwelt in the land of Nod* (i.e., wandering, but not a fugitive). From this you may learn how great is the efficacy of prayer before God.

Deut. R. 8. T.S. 4, 98.

55. **Thou shalt be *na* and *nad* (AJV: a fugitive and a vagabond).**

Na means that he was condemned to wander from his native place; *nad,* that he would nowhere be at rest, for his body would ceaselessly reel, like a drunkard. However, when he re-

§ 52 [1] This was understood as a curse upon the earth, not simply upon Cain, for receiving Abel's blood.

§ 53 [1] Thus was the curse mitigated; indeed it became a blessing in disguise. Not idleness but a life of fruitful activity — this was in effect God's declaration.

be in the earth.' [13]And Cain said unto the Lord: 'My punishment is greater than I can bear. [14]Behold, Thou hast driven me out this day from the face of the land; and from Thy face shall I be hid; and I shall be a fugitive and a wanderer in the earth; and it will

COMMENTARY

and the soil will be barren for him. The remainder of his existence will consequently be an unceasing vagabondage.[59] **a fugitive and a wanderer.** Trembling and driven from place to place.[60] **[13]My punishment is greater than I can bear. a.** Is my sin too great to be borne?" i.e., to be forgiven.[61] **b.** My sin is indeed too great to be forgiven, yet why should I be punished more than Thou hast decreed?[62] **c.** My punishment is too great to be borne, the Heb. *awon* meaning both sin and punishment for sin.[63] **[14]from the face of the**

ANTHOLOGY

pented, one sentence was remitted, as it says, *And he dwelt in the land of Nod, on the east of Eden*, but *na* is no more mentioned.

Gen. R. cited in RaDaK. T.S. 4, 99.

56. **And Cain said unto the Lord: "Is my iniquity too great to be borne" (pardoned)?**

For four sins, idolatry, adultery, bloodshed, and calumny, man will pay a penalty in this world and yet be arraigned therefor in the Hereafter; and calumny is more heinous than all the others. How do we know that it is more reprehensible than murder? Here we read, *And Cain said unto the Lord: "Is my iniquity too great to be borne?"* But when Scripture speaks of slander, it does not describe it simply as *a* great offense, but employs the plural form, viz., *May the Lord cut off all flattering lips, the tongue that speaketh great* wrongs (Ps. 12:4).[1]

J. Peah 1:1. T.S. 4, 101.

57. AND CAIN SAID UNTO THE LORD: "IS MY SIN TOO GREAT TO BEAR?" Thou bearest the heavenly and the earthly, yet Thou canst not bear my transgression!

Gen. R. 22. T.S. 4, 103.

58. MY SIN IS TOO GREAT. It is greater than my father's. My father transgressed but a slight command and was expelled from the Garden of Eden; how much more then, in this terrible crime of murder, is *my sin too great!*

Gen. R. 22. T.S. 4, 104.

59. MY SIN IS GREATER THAN I CAN BEAR. Great indeed is my sin, that I cannot bear it. This coincides with the text: *Happy is he whose transgression is forgiven, whose sin is pardoned* (Ps. 32:1). Yea, happy is he who can *bear* his transgressions, but woe to him whom his sins bear. This is in line with the verse, *And our iniquities, like the wind, bear us away* (Isa. 64:5); similarly it is written, *I am weary to bear them* (ibid. 1:14), as if to say, even His power has become too feeble to bear them.

Midrash in Introduction to Tanhuma Yashan. T.S. 4, 106.

60. **And I shall be a fugitive and a wanderer.**

R. Judah b. R. Hiyya said: Exile atones for the half of one's sins. Earlier in the Cain narrative it is written, *And I shall be a fugitive and a wanderer;* but subsequently we read, *And Cain dwelt in the land of Nod.*[1]

Sanhedrin 37b. T.S. 4, 107.

61. **And from Thy face shall I be hid.**

Said Cain: "Should I desire to dwell where Thou wilt not know what I do, can I be hidden from Thy face? Surely not, for everything is

§ 56 [1] I.e., slander. "Wrongs" is not in the original, which reads *g'doloth* (plural of *gadol*), implying that slander constitutes a multiplicity of great offenses.

§ 60 [1] I.e., wandering: he became a wanderer, but not a fugitive. The latter half of his sentence was remitted because he became a wandering exile.

come to pass, that whosoever findeth me will slay me.' [15]And the Lord said unto him: 'Therefore whosoever slayeth Cain, vengeance shall be taken on him sevenfold.' And the Lord set a sign for Cain, lest any find-

COMMENTARY

land. From the choice land of Eden,[64] thereby depriving me of any livelihood.[65] **and from Thy face shall I be hid. a.** Shall I be able to hide myself from Thy face?[66] **b.** I must hide in shame from standing before Thee in prayer and sacrifice.[67] **c.** I shall be removed from the protection of Thy divine providence.[68] **d.** *and from Thy face.* This anguished cry of Cain reveals him as a man not wholly bad, one to whom banishment from the Divine presence is a distinct ingredient in his cup of misery.[69] **whosoever findeth me. a.** Cain feared death at the hands of some future "avenger of blood"; cf. Num. 35:10 f.[70] **b.** Better, *whatsoever,* this referring to wild beasts: since I am expelled from the land and doomed to be a wanderer, I cannot build a house for my protection, and with Thy protection also withdrawn from me, I shall be at the mercy of the wild beasts.[71] **will slay me.** Which exceeds the punishment Thou hast decreed.[72] [15]**Therefore whosoever slayeth Cain, vengeance shall be taken on him sevenfold. a.** Whoever slays Cain shall be punished (this clause being understood); as for Cain, vengeance shall be taken on him after seven generations, but until then he is immune.[73] **b.** Whoever would slay, give heed! Vengeance will be taken on Cain only after seven generations, but not now.[74] **c.** Whoever slays Cain shall suffer a sevenfold vengeance, for Cain did not know the heinousness of murder, whereas those who may follow him already know how abhorrent it is in God's eyes.[75] "Seven" simply means many times over. **a sign. a.** He gave him courage; or some sign to allay his fears.[76] **b.** He gave him safety directions for his enforced itinerary so fraught with peril and insecurity.[77] **c.** This is an idiomatic expression, implying an unqualified assurance.[78] **d.** He engraved a letter of His Name on his forehead. Another interpretation is:

ANTHOLOGY

known to Thee. Therefore I cannot escape the doom to which Thou hast sentenced me, to become a fugitive and a wanderer in the earth, and so *it will come to pass, that, whosoever findeth me will slay me*, for all Thy creatures will know that I deserve to die."

Midrash Aggadah B'reshith. T.S. 4, 111.

62. **And the Lord said unto him: "Therefore whosoever slayeth Cain," etc.**

R. Judah said: Cattle, beasts, and birds assembled to exact retribution for Abel's murder.[1] Said God to them: "Therefore I say, whosoever slayeth Cain shall be slain." R. Levi said: It was to the primeval serpent, who came to demand justice for Abel, that He spake thus. R. Nehemiah said: The Almighty declared: "Cain's sentence is not the same as that of other murderers who may follow him. Cain slew, but he had none from whom to learn the heinousness of murder. Henceforth, however, whosoever slayeth Cain shall be slain."

Gen. R. 22. T.S. 4, 112.

63. **And the Lord set a sign for Cain.**

"Sovereign of all worlds!" Cain pleaded, "*My sin is too great to be borne*, for it has no atonement." This confession was accounted to him as repentance. "Moreover," he continued, "one will arise and slay me by pronouncing Thy great Name against me." What did the Holy One, blessed be He, do? He took one letter from the twenty-two letters in which the Torah is written and set it upon Cain's arm, that he should not be killed, as it is said, *And the Lord set a sign for Cain.*

Pirke d'Rabbi Eliezer Ch. 21. T.S. 4, 119.

64. AND THE LORD SET A SIGN FOR CAIN. R. Judah said: He caused the orb of the sun to shine on his account. Said R. Nehemiah to him: For that evildoer He caused the orb of the sun to shine! Rather, He afflicted him with leprosy, which is called a sign in the verses, *And when he* (Moses) *took it out, behold, his hand was* leprous . . . *And He* (God) *said . . . if they will not believe thee . . . they*

§ 62 [1] This explains whom Cain feared, viz., the animals, etc., since there were as yet no other *humans* on earth.

ing him should smite him. [16]And Cain went out from the presence of the Lord, and dwelt in the land of Nod, on the east of Eden. [17]And Cain knew his wife; and she conceived, and bore Enoch; and he builded a

COMMENTARY

since Cain now feared the wild beasts, God restored their natural fear of man.[79] [16]**from the presence of the Lord. a.** From the environs of the Garden of Eden, where God revealed Himself to him and to his parents.[80] **b.** The verb implies that he never stood again in His presence.[81] **Nod.** I.e., the land of wandering, where all exiles are doomed to wander.[82] [17]**and bore Enoch; and he builded a city. a.** He first thought that he would be doomed to

ANTHOLOGY

will (surely) *believe the voice of the latter* sign (Exod. 4:6-8). Rab said: He gave him a dog. Abba Jose said: He made a horn grow out of him. Rab said: He made him an example to penitents. R. Levi said in the name of R. Simeon b. Lakish: He suspended his judgment until the Flood came and swept him away, as it is written, *And He blotted out every living substance*, etc. (Gen. 7:23).

Gen. R. 22. T.S. 4, 116.

65. AND THE LORD SET A SIGN FOR CAIN. Some say that the Sabbath barred the way to punishment, *"sign"* referring to the Sabbath, as it says, *Wherefore the children of Israel shall keep the* Sabbath . . . (for) *it is a* sign *between Me and the children of Israel for ever* (Exod. 31:16-17). Just as the Sabbath pleaded on behalf of Adam,[1] so it pleaded on behalf of Cain.

Tanhuma B'reshith Par. 10. T.S. 4, 118.

66. **And Cain went out, etc.**

In which state of mind did he go out?[1] R. Judan said, citing R. Aibu: He spurned God's words, throwing them behind him, and went out like one who would deceive the Almighty. R. Berekiah said in the name of R. Eleazar b. R. Simeon: He went forth like one who shows the cloven hoof and would deceive his Creator.[2] R. Hanina b. Isaac said: He went forth in gladness, *"went out"* having the same meaning as in the text, *He* goeth forth *to meet thee, and when he seeth thee, he will be* glad *in his heart* (Ex. 4:14). Adam met him and asked him, "How did your case go?" "I repented and am reconciled," replied he. At these words Adam beat his face in grief that he too had not repented, crying out, "So great is the power of repentance, and I knew it not!" Forthwith he arose and exclaimed, *"A psalm, a song for the Sabbath day: It is a good thing to make confession unto the Lord"* (Ps. 92:1).

Gen. R. 22. T.S. 4, 120.

67. **On the east of Eden (kidmath Eden).**

He was the first man who sought nothing but selfish pleasure.[1] Another interpretation: Before Cain slew his brother the earth was like the Garden of Eden. But after the Holy One, blessed be He, sent him forth to be a wanderer and cursed him, saying to him, *"It* (the earth) *shall not henceforth yield unto thee her strength"* (verse 12), he no longer prospered when he sowed the ground.

Midrash Aggadah. T.S. 4, 125. 126.

68. **And he builded a city.**

This building of cities was a godless deed, for he surrounded them with a wall, forcing his family to remain within. He also introduced a change in the ways of simplicity wherein men had lived before, and he was the author

§ 65 [1] See Chap. II, par. 37.

§ 66 [1] Since one cannot go out from God's omnipresence, it is assumed that "went out" is meant figuratively in the sense of a mental or spiritual departure.

[2] The swine is an unclean animal, since it does not chew the cud. But it has a cloven hoof, which is one of the signs of cleanness; this it ostensibly displays, as though to say, "See! I am clean!"

§ 67 [1] This renders *kidmath* "the first of" (which it can mean), and connects Eden with *hith-aden,* to take pleasure. Selfish hedonism, without thought or care for others, can lead to the gravest crimes.

city, and called the name of the city after the name of his son Enoch. [18]And unto Enoch was born Irad; and Irad begot Mehujael; and Mehujael begot Methushael; and Methushael begot Lamech. [19]And Lamech took unto him two wives; the name of the one was Adah, and the name of the other Zillah. [20]And Adah bore Jabal; he was the father of such as dwell in tents and have cattle. [21]And his

COMMENTARY

childlessness; when he saw that this was not so, he built a city. Knowing himself to be accursed, he named it after his son. Further, Scripture declares that he "was building" (so literally) and not "he built," because owing to his wandering he erected it only a little at a time, perhaps, indeed, he never finished it.[83] **b.** Cain attempts to build his life without God. As the soil does not support him, he becomes the father of an urban culture that is independent of the soil.[84] [19]**two wives.** This is especially mentioned, as it was a departure from the ideal expounded in 2:14.[85] [20]**the father.** The teacher and originator.[86] **cattle.** Heb. *mikneh,* root *kanah,* "to possess." Cattle was so termed, because it constituted the medium of exchange of possessions.[87] **the father,** etc. I.e., the originator of grazing in fixed pastures, as distinct from nomadic sheep-breeding.[88]

ANTHOLOGY

of measures and weights. And whereas men lived innocently and generously while they knew nothing of such arts, he changed the world into cunning craftiness.

Josephus Art. 1:22. Ginzberg Legends, 1, 115.

69. AND HE BUILDED A CITY, AND CALLED THE NAME OF THE CITY AFTER THE NAME OF HIS SON ENOCH. Because he had heard from the Almighty that his descendants would be extinct after seven generations, he called the city after his son's name in order to perpetuate it, as it is written, *They call their lands after their own names* (Ps. 49:12).

Midrash Aggadah B'reshith. T.S. 4, 129.

70. **And called the name of the city after the name of his son Enoch.**

It is written, *Their inward thought* (kirbam) *is, that their houses shall continue for ever,* etc. (Ps. 49:12). R. Judan interpreted: What do the wicked think? *That within their houses* (they shall live) *for ever, and their dwelling-places* (shall exist) *to all generations, and they call their lands after their own names,* e.g., Tiberias after Tiberius, Alexandria after Alexander, Antioch after Antiochus. R. Phinehas observed: *Their houses are* (indeed) kirbam *for ever,* i.e., tomorrow their houses become their sepulchers (*kibram*), and *their dwelling-places to all generations,* i.e., they will neither live (i.e., be resurrected) nor be judged. Yet *they have* (impudently) *called their lands after their own names!* Thus it is written, *And he builded a city, and called the name of the city after the name of his son Enoch.*

Gen. R. 23. T.S. 4, 128.

71. **And Lamech took unto him two wives; the name of the one was Adah, and the name of the other Zillah.**

One wife was named Adah because Lamech luxuriated (*mith-aden*) in her bodily attractions. The other wife was called Zillah because he dwelt in the shadow (*zel*) of her children.[1]

J. Yebamoth 6:5. T.S. 4, 131.

72. **He was the father of such as dwell in tents and have cattle.**

He was the first to build tents; the first to engage in pastoral pursuits; and the first to practice the science of the veterinary.

Midrash Aggadah B'reshith. T.S. 4, 135.

§ 71 [1] I.e., the former was solely for his carnal pleasure, the latter for childbearing.

brother's name was Jubal; he was the father of all such as handle the harp and pipe. [22]And Zillah, she also bore Tubal-cain, the forger of every cutting instrument of brass and iron; and the sister of Tubal-cain was Na-

COMMENTARY

[21]**handle.** Heb. *tofes,* literally "grasps," "seizes," i.e., one eager to perform his task and devoted to his calling.[89] **harp and pipe.** Music, according to Hebrew tradition, is thus the most ancient art, dating from the beginnings of the human race.[90] [22]**the forger,** etc. **a.** Polisher of all tools.[91] **b.** The sharpener of all cutting instruments, such as swords, knives, etc.[92] **c.** Here too *the father of* is to be understood in the text, i.e., he was the first to make these implements.[93] **d.** Special attention is drawn to these originators of arts and crafts in order to emphasize, in contrast to pagan mythologies, that they were human, and not gods. Thus the Greek Hephaestos, the Roman Vulcan, and the recently unearthed Canaanite H Y N, are all gods, whereas Jubal and Tubal-cain are distinctly human.[94] That Scripture hinted here at the purity of the Hebrew conception of the beginnings of history, as opposed to the weird and sordid pagan representations thereof, is further attested by the fact that Naamah is described as the sister of Tubal-cain. This stands in happy contrast to Hephaestos' lewd relations with Aphrodite in Greek mythology.[95] **brass.** The Heb. is more accurately translated "copper," since it was a metal dug from the earth (Deut. 8:9).

ANTHOLOGY

73. THE FATHER OF SUCH AS DWELL IN TENTS, etc. The wicked Lamech had two wives, Adah and Zillah, and *Adah bare Jubal; he was the father of such as live in tents and feed the cattle* (4:20). He discovered the work appertaining to shepherds, and made tents and pens for the cattle, one for the sheep, and another for the oxen, distinct from each other. He also invented the locks which are made to prevent thieves entering the house, which are like unto this, *And the name of his brother was Jubal, the father of all who play on the harp and the reed-pipe* (ibid. 21).

At this time the inhabitants of the earth began to commit violence, to defile each other, and kindle the anger of the Lord. They began to sing with the harp and the reed-pipe, and to sport with all kinds of song corrupting the earth. This Jubal discovered the science of music, whence arose all the tunes for the above two instruments. This art is very great. And it came to pass, when he heard of the judgments which Adam prophesied concerning the two trials to come upon his descendants by the flood, the dispersion and fire, he wrote down the science of music upon two pillars, one of white marble, and the other of brick, so that if one melt and crumble away on account of the water, the other would be saved. And Zillah bare Tubal-cain, who forged all the iron implements of war, and was an artificer in all kinds of iron work. He also discovered the art of joining lead and iron together, in order to temper the iron and to make the blade sharper. He also invented the pincers, the hammer, and the axe, and other instruments of iron. Tubal was a worker in all kinds of tin and lead, iron and copper, silver and gold.

Chronicles of Jerahmeel. Gaster pp. 50-51 (XIV:5-8).

74. **And Zillah, she also bore Tubal-cain, the forger of every cutting instrument of brass and iron, etc.**

R. Joshua of Siknin said in R. Levi's name: This man perfected (*tibbel*) Cain's sin: Cain slew, yet lacked the weapons for slaying, whereas he was *the forger of every cutting instrument of brass and iron.*

Gen. R. 23. T.S. 4, 140.

75. **And the sister of Tubal-cain was Naamah.**

R. Abba b. Kahana said: Naamah was Noah's wife; and why was she called Naamah? Because her deeds were pleasing (*n'imim*). The Rabbis said: Naamah was a different woman, who was called Naamah (from *naim,* sweet) because she played sweet music on the timbrel in honor of idols.

Gen. R. 23. T.S. 4, 141.

amah. [23]And Lamech said unto his wives:

Adah and Zillah, hear my voice;
Ye wives of Lamech, hearken unto my speech;

COMMENTARY

Brass is an alloy. The discovery of the use of metals forms an important step in the progress of civilization.[96] [23]**and Lamech said,** etc. This is an ancient poem, whose meaning is obscure. The following interpretations have been proposed: **a.** Lamech, who was blind, had accidentally killed Cain and his own son (see Anthology, Chap. IV. par. 78). When his wives denied him conjugal rights on that account, he sought to placate them by pleading: Am I responsible for this unfortunate result of my blindness?[97] **b.** He reassured his wives, who feared that he or his progeny would die for the sin of Cain. The verse is rendered: Have I slain a man, that I should bear guilt on his account, or a young man, that the guilt should be laid to my descendants? This connects *haburathi* (AJV: bruising) with *haburah*, a company, hence, "those attached to me," viz., my posterity.[98] **c.** Lamech's wives feared that he would be held to Divine account for having taught his son Tubal-cain to forge the implements of war. He therefore assured them that they had nothing to fear, since he had not committed murder. God would therefore surely protect him, even more than Cain.[99] **d.** Lamech's wives dreaded the prospect of giving birth to the seventh generation that was to pay the penalty of death for Cain's crime. Said Lamech: It is I who belong to the seventh generation, and not your children, for the count begins with Adam, not with Cain. Should a man wound me, or a young man bruise me, I will not fear to

ANTHOLOGY

76. AND THE SISTER OF TUBAL-CAIN WAS NAAMAH. R. Isaac asked: What is the purpose of this statement? To teach that she was a noble woman, lovely in her deeds as her name suggests. R. Abbahu said: The plain meaning is that she too was a skilled artificer in iron as was her brother. For thus it is written, *Tubal-cain was the instructor of all the artificers in brass and iron, and* (so was) *Naamah, the sister of Tubal-cain.* He created the art and she collaborated with him: hence the expression, *And* (so was) *Naamah, the sister of Tubal-cain,* implying that she was as skilled as he, for the conjunction "*and*" refers back to the beginning of the verse (i.e., he was the instructor, etc., and so was his sister Naamah). R. Ba said: On the contrary, she was the mother of demons, the proof being that Naamah is the name of the mother of Ashmedai, king of the demons. R. Isaac said in the name of R. Johanan: She was called Naamah (i.e., lovely) because of her beauty. She was the progenitress of those of whom it is written, *The sons of God saw the daughters of men, that they were fair* (6:2).

Midrash Haneelam Zohar Hadash 19.
T.S. 4, 142.

77. **And Lamech said unto his wives, etc.**

R. Jose b. R. Hanina said: He summoned them to their conjugal duties. Said they to him: "Tomorrow the Flood will come — shall we bear children for a curse?" He answered: "*For have I slain a man for my wounding* — that wounds should come to me on his account! *And a young man-child for my bruising* — that bruises should come upon me! Cain slew, yet his judgment was suspended for seven generations; I did not slay; surely my judgment will wait seventy-seven generations!" Rabbi said: This is a reasoning of darkness (i.e., fallacious): for if so, whence is the Holy One, blessed be He, to exact His bond? R. Jacob b. Idi asked R. Johanan: If Lamech's victim was a man, why is he also called a child; if a child, why a man? His limbs were fully-grown, as a man's, but he was a child in years.[1] Said he (Lamech) to them: "Come, let us go to Adam and put our case before him." When they came before him he bade them: "Do you do your duty, while the Holy One, blessed be He, will do His." "Physician, physician, heal thine own limp!" they retorted. "Have you kept apart from Eve a hundred and

§ 77 [1] This comment assumes that he had slain someone.

For I have slain a man for wounding me,
And a young man for bruising me;
[24]If Cain shall be avenged sevenfold,
Truly Lamech seventy and sevenfold.

COMMENTARY

slay him. For if Cain's punishment was deferred to the seventh generation, surely mine will be deferred to the seventy-seventh.[100] **e.** He had slain a youthful enemy of his for bruising and wounding him. He then allayed his wives' fears of punishment by pleading that he had justly killed him, since he had struck the first blow.[101] **f.** His wives were given to continual wrangling. He pleaded with and threatened them: What is my sin that I should have no peace in my house? Have I slain man or child?[102] If God pardoned Cain's sin and declared that He would visit retribution upon his slayer, all the more will He visit retribution upon you who have made my life unbearable by your constant altercations.[103] **g.** Lamech said to his quarreling wives: If you will not desist, I will slay you without fear. For were I even to slay an adult or a child, God would delay my punishment longer than Cain's, for I am a better man than he.[104] **h.** Lamech sang a song of triumph on the weapons invented by Tubal-cain,[105] boasting: Should anyone even touch me with evil intention, I will kill him without mercy. For whoever would attack me will suffer far greater retribution than that which was stated in connection with Cain.[106] **i.** Lamech was the father of seventy-seven sons (Josephus, Antiquities, Bk. 1, ch. 2), yet only these inventors mentioned in the Bible. We may accordingly surmise that his wives were apprehensive lest woe betide their offspring because of Cain's transgression. But he consoled them, saying: Would I, a morally infirm and imperfect mortal, slay a man for a mere wound,

ANTHOLOGY

thirty years for any reason but that you might not beget children by her!" On hearing this, he (Adam) resumed his duty of begetting children.

Gen. R. 23. T.S. 4, 144.

78. **For I have slain a man, etc.**

How was Cain slain? Cain was metamorphosed into the Angel of Death for 130 years, what time he was a fugitive vagabond, accursed. Lamech was his great-grandson of the seventh generation, and blind. When he (Lamech) went hunting his son would guide him, holding his hand, and tell him when he saw the horns of a beast, whereupon Lamech would draw his bow and kill it. Once he saw Cain's horns between two mountains, but not Cain himself. "I see an animal's horns!" he exclaimed, and Lamech shot and killed him. But when they went to take it the child cried out, "It is my grandfather!" In grief Lamech beat his hands; accidentally he dealt his child a blow on the head and killed him. Thus it is written: *And Lamech said unto his wives: " . . . I have slain a man by my wounding, and a child by my bruise."* Thus the three, Cain, the dead child, and the blind Lamech, were left together. At that moment the earth opened and swallowed up four families: Enoch, Irad, Mehujael, and Methusael. Now Lamech became metamorphosed into the Angel of Death, thus fulfilling the prophecy, *If Cain shall be avenged sevenfold, truly Lamech seventy and sevenfold.*[1] When Lamech returned home, he invited his wives to share his couch, but they demurred: "You killed our grandfather Cain and our son, Tubal-cain. We will no longer wive you." Lamech pleaded: "Behold, Cain has received his penalty, but only after seven generations. Surely then mine must be postponed for seventy-seven!"[2] But they persisted in their refusal, saying, "Shall we bear children for a curse?" "Then let us submit our case before Adam," he proposed.

Tanhuma B'reshith Par. 11. T.S. 4, 146.

§ 78 [1] The connection is not clear. Perhaps it means that as the Angel of Death he would now be able to take unlimited vengeance (*"seventy and seven-fold"*) upon all who sought to harm him.
[2] Since he killed deliberately, whereas I killed unintentionally.

[25]And Adam knew his wife again; and she bore a son, and called his name Seth: 'for God hath appointed me another seed instead of Abel; for Cain slew him.' [26]And to Seth, to him also there was born a son; and he

COMMENTARY

or a child for a blow? Much less would the Righteous Judge of the whole earth condemn seventy-seven souls to destruction for the crime of a single person. Though He has indeed declared, "*Vengeance shall be taken on him seven-fold*" (verse 15), yet since my household consists of so many, He must certainly have annulled the decree of evil.[107] [25]**hath appointed me.** As an abiding gift (unlike Abel, who was taken from me).[108]

ANTHOLOGY

79. **And Adam knew his wife furthermore.**

Desire was added to his desire. Formerly he had experienced no desire when he did not see her, but now he desired her whether he saw her or not. R. Abba b. Judan said in R. Aha's name: This is a hint to seafarers to remember their homes (i.e., their wives) and repair thither immediately on returning home from a journey.

Gen. R. 23. T.S. 4, 151.

80. AND ADAM KNEW HIS WIFE AGAIN. What is the implication of "*again?*" When he repented Seth was born to him in his own image and form.[1]

Midrash Habiur. T.S. 4, 152.

81. AND ADAM KNEW HIS WIFE AGAIN. When the son of R. Johanan b. Zakkai died, his disciples came to console him. R. Eliezer entered, sat down before him, and said: "Revered teacher, may I say a fitting word?" "Speak," he replied. R. Eliezer resumed: "Adam lost a son, yet allowed himself to be comforted. We know this from the verse, *And Adam knew his wife again.* So do you too accept consolation." R. Johanan replied: "Is not my own grief enough, that you must remind me of Adam's grief too!"

Aboth d'Rabbi Nathan Ch. 14. T.S. 4, 150.

82. **And she called his name Seth: "for God hath appointed me another seed," etc.**

R. Tanhuma said in the name of Samuel: She hinted at that seed which would arise from another source, viz., the king Messiah.

Gen. R. 23. T.S. 4, 153.

83. **For God hath appointed me another seed instead of Abel.**

When Cain slew Abel, all lives and all seeds were smitten, save those in Abel's portion. They mourned and languished and ceased to yield aught but one single edible fruit. When Seth was born, he took that as his portion, the rest being hidden away in the vine, as it says, *And the vine said unto them: "Should I leave my wine?"* (Jud. 9:13). Why did it emphasize, "my *wine?*" Because when Abel was slain, the vine ceased producing 926 kinds of fruit, leaving only the wine, *tiroshi* (the Heb. for "my wine") having the numerical value of 926. The rest was hidden away, being preserved for the Messianic era. Then will all the other species of trees and grasses and herbs be restored too.

Midrash quoted in Ms. Introduction to Tanhuma Yashan. T.S. 4, 156.

84. **And to Seth, to him also there was born a son; and he called his name Enosh; then began men to call upon the Name of the Lord.**

R. Jose said: Why are idols called "other *gods?*" Lest people say, "Had *they* been designated *gods,* as He is, they too would have been necessary"; therefore they were named as

§ 80 [1] Before his sin Cain and Abel were born in his God-given image. But after his sin he separated from Eve and begot demons (see Chap. V, par. 21); now that he had repented, he again begot children in God's image.

called his name Enosh; then began men to call upon the name of the Lord.

COMMENTARY

[26]**Enosh. a.** In Heb. poetry *enosh* means "man."[109] The verse as a whole is given diametrically opposite interpretations, some interpreting it in the sense of a renewed worship of the Almighty; others as a statement of man's degradation in now turning to idolatry (see further on). The following comments on "Enosh" are based on these respective views: **b.** The Hebrew name for him (who seeks God) is Enos, and Enos translated is man. He takes the name which is common to the whole race as his personal name, a reward of special distinction implying that no one should be thought a man at all who does not set his hope on God.[110] **c.** Contrary to Adam, the pure man, Enosh describes the sick man in his depravity. And Moses characterizes this deepening estrangement with these words: "In those days it became necessary to call in the name of God." Chacham Bernays explains this as follows: Of Abraham's life it says repeatedly: "He called in the name of God," i.e., he made mankind, which had completely forgotten God, again conscious of God and His significance for human life. But the immeasurable significance of Abraham's life which made possible the rebirth of mankind were, in the days

ANTHOLOGY

He, and yet they are utterly worthless. Now, when were the idols first so designated? In the generation of Enosh, as we read, *And he called his name Enosh; then began men to call* (idols) *by the name of the Lord.* It was then that the Ocean (the Mediterranean) rose and flooded a third of the world. For God spake thus to them: "Ye have made a new thing (an idol), and given it My name. So I too will make something new and call it by My name." Hence it says, *He calleth the waters of the sea, and poureth them out upon the face of the earth; the Lord is His name* (Amos 5:8).[1]

Sifre Ekeb Par. 43. T.S. 4, 158.

85. AND TO SETH, TO HIM ALSO THERE WAS BORN A SON; AND HE CALLED HIS NAME ENOSH. Abba Cohen Bardela was asked: Why does Scripture enumerate Adam, Seth, Enosh, and then become silent?[1] Hitherto they had been created in the likeness and image of God, he replied, but from then onward centaurs were created.[2] Four things changed in the days of Enosh: The mountains became barren rocks, the dead began to feel the worms, men's faces became ape-like, and they became a prey to demons. Said R. Isaac: They were themselves responsible for this, as a punishment for arguing, "What is the difference whether one prostrates oneself before an image or before man?"

Gen. R. 23. T.S. 4, 161.

86. THEN BEGAN MEN TO CALL (IDOLS) BY THE NAME OF THE LORD. On three occasions God overlooked idolatry, but would not forgive quarrelsomeness and strife. Once in the days of Enosh, when it says, *Then began men to call* (idols) *by the name of the Lord,* i.e., they began to practice idolatry, yet He did not punish them until the Generation of the Flood, when men quarrelled, robbed and oppressed one another. This He could not overlook, and then He pronounced their sentence: "*The end of all flesh is come before Me*" (6:13).

Midrash quoted in Reshith Hokmah, referring to a Ms. of M'norath Hamaor. T.S. 4, 167.

87. THEN MEN BEGAN TO CALL (IDOLS) BY THE NAME OF THE LORD. His contemporaries came and asked Enosh what was his father's name. "Seth," he replied. "And your grandfather's name?" they pursued. "Adam." "And *his* father's name?" "He had no father," replied he, "for God created him first as a life-

§ 84 [1] This vast flooding by the Ocean was a new phenomenon, and it was called by the name of God, i.e., God's Ocean. This is the most likely meaning of the passage.

§ 85 [1] Instead of continuing the genealogical list, Scripture recommences with Adam.

[2] Centaurs were mythical creatures, half-man half-horse. This symbolizes the brutalization and spiritual decadence which now set in.

COMMENTARY

of Enosh, signs of a sad decay. How "sick" men must have become that it was necessary to announce to men the name of God! What should have been self-evident, now had to be *taught*.[111] **then began (huhal) men. a.** Then did the righteous begin to teach the Name of the Lord, and to pray to Him in adversity.[112] **b.** *Huhal* is connected with *hol,* "profane," and the verse reads: Then was the profane called by the Name of the Lord, i.e., men and lifeless objects were called "god," and idolatry began.[113] **c.** Then began the true worship of the Lord.[114] **d.** Once again men called upon God under His true name, Adonai, Lord, which Cain's descendants apparently had forgotten.[115] **e.** By a further extension of the meaning given in **b.** we can render: Then was the calling upon the name of the Lord profaned, i.e., men ceased to call upon His name.[116]

ANTHOLOGY

less form, and then breathed into him the breath of life." "But how did He make him?" they persisted. Thereupon he took a clod of earth and kneaded it into a human shape; a demon entered its nostrils, and endowed it with life. On seeing this they exclaimed, "This is our god!" and they believed in it.

Midrash; T.S. 4, 168. See also refs. in Ginzberg Legends, Vol. 6, p. 150, ref. 54.

88. THEN WERE MEN DEGRADED, THAT THEY CALLED NOT UPON THE NAME OF THE LORD.

When Cain arose and slew his brother Abel, the Shekinah withdrew from the first heaven to the second. Then the generation of Enosh arose and practiced idolatry, as we read, *Then were men degraded,* etc.; thereupon the Shekinah retired further to the third heaven.

Targum Jonathan Naso Par. 24. T.S. 4, 165.

GENESIS

CHAPTER V

[1]**This is the book of the generations**

COMMENTARY

[1]**This is the book.** Heb. *Sefer* does not always mean a volume; it may be used of any written document. Rabbinic tradition states the Torah is not one continuous work, written at one definite moment. "The Torah was given to Moses in separate scrolls" (תורה מגילה מגילה נתנה).[1] **the book of the generations of Adam. a.** A list of the generations through a single line of descent from Adam to Noah.[2] **b.** The meaning of the phrase is: the history of the events which befell the human race.[3] **c.** The whole Torah *is the book of the generations of Adam,* for which reason "book" is specifically mentioned.[4] **d.** The formula, "These are the generations," which occurs ten times in Genesis, each time beginning a new section, would mark the beginning of such scroll or "book." This explains why some sections, as this Chapter, have introductory verses *which recall or summarize facts*

ANTHOLOGY

1. **This is the book of the generations of Adam.**

R. Akiba declared: The dictum, *But thou shalt love thy neighbor as thyself* (Lev. 19:18), is a great principle in the Torah. Ben Azzai said: *This is the book of the generations of Adam* is a greater principle.[1]

Torath Kohanim Kedoshim 4:12. T.S. 5, 1.

2. THIS IS THE BOOK OF THE GENERATIONS OF ADAM. This teaches that the Holy One, blessed be He, conjured up for Adam all the generations that were destined to descend from him. He passed in review before him every generation with its guides and prophets, interpreters and sages; every generation with its leaders, judges and warriors; the righteous of each age and the wicked of each age; as we read, *The wicked are estranged from the womb* (Ps. 58:4).[1] God unfolded to Adam the number of their years and days, the count of their hours, and the very sum of their steps, as it says, *But now Thou numberest my steps* (Job 14:16); it is also written, *Thine eyes did see mine unformed substance, and in Thy book they were all written — even the days that were fashioned, when as yet there was none of them* (Ps. 139:16).

Seder Olam Ch. 30. T.S. 5, 2.

3. THIS IS THE BOOK, etc. R. Nehemiah said: How do we know that a single man is equal to the entire Creation? Because our text reads, *This is the book of the generations of Adam. In the day that God created man, in the likeness of God made He him.* Now, another verse says: *These are the generations of* the heaven *and of* the earth *when they were created, in the day that the Lord God* made earth *and* heaven (2:4). Just as creating and making are stated in the case of the latter (heaven and earth), so are they stated in connection with the former.[1]

Aboth d'Rabbi Nathan Ch. 31. T.S. 5, 3.

4. THIS IS THE BOOK OF THE GENERATIONS OF ADAM. Scripture writes, *For I will not contend for ever* (Isa. 57:16): this means, with Adam; *neither will I always be wroth* (ibid.) — with his descendants. The text continues: *For the spirit that enwrappeth itself* (is) *from Me, and the souls which I have made* (ibid.). Our

§ 1 [1] Because by stating clearly that all "generations" are descended from Adam it emphasizes more strongly the Brotherhood of Man.

§ 2 [1] This rendering follows AJV. It is probably understood in the sense of the womb of time, i.e., from the very beginning of time it was known that they would be wicked. But perhaps he renders: *the wicked are* spread out (before Adam) *from the womb.*

§ 3 [1] The use of the identical words in connection with each indicates that they are of equal importance.

COMMENTARY

mentioned in earlier sections.[5] **e.** This book of mankind's history shows nothing but the development (תולדות) of man (אדם), whom God has created in His image. You behold pure noble men — but also perverted and crooked ones who are worse than the devil; opposite types, yes, but pre-conceived with the creation of "Adam" whom God gave a Divine Soul! The gift of freedom may raise him to towering heights, but may also throw him into the abyss of fearful degradation.[6] **f.** "This is the book of the generation of Man" — not black, not white, not great, not small, but *Man*. In these Scriptural words we have a concept quite unknown in the ancient world — Humanity. And only the belief in One God could lead to such a clear

ANTHOLOGY

Rabbis said: The royal Messiah will not come until all the souls which the Divine Mind conceived to be created shall indeed have been created. What is the proof? The text, *and the souls which I have created,* which means for the sake of the souls which I have made.[1] And the souls are referred to in the Book of Adam[2] in our text, *This is the book of the generations of Adam.*

Gen. R. 24. T.S. 5, 6.

5. THIS IS THE BOOK OF THE GENERATIONS OF ADAM. It is written, *Then did He see it, and declare it; He established it, yea, and searched it out* (Job 28:27). R. Judah b. R. Simon said: It was fitting that the Torah should have been given through Adam. Whence does this follow? From our text: *This is the book of generations of Adam.* Said the Holy One, blessed be He: "He is the creation of My hands; shall I not to give it to him!" Subsequently, however, He said: "I gave him six commandments, and he did not remain loyal to them; how then shall I give him six hundred and thirteen precepts, viz., two hundred and forty-eight positive precepts and three hundred and sixty-five negative precepts?" Hence it is written, *And He said la-adam,* which is read *lo Adam:* I will not give it to Adam. But to whom will I give it? To his descendants. Hence, *This is the book of the generations of Adam.*[1]

Gen. R. 24. T.S. 5, 7.

6. THIS IS THE BOOK OF THE GENERATIONS OF ADAM. R. Jacob of Kefar Hanan said: It was fitting that the Twelve Tribes should have sprung from Adam. What is the proof? *This* (zeh) *is the book of the generations of Adam,* implying that the Twelve, the numerical value of *zeh,*[1] should have been his generations (descendants). However, the Almighty declared: "I gave him but two sons, and one arose and slew the other; how then shall I give him the Twelve Tribes?" Hence Scripture writes, *And He said* la-adam (Job 28:27), which may be read, *lo Adam,* meaning, not to Adam will I give them, but to his descendants.

Gen. R. 24. T.S. 5, 8.

7. THIS IS THE BOOK. R. Tanhuma said in R. Eleazar's name: Adam taught all forms of craftsmanship. What is the proof? *And they are crafsmen from Adam* (Isa. 44:11), i.e., from the first Adam. Our Rabbis said: Adam even taught how to rule the parchment for the Scroll (sc. the Pentateuch), as it says *This is the book,* which means, This Book (the Pentateuch), and the manner of its ruling, is of the generations of Adam, i.e., the result of his instructions.

Gen. R. 24. T.S. 5, 10.

8. THIS IS THE BOOK OF THE GENERATIONS OF ADAM. R. Simon said: Adam alienated himself from Eve for 130 years after Abel was killed, saying, "Why should I beget children

§ 4 [1] The verse is now translated: For the spirit (the Messiah) shall be detained before Me until the souls which I have made have been created.
[2] Theodor assumes that an actual work called The Book of Adam is meant.
§ 5 [1] Rendering: This book (the Torah) shall be for the generations (descendants) of Adam, but not for him.
§ 6 [1] "*Zeh*" consists of two letters, *zayin* and *he,* whose numerical value are 7 and 5 respectively, totalling 12. — Hebrew letters are also numerals.

ANTHOLOGY

who are accursed?" But when Seth was born Adam addressed his sons:[1] "I did not give the genealogy of my first sons (Cain and Abel), because they were under a curse. But this one's genealogy I will give, because he ranks first of the generations that are to follow." This we learn from our text: *This is the book of the generations of Adam . . . And Adam lived a hundred and thirty years, and begot a son . . . and called his name Seth.*

Tanhuma Yashan B'reshith Par. 26. T.S. 5, 12.

9. THIS IS THE BOOK OF THE GENERATIONS OF ADAM. Whenever the Omnipresent intended to raise up a nation or a genealogical tree from one, He employed the term, "generations." Consequently you find this term used twelve times in Scripture. It is first found in the sentence "*These are the generations of heaven and earth*" (2:4). Then in the following cases: *This is the book of the generations of Adam; These are the generations of Noah* (6:9); *These are the generations of the sons of Noah* (10:1); *These are the generations of Shem* (11:10); *These are the generations of Terah* (11:27); *These are the generations of Ishmael* (25:12), *of Isaac* (ibid. 19), *and of Jacob* (37:2). Through these ten "generations" the Holy One, blessed be He, labored to create the world and evolve the nations.

Num. R. 2:21. T.S. 5, 11.

10. THIS IS THE BOOK OF THE GENERATIONS OF ADAM. What did God do to Adam?[1] He threw him into a sleep, in which He showed him Noah and all the upright, Abraham and all proselytes, Isaac and all who would sacrifice burnt-offerings, Jacob and all who dwelt in tents, Moses and all the meek, Aaron and all priests, Joshua and all leaders, David and all kings, Solomon and all judges.[2] After beholding all these Adam awoke and God spake to him: "Thou hast seen them. As thou livest, all these righteous men will be thy descendants." On hearing these words, Adam was content.[3]

Tanhuma Yashan B'reshith Par. 2. T.S. 5, 13.

11. THIS IS THE BOOK (SEFER), etc. On the 28th of Ellul the sun and the moon were created. The number of years, months, days, nights, terms, seasons, cycles, and intercalations were before the Holy One, blessed be He, and He intercalated the years and then delivered the calculations to the first man in the Garden of Eden, as it is said, *This is the* calculation (sefer)[1] *for the generations of Adam:* the calculation of the world is therein for the generations of the children of Adam. Adam handed on the principles of intercalation to Enoch. Thus initiated, he intercalated the year, as it is said, *And Enoch walked with God,* which means that he walked in the ways of the seasonal calculations which God had delivered to Adam.[2]

Pirke d'Rabbi Eliezer Ch. 8. T.S. 5, 15. 56.

12. THIS IS THE BOOK OF THE GENERATIONS OF ADAM. When God showed these generations to Adam, among them he saw David, to whom but three hours of life had been allotted. Adam then turned to God, asking, "Cannot his fate be altered?" "Thus have I decreed," was His reply. "What is the span of my life?" he asked. On being told that it was one thousand years, he asked whether he would be permitted to make a gift, and when he was answered in the affirmative, he exclaimed, "I

§ 8 [1] Presumably this means Cain and his children. This passage explains why the generations are traced from Adam through Seth, and not through Cain.

§ 10 [1] Probably, in order to induce him to resume his marital relations with Eve.

[2] All these enumerated are regarded as prototypes. Thus, Abraham was the first proselyte, Isaac the first to offer a burnt-offering, etc. Jacob is described in 25:27 as "*dwelling in tents,*" which in Rabbinical parlance meant a student of the Torah.

[3] He no longer feared that he would bring children into the world for a curse.

§ 11 [1] By a play on words *sefer* is connected with *safar,* to count or calculate.

[2] The Jewish year is primarily lunar, consisting of twelve lunar months, which is just over 354 days. Since this is about 11 days short of the solar year, an additional month is intercalated in the year at certain intervals.

of Adam. In the day that God created man, in the likeness of God made He him; [2]male and female created He them, and blessed them, and called

COMMENTARY

affirmation of the unity of mankind.[7] **In the likeness of God made He him. a.** This is mentioned to indicate that unlike his descendants he had no father or mother, but issued direct from the hand of God.[8] **b.** The point is that man possesses free will which justifies his punishment when he sins.[9] **c.** A reminder of the dignity of man's nature.[10] [2]**and blessed them.** With the power of begetting children like themselves, who in turn would have the same power for all time.[11] **called their name Adam** (man). Since *Adam* is a general term for the whole human race, it is stated here that God so named them. Hence the introductory words of the

ANTHOLOGY

give to David 70 years of my own life!" He then proceeded to document this offer, God, Metatron, and Adam signing it. Adam then cried: "O Master of the world, how beautiful is his reign and the gift of song given him, the bard, for seventy years to hymn Thy glory!" This is what is meant in the Psalms, when David declared, "*Lo, I am come with the roll of a book which is prescribed for me*" (Ps. 40:8).

Midrash quoted in Yalkut Shimoni Par. 247. T.S. 5, 23.

13. **In the day that God created man.**

This supports the statement of R. Eleazar b. Azariah: Three miracles were performed on that day: on the selfsame day they were created, they cohabited, and produced offspring.[1]

Gen. R. 24. T.S. 5, 18.

14. **Male and female created He them.**

Mishnah. A man may not abstain from procreation unless he already has children. Beth Shammai ruled: Two males. Beth Hillel ruled: A male and a female, for it says, *Male and female created He them.*

Yebamoth 61b. T.S. 5, 24.

15. MALE AND FEMALE CREATED HE THEM. For King Ptolemy[1] the seventy-two elders wrote, *Male and female He created* him (not *them,* lest it be thought that they were separately created from the very beginning).

Megillah 9a. T.S. 5, 25.

16. MALE AND FEMALE CREATED HE THEM. R. Eleazar said: A man without a wife is not a man; for it is said, *Male and female created He them . . . and called their name Man.*[1]

Yebamoth 63a. T.S. 5, 26.

17. MALE AND FEMALE CREATED HE THEM. R. Jeremiah b. Eleazar said: The Holy One, blessed be He, originally created Adam an hermaphrodite (bi-sexual), for it is said, *Male and female created He them and called their name Adam* (i.e., both sexes were united in Adam).

Gen. R. 8. T.S. 5, 27.

18. MALE AND FEMALE CREATED HE THEM. R. Samuel b. Nahmani said: What is meant by the expression, *Thou hast formed me behind and before* (Ps. 139:5)? It refers to the two visages, male and female, with which Adam was created, as it says, *Male and female created He them . . . and called their name Adam.*[1]

Tanhuma Tazria Par. 1. T.S. 5, 28.

19. **And blessed them.**

From whom did our Patriarchs learn to bless their respective generations? Their Teacher was God. For when God created man He

§ 13 [1] Rendering: *This is the book of the generations of Adam* (which were born) *in the day that God created man.*
§ 15 [1] See Cap. I, par. 37.
§ 16 [1] Only when *together* as man and wife is he called Man.
§ 18 [1] I.e., together, male and female, they originally constituted the one man (Adam).

their name Adam, in the day when they were created. [3]And Adam lived a hundred and thirty years, and begot a son in his own likeness, after

COMMENTARY

chapter, *This is the book,* etc., refer not only to Adam, but also to his descendants.[12] [3]**a hundred and thirty years.** During this period he held aloof from his wife.[13] **in his own likeness.** Resembling him facially.[14] **after his image.** Similar to him in build.[15] *In his own likeness, after his image.* **a.** He was as like his father as though he were his image, that is to say, he was an upright man. The phrase is a tribute to Seth with whose descendants the world was re-populated after the flood through the line of Noah.[16] **b.** Who like himself had the capacity for spiritual exaltation, that his deeds might be like those of God.[17] **c.** Although all are born in the likeness of their begetters, it is here particularly pointed out that since Adam was created in God's image and it

ANTHOLOGY

blessed him, as it says, *Male and female created He them, and blessed them.*

Tanhuma V'Zoth ha-B'rakah Par. 1. T.S. 5, 29.

20. **And called their name Adam.**

Adam has seven different meanings. (1) It is the name of the first man. (2) It is the name of his wife and (3) all his children. (4) The common people too are called Adam. (5) It signifies man as opposed to a woman, (6) and woman as opposed to man. (7) It is also the name of a city (Josh. 3:16). That it signifies the first man and his wife we know from the Scriptural verse, *And God called* their *name* Adam.

Midrash Sh'loshah V'Arbaah. T.S. 5, 32.

21. **And Adam lived a hundred and thirty years, and begot a son in his own likeness.**

R. Jeremiah b. Eleazar stated: In all those years during which Adam was under the ban[1] he begot wraiths and male and female demons, for it says; *And Adam lived a hundred and thirty years, and begot a son in his own likeness, after his image,* whence it follows that until then he did not beget after his own image. An objection was raised: R. Meir used to say: Adam was extremely pious. When he saw that through him death was ordained, he spent a hundred and thirty years in fasting, shunned his wife, and wore clothes of fig-leaves on his body for 130 years. (How then could he have begotten anything at all?) His statement referred to the semen emitted unintentionally.[2]

Erubin 18b. T.S. 5, 33.

22. AND BEGOT A SON IN HIS OWN LIKENESS, AFTER HIS IMAGE. This teaches that Seth too (like Adam) was born circumcised.[1]

Aboth d'Rabbi Nathan Chap. 2. T.S. 5, 34.

23. AND BEGOT A SON IN HIS OWN LIKENESS, AFTER HIS IMAGE. R. Joshua b. Nehemiah said: The third child is always the most beloved. Adam had three sons, Cain, Abel and Seth, of whom Seth was the most beloved. For it says, *This is the book of the generations of Adam;* and it continues, *And* (he) *begot a son in his own likeness, after his image, and called his name Seth.*[1]

Tanhuma Jethro Par. 10. T.S. 5, 37.

24. AND ADAM LIVED A HUNDRED AND THIRTY YEARS, AND BEGOT A SON IN HIS OWN LIKENESS, AFTER HIS IMAGE. From this you learn that Cain was not of Adam's seed, nor after his likeness, nor in his actions did he emulate Abel his brother. Thus Adam had no worthy progeny until Seth was born, who was indeed of his seed and in his own likeness,

§ 21 [1] For his disobedience.
[2] The Rabbis believed that from semen which does not serve its proper function demons are created.
§ 22 [1] Since he was born exactly like Adam, who was also created circumcised; see Chap. I, par. 256.
§ 23 [1] Thus, only his third son did he regard as being in his own likeness, because he was his most endeared.

his image; and called his name Seth. [4]And the days of Adam after he begot Seth were eight hundred years; and he begot sons and daughters. [5]And all the days that Adam lived were nine hundred and thirty years; and he died. [6]And Seth lived a hundred and five years, and begot Enosh.

COMMENTARY

might be thought that such a privilege could only belong to one directly created by Him, his children were begotten in the same Divine image.[18] [4]**eight hundred years.** The ages both before and after begetting are given because of the extreme longevity, the reason of which was that Adam, as God's handiwork, was physically perfect, and the same applied to his children. After the Flood, however, a deterioration in the atmosphere caused a gradual shortening of life. The view of Maimonides that those enumerated in the chapter were exceptions, others living the ordinary span of life, is untenable.[19]

ANTHOLOGY

while at the same time emulating the noble deeds of his brother Abel.

Pirke d'Rabbi Eliezer Ch. 22. T.S. 5, 40.

25. **And he called his name Seth.**

He named him thus because he became the *basis* of the world, since Cain and Abel disappeared from the scene.[1]

Bamidbar 14:24. T.S. 5, 39.

26. SETH. This was to indicate that *he* would rank as his offspring (lit., shoot, deriving Seth from *shathal,* to plant) instead of Abel.

Ms. in Aggadath B'reshith, cited in T.S. 5, 39, note.

27. **And eight hundred years.**

Throughout Scripture the word *meoth* (hundreds) is spelled in full; but in the texts relating to Adam and Lamech it is spelled defectively, with the letter *waw* which should follow the *alef* missing. The reason for the former is that Adam and Enoch died in the same year, and thus two righteous men were lost to the world. Again, in the verse referring to Lamech the word *meoth* is defective, because the catastrophe of the Flood occurred in the year of his demise.[1]

Midrash Habiur Ms. T.S. 5, 46.

28. **And all the days that Adam lived were nine hundred and thirty years; and he died.**

Three resisted the Angel of Death when he came to take their lives: Adam, Jacob and Moses. When the Angel of Death came to take Adam's life, he protested, "From God's own mouth I heard with my own ears that I would live a thousand years; but I have lived only nine hundred and thirty." Then the Angel of Death ascended before the Almighty and repeated what Adam had said. The Almighty gave him the written deed (in which Adam had assigned 70 years to David), and bade Gabriel, Michael and Sarfiel to accompany him. They went down to Adam and saw his countenance changed, his limbs wrenched apart, his heart fiercely palpitating from his right ribs to his left ribs, and they heard him crying: "Happy were I had God never created me!" Said the angels accompanying the Angel of Death to him: "Why weep and cry because of death? All must die save Him who lifted His hands to heaven," as it says, *For I lift up My hand to heaven and say: "I live for ever"* (Deut. 32:40). Gabriel recalled to him the 70 years which he had assigned to David the son of Jesse, Michael

§ 25 [1] Deriving Seth from *shath,* to found or place.

§ 27 [1] The defective spelling is interpreted in both cases as indicating a great loss. The dating is difficult, since from Scripture it does not appear that Adam and Enoch died in the same year, nor that the Flood occurred in the year of Lamech's death.

[7]And Seth lived after he begot Enosh eight hundred and seven years, and begot sons and daughters. [8]And all the days of Seth were nine hundred and twelve years; and he died. [9]And Enosh lived ninety years, and begot Kenan. [10]And Enosh lived after he begot Kenan eight hundred and fifteen years, and begot sons and daughters. [11]And all the days of Enosh were nine hundred and five years; and he died. [12]And Kenan lived seventy years, and begot Mahalalel. [13]And Kenan lived after he begot Mahalalel eight hundred and forty years, and begot sons and

ANTHOLOGY

and Sarfiel adding, "We were signatories to the deed." Then said Adam: "Now, indeed, I must die on the testimony of the three of you," as it says, *At the mouth of two witnesses, or three witnesses, shall he that is to die be put to death* (Deut. 17:6).

B'reshith Rabbathi Ms. T.S. 5, 45.

29. AND HE DIED. God called unto the body of Adam, "Adam! Adam!" and it answered, "Here am I, Lord!" Then God said: "I told thee once, 'Dust thou art, and unto dust shalt thou return.' Now I promise thee resurrection. I will awaken thee on the day of judgment, when all the generations of men that spring from thy loins shall arise from the grave." God then sealed up the grave, that none might do him harm during the six days to elapse until his rib should be restored to him through the death of Eve.

Apocalypse of Moses 41-45. Ginzberg Legends, Vol. 1, p. 101.

30. **And he begot Kenan.**

Why was he called Kenan? Because he brought (*hiknah,* same root as Kenan) misfortune on his generation by leading them astray.

Midrash printed in Aggadath B'reshith from Ms. T.S. 5, 47.

31. AND HE BEGOT KENAN. Enos was ninety years old when he begot Kenan. The lad grew up and was intelligent and clever, and he understood that the deeds of his father were evil. God gave him abundance of wisdom and knowledge and he became exceedingly wise. He gathered to him multitudes of people, and instructed them and taught them to do what was right in the sight of the Lord, and when the people heard his words of wisdom, they said to one another, "Let us make him King over us." And they did so. And Kenan reigned over all the earth.

Sepher Ha-Yuchasin; Gen. R. 23:11. Levner, Legends of Israel, p. 35.

32. **And Kenan lived seventy years.**

He was the fourth generation of the first civilization (i.e., that which preceded the Flood). Two begot at the age of seventy: Kenan, who belonged to the first civilization; and Terah, who belonged to the second (that which was built up after the Flood).[1]

Midrash Tadshe Ch. 10. T.S. 5, 48.

33. **And begot Mahalalel.**

Why was he so called? Because he was the first to repent and render praise (*hallel,* same root as Ma-halalel) to God.

Midrash printed in Aggadath B'reshith from Ms. T.S. 5, 49.

§ 32 [1] The point apparently is this: Just as Kenan at the age of 70 begot Mahalalel, who led men back to God (see par. 33), so did Terah at the age of 70 beget Abraham, who likewise taught men the worship of the true God.

daughters. [14]And all the days of Kenan were nine hundred and ten years; and he died. [15]And Mahalalel lived sixty and five years, and begot Jared. [16]And Mahalalel lived after he begot Jared eight hundred and thirty years, and begot sons and daughters. [17]And all the days of Mahalalel were eight hundred ninety and five years; and he died. [18]And Jared lived a hundred sixty and two years, and begot Enoch. [19]And Jared lived after he begot Enoch eight hundred years, and begot sons and daughters. [20]And all the days of Jared were nine hundred sixty and two years; and he died. [21]And Enoch lived sixty and five years, and begot Methuselah. [22]And Enoch walked with God after he begot Methuselah three hundred

ANTHOLOGY

34. **And begot Yared.**

He was so called because his generation degenerated (*yarad*) to the lowest level. A contrary reason is that in his days angels descended (*yardu*) from heaven and taught men how to serve God.

Midrash Aggadah B'reshith. T.S. 5, 50. 51.

35. **And Enoch walked with God.**

When Enoch, the son of Jered, saw the evil ways of mankind, he turned away from them, and built a house for himself where he worshipped the Lord with all his heart, and prayed to him, saying, "O Lord God, create in mankind a pure heart, to love good and hate evil, that men may serve You and do what is right in Your sight." And as Enoch was praying to God and pleading with Him for the people of his generation, an angel of the Lord called to him, "Enoch! Enoch!" and Enoch answered, "Here I am!" And the angel said to him, "God has sent me to say to you, 'Arise, come out of the place in which you have hidden yourself and go to the people of your generation and teach them how they should live.'" Then Enoch came out from his hiding-place and went to the people and taught them the ways of lovingkindness, righteousness and mercy.

At that time all the hundred and thirty kings of the earth gathered together and came to Enoch, and bowing before him, said, "We have seen that God is with you, and has given you of His wisdom, therefore come and reign over us." And he was persuaded by them and made them acquainted with the ways of God, and made peace between them, and there was peace throughout the whole earth all the days of Enoch, who reigned over all mankind two hundred and forty-three years and executed justice and righteousness over all the people and led them in the path of the Lord.

Book of Jubilee; Baraitha di Rabbi Ishmael, 23, 11. Levner, Legends of Israel, pp. 36-37.

36 AND ENOCH WALKED WITH GOD. All sevenths are favorites in the world. (After stating and proving that the seventh heaven is the most favored, and also that *tebel*, the seventh name for the earth, shows it under its most favorable aspect, the Midrash continues:) The seventh is the most-favored among the generations. Thus: Adam, Seth, Enosh, Kenan, Mahalalel, Jared, Enoch, and of him, the seventh, it is written, *And Enoch walked with God.*

Lev. R. 29. T.S. 5, 53.

37. AND ENOCH WALKED WITH GOD. God's way is unlike man's. When a land rebels against a mortal king, he penalizes it by destroying the good alike with the evil. Not so is it with God. When a generation provokes Him, He delivers the good and destroys the

years, and begot sons and daughters. [23]And all the days of Enoch were three hundred sixty and five years. [24]And Enoch walked with God, and

COMMENTARY

[22]Enoch walked with God. a. He lived righteously.[20] **b.** He walked in God's ways, doing good to others by practice and precept.[21] **[24]and he was not. a.** He was tempted to become wicked, whereupon God cut his life short so that *he was*

ANTHOLOGY

wicked. When the generation of Enoch sinned, God destroyed the sinners but saved Enoch, as Genesis narrates, *And Enoch walked with God*. In like vein Scripture writes, *The Lord is good, a stronghold in the day of trouble, and He knoweth them that take refuge in Him* (Nahum 1:7).

Num. R. 5:4. T.S. 5, 54.

38. AND ENOCH WALKED WITH GOD. Enoch was one of the thirteen who were born circumcised. Here it says, *And Enoch walked with God;* while it is also written, *Noah* walked *with God:* the employment of "*walked*" in both cases implies that they were alike (and Noah was born circumcised).

Midrash on Psalms Chap. 9. T.S. 5, 55.

39. AND ENOCH WALKED WITH GOD. The companionship of the righteous with God is described in three ways. Of Noah we are told, *Noah walked* with *God* (6:9). Jacob said: "*The God* before *Whom my fathers Abraham and Isaac* walked" (48:15). And finally, Moses bade the children of Israel: After *the Lord your God shall ye walk* (Deut. 13:5). This may be illustrated by the case of a man who has three children: the oldest walks *before* his father; therefore the Patriarchs, who were indeed great[1] in good deeds, are described as walking *before* God. The middle son walks *behind* him. Therefore the Israelites were bidden, After *the Lord your God shall ye walk,* which means, emulate Him in His humility, His enduring patience, and His love. But the youngest walks *by the side* of his father, so as not to go astray. Therefore of the earlier generations it is said, *And Enoch walked* with *God; and Noah walked* with *God*.

P'sikta Zuta B'reshith. T.S. 5, 57.

40. AND ENOCH WALKED WITH GOD. That means that he was absorbed in the service of God to the exclusion of all other interests.

Midrash Habiur. T.S. 5, 59.

41. **And he was not; for God took him.**

R. Ishmael related: When I scaled heaven to gaze at the vision of God's chariot, I passed through palaces. I met Metatron and asked him: "Why are you called by the seventy names which belong to your Creator? Moreover, you are the greatest of all the heavenly princes, higher than all the angels, the most beloved of all His ministers, the most honored of all the hosts, and greater than all the mighty in honor, majesty and glory. Why then do they call you a young lad in the highest heaven?" He answered: "Because I am Enoch, son of Jared. When the Generation of the Flood sinned and hurled defiance at God, '*Depart from us, for we desire not the knowledge of Thy ways*' (Job 21:14), He delivered me before their very eyes (another version: He removed me from them and translated me to Heaven) that I might be a witness in the high heavens to every human being, that none might say that the Merciful One is cruel, for what grievous sin did those masses commit? Therefore He translated me while they still lived, before their very eyes, so that I be a witness against them in the future world. Then God made me a ruler and a prince among the ministering angels."

The Book Hekaloth (Palaces), which is called the Book of Enoch. T.S. 5, 65.

§ 39 [1] In Heb. "the oldest" and "great" are the same word, *gadol*.

he was not; for God took him. [25]And Methuselah lived a hundred eighty and seven years, and begot Lamech. [26]And Methuselah lived after he begot Lamech seven hundred eighty and

COMMENTARY

not — this phrase being used rather than the normal "and he died."[22] **b.** He disappeared, and his contemporaries knew not what became of him.[23] **for God took him. a.** Before his time.[24] **b.** His death is described in these terms as a special mark of honor.[25] **c.** This description of death is profoundly significant. We come from God, and to Him do

ANTHOLOGY

42. AND HE WAS NOT; FOR GOD TOOK HIM. Because Enoch was a righteous man God removed him from the world of mortals and translated him into the Angel Metatron. R. Akiba and his colleagues disagree on this subject. The latter maintained: Enoch was righteous only intermittently, vacillating between righteousness and sinfulness. Said the Holy One, blessed be He: "I will remove him from the earth (that is to say, I will let him die) while he is righteous." R. Hama b. R. Hoshaya said: *And he was not* means that he was not inscribed in the register of the righteous but in that of the wicked. R. Aibu said: Enoch was changeable, at times righteous, at others wicked. Said the Holy One, blessed be: "While he is righteous I will remove him from the world, so that he will be judged as a righteous man." R. Aibu also said: He judged and condemned him on New Year, when He judges the whole world.

Midrash B'reshith; Gen. R. 25. T.S. 5, 52. 62.

43. AND HE WAS NOT; FOR GOD TOOK HIM. Thus it happened with Enoch. While he was yet righteous and his whole generation was wicked, God prematurely removed him from the world, lest he learn the wicked ways of his age and himself be corrupted and lose his good name. This is what is meant by the text, *And he was not; for God took him.* This was a way of saying, He was no more in this world to complete his allotted time, God having removed him prematurely in order to deal lovingly with him by bestowing on him the life of the Hereafter.

Midrash Haneelam Zohar Hadash 20. T.S. 5, 66.

44. FOR GOD TOOK HIM. The Seraphim and the Cherubim became very agitated and trembled, and they cried out to God, saying, "Lord of the Universe! How can one born of woman mingle among us, and come up to heaven to minister to you?" And God answered them: "Know you, My ministers, My hosts, My Cherubim and My Seraphim, that mankind forsook Me and worshipped wood and stone and they caused Me to keep far from them, by reason of their evil deeds, and Enoch was the only man who exalted My name, and praised My works and told of My righteousness, and brought back many from their evil ways."

Book of Jubilee; Baraitha di Rabbi Ishmael, 23, 11. Levner, Legends of Israel, pp. 38-9.

45. AND HE WAS NOT; FOR GOD TOOK HIM. Enoch walked in the ways of Heaven, and to him apply the words of the Psalmist, *Happy is the man whom Thou choosest, and bringest near, that he may dwell in Thy courts* (Ps. 65:5). Hence it says, *And Enoch walked with God, and he was not; for God took him:* this teaches that He took him and hid him.

Midrash printed in Introduction to Aggadath B'reshith. T.S. 5, 63.

46. AND HE WAS NOT; FOR GOD TOOK HIM. It was taught: Three men ascended to heaven and ministered there before God. They were Enoch, Moses and Elijah. The proof lies in the following texts: Enoch: *And he was not, for God took him.* Moses: *And he ascended from the plains of Moab . . . And no man knoweth* of his sepulcher *unto this day* (Deut. 34:1, 6.).

two years, and begot sons and daughters. [27]And all the days of Methuselah were nine hundred sixty and nine years; and he died. [28]And Lamech lived a hundred eighty and two years, and begot a son. [29]And he called his

COMMENTARY

we return. To die is to be taken by God, in Whose Presence there is life eternal.[26] **[28]and begot a son** (*ben*). I.e., one by whom the world would be rebuilt.[27] (This connects *ben* with *banah*, "to build"; otherwise Scripture would merely have stated, "he begot Noah." — Ed.) **[29]shall comfort us in our work. a.** Said prophetically in reference to the invention of the plow, which was attributed to Noah.[28] **b.** This should rather be rendered: May

ANTHOLOGY

And Elijah ascended into heaven by a whirlwind (2 Kings 2:11).[1]

Midrash Hagadol B'reshith. T.S. 5, 64.

47. FOR GOD TOOK HIM. Sectarians asked R. Abbahu: "We do not find that Enoch died?" "How so?" inquired he. "Scripture speaks of God's taking him," they replied, "whilst the same is said in connection with Elijah, *Knowest thou that the Lord will* take *away thy master from thy head today*" (2 Kings 2:3).[1] "If you interpret the word 'taking,'" he answered, "then 'taking' is employed here, while in Ezekiel it says, *Behold, I* take *away from thee the desire of thine eyes* in a plague" (Ezek. 24:16 — there it obviously means death). R. Tanhuma observed: He answered them well. A matron asked the same question of R. Jose, to which he replied: "If Scripture only said, *And Enoch walked with God,* and nothing more, your deduction would be correct. Since, however, it adds, *And he was not, for God took him,* it means that he was no more in this world (having died), for God took him."

Gen. R. 25. T.S. 5, 60. 61.

48. **And all the days of Methuselah were nine hundred sixty and nine years; and he died.**

According to tradition he was a truly righteous man. He was named Methuselah because every utterance of his contained 230 parables (*mashal,* here connected with his name). Moreover, he learned in praise of God 900 halakot (laws) in the Books of the Mishnah, 300 teachings on the thousands of years when the earth was tohu (formless), and 300 on the two thousand years by which the Torah and the Messiah preceded the creation of the earth.

When he departed a sound as of a mighty storm arose in heaven, and a choir of 900 ministering angels eulogized him, the number corresponding to the 900 Orders of the Oral Law which he had studied. The holy celestial beings (Ezek. 1:5 ff.) from whose eyes tears streamed down upon the spot where he departed, did likewise. When the mortals saw this, they too eulogized him below.

Aggadath B'reshith. T.S. 5, 68.

49. **And Lamech lived a hundred eighty and two years, and begot a son.**

From Adam to the Flood there were 1656 years. The calculation is as follows: Adam became a father at 130 years, Seth at 105, Enosh at 90, Kenan at 70, Mahalalel at 65, Jared at 162, Enoch at 65, Methuselah at 187, and Lamech at 182, when he begot Noah. Noah was 600 years old when the Flood commenced (7:11), which gives a grand total of 1656. Enoch buried Adam and lived 57 years after that. Methuselah rounded out his full tale of years before the Flood.

Seder Olam, Chap. 1. T.S. 5, 70.

§ 46 [1] This passage apparently means that these never died, but were bodily translated into Heaven. In the proof-text for Moses *"ascended"* is understood in that sense, since *"no man knoweth of his sepulcher,"* which is taken to mean there was no sepulcher to know, because he never died.

§ 47 [1] He was taken up in a whirlwind, but did not die in the ordinary way (ibid., verse 11).

name Noah, saying: 'This same shall comfort us in our work and in the toil of our hands, which cometh

COMMENTARY

he comfort us.[29] **c.** This name was given to him when he grew up by his contemporaries, because he invented wine, which comforts and cheers the worker in his toil. "And he called" should then

ANTHOLOGY

50. AND BEGOT A SON. This is stated because from this son (Noah) the world was recreated anew.

Tanhuma B'reshith Par. 11. T.S. 5, 69.

51. AND BEGOT A SON. Why is he not straightway called by his name, as, e.g., in the case of Mahalalel and Jared, where we read, *And begot Jared . . . and begot Enoch* (verses 15, 18)? Methuselah was a very wise man, and he warned his family not to call him by name, lest the people of the Generation of the Flood kill him with their witchcraft, of which they were adept practitioners.[1] When he (Lamech) grew up, married, and begot a son, he went to his father and informed him, "A son has been born to me." "Then call him Noah," he advised, "for he will comfort the generations."[2] When the Generation of the Flood heard this, they too called him Noah, *saying: "This one shall comfort us in our work and in the toil of our hands."* Said he to them: "If you repent, he will comfort you; if not, he will not comfort you."

Ms. quoted in Introduction to Aggadath B'reshith. T.S. 5, 71.

52. AND BEGOT A SON. There were ten generations from Adam to Noah. This demonstrates how long-suffering was the Almighty. For all these generations angered Him continuously until He brought the Flood upon them.

Aboth 5:2. T.S. 5, 72.

53. **And he called his name Noah, saying: "This same shall comfort us (y'nahamenu fr. nahem) in our work," etc.**

R. Johanan said: The name does not correspond to the interpretation, nor does the interpretation correspond to the name. The text should either have stated, "This same shall give us rest (*yanihenu*)," or, "*And he called his name* Nahman, saying: '*This same* y'nahamenu;' " but does Noah correspond to *y'nahamenu?* The truth is that when the Holy One, blessed be He, created Adam, He gave him dominion over all things: the cow obeyed the plowman, the furrow obeyed the plowman. But when he sinned, they rebelled against him: the cow no longer obeyed the plowman, nor did the furrow obey the plowman. But when Noah arose, they ceased to rebel. Whence do we know it? Scripture uses the word Noah here (root *nah*); whilst elsewhere it says, *That thine ox and thine ass may cease* (from labor—*yanuhu,* same root) (Exod. 23:12): just as the cessation stated there means the cessation of the ox (from work), so the cessation mentioned here implies the cessation of the ox (from rebellion).

Resh Lakish gave this interpretation: Before Noah was born the waters used to ascend and inundate the dead in their graves. For it is twice stated, *He calleth for the waters of the sea* (Amos 5:8; 9:6), corresponding to the two times daily, morning and evening, that the waters came up and inundated them in their graves. Thus it is written, *Like the slain that lie in the grave* (Ps. 88:6), i.e., even those who

§ 51 [1] It was believed that witchcraft could not be practised against a person unless his name was known and pronounced in the incantation or spell. It is not altogether clear whose name was suppressed. Apparently Methuselah warned his family not to call him (Methuselah) by name. Or perhaps he warned his family not to call his son Lamech by name. Consequently, when a child was born to Lamech he feared to name him until he consulted his father. Frazer in "The Golden Bough" cites many instances of the fear amongst primitive peoples of calling a person by name.

[2] By popular etymology Noah is derived from the verb *nahem,* to comfort. According to another version Methuselah called him Noah, but advised his father (Lamech) to call him Menahem, the comforter.

ANTHOLOGY

died naturally were like the slain (without rest in the grave). But when Noah was born, they had rest; for "resting" is mentioned here (Noah, root *nah,* to rest), and also elsewhere, viz., *He entereth into peace, they* rest *in their beds* (Isa. 57:2): just as there the rest of the grave is meant, so does it here too. R. Eleazar said: He was so named on account of his sacrifice, as it is written, *And the Lord smelled the sweet* (nihoah) *savor* (Gen. 8:21). R. Jose b. Hanina said: On account of the resting of the ark, as it is written, *And the ark rested — wattanah* (ib. 4).

Gen. R. 25. T.S. 5, 74-76.

54. AND HE CALLED HIS NAME NOAH, SAYING. Whence do we know that when the righteous come into the world good arrives and suffering disappears from the earth? From the verse, *And he called his name Noah, saying: "This one will comfort us in our work and in the toil of our hands."*

Tosefta Sotah Chap. 10. T.S. 5, 73.

55. AND HE CALLED HIS NAME NOAH. It is noteworthy that whenever God descried that a righteous man was born He Himself, in all His Majesty, named him. Thus *He* named Noah, because he was righteous, as we read, *And He called his name Noah.*

Tanhuma Yashan B'reshith Par. 30. T.S. 5, 77.

56. AND HE CALLED HIS NAME NOAH, SAYING: "THIS SAME SHALL COMFORT US," etc. How did he know that he would comfort them: was he then a prophet? Said R. Simeon b. Jehozadak: They were indeed instructed in the matter. For when the Almighty said to Adam: *"Cursed is the ground for thy sake, in toil shalt thou eat of it all the days of thy life"* (3:17), Adam pleaded: "O Master of the Universe, how long is that to last?" And he was told that it would last until a man was born circumcised. Hence, when Noah was born circumcised, Lamech immediately exclaimed, *"This same shall* certainly *comfort us!"* What does *in our work and in the toil of our hands* mean? Before Noah's birth men would sow one thing and reap something totally different. They would sow wheat and reap thorns and thistles. But when Noah was born the world returned to its proper course. They sowed wheat and reaped wheat; barley, and reaped barley. Moreover, before Noah all the work was done by hand; therefore it says, *in the toil of our* hands. But Noah provided them with plows, scythes, axes and all manner of tools.[1]

Tanhuma B'reshith Par. 11. T.S. 5, 78.

57. THIS SAME SHALL COMFORT US. All who were born before Noah had their hands in one piece, undivided into fingers, because they did not need to till the ground. But Noah was born with his digits separated and clearly defined. From this Lamech understood that Noah would need his hands so shaped in order to cultivate the soil.[1]

Midrash Abakir. T.S. 5, 79.

58. THIS SAME SHALL COMFORT US. Lamech was indeed a great prophet to be able to speak thus. For how could he have known it otherwise?

Midrash quoted by Kimchi. T.S. 5, 80.

59. THIS SAME SHALL COMFORT US. Because the earth had been cursed on account of Adam; when he died Noah took his place,[1] and he made an end to the curse.

P'sikta (or: Pirke) d'Rabbi Eliezer. T.S. 5, 81.

§ 56 [1] Though it is stated in 4:22 that Tubal-cain was the "forger" (inventor?) of every cutting instrument of brass and iron, this Midrash assumes that for some reason they did not use them until Noah.

§ 57 [1] Those before him did not till the ground because it was accursed. Through Noah being born with hands suitable for husbandry Lamech understood that with him the curse would be lifted.

§ 59 [1] It is not clear how Noah took his place. Possibly, as the first of a 10-generation epoch, into which early humanity is elsewhere divided (cf. Aboth 5:2: There were ten generations from Adam to Noah . . . and ten generations from Noah to Abraham). This passage probably assumes that the curse was limited to the Adam epoch, and was therefore lifted when Noah was born.

from the ground which the Lord hath cursed.' [30]And Lamech lived after he begot Noah five hundred ninety and five years, and begot sons and daughters. [31]And all the days of Lamech were seven hundred seventy and seven years; and he died. [32]And Noah was five hundred years old; and Noah begot Shem, Ham, and Japheth.

COMMENTARY

rather be, "And one (indefinite subject — i.e., his contemporaries) called him Noah."[30] [32]**five hundred years old.** Why did he beget so much later that his contemporaries? God said: "If his children are wicked, they will have to be drowned in the Flood, which will grieve Noah. If they are righteous and grown up, they will each need an ark." Therefore He withheld children from him until an advanced age, so that the eldest was less than a hundred years old at the time of the Flood, and at that period one less than a hundred years old was considered irresponsible and not liable to punishment for his sins.[31] **Shem, Ham, and Japheth.** Japheth was the eldest. Shem is mentioned first because he was righteous, born circumcised, and the ancestor of Abraham.[32]

ANTHOLOGY

60. **And Noah was five hundred years old.**

It is written, *Happy is the man that hath not walked,* etc. (Ps. 1:1). "*Happy is the man*" refers to Noah: "*That hath not walked in the counsel of the wicked,*" etc. R. Judah said: It means through the three generations of Enosh, the Flood, and the Separation of Tongues.[1] R. Nehemiah said: It means through the generations of the Flood and the Separation; but during the generation of Enosh he was but a child. The text continues: *But his delight was in the law of the Lord* (ib. 2): this alludes to the seven precepts which he was commanded.[2] *But in His law doth he meditate:* he studied His Torah, deducing one law from another.

Gen. R. 26. T.S. 5, 87.

61. AND NOAH WAS FIVE HUNDRED YEARS OLD, etc. R. Judan observed: Why did all the generations beget at a hundred or two hundred years, while he begot at five hundred years? Because the Holy One, blessed be He, said: "If they (Noah's sons) are destined to be wicked, I do not desire them to perish in the flood; and if righteous, am I to burden him with the building of many arks?" Therefore the Lord denied him children until he was five hundred years old. R. Nehemiah said in the name of R. Eliezer b. R. Jose the Galilean: Thus even Japheth, the eldest, would not be a hundred years old at the time of the Flood, and therefore not subject to punishment.[1]

Gen. R. 26. T.S. 5, 85.

62. **And Noah begot Shem, Ham and Japheth.**

It may be proved that Scripture enumerates them in order of their wisdom (not age). For it is written, *And Noah was* five hundred *years old; and Noah begot Shem, Ham, and Japheth.* Now, if the order is according to age, Shem was at least a year older than Ham, and Ham a year older than Japheth, so that Shem was two years older than Japheth. Now it is written, *And Noah was* six hundred years *old when the flood of waters was upon the earth* (7:6); and it is written, *These are the generations of Shem. Shem was* a hundred *years old, and begot Arpachshad* two years *after the flood* (11:10). But was he a hundred years old? He must have been a hundred and two years old. Hence you must say that they are enumerated in order of their wisdom.

Sanhedrin 69b. T.S. 5, 84.

§ 60 [1] Though Noah lived through these wicked generations, he remained uncorrupted.
[2] See Chap. II, par. 134.

§ 61 [1] It was held that before the Flood one remained a minor in respect of Divine punishment until the age of a hundred.

ANTHOLOGY

63. AND NOAH WAS FIVE HUNDRED YEARS OLD; AND NOAH BEGOT SHEM, HAM, AND JAPHETH. Consider: all the wicked before Noah begot child at the ages of seventy, eighty and a hundred years, whereas Noah begot child only when he was five hundred years old. Why was this? Noah observed his fellow-men and saw how they would rise up and anger the Lord. Said he: "Why then should I beget children?" For that reason he had none until he was five hundred years old. But then he reflected: "Shall I then die childless, whereas the Holy One, blessed be He, commanded Adam to propagate his species, as it says, *And God blessed them; and God said unto them: 'Be fruitful and multiply'* (1:28). Yet I would die without child!" Therefore after five hundred years he decided to have children, and Shem, Ham, and Japheth were born to him.

Tanhuma Yashan B'reshith 39. T.S. 5, 86.

64. AND NOAH BEGOT SHEM, HAM, AND JAPHETH. Surely Japheth was the eldest? Shem takes precedence for a number of reasons: he was righteous; he was born circumcised; the Holy One, blessed be He, set His name particularly upon him; Abraham was destined to be his direct descendant; he was to minister in the High Priesthood; and the Temple would be built in his territory. Simeon b. Huta said: The reason is because the Holy One, blessed be He, suspended the punishment of the generations from the Flood until the Separation for 340 years, which is the numerical value of his name.

Gen. R. 26. T.S. 5, 88.

65. AND NOAH BEGOT SHEM, HAM, AND JAPHETH. It is written, *Better is a little that the righteous hath than the abundance of many wicked* (Ps. 37:16). Those three sons of Noah were better to him than all the multitudes of the generation of the Flood, when every mother bore quadruplets or quintuplets. See then how vast were their multitudes, and through their very prolificness they provoked the Lord![1] But of Noah it is merely written, *And Noah was five hundred years old* (*and Noah begot Shem, Ham and Japheth*),[2] but not "and he begot sons and daughters," as in the case of the others.

Aggadath B'reshith Ch. 10. T.S. 5, 91.

§ 65 [1] Because their vast numbers gave them a feeling of security and independence of God.
[2] The bracketed words are not in the text, but have been added because the whole point apparently lies in the contrast between his three sons and the "sons and daughters" whom the others begot in abundance. Possibly, however, the point is that since he had children only at 500 years, they could not be so numerous, in which case the addition is unnecessary.

GENESIS

Chapter VI

[1]And it came to pass, when men began to multiply on the face of the earth, and daughters were born unto them, [2]that the sons of God saw the

COMMENTARY

[1]when men began to multiply. The birth of Noah and his sons introduces the story of the Flood. Therefore Scripture now tells us that as soon as men began to multiply they began to sin.[1] **and daughters were born unto them.** This is stated parenthetically: and daughters too having been born unto them.[2] **[2]the sons of God.**, etc. **a.** I.e., the sons of princes and judges saw the daughters of the common people ("men"), *Elohim* always implying rulership (cf. *and thou shalt be to him in God's stead* [lit., "for

ANTHOLOGY

1. **And it came to pass.**

R. Levi — some say, R. Jonathan — said: The following is a tradition handed down to us from the Men of the Great Assembly: Wherever we find the term "*and it came to pass*" in Scripture, it indicates the approach of trouble. Thus, *And it came to pass when men began to multiply* leads up to, *And the Lord saw that the wickedness of man was great* (6:5).

Megillah 10b. T.S. 6, 1.

2. **And it came to pass, when men began (hehel) to multiply.**

The Hebrew *hehel* is derived from *hulin*, meaning profane, and the text reads: *And it came to pass, when men became profane to excess* — because they were wicked.

Midrash Aggadah B'reshith. T.S. 6, 4.

3. **To multiply (la-rob).**

R. Johanan said: This means that the world increased abundantly. Resh Lakish maintained: It implies that strife (*meribah*, which he connects with *la-rob*) then came into the world.

Baba Bathra 16a. T.S. 6, 2.

4. **To multiply on the face of the earth.**

This teaches that they spilled their semen upon the trees and stones; and because they were steeped in lust the Holy One, blessed be He, gave them many women, as it is written, *And it came to pass, when men began to multiply . . . and daughters were born unto them.*

Gen. R. 26. T.S. 6, 5.

5. R. Simeon b. Ammi's wife gave birth to a daughter. When R. Hiyya the Elder met him, he said to him: "The Holy One, blessed be He, has begun to bless you." "What is the proof?" inquired he. "The verse, *And it came to pass, when man began to multiply . . . and daughters were born unto them*," he replied. When he (R. Simeon) went to his father he asked him, "Did the Babylonian congratulate you?" "Yes," he answered, and related their conversation. "Nevertheless," observed his father, "though wine and vinegar are both needed, yet wine is more necessary than vinegar; wheat and barley are both needed, yet wheat more so than barley. When a man gives his daughter in marriage and incurs expense, he says to her, 'May you never return hither.'"

Gen. R. 26. T.S. 6, 6.

6. **The sons of elohim (AJV: God).**

R. Simeon b. Yohai called them the sons of judges,[1] and cursed those who called them the sons of God. R. Simeon b. Yohai said: If demoralization does not proceed from the leaders, it is not real demoralization.

Gen. R. 26. T.S. 6, 9.

§ 6 [1] For this meaning of *elohim*, see Chap. III, par. 9.

daughters of men that they were fair; and they took them wives, whomsoever they chose. [3]And the Lord said: 'My spirit shall not abide

COMMENTARY

Elohim"], Exod. 4:16; cf. also Exod. 7:1).[3] **b.** Or, the virtuous sons of the house of Seth saw the wicked daughters of the line of Cain.[4] Thus *"sons of God"* means those who serve God and obey Him, those nourished and brought up in the love of Him as their Father and Benefactor (Exod. 4:22; Deut. 14:1; 32:5; Isa. 1:2; Hos. 2:1). It is quite in accord with Biblical usage that those who adhered to the true worship of God — the children of Seth — are called *"sons of God"*; and that, in contrast to these, the daughters of the line of Cain should be spoken of as *"daughters of men."* Verses 1-4 would then point out the calamitious consequences to mankind when the pious sons of Seth merged with those who had developed a Godless civilization and who, with all their progress in arts and inventions, had ended in depravity and despair. Through intermarriage, the sons of Seth sank to the level of the ungodly race; and likewise deserved the doom that, with the exception of one family, was to overtake mankind. These verses are thus the first warning in the Torah against intermarriage with idolaters.[5] **c.** Conversely, the iniquitous male descendants of Cain (called *b'nei elohim* because they were giants) saw the righteous women of the stock of Seth; or the uncouth barbarians saw the refined daughters of civilized men.[6] **and they took.** By force.[7] **[3]My spirit shall not abide** (or, strive — Heb. *yadon*),

ANTHOLOGY

7. The sons of elohim (AJV: God). These were the sons of Cain, who were strikingly beautiful and tall in stature; and *so they took them wives, whomsoever they chose,* even married woman leaving their husbands for them.

Introduction to Aggadath B'reshith. T.S. 6, 13.

8. The sons of elohim. The celestial beings are called elohim, as in our text, *The sons of elohim saw the daughters of men.* Israel too is so designated in the verse, *I said: "Ye are elohim"* (AJV: godlike beings).

Yelamdenu. T.S. 6, 19.

9. **That the sons of elohim saw the daughters of men.**

R. Aibu commented: It is written, *Let the eyes of the wicked be darkened, that they see not* (Ps. 69:24). For it is the lust of their eyes that drags them down to Gehinom, as our text relates, *That the sons of elohim saw the daughters of men,* etc.[1]

Est. R. 7; Abba Gurion 12. T.S. 6, 11.

10. The sons of God saw the daughters of men. They were the angels Uzza and Uziel whose abode was above, but descended to the earth to try their constancy. While in heaven, they heard God say, *"I will blot out man whom I have created from the face of the earth"* (6:7). Said they to Him: "Sovereign of the Universe! *What is man, that Thou art mindful of him, and the son of man, that Thou thinkest of him?"* (Ps. 8:5)[1] God answered them: "If ye lived on earth and saw the beauty of their women, the Evil Tempter would master you too and drive you to sin." "We will descend," they rejoined, "and yet not sin." Straightway they descended, so Scripture narrates that *the sons of God saw the daughters of men.* On seeing them they desired to return to heaven, pleading, "Let this trial suffice!" But He answered: "Ye have already become defiled, and can never again be pure."

Introduction to Midrash Aggadath B'reshith. T.S. 6, 16.

11. **My spirit shall not judge man, etc.**

R. Akiba interpreted: The Holy One, blessed be He, said: "These men, not realizing that

§ 9 [1] In this and the next passages *elohim* is understood not as God, but as great men who wickedly took advantage of their position and strength to seduce and rape.

§ 10 [1] They said this in agreement with God, adding (as is suggested by parallel midrashim) that man should never have been created.

in man for ever, for that he also is flesh; therefore shall his days be a hundred and twenty years.' [4]The

COMMENTARY

etc. Many interpretations of this difficult verse have been proposed. **a.** Let not My spirit which I have placed in man (i.e., the soul) be in eternal strife with the body which draws him to earthly desires.[8] **b.** *Yadon* is derived from *n'dan* ("scabbard"), hence: Let not My spirit (i.e., the soul) abide for ever in its sheath, i.e., the body.[9] For he too is but flesh like every other creature, and does not deserve to have My spirit in him.[10] Or, because through his having utilized his freedom of choice to choose evil, even the spirit within him has turned to flesh.[11] **c.** My spirit will not for ever rule over man's body, since in respect to his erroneous course of conduct he is but flesh. This connects *yadon* with an Arabic root meaning to rule, subjugate; and *b'shaggam* (AJV: for that also) with *shagag*, to err, the *mem* at the end being adverbial, as in *omnam*.[12] **d.** Not for ever will My spirit deliberate within Me whether to destroy man or to spare him,[13] for though he is but flesh, he has not submitted to My rule. **e.** I shall not for ever keep on debating with Myself whether to destroy him; for in spite of having been

ANTHOLOGY

they are but flesh and blood, have hurled defiance against Heaven, *and said unto God: 'Depart from us'* " (Job 21:14). R. Meir gave this exegesis: "That generation," said the Almighty, "has averred, 'The Lord will not judge; there is no Judge, for the Omnipresent has abandoned the world.' " Rabbi (i.e., R. Judah ha-Nasi) interpreted it: The Almighty declared: "They have not established courts of law on earth; I will therefore set up a Celestial Court to judge them."

Aboth d'Rabbi Nathan Chap. 32. T.S. 6, 27. 28. 29.

12. MY SPIRIT SHALL NOT JUDGE MAN, etc. Scripture says: *Thy right hand, O Lord, is glorious in power* (Exod. 15:6). Glorious and majestic art Thou in Thy power: long indeed didst Thou wait for the Generation of the Flood to repent, but they did not repent; thus it says, *My spirit shall not judge man* (immediately). Yea, Thou didst not finally determine their doom until their wickedness reached the very brim.

Mekilta B'shallah Ch. 85 on the Song of Moses. T.S. 6, 31.

13. MY SPIRIT SHALL NOT ALWAYS STRIVE WITH MAN. R. Levi said: On three occasions the ministering angels desired to hymn the Almighty, but He would not permit them, viz., in the generation of the Flood, at the Red Sea, and at the destruction of the Temple.[1] Of the generation of the Flood Scripture relates: *And the Lord said: "My spirit shall not always strive with man."*[2]

Introduction to Lam. R. 24. T.S. 6, 32.

14. AND THE LORD SAID: "MY SPIRIT SHALL NOT ENTER INTO JUDGMENT WITH MAN FOR EVER." The generation of the Flood has no portion in the future world, nor will they stand for Judgment, as it is written, *My spirit shall not enter into judgment with man for ever* — there will be neither Judgment for them, nor My spirit, by which alone they might attain to the Hereafter.

Sanhedrin 107b. T.S. 6, 20.

15. **For that he also is flesh.**

Men cannot grasp the fact that they too are but flesh, just as cattle, even as Scripture writes, *Man hath no pre-eminence above a beast; for all is vanity* (Eccl. 3:19).

P'sikta Zuta B'reshith. T.S. 6, 40.

16. **Therefore shall his days be a hundred and twenty years.**

It is written, *That which is crooked cannot be made straight, and that which is wanting*

§ 13 [1] These were three occasions when God visited sinners with punishment. But He would not permit the angels to sing His praises: though sinners they were still His children, and their deserved punishment was not a proper occasion for hymns.

[2] Though I must judge them, yet I have no pleasure in it.

COMMENTARY

created in My image, he is also flesh, which brings him to sin.[14] **f.** Let not My spirit dwelling in man be permanently disgraced by man who erroneously (equating *be-shaggam* with *be-shoggam*) maintains that he is wholly flesh, i.e., matter.[15] **g.** Disregarding the pausal accent on *l'olam,* the phrase may mean: I must not for ever busy Myself (cf. Syriac *shegam,* "to be engaged") thinking that, because he is but flesh, I must show him pity.[16] **h.** My spirit shall not contend with and vex Me on account of man.[17] **i.** The interpretation of "*sons of God*" as referring to men and not to angels, as some maintain, is borne out by this verse. For, if fallen angels were in question, and if it was wrong for them to marry human women, the angels surely were the chief offenders; and yet the sentence falls exclusively upon *man.* "In God's judgments there is no unrighteousness, partiality, or even the appearance of partiality" (Keil).[18] **a hundred and twenty years. a.** This is the period

ANTHOLOGY

cannot be numbered (Eccl. 1:15). *That which is crooked cannot be made straight* alludes to the generation of the Flood: once they had become crooked in their deeds, they were never again made straight; *and that which is wanting:* once the Almighty had reduced their years, their former longevity was never restored.

Eccl. R. 1:37. T.S. 6, 37.

17. THEREFORE SHALL HIS DAYS BE A HUNDRED AND TWENTY YEARS. There were twenty-four beneficent powers in the world, and all were lost through sin; yet will God restore them to Israel at the End of Days. Four were lost on account of the Generation of the Flood. They are: physical strength, longevity, prolific propagation, and peace. Longevity: It is written, *And all the days that Adam lived were nine hundred and thirty years* (5:5). But when the generation of the Flood sinned, God declared: "*Therefore shall his days be a hundred and twenty years.*" Yet will God restore this to Israel, for it is written, *They shall not build, and another inhabit; they shall not plant, and another eat; for as the days of a tree shall be the days of My people, and Mine elect shall long enjoy the work of their hands* (Isa. 65:22).

Midrash Hagadol B'reshith. T.S. 6, 42.

18. THEREFORE SHALL HIS DAYS BE A HUNDRED AND TWENTY YEARS. Thus did Moses plead with the Lord: "The angels are immortal, yet though they constantly hymn Thy glory, they never see nor know the place of Thy abode; whereas I have communed with Thee face to face." God replied: "I can do no otherwise, for I decreed your span of life from the very earliest days," as it says, *My spirit shall not abide in man for ever, for that he also is flesh; therefore shall his days be a hundred and twenty years.*[1]

Yalkut Shimoni 1:815. T.S. 6, 38.

19. THEREFORE SHALL HIS DAYS BE A HUNDRED AND TWENTY YEARS. You say this in the face of Adam's life of nearly a thousand years! It means that in 120 years (in the grave) the body becomes but a single spoonful of dust.

J. Nazir 7:2. T.S. 6, 34.

20. THEREFORE SHALL HIS DAYS BE A HUNDRED AND TWENTY YEARS. It is written, *In the six hundredth year of Noah's life . . . were all the fountains of the deep broken up, and the rain descended* (7:11-12). How can this be reconciled with our text?[1] We must assume that their doom had been determined one hundred and twenty years earlier.[2]

Seder Olam Chap. 28. T.S. 6, 33.

§ 18 [1] The 120 years are understood as an allusion to Moses' life-span.

§ 20 [1] The Rabbis understood the text to mean that man would be given another 120 years on earth, to repent. But this was said when Noah was 500 years old (5:32); therefore the Flood should not have commenced until he was 620 years old.

[2] I.e., although Scripture tells of this decree *after* the birth of Noah's children, which took place when he was 500 years old, in fact it had been determined twenty years earlier (the Torah not being in chronological order). A variant does read: Their doom had been determined *twenty* years earlier.

Nephilim were in the earth in those days, and also after that, when the

COMMENTARY

of grace for mankind to repent before God brings the Flood upon them. Since Japheth, Noah's oldest son, was born a hundred years before the Deluge (see 5:32 and cf. 7:11), mankind must have been warned of its doom twenty years before Noah became a father.[19] **b.** The duration of the individual's life is not to exceed 120 years.[20] [4]**Nephilim. a.** A race of giants, exercising tyrannical sway over their contemporaries.[21] **b.** They were so named because they "fell' (*naphal*) and caused the world to fall.[22] **c.** The heart of all who beheld them fell in wonder at their enormous stature.[23] **d.** They existed before the intermarriages took place. The mention of Nephilim in Num. 13:33 is

ANTHOLOGY

21. **The Nephilim were in the earth.**

They were called by seven names: *Nephilim, Emim, Refaim, Gibborim, Zamzumim, Anakim,* and *Awim. Nephilim* denotes that they hurled (*hippilu*) the world down, themselves fell (*naflu*) from the world, and filled the world with abortions (*nephilim*) through their immorality.

Gen. R. 26. T.S. 6, 43.

22. THE NEPHILIM WERE IN THE EARTH IN THOSE DAYS. This teaches that they observed the sun and the moon and then performed witchcraft. It is of them that Scripture writes, *These are of them that rebel against the light* (Job 24:13). They were indeed the mighty and stiff-necked, who rebelled against God and practiced witchcraft.[1]

Tanhuma B'reshith Par. 12. T.S. 6, 44.

23. THE NEPHILIM WERE IN THE EARTH. R. Zadok said: From them were born the giants (Anakim), who walked with pride in their heart, and who stretched forth their hand to all kinds of robbery, violence, and bloodshed, as it is said, *And there we saw the Nephilim, the sons of Anak* (Num. 13:33); and it says, *The Nephilim were on the earth in those days.*

Pirke d'Rabbi Eliezer Chap. 22. T.S. 6, 46.

24. THE NEPHILIM WERE IN THE EARTH. They were the sons of Cain who were the greatest and most renowned of that generation. Whence do we know that Nephilim means great and ruling personalities? From the verse, *So that we are distinguished* (v'niflinu), *I and Thy people* (Exod. 33:16). Thus the text continues: *And also after that, when the sons of elohim*[1] *came in.* They were the grandchildren of Cain, born of the daughters of men,[2] more handsome, taller, stronger and more distinguished-looking than their parents. *And they bore children unto them* — yea, like unto them in beauty and general appearance. *The same were the mighty men that were of old:* they are described in these words because they were the first of the human race, existing from the very creation of the world. *Men of renown* (better, notoriety): murderers and the sons of murderers: Cain slew Abel, and Lamech slew Cain and his sons.

Introduction to Aggadath B'reshith. T.S. 6, 47. 51.

25. **And also after that.**

R. Judah b. Ammi commented: The later generations would not learn from the earlier ones, i.e., the generation of the Flood from that of Enosh, and the generation of the Separation from that of the Flood. Hence Scripture says, *And also after that* they had the

§ 22 [1] On the present reading the connection with the text is obscure. By a slight change, which is the variant in other texts, it reads: They were the mighty . . . who brought down (the powers of the sun and the moon) and practised witchcraft by means of them. This will be based on the word Nephilim, which is connected with *nafal,* to fall, in the sense that they made the powers of the sun fall to the earth.

§ 24 [1] See pars. 6 and 7.

[2] I.e., of human mothers. The phrase is from our text: *When the sons of* elohim *came in unto the daughters of men.* Perhaps the idea is to emphasize their human descent, in contrast to the demons who were born during the 130 years of the separation of Adam from Eve (see Chap. V, par. 21).

sons of God came in unto the daughters of men, and they bore children to them; the same were the mighty men that were of old, the men of renown. [5]And the Lord saw that the

COMMENTARY

no reason to assume that they survived the Flood. The excited imagination of the Spies expresses its terror at the men of great stature whom they saw at Hebron, by saying that they must be the old antediluvian giants (W. H. Green).[24] **in those days. a.** In the days of the generation of Enosh and the children of Cain.[25] **b.** During the period of grace given by God for their repentance; whilst *and also after that* means that they did not repent.[26] **and also after that. a.** Although they saw the destruction of the generation of Enosh, the ocean having overflowed its bounds and drowned a third of the world (according to an old legend), they still did not repent.[27] **b.** After the Flood.[28] **c.** It has also been held that either they were the forbears of the wives of Noah's sons, and the children they bore after the Flood were giants; or this agrees with the tradition that Og, king of Bashan, was one of them and that he escaped the Flood and many with him.[29] **came in.** And begot giants like themselves.[30] **the mighty men.** They were mighty in their rebellion against God.[31] **the men of renown** (*shem*). **a.** They brought desolation (*shimamon*) upon the world.[32] **b.** By reason of their abnormal physical strength, they gained for themselves a reputation as heroes. But enduring fame does not rest upon such qualifications as these Nephilim possessed. Their fate was to disappear from the earth, and humanity was to continue through Noah, "a righteous man, and blameless in his generations."[33]

ANTHOLOGY

dread example before their eyes, they persisted in sinning.

Gen. R. 26. T.S. 6, 49.

26. **When the sons of God, etc.**

R. Joshua b. Karcha said: The Israelites are called sons of God, as it is said, *Ye are the sons of the Lord your God* (Deut. 14:1). The angels are called sons of God, as it is said, *When the morning stars sang together, and all the sons of God shouted for joy* (Job 38:7); and these (of our text) whilst still in their holy place, in heaven, were called sons of God, as it is said, *And also after that, when the sons of God came in unto the daughters of men.*

Pirke d'Rabbi Eliezer Chap. 22. T.S. 6, 56.

27. **The same were the mighty men.**

R. Berekiah said: They were very fierce, and men of great stature — that is the meaning of the text. Had He not liquidated them with fire from heaven above, none could have prevailed against them.

Tanhuma Noah Par. 7. T.S. 6, 52.

28. **Men of renown.**

R. Aha said, citing R. Joshua b. Levi: Dissension is as great an evil as the sin of the generation of the Flood. It says here, *Men of renown;* whilst elsewhere it says, *They were princes of the congregation, the elect men of the assembly,* men of renown (Num. 16:2). Just as the offense of the "*men of renown*" in the latter instance was dissension, so was that of the "*men of renown*" in our text.

Gen. R. 26. T.S. 6, 55.

29. **And the Lord saw, etc.**

The wicked say: God does not see us when we sin, because He is far, and seven heavens lie between Him and us. God answers them: Ye sinners! *He that planted the ear, shall He not hear? He that formed the eye, shall He not see* (Ps. 94:8)? Behold, He surveys all! Indifference has indeed been attributed to Me, as it says, *For He knoweth base men; and when He seeth iniquity, He doth not consider it* (Job 11:11). But this I have done for your sake, as it says, *And the Lord saw that the wickedness of man was great.*[1]

Aggadath B'reshith Ch. 1. T.S. 6, 63.

§ 29 [1] The meaning is not clear. Probably: This apparent disregard of sin is for man's sake, to give him time to repent, but not because He does not see it, for He certainly does.

wickedness of man was great in the earth, and that every imagination of

COMMENTARY

c. The whole passage has been interpreted on the supposition that Adam and Eve are designated *the sons* (children) *of God* (verse 2), as well as Seth and Enosh; their children are the *Nephilim* who, though no longer bearing the visible impress of God's creation, nevertheless stood out from their fellow-men. *Nephilim* then signifies the "inferior ones," i.e., inferior to their parents.[34] [5]**wickedness.** This verse and the two that follow form the climax to the previous four verses in which the moral depravity of the age is depicted. Retribution is swiftly coming.[35] **was great.** In the past.[36] **every imagination** (*yetser*) **of the thoughts of his heart. a.** In the future; there was no hope of repentance.[37] **b.** The Heb. *yatsar* means to form (it therefore has nothing to do with the "Evil

ANTHOLOGY

30. **The wickedness of man was great.**

R. Hanina said: This means that their wickedness waxed ever greater and greater. R. Berekiah observed in the name of R. Johanan; We know from Scripture that the generation of the Flood was punished by water, and that the Sodomites were judged by fire. How do we know that each in addition received the punishment of the other? Because they were equally wicked, for "great" is stated in the case of each,[1] which teaches that both were judged in like manner.

Gen. R. 27. T.S. 6, 58.

31. AND THE LORD SAW THAT THE WICKEDNESS. It is written, *There is an evil of man which I have seen under the sun which is great* (Eccl. 6:1). The Holy One, blessed be He, saith: See what the wicked are doing! When I created man I gave him two ministers to serve him, one good, the other bad. But they leave the good and associate with and cleave to the evil one! Not alone have they failed to turn the bad minister good, but have actually made the good one evil! This is what Scripture says, *And* every *imagination of the thoughts of his heart* (even the good impulse) *was only evil continually.*

Aggadath B'reshith Ch. 1. T.S. 6, 64.

32. AND THE LORD SAW THAT THE WICKEDNESS OF MAN WAS GREAT. Scripture writes: *For to every matter there is a time and judgment; for the wickedness of man is great upon him* (Ecc. 8:6). The wicked anger God and say: The Almighty has sworn not to bring a flood upon earth again; therefore we can do whatever we desire with impunity. But God replies: Seeing that the wicked speak thus, as you live, I have other means of retribution. Thus, e.g., he drowns them in the oceans, rivers, and seas. Hence Scripture writes, *And the Lord saw that the wickedness of man was great.*[1]

Tanhuma Yashan B'reshith 36. T.S. 6, 61.

33. AND GOD SAW THAT THE WICKEDNESS OF MAN WAS GREAT IN THE EARTH. Thus Scripture says, *Evil men understand not justice* (Prov. 28:5), which alludes to the generation of the Flood who sinned and disregarded their inevitable retribution. *But they that seek the Lord understand all things* (ibid.) alludes to Noah and his sons, who began to fear God when they heard from Him that He would bring a flood.

Tol'doth Yitzhak B'reshith 37. T.S. 6, 62.

34. THE WICKEDNESS OF MAN. When the world was first created the Shekinah abode in the lower heavens. When the generation of the Flood sinned, as it says, *And the Lord saw that the wickedness of man was great,* it departed to the fourth heaven. When the generation of the Separation of Tongues arose, the Shekinah departed still further to the fifth heaven.

P'sikta Rabbathi Chap. 5. T.S. 6, 65.

§ 30 [1] In the case of the Sodomites it is written, *Verily, the cry of Sodom and Gomorrah is very great* (18:20).

§ 32 [1] The point is not clear, but apparently it emphasizes that retribution can never be escaped, God having many judgments (punishments) at His command, which are necessitated by the great prevalence of sin and the evil doer's confidence in escaping his just deserts.

the thoughts of his heart was only evil continually. [6]And it repented the

COMMENTARY

Inclination" that "impels" man); *yetser* (passive) is something that is formed by man; they are the conceptions and intentions which are created by men's thoughts and whose goal is the good or evil. In this generation all "structures" of the thought of man pointed solely towards evil.[38] *heart.* In Heb. the heart is the seat of mind, intellect, purpose.[39] **[6]And it repented**

ANTHOLOGY

35. **Was only evil.**

Resh Lakish said: Satan is identical with the Evil Inclination and the Angel of Death. It is he who is referred to in the verse, *So Satan went forth from the presence of the Lord* (Job 2:7). He is identical with the Evil Inclination; for here it is written, *Was only evil continually,* whilst there it says, Only *upon himself put not forth thy hand* (ibid. 1:12 — spoken to Satan). He too is the Angel of Death, for to the self-same Satan God said, "*Only spare his life*" (ibid. 2:6), which proves that it lay in his hands (which is true only of the Angel of Death).

Baba Bathra 16a. T.S. 6, 67.

36. **Was only evil the whole day.**

R. Isaac stated: From this we learn that a man's Evil Inclination increasingly masters him from day to day.

Sukkah 52a. T.S. 6, 66.

37. WAS ONLY EVIL ALL DAY. It is written, *For all his days are pains* (ib. 23): this means that they pained the Holy One, blessed be He, with their evil deeds; *and his occupation vexation* (ib.): they vexed the Holy One, blessed be He, with their evil deeds. *Yea, even in the night his heart taketh no rest* (ib.) — from sin. How do we know that by day too they did not cease from evil? From our text, *was only evil all* day.

Gen. R. 27. T.S. 6, 68.

38. WAS ONLY EVIL ALL DAY. From the rising until the setting of the sun there was no hope of good in them, as it is written, *The murderer riseth with the light, to kill the poor and needy; and in the night he is as a thief* (Job 24:14).

Gen. R. 27. T.S. 6, 69.

39. **And it repented the Lord, etc.**

R. Aibu said: God soliloquized: "I regret exceedingly that I created the Evil Inclination in man. Had I not created it in him, he would not have rebelled against Me." R. Levi said: He declared, "My consolation is that I formed man, but made him mortal."

Gen. R. 27. T.S. 6, 74.

40. **And the Lord was comforted that He had made man in the earth.**

When R. Dimi came from Babylon to Palestine he taught: The Holy One, blessed be He, exclaimed: "I did well in preparing graves for them in the earth." How do we know this? Here it is written, *And the Lord was comforted;* whilst elsewhere it is stated, *And he comforted them, and spake kindly unto them* (50:21). Others say: He exclaimed: "I did *not* do well in preparing graves for them in the earth." This follows from the fact that here it is written, *And it repented the Lord;* whilst elsewhere it is written, *And the Lord repented of the evil which He had said He would do unto his people* (Exod. 32:14).[1]

Sanhedrin 108 a, b. T.S. 6, 71-2.

§ 40 [1] The proof-texts in the two versions merely show the meaning of *vayinahem* ("repented"), for both have verbs of the same root, but in the former it means comforted and in the latter repented. But the meaning, particularly of the second version, is rather obscure. According to the first, since man was so evil, God was at least comforted in the knowledge that He had decreed death for man, so that there would be some limitation of his evil. The text then reads: *And the Lord was comforted* (in that) *He had made man* in the earth, i.e., had provided graves for him. But the second version is much more difficult to explain. Possibly it means: The Lord repented that He had made man in the earth, i.e., mortal, for had man been immortal he might have triumphed over the power of sin. Other explanations have been offered, but like this one, they are only conjectural, with varying degrees of probability.

Lord that He had made man on the earth, and it grieved Him at His

COMMENTARY

(*vayinahem*) **the Lord. a.** God reversed His stand from that of upholding the world to that of destroying it.[40] **b.** It was a consolation (*nehamah*) to Him that He had not created man a celestial being, for then he would have instigated revolt among the angels.[41] **c.** The meaning is "repented," the phrase being an anthropomorphism; the same is true of "*for it repenteth me*" in v. 7.[42] **d.** He who destroys his own work seems to repent of having made it.[43] **and it grieved Him at His heart. a.** Because He does not desire the death of the wicked.[44] **b.** *At His heart* implies that He kept it within Himself and did not send a prophet to rebuke them.[45] **c.** A touching indication of the

ANTHOLOGY

41. **And it grieved Him at His heart.**

An unbeliever asked R. Joshua b. Karhah: "Do you not maintain that the Almighty foresees the future?" "Yes," replied he. "But it is written, *And it grieved Him at His heart?*" "Was a son ever born to you?" he asked — "Yes." "And what did you do?" — "I rejoiced and made all others rejoice." "Yet did you not know that he must die one day?" "Rejoicing in the time of rejoicing, and mourning in the time of mourning," replied he. "Even thus was it with the Holy One, blessed be He," was his rejoinder.

Gen. R. 27. T.S. 6, 76.

42. AND IT GRIEVED HIM AT HIS HEART. R. Berekiah said: If a king has a palace built by an architect and it displeases him, against whom is he to complain? Surely against the architect! Similarly, *It grieved Him at His heart.* R. Assi said: It may be compared to one who traded through an agent and suffered loss. Whom must he blame? Obviously, the agent. So here too, *it grieved Him at His heart.*[1]

Gen. R. 27. T.S. 6, 75.

43. AND IT GRIEVED HIM AT HIS HEART. R. Abbahu observed: He grieved at *man's* heart, like one who commits an error and realizes that he made a mistake, and blames himself, saying, "What have I done?" Even so did the Almighty, blessed be His name, declare: "It was I who put the leaven in the dough,[1] *for every imagination of the thoughts of his heart are only evil continually*" (verse 5).[2] Hence, *And it grieved Him at his heart* can only mean that He was grieved at the heart of man.

Tanhuma Yashan Noah Par. 4. T.S. 6, 78.

44. AND IT GRIEVED HIM AT HIS HEART. God was rapt with joy when the world was created, as it says, *And God saw everything that He had made, and, behold, it was very good.* (1:31). Yet, in the end *it repented the Lord that He had made man on earth, and it grieved Him at His heart.* Hence Scripture writes, *I said unto the revellers: "Revel not"* (Ps. 75:5): If the rejoicing of the Almighty did not endure, how much more so that of mortal man!

R. Bachaya on Sh'mini quoting Tanhuma a.l. T.S. 6, 80.

45. AND IT GRIEVED HIM AT HIS HEART. This means that He grieved for the righteous Noah who would be sorely tried by the Flood. For we find the righteous referred to as the *heart,* in the verse: *I sleep, but my* heart *waketh* (Song of Songs 5:2). *I sleep* (says the Community of Israel), sunk in the torpor of Exile, *but my* heart *waketh:* the prophet (the righteous man) is awake to rouse them to repentance.

P'sikta Zutrathi B'reshith. T.S. 6, 81.

§ 42 [1] "*His heart*" is understood to mean an intermediary agency which created the world and man (according to the mystic idea that the creation of the world was also through an intermediary). The verse in then rendered: And He experienced a spirit of resentment against His heart.

§ 43 [1] A common metaphor for the evil impulse.
[2] And for that I (the Lord) am responsible, for thus I created him. Therefore He grieved at the way in which He had made man's heart.

heart. [7]And the Lord said: 'I will blot out man whom I have created from

COMMENTARY

Divine love for His creation. God is grieved at the frustration of His purposes for the human race — the possibility of such frustration being the price of man's freedom of will. According to Biblical thought, God glories in the beauty of His handiwork; how great then must His grief be, when His handiwork is soiled through human wickedness![46] **[7]And the Lord said. a.** In His heart, i.e., He decided.[47] **b.** To Noah.[48] **I will blot out man.** In the Divine economy of the universe, men or

ANTHOLOGY

46. AND IT GRIEVED HIM AT HIS HEART. He was angry with them in His heart, but did not reveal His anger to them by prophet or messenger. You find an analogy for this meaning of "*at His heart*" in the text, *And the Lord said* in His heart (8:21): He said *in His heart*, but not to others.

Midrash Hagadol B'reshith. T.S. 6, 82.

47. AND IT GRIEVED HIM AT HIS HEART. Moses exhorted Israel: Keep God's charge, for He observed seven days of mourning before He brought the Flood.[1] Whence do we know it? From our text, *And it repented the Lord . . . and it grieved Him at His heart: "grieved"* means nought else but mourning.

Tanhuma Yashan Shemini. T.S. 6, 79.

48. **And the Lord said.**

R. Samuel b. Nahman said: Woe to the wicked who turn the Attribute of Mercy into the Attribute of Judgment. Wherever the Tetragrammaton ("Lord") is employed it connotes the Attribute of Mercy, as in the verse, *The Lord, the Lord, God, merciful and gracious* (Ex. 34:6). Yet it is written, *And the* Lord *saw that the wickedness of man was great . . . and it repented the* Lord *that He had made man . . . And the Lord said: "I will blot out man"* (ib. 7).

Gen. R. 33. T.S. 6, 84.

49. AND THE LORD SAID. In the Creation narrative only *Elohim* (God) is used, but not *Adonai* (the Lord). In the story of Cain the reverse is found. It is likewise in the present passage, where only *Adonai* is employed: *And* Adonai (*the Lord*) *saw that the wickedness of man was great . . . And it repented* Adonai *that He had made man . . . And* Adonai *said: "I will blot out man."*[1]

Midrash Tadshe Chap. 20. T.S. 6, 85.

50. **I will blot out man.**

It does not say, "I will cut off, destroy, or annihilate," but "blot out," (Heb. *emheh*, lit., dissolve). Therefore R. Berekiah remarked: The sky above is the realm of water, the sphere below is the realm of dust and ashes; and it is the nature of water to dissolve dust. Said the Almighty, Since the earth has rebelled against Me, I will loose[1] the waters upon the earth to dissolve and blot it out.

Tanhuma Yashan Noah 4. T.S. 6, 86.

51. I WILL BLOT OUT MAN. The Holy One, blessed be He, is long-suffering in everything but immorality. What is the proof? Scripture says, *And it came to pass . . . when the sons of God saw the daughters of men that they were fair . . . that they took them wives, whomsoever they chose* (verse 1-2);[1] and this

§ 47 [1] So should you too observe seven days of mourning for the death of a close relation.

§ 49 [1] *Adonai* and *Elohim* were always interpreted by the Rabbis as meaning the God of Mercy and the God of Judgment respectively. The point of the par. is not clear, but there are two possibilities: (1) Man's wickedness was now so great that even in His capacity as the God of Mercy He had to decree their destruction. (2) Whilst it would appear that He was now acting as the God of Judgment, in truth, that very judgment, stern though it was, would ultimately prove to be an act of mercy, for thereby a higher humanity was enabled to arise.

§ 50 [1] In the Heb. the word is of the same root as that for rebellion, so that the Flood is conceived of as measure for measure.

§ 51 [1] Even married women; see par. 7.

the face of the earth; both man, and beast, and creeping thing, and fowl

COMMENTARY

nations, or generations, that thwart God's purpose, have no permanent title to life.[49] **both man, and beast. a.** The latter, too, had corrupted their way. Alternatively, the beasts had been created for man's use; since man was to be destroyed, there was no need for them.[50] **b.** Rashi remarks: "Beast and creeping thing and fowl were all created for man's sake. When, therefore, man disappears, what necessity is there for preserving the animals alive!" But a comparison with Jonah 4, 11, where the innocence of the animals as well as of the little children is invoked by the Prophet

ANTHOLOGY

is immediately followed by, *And the Lord said: "I will blot out man."*

Gen. R. 26. T.S. 6, 87.

52. I WILL BLOT OUT MAN. Whenever man willfully follows his own desires disregarding the will of God, let him know that he will be held accountable for it. Though retribution is not immediate, let him not delude himself that God will overlook his transgression: God is indeed long-suffering, yet He collects what is due to Him. He punishes when judgment is ripe. Thus it is written, *In the fullness of his sufficiency he shall be in straits* (Job 20:22). Hence Scripture declares: *For the evil of man is great upon him* (Eccl. 8:6). He does not punish while man's evil is yet small, but waits until it is great, just as He did to the generation of the Flood: He granted them a long time of apparent immunity, yet at last called them to account. Thus we read, *And the Lord saw that the wickedness of man was great in the earth;* and after that, *And the Lord said: "I will blot out man."*

Num. R. 14. T.S. 6, 89.

53. I WILL BLOT OUT MAN. At first the praise of the Almighty ascended from nought but the waters. Said the Holy One, blessed be He: "If these, which have neither mouth nor speech, do thus, how much more will I be praised when I create man!" But the generation of Enosh, the generation of the Flood, and the generation of the Separation of Tongues rose up and rebelled against Him. Thereupon the Holy One, blessed be He, decreed: "Let these be removed, and their place be taken by those who preceded them (sc. the waters). Hence it is written, *And the Lord said: I will blot out man.* What think they? That I need armies? Did I not create the world with a word? I will but utter a word and destroy them!"

Gen. R. 28. T.S. 6, 91.

54. I WILL BLOT OUT MAN. R. Johanan said: We may liken this to a king who had a garden where he planted all kinds of luscious fruits, and appointed a steward to tend it. But the steward was lazy; not only did he not tend it; he actually destroyed it! Said the king: "Did I entrust the garden to him to improve it or to spoil it?" What did the king do? He set it on fire. So too was it with God. He created a world abounding with all sorts of delights, and delivered it into the hands of man to enjoy and to improve it. But instead there arose the generation of the Flood; they provoked Him to anger, corrupted the world, and denied God, saying, *What is the Almighty, that we should serve Him* (Job 21:15)? Thereupon God decreed: *"I will blot out man."*

Midrash Hagadol B'reshith. T.S. 6, 98.

55. **Both man, and beast, etc.**

R. Judan said: This may be compared to a king who entrusted his son to a teacher who led him into evil ways, whereat the king became angry with his son and slew him. Said the king: "Who but this man led my son into evil ways: my son has perished; shall this man live?" Therefore God destroyed *both man, and beast, and creeping thing, and fowl of the air.*[1]

Gen. R. 28. T.S. 6, 94.

§ 55 [1] Because the abundance of wealth which man enjoyed through these led to his moral downfall.

of the air; for it repenteth Me that I have made them.' [8]And Noah found grace in the eyes of the Lord.

COMMENTARY

in his plea for Nineveh, suggests that in the Biblical view all life, whether human or animal, forms one organic whole; see v. 12 of this chapter.[51] **[8]found grace. a.** He found mercy.[52] **b.** His deeds found favor in God's sight, the reason being stated in the next verse.[53] **c.** *"Finding grace"* is not as some suppose equivalent only to being well-pleasing . . . The righteous man exploring the nature of existence, makes a surprising find, in this one discovery, **that all**

ANTHOLOGY

56. BOTH MAN, AND BEAST, etc. R. Phinehas said: This may be compared to a king who gave his son in marriage and prepared a nuptial chamber for him, plastering, painting, and decorating it. Subsequently the king became angry with his son and slew him, whereupon he entered the nuptial chamber and broke the rods, tore down the partitions, and rent the curtains, exclaiming: "I prepared these for none other than my son: he has perished; shall these remain!" Therefore God destroyed *both man, and beast, and creeping thing, and fowl of the air.* Thus it is written, *I will consume man and beast,* etc. (Zeph. 1:3).

Gen. R. 28. T.S. 6, 95.

57. BOTH MAN, AND BEAST. Just as man was punished when he sinned, so too were the cattle, beasts, and fowl punished for their misdeeds. Whence do we know it? From our text, *And the Lord said: "I will blot out . . . both man, and beast,"* etc. Why were they punished? Because they copulated promiscuously, members of one species mating with members of another.

Tanhuma Yashan Noah Par. 11.
T.S. 6, 97.

58. BOTH MAN, AND BEAST. When God contemplated destroying His world in the generation of the Flood, which had become corrupt, He weighed man in one balance with the cattle, punishing both, as the Bible states: *And the Lord said: "I will blot out . . . both man, and beast,"* etc. Therefore, when the time for appeasement came, just as He became reconciled to man and had compassion upon him, so did He have compassion upon the cattle too, as we read, *And God remembered Noah, and every living thing, and all the cattle that were with him in the ark* (8:1).

Tanhuma Yashan Noah Par. 7.
T.S. 6, 96.

59. **It repenteth Me that I have made them.**

The School of R. Ishmael taught: The doom of destruction was decreed against Noah too, but that he found favor in the eyes of God, as it is written, *It repenteth Me that I have made them. But Noah found grace in the eyes of the Lord.*

Sanhedrin 108a. T.S. 6, 100.

60. **But Noah found grace in the eyes of the Lord.**

R. Johanan said: It may be compared to a man walking on a road, when he saw someone whom he attached to himself. How far did his attachment go? So far that he became bound to him in love. Even so, *"grace"* is said here; while elsewhere we read, *And Joseph found* grace *in his sight* (39:4).[1] R. Simeon b. Lakish said: It went so far that He conferred dominion upon him. For *"grace"* is said here, while elsewhere it says, *And Esther obtained* grace *in the sight of all them that looked upon her* (Est. 2:15).[2] The Rabbis said: It may be compared to one who was walking on a road, when he saw a man whom he attached to himself so strongly that he gave him his daughter in marriage. Similarly, *"grace"* is said here, while in another verse we read, *And I will pour upon*

§ 60 [1] It is clear that the "grace" there was love and affection.
[2] That "grace" made her a queen.

COMMENTARY

things are a grace of God, and that creation has no gift of grace to bestow, for neither has it any possession, since all things are God's possession, and for this reason grace too belongs to Him alone as a thing that is His very own. Thus to those who ask what the origin of creation is, the right answer would be that it is the goodness and grace of God, which He bestowed on the race that stands next after Him. For all things in the world and the world itself is a free gift and act of kindness and grace on God's part.[54]

ANTHOLOGY

the house of David and upon the inhabitants of Jerusalem the spirit of grace (Zech. 12:10).[3] How far did God's favor to Noah extend? Until he knew to distinguish which animal must be fed at two hours of the day and which beast must be fed at three hours of the night.

Gen. R. 29. T.S. 6, 103.

61. BUT NOAH FOUND GRACE IN THE EYES OF THE LORD. R. Simon said: The Holy One, blessed be He, found three treasures, Abraham, David, and Israel. (A proof-text is cited for each, in which the word "found" occurs.) His colleagues objected: Surely it is written, *But Noah found grace in the eyes of the Lord? He* found, replied he, but the Holy One, blessed be He, did not find.

Gen. R. 29. T.S. 6, 102.

62. BUT NOAH FOUND GRACE. R. Simon said: We find that the Holy One, blessed be He, shows mercy to the descendants for the sake of their forbears. But how do we know that the reverse too is true? Because it says, *But Noah found grace,* which was for the sake of his offspring, as it is written, *These are the generations of Noah.*

Gen. R. 29. T.S. 6, 104.

[3] Which would find expression, as it were, in the bethrothal of Israel to God. — It is, however, probable that the text is in disorder. The proof-text cited by R. Johanan is more fitting for Resh Lakish's view, since the "grace" of Joseph resulted in his being appointed steward over his master's household. Conversely, the latter's proof-text is more suitable for the Rabbis' dictum, Esther's "grace" being that Ahasuerus married her. Likewise, the verse cited by the Rabbis is not particularly relevant, save on the explanation given here, which, however, is absent from the actual text. It would make better sense if they were transposed, thus: The Rabbis' proof-text to R. Johanan, R. Johanan's to Resh Lakish, and Resh Lakish's to the Rabbis.

APPENDIX

1.

CONCEPT OF TIME IN BIBLICAL AND POST-BIBLICAL LITERATURE

2.

THE ATOM IN JEWISH SOURCES

3.

CREATION AND THE THEORY OF EVOLUTION

4.

CREATION AND HUMAN BROTHERHOOD

5.

Addenda to the Commentary

(i) *The Creation Chapter* (Hertz)

(ii) *The Nephilim* (Malbim and Cassuto)

1.

THE CONCEPT OF TIME

IN BIBLICAL AND POST-BIBLICAL LITERATURE

Referring to page 1, commentary on verse 1: "In the beginning" (**d.**) *on the creation of time.*

Time is one of the most obscure riddles of the human consciousness, a riddle whose solution has been sought by thinkers for the last 2,500 years.

What is Time? Has it an independent existence as a created entity perceptible to the senses; or is it a concept existing only in the human mind, in which case it is eternal? If Time is something created, what kind of Time existed before?

Maimonides[1] asserts that Time was created simultaneously with the world. This, he maintains, "is undoubtedly a fundamental principle of the Law of Moses, next in importance to the principle of God's Unity."

In the present study my purpose is to explain the views of our Sages as expressed in the Talmud, Midrash, and Biblical exegesis, which I shall preface by a brief review of the main lines of thought on the subject. Contemporary scientists, headed by Professor Einstein, concur in Maimonides' view that Time is a perceptible entity which constitutes a fourth dimension, the other three, of course, being Length, Breadth and Height. When we measure the length, breadth and height of a growing tree, we should also consider the time of its growth as an intrinsic measurement. When we draw a line on paper we should measure the time it took to draw, just as we measure its length. This applies to all things.

Plato holds that Time is related to the motion of matter. Before the creation of the universe Time in our sense did not exist. It was rather in the nature of eternity. This he calls aeon, and this eternal time has no motion and neither before nor after.[2]

Aristotle[3] follows Plato in relating time to motion, defining it as follows: Time is the number of motion — divided into anterior and posterior. It exists both within and without the mind. In its quality of number it is in the mind, for without that which counts (the mind) there can be no count, and without the present there can be no before or after. But motion itself is outside the mind . . . If you thus conceive of Time, it is in the mind, but its matter is outside it.

Crescas[4] briefly states Aristole's theory thus: "Time is an accident, which is both consequent to, and conjoined with motion. Neither can exist without the other. Motion does not exist without time, and time is unintelligible save in conjunction with motion. Whatever is not subject to motion does not come under the category of time."

Aristotle dwells at length on the above four premises and other problems involved in this theory. The difficulty raised first by Straton,[5] an early Greek philosopher, and then by Crescas, that the state of continued rest also comes under the category of time, is anticipated and answered by Aristotle himself. Aristotle holds that the universe is eternal, and so is motion and Time. The Stoics,[6] too, follow Aristotle and Plato in reference to Time.

Philo,[7] the first Jewish philosopher to deal specifically with this question, writes: "Time came into existence together with, or after, the creation of the world." "The world preceded

[1] Guide of the Perplexed II, ch. 13. [2] Timaeus, 37c - 39e. [3] Physics IV, II, 219a, 1-220a, 26; IV, 12, 221. Intermediate Physics IV, III, 7. [4] Or Hashem, ch. 16. [5] Zeller, E., II, 2, 911. [6] Arnim II, 509-521. [7] Opif., 7, 26; Leg. All. I, 2, 2; Sacr., 18, 68; Immut., 6, 31; Wolfson, *Philo* I, p. 311.

Time." "God created Time." He agrees with Plato's assumption of a kind of eternal time before creation.

Augustine:[8] "There was no time prior to creation. With creation time too came into being. With respect to God all time is like one day. The term yesterday, or tomorrow, is not applicable to Him."

Saadya Gaon:[9] "Time is nothing but the measurement of the duration of corporeal bodies, and that which is not body is beyond time and measurement of duration."

R. Abraham bar Hiyya:[10] "Time is naught but a term signifying the duration of existent things. If there be no existing things, there is no term to describe time." "For time is nothing but the number of cycles or spheres which pass on existent things, according to anterior and posterior." "Time exists only in the mind and as it is comprehended by the intelligence; before the Six Days of Creation there was no Time."

Maimonides[11] elaborates on this subject, stating: "Since the nature of time embarrasses the greatest philosophers, some of them being altogether unable to comprehend it, what can be expected of those who do not probe the nature of things?" Again: "Those who believe in the Torah of Moses believe that everything has been brought by the Eternal into existence out of non-existence. *Even time itself is among the things created,* for time depends on motion. Now, motion is an accident in the mover, whilst the mover himself, upon the motion of whom time depends, is himself a created entity, which has passed from non-existence to existence. We say that God existed before the creation of the Universe, though the verb 'existed' appears to imply the notion of time; we also believe that He existed for an infinite time, before the Universe was created; but in these cases we do not mean time in its true sense. We only use the term to signify something analogous, a semblance of time."

Efodi suggests that this means that there was no time in existence at all, the mind only *assuming* such a state. Maimonides himself does not explain what he means by "semblance of time."

Albo in *Ikkarim* 2:18 explains the phrase by stating that there are two kinds of time:

1. That which is measured and numbered by the motion of the sphere, and in which there are the distinctions of anterior and posterior, equal and unequal. This is called the "Order of Time," as explained in Genesis Rabbah: "This teaches that the Order of Time existed previously," meaning from the first day of the creation of the sphere.

2. Unmeasured duration conceived only in thought as eternal, having existed before the creation of the World, and continuing to exist after its passing. However, in that duration there was no apparent order of time due to the motion of the sphere, since there was no motion or existence of the sphere. This is called "Time," and not "Order of Time." This Maimonides called "semblance of time," and this kind of time is possibly eternal. On the other hand, the Order of Time is itself within Time.

R. Menahem Azariah de Fano[12] rejects Albo's idea that there was unmeasured time before creation. It is impossible to entertain any concept of time before the creation of the world. The eternity of God, Who is infinite, cannot

[8] Confessions, I, 336-342. See *V'zot Li-Y'huda,* p. 35, and Wolfson, *Spinoza,* p. 342. Note Isserles in *Torath Haolah,* III, 59, on the verse *And He rested on the seventh day.* He comments: Prior to the creation of the world time was not in existence, and the numbering of days and years could not apply. All was but duration and considered as one day . . . Perhaps it is for this reason that Scripture states, in referring to the first day, *And there was evening and there was morning, one day* — not *first day,* because there was no day preceding this. See T.S., ch. 1, par. 430. [9] Emunoth V'deoth 2,5. [10] *Higayon Hanefesh* and *M'gillat Hamegaleh,* p. 8 ff. See also the preface *op. cit.* [11] Guide, II:13, I:73, II:30. Crescas' commentary on *Guide of the Perplexed, loc. cit.,* writes: "And if it is something very difficult to imagine, and our faculties are too limited to apprehend it, then we can only rely on the prophets who recount to us the word of the Almighty, since by our own understanding we cannot grasp such theoretical speculation." *Ikkarim* 2 18 writes that "the difficulty of understanding how there can be duration before creation of the world, which has in it neither *before* nor *after* such as applies to the present order of Time, accounts for the statement of the Rabbis that *one must not ask what is above, what is below, what is before and what is after . . . Before* and *after* refer to the duration, which is prior to the creation of the world, and which will follow its cessation . . ." [12] *Assarah Ma-amarot,* second essay, I, par. 16.

properly be described by time, even unmeasured.

Gersonides[13] explains that time was created as well as motion; it is a continuous quantity, existing partly in a subject and partly independently. The particular instant stands between the potential and the actual. Gersonides gives ten proofs that time cannot be infinite. Time is posterior to motion because motion gives time its quantitative aspect, according to its anterior and posterior state.

All these writers accept the view that time is related to motion.

Another school of thought rejects this conception completely. Plotinus asserts that time is not connected at all with the motion of matter, but exists also in the spiritual realm of ideas. According to Aristotle time is *generated* by motion, whereas Plotinus holds that time flows and *is manifested* through motion. In Aristotle's view time *measures* motion, while Plotinus considers motion as a measure of time. In his opinion the world was created in time.

Crescas[14] in *Or Hashem* agrees with Plotinus, opposing the views of Aristotle, Maimonides, and other early philosophers. He refutes Aristotle's main proposition and the four premises on which they are based. He holds that time, in its essence, is duration, independent of motion, existing in the mind alone. A finite portion of duration which is measured by motion is called Time.

Aristotle cites other opinions of the ancients on the concept of Time: One view is that Time is the motion of the universe, that is, the rotation of the heavens. Another is that we are all in Time and that all things are in Time. According to the first theory motion is Time.

Simplicius[15] explains that the second theory is that of the Pythagoreans, who derived it from Archytas, that time is the locus of the universe. Further, Altabrizi records that the ancients held the following views regarding the essence of time: 1. Time exists in itself, is not a body, but an entity whose existence is necessitated by itself. 2. Time is a body which comprehends all the bodies of the Universe; namely, the celestial equator. 3. It is the motion of the celestial equator.

Again, some maintain that time is not related to nor dependent upon anything, but like a stream flows endlessly: for them time always was, and always will be. Others hold that time has no true existence at all. Some believe that time embodies two distinct concepts, namely, quantitative time and qualitative time. The former is a mathematical concept linked with matter. The latter is qualitative, a swiftly flowing stream passing on, in which events of history are recorded.

R. Isaac Arama,[16] noted biblical commentator, holds that the concept of time has three aspects. 1. The spiritual realm is above time. 2. The heavenly bodies are on the same level with time, in the sense that with the beginning of motion began Time too. 3. The terrestrial world of the elements is completely under the dominion of Time. He writes as follows:—"The Sage (Solomon) in Ecclesiastes frequently uses the expression 'under the sun,' i.e., under the celestial motion. For the superior entities (existing in the higher spiritual realm) above the heaven, being incorporeal and having no force, have none of the various types of motion either; hence time does not exist in their sphere. They are not in time, and time neither limits nor rules them. On the contrary, time and its substratum are subject to them. However, the heavenly bodies themselves, in which that motion was newly generated from which Time first flowed, by virtue of their being bodies in motion, are co-eval with time, for with the beginning of motion Time was generated."

[13] *Milhamot Hashem,* chapters 10, 11, 12. [14] See Prof. H. Wolfson in his exposition of Crescas' *Or Hashem,* proposition 15 (Cambridge, 1929) where the system of Crescas and all the other above-mentioned systems are dealt with at length. He mentions that the early philosophers, Simplicius, Seno, and Chrysippus, hold that time is the extension of the motion of the world; and that Algazali defines time as a "term" signifying the duration, that is to say, the extension, of motion. He also notes that the above quotations from Saadya and Abraham bar Hiyya harmonize with these views. See his book on Spinoza (Harvard, 1934), chap. 10; *Philo* (Harvard, 1947), 217, 311; *Jewish Quarterly Review,* new series, 10, 1-17; and his article in *Jewish Studies in Memory of Israel Abrahams,* 1927. [15] Wolfson, *op. cit.*
[16] *Akedat Yizhak,* v. 4, *Matoth.*

TIME IN THE TORAH

On the first verse of Genesis, *In the beginning* (b'reshith) *God created the heaven and the earth,* Philo[17] comments: *B'reshith* is similar to *barishona* (at first), the verse referring to the order of creation, but not to the order of time, since time was then non-existent. This significant exegesis is also found in *Seder Rabbah,* as cited in T.S. Genesis chap. I, par. 78, and in *Lekah Tob*: "*B'reshith,* i.e., at the head of all His work, God created the heaven and the earth." R. Bahya too understands it as "*barishona.*" Targum Jonathan translates it "*min avla,*" meaning at first. *Midrash Aggadah,* likewise, renders *b'reshith* in the sense of at first. Rashi, however, rejects this interpretation.

Maimonides[18] states in the Guide of the Perplexed: "Time itself was created. Therefore Scripture employs the term *b'reshith* (in a principle), using the '*beth*' prepositionally, denoting 'in,' the true explanation of the first verse of Genesis being as follows: In [creating] a principle, God formed the beings above and below. This interpretation is in accord with the theory of a newly created world" (in opposition to the view that it was eternal). See commentaries *ad. loc.*

Mikhlal Yofi remarks: "Some maintain that *b'reshith* is in the construct state, its complement, time, being omitted [so that it means: 'in the beginning of time']." The author of the Guide explained the term *b'reshith* to mean that with the principle of primacy and matter God created the heaven and the earth, and there was no prior material. R. Isaac Abrabanel writes similarly: "In the beginning (of the newly-created time) God created. If it is characteristic of our language occasionally to omit the absolute complement even in matters patent and palpable, how much the more is it fitting to omit it here, since time is something so difficult to comprehend and so intangible an essence." Isaac Caro writes in *Tol'doth Isaac*: "At the beginning of 'time' the Holy One, blessed be He, created a new formation *ex nihilo.*" Sforno interprets: "*B'reshith* i.e., in *the first,* indivisible instant."

Elijah Gaon states in *Adereth Elijah*: "The *beth* of *b'reshith* is temporal, as in *bayom* (in the day), since time itself was created. The *beth* thus indicates the time of creation, namely, that it occurred in the first portion of created time. *Reshith* thus implies absolute beginning, prior to which nothing can be conceived as existing, in order to refute the heretics who say that— Heaven forbid!—two kinds of primordial matter existed."

This is more fully explained in *Boser Ol'loth* by Meir Santo: "*B'reshith* means prior to any existing entity. For the concept of beginning (*reshith*) is a temporal one, and there is neither season nor time before the Holy One, blessed be He. Only to us mortals is everything limited in time and space. The sense of *reshith* is therefore, 'when time came into existence,' for time is a necessary element in the existence of every wrought thing under the sun, and without the thing wrought there is no time. This then is what Scripture says: In the beginning of all time."

A source for this interpretation is to be found in the Babylonian Talmud in Megillah 9a, where it is narrated that the seventy elders who translated the Pentateuch for King Ptolemy altered the text and wrote: "God created *b'reshith,*" on which Rabbi Jonathan Eibeschutz comments:[19] "Their purpose was to interpret the text as meaning that God created the beginning of time, which is '*b'reshith,*' for time is included in the things created; and previously there was no time at all."

The passages in the Liturgy, "It is our duty to ascribe greatness to the Creator of *b'reshith,*" "Our Creator and the Creator of *b'reshith,*" and "Blessed is He who made *b'reshith,*" are similarly rendered, that is, that He created the *b'reshith,* meaning, Time.[20]

[17] Opif, 7, 26. See T.S., chap. I, par. 230, 251. [18] *Ibid.* See R. Shmuel ibn Tibbun, *Yikavu Hamayim,* p. 216. See also Al-harizi's translation of the *Guide,* which differs from that of Ibn Tibbun. See above, *Commentary,* p. 1.
[19] *Ya-arot D'bash.* See glosses of R. Zvi Hirsh Hayoth to Megillah 9a. See Torah Shelemah, v. I, par. 197, and appendix to 3rd ed., p. 183. [20] See commentary of R. Jacob Emden in his *Siddur Beth Ya-akob, ad. loc.* See also R. Moses Isserles, *Torath Ha-Olah,* end.

In Gen. R. 3:5 on the verse, *And there was evening and there was morning,* R. Judah b. R. Simon commented: It is not written, Let there be evening, but "*there was evening,*" which proves that the order of the divisions of time existed previously. R. Abbahu observed: It shows that God created worlds and destroyed them, until He created ours, saying, "*These* please Me, and those did not please Me."

Maimonides (in Guide of the Perplexed, 2:30) writes about the above-quoted *midrash:* "Some of our Sages reportedly held the opinion that time existed before the Creation. This is dubious, because the theory that time cannot be conceived to have had a beginning was taught by Aristotle, as shown, and is objectionable. Those who made this assertion were led to it by the phrases, 'one day,' 'a second day.' Taking these terms literally, they asked, 'What determined the first day, since there was no rotating sphere, and no sun?' The answer to this question they found in the above-mentioned Rabbinical dicta. We can understand that they said this in order to answer the difficulty which naturally presents itself, viz., how could time exist before the creation of the sun? However, our Sages, speaking of the light created on the first day, explicitly state: 'These are the self-same luminaries which were created on the first day, but were not fixed in their places until the fourth day.' The purpose of this comment was indeed to answer that very difficulty."

I have given several expositions of this Rabbinical passage in T.S. I, par. 422. Some hold that R. Judah meant that the order of the divisions of time existed *in the worlds created and subsequently destroyed,* in accordance with R. Abbahu's dictum, which they understand literally, viz., that they had *actually* been created. Others maintain that even according to the interpretation that worlds were created and destroyed only *in thought,* his statement that the order of the divisions of time existed previously, refers to the point when these were fashioned in thought, but not to a prior period. Others again relate it to the 2,000 years preceding the creation of the world, when the Torah was conceived, that is, when it was born in the Divine Mind, the order of time thenceforth being established. R. Bahya declares that the order of time [Hebrew—"times"] existed previously; although time was created, and prior to creation time did not exist, the Midrash employed the term "*times*" in reference to those 2,000 years. In that time God conceived the intention of creating 1,000 generations, of which 974 generations were blotted out, i.e., in thought, and this transpired between *b'reshith* until the moment of which it is written, "*and there was light.*" According to these views R. Judah too might hold that time was created.

Crescas, following his own views that time is not bound up with motion, and that the category of time applies to the separate intellects also, declares (*op. cit.,* chap. 15): "And therefore is the statement of R. Judah b. R. Simon verified in accordance with its literal meaning."

From the foregoing it is clear that the passage in Gen. R. is not conclusive in favor of either view. (See my comments in T.S. *ad. loc.*)

Commenting on the verse, *For six days the Lord made* (Exodus 20:11—literal translation), R. Bahya wrote: "It is reasonable to infer that the Lord made the six days, and that they are included in the Creation, thus indicating that time was created. Had Scripture stated, *In six days,* it would suggest that time is eternal." The same is stated in *Torath Ha-Olah* in the name of Ibn Ezra; by an enquirer mentioned in the Responsa of Rashba (I, 423); and in *Tol'doth Isaac* of Isaac Caro on Sidrah (pericope) Jethro, *loc. cit.*[21]

Genesis 2:2 reads: *And on the seventh day* (ba-yom) *God finished.* Commenting on the fact that Scripture does not say "on the *sixth* day," Ibn Ezra observes: Some maintain that the days themselves were created; the text therefore means that *with* the creation of the seventh day God finished His work, the *beth* of *ba-yom* being instrumental, not temporal.

[21] See Nahmanides to Exodus 20:11; *Sefer Hababir,* par. 29, 36 and 51; Zohar, v. 1:264, 247; v. 2:89; v. 3:94, 103; *Torah Shelemah,* v. 1, appendix, p. 179.

The same is conjectured in the commentary of *Tur* on the Pentateuch, and in *Lekah Tob*: "*And on the seventh day God finished.* Since He did not do anything on the seventh day, why does Scripture write, on the *seventh* day? It means, however, that by the very coming into existence of a seventh day the world was finished, for the (creation of the) seventh day itself was one of God's works, though no work was actually performed on that day; yet the hours of the seventh day are designated as work, since they are counted in the seven days to be called a week."

Thus may be explained a passage in *Midrash Aggadah* on the beginning of Genesis: "*And on the seventh day God finished*: This teaches that He ordered the measure of day and the measure of night on the seventh day." Buber in his annotations remarks that this is unintelligible. But it is clear that the reference is to the view of Ibn Ezra quoted previously. The meaning of the *Midrash Aggadah* then is that the actual time of the seventh day was created on the seventh day.

In this manner one may explain the text of the *Midrash Hagadol*, Genesis 1:8: "*And there was evening and there was morning, a second day.* This teaches that time is included in the work of Creation." This means that the reason for the Torah's repetition of *And there was evening*, etc., in connection with each of the six days of Creation, instead of stating it only in connection with the first and letting it be understood that the same applied to the other days, is to inform us that the *time* of the six days of Creation was created each day, and the time of the seventh day was itself created on the seventh day, the work thus becoming completed therein.

In consonance with the above quotation from the *Midrash Aggadah* the source for the theory of the creation of time may be found in Hagigah 12: "Rab Judah said in the name of Rab: Ten things were created on the first day, namely, heaven and earth, light and darkness... and the measure (or nature) of day and night (their combined length being 24 hours—Rashi), as it is written, *And there was evening and there was morning, one day.*" Maharsha propounds: "By 'the nature (*midath*) of day and night' is meant the accident of time which inheres in every material body." But on the basis of the *Midrash Aggadah* we may say that the phrase refers to time itself, which was created on the first day, in the first instant when the elements of heaven and earth were created. This will agree with the theses already mentioned that time is an independent entity, while the measure of the hours of day and night, dependent on the motion of the spheres, is the created time. I have likewise cited Saadyah *supra*: "Time is nothing but the measurement of the duration of corporeal bodies." This too is the interpretation of the words "the measure" (or nature) in the Talmud.

The statement that the six days were created, and that regarding the creation of the seventh day, require further illumination. If they refer to that time which is bound up with matter, that surely was created only in the first instant in which matter was created and in which motion began, after which one cannot speak of its further creation, since time had already begun to flow. How then can it be said that all the seven days were created?

To explain this we must first state a major principle pertaining to the concept of time, which many physicists, headed by Prof. Einstein, accept, namely, that all conceptions of the measurements of time are relative to frames of varying velocities. For example, our day, consisting of a day and a night, comprises the time the earth rotates on its axis, covering about 24,000 miles at the rate of 1,000 miles an hour. Our year is 365 days—the time in which the earth revolves around the sun. If we could imagine that we are living on the planet Neptune which takes 164 years and 68 days to revolve around the sun, besides its own rotation, then as inhabitants of this planet we should have a different conception of the time of one year, which is 164 times as long as our year on earth. Conversely, the year of an inhabitant of the planet Mercury, which revolves around the sun in 88 days, is shorter, measuring about one-fourth of our year.

Everyone can himself experience the coursing of time in various degrees. When a man is in distress or in pain, every minute seems a day to him, the minutes and seconds passing slowly. The Sages found this idea expressed in the Torah in Exodus 2:23 in the words: *And it came to pass, in the course of those many days...* Their comment is: Those were days of sorrow; therefore does Scripture call them "many." Not so, however with joy or pleasure. Then time speeds and we hardly notice its passing. Scripture says of Jacob: *And they* (the seven years) *seemed unto him but a few days* (Gen. 29:20). The seven years are characterized as "a few days," because each day brought him closer to his goal. He felt pleasure in his work, and the time passed rapidly. (See T.S. *ad. loc.*)

The measure of time is thus relative to and dependent on one's state of being; in the main, however, it is bound up with the category of place.

This reflection may be illustrated by a clock, where a minute is subdivided into sixty seconds. Custom makes a second appear as the smallest unit of the measurement of time. But there are clocks on which we can see the pendulum pass 10,000 units in the course of a minute. There even exists a clock on which we can see the pendulum pass 1,000,000 units a minute. Of course, we then conceive of a minute as a long time. Or, to take another example: the speed of light coming from sun to earth is 186,000 miles per second. Then if one were able to travel so fast and pass over that distance in one second, that second would appear to him much as a month now appears to us.[22] From what has been said above it will readily be understood that the conception of time is not something fixed and determined, but only relative to position, mind, and place. How many more variant outlooks must there be in the spiritual world! There is a measure of time whereby an infinite number of years is but as one day. And there is a measure whereby one second is longer than a thousand years of ours.

Dr. Grunwald, a disciple of Einstein, writes in explanation of the theories of relative time:[23] "Newton and his school taught that there is absolute time, flowing with unvarying speed, and that we can measure its rate of flow by means of units of time arbitrarily chosen. Furthermore, we can fix time-differences and increments equally for all with complete absoluteness.

"Mach says that we cannot observe absolute time: such time does not exist in Physics. And if we do fix the rate of time-flow, according to our convention, and by comparison with the rotation of the earth about its axis, then we already have a measure of time usable by every one.

"Einstein asserts that absolute time does not exist, and that its rate of flow, that is to say, the measure of time-differences and increments, is not necessarily equal in different co-ordinate systems."

The concept of relative time is also found in Scriptural commentaries regarding the Six Days of Creation.

In *Sefer Ha'ibbur* and in *M'gillat Hamegaleh* Abraham bar Hiyya maintains that before the creation of the sun the earth was in darkness for three days. Proof of this interpretation may be found in *Midrash Tadshe,* quoted in T.S. Chap. I, par. 606. The thesis of *P'sikta Rabbathi,* ch. 46, is just the opposite, namely, that during the first three days there was only light and no night, and the light created on the first day served till the fourth day.

In his commentary on *Sefer Y'tsirah,* p. 33, R. Judah Albarceloni states that the light which the Holy One, blessed be He, created on the first day, whereby a man could view the universe from end to end, served until the sixth day, when man appeared.

[22] Much has been written in scientific literature about the measurement of time-space in relation to the position of the observer. For instance, if two planes pass each other, each pilot will see the other going at a speed quite different from that perceived by someone standing on the ground. If two planes travel together at exactly the same speed and in the same direction, each pilot will see the other as being perfectly stationary. Time-space, then, seems to be subjective, differing for each individual. The same can be seen with ships and elevators, where speed, space and time are relative, and depend on the position of the observer. Much has also been written about man's conception of time in dreams and in thought, where the human mind covers great stretches of time in seconds.

[23] *Ha-T'kufah,* v. 18, p. 276.

Sefer Hab'rith (Part I, Chapters 4 to 10) elaborates on the statement of Rashi that "light and darkness functioned in confusion." Thus, during the first three days the light would undulate once every minute, so that any site would be illuminated for half a minute and in darkness for half a minute. This would be so, if instead of making the rotation about its axis in 24 hours, as at present, the earth at that time made it every minute.

A similar exposition is made in Gen. R. 10, 4 that before Adam sinned the planets moved in abbreviated paths and with (much greater) speed.

In T.S. Chap. I, par. 448 I quote *Aggadath Sh'muel,* who cites the *Glosses of R. Obadiah* to Rashi, Isaiah 23:15 (Amsterdam, 1698): "In the works of Creation the Holy One, blessed be He, used the expression '*And there was evening and there was morning*' with reference to each day, in order to intimate that each complete day was a thousand years, as it is said, *For a thousand years in Thy sight are but as yesterday when it is past* (Ps. 90:4). Now, from the Scriptural formulation respecting the second day, we may draw inferences regarding all the other days, for the first day also is on a par with it. For if it said: 'And there was evening and there was morning' respecting the first day alone, we might say: 'Who knows how many thousands of years the first day included?' Therefore was the formula particularized for each individual day, to show that as the second day was a thousand years, so was each of the others. For this verse, *For a thousand years,* etc., refers primarily to our *second* day, since it states, *are but as yesterday when it is past,* which implies that that day is meant which had a yesterday but not a day before yesterday, viz., the second." An exposition of a similar nature is found in *B'reshith Rabbathi* of R. Moses Ha-Darshan, p. 10. See T.S. *ad. loc.,* Addenda, p. 181.

This thought which the formulation of the second day is intended to negate,—the possibility of saying, "Who knows how many thousands of years the first day included?"—is actually propounded as a fact by R. Bahya in his commentary on the beginning of Genesis: "Consider that the Torah antedated the world by a period extending from *b'reshith,* which means in the beginning, to the utterance '*Let there be light*!' So do we find Gen. R. remarking: 'Hence we learn that the order of time existed previously.' Although time was created, and did not exist prior to creation, the Midrash employed the term '*times*' in reference to those 2,000 years, for those days are not as the days of man. Rather are they days of those years which are unsearchable, and of which it was written in Job 36:26, *Behold, God is great, beyond our knowledge; the number of His years is unsearchable;* also, *Are Thy days as the days of man* (ibid. 10:5)? Again, the same thought recurs in Psalms 102:28: *And Thy years shall have no end.* It was in the time thus described that the thought of creating 1,000 generations was divinely born, of which 974 generations were blotted out—likewise in thought." In T.S. vol. 1, p. 178 (*q.v.*) I cite *Midrash Shohar Tob* on Psalm 90 as a source.

It is clear from his words that from the point of *b'reshith,* when time was created, until the Divine fiat, "Let there be light," when the standard length of our day was created, the day was of the class of the days and years referred to as unsearchable. According to this, then, even in this world, after time had been created, there was a period of an entirely different concept of time-length.

Strong corroboration of the above view may be brought from Onkelos, who interpreted *b'reshith* as *b'kadmin*; and in *Simlath Ger,* p. 100: The rendering *b'kadmin* has the sense of "of old" (*l'fanim*), as in the words of King David in Psalms: "*Of old Thou didst lay the foundation of the earth.*" This is time which cannot be limited by a given date. We also find in the scriptural text: "Before time (*l'fanim*) in Israel" (I Samuel 9:9) which is undefined time except that it signifies a very long period. Targum Jonathan renders *l'fanim* as *b'kadmin. Cf.* Joseph Caspi's *Mishneh Kesef,* Krakow, 1906.

Note should be made of the text of the liturgy of the Sabbath and New Moon: "Thou didst form Thy world from 'of old' (*mikedem*); Thou didst finish Thy work on the seventh day." Apparently, the meaning of *mikedem* accords with the rendering of Onkelos, "*mil'kadmin*." And so in Genesis 2:8, "And the Lord God planted a garden in Eden *mikedem*," Onkelos translates the last word as *mil'kadmin*. This is based on the scriptural text: "Of old Thou didst lay the foundation of the earth." R. Menahem Azariah in *Imre Binah* ch. 25 has the same interpretation on *b'reshith*.

According to the thesis of R. Obadiah, mentioned above, each of the days of Genesis was a thousand years. *Anafim*, a commentary on *Ikkarim* 2:18, explains why according to R. Bahya Scripture writes *one day* and not *first day*. The reason is that *one day* refers to those days and years that are unsearchable. Those days were joined into an absolute unity, having no distinction or separateness whatsoever, so that we may refer to them only as "one day." The meaning here is that since we cannot comprehend the magnitude and nature of those days and years, and since it is only the subsequent creation of the world which ended this period of days, we can speak of it at least as "one day," for the period has now been made whole, a unit. Scripture does not say *first day*, because there is no second that is analogous to it.

From the above discussion it is clear that there are various views on the length of the day of the Six Days of Creation before Creation had been completed, and as a matter of course a different conception was applied to the category of time: for, if we say that the sphere of the earth, which now rotates about its axis in 24 hours, then made the rotation in one minute, then, from one aspect, the length of the day was short; from another aspect, however, a minute was conceptualized as immeasurably long, since it was possible for the sphere to rotate about its axis in that time. And we may say this for all other phases of the day.

Accordingly, the following passage in Gen. R. 9, which the commentators found so difficult, may be explained thus:—The text says: "*And there was evening and there was morning, the sixth day:* R. Simon b. Martha said: Up to here the reckoning is as the world counts. Henceforth, the count is made by a different standard." What is meant is that the system of temporal time-measurement, valid for the Six Days of Creation, was based on a perception of the newly created time implying other categories, whereas our system of time-reckoning begins after the creation of heaven and earth was finished—on the seventh day.

In the light of all this we may explain that the statement above that the time of the seven days of Creation was created on each day, postulates a separate and relative time for each day.

In Gen. 21:33 we read: *And he* (Abraham) *called there on the name of the Lord, the God of olam* (AJV: *the Everlasting God*). (Now, *olam* means "world" or "everlasting," *ha-olam*, with the definite article, means "the world"). Commenting on the fact that Scripture does not say, the God of the world, Maimonides explains that time itself was created, and that Abraham began to teach that doctrine, at which he arrived through speculation. Therefore he called there on the name of the Lord, the God of Everlasting (i.e., the God who is Master even over everlastingness, i.e., of time). Nahmanides *ad. loc.* explains: "He called on the name of the Lord, who controls Time in His Might." He adds, "The teacher [Maimonides] states in the 'Guide' that this points to God's eternity, predating the existence of time." Sforno *loc. cit.* explains: "He proclaimed and made known to the many that God is the God of Time, which He brought into being, thus refuting the doctrine of the heretics, both modern and ancient."

Thus *olam* here denotes not merely place but also time, the phrase meaning the Eternal God. This dual meaning of *olam* indicates that time is bound up with space, as will be explained further on. Similarly, when our Sages of the Mishnah applied the designation *makom* (Place) to the Creator on the basis of various verses in the Torah, they pointed to the same idea. Just as the Tetragrammaton indicates eternity, that is, that He created time, He being in the category of "He was, He is, He shall be," so does the designation *makom* indicate that He created space—and the two concepts are one. Again, the word *olam* is linguistically connected with *haalamah*, hiding, because the essential nature of the matter is hidden from human understanding. The same thought is hinted at in Isa. 40:28: *Hast thou not known? Hast thou not heard that the everlasting God, the Lord, the Creator of the ends of the earth, fainteth not, neither is weary? His discernment is past searching out.*[24]

This novel interpretation of *olam* by the early exegetes as signifying both space *and* time, is also expressed by a modern thinker. Dr. Grunfeld writes:[25]

"In Physics place (space) and time must fuse and coalesce into one concept. In this sense Minkowski used the term 'world' to designate the entirety of events in Physics. By this he meant that the basis of all order and system of the realities of the universe is not space alone nor time alone, but the events themselves, which Minkowski calls 'the points of the world,' that is, the position of a given event associated with a defined and given instant of time, etc. This world of Minkowski is a four-dimensional one, of space and time fused together to define the phenomena of Physics. . .

"In the earlier physics preceding the Relativity Theory time was considered an absolute quantity, self-sufficient and completely independent of the coordinates of space, etc. However, according to the relativity theory, as said before, the 'world' is four-dimensional, for time is not an independent, absolute quantity, but as Minkowski states: 'Henceforth [after the Theory of Relativity] space (or extension) and time cease to be independent entities and are reduced to the position of the passing shadow, and only by coalescing do they assume a position of independence.' Again: 'We see clearly that only in abstract thought can we separate space (extension) and time from the objects and phenomena of Physics; apart from such abstraction they in fact cohere and join, having existence only when they form a complete unity. By itself, each is no more than an abstraction.' "

It is interesting to note that this idea is already found in the *Tifereth Yisrael*, Chap. 26, by Maharal of Prague (1515-1609): "Time and place are but one, as is known to the wise."

The above may be summarized in the following three propositions: 1. Time was created. 2. Our standard of time is relative, not absolute. 3. Time and space are two concepts which essentially are but one.

The above researches into the nature of time enable us to shed light on many fundamentals of the Torah and on many Rabbinical dicta.

TIME, SPACE AND GOD'S UNITY

In the reciting of the Shema, *Hear, O Israel: The Lord Our God, The Lord is One*, the Jew is enjoined to accept the yoke of the Kingdom of Heaven, and to attest his belief in the One God. The Sages explain[26] that one must affirm His sovereignty as the One God over oneself, over heaven and earth, and over the four points of the compass. *Sifre*[27] comments: *The Lord our God*—over us; *the Lord is One*—over all the inhabitants of the earth. *The Lord our God*—in this world; *the Lord is One*—in the Hereafter. And so Scripture says: *And the Lord shall be King over all the earth; in that day shall the Lord be One, and His name one* (Zech. 14:9).

Apparently, according to the first interpretation in *Sifre* and in both *Talmudim* we affirm His Sovereignty spatially, i.e., over all the inhabitants of the earth, over heaven and earth, and over the four quarters of the universe. Thus Scripture states: *Know this day, and lay it to thy heart, that the Lord, He is God in heaven above and upon the earth beneath; there is none else* (Deut. 4:39). (*Sifre Pin'has* 134, comments: even in open space; Deut. R. 2:27: even in the empty space of the universe). And it is

[24] See Psalms 89: 2-3, Midrash T'hillim ad. loc., and Exodus Rabba, ch. 15, 31. [25] *Ha-T'kufah*, v. 18, p. 276.
[26] Talmud B. *Berakoth* 13, Yerushalmi, ibid., 2, 1. [27] Va-et'hanan. See *Midrash Tannaim* and *Midrash Hagadol*, ad. loc.

written: *The Lord of hosts, the whole earth is full of His glory* (Isa. 6:3), on which the comment is made in Exod. R. 1:9: There is no place devoid of the Shekinah. And it is written: *Do not I fill heaven and earth?* (Jer. 23:24) which the Sages explain: The Holy One, blessed be He, is the place of the universe. (Vid. T.S. v. 8, Exodus Addenda, 15.)

All these verses speak of the Kingship of God from the aspect of *space.*

According to *Sifre's* second interpretation (quoted in Rashi) the sense is to affirm His Kingship from the aspect of *time,* in the past, present, and future, and as proclaimed in the Liturgy, "The Lord is King, the Lord was King, the Lord shall be King for ever and ever" (*l'olam vaed*)—i.e., past, present and future (and in *Erubin* 54a: "Wherever Scripture employs the term *vaed,* eternal and unbroken continuity is indicated"). Similarly for the meaning of the Tetragrammaton: He was, He is, and He shall be. Further, the verse, *Blessed be the Lord, the God of Israel, from everlasting even to everlasting,* is the profession of God as King from the aspect of time. This too is the spirit of the hymn: "Lord of the Universe, who reigned before anything formed was created. . . And after all things shall have ceased to exist, He alone, the revered One, will reign."

So too in J. Berakoth 9:1:[28] "When the Israelites enter the synagogues and houses of study in the morning and assert the unity of His name, proclaiming, 'Hear O Israel: The Lord our God, the Lord is One,' all the ministering angels gather before the Holy One, blessed be He, and declare: 'Thou wast while yet the world had not been created; Thou art from when the world was created. Thou art in this world; Thou shalt be in the World to come'—thus professing His Kingship temporally—in the past, present, and future."

In *Hizkuni,* "*Hear O Israel*—hear and understand this thing: the Lord Who was from of yore, without beginning, He is the Lord of the present, and He is the everliving Lord, without end and limit. In this respect He *is One,* viz., in Him alone there is a unity such as was not nor shall be in anything in the universe."

R. Bahya, quoting Eliezer of Worms, gives this interpretation: "*Hear O Israel, the Lord* —anterior to the world—*our God*—contemporaneous with the world—*the Lord*—posterior to the world—*is One*—in all the worlds." Thus, on this interpretation, the verse affirms His unity both spatially and temporally. The explanation of the early exegetes that the Tetragrammaton implies *is, was* and *shall be,* permits the interpretation of the verse in accordance with its obvious sense, and in a manner analogous to what R. Eliezer of Worms wrote: " '*The Lord*' (i.e.; Who was, is, and shall be), He is '*our God*'—from point of view of time, '*the Lord is One,*' in heaven and earth and the four quarters of the universe,"—a spatial affirmation.

And perhaps the statement of Maimonides in Guide of the Perplexed quoted above, that the knowledge of time's having been created is a fundamental of the Faith, ranking second to the belief in the Unity, is based on the fact that both are included in the verse *Hear, O Israel. . .,* as I have explained the meaning of *Sifre.*

Numerous Biblical verses express the thought of His kingdom and eternity from the aspect of time and space. Here are some examples. *Blessed be the name of the Lord from this time forth and for ever* (time) (Ps. 113:2). *From the rising of the sun unto the going down thereof, the Lord's name is to be praised* (space) (ibid. 3). *Thy kingdom is the kingdom of all the worlds* (space), *and Thy dominion endureth throughout all generations* (time) (ibid. 145:13). And so the formula of the benediction: "Blessed art Thou, O Lord our God (time in the aspect of *was, is,* and *shall be*), King of the Universe (space) . . . "

FOREKNOWLEDGE AND FREE WILL

The difficult question of Foreknowledge and Free Will is considered by Maimonides in *Hilkoth T'shuba* 5:5. His answer is: "Man cannot apprehend the mind of the Creator. This is what the prophet said: *For My thoughts are*

[28] Cited in *Yalkut Shim'oni, Va-et'hanan,* par. 836, but missing in our text.

not your thoughts, neither are your ways My ways, saith the Lord (Isaiah 55:8). And since this is so, we cannot know how the Holy One, blessed be He, can have knowledge of all creatures and acts. But we do know indubitably that a man's actions are in his own hands, which the Holy One, blessed be He, neither compels nor decrees." (See Maimonides, *Sh'moneh P'rakim,* end of Chapter 8. Guide of the Perplexed 3:20; and Tos. Yomtob on Aboth 3:15). The Maharal (in *G'buroth Hashem,* Preface 2) and the author of *Tsemah Tsedek* in the *Taame ha-Mitzvoth,* explain this statement in accordance with what Maimonides wrote in Guide of the Perplexed, Part 1; namely, that there is a qualitative, and not only a quantitative difference between His knowledge and ours, the two being entirely distinct; and this is implied in the verse. . . . *My thoughts are not your thoughts* (Isa. 55:8). See also Saadya Gaon in *Emunoth v'Deoth,* chap. 4.

The problem of Foreknowledge and Free Will is connected with the concept of Time, in accordance with R. Bahya's remarks on Exod. 15:18, quoted above: ". . . because all periods of time, past and future, are as the present to Him, for He was while yet time did not exist, and time shall not pass Him."

Commenting on "The day of the Holy One, blessed be He, is one thousand years," *Y'fe Toar* (Num. R. 5:4) remarks: "Far be it from us to think that time counts with Him, for a thousand million years are to Him but as a moment, because He is not in any relationship to time. The expression must be understood figuratively only, as being couched in terms of human comprehension. Its real meaning is this: When the Holy One, blessed be He, mentions 'day,' He means 1,000 years, as when He said to Adam, '*In the day that thou eatest thereof, thou shalt surely die*'" (Genesis 2:17).

All this is implied in *My thoughts are not your thoughts,* for according to our perception of the essential nature of time it is impossible to dissociate it from past, present, and future. Nevertheless, the rational disciplines lead us to understand that He is above time, and that the above-mentioned matters, as understood by our human intelligence, are not really relevant to Him. This then is the main point to be considered for the understanding of the question of Foreknowledge and Free Will, to which Maimonides found the solution in the words, *For My thoughts are not your thoughts.*[29]

TIME AND THE SABBATH

In a lengthy article (*Talpioth,* 1st year, v. 2, p. 415 ff.) I discuss in great detail the first Sabbath of the world. (See Torah Shelemah, v. 14, p. 306.) The Bible reads: "*And on the seventh day God finished His work*" (Genesis 2:2). The Sages comment on this: "He finished His work at the very last moment of the sixth day, so that at the very instant that He finished it was the seventh day." (See T.S. v. 2, ch. 2, par. 24.) There I raise the question: How are we to understand this? The world is a globe, and the Sabbath does not begin everywhere at the same time. How, then, can the first Sabbath have begun at one instant for the entire world? When Sabbath commences in Israel, at a point 270 degrees away it is still Thursday midnight.

There is also a Rabbinic tradition that when it is the Sabbath on earth, it is Sabbath in Heaven.[30] The same difficulty arises. Since the world is round, from the time that the Sabbath commences until it ends in the entire globe, an interval of 48 hours is required. How then can we visualize Sabbath in Heaven at the same time? Besht in *Kether Shem Tob* seems to supply a satisfactory answer in a comment on a passage in the Zohar (v. 2, 88): "What is the Sabbath?— The name of the Holy One, blessed be He." On this Besht observes: "In this sense our great Sages said: 'With the Sabbath came rest—*m'nuhah*— meaning thereby that the Holy One, blessed be He, is called *M'nuhah,* for motion cannot be ascribed to Him, since motion pertains only to that which is in time and space. However, the Holy One, blessed be He, is infinite, and

[29] See *Or Same-ah,* commentary to *Yad Hahazaka,* loc. cit.
[30] See T.S., Genesis, ch. 2, par. 49; Exodus, ch. 16, par. 137; and *Midrash T'hillim,* ps. 94.

is not moved from place to place, neither does He come within the category of time.

"In an essential sense the Sabbath is the revelation of the root and the yearning of the branches therefor. This means, the Sabbath is the holy day which reveals and radiates bright light from the Holy One; for He, blessed be His Name, is the most Holy of the holy, illuminating all the created, i.e., the spirituality of everything is that which emanated from the Primordial Thought. This is the life-essence of all, yet subsequently, when by the process of unfolding, Creation became an actuality, this spirituality still remained above, hidden within its root. The life-essence in the created beings was extremely small, since it had undergone contraction in order to be vested with corporeality. If the world had remained in this manner after everything had been finished on the sixth day, Creation could not have endured. Therefore, after all the work of Creation was finished, He radiated a splendor from the hidden Creation; that is, the extremely spiritual state of existence, characteristic of the beings created in His thought. He thus beamed the lustrous glory of His majesty from end to end of the universe on all the works of Creation. But principally on man, the crown of Creation, shone this effulgence which proceeded from the hidden roots in His thought.

"This is the meaning of the passage: 'What did the world lack? — It lacked *m'nuhah*' — i.e., it lacked the spirituality of the Godhead, Who is called *m'nuhah,* and 'with the Sabbath came *m'nuhah*,' viz., the hidden brightness of the being of the created things, which is of the essence of God, blessed be His name. This filled men with love and desire for God, like a child engaged in play that forgets his father; yet when he sees him, throws everything aside and runs and cleaves to him out of love for him, being a part of his body. So, figuratively, when the Blessed Name of God makes the splendor of His Majesty shine upon His creatures, their faces yearningly turn toward Him. This is His Will: This He expects from them, and this is the cause of their continued existence. This too is the essence of the Sabbath—it is a return to the root. The root illumines the branches, and the branches in turn long and yearn for it; in this yearning consists the unity of the Blessed Name of God.

"The Zohar (v. 2, T'rumah, 135) avers: 'The mystery of the Sabbath is the Sabbath that becomes a unity through the mystery of the *ehad* . . . for God's Throne of Glory becomes a unity through the mystery of *ehad.*' This means that the created in their collectivity are deemed a throne for the Almighty, as it is written, *The heaven is My throne and the earth is My footstool* (Isa. 66:1). The created beings are multiple externally, but are one internally. However, they are one only when their entire desire and attachment are dedicated to the one thought of cleaving to the Blessed Name of God. This cleaving unites and binds Him to His creatures, and in turn makes them endure through the Blessed Name of God Who is One: this attachment is called 'covenant.' Hence the Sabbath is called an 'everlasting covenant.'

"As it was at the beginning, so does God ever revive His spirit in us perpetually. Particularly in the matter of the sacred Sabbath must it always be so, for in His goodness He reneweth the creation every day continually. Every day a day is created, and every day are the created things (re)created from matter inorganic and organic, from the category of the animal and the human, until the advent of the Sabbath day. Then the Almighty rouses Himself, if it were possible to say so, to endow them with a life-force, as it was at the time of the Creation."

To sum up: In the spiritual world above there is no time at all, and the Almighty is called *m'nuhah.* But when the seventh day is observed as the Sabbath in the terrestrial world, *whatever the time,* spiritual channels are opened, through which streams down a vivifying force of holiness from the Almighty, the brilliant light of His holiness. This our Sages called "the additional soul" which the observer of the Sabbath then enjoys. That is what they mean by: "with the Sabbath came *m'nuhah*"—the indwelling of the Shekinah, which is the soul of the universe.

The source of this idea may possibly be found in the Mishnah (end of *Tamid*):

"*A Psalm, a Song for the Sabbath-day* (Ps. 92:1). This means: A psalm, a song for the future to come, for the day (lec. var. the world) which is altogether Sabbath, *m'nuhah*, in the everlasting life." The same thought is expressed in the Grace after meals: "May the All-merciful let us inherit the day which shall be wholly a Sabbath and rest in the life everlasting." That is to say, the Hereafter is wholly Sabbath because it is rest—*m'nuhah*.

This explanation affords a solution to the problem of how the celestial Sabbath can be linked with the terrestrial Sabbath, seeing that the latter lasts 48 hours over the whole globe, as stated above. The answer is that in the upper spiritual world there is no motion; consequently it is *always* in the state of Sabbath and *m'nuhah* (rest), as it was before creation. The connection lies in the fact that when the Sabbath is observed in the lower world, the gates of the upper world are opened and a stream of the Sabbath light and rest pours down upon those who observe the Sabbath, each locality in its own seventh day. This explains as well the problem of the first Sabbath. As the sixth day came to an end — in each locality in its own time — Sabbath began, and brought rest and holiness from the "Sabbath in Heaven" — again to each locality in its own time.

This solution may be hinted at in the phrase of the Zohar: "The mystery of the Sabbath" — the secret of understanding the link between the Sabbath above and the Sabbath on earth. Concerning this it is stated: "It is the Sabbath that became a unity through the mystery of *ehad*," as explained above.

This thesis may explain the passage in Mekilta, Thisa: "R. Eleazar b. P'rata says: Whoever keeps the Sabbath, it is accounted to him as if he *made* the Sabbath, as it says, *Wherefore the children of Israel shall keep the Sabbath, to* make *the Sabbath*" (Exod. 31:16—lit. translation). Presumably R. Eleazar wished to answer the difficulty which his proof-text raises, viz., how can one "make" the Sabbath, seeing that its advent is automatic? (This is unlike the festivals whose observance is dependent on man, in so far as the Beth Din fixes the calendar: hence they can be said to be "made" by those who observe them. Not so the Sabbath, however.) In the light of the above, notwithstanding that its advent is automatic and independent of man, it nevertheless requires preparation and awareness on the part of human beings in order that it may receive the stream of holiness from above, whereby the two Sabbaths, terrestrial and celestial, are linked. In that sense one who properly observes the Sabbath may truly be said to "make" it.

SPACE-TIME IN RELATION TO THE SABBATH

Accordingly, we see that just as the holiness of the Sabbath attaches to time, it also attaches to the spatial universe and to the entire creation. This space-time sanctity of the Sabbath is made all the more manifest when we bear in mind, as stated above, that over the whole globe it lasts 48 hours. Hence the actual observance of the 24 hours is dependent on locality, i.e., space.

To repeat the quotation from the Besht: "He thus beamed the lustrous glory of His majesty from end to end of the Universe on all the works of Creation, but principally on man." Thus we see that time and space are integrally one as regards the Sabbath.

This concept that for the Sabbath time and space are interlinked, is hinted at in the Zohar 2, 63 (cited in Torah Shelemah, v. 14, pp. 234, 249), which explains the Scriptural exhortation, *Let no man go out of his place on the seventh day* (Exod. 16:29) as alluding to the Scriptural verses, *Blessed be the glory of the Lord* from His Place—*The* place *whereon thou standest is holy ground* . . . By this the Zohar meant that space and time are interlinked, and as *Maharal* said (above, p. 206), are one.

The violator of the Sabbath therefore departs from holiness in time and space. This is intimated in the Biblical sentence, *Let no man go out from his place on the seventh day.*[31]

[31] See Abraham J. Heschel in *Judaism*, v. 1, no. 3, pp. 262-269.

TIME AND REPENTANCE

Thou turnest man to contrition, and sayest, "Return, ye children of men" (Ps. 90:3). *Targum Jonathan* comments: "Thou dost requite man for his sins until his death, and sayest: *'Return, ye children of men'; for a thousand years in Thy sight are but as yesterday when it is past, and as a watch in the night.*" The exegetes had difficulty in finding a connection between the two verses.

In accord with our elucidation we would say that the first two verses, *Thou hast been our dwelling-place . . . before the mountains were brought forth, even from everlasting to everlasting,* preface the declaration that God is above space and time. "*Thou hast been our dwelling-place,*" as interpreted by the Sages in *Midrash T'hilim,* conveys the idea that "the Holy One, blessed be He, is the dwelling-place and site of the universe, but the universe is not His site." Again, "*before the mountains were brought forth*" states that God existed before the universe was created. This is followed by the exhortation to repent: "*and sayest, 'Return, ye children of men.'*" The same is expressed in the liturgy: "Until the day of his death dost Thou wait for him"; and in Kiddushin 40b: "Even if one has been an inveterate evil-doer all his days, if he repents at the end, his evil is no longer charged to him." Similarly Maimonides in *Hilkoth T'shuba* 2: "Even if one transgressed all his days but repented on the day of his death and died penitent, all his iniquities are pardoned."

At first sight it is hard to understand why a man who sinned for seventy years should have his iniquities pardoned because he repented on the day of his death! Is this logical? How can one hour of repentance undo the wicked deeds of seventy years? But the verse, "*for a thousand years in Thy sight,*" etc., answers this by explaining that our conception of the nature of time is not the same as God's, as it is written: "*My thoughts are not your thoughts.*" A thousand years are to God as yesterday, or as a watch in the night. (Since a "watch" consists of 3 hours, the "watches" of a thousand years will equal approximately 120 years, the ideal span of life—See Gen. 6:3.)

The above difficulty is thus resolved; for man's bodily life, though seeming to us to cover a long period of 70 years, is but as a day or a few hours in duration. This was stated in *Midrash T'hillim,* (ed. Buber, Ps. 90), namely, that 974 generations swept forward and disappeared in the twinkling of an eye.

It is plain then that repentance is measured by a different standard, by a sort of a qualitative clock: A single hour of repentance may equal a period so long that one can thereby amend the misdeeds of a lifetime.

In this spirit we may explain Isa. 55:7ff: *Let the wicked forsake his way, and the man of iniquity his thoughts; and let him return unto the Lord, and He will have compassion upon him, and to our God, for He will abundantly pardon. For My thoughts are not your thoughts, neither are your ways My ways, saith the Lord. For as the heavens are higher than the earth, so are My ways higher than your ways, and My thoughts than your thoughts.* Thus here too repentance is linked with the concept of time-space.

In Abodah Zarah 10 we find a similar statement: "A man may acquire his Hereafter in a single hour." Thus by a single action, such as fulfilling a particular precept or withstanding a trial, he attains that spiritual stature which earns him his Hereafter, and that one hour is more important and longer than a lifetime of seventy years.

LENGTH OF DAYS

"It was taught in a Baraitha: R. Jacob says: There is not a single commandment in the Torah promising reward, which reward is not made dependent on the resurrection of the dead, in order to teach that there will be reward only in the World to Come. In the matter of honoring father and mother it is written, *That thy days be long, and that it may go well with thee* (Deut. 5:16). In connection with freeing the mother-bird when one takes the nest, Scripture likewise says, *That it may be well with thee, and that thou mayest prolong thy days* (ibid. 22:7). But consider: A father once bade his son, 'Go up to the top of the castle and bring me fledglings from the nest.' The son climbed up to the top of the castle, let the mother-bird go and took the young. Returning, he fell and died. Where, then, was his promised well-being and his prolongation of days? We therefore conclude that the reward of well-being—'*that it may go well with thee,*'—must refer to a world that is wholly good, and that the promise, '*that thy days may be long,*' refers to a world that is wholly long" (Kiddushin 39a).

This requires elucidation. Scripture explicitly states, *That thy days may be long, and that it may go well with thee,* upon the land *which the Lord thy God giveth thee* (ibid. 5:16). How then can we say that it refers to the Hereafter? Furthermore, what is meant by the expression, "in a world that is wholly long?" We can understand the phrase "a world that is wholly good," for the World to Come is indeed so called, as Rashi comments, for there injury and pain will be absent and it will contain only good. The Hereafter is also thus designated in J. Hagigah 2:1. But what are we to understand by "a world that is wholly long?"

Now, we have established the fact that our measure of time is relative. In the spiritual worlds in particular there is certainly an entirely different conception of the nature of time and a different standard of measurement.

In the light of this the Rabbinical interpretation may be explained thus: *That thy days may be long* "in a world that is wholly long" *upon the land,* etc., i.e., if you fulfill this precept, the very minutes of the days you live upon the land will be long, quite literally. For, when a man fulfills a command of the Torah he cleaves to God, Who lives forever; therefore those moments are told out on an hour-glass transcending the quantitative. Those moments are *actually* very long, verily, longer than all the seventy years of one's material life, measured by a clock of a quantitative nature. This is the sense of "a world that is wholly long," namely, a world in the upper spheres, where our moments are passed in "a world that is wholly long."

This may also be the idea in Deut. 30:20: *To love the Lord thy God, to hearken to His voice, and to cleave unto Him; for that is thy life, and the* length of thy days, *that thou mayest dwell* in the land, etc. This too states that the reward for fulfilling God's commandments and cleaving to Him, is length of days *in the land.* Again, Scripture says . . . *to observe to do all the words of this law . . . and through this thing ye shall make your days long* upon the land (ibid. 32:46). Similarly the liturgical passage: "For they (the commandments) are our life and the length of our days." In all these the meaning of lengthy days is that given in our present discussion.

Likewise in Deut. 11:21: *That your days may be multiplied . . . as the days of the heaven above the earth.* The meaning of this, in accordance with our thesis, is that the Torah tells us: If you fulfill the commands of the Torah, you shall have length of days, as the days of the heaven above the earth; for your days, namely, the seconds, minutes, and hours, spent in fulfilling the commands of the Torah, are then measured according to the time-standards of Heaven, by a qualitative and not a quantitative clock. A minute then becomes a "*long world*"; that is the true length of days. We may apply the same interpretation to the passage, "for this is a great and holy day," which is recited on the Sabbath in the Grace after Meals. "Great" can be interpreted in consonance with the above thesis, that time is not absolute but relative. Consequently, the holy Sabbath Day being sanctified ever since the Six Days of Creation, the standard of its time is relatively longer than the other days, because time of holiness is measured qualitatively.

TO DISTINGUISH BETWEEN DAY AND NIGHT

In the morning service there is a benediction: "Blessed art Thou . . . Who hast given to the *sekvi* (which means mind, heart, or rooster) understanding to distinguish between day and night." This formula is derived from Job 38:36: (see Rosh Hashana 26a) *Who hath given the* sekvi *understanding?* R. Asher b. Yechiel comments (Berakoth 9:23): "The heart is called *sekvi,* and by means of understanding a man distinguishes between day and night. Now, since the cock, which is called *sekvi* in another Semitic language, also has this understanding, it was decreed that this benediction should be pronounced upon hearing the cock crow."

However, in actual practice we recite the blessing even if no cock is heard. Then the question arises, what is its purpose? The view of Maimonides stated above, that a cardinal article of faith, second only to God's Unity, is the doctrine that time came into existence simultaneously with the creation of the world, and that the Holy One, blessed be He, is anterior to our time, may enlighten us. The idea of time becomes most vivid to us, and its flight is most acutely sensed, when night yields to day and one actually sees with one's own eyes the distinction between night and day. This leads to the realization that time is bound up with motion, and that it was created when primordial matter was created. The purpose of the benediction, then, is to offer thanks to the Almighty for giving us his deeper understanding into the true nature of time as evinced by the distinction between night and day. It is therefore fitting that this blessing should precede the benediction "who hast not made me a heathen," i.e., who hast given me clear insight into the unity of God, Who is the Only One and Unique, above Time and Space, an insight whereby we are distinguished from the idolaters.

In this way too we may explain why the Sages instituted a benediction for the Sanctification of the new moon. Just as the power to distinguish between day and night leads to the understanding of the flight and nature of time, so even in greater measure does the viewing and observing of the rebirth of the moon, which is associated with a period of a month of days.

The same applies to the benediction of the sun, recited once in 28 years. Perhaps this thought is also implied in the words of the Evening Prayer, "Thou changest times and variest the seasons," for in the setting of the sun we distinguish the passage of time and its change.

2.

THE ATOM IN JEWISH SOURCES

Referring to Chapter I, verse 2, page 15: "Now the earth was tohu *and* bohu *(AJV: unformed and void)."*

I

We are living in days of great scientific discoveries—electricity, radio, television, the airplane, and numerous others. None, however, has made so deep an impression as the discovery of atomic energy. The explosion of the first atom bomb over Nagasaki in 1945 heralded the birth-pangs of a new world. Not only did it overwhelm and conquer the Japanese; the whole world was profoundly shaken and astounded at this development of Science, and the genius of human reason which had penetrated the innermost secrets of Nature — and thought fearfully and apprehensively whither this might lead.

It is widely realized that we have entered upon a new era, and that this discovery will in the near future revolutionize the world, completely rebuild it—or destroy it.

What do the Bible and our Sages have to say about these hitherto undreamt-of forces? In the present study I will attempt to answer that question; in the course of so doing I hope to prove that these world-shaking discoveries fully confirm their teachings, with the consequent strengthening of our Faith. This study will be facilitated by a brief résumé of what science teaches and has taught on this subject.

The atom system was first expounded by the Greek philosopher Democritus (566-469 B.C.E.). He taught that the universe is composed of varying combinations of minute indivisible particles (atoms), much too small to be perceptible to the senses, and differing only in size and form. He held that the universe was created out of a primordial matter which he termed the simple principle, the element, the father, the original substance—(the *hyle*).[1] Newton (1664-1727) carried this much farther. According to him all matter is composed of small molecules; the smallest, which is not capable of further division, is the atom. This atom is so small that it is invisible even under the most powerful microscope; we only *know* of its existence. When these tiny particles combine in varying proportions, different substances are formed; thus there are atoms of copper, tin, lead, etc. To date over ninety kinds of atoms have been found, and classified according to their weight. These atoms consist of a nucleus of protons and neutrons, about which revolve electrons, much as the planets revolve about the sun. From Newton's day to the present physicists have studied the nature of the atom.

Contemporary scientists, and notably Prof. Einstein, have developed the theory that the material atom may be transformed into energy, matter being merely highly concentrated energy.

Until recently it was accepted that all substances could be decomposed into their constituent elements, but no matter how far one might proceed with the process of decomposition, a material residue must always remain, for matter can be neither created nor destroyed. But according to the modern outlook matter, an existent, could cease to exist. If transformed into energy, a substance will lose material exist-

[1] R. Saadya Gaon in *Emunoth v'Deoth* and in his commentary on *Sefer Y'tsirah* rejects and refutes the notion of a primordial matter, and proves the truth of the Jewish belief that the universe was created *ex nihilo* and that only by the will of the Creator was the original matter created.

ence completely. This theoretical conclusion finds confirmation in the disintegration phenomena of radium which occur in consonance with the new principles. A method has now been devised to bring about fission of the atom of uranium, the heaviest of the elements, transform the matter of the atom into more energy, and utilize this energy. Scientists have thus confirmed the view that matter is energy in a different form, and that the primary source out of which matter has been formed is energy, which has been concentrated into tiny electrical particles termed ions.

Having summed up the major results of modern scientific research, we may now turn our attention to what Jewish sources have to say. It should be noted at the outset that the lore of the Sages does not consist of works directly devoted to the subjects of science, but of ideas, insights, perceptions and observations arising out of their interpretations and explanations of Scripture.

II

The Bible commences with the creation of the Universe. Its first two verses read: *In the beginning God created heaven and earth. Now the earth was* tohu *and* bohu (AJV: *unformed and void*) and darkness *was upon the face of the* t'hom (AJV: *deep*); *and the spirit of God hovered over the face of the waters.* What is the meaning of *tohu* and *bohu*? Onkelos and Jonathan translate: "desolate and void." Rashi relates them to the Hebrew words designating desolation and emptiness. Similarly Ibn Ezra rejects Saadya's interpretation of *tohu* as derived from *t'hom* (deep).

The Sages of the Talmud, however, hint that *tohu* and *bohu* are not terms designating negation and non-existence, but positive and real entities. "Rabbi Judah said in the name of Rab: 'Ten things were created on the first day, and they are as follows: Heaven and earth, *tohu* and *bohu,* light and darkness . . .' " (Hagigah 12). Thus *tohu* and *bohu* are not negative concepts but real entities, since they were created. The Talmud then explains the terms thus: "*Tohu* is a green line surrounding the universe, from which darkness emerges; *bohu* is the smooth stones. . ." This explanation still leaves the matter in obscurity.[2]

Gen. R. 1:9: "A philosopher asked R. Gamaliel: 'Your God is a great artist, but surely He found good materials to assist Him, viz., *tohu, bohu,* darkness, water, wind (*ruah*) and the deep.' R. Gamaliel answered him: 'Scripture records that all these were created. *Tohu* and *bohu* were created, as it says, *I make peace, and create evil . . .* ' " (Isa. 45:7) (quoted in vol. 1, ch. 1, par. 65, q.v.).

Thus here too *tohu* and *bohu* are not concepts of negation and non-existence. The proof-text, however—*I make peace and create evil*—is obscure and requires further elucidation. *Sefer Habahir* 9, comments: "Evil from *tohu* and peace from *bohu.*"

Sefer Y'tsirah 2:6: "He formed (created) a substantiality out of *tohu,* and made the non-existent existent." Most commentators explain this as meaning that He created substance out of nothingness (positive out of the negative). Judah Albarceloni explains the words "substantiality out of *tohu*" as referring to the wind (*ruah*), which is something of the attenuated nature of *tohu* converted into a more solid substance. *Sefer Habahir* 2: "R. Berekiah said: 'What is *tohu*? Something which confounds men . . . a substance beyond human comprehension . . . What is *bohu*? Something which exists, since *bohu* is really two words, *bo hu* (it is therein).' ' . . . it was *tohu* and was transformed into *bohu.*' "

The identification of *tohu* and *bohu* with matter and form respectively is elucidated in *Higayon Hanefesh* 3 by Abraham bar Hiyya; (see also his *M'gilath Ham'galleh,* p. 16). Abrabanel and *Zohar* I, 16, state: "*Tohu* is a place that has neither color nor likeness; *bohu* has shape and image."

In his commentary on *Sefer Y'tsirah* I, 11 Ibn Daud writes: "Hence it follows that *tohu* is neither desolation, emptiness, nor waste, but

[2] For a further discussion see A. Altman, "Gnostic Themes in Rabbinic Cosmology," in *Essays Presented to J. H. Hertz,* p. 20.

subtle *entities* so intangible that no name or word can be applied to them; for that reason they are described by a term denoting astonishment or incomprehensibility. . . *Bohu,* however, is matter invested with form; yet it is still too subtle to be designated with a specific term. Therefore the designation *bohu,* whose components are *bo-hu* which denote 'it is therein,' is a fitting one." So also R. Moses Botarel in his commentary on *Sefer Y'tsirah* I, 11.

Nahmanides in his commentary on Gen. 1:1, explains the passage of *Sefer Habahir* thus: "The Holy One, blessed be He, extracted from the complete and absolute nothingness an extremely tenuous element; this was devoid of substantiality, but it possessed the potential to receive form and to emerge from a latent to an active state. This was the primal substance called by the Greeks *hyle.* Thereafter He created nothing new *ex nihilo,* but formed and made everything out of this *hyle,* which He invested with their forms, and then perfected them. . . This *hyle* is termed *tohu* . . . for it had not yet assumed a form that would in any way have permitted a symbolic representation. The form with which this matter is invested is called *bohu.*"[3]

R. Samuel Masnuth states in *Yalkut* MS:[4] "Wherefore does the Torah begin with the letter *beth*? In order to point out that the Blessed and Supreme Name is One, but the things created are two, viz., matter and form."

Gersonides holds the original viewpoint that *tohu* is form and *bohu* matter. This interpretation he bases on the above quotation from Hagiga 12a.

Sforno: " . . . *tohu* is pure potentiality only . . . and the form borne by that primal compound is called *bohu.*"

Now, all these interpretations are based on the philosophical system of Aristotle, which divides all the existents of the universe into matter and form. But the main idea that *tohu* and *bohu* are not terms indicating negation only, but positive entities, is founded on views of the Rabbis as expressed in the Talmud, in Gen. R., and in *Sefer Habahir.*

To sum up: Genesis 1:2 is thus explained: *Now,* in the evolutionary creation of *the earth,* "*tohu*" was created first (an extremely fine entity without any shape or form whatever, but only of the nature of what we call "energy"); *and bohu*; out of the *tohu* the Creator made *bohu* by concentrating this force or energy and investing it with form, the two constituting matter. *Bohu,* however, is as yet invisible to the human eye because of its extreme minuteness. *Tohu,* as pure energy, is a destructive and devastating force, and is called "evil"; while *bohu* is the case within which *tohu* is restrained and confined so that it may endure; this is today called "atom." In brief, *tohu* is energy, and *bohu* is atom.

The Sages make a remarkable statement in Baba Bathra 74b: "Rabbi Judah said in the name of Rab: Everything which the Holy One, blessed be He, created in His universe, He created male and female. . ." The expression "everything" is specifically intended to include even the vegetable and mineral kingdoms. As for the former, it has long been known that there are male and female potencies in plants; see Gen. R. 41; Pesahim 53a, Rashi *s.v. bid'nishane: Aruch, s.v. nisan;* R. Bahya *Tazria, Zohar, Vay'hi* 238. With reference to the mineral kingdom, Ibn Daud in his commentary on *Sefer Y'tsirah* 3:45 writes that even in the mineral kingdom just as among plants, animals, and human beings, there are male and female.

So also in *Hakmuni,* a commentary on *Sefer Y'tsirah,* chap. 3: " . . . thence issue fire, water, and wind, and become divided into male and female, for everything that has been created in the universe, be they stars or planets, all creatures on land or sea, all plants and fruits, are male and female."

Judah Albarceloni comments on *Sefer Y'tsirah,* p. 226: "When the *Sefer Y'tsirah* avers

[3] Cf. Kuzari 4.25 and 5.2, and commentaries *ad. loc.,* explaining *tohu* and *bohu* as being the primal substance, devoid of quality. See also Kimhi, quoting R. Isaac ben Solomon Israeli, where *tohu and bohu* are defined as the static resting air (ether) before its assumption of motion at the will of God, and the static air (ether) before Creation. Also T.S. chap. 1, p. 325. [4] Quoted at length in T.S., Part I: Addenda, p. 183, par. 38.

that 'they issue and become divided into male and female' it means this: 'Heaven issues from fire: the latter is female, the former male; earth from water: earth is female, water is male. Similarly, all objects in the universe are male and female, and the wind aids all objects.' "

These dicta, asserting a male and female urge in everything, may be elucidated with the aid of our thesis that *bohu* was created out of *tohu*. That is to say, when the Holy One created *bohu* out of *tohu*, He divided *tohu* into two potentials, a male potential and a female potential, joined to each other. This is also the force of attraction and repulsion present in all bodies. It is thus that all bodies and all matter in the universe remain integrated.

This definition of *tohu* and *bohu* clearly harmonizes with the results of present-day scientific research. The *tohu* of the Torah is the primal force formerly called formless matter, pure potentiality, an evil and destructive drive causing desolation. This is what we call "energy." *Bohu* is matter, subtle and minute, invisible to the human eye, but already possessing form and the power to contain the *tohu*, which is what is today called "atom." The protons and the electrons are the male and female potentialities: the former, being positive, male; the latter, female.

In this same line of thought the *Zohar*, quoted above, gives a novel interpretation of the continuation of the verse, *and darkness was upon the face of the deep*, which is described as a "black fire." In T.S. I, 284, 325, 327 and 331, I indicated that such too is the view of Maimonides in the Guide of the Perplexed, chap. 30, and of Nahmanides in the beginning of Genesis. In their opinion the "darkness" in verse 2, which we are discussing, is not identical with the "darkness" in verse 4: *And God divided the light from the darkness*. By the former is meant an elemental, non-luminous fire, black, not red like the fire with which we are familiar; hence it is called darkness. This darkness was a *positive* entity, as Scripture writes, *I form the light and create darkness*. Saadya in *Emunoth v'Deoth* 1, dissents from this view, holding that darkness is but negativity, the *absence* of light. See also Kuzari 5. In the passages in Torah Shelemah I supported the views of Maimonides and Nahmanides with many proofs from Hagigah 12a and the *Zohar*, where darkness is counted among the ten things which were *created* on the first day.

As to the essential fact of the existence of elementary fire, held in doubt by many, the author of *Keseth Hasofer*, a commentary on Genesis, notes that the discovery of electricity in 1799 and radium in 1898 has demonstrated the truth of the existence of an elemental fire-energy. However, he does not refer to the *Zohar*.

According to the modern scientific theory of cosmic evolution, both matter and light originated in activity of the electromagnetic medium. This corresponds to our interpretation of *tohu, bohu*, and darkness, the last-named being elemental fire—"black fire," as it is called. Following upon this, the next verse, *And God said: "Let there be light,"* was a decree that this matter and energy should now become manifest and actualized; and thus was born light.

In Hagiga *l.c.* it is stated that by the light created on the first day one could see from one end of the universe to the other. Many commentators maintain that this was a conceptual light only, not a sensible one. Judah Albarceloni, however, in his commentary on *Sefer Y'tsirah*, p. 20, holds that this was sensible light which functioned for but a fraction of the first day, and then was secreted away.[5] Had man been created on that day he would have been able to see from one end of the universe to the other. These interpretations are in harmony with the above-noted thesis of the *Zohar*. We may add that this was that same elemental fire which became manifest and was transformed into sensible light. Perhaps we have an allusion here to television, which is indeed a light whereby one can see "from one end of the earth to

[5] *Vid.* my article, *The Sabbath of Creation and the Sabbath of Sinai*, in Talpioth, 1-2, p. 381, on the various views held by the Sages regarding the nature of the light created on the first day, prior to that light which streamed forth from the luminaries which were suspended on the fourth day.

the other," the light which for a fraction of the first day, at the time of the creation of the world, functioned palpably, the light which is the elementary fire. A passage in *Midrash Hane'elam* states: "There is a place in the region of the sea-towns where fire is called *tohu.* And this is the primary element" (quoted in T.S. chap. I, par. 337). Again: "*Tohu, bohu,* darkness and *ruah* (wind, air, or spirit) are the four elements by means of which the world was established" (*loc. cit.* 329). Further: "Fire conceived and bore light" (*loc. cit.* 242, citing Exod. R. 15). Also: "Fire — that is the darkness. Hence, *And thou didst hear His words out of the midst of the fire,* means out of the midst of the darkness." (T.S. 2nd ed. 1, Add. 337, citing the Yalkut of Samuel Masnuth 79.)

III

The great discovery basic to the atomic bomb which the natural scientists of our day have made, is that a small particle of matter contains incredible power and incalculable energy, a force that can destroy an entire world! We no more believe, as we did until recently, that once energy is transformed into matter it loses its original potency and remains permanently matter and corporeality. We now know that the original energy remains provisionally encased in its material sheath, requiring only the stimulation of some external force for it to be re-transformed into its original state of gigantic power. This fact may greatly aid our understanding of and belief in two fundamentals of Judaism, viz., Immortality and Resurrection.

The savant Hayim Selig Slonimsky wrote a special monograph to prove immortality on the basis of natural science. It is a fundamental law of natural science that matter cannot be destroyed. Only the *form* may change, e.g., from solid to liquid, from liquid to gas; but the transformation leaves the material content unchanged. If so, it is clear beyond any doubt that this law holds good also in the realm of man's spirit; it clearly remains after man's death, and returns to its origin.

It is now possible to view the same matter in another way. We see clearly that it is impossible to annihilate matter, but it is possible to restore it to its root, to its original status prior to its transformation into matter, i.e., to a state of pure energy. As such its power is infinitely multiplied—increased beyond human comprehension. If this be true of crude matter, how much the more must it be true that the fundamental force in the life of the rational being (the soul of man, the divine portion within him) after leaving the body, returns to its source and rises in spiritual stature, exalted and elevated beyond measure and beyond compare, each man according to his spiritual mould.

In a similar manner, the discovery of the reversion of a minute particle to so tremendous a force enables us to comprehend rationally the belief in the resurrection of the dead—a belief which admittedly it is difficult for the human understanding to grasp. We notice that from a drop of human semen a child complete in body is born; moreover, this drop contains within it hereditary, biological and psychological characteristics, which will appear in the child. Here is heredity, operating in some mysterious way that baffles our understanding. In exactly the same way we can imagine a tiny point in the human body, in some particle of which are stored all the powers and characteristics of the individual, and that in God's proper time He will create an external force which will effect the metamorphosis of this particle back into the former shape of its owner. The individual will be "reborn." For this is precisely what happens to the drop of semen and to the uranium atom, transmuted into a mighty force, the essence of which is beyond our comprehension. Nothing remains for us but to accept the established fact.

In the light of this we may understand and interpret the verse, *Thou hast made heaven, the heaven of heavens, with all their host, the earth and all things that are thereon, the seas and all that is in them, and Thou preservest them all*— (Heb. *m'haye,* keepest alive or makest live) (Neh. 9:6). Many interpret the word *m'haye* literally, in accordance with the Scriptural text, *For ever, O Lord, Thy word standeth fast in heaven* (Ps. 119:89), as expounded by the Sages in *Midrash on Psalms* 119: "Which word then stands fast in heaven? (the *Midrash* asks). The meaning is this: God said, 'On what does heaven stand? Surely on the strength of My decree: *Let there be a firmament . . . and it was so.*' Thus it is written, *For He spoke, and it was* (Ps. 33:9)—that which He said, He accomplished. Therefore Scripture continues, *He commanded, and it stood.* By God's word were the heavens formed, and by the same word wherewith He created them, by that very word do they stand forever. Therefore it says, *For ever, O Lord, Thy word stands fast in heaven*" (quoted in Anthology 1, 140). By God's speech is meant His will, whereby He created the universe *ex nihilo,* and it is this same speech (will) which makes them endure. Spirituality is the life-force of the universe and the source of its vitality. To quote the *Zohar*: "Thou art He who binds them and unites them." Now, it has been shown above that when the primal matter, which the Torah calls *tohu,* became *bohu,* in being transformed into dense and coarse matter through countless processes of unfolding, contraction, and evolution, it did not thereby become irrevocably corporeal, but always retained its original potentiality—its *tohu,* which is called energy. Furthermore, as we see now, it can revert to its primal state, cease being matter and become energy once more. Consequently, we can interpret the text, *and Thou makest them all live,* to mean that *tohu,* the primal matter which God created *ex nihilo*—the "soul" (life force)—gives life through the will of God to all things that exist in the form of *bohu.* It is this *bohu* that is now termed atom, and it is by the will of God that these atoms have been built up into elements and into more complex bodies.

This approach enables us to explain a remarkable statement of Maimonides in *Hilkot Y'sode Torah* 3:9 and in the Guide of the Perplexed 2 (quoted in T.S. 1, 643): "The revolving heavenly bodies are not inert matter but living beings that serve their Lord"; and in *loc. cit.*: "For they are beings possessed of soul, knowledge, and discernment; and their intelligence is less than that of the angels but greater than that of men."

To prove his assertion Maimonides cites Gen. R. 2, where the earth is made to say: "The upper and the lower were created simultaneously; those above, living, and those below, dead."

This view is clearly indicated by the wording of the Benediction on the Moon: "Joyous and happy are they to do the will of their Master," and in the Sabbath Prayers: "They perform with awe the will of their Master." This is also Philo's view in his work on the special commandments, 1, 13. Abrabanel comments at length on this in Genesis 1. *Maharal* of Prague, in the Preface of his book *G'buroth Hashem,* strongly criticizes this view, which he characterizes as "words of folly." The *Maggid* of Kosnitz, however, in his essay *G'ulath Israel,* defends Maimonides, declaring "that the heavenly bodies are intelligent beings devoid of free will." *Vid. Sefer Hab'rith* 1:44. In T.S., ch. 1, par. 643, we read: "In the future the Holy One, blessed be He, will say to the heavens: 'The kings of the East and the West, wearing their royal crowns, came and worshipped you, yet ye did not say: "Are we not sherds as the sherds of the ground? Do not worship us."' How do we know that they are called sherds? From the verse: *Who commandeth the* heres (sun or sherd in Heb.) *and it riseth not; and sealeth up the stars* (Job 9:7)." This confirms the view of *Maharal* and the natural scientists who maintain that the celestial bodies are lifeless masses like our own earth. See Gen. R. 12, where R. Nahman expounded the scriptural text, *all are of the dust,* as meaning even the sphere of the sun, as it says, *Who commandeth the* heres, *and it riseth not.* The Babylonian Talmud, Berakoth 32b appears to coincide with the view of *Maharal.* As for the phrase *supra* "those above, living," it must be understood as a metaphor denoting permanence, for a similar style is employed in the context, where it is stated that the earth "said," "wept." See Anthology 1, 59:60 and T.S. *ad. loc.*

To obviate the difficulties of the thesis of Maimonides an exposition on the basis of Kabbalistic principles made by Hayim Vital in his book *Sha'are K'dusha* III, 1, should be mentioned. The idea developed there is that just as a living being has a soul, so does inert matter have a "soul," and this soul is the power that fused and combined the four elements, air, fire, water and earth, out of which, according to ancient philosophy, the universe was formed. *Keseth Hasofer,* a later work, states that this view of Hayim Vital revealed the nature of electrical energy. Now, Maimonides' view that the angels possess intelligence and understanding refers not to our understanding, which is linked to the five bodily senses, but to a spiritual understanding varying according to their different levels. So too is it with *tohu,* the primal power created by the decree and will of God, which always persists in matter in its various forms, at first in *bohu,* i.e., in the atom, and subsequently in the elements and more complex substances. This power is called *malakh* (generally rendered angel, but actually a messenger or emissary), because it is a real emissary of the Creator for the mission of being transformed into matter. It is not at all impossible that this power possesses intelligence and a rule of law of its own, determined by its nature, and knowledge of its Lord who formed it. In the words of Maimonides, they "serve their Lord." Seeing the gigantic forces hidden in one particle, we can imagine what tremendous force is compressed and imprisoned in the celestial spheres. It is of those powers, which are called "the soul of inert matter," to quote Hayim Vital, that Maimonides wrote that they possess soul, knowledge, and discernment. None can positively deny this, since human understanding is too limited for dogmatic assertions on the mysteries of Creation; what once seemed sheer folly, are today established facts. In a well-known passage in *Sh'moneh P'rakim* Maimonides speaks of the impossibility of an iron ship flying in the sky. Such a thing was then thought folly. Today it is simple and natural.

How true are the words of the Sages in *Aboth*: "Say thou not regarding a thing that it is impossible of comprehension, for in the end it shall be comprehended." One cannot categorically reject anything as impossible, for everything is very definitely possible. Man lives in a world full of mysteries and secrets of Creation. From generation to generation Heaven moves man to discover these secrets of Creation. What formerly was impossible is today possible.

3.

CREATION AND THE THEORY OF EVOLUTION

Referring to Chapter I, verse 26, page 58: "Let us make man."

I have often been asked for an opinion on the view of the late Chief Rabbi of Israel, Abraham Isaac Hacohen Kook, of blessed memory, expressed in the second volume of *Oroth Hakodesh* (Jerusalem 1938, pp. 559f) that it is possible to harmonize Scripture and the views of our Sages with the theory of evolution, by adding to it the concept of Divine Providence.* For undoubtedly the relevant Biblical passages in Genesis in their literal meaning, and a wealth of statements by our Sages, definitely contradict this theory *in toto,* and most believing Jewish scholars completely reject it.

Rabbi Kook does not attempt a *detailed* interpretation of the relevant passages in accordance with his views, and contents himself with the broad principle of Divine Providence, as stated.

Before treating the subject in full, I present the following article by Dr. S. B. Ulmann (translated from *Torath Habriah v'Torath Hahithpathuth,* printed in Sinai, 1943, vol. 12, Jerusalem), which deals with the matter from the strictly scientific standpoint.

EVOLUTION vs. CREATION

by DR. S. B. ULMANN

I

For an entire century the doctrine of evolution has ruled the science of biology, completely displacing the doctrine of creation. In all university textbooks, such as Strasburger's,[1] as well as in popular works, like *Science of Life* by Wells and Huxley,[2] this theory enjoys complete supremacy. It has won an absolute victory in the field of biology, as has also the descent theory. The doctrine is not new: It was already familiar to the Greeks, and is found in Democritus and Leucippus. But it was given a powerful stimulus in modern times by the active and enthusiastic support of a group of atheistic materialists, including Haeckel,[3] Buchner,[4] and Huxley, thanks to whom it has triumphed so completely.

Some, like Darwin[5] or Spencer,[6] were agnostics in the religious sense. But all took a negative attitude toward religion. Through the influence of Spencer, in particular, the idea of evolution has penetrated all strata of science as well

* See also notes 56* and 58, below.

1 Strasburger, C. S., Lehrbuch der Botanik für Hochschulen, Jena, 1923. 2 Wells, H. G., and Huxley, J. S., Science of Life. 3 Haeckel, E., Natürliche Schöpfungsgeschichte, 1868; Anthropogenie oder Entwicklungsgeschichte des Menschen, 1874. 4 Buchner, L., Kraft und Stoff. 5 Darwin, C., On the Origin of Species by Means of Natural Selection, 1859; Naturalist's Voyage Around the World, 1870; The Descent of Man and Selection in Relation to Sex, 1871. 6 Spencer, H., Principles of Psychology, 1855; A System of Synthetic Philosophy, 1860-1896.

as literature, jurisprudence, and even religion itself. Spencer had stated it before Darwin, but the latter is responsible for its almost universal acceptance.

II

Most writers present this theory as indubitably true, and one which affords a correct and precise explanation of all phenomena of life. Some biologists do add some mild criticism and admit that a few "small" difficulties remain, but uniformly ignore the contradictions involved in this theory. Others are deliberately silent on its failings and shortcomings.

The matter is worse with regard to Wells and Huxley. They would *compel* belief, and do not refrain from coarsely assailing any who dare doubt the truth of the theory of descent, stigmatizing them as "perverse, fanatic, and small-minded" (*Science of Life*).

The doctrine of evolution has appeared in various forms in the course of the century — Lamarckism, Darwinism, and the mutation theory. It is my wish to show what remains of these three schools of thought, and to state the criticism of them by distinguished scientists and biologists. This criticism affects the doctrine *at all points,* in all *its different forms.* It is strange that few of these scientists are consistent enough to abandon entirely the idea of descent, despite their rejection of the three forms which dominate the science of biology.

III

The first to formulate the theory of descent in our era was the French zoologist Lamarck.[7] He concluded, on the basis of his repeated researches in comparative anatomy, that all appendages, for example, have a common basic structure which changes with each species. In one animal it is adapted for digging; in another, for swimming; in a third, for running. Lamarck thought that these variations in basic structure arose through need, use, and training. If an animal uses a part of its body, that part will develop; if not, it will atrophy. After it has achieved a special structure, this is transmitted to its offspring by heredity. He spoke of "acquired characteristics passing in inheritance from generation to generation." The most popular illustration is: "How did the giraffe get its long neck?" The Lamarckists answer that this animal sought its food in high trees, and therefore, through training and adaptation, developed the elongation.

Now let us note the criticism of some scholars who still support the doctrine of descent. Bertalanffy[8] writes: "Where are the *assured facts* from investigation of organisms for Lamarck's assumptions? It is impossible to forbid anyone to believe in adaptation and in inheritance of 'acquired characteristics.' But *this is only a theory, lacking in proof!*" *This* scholar, *summarizing all investigations* in the matter, asks: "Perhaps this theory is utilitarian and purposivistic?" But he is obliged to give a clear answer: "No!"

The second critic is Prof. Goldschmidt,[9] quoted by Boker:[10] "In the doctrine of evolution according to Mendel there is no place for 'inheritance of

[7] Lamarck, J., Philosophie Zoologique, 1809. [8] Bertalanffy, L., Kritische Theorie der Formbildung in Abhandlungen der Theoretische Biologie, 1925. [9] Goldschmidt, R., Einfuehrung in die Vererbungswissenschaft, 1928. [10] Boker, H., Folia Biotheoretica, Form und Funktion, 1926.

acquired characteristics.' Within the framewrok of the doctrine of genotypes it is *impossible and illogical.*" Today many students agree that the adaptations of Lamarck are possible only *under very limited conditions,* and they call these "modifications."

IV

After Lamarck came Darwin with his theory of "natural selection." His doctrine won over the scientific world and the world in general. Darwinism became a basic faith, a religion in itself. As an example we may note the book of Prof. Dodel,[11] *Moses or Darwin,* in which he would have Darwinism replace the Bible in the Christian schools of Switzerland! One cannot readily discover a parallel to the victories of Darwin. The edifice he erected attracted and overwhelmed all men of science. Darwinism became synonymous with the theory of descent, indeed, with the entire doctrine of evolution. Most people do not know that Darwinism is only *one* form of this theory.

How did Darwin arrive at his teachings? First, he observed that breeders of sheep and other animals know how *to select,* and through *selection* over a period *of many generations, develop types* which vary *somewhat* from their ancestors. He thought that in nature too such changes took place. Nature selects from the offspring of a single individual the better and the more fit (survival of the fittest). Only the winners in the struggle for existence remain alive. These two factors have brought about permanent changes. And thus new species have been formed from the old.

He drew the attention of investigators to the fact that if all the descendants of a single animal pair remained alive, they would fill the world entirely and leave no room for others. Therefore nature had to be selective, choosing for survival only the strongest, those best able to adapt themselves to the requirements of their environment. By this conception, "natural selection," Darwin now sought to explain *the origin of species.* Until his time, most scholars had held, on the basis of the doctrine of creation, that the species were fixed and had not undergone modification. During his famous voyage on the "Beagle," he observed that animal species in the Galapagos Islands resembled others in South America, but with slight variations in each individual species. To explain these variations he put forward the theory that all members of a species (varying in different locations) were of one origin, but had developed differently; hence the differences. Later, he went further and maintained that *all* the different species (millions!) had been formed in such a fashion. *Evolution* from species to species, beginning from a unicellular organism, through the invertebrates, and terminating in man, had taken place, in his opinion, through *natural selection.*

First, let us note the criticism of the fundamentals of Darwinism and the theory of descent in general. Prof. de Vries,[12] the celebrated Dutch investigator, writes on natural selection: "I believe *on the basis of my researches* on the mutation theory, that the 'struggle for existence' and 'natural selection' would not lead to different species, but on the contrary, to perdition!" The distinguished physiologist Pfeffer, quoted by Price, says: "*Artificial* selection (through human hands) selects for life; *natural* selection, for death." He

[11] Dodel, A., Moses oder Darwin; eine Schulfrage, 1895.

[12] De Vries, H., Die Mutationstheorie, 1903.

quotes E. Lehman: "The doctrine of selection cannot prove the creation of new variants. On the contrary, *experiments* have placed this in great doubt." Prof. Fleischman,[14] who at first was a supporter of Darwinism but later turned from it, speaks very sharply: "*Darwin's doctrine of natural selection is built entirely on theory in an* a priori *fashion, and it changes and twists the facts according to its will!*"

Krapotkin[15] made extensive researches on *reciprocal aid* among living creatures. In complete contrast to Darwin's theories, he showed that this factor also wielded a great influence in nature. Otto sums up his results in these words: "*He demolishes the foundation of Darwinism* and shows by many fine examples from actual life how much *more important in nature is the factor of reciprocal aid than that of the struggle for existence.*" Everyone knows the phenomenon called symbiosis. Let us give a few examples. On the roots of leguminous plants live all kinds of microorganisms. They receive organic food, and provide the plant with inorganic food which they are able to compound from the nitrogen in the air. One *helps* the other! In the lichens, we see plants of the mushroom family and algae living together. Each alga (which is green) produces organic nutritive materials through assimilation, and each fungus gives the alga inorganic materials and water. *Mutualism* may be found in many other instances in nature.

Now let us pass to criticism of Darwinism in general, and see what remains of this splendid edifice after many years of energetic research. Losty[16] epitomizes the facts in such wise:

"*Researches in heredity* have reduced Lamarckism and Darwinism to the level of *highly problematic theories.* I remain loyal to the teachings of Linnaeus that species are fixed, and I believe that Darwin erred in his attack on the fixity of species."

Bertalanffy writes: "*The new era has destroyed the Darwinian dreams.*" More sharply than all of them speaks Uexküll:[17] "There is no need to wonder at the confusion rampant in the basic integration of our knowledge of nature. It is a consequence of the distortions and dishonest subtleties of Darwinism." With complete justification the same author notes: "Thus has the idea of evolution become a faith of thousands, *having no connection whatsoever with unprejudiced investigation of nature.*" Elsewhere he writes: "*Darwinism is more faith than science.*"

It is highly interesting that Dinger,[18] after deep and extensive study, arrived at the same conclusion: "This principle [evolution] is not a law but a dogma, like every creed. This new faith, garbed in scientific form, found its prophets in Haeckel and Huxley. Haeckel, especially, brought the new monistic doctrine to flower, and led to its widespread acceptance." Here we shall content ourselves with showing only the harm the doctrine has done to *biology and science* in general. The spiritual damage wrought by Darwinism is thus described by Otto:[19] "With the theory of the struggle for existence, dependent on the play of chance forces, Darwinism would deliver the world of life, which displays

[14] Fleischman, A., Die Darwinische Theorie, 1903; Die Deszedenztheorie, 1909. [15] Krapotkin, P., Gegenseitige Hilfe in der Entwicklung, 1908. [16] Losty, J. F., Evolution im Lichte der Bastardierung Betrachtet, 1926. [17] Uexküll, J., Theoretische Biologie, 1920. [18] Dinger, H., Das Prinzip der Entwicklung; Der Zusammenbruch der Wissenschaft unter der Primat der Philosophie, 1926. [19] Otto, R., Naturalistische und Religiose Weltansicht, 1909.

the wonders of plan and design, to base instinct and factors that are without plan or order. With the doctrine of evolution and development from lower to higher it would destroy the majesty of the human spirit, all the freedom and nobility of logical thought, free will, and the aesthetic sense, and drag all this down to the forces of an Evil Genius, to animal passions and base emotions."

Prof. Boker, quoting Russel[20] in *Acta Biotheoretica,* makes it clear that dogmatic materialism and a rigid evolutionary theory have completely blinded man to the rich forms, the many secrets and mysteries, of the phenomena of life. At the same time that Darwin and his devotees created a world tempest with their unfounded imaginings, a serious investigator, Gregor Mendel,[21] labored in Brünn, and discovered important laws of heredity. However, when he published his outstanding studies in 1866, he found no response. He was deeply disappointed. Only after his death did three investigators, de Vries, Correns,[22] and Tschermak,[23] rediscover Mendel's work and laws. Without doubt, the great tumult centering about Darwinism was one of the factors that concealed the important discovery of Mendel—which has been confirmed many times, and which is based on facts, in contrast to Darwinism.

V

As is known, Haeckel was one of Darwin's ardent admirers. He proclaimed the biogenetic law. This law was to have been proof decisive for the idea of descent. Haeckel said that ontogenesis (the development of the embryo from a single cell into a mature creature) is an abridged recapitulation of phylogenesis (the evolution from remote one-celled ancestors to the highly complex creatures of the present day). It may be well to mention that the adherents of the descent theory thought that from unicellular organisms emerged various invertebrates, which, in turn, produced the vertebrates. Evolution proceeded by way of fishes, reptiles, and mammals to the ape. From the ape there emerged the ape-man, and from him, finally, man. This process, in their opinion, extended over millions of years. Now, the embryo of man, in a marvelous abridgement, during the meager nine months of pregnancy, recapitulates the major portion of the history of his remote ancestors. So much for Haeckel.

Let us see what some of the critics say. Hamman[24] writes: "It is impossible for an evolution to have taken place from protozoa to metazoa (from unicellular to multicellular organisms). The amoeba is already organized and specialized in its structure and in the physiology of the conditions of its existence; it is a complete and finished type."

Kölliker,[25] quoted by Otto, writes: "As in the case of the generality, so it is possible also to see in the case of the individual, in embryology, *in contradiction to the law of biogenesis,* that there is a development from the general to the particular, from the incomplete to the complete, from the transient to the fixed."

[20] Russel, E. S., Form and Function, 1916; Folio Biotheoretica No. 1, 1936. [21] Mendel, Gregor, 1832-1884. [22] Correns, Gesammelte Abhandlungen der Vererbungswissenschaft, Prague, 1927. [23] Tschermak, A. V., Allgemeine Physiologie, 1914. [24] Hamann, O., Entwickelungslehre und Darwinismus, 1892. [25] Koelliker, A. V., Handbuch der Gewebelehre; Entwicklungsgeschichte d. Menschen und den höhern Tieren, 1872-1876.

Steiner[26] develops the same idea. Price[27] draws attention to the fact that even the lowest form of life cannot continue by itself for even one minute. All are dependent on the products of other living organisms, high or low. How is it possible to maintain that once there was only one unicellular organism or one species of unicellular organisms?—asks this writer. Bertalanffy attacks the law in another way: "It is impossible to compare in any manner whatever the human ovum, with the infinite possibilities hidden within it, with the primordial ovum from which evolution began. It may be declared that ontogenesis cannot recapitulate the life of ancestral series in any essential manner, since the embryo of a more highly developed animal is distinct from that of an animal lower than it." The same thought is expressed by Fleischman: "The one-celled egg is entirely distinct and absolutely different from one-celled living organisms of the level of Protista."

Price relates that Haeckel wished to prove that the human embryo resembles a fish at a certain time; afterward, a reptile; and so on. When he did not succeed in finding the facts in accordance with his desire, he falsified the sketches! Of course he called this alteration "according to scientific imagination." Prof. Haeckel always spoke of the evil deeds of the Christian clergy, of *fraus pia*. But he himself employed *fraus pia* to prove (!) his doctrine. Uexküll speaks more critically of the biogenetic law: "When they saw that it was impossible to learn anything from phylogenesis, they began to draw inferences from ontogenesis." The author speaks of "conclusions twisted" and reversed by adherents of the theory of descent, in their application of the biogenetic law of Haeckel.

In contrast, Hertwig,[28] though he speaks calmly, is compelled to declare: "Proofs such as are demanded by the exact sciences have not been produced by Haeckel, nor can they be." In general, almost all biologists today agree that the biogenetic "law" is not a law! *Nevertheless, it remains in most university textbooks,* at times with slight limitations, but no more. It is most interesting to note how Haeckel influenced and veritably bewitched his readers. One finds the law of biogenesis in all university textbooks on botany, e.g., in Strasburger's, written by seven great researchers: Noll, Schenk, Schimper, Fitting, Jost, Karsten, and the editor. One might assume that some basis for the biogenetic law is to be found in zoology. But in botany it is difficult to discover even a hint of the law; the higher plant in its development resembles neither mushroom nor alga nor fern.

VI

Let us not think that in Haeckel's time there were no scholars to foresee the outcome and warn the scientific world. Immediately after Haeckel launched his powerful propaganda, Wigand[29] and Bastian[30] issued warnings. The latter wrote in opposition to Haeckel: "The embryo resembles neither starfish, insect, snail, nor worm. Their structure differs absolutely from that of the vertebrates." He quotes Wigand: "*Darwin builds his theory within limits absolutely unknown to us.*" Bastian writes elsewhere: "Man does not

[26] Steiner, B., Ueber das Biogenetische Grundgesetz. Acta Biotheoretica, 1939. [27] Price, G. M., Naturwissenschaft und Schöpfungslehre. [28] Hartwig, R., Abstammungslehre und Neuere Biologie, 1927. [29] Wigand, Albert, Der Darwinismus ein Zeichen der Zeit, Heilbronn, 1878. [30] Bastian, A., Schöpfung oder Entstehung, 1875.

at a given time resemble (in his bodily structure) fish, amphibian, or bird, but rather resembles fish *and* amphibian *and* bird, because they are all vertebrates." He quotes from the celebrated physiologist, Johann Müller:[31] "Fish, amphibian, bird, mammal, and man, have in their origin a common body-structure, a basic type, but in their development they diverge from one another."

The advocates of the theory of descent well knew that they lacked decisive proofs that man descended from the ape. They had no ape-man, which would provide the missing link in the transition from ape to man. In 1892 Dubois,[32] an army doctor in the Dutch Indies, discovered several bones which he concluded were of an ape-man who had walked erect. This was the tie between man and the animals.

However, the great scholar Virchow,[33] whom Haeckel and the rest were obliged to accept as the greatest pathologist of his time, strongly opposed Dubois. On many questions he assailed the interpretation of Dubois. He cast doubt on whether these bones belonged to one animal. The skull, he believed, came from a half-erect ape (of the genus *Hylobates*). He had already declared in the year 1882 that the Neanderthal skull was only that of a pathologic human individual; variations such as these appear among abnormal human beings, who nevertheless undoubtedly belong to *homo sapiens!*

Through much scientific work Virchow proved that the skull of man differs completely from that of the beast. He pointed out fundamental differences in all the minute details, and particularly in internal structure. He dwelt on basic differences in the constitution of the entire body, its development, and its structure. In opposition to advocates of the theory of descent, who sought to explain any number of phenomena in terms of atavism (regression to lower forms), he wrote: "Abnormal forms among human beings, microcephaly or idiocy, are not atavisms (regression to their distant ancestors, the apes) but pathologic variations. A man in whom pathologic changes have occurred remains a man, and is not a monkey. . ." He will not admit the possibility of evolution from species to species. "The Negro remains a Negro also in America, under entirely different conditions."

"Can the Ethiopian change his skin, or the leopard his spots?" was long ago spoken by the prophet Jeremiah (13:23). Long ago the prophet knew and understood nature well! It is highly interesting to note this agreement between Jeremiah and that great scholar who was the very personification of science!

Not Virchow alone opposed the theory of descent. Fleischman writes: *"Modern zoology* posits seventeen major form-groupings, *and it is impossible to find a transition from one to the other.* Such is the case with the lower divisions of fishes, birds, and mammals. *There is no bridge and no transition between them."*

Bastian too holds that the species are fixed, and says: "The attestations of geology prove that the species remain fixed despite the long aeons of natural history." Dürken[34] wrote in 1935: *"It is impossible to cross the boundaries of species,* and it is certainly impossible to cross those of classes or orders—either

[31] Müller, Johann, 1801-1858, professor of physiology. [32] Dubois, E., Pithecanthropos Erectus, 1894. [33] Virchow, R., Vortrage Heft 96, 1870; Rassenbildung und Erblichkeit, 1895; Archiv, Bd. 7, 1855. [34] Duerken, R., Entwicklungsbiologie und Ganzheit, 1936.

by combinations or by fusion of characteristics through artificial selection! Selection has been practised on the horse for the longest time. All kinds of races have been formed under the influence of artificial selection, pairing, and domestication, all of them strikingly different from one another. *But the horse remains a horse and will forever remain a horse!* The same thing is true of dogs. Here the differences are even greater, but they have *always remained dogs.*"

The horse is the favorite child of all the votaries of the theory of descent. In this case, they argue, it is possible to see the evolution from a five-toed animal to one with a single toe. In America there have been found in excavations all transitions from *Coryphodon* through Eo-hippus-Hippodon, etc. up to Equus, i.e., the horse. So writes Haeckel. Now let us see what the paleontologist Schindewolf,[35] who in respect of the horse still supports the descent theory, writes: "Now that the science of paleontology has gathered much material, it has become definitely clear that the evolution and perfection of permanent typical characteristics proceed in a single straight line. *But nowhere do we see transition forms that are capable of demonstrating the origin of types entirely new.* So *also with the horse.* We can find numerous transition forms from *Eo-hippus* to the modern horse, but prior to this evolution is not to be seen." He explains that all manner of horses have been found, but a transition from a horse to some other five-toed animal cannot be discovered.

He continues: "In case of the horse only the second developmental stage has been found. *This point speaks definitely against the Darwinian outlook on evolution.*" In order to escape difficulties he concludes that the earlier development did not take place when the animals were already matured, but at an early stage, through differentiation of the endoderm; therefore there is no *visible* evidence of the transition to be found. He writes with unmistakable emphasis: "The first bird emerged from the egg of a reptile!"

Among the many critics of Darwinism there is also Metalman:[36] "Natural selection and the struggle for existence cannot elucidate the theory of descent." M. Hartman[37] summarizes his views thus: "*Experiments in the study of heredity* partly confirm the Darwinian explanation of evolution, but the theory of natural selection does not explain *new* species; rather, only the survival of the fit and strong *of species that already exist,* which is proved by experience as well. The main problem remains without a solution."

The proponents of the theory of descent point out very strongly that there are in the human body many parts that are vestiges or without any useful function. How can the doctrine of creation explain the existence of these vestiges? Only their theory could explain things that have no function. Haeckel enumerates in *Anthropogenie,* p. 693, many parts that serve no purpose. Among these he counts the thyroid gland. Today every one knows that this gland has important and vital functions in the physiology of the body. Is it not possible, then, that further study will reveal functions of other so-called "useless organs"? But the devotees of the descent theory have refused to learn, and to this very day we find in Strasburger's textbook the concept of useless organs!

[35] Schindewolf, O. H., Beobachtungen und Gedanken zum Deszedenzlehre, 1937. [36] Metalman, J., Der Kampf um die Autonomie des Lebens, 1939. [37] Hartman, M., Philosophie der Naturwissenschaften, 1937.

VII

In spite of *defeats and reverses* suffered by the theory of descent in its Lamarckian and Darwinian forms, it has not yielded nor lost its factitious eminence. The Dutch biologist, Hugo de Vries, introduced a further variation of evolutionary theory—mutation. It was already known before him that sometimes plants suddenly appear which vary a bit from their ancestors. Thus there was discovered in 1540 *Chelidonium laciniatum,* and several more variants thereafter. But it was de Vries who demonstrated with precision, by his experiments with *Oenothera lamarckiana,* that new and varying forms had arisen. On the basis of his work de Vries sought to prove that evolution unfolds through variations such as these. He called them mutants, "saltatory variations." When it became apparent that this phenomenon occurs only in small numbers from among hundreds of thousands of animal or plant species, he developed the theory that every species of plant or animal passes through a mutation period at a certain time. After the changes have taken place in this species the plant or animal returns to its quiescent state.

Let us recapitulate the criticism. Prof. Boker quotes O. Naegeli:[38] "Most known mutations represent only injury to heredity; i.e., they create pathologic states. It is obvious that they are not to be reckoned with in the matter of formation of new species. For the most part the mutant is not capable of survival, and perishes. For the most part, too, the mutation does not appear among wild life or wild vegetation, but among domesticated plants or domesticated animals. Mutations which succeed alter only secondary signs of body integument, such as changes in color or in skin, their biologic function being only for recognition and delimitation." He bases this summation on the investigations of E. Stresemann[39] in 1926, encompassing twenty-four mutations among birds; and on the investigations of H. M. Keyle, of the same year, on the fish *Lebistes*: "All mutations embrace anatomical signs that are entirely unimportant for the lives of these living creatures." Bertalanffy in his work sums up all that is known up to his time: "With regard to the question of *the factors of evolution* we see *that all three theories, the Lamarckian, the Darwinian, and the mutation theories, cannot explain them.* The negative attitude towards problems of evolution assumed by investigators of genetics, among them Johansen,[40] the great researcher, is well known." Plate,[41] the heir of Haeckel, writes: "Many researchers in genetics have concluded that perhaps it would be best to give up the deductive theory of evolution. This would be the only consistent solution in view of all the contradictions in this science."

VIII

Thus has the doctrine of descent passed through many transmigrations, each time with a dazzling beginning and with assurance of victory. Haeckel wrote that it was on a par with the gravitation theory of that genius of physical science, Newton,[42] and that it even rose above it! However, we have already seen that *the pungent criticisms* of the greatest authorities have to a large extent destroyed the value of the descent theory in its various forms.

[38] Naegeli, Karl Wilhelm, 1817-1891, Swiss botanist. [39] Stresemann, Erwin, Die Entwicklung der Ornithologie von Aristotle bis zur Gegenwart, Berlin, 1951. [40] Johansen, Anders C.J., 1867-, Danish marine biologist. [41] Plate, L., Vererbungslehre, 1933. [42] Newton, I., 1643-1727, British physicist.

Regarding the theory of evolution Russel writes that it has made one thing clear: the true meaning of the unity, the single plan of this world, seen in all forms of nature.[43] These words must recall to the mind of the reader the words of Ibn Gabirol about *the unity of the forms.* If the theory of evolution is not a biologic theory but a philosophic one, as many already think today, then numerous writers antedated it when they depicted *the unity of creation* and its unique plan.

Let us return to the doctrine of evolution as a biologic theory. Is it true that there is an evolution from "lower forms" to "more highly developed forms"? Do "lower forms" truly exist? Let us take as an example of the latter, the "yeasts." How many thousands of scientific projects have been published; how many great researchers, beginning with Pasteur,[44] have spent a great part of their lives in these projects? Yet they have not succeeded in explaining all *the extensive and extremely important activities* of these one-celled organisms, their mighty power, employed in many branches of industry from the time of Noah's production of wine to the present day.

The advocates of the theory of evolution would explain that in all branches of life there has been an evolution from low to high. Yet these men of science forget that many hold that truly great scientists arise at the *inception* of the development of a science—precisely as Moses, greatest of the prophets, *began* the era of prophecy. In a science as young and modern as bacteriology the eminent Pasteur and Koch[45] were the first, yet greatest; and there has been no evolution from the "lower" to the "more highly developed."

IX

If all the facts and the many proofs presented by scientific criticism against the theory of descent are reviewed, and if most *scientists nevertheless remain loyal to it,* then one understands well what N. Hartman[46] wrote (quoted by H. Hartman): "In all changes in outlook the theories remain built up in an *a priori* manner, even where they have resulted from experimental fact! The investigators do not realize the extent to which bias influences scientific theories. Yet the *a priori* constitutes a genuine portion of every perception. Only rarely is it innocent, and it is not lacking anywhere." This view, that the doctrines of the advocates of the descent theory are only *a priori,* we have already noted in the statements of Fleischman and Uexküll. Criticism in biology is gradually making headway.

The conclusions of the great scientists we have presented above, as well as the studies of Kohlbrugge,[47] Jordan,[48] and Schwarz, show that the true value of the theory of descent is beginning to be understood. The very fact that a scientific book has appeared with the title *Evolution, Fact or Fiction,* proves that a change is taking place.

We have noted that *among all supporters of the theory of descent there are basic contrasts and vigorous disagreements.* There are bitter disputes be-

[43] Russel, E. S., Folio Biotheoretica, No. 1, Form and Function, 1936. [44] Pasteur, Louis, 1822-1895, French bacteriologist. [45] Koch, Robert, 1843-1910, German bacteriologist. [46] Hartman, N., Das Problem des Apriorismus in der Platonischen Philosophie. [47] Kohlbrugge, Jacob Hermann Friedrich, Die Morphologische Abstammung des Menschen, Stuttgart, 1908. [48] Jordan, David Starr, Evolution and Animal Life, N. Y., 1907.

tween morphologists and geneticists, between mechanists and vitalists, and between neo-Lamarckists, Darwinists and followers of other trends in biology. These controversies are found in all aspects of the problem. Although they all believe in the descent theory, they have no common ground. Bertalanffy thus describes the situation in biology, making use of a quotation of Dinger: "Diverse and bizarre theses have appeared, of which each protagonist believes that only he is right, while casting doubt in the process on all the laws of science. The old laws are overthrown. New ones come in their place. In ever-shortening periods everything in science is overturned, and in the end a situation arises in which nothing is certain. Everything is possible, everything is worked out, everything is computed; but there is no basis, there is no foundation, and there is no direction. In other words—*chaos!*"

X

Now that we have reached this point, the question arises: would it not be more proper *to forsake entirely the doctrine of evolution,* the fruit of ancient and modern paganism, pantheism, and mechanical materialism, *and return to the doctrine of Creation* as based and accepted on the authority of the Bible? Certainly there remain and will remain many questions and many mysteries. Prof. Price quotes scientists who agree *that man cannot know anything whatsoever concerning the origin of the universe and the formation of organisms.* These scientists admit that creation remains an insoluble riddle. O. W. Fraas[49] properly asserts that science can provide no information on the origin of the universe, just as a man cannot offer personal testimony affirming his own birth. He does not content himself with specialists in his own field, but adduces support from such great physicists as Lord Kelvin.[50] Prof. Schaxel[51] sums up his opinion in this matter: "After all, life appears to the scientific investigator so mysterious and secret, that he feels strongly impelled to forego the solution of the basic problems."

In contrast to the mechanists who wished to solve everything in their own mechanistic manner, Reymond Du-Bois[52] reached a different conclusion in his famous lecture where he debated the possibility of recognition and knowledge. He there demonstrates our disabilities in this manner. Even if we could open up the eye and see with complete exactness how an image is formed on the retina, and even if we could see the minute details of the passage of light along the nerves to the brains, and if we could mark all the motions of the molecules and atoms within the brain, we could still not actually understand how an image is formed in our brain or a concept in our thought.

And he reaches the conclusion, *ignoramus ignorabimus!* (We know not and we shall never know). These words remind one of the verse in Ecclesiasticus: "A man, when he has made an end of inquiring, has hardly begun, and when he ceases, gropes in darkness." We have already seen above the complete agreement between Jeremiah and Virchow. Here we see the same

[49] Fraas, Oscar, Die Alten Höhlenbewohner, Berlin, 1872. [50] Kelvin, Baron William Thomson, Treatise on Natural Philosophy, Cambridge, 1879-1883. [51] Schaxel, J., 1866, Erscheinung, Bestimmung und Wesen des Geschlechts, 1926. [52] Du-Bois, Reymond, Ueber die Grenzen des Naturerkenntniss.

rapport between Reymond Du-Bois and Ben Sira! Things have not changed much in two thousand years!

Of course, many scientists will hesitate to take this step, to give up the doctrine of evolution and return to the doctrine of creation. For their sake it is perhaps of value to add here what was said on the Creation narrative by two mechanist-atheist adherents of the doctrine of evolution, whom it is surely not possible to accuse of one-sidedness or religious bigotry. Said Haeckel: "Two important and basic ideas of the theory of descent appear in Moses' theory of creation: — differentiation and completion." Boelsche[53] calls the Narrative of Creation "the most exalted picture of the origin of our civilization." If these men speak in such a manner, then we are permitted to see absolute truth in it.

I shall conclude with a quotation from Virchow, who expresses the opinion of many distinguished investigators and great scholars: "I have explicitly said *that the natural sciences cannot solve the problem and the riddle of creation.* I admit and confess that our investigations do not permit us to debate that which may not be counted and calculated, and that which may not be seen and observed."

* * *

In the preceding article we have seen that according to Dr. Ulmann there is no room in the ideology of Torah for the doctrine of evolution. He is opposed to those who would accept both the Torah's account of creation and evolution. Their idea is that it is possible to compromise, to show that there is no contradiction between the doctrines of creation and evolution, by eliminating the element of chance. In other words, it is true that everything evolved from lower forms, *but not by chance*, for this very evolution the Creator predetermined by establishing the laws of nature. Every relevant passage in Genesis is explained as creation of forms and structure through evolutionary development.

Dr. Ulmann[54] explains this approach, and rejects it for two reasons. In his view the doctrines of creation and evolution are irreconcilable opposites.

For the focal point and main value of the theory of evolution is just this—that it removes all higher, supernatural power from the world of nature. Furthermore, it is totally unnecessary to seek to harmonize science and Torah. His reason is that the Torah is accepted by us as eternal; it is true and valid forever. Not so science. Anyone at all familiar with scientific thinking knows that in science nothing is ever fixed. Its theories change from generation to generation. What was once accepted as final truth, others will later proclaim null and void. This is so in every generation, and in every branch of science—later discoveries and findings bring new viewpoints. Many things held as certain by early investigators were rejected by later scholars, only to be re-accepted in our own days. As one great scientist wrote, supporting his statement by many examples: "What is regarded today as basic truth can be discarded tomorrow. What we saw yesterday as a truth, today becomes a total error of the past."[55]

That being so, there is certainly no necessity to seek a middle way between the Torah and evolution, which many important scientists reject completely, and many of whose hypotheses are undermined from time to time. For it is entirely possible that at some later date this theory will be completely invalidated and for-

[53] Boelsche, Abstammung der Menschen, 1900. [54] *Madaei Hateva Ub'riath Haolam*, Tel Aviv, 1944, pp. 31, 50. I am grateful to Dr. Arthur Hyman, who first brought this book to my attention, and made his copy available to me.
[55] K. E. v. Zittel, quoted by Ulmann, ibid., p. 46.

gotten, as has happened with many other theories.

In his basic thinking Dr. Ulmann is certainly correct. The plain meaning of Scripture as well as rabbinic exegesis thereof, is decidedly opposed to the theory of evolution. The verses of Genesis speak clearly about the creation of the third day (*fruit-tree bearing fruit of its kind, wherein is the seed thereof*); the fifth day (*wherewith the water swarmed after its kind, and every winged fowl after its kind*); the sixth day (*the living creature after its kind, cattle, and creeping things, and beast of the earth after its kind . . . and everything that creepeth upon the ground after its kind*).

The Torah specifies for each creature *after its kind*—to teach that the species are *fixed;* there is no transition from one to another, as the theory of evolution posits for all nature—the *descent* of species. See T.S. *ad. loc.* quoting the rabbinic exegesis on these verses as teaching that it is forbidden for all time to cross different species.[56]

This is in agreement with the views of many great scientists quoted by Dr. Ulmann (*ibid.* p. 36), that it is impossible to find in nature a transition from one kind to another, and certainly not from species to species or from genus to genus. Only minor variations within one kind are possible. But an organism cannot be changed into an organism of another *kind.*

Especially as regards the creation of man, the verses of the Bible (Gen. 1:26; 2:7) — *And God said, 'Let us make man in our image' . . . Then the Lord God formed man of the dust of the ground*—literally contradict the theory of evolution. And so does the viewpoint of the Rabbis as cited in T.S., Genesis, on the above verses. I offer two of these passages:

1. Hullin 60a: "R. Joshua b. Levi said: Every thing in creation was created in its full structure, mind, and form." Rabbenu Hananel comments: *In its full structure,* full-grown and filled out; *mind*: not with infantile powers of cognition, but with adult mind; *form*: in final appearance and beauty. Maimonides writes similarly in Guide of the Perplexed II, 30: "All that He created was made as complete as He is, in final form, in the most beautiful form possible. And know that this is an important principle." See also T.S., Genesis, Chap. II, par. 16, on the details of this exegesis. In *Midrash Hagadol,* Genesis (quoted in Anthology, chap. I, par. 162) this view is expressed in regard to plants as well, on the basis of the verse, *Let the earth put forth grass* (Gen. 1:11). "This teaches," the Midrash states, "that they all issued forthwith complete and perfect." This view is also evident in Rosh Hashanah 11a.

2. Gen. R. 14: "R. Johanan said: Adam and Eve were created as at the age of twenty." See Anthology 2, 87. It is not at all necessary to multiply rabbinic proofs for the plain meaning of the Biblical passages.

It has been mentioned, however, that some seek a middle road, and endeavor to explain away the differences between Torah and the doctrine of evolution. The reason is that it has captured many adherents of Torah who observe its precepts; for the doctrine as fully elaborated

[56] Maimonides, *Yad Hahazaka, Kilayim,* 3: Of two plants of the same species, one may become so different from the other through change of location and special conditions of cultivation, that they cease to resemble each other and appear to be two completely different species. Nevertheless, they still belong to the same species, and the prohibition of mixed seeds does not apply to them. On the other hand, some plants resemble one another; they almost seem to be of one shape and form. Nevertheless, since they are of two distinct species, they may not be "mixed." Ibid., 4: "Two animals or beasts of different species may resemble each other, and even be able to interbreed; yet since they are of two species they rank as *kilayim* (diverse, heterogeneous), and may not be mated. A species which contains both undomesticated and domesticated varieties . . . the two varieties may be mated, for they are of one species."

Nahmanides, Commentary to Leviticus, 18:19: The reason for the *laws of diverse species* is that God created species of all living things, plant and animal, and gave them reproductive power, that each species may continue to exist forever so long as He wills the continuation of the world. He endowed them with the power to reproduce their *own,* and they will never change to another kind, for *l'minehu* (after its kind) is written for each one. . . . Furthermore, an animal cannot impregnate another animal of a different kind. And even among those which are so closely akin, that they can produce hybrids, these will die out, for they cannot give birth themselves. These considerations, then, indicate that mating of different species is a repugnant and futile act. Among plants, too, different species which can be interbred, will produce hybrids which cannot reproduce themselves. (See Rabbi M. Abusaula, commentary on Nahmanides, and Shem Tob Palquera's commentary to Maimonides' Guide of the Perplexed, III, 49.)

is not only a theory of development from lower to higher forms; in its way it explains many other phenomena, such as the development of the group and relations between man and man and between nation and nation, and so on. The basic idea here is Jewish—the belief in the coming of the Messiah and the reconstruction of the world through God's will. *And all wickedness shall vanish. And the earth shall be filled with knowledge of the Lord.* . . Thus did all the prophets predict. From this there has developed the idea that the world is constantly becoming better, until it will ultimately attain perfection. Maimonides writes toward the end of his *Yad Hahazakah* (found in manuscripts and the first printed edition, and later deleted by censorship) that the world is slowly approaching its complete "repair"; as it is written, *For I will turn a clear speech to summon them all in the name of the Lord to serve Him shoulder to shoulder.* He writes that in his own time it can be seen that the ideas of the Bible are continuously spreading, even among nations "with covered hearts." And when the true Messiah arises, all will acknowledge him and perceive that they have erred.

To our sorrow, we have in our own time witnessed the very opposite—the development of human perfection to the state of Nietzche's superman, whom Hermann Cohen dubbed "this inhuman superman," and whom we can now call by his true name: *savage beast.* While we have made great progress in physics and the other natural sciences, we have achieved very little advancement of the spirit. We have witnessed the regression of a segment of humanity —a descent without parallel in human history.

We are inclined to think that the perfection of this world will come about only through revelation and emanation from above to all mankind, when it becomes the will of the Creator—and not through a transitory development. This does not mean that mankind lacks the means for its improvement. Man ever has free will, and can ever change. But insofar as we can see ahead man's ultimate salvation will come from on high, rather than from his own efforts. In the words of the prophet (Ezekiel 36:26, 27): *A new heart also will I give you . . . and I will take away the stony heart out of your flesh . . . And I will put My spirit within you.* . . . But in any case, the evolution of the human spirit has no connection at all with the development of species on which the theory of evolution is based.

There is another reason for the attempt of some scholars of traditional Judaism to find a compromise between evolution and creation.[56*]

[56*] The point of view is developed by the late Chief Rabbi J. H. Hertz in his commentary on Genesis. The following is an excerpt from his *Pentateuch*:

JEWISH ATTITUDE TOWARDS EVOLUTION. In face of this great diversity of views as to the *manner* of creation, there is, therefore, nothing inherently un-Jewish in the evolutionary conception of the origin and growth of forms of existence from the simple to the complex, and from the lowest to the highest. The Biblical account itself gives expression to the same general truth of gradual ascent from amorphous chaos to order, from inorganic to organic, from lifeless matter to vegetable, animal and man; *insisting, however, that each stage is no product of chance, but is an act of Divine will,* realizing the Divine purpose, and receiving the seal of the Divine approval. Such, likewise, is in effect the evolutionary position. Behind the orderly development of the universe there must be a Cause, at once controlling and permeating the process. Allowing for all the evidence in favour of interpreting existence in terms of the evolutionary doctrine, there still remain facts—tremendous facts—to be explained: *viz.* the origin of life, mind, conscience, human personality. For each of these, we must look back to the Creative Omnipotence of the Eternal Spirit. Nor is that all. Instead of evolution ousting design and purpose from nature, 'almost every detail is now found to have a purpose and a use' (A. R. Wallace). In brief, evolution is conceivable only as the activity of a creative Mind purposing, by means of physical and biological laws, that wonderful organic development which has reached its climax in a being endowed with rational and moral faculties and capable of high ethical and spiritual achievement; in other words, as the activity of a supreme, directing Intelligence that has planned out, far back in the recesses of time, the ultimate goal of creation—'last in production, first in thought.' Thus evolution, far from destroying the *religious* teachings of Genesis 1, is its profound confirmation.

As a noted scientist well remarks: 'Slowly and by degrees, Science is being brought to recognize in the universe the existence of One Power, which is of no beginning and no end; which has existed before all things were formed, and will remain in its integrity when all is gone—the Source and Origin of all, in Itself beyond any conception or image that man can form and set up before his eye or mind. This sum total of the scientific

They seek to follow Maimonides (Guide of the Perplexed) and his successors—great men who sought to explain that there is no contradiction between science, philosophy, and Torah. Though evolution and creation are worlds apart, present-day scholars attempt to build a bridge between the two.

The words of Rashbam[57] (on Gen. 37:2) are well known. He quotes his grandfather, Rashi, as having told him that if he (Rashi) had the time, he would re-write his commentary on the Torah, "according to the new interpretations forthcoming every day." This, then, is held to apply to the sages of each generation—to interpret everything according to contemporary findings.

The advocates of compromise cite the following rabbinic passages to support their views:

1. Gen. R. 14: "*And the man became a living soul* (l'nefesh hayah) (Gen. 2:7). Said R. Judah: This teaches that He made man with a tail, which He subsequently removed for the sake of his dignity." The midrashic commentary *Matnath K'hunah* gives as source for this opinion the word *hayah* (ibid.), which might literally mean "animal-like." Similarly, Berakoth 60: "*The rib* (appendage) *which He had taken from the man* (ibid. 2:22)—one opinion is that it was a tail." See T.S., chap. 2, par. 155, commentary.

2. Genesis 1:24: *And God said: "Let the earth bring forth the living creature* (nefesh hayah) *after its kind, cattle . . .* " on which R. Eleazar observed (Gen. R. 7 *seq. Yalkut Shim'oni*): "*Nefesh hayah* means the life of Adam; and thus it is written, *and the man became a* nefesh hayah" (ibid. 2:7). R. Eleazar, then, interprets the verse that when animal souls were created, the life of man also came into being. In Gen. R. 8:1 and Tanhuma Tarzia 1 this is explained further—that on the sixth day man's life came into being prior to the animals, and was later developed further. Obviously, this agrees with the first passage.[57*]

Dr. Aaron Marcus in *Keseth Hasofer* (Krakow, 1912), p. 20, quotes many passages from 138 Doorways to Wisdom by Rabbi Moshe Hayim Luzzatto (author of *M'sillat Y'sharim*). I reproduce one such passage from chap. 36: "As a craftsman fashions a utensil from a piece of wood; at first it is formless, and then, after its form is completed, its beauty is seen in its proper shape. . . That is to say that the Infinite One, blessed be He, did not wish to fashion this matter in its final, perfect form all at once, but gradually; He fashioned it a little at first, and

discoveries of all lands and times is the approach of the world's thought to our *Adon Olam,* the sublime chant, by means of which the Jew has wrought and will further work the most momentous changes in the world' (Haffkine).

Nor is the Biblical account of the creation of man irreconcilable with the view that certain forms of organized being have been endowed with the capacity of developing, in God's good time and under the action of suitable environment, the attributes distinctive of man. 'God formed man of the dust of the ground' (Gen. 2:7). Whence that dust was taken is not, and cannot be, of fundamental importance. Science holds that man was formed from the lower animals; are they not too 'dust of the ground'? 'And God said, *Let the earth bring forth the living creature*'—this command, says the Midrash, includes Adam as well, תוצא הארץ נפש חיה, זו רוחו של אדם הראשון. The thing that eternally matters is the breath of Divine and everlasting life that He breathed into the being coming from the dust. By virtue of that Divine impact, a new and distinctive creature made its appearance—man, dowered with an immortal soul. The sublime revelation of the unique worth and dignity of man, contained in Gen. I, 22 ('And God created man in His own image, in the image of God created He him'), may well be called the Magna Charta of humanity. Its purpose is not to explain the biological origins of the human race, but *its spiritual kinship with God.* There is much force in the view expressed by a modern thinker: '(The Bible) neither provides, nor, in the nature of things, could provide, faultless anticipations of sciences still unborn. If by a miracle it had provided them, without a miracle they could not have been understood'.

It should be noted that the previous statement, "Such, likewise, is in effect the evolutionary position," is inaccurate, as we will see further on. The doctrine of evolution, *as presented by its founders,* definitely opposes the viewpoint of Judaism. Were evolution definitely proven, so that it must be accepted (which it is not, as shown further), there would have to be added to it the fundamental principle that evolution occurred through Divine Providence, and not by chance, as the founders of the doctrine would have it.

[57] R. Samuel b. Meir (1058-1124), Tosafist and exegete, France.

[57*] This passage has been omitted from the Anthology through an oversight.

then more, until it was complete. Therefore that which it was finally it was already at the beginning, but it lacked completion of its proper form—as in the case of a craftsman who makes a utensil. In other words, the Infinite One, blessed be He, did not wish to act as Himself—to make the matter perfect all at once—but as a craftsman who can work by stages only; he (the craftsman) takes the piece of material and forms it a bit, and then it passes through many transformations of shape and appearance until it is completed in its final form. At first the object is a formless lump, and whoever sees it then or in its early shapes will behold only an ugly thing; but finally the beautiful form appears, and proves that all this (process and development) was necessary for the attainment of its beauty." Again: "But the parts were not arranged in any workable way. . . Then the things were done gradually; the parts were arranged a different way, and the creatures themselves were given a new existence, more select and improved" (*op. cit.* chap. 47).

Dr. A. Marcus emphasizes that Luzzatto had as early as 1705 presented the idea of evolution in creation from lower to higher forms, specifically at the end of the passage: "And the creatures themselves were given a new existence, more select and improved."[58]

It is interesting to note that Luzzatto's thought, including the example of the formless piece of wood and the utensil, is found in Aboth d'Rab. Nathan, chap. I: "How was the first man created? The first hour, his earth was gathered; the second, his form was created; the third, he was made into a crude shape; the fourth, his limbs were joined together; the fifth, his body-passages were opened; the sixth, he was given life; the seventh, he stood on his feet . . ." Lev. R. and Sanhedrin 38b: "R. Johanan b. R. Hanina said: . . . The first hour, his earth was gathered; the second, he became a crude form; the third, his limbs were spread out; the fourth, life was put into him; the fifth, he stood on his feet . . . " *P'sikta Rabbathi* chap. 46: " . . . the sixth hour, He raised him to his feet; the seventh, He breathed life into him."

Aside from variations about the hours, there is one significant difference of opinion here. According to the Talmud and *Aboth d'Rabbi Nathan,* man was given life *before* he rose to his feet. In *P'sikta Rabbathi* it is stated that man was made in crude form and raised to his feet before he was given life.[59] These views would correspond to two different interpretations of the verse: " . . . *and breathed into his nostrils the breath of life* . . . " (Genesis 2:7). According to Onkelos as paraphrased by Nahmanides, man had life and mobility like all animals at the time of his creation; then the Lord instilled into him a "soul of intelligence" and "a soul of growth." Others explain the verse to mean that man was at once given the "souls of mobility, growth, and intelligence." The view of the *P'sikta* that man was made in crude form and put on his feet, would mean that he had the "soul of mobility" (power of locomotion) before he was given intelligence. The other view—that he was first endowed with a soul and then raised to his feet—would agree with the second interpretation that he was given all his powers and faculties simultaneously.

In a responsum of R. Joseph Gaon M'hassya, published in *Ginze Kedem,* v. III, p. 60, there is a marginal note about the stages of

[58] In an article by Rabbi David Hacohen in *Sinai,* Jerusalem, Nissan, 1946, the writer states that the view of his revered teacher, Rabbi Kook, of blessed memory, on the reconciliation of evolution and creation (see above, p. 221), is based on many passages in the writings of Rabbi Moses Hayim Luzzato, as I have here noted in the name of Dr. A. Marcus. Hacohen was not aware that Dr. Marcus had already discussed the relevance of R. Luzzatto's views to the theory of evolution. He also states, *ad. loc.,* that his revered teacher's views on evolution were similar to those of the well-known French-Jewish philosopher Henri Bergson, who likewise attempted to reconcile the doctrines of evolution and creation; but that Rabbi Kook differed from Bergson on the question of ultimate perfection.

[59] The view of *P'sikta Rabbathi* is also in *P'sikta d'R. Kahana,* ch. 23. However, *Midrash T'hillim,* Ps. 92 and *Pirke d'R. Eliezer,* ch. 11, agree with *Aboth d'R. Nathan* and *Sanhedrin* 38b. Another version of this midrash is found in *Midrash Tanhuma, Sh'mini* 8: "The first hour, he was conceived in (God's) thought; the second, He consulted with the ministering angels; the third, He gathered the earth; the fourth, He kneaded him; the fifth, He formed the limbs; the sixth, He made him into a crude image; the seventh, He breathed life into him. . . ."

man's creation: "It seems to me that at the end of the second hour his creation was finished, and he was a rough, crude man with animal-like life, as it is written, *When a wild ass's colt is born a man* (Job 11:13). The Talmud (Sanhedrin 38b) writes: 'In the second hour he was fashioned into a crude shape; in the third, his limbs were formed; in the fourth, life was breathed into him . . . Perhaps by this *life* a soul of wisdom is meant . . . but life itself was in him as soon as he was made—formless and crude.' " According to this, even the Talmud and the other sources hold that man first possessed life and mobility, and only later was he given intelligence.

Apparently, then, there is one rabbinic view that when man was created there was a definite period during which he was, as it were, crude and formless—possessed of life and movement like all animals, but without human intelligence. In The Concept of Time (Appendix p. 204f) I have shown that the measure of time in the "six days of creation" was of a different kind from our measure. Perhaps the hours listed in the creation of man are also of a different sort.

According to this view man was created by evolving from one stage to another—just as an object fashioned by a craftsman takes on different shapes and forms until it is completed—unlike the opinion that man was created at once, complete. Moreover, R. Judah (see above, p. 235) holds that man had a tail. Combining these views we arrive at the conclusion that he was certainly an animal at first, and only later became man, and then God removed the tail for the sake of human dignity.

Dr. Marcus (*Keseth Hasofer,* p. 66) cites the following passage in Zohar, v. 1, 134: "There is not a single organ in man to which some creature in the world does not correspond. The human being is divided into parts and organs; all exist at different levels, and all join together to form one body. So also is the world. All the creatures are parts and organs, and all exist and add up together to form the body." He (Dr. Marcus) quotes *M'irat Enayim* by R. Menahem Azariah de Fano that man has in himself all the levels of earthly life and existence which have preceded him, for he is a microcosm, the image of the macrocosm.

This basic idea—that man has within him faculties of all creatures—is often mentioned in Midrashim and Zohar.

Aboth d'Rabbi Nathan, chap. 31: "R. Jose Hag'lili says: 'All that the Holy One, blessed be He, created on earth, He created in man. He created bushes in the world and bushes in man—his hair. He created wild beasts in the world and wild beasts in man—vermin; deer in the world and deer in man—his thighs; horses in the world and horses in man—the hind-parts of man. Thus we learn that whatever the Holy One created on earth He created in man.' " It is clear then that within man are the powers of various animals.

Aggadath Olam Katan (printed in *Beth Hamidrash* V): "Our Rabbis learned: The creation of the world was similar to the creation of man, for whatever the Holy One created in His world, He created in man. . ."

Zohar Hadash v. III, 48: "*Then the Lord God formed man* (Genesis 2:7)—with the full Holy Name, since we have established that he (man) is the perfection of all and the sum total of all. . . We have learned: On the sixth day man was created . . . he was made complete, whole, and so was all that had gone before and that was lower than he; and all were included in man. It was learned: R. Jose said: It is written: *And as for the likeness of their faces, they had the face of a man* (Ezekiel 1:10)—the sum total of all; and all are included in this image."

Zohar v. 3, 219: "*And God said: 'Let us make man'* (Genesis 1:26). After each craftsman had finished his work, the Holy One, blessed be He, said to them, 'I have one task to do, which will be done by all of us. Let us all join together, so that each one will do his share, and I will do Mine.' And that is the meaning of: *Let us make man in our image, after our likeness.*"

Rabbi Elijah, Gaon of Vilna, writes on Genesis 1:26 (in *Adereth Eliyahu*): "*And God said: 'Let us make man.'* The meaning is that man was created after all the other creatures, and therefore the Holy One, blessed be He, bade all the creatures to give part of their characterstics to man's body.[60] For strength is ascribed to the lion, swiftness to the deer, lightness to the eagle, cunning to the fox, and so on. Man also has both plant and animal properties within him. The word *image* means form and final appearance; living creatures are more advanced than plants because they possess animal life; this animal life is their image. Plants are equally superior to inanimate objects. Therefore *in our image* means that the images of all species are to unite in man, so that they will all be beneath him—inanimate life, plant life, animal life, and human life—and through their natural powers and minds he will rule over all. And He gave man a divine element from on high, that man might serve Him."[61]

It should be emphasized that all these passages treat only of "powers of the soul" of living beings that were included in man at his creation. There is no mention at all about physical evolution.

Let me add, however, an interesting paragraph from the Talmud which describes a series of metamorphoses so extensive and bizarre that we cannot but be impressed that here we are confronted with an awareness of evolution as a factor in nature (Baba Kama 16a): "It was taught: A male *zabua* (viper) becomes an *atalef* (a kind of bat) after seven years; after seven years the *atalef* becomes an *arpad;* the *arpad* after seven years becomes a thistle; a thistle after seven years becomes a brier; a brier after seven years becomes a demon. The human spine after seven years becomes a serpent."[62]

And in J. Shabbath 1, 5: "R. Jose b. Bun said in the name of R. Z'vid: 'Once in every seven years the Holy One, blessed be He, changes His world.' " (The passage continues like the Talmud Babli, though with differing names of creatures.) We see that the Talmud Jerushalmi states explicitly, "The Holy One changes His world"—not by accident or chance but by intention.

In *Tur Orah Hayyim,* par. 121, the passage of Baba Kama is quoted as reading: "Once every *seventy* years." Perhaps seventy is a symbol for a long period.[63]

* * *

I will now cite Rabbinic sources relevant to six aspects of the doctrine of evolution:

1. Lamarckism;
2. The biogenetic law;
3. Vestiges;
4. The missing link;
5. Atavism;
6. Spontaneous generation.

1. Lamarck explains that changes in living beings are caused by need, use, and adaptation. If an animal makes excessive use of one particular limb, that limb develops and evolves.

[60] See T.S., Genesis, ch. 1, par 756 (Anthology, I, par. 233) and Tikkune Zohar 69. Similarly in Zohar, v. 1, p. 19 (T.S., v. 1, par. 572), that man's image includes all images. In Zohar, v. 2, p. 178 (T.S., v. 1, par. 720), we read: "Animal is in the generalization of man."

[61] The following is taken from *Ahavath Jonathan* on Genesis by the renowned 18th-century rabbi, Jonathan Eibeschutz: ". . . The sum of the matter is that all powers and character traits, both good and bad, were distributed among the creatures below, so that each should make use of those faculties and traits which belong to its nature. As the rabbis say: 'If Torah had not been given, we would have learned modesty from a cat. . . .' Man possesses all their powers and traits, and him alone has the Holy One, blessed be He, given freedom of choice, to select for use whatever he wishes. We further know that the name of each creature is in accord with its individual nature and traits. The rabbis say: 'Why was this bird named *hassidah* (merciful)? Because it acts in loving-kindness toward its fellows. That bird was named *anafah* because it commits adultery. . . .' Since man is a summation of them all, all the names of the lower creatures were ready for his use. . . ." In *Malbim* to Genesis 1:24: "*Let the earth bring forth* nefesh hayah *after its kind*—this means the spirit of the first man. Although the intelligent soul of man was created separately, for there is nothing like it among the animal souls, the spirit of life, and the faculties of human life, are akin to those found in other living beings. Scattered amidst the souls of living beings are many traits, sparks of powers later gathered to illuminate the chambers of the human soul." See further *ad. loc.* [62] Rashi *ad. loc.*: "A male *zabua*—the *Arukh* explains this to mean a viper. 'The valley of *Zebuim*' (I Samuel, 13:18) is translated in the Targum as 'the valley of vipers.' *Arpad*: The Targum Jerushalmi translates *et ha-atalef* (Leviticus 11:10) as *yat arpada.*" [63] In *Likutim Misefer Ham'lizah,* printed in *Ozar Hag'onim,* it reads: every *sixty* years. See also Bekoroth 8b: "The viper conceives seventy years after its birth." In the Commentary to *Sefer Yetsirah* by R. Judah b. Barsilai, p. 26, there is a quotation from R. Saadyah that seven, seven times seven, and seventy occur frequently in the Torah as expressions for a large number. See also Arukh, s.v. *Guzma.*

When the animal has perfected the proper structure of the limb, it transmits this to the offspring. An illustration of this is the horse, which has one toe per foot. According to Lamarckians fossils have been found in North America of all the stages of transition from a horse with five-toed feet. It is presumed that gradually the toes atrophied, until the horse with one-toed feet was born.

Interestingly enough, there is an old Rabbinic statement in *Midrash Abakir* (quoted in *Pa-aneah Raza,* Genesis) as follows: "All those who were born before Noah had completely joined (webbed) hands, without any separation or division between fingers, and Lamech understood that such fingers would be needed for working the earth. This is the meaning of the verse: *This same shall comfort us . . . in the toil of our hands*" (Gen. 5:29). In T.S., chap. 5, I cite other sources, that before Noah man had no separation of fingers, and plowed with his hands. This is evident from *Midrash Tanhuma* Genesis 6. The version of the *Tosafot ha-Rosh* is that man had separated fingers, but they were joined at the top.

This *midrash* then clearly indicates a tradition that at one time man's fingers were joined together, either entirely or at the ends, and Noah was the first to be born with divided fingers. The theory of Hugo de Vries is that some animals and plants will all at once acquire a new form; suddenly there will appear plants which differ from their predecessors. According to de Vries this occurs with all animals and plant species. Our midrashic passage—that Noah was born with a totally different kind of hands (separated fingers)—would support this theory. However, this seems to be a Rabbinic tradition in but a single instance, to which there is an allusion in the Bible; it does not appear to be a general rule of nature, operative elsewhere.

According to the doctrine of descent, a chance occurrence or accident can change the structure of an animal. Haeckel considers it likely that at one time the tail of an animal was cut off, and forever after the animal produced tail-less offspring. It was in this way that man lost his tail. Others reject this, and point out that Jews have been circumsizing their children for the past 3,500 years, and yet no greater percentage of circumcized children is born to Jews than to non-Jews who do not practice the rite. See also Hullin 69a. According to the Sages, however, there is no problem whatsoever here, and we need not seek theories as to how he (man) lost his tail; as explained above, there was a human tail, and it was removed from him for the sake of his dignity.

2. The biogenetic law was formulated by Haeckel. It was to be the final proof of the idea of descent—that every embryo, in developing from a single cell to the finished creature, passes through all the stages through which its predecessors passed during millions of years of development from a one-celled organism—such as the sequence of starfish, snail, crab, fish, reptile, mammal, primate, until man. Haeckel tried to prove that the human embryo resembles a fish for a certain time, then a reptile, and then some other kind of animal. This hypothesis, investigated by many scientists, encountered much evidence to contradict it. Nevertheless the biogenetic law remains in the university textbooks.

In an ancient source we find that the Sages did discuss the occasional resemblance of a human fetus to an animal. In the Mishnah *Niddah* III, 2 we read: "If a woman gives abortive birth to a flat fish (sandal) or a placenta, she is unclean as for both a male and female child." The Gemara *ad. loc.* (25b) states "*Sandal* [the fetus] resembles a fish. At first it was a fetus, but it was crushed." R. Meir and other Sages hold different views thereon.

"Whoever gives abortive birth to a snake-like object . . . is unclean . . . since the eyeball is oval like that of a human." So also in *Sifra Tazria* 12, 2: "You might think that if a woman drops an object like a fish, an insect, a creeping or a crawling thing, she shall be unclean; therefore it is written *male* . . . " Obviously the Sages were aware that the fetus sometimes has such shapes and forms. When the fetus is prematurely dropped, it is pounded; sometimes, however, it retains its intra-uterine shape. But this does not mean that they share Haeckel's views.

3. Vestiges. Another proof of the theory of descent is the existence of vestigial organs in

the human being, i.e., organs supposedly carried over from an earlier period, but useless at present. If man was created as he is now, and did not evolve, whence and why these vestigial organs? According to the theory of evolution they are remnants of his development. Others, however, maintain that because we do not know an organ's function, that does not mean that it has no function. For instance, the thyroid gland was considered purposeless at one time; now we know it to be vitally needed for the body's health.

On this, too, there is a Rabbinic statement. Gen. R. 8: "The Holy One, blessed be He, created man with two fronts (as two people, joined back to back), then split him into two, each with a back." *Midrash T'hillim* on Psalm 139: "*Thou hast hemmed me in front and back* (ibid. 5)—two fronts joined together were created; this was Adam. At his back was the form of Eve." Plato and Philo write similarly. See T.S., Genesis chap. 2, par. 281; chap. 5, par. 27. R. Hananel, in his commentary on Berakoth, writes: "They were two joined fronts; then they were split and separated, and each front was completed with new flesh in place of its missing part." Thus according to this view Adam changed from a two-fronted to a one-fronted person. Another opinion in Gen. R. *ad. loc.* is that Adam was created androgynous, i.e., bi-sexual. In *Ma'amar Hap'siyoth* R. Hayyim Vital writes that the male's vestigal breasts are remains from the time of creation, when man was "two-fronted"—that is to say, androgynous.

A similar idea is found in Hullin 27b, in reference to birds, where the Rabbis remark that birds have fish-like scales on their legs, which indicates that they were created, like fish, from water. See *Tosafot ad. loc.* and *Keseth Hasofer*, p. 30.

4. The missing link. The theory of evolution lacked evidence of any transition from ape to man; the differences between man and the most highly developed ape known to us are very great. Bones of an ape were found and proclaimed to belong to an ape-man; others vigorously denied this.

Interestingly enough, an allusion to such a missing link is found in Zohar, v. 2, 167. Commenting on the verse, ". . . *and she conceived and bore Cain*" (Genesis 4:1) Zohar states: "Together with Adam's energy it was that which had been left of the ape element in her which produced Cain." In other words, the serpent was the primal ape who was punished by being changed to a snake, and he was called serpent in anticipation of his ultimate form. See T.S., Genesis 3, 9 and 4, 14, that the serpent spoke to and cohabited with Eve. See Bekoroth 8a about the dolphin (sea-serpent).

5. Atavism. One great scientist who supported the theory of evolution, Prof. K. Vogt (1817-1895), held that abnormal human beings, e.g., morons, idiots, and imbeciles, are throwbacks, regressions to an earlier period or stage of development—a return to the level of apes. Prof. Virchow rejects this. The abnormal human differs psychologically from his fellow-humans, but he remains a human being, and is not an ape.

This idea of atavism too can be found in the writings of the Sages, in Gen. R. 23: "Four things were altered in the days of Enos . . . and their faces became ape-like." Sanhedrin 109a: "Those who said, 'Let us go up and do battle' (in the age of dispersal) were turned into apes, spirits, devils, and night-demons." So also in a midrashic passage quoted in T.S., Genesis 1, 792: "And their appearance was changed to that of an ape in the age of dispersal." Erubin 18: "All the years that Adam spent in banishment, he gave birth to spirits, devils and night-demons." In *Midrash Hagadol* the reading is "monkeys and night-demons." R. David Kimchi explains in the name of R. Sh'rira Gaon that they were strange creatures, similar in facial ugliness and stature to devils and night-demons. See also Maimonides, Guide I, 7, and T.S., Genesis 5, 33.

6. Spontaneous generation. Ulmann writes:[64] "(For those who do not accept the

[64] *Madaei Hateva U'briath Haolam*, Tel Aviv, 1944, p. 21.

Torah's account of creation) there has ever been one pressing question—what is the origin of life on earth? A few hundred years ago many scientists held that animate matter or a live body can arise out of inanimate matter. In 1668 Redi proved that it is impossible to get flies from meat (an accepted belief at the time) unless the eggs or larvae of flies were in the meat. As late as 1652 the Dutch chemist Helmont gave instructions for the creation of mice from a bundle of rags steeped in corn.

"Paul de Kruif in his Microbe Hunters gives an excellent account of the disagreement between those who believed in spontaneous generation and those who held that only the living beget the living. It is well worth while to read the details of the debate between Spalanzani and Needham (both priests).

"This argument remained unresolved until Pasteur apparently settled the matter. By a series of brilliant experiments he proved that only living creatures can produce living creatures. And the Englishman Tyndal confirmed his findings. He proved that microbes and bacteria can grow only where germs exist. No life can ever come into being in sterile matter. Pasteur's experiments cannot be disproved. They were simple and irrefutable, and showed conclusively that only living beings give birth to living beings. And yet, several years after Pasteur's experiments had established that truth, Haeckel came and revived the old conjecture. At some point in time, he claimed, a living being had arisen from inanimate matter. The theory of descent required this postulate; it had to believe in spontaneous generation, in spite of the scientific proof against it. Not only Haeckel accepted this postulate. Many serious researchers wrote that we must accept the idea that long ago in the very remote past, life came out of inanimate matter, even though this is in opposition to present-day scientific thinking."[65]

It is of interest to note that the schools of Shammai and Hillel debated this very point too. In Shabbath 12 there is a question as to whether vermin may be killed on the Sabbath. The school of Shammai forbids; the school of Hillel permits. According to the Talmud *ad. loc.* 107, the difference of opinion depends on the origin of vermin: do they come only from vermin eggs or not—i.e., can a living creature come from a non-living source? According to the Hillelites they can derive from perspiration as well, and also from other inanimate sources. See T.S., Genesis, v. 1, par. 706 for a fuller discussion of this matter.

SUMMARY

Concerning the theory of the evolution of species, the literal meaning of biblical verses and the views of the Sages are opposed to it. According to the latter, all plant and animal life was created in the "six days of Creation." From then on for all of existence the species are permanent. If certain changes occur from time to time, these remain within the bounds of the species, for they were included in the plan of creation; but there can be no descent or mutation from one species to another. Especially is this true of man, who was created last, by the will of the Creator, with adult mind and character.

Nevertheless, some who believe in Torah and its precepts have also accepted the doctrine of evolution, but with the qualification that evolution was a law of nature by the Creator; such was His will. To them we might repeat the words of Maimonides, in Guide of the Perplexed, v. II, chap. 25: "We do not reject the eternity of the universe because certain passages in Scripture confirm the Creation; for such passages are not more numerous than those in which God is represented as a corporeal being; nor is it impossible or difficult to find for them a suitable interpretation. We might have explained them in the same manner as we did in respect to the incorporeality of God. We should perhaps have had an easier task in showing that the Scriptual passages referred to are in harmony with the theory of the Eternity of the Universe, if we accepted the latter, than we had in explaining the anthropomorphisms in the

[65] *Vid. loc. cit.*, p. 55, note 23a, that others accept spontaneous generation as a possibility because "we have recently become aware of the existence of transitional forms between inanimate and animate, or lower, forms of life."

Bible, where we rejected the idea that God is corporeal. . . However, we have not done so . . . [as] the Eternity of the Universe has not been proved; a mere argument in favor of a certain theory is not sufficient reason for rejecting the literal meaning of a Biblical text and explaining it figuratively, when the opposite theory can be supported by an equally good argument. . .

"As there is no proof sufficient to convince us . . . we take the text of the Bible literally."

Paraphrasing Maimonides we might say, "Were the theory of evolution conclusively proved, then it need not contradict the fundamental view of the Torah, for the Scriptural verses can be explained accordingly."

For example, a certain midrashic passage would seem to contradict the plain meaning of the verse in the Bible that Adam's creation began the sixth day. *Yalkut Shim'oni*, Genesis, par. 34, in the name of *Midrash Abakir*: "When the Holy One, blessed be He, sought to create the world, He began with man, and made him a formless lump. But when He came to put life into man, He said, 'If I bring him to life now, it will be said that I had a partner in the work of creation. I will leave him as he is until everything is created.' After everything was finished, the ministering angels said to Him, 'Wilt Thou not make the man, as Thou didst say?' He replied, 'I have already made him. He lacks nothing but life.' Thereupon He brought man to life and included all the world in him. The Creator began with man, and ended with man, as it is written, *Thou hast hemmed me in before and behind* (Psalms 138:5)."

Similarly, this text was in the manuscript of *Midrash Ruth* that was before the author of *Oth Emeth*, who copied it into his glosses: "The *aleph* of the word *Adam* is larger than every other *aleph* in Scripture; for with Adam did the Holy One, blessed be He, begin to create everything, and with him everything was completed. It was thus: He created him and left him a formless lump; on the sixth day He breathed into him a living spirit. He (the Creator) did not breathe life into him the first day lest one say that Adam created the world with Him . . ."[66]

The probable basis for this view is the statement of R. Nehemiah in Gen. R. 12, which is elaborated further in *Midrash Tanhuma*, ed. Buber, Genesis 1, 1. There R. Nehemiah says: "On the first day the entire world was created. . . . *Let the earth bring forth*—implies that which was prepared at the very beginning." (See T.S., 1, 205; 584 — Anthology 1, 172 and Hullin 60b: "The grass came up and waited at the 'entrances' of the earth.") Perhaps the intention of the above *midrash* is to negate completely any idea of evolution; for it stresses that both the body and the spirit of man were created the first day, before all other forms of life. In any case, we find individual points of view about creation, which differ from the literal meaning of the Scriptural verses and the views of other Sages in the *midrashim*.

All that is certain is that we have no single definitive, accepted interpretation of the Biblical account of creation. One glance at the numerous passages in T.S. on the Creation narrative will show a wealth of interpretations, rabbinic and medieval, on every detail. I refer not to homiletic interpretation, but to the simple meaning of the Biblical text, for as it is said, "Torah has seventy faces."[67]

We have also seen that some Sages held that for a time Adam was a crude, rough being, and had a tail before he was endowed with human reason; he was created "two-fronted" or androgynous. Another view was that all humans before Noah had hands with undivided fingers. Further, there is an opinion that the Creator changes creatures every seven years (or, seventy —probably a round figure denoting a long

[66] This passage is also in a manuscript, *Yalkut Talmud Torah*, where *Midrash Ruth* is given as its source. See *Hazofeh Me-eretz Hagar*, 1914, where the manuscript is cited. The author there finds no source for the midrashic passage, and surmises that it is originally from some non-Jewish source, and was later incorporated in the Midrash. But it is difficult to agree with him, since we have *two* sources—*Midrash Ruth* and *Midrash Abakir*. [67] See *Talpioth*, I, p. 385, N. Y., 1944, where I list ten points of creation about which rabbinic opinion is divided. Concerning the creation of the lights, when they were created and how they functioned, there are almost twenty views.

time). Similarly, there are statements by the Sages that man includes within himself all animal characteristics.

All this would provide a basis for those traditional Jews who accept, or rather, who *believe* in the theory of evolution. For it has not been scientifically proven, and many great scientists reject it as completely invalid. That being so, the theory of evolution need not cause us to interpret the Bible in any especial way.

I quote briefly, from Ulmann, *ibid.*, statements of several scientists who are irreconcilably opposed to the theory of evolution.

Linnaeus (biologist, 1707-1778; laid the foundation for the classification of plant and animal life): His conclusion is that there is no other explanation for the force in nature which produces an infinite number of plants and animals, other than the concept that the Eternal created everything, and continues to create until the end of time. We must seek to explain the one, single force, that ceaselessly creates in the living world—this omnipotent, all knowing word—Creator. Linnaeus regards all species as fixed.

Agassiz (professor of natural science, 1807-1873) writes that the species are the materialization of the Creator's plan.

Plate (professor of zoology): "The most important fact that the natural scientist can establish is that nature is not chaotic . . . there is a fundamental non-physical determinant of law and order that we call God."

Schleiden (professor of botany and pharmacognosy, 1804-1881): "No investigator, no matter how deep his probing, can arrive at a higher principle than the idea that God is the *causa causalis;* that His knowledge and love have created the world. This is a truth which needs no further investigation."

The great biologist Pasteur wrote that we see in nature hundreds of thousands of miracles which reveal the working of God.

Schonbein (professor of chemistry, 1799-1868): "It cannot be denied that within the bounds of organic life there exists order, plan, and intention. We can see in nature the power of the Eternal functioning according to these principles."

In view of all this, why reinterpret the plain meaning of the Bible for the sake of an unproven theory?

The words of Saadya Gaon (T.S., Exodus chap. 8, par. 50) are fitting here: "We find the metaphor *finger* used in Scripture three times. It is used with reference to the heavenly spheres, which are exceedingly great: *When I see Thy heavens, the work of Thy* fingers, *the moon and stars which Thou hast fixed firm. . .* (Psalms 8:4). It is used about the Tables of the Law, which were unmatched for radiance . . . *written by the* finger *of God* . . . (Exodus 31:18). It is used also with reference to vermin, which are exceedingly small and insignificant: *It is the* finger *of God* (ibid. 8:15) is written about the third of the ten plagues in Egypt. The use of the same word in Scripture for all three things teaches us that He manifested the same powers in the creation of this globe as in the creation of a tiny insect."

This constitutes a reply to the doctrine of evolution. Those who maintain it and seek to explain by it the creation of complex man, ignore the fact that to the Creator there is no difference between the creation of the entire world and that of the tiny mosquito. He who created the former also created the latter, as well as man with all his perfection of character and intelligence. On the other hand, the structure of the tiny ant may afford us more cause for wonder than that of the elephant. We say in admiration, "How great are Thy works, O Lord;" but we can also say, "How wonderful are Thy small works, O Lord!"

I will conclude with a midrashic passage in Lev. R. 14: "If a man has merit, we say to him, 'You preceded all creation.' If not, we say to him, 'A fly was made before you, a gnat, a worm preceded you.'" The commentaries explain that if he has merit—in other words, if he has achieved perfection—he is first in creation, for the spirit of man was created the first day; the phrase '*the spirit of God*' is interpreted as the soul of the first man. If not—

if he is without human spirit—the human body was created the last day. We might add homiletically: If a man succeeds in recognizing the greatness of his own self as a fragment of the divine—a Godly creation—if he recognizes the spiritual qualities with which the Creator has endowed him, he then perceives the closeness of God, and the divine element of himself, as we say in prayer, "The soul is Thine, and the body Thy handiwork." Then he is told, "You were first in creation." If not—if he wallows in materialism, and is not at all aware of the soul within him; if he is detached from his roots in the Divine—then he is told, "According to your own concepts and understanding, a worm preceded you. You are a descendant of a worm." For such we pray, "Let every living form know that Thou hast formed it, and let every living creature understand that Thou hast created it."

4.

CREATION AND HUMAN BROTHERHOOD*

The Biblical account of the creation of man seeks to teach one grand lesson valid for all times: The foundation of the world is belief in One God as Creator and Father, and its corollary, brotherly love, accompanied by a constant awareness that all human beings are of one human father (Adam). The prophet Malachi asked of us: "Have we not all one father? Hath not one God created us? Why do we deal treacherously every man against his brother?" (Malachi 2:10). Man's failure to realize this breeds misunderstanding, prejudice, and ill-will leading to fratricidal hate; it is the great illness which produces suicidal strife, ruin and desolation, and has brought us to our present all-too-justified fear of total destruction.

This one fundamental idea is familiar to all; we know it well. Yet we are far from accepting it in practice. Our physical and material progress goes on apace with tremendous speed; but our moral progress lags woefully behind. It is our task to speak to the heart of man. This profoundly true principle which is so clearly enunciated in the Bible, and in the Prophetic writings, has been constantly studied and emphasized by our Sages. In the following pages I present the thought of our great teachers and scholars on this subject, as manifested in our Talmudic-Midrashic literature.

Talmud Jerushalmi, Nedarim, ch. 9, 41c, reports an interesting and highly significant discussion between two of its most outstanding scholars, R. Akiba and Ben Azzai. The former declared: "*Thou shalt love thy neighbor as thyself* (Lev. 19:18) is the greatest principle of the Torah." Whereupon Ben Azzai observed: "*This is the book of the generations of Adam* (man) (Gen. 5:1) is an even greater principle."

R. Akiba's statement is self-explanatory. Ben Azzai's, however, is not so self-evident. Nevertheless it lays down a fundamental tenet of Judaism. For in the verse quoted the scholar saw the basic declaration of human brotherhood: by tracing back the whole of the human race to one single ancestor, created by one God, the Bible taught that all men have *one* Creator — the heavenly Father — and *one* ancestor — the human father. Thus all men, notwithstanding differences and variations produced by external conditions, are brothers. If, then, R. Akiba saw in the command to love one's neighbor the prime motivation of Judaism, Ben Azzai went behind this precept, as it were, seeking the basis upon which it rests and the sanction which gives it validity, and he found it in this Biblical account of Creation.[1]

Korban Aaron comments: "A still greater principle is that all human beings have God for Father. The Holy Writ intends to say: This is the book of the Torah which tells of the generations of the first man, and teaches that all are the children of one Father, that they are all made in one image and one imprint, the form of God. Wherefore men should not be haughty towards nor hate one another."

R. Yehuda Gedaliah writes on the same passage (Gen. R., ed. Saloniki): "Our sacred Torah is a book for all the generations of man; for we all have one father (Adam), and the Holy One, blessed be He, created all human beings in His likeness and image. Therefore should all endeavor to cling to His attributes (lovingkindness, compassion, and justice); every man should love his neighbor even as

* This essay is a chapter of an unpublished manuscript of mine, *Israel and the Nations,* which deals at length with this topic.

[1] Ben Azzai also links this with the end of the verse, *in the image of God made He him,* on which he comments: "Do not say, since I myself have been put to shame, or am in an evil plight, I may treat my neighbor in like manner (for *thou shalt love thy neighbor as thyself* does not imply that I am to be *more* considerate of him than of myself)." R. Tanhuma explains the connection thus: "For if you do act in this manner, know that you are degrading the image of God." (See Theodor's ed. of Gen. R., chap. 24, p. 237 and commentaries *ad. loc.*)

his own self, and assist him to observe the Commandments and practice good deeds, and so attain to holiness."

A manuscript commentary on Gen. R. quoted by Theodor (p. 237) writes: "Since all nations are one, and all human beings are descended from one man, humanity is like a single body divided into many organs; as the organs of a body are mutually helpful to one another, so should all human beings be mutually helpful to each other. That is why one Sage held that *This is the book of the generations of Adam* is a greater principle."

Thus our Rabbis say: "For this reason was man created alone, to teach that whosoever destroys a single soul[2] is as guilty as though he had destroyed a complete world; and whosoever preserves a single soul[2] is as meritorious as though he had preserved the whole world" (Sanhedrin 37a). It is hard to imagine a more emphatic assertion of human worth. From this it is a natural step to insist first upon peace and then upon the essential equality of humanity: "God created only one man at first. Why? Lest the righteous boast that they are the descendants of a righteous first man, whilst the wicked plead that their first progenitor was evil." (It is interesting to note how this ancestral equality is made to serve the cause of righteousness by depriving the wicked of the plea of a hereditary disposition to evil.) Another reason: "So that families should not quarrel with each other" (Sanhedrin 38a).

Thus the precept, *Thou shalt love thy neighbor as thyself*, follows as a *natural* corollary to this conception of a humanity united in and through a common ancestor. In keeping with this Hillel gave his famous reply to the heathen who wished to learn the whole Torah whilst he stood on one foot: "That which is hateful to thyself, do not unto thy neighbor; that is the whole Torah. The rest is commentary; go and learn it" (Shabbath 31a).

This, of course, was a paraphrase of the Golden Rule. Let us now examine the text more closely. Its significant words are "love" and "neighbor": what does love imply, and who is "thy neighbor"?

R. Israel Al-Nakawa (*Menorath Hamaor* IV, 305) points out that "thy neighbor" is in the dative instead of the accusative (*l'reacha* instead of *eth reacha*), so that the text actually reads, *Thou shalt love* for *thy neighbor as* for *thyself*; in other words, whatever you would love or desire for yourself, that you should desire for your neighbor too. The famous mediaeval moralist R. Bachya writes in a similar vein, but with more detail: "Inasmuch as a man associates with his fellow-men in all that pertains to social welfare, such as sowing, plowing and reaping, or in labor or commerce, he should make a spiritual accounting with himself, to what extent his own activities have contributed thereto. In all these matters he should love for his neighbor what he loves for himself; hate for others what he hates for himself; have compassion upon his fellow men and save them, insofar as it lies within his power, from aught that might harm them. That is the meaning of the Scriptural injunction, *Thou shalt love thy neighbor as thyself*" (Duties of the Heart, on "A Spiritual Accounting," par. 22).

R. Bahya b. R. Asher points out that "thy neighbor" includes even the people *at whose hands one has suffered injury*. He proves this by referring his reader to Exod. 1:2: "*Speak now in the ears of the people, and let them ask every man of his* neighbor, *and every woman of her* neighbor," etc. Thus were the Israelites bidden before they departed from Egypt. The "neighbors" referred to were the Egyptians who, as their taskmasters, had embittered their lives with rigorous and cruel slavery. Yet they are called their neighbors. It should be noted that the Sages' conception of *thy neighbor* included the most wicked and contemptible, even those condemned to death. Their feelings and dignity had to be respected as far as possible even in the act of execution (Sanh. 45a).

The demand for such consideration and

[2] Such is the version in the Munich Manuscript. *Dikduke Soferim* maintains that this is the correct version in all the Talmudic *aggadot*. The addition of *in Israel* was made by printers.

respect for human dignity stemmed from the Biblical conception of man as created in the image of God. Thus we read: "Rabbi Akiba said: Beloved is man, for he was created in the divine image. He is granted an exceeding great love, for he was created in the divine image. As it is said (Genesis 9:7), *For in the image of God did He make man*" (Aboth 3:14). This has been explained thus: "The form in which man was made is called the image of God, to teach that it is the most excellent of all. In the same way the man honored above all men was called the man of God; the Temple, too, is called the House of God, since it is exalted above all houses for the acceptance of prayer . . . *And in the matter of being created in God's image, all human beings are equal,* the righteous as the wicked" (Simeon Duran in *Magen Aboth ad. loc.*)

Tosephoth Yom Tob (in Aboth *ad. loc.*) writes the following on Rabbi Akiba's saying: "Rabbi Akiba applies this to all human beings. That is evident from the fact that in support of his statement he quotes a passage spoken *to the children of Noah, and not to the children of Israel.* Rabbi Akiba mentions *all* human beings favorably, not merely Israel, so as to attract their hearts to do the will of their Creator. When he says that they are beloved, for they were created in the divine image, he means that they can be educated and led to divine ways."

It was shown *supra* that "*thou shalt love thy neighbor as thyself*" applies even to the sinner. Whence did this conception arise? It stemmed from the teaching that "God is long-suffering towards and patient with the sinner, desiring his repentance rather than his death"; indeed, therein lies His essential greatness. This led to the principle that we ourselves must not hate the sinner — a humanitarian principle that many find it particularly difficult to learn.

The former teaching is expressed with remarkable clarity in the following passage: "R. Joshua b. Levi said: 'Why were they (the members of the Synod convened by Ezra and Nehemiah) called the Men of the Great Assembly? Because they restored the crown (of the Almighty) to its pristine greatness. Now, Moses had described Him as *the great God, the mighty, and the awe-inspiring* (Deut. 10:17). When, however, the Temple was destroyed, the Prophet Jeremiah exclaimed: "Idolaters are dancing in His Temple! Where then is His awe?" Thus he omitted "awe-inspiring" as one of His attributes. Then came Daniel and complained: "Idolaters have enslaved His children: where then is His might?" And so henceforth he omitted "mighty." Then came the Men of the Great Assembly and taught: "On the contrary. Therein He shows His might and awe. He shows His might in suppressing His anger and in being long-suffering with the wicked. And He proves His awe-inspiring nature, for but for that, how could one nation (Israel) maintain itself among seventy nations?" Thereupon they restored the epithets, and decreed that He should again be thus described in the daily services' " (Yoma 69b).

It is of interest to observe that in this passage God is described as being long-suffering with the wicked *heathens,* to whom it refers. In that same spirit the Midrash Rabbah on Ruth (3:2) writes: "We have learned: When a person sees an act of idolatry performed, what must he say? 'Blessed be He who is long-suffering toward those who transgress His will.' " Again, in Berakoth 9:1 we read that when one sees the shrine of the idol Mercurius he should recite a similar blessing. Maimonides formulates the ruling thus (*Hilkot Berakoth* 10:9): "When one sees a place where idols are worshipped he must recite this benediction: 'Blessed art Thou, O Lord, King of the Universe, who art long-suffering toward those who transgress Thy will.' "

"Come and behold the mercies of the Holy One, blessed be He!" exclaims a teacher in Exod. R. 12, 3: "Even in the hour of His anger He takes pity on the wicked and on their cattle."

Justice and social stability may demand that the wicked be punished, even destroyed; but the Almighty takes no pleasure therein. So He is pictured as rebuking the angels who sought to sing praises to Him when the Egyptians who pursued the Israelites were engulfed by the returning waters of the Red Sea: "My creatures, the work of My hands, are drowning in the sea, yet ye would utter song!" (Sanhedrin 39b).

In Megillah 10b we read: "R. Joshua b. R. Hananiah commenced his lecture with the text: *And it shall come to pass, that as the Lord rejoiced over you to do you good, and to multiply you; so the Lord will rejoice over you* (yasis) *to cause you to perish, and to destroy you* (Deut. 28:63). (This occurs in the chapter of "Rebuke"—a prediction of the disasters which would befall the people in the event of disloyalty and national apostasy.) Does then the Lord rejoice over the fall of the wicked? Surely it is written, *As they* (the Temple singers) *went out before the army they said: 'Give thanks unto the Lord, for His mercy endureth for ever'* (2 Chron. 20:21). R. Johanan commented thereon: 'For He is good' is omitted here, though elsewhere it is used often in the expression of gratitude to the Almighty, as it says, *Give thanks unto the Lord,* for He is good, *for His mercy endureth for ever* (Ps. 106:1). Why then the omission here? Because the occasion of that thanksgiving was the defeat of the Ammonites, and the Holy One, blessed be He, does not rejoice in the fall of the wicked." Thus this contradicts our first text. The answer was given by R. Jose b. R. Hananiah: "He does not, indeed, rejoice Himself, but causes others to rejoice. For the Writ does not say *yasus,* which means, He will rejoice, but *yasis,* which can be regarded as the *hifil,* causative, and means, He will make others to rejoice."

In this last passage we have a concession to, or rather, a recognition of human weakness. Only those who rise to the loftiest spiritual heights will refrain from rejoicing at the downfall of the wicked; and alas! not many do reach those heights. Consequently God's punishment does cause the average man to rejoice. But one should seek to overcome this weakness, and in imitation of God (a vital principle in Judaism) suppress his desires for the destruction of the wicked, and rather pray for their repentance and reformation.

The three major festivals, known as the Three Pilgrimage Festivals (*Shalosh R'galim*) are Passover (commemorating the Exodus from Egypt); Weeks (the Feast of the First-fruits, also celebrated as the Feast of Revelation); and Tabernacles (the Feast of Ingathering — the Harvest Festival). The Sages observed that Scripture bids the Jew rejoice on the latter two festivals: . . . *and thou shalt keep the feast of weeks . . . and thou shalt rejoice before the Lord thy God* (Deut. 16:10 f). *Thou shalt keep the feast of Tabernacles seven days . . . and thou shalt rejoice in thy feast . . . and thou shalt be altogether joyful* (ibid. 13-15). But Scripture does not order rejoicing on Passover, although as the festival of Liberation it was certainly no less a joyous occasion than the other two. Why was this? Because it involved the punishment of the Egyptians. For the same reason the full Hallel (Doxology—a liturgical service of Praise which is recited in its entirety every day of the other two festivals), is only recited on the first two days of Passover, but not after (for the Egyptians were drowned on the seventh day). As Samuel explained it, citing Prov. 24:27: *Rejoice not when thine enemy falleth* (P'sikta d'R. Kahana, p. 189). We do not sing full praises, for human beings died, their enmity to us notwithstanding. (See T.S., v. 9, p. 136, for a lengthier discussion.)

Here we find a contradiction. Whilst Samuel, on the basis of Proverbs, emphatically repudiates rejoicing at the downfall of the wicked, Midrash T'hillim on Ps. 94 states: "David composed 103 Psalms, yet did not say Hallellujah (*Praise ye the Lord*) until he beheld the fall of the wicked."

Seder Elijah Rabbah (chap. 18) long ago grasped the contradiction between the two views, which appears, moreover, in Proverbs itself. Thus this work observes: "The Writ says: *When thy enemy falleth, do not thou rejoice.* Yet further it says: *When the wicked are destroyed, there is joyous song* (Prov. 11:12). How can the two be reconciled? It seems to me that the joyous song mentioned in the latter verse, and the statement, *Let the righteous one rejoice, for he has beheld vengeance,* refer to the time when the event is taking place. But one should not set a festival for generations because an enemy has fallen. Perhaps that is the reason why the Sages preferred to ascribe the festival of Hanukah primarily to the miracle of the cruse of oil, rather than to the downfall of the Greek Syrians in the Maccabean war. On Purim we commemorate not so much Haman's downfall as the delivery of the Jewish people through Esther from the extermination which his evil machinations had sought to bring about.

The Talmud relates some actual instances. Wicked men living in the vicinity of R. Meir tormented him so grievously that he prayed for their death. But his wife Beruriah chided him: "Why do you pray for their death? Is it because Scripture writes, *Let sinners* (hataim) *cease out of the earth*? (Ps. 104:35). But Scripture does not write *hotim,* sinners, but *hataim,* sins, so that the verse reads: *Let* sins *cease,* etc. Consequently it continues, *so the wicked shall be no more,* for when sins cease they will automatically be wicked no longer. Rather, then, pray that they should repent." R. Meir did so, and they did indeed repent (Berakoth 10a).

A heretic used to vex R. Joshua b. Levi so much with his arguments on the Bible that he determined to curse him at a moment when a curse would be most efficacious. . . But when the propitious moment came he fell asleep. On waking he remarked: "This teaches that what I sought to do was improper, for it is written, *The Lord is good to* all; *His tender mercies are over* all *His works* (Ps. 145:9); and it is also written, *There is punishment for the righteous too who is not kind*" (Prov. 17:26) (Berakoth 7a).

In mutual love and harmony our Sages saw the well-being of Society; in dissension, schism, and mutual hate, its dissolution. They gave expression to this in some remarkable passages. As to the former, the following is instructive. In Aboth d'R. Nathan, chap. 16, (ed. Schechter p. 64) R. Simeon b. Eleazar, commenting on the verse which we have quoted so often, *Thou shalt love thy neighbor as thyself,* observed: "This injunction was accompanied by a great oath, for it is immediately followed by, *I am the Lord.* This means, 'I, the Lord, have created him. I swear, if thou lovest him, I am thy faithful Employer to pay thee thy reward; but if thou dost not love him, I am a Judge to punish thee.' Hence we learn that we must not hate our fellow-creatures."

Intent on seeking the ethical purpose of the Torah, the Rabbis found sermons literally in stones. The Bible enjoins: *Neither shalt thou go up by steps unto Mine altar, that thy nakedness be not uncovered thereon* (Exod. 20:23). This would certainly appear to have no connection whatever with human relations, yet the Rabbis found even here a warning to respect human dignity and worth. By exposing his nakedness a man would fail in respect for the dignity and prestige of the altar. That the stones of the altar were consecrated did not prevent the Rabbis from commenting: "The stones of the altar have no consciousness of either good or evil, yet the Almighty bade us respect their dignity; how much the more must you show the fullest consideration for and avoid shaming your neighbor, who was made in the image of Him who created the world by His command!" (Mekilta, Jethro Chap. 11).

From that follows almost as an obvious corollary their dictum (Aboth, chap. 4): "Who is honored? He who honors all human beings, as it says, *For they that honor Me I will honor, and they that despise Me shall be held in contempt*" (1 Sam. 2:30). Now, the proof-text speaks of honoring or despising not one's fellow-man, but God! Yet it is automatically applied to man. The implication is obvious (so much so that he does not even state it): honor or contempt of the Almighty is identical with honor or contempt of one's fellow-creatures.

The thought is clearly expressed and with more detail in the following passages:

"*And Jacob said unto them: 'My brethren, whence are ye?'* (Gen. 29:4). From this the Sages learned: A man should always be sociable and affable towards his fellow-men, call them his brothers and companions, and be first to enquire about their health and well-being, so that the Angel of Peace and the Angel of Mercy may walk before him." (Midrash Hagadol *ad. loc.*; see also T.S. *ad. loc.* and comments thereon). Taking this teaching to heart, Abaye (a fourth-century teacher) was fond of repeating:

"A man should always be . . . soft of speech and seek to remove anger; he should speak peace with his brethren and relations, yea, with every man, even with the idolator in the market-place. If he does so he will be beloved in heaven and on earth, and find favor in the eyes of all. It was told of R. Johanan b. Zakkai that no man anticipated him in extending a greeting, not even an idolator, for he was careful always to be first to greet" (Berakoth 17a). Maharsha, a late commentator, linked this with a similar passage in Aboth (3, 13): "He in whom the spirit of his fellow-creatures takes delight, in him the spirit of the Omnipresent takes delight." From this it follows that a man's superiority depends not on birth or race, but upon his actions.

Recognizing that man's tendency, however, has always been to look down upon the stranger and to oppress him in greater or lesser degree (a tendency which, alas! history has all too amply proven), the Torah demanded not merely that he should be respected and protected against discrimination, but that he should be loved too: *And if a stranger sojourn with thee in your land, ye shall not do him wrong. The stranger that sojourneth with you shall be unto you as the home-born among you, and thou shalt love him as thyself; for ye were strangers in the land of Egypt: I am the Lord your God* (Lev. 19:33f).

This "love" was not to lose itself in the abstract, but to be given concrete expression in our daily dealings with the alien. Thus *Sefer Hahinuk* writes (*Mitsvah* 431): "We were commanded to love aliens. This means that we may not cause them to suffer hurt in anything, but treat them kindly with acts of benevolence, even as is seemly and as lies within our power. Moreover, this noble commandment exhorts us to have compassion on *any human being* who is not in the city of his home and birthplace, or in the dwelling-place of his parents or family. When we find a stranger alone and far from those who might help him, we must not mislead him on the way, for the Torah has commanded us to have compassion on anyone in need of assistance. If we carry out this commandment faithfully we shall be privileged to enjoy His mercy too, and the blessing of Heaven will rest upon our heads.

"The Holy Writ has indicated the reason for this commandment: *For ye were strangers in the land of Egypt.* It reminds us that we ourselves have been seared by the great torment which befalls every person who finds himself among a strange and alien folk. We must bear in mind the depth of anxiety and distress pertaining to this condition, for grievously has our nation experienced it, until the Almighty delivered us in His love and favor. Since this is so, we should feel warm pity for any human being in that condition."

Such love stems from a passionate inability and refusal to brook injustice, against whomsoever directed. Maimonides, one of the greatest Jewish philosophers that ever lived, finds in this the source of prophecy, which is the highest spiritual state to which man can attain. He writes: "The beginning of prophecy is this: Divine help begins to accompany a man, and this compels and urges him to great good deeds. . . . This compulsion did not forsake Moses from the time he arrived at man's estate. Therefore he was aroused to kill the Egyptian, and to restrain the guilty one of the two who quarreled. Fearing Pharaoh's wrath, he fled to Midian, where he was but a miserable stranger. Nevertheless, when he saw an injustice he could not control himself and had to remove it, for he could brook no injustice. Thus it is said: *And Moses arose, and helped them*" (Jethro's daughters) (Guide of the Perplexed, II, 45; T.S., Exodus, ch. 2, par. 144.)

These noble sentiments, so lofty and in advance of their time (for many peoples and nations are still very far from them), need not surprise us, when we consider that since its earliest days Judaism has emphasized the rights even of dumb creatures. (Kindness to animals as a recognized and avowed obligation is little more than a hundred years old even amongst civilized nations.) Thus the Ten Commandments, Humanity's Charter, not only thinks of the lowly slave, but extends its protecting care even to animals: . . . *but the seventh day is a Sabbath unto the Lord thy God; in it thou shalt not do any work, neither thou, nor thy son, nor thy man-servant, nor thy maid-servant, nor thy cattle. . .* (Exod. 20:10).

Why was Moses chosen to lead the Israelites, and how did the Almighty test his fitness for this task? In a passage brimming with love for the dumb creatures the Sages in Exod. R. 2, 2 give the answer: "Moses too was tested by the Holy One, blessed be He, by his love and care for his flocks. While he was tending the flocks of Jethro in the desert, a kid ran away from him. Moses pursued and overtook it at a pool of water, where the kid stopped to drink. 'I did not know that you ran away because you were thirsty,' he cried out; 'you are tired.' And so he carried the kid back on his shoulder, and rejoined his flock. The Holy One, blessed be He, then said: 'Thou hast shown compassion on the flocks of one who is flesh-and-blood. So, by thy life, wilt thou tend My flock Israel" (T.S. *loc. cit.* ch. 2, par. 2).

One of the outstanding scholars and leaders of the Talmudic age was the Patriarch R. Judah the Prince, the editor and compiler of the Mishnah. Yet the Talmud did not hesitate to ascribe his physical sufferings through an internal illness, and his subsequent recovery, to the lack of pity he showed for a dumb animal at first, and his compassion later on:—"The sufferings of R. Judah the Prince came to him on account of an incident, and they departed on account of an incident.

"*They came on account of an incident.* A calf which was being led to the slaughter escaped, and sought to hide under the Rabbi's cloak, whilst bleating piteously, as if to say, 'Save me.' But the Rabbi said to it, 'Go; for this you were created.' They said (in Heaven), 'He does not pity a fellow-creature; let suffering come upon him.'

"*And they departed on account of an incident.* Once his maid-servant, who was sweeping the house, was about to sweep away some small kittens lying there; said the Rabbi to her, 'Let them be. It is written, *And His tender mercies are over all His creatures*' (Ps. 145:9). They said (in Heaven), 'Since he pities his fellow-creatures, let us have pity upon him.' Thereupon he was healed" (*Baba Metsia* 85a).

Sefer Hassidim (ed. Berlin 1891, p. 63, par. 138), reads: "A man will be punished for any suffering he may have caused his fellows; yea, even for needless suffering to animals. He will be held to account if he puts a burden on a beast heavier than it can bear, or goads it with a whip when it cannot move. An exhortation against cruelty to animals is found in the angel's rebuke to Balaam: '*Wherefore hast thou smitten thine ass these three times?*' (Num. 22:32). Because Balaam raged against his ass, saying, '*I would there were a sword in my hand, for now I had killed thee*' (Num. 22:29), he perished by the sword, as it is said, *And Baalam the son of Beor they slew with the sword*" (Num. 31:8).

Unwittingly, that very Balaam, who had come to curse Israel but had remained to bless, furnished the lofty opening of Israel's daily devotions: *How goodly are thy tents, O Jacob, thy dwellings, O Israel!* (Num. 24:5). For from the tents and dwellings of Israel, from their houses of prayer and houses of study, have issued humanity's essential teachings of universal brotherhood and universal love.

Mankind's one-ness becomes more and more evident—a unity of all humans which is paralleled and strengthened by a growing realization of a basic one-ness in nature as well. Science has taught us that time and space, hitherto regarded as separate and distinct, are one indissoluble concept. And now scientific thinking is on the verge of adding that energy too is an integral part of the single concept of time-space.

Thus, in the natural world which surrounds him, and in the universal community of humans among whom he lives, man must realize ever more intensely and irrevocably their basic one-ness, which mutely attests to one Creator and one human ancestor. This is Israel's fundamental teaching to humanity—the reality of universal brotherhood, which will eventually bring the Messianic Era and the kingdom of God on earth.

5.

ADDENDA TO THE COMMENTARY

(i) THE CREATION CHAPTER

Genesis 1:1—2:3 is a worthy opening of Israel's Sacred Scriptures, and ranks among the most important chapters of the Bible. Even in form it is pre-eminent in the literature of religion. No other ancient account of creation (cosmogony) will bear a second reading. Most of them not only describe the origin of the world, but begin by describing how the gods emerged out of pre-existent chaos (theogony). In contrast with the simplicity and sublimity of Genesis 1, we find all ancient cosmogonies, whether it be the Babylonian or the Phoenician, the Greek or the Roman, alike unrelievedly wild, cruel, even foul.

Thus, the Assyro-Babylonian mythology tells how, before what we call earth or heaven had come into being, there existed a primeval watery chaos — Tiamat — out of which the gods were evolved:—

> "When, in the height, heaven was not yet named,
> And the earth beneath did not bear a name,
> And the primeval Apsu (the Abyss), their begetter,
> And Chaos (Tiamat), the mother of them both,
> Their waters were mingled together,
> Then were created the gods in the midst of heaven."

Apsu, the Abyss, disturbed at finding his domain invaded by the new gods, induced Tiamat (Chaos) to join him in contesting their supremacy; he was, however, subdued by the cunning of Ea; and Tiamat, left to carry on the struggle alone, provides herself with a brood of hideous allies. The alarmed gods thereupon appoint Marduk as their champion. With winds and lightnings, Marduk advances; he seizes Tiamat in a huge net, and "with his merciless club he crushed her skull." The carcass of the monster he split into two halves, one of which he fixed on high, to form a firmament supporting the waters above it. In the same grotesque way, the story continues to describe the formation of sun, moon, plants, animals and man . . .

The infinite importance, however, of the first page of the Bible consists in the fact that it enshrines some of the fundamental beliefs of Judaism. Among these are:—

I. GOD IS THE CREATOR OF THE UNIVERSE. Each religion has certain specific teachings, convictions, dogmas. Such a dogma of Judaism is its belief that the world was called into existence at the will of the One, Almighty and All-good God. And nowhere does this fundamental conviction of Israel's Faith find clearer expression than in Genesis 1. When neighboring peoples deified the sun, moon and stars, or worshipped sticks and stones and beasts, the sacred river Nile, the crocodile that swam in its waters, and the very beetles that crawled along its banks, the opening page of Scripture proclaimed in language of majestic simplicity that the universe, and all that therein is, are the product of one supreme directing Intelligence; of an eternal, spiritual Being, prior to them and independent of them.

Now, while the *fact* of creation has to this day remained the first of the articles of the Jewish Creed, there is no uniform and binding belief as to the *manner* of creation, *i.e.*, as to the process whereby the universe came into existence. The manner of the Divine creative activity is presented in varying forms and under differing metaphors by Prophet, Psalmist and Sage; by the Rabbis in Talmudic times, as well as by our medieval Jewish thinkers. In the Bible itself we have at least three modes of representing the overwhelming fact of Divine Creation. Genesis 1 gives us the story of Creation in the form of a Divine drama set out in six acts of a day each, with a similar refrain (*And there was evening, and there was morning, etc.*) closing the creative work of each day. The Psalmist, to whom Nature was a continual witness of its Divine Author (Ps. 19) gives in Psalm 104 a purely poetic representation of the Creation story:—

"O Lord my God, Thou art very great;
Thou art clothed with honor and majesty.
Who coverest Thyself with light as with a garment;
Who stretchest out the heavens like a curtain . . .
Who maketh the clouds his chariot;
Who walketh upon the wings of the wind:
Who maketh winds his messengers . . . "

Again, Proverbs 8:22-31, shows forth Divine Wisdom presiding at the birth of Nature.

The mode of creation continued to engage Jewish minds after the close of the Bible and throughout the Rabbinic period, even though the Mishnah warns against all speculation concerning the beginning of things. To some, the relation of God to the universe was that of a mason to his work, and they accordingly spoke of God's "architect's plans"; others lost themselves in heretic fancies as to what constituted the raw material, so to speak, of Creation; while to Philo of Alexandria, Creation was altogether outside time. Several of the ancient Rabbis, followed by the later mystics, believed in successive creations. Prior to the existence of the present universe, they held, certain formless worlds issued from the Fountain of Existence and then vanished, like sparks which fly from a red-hot iron beaten by a hammer, that are extinguished as they separate themselves from the burning mass. In contrast to these abortive creations, the medieval Jewish Mystics maintain, ours is the best of all possible worlds. It is the outcome of a series of emanations and eradiations from God, the Infinite, *En Sof*. Furthermore, Rashi, the greatest Jewish commentator of all times, taught that the purpose of Scripture was not to give a strict chronology of Creation; while no less an authority than Maimonides declared: "The account given in Scripture of the Creation is not, as is generally believed, intended to be in all its parts literal." Later Jewish philosophers (Levi ben Gershon, Crescas, Albalag) made dangerous concessions to the Aristotelian doctrine of the eternity of matter; which doctrine Yehudah Hallevi, among others, strongly opposed as both contrary to Reason and as limiting God's Omnipotence.

Rabbi Dr. Joseph Herman Hertz,
The Pentateuch and Haftorahs with Commentary

(ii) THE NEPHILIM

(*on Gen.* 6:4, *p.* 186)

Two interesting excursi on the whole passage regarding the *Nephilim* (Gen. 6:4) are appended:—

1. All ancient mythologies tell of celestial being, sons of gods, who, attracted by the beauty of women, came down to earth, mated with them and begot a race of supermen, semi-gods, who in time were accorded divine honors. Our passage refers to these myths, only, however, to emphasize their utter falsity; and the evil consequences that flowed from them. Thus it relates: *And it came to pass, when men began to multiply . . . and daughters were born to them, that the* [so-called] *sons of God* took the most beautiful women, *whomsoever they chose,* even against their will, even married, and begot children by them. Now, *these* "sons of God" *were* in fact *the Nephilim,* a race of giants, who were in the earth in those days, and even much later, i.e., *after that*. These giants were believed to be of divine origin, who in time became the legendary founders of

dynasties of god-kings, to whom superhuman deeds were ascribed. These, then, were *the sons of God who came in unto the daughters of men and they bore children to them.*

However, such stories and legends were utterly false, for in fact *they referred to* nothing more *than the mighty men that were of old, the men of renown.* The attribution of divinity to such men, or to any who excelled in any particular branch of human endeavor, led to the growth of idolatry and widespread evil and corruption, since, as we have seen, their prowess was accompanied by rape and unbridled license. Hence Scripture continues: *And the Lord saw that the wickedness of man was great in the earth,* etc.

R. Meir Leibush Malbim,
Hatorah v'Hamitsvah

2. Ch. 6:1-8 takes a definite stand against the stories of the connubial relations between gods and mortals so current in the mythologies of the Ancient Near East. However, before enlarging upon this subject, we must dismiss from consideration the purely tendentious interpretation that identifies the *benei Elohim* with the men of the upper strata and the *benoth ha-adam* with the women of the lower strata of society. Both the immediate context and the historico-social background of the passage as a whole militate against such a cavalier interpretation of *benei Elohim* . . .

Some of our greatest philosophers, thinkers in the Middle Ages have looked upon these non-human beings as personifications of the physical and mental forces in nature. Accordingly, it might well be that the *benei Elohim* spoken of in Ch. 6 were produced merely by the pre-natal influences exerted on them, which, as is well known, have constituted a subject of inquiry in both ancient and present-day literatures . . .

The Hebrew masses, dazzled by the richly appointed celebrations of the so-called sacred marriages between gods and certain mortals, could not very well conceive how nations could lavish enormous wealth on rites utterly devoid of a realistic background. So in their limited understanding they deluded themselves into thinking that perhaps there was some measure of truth in this claim of the pagans. But the Torah in Chapter 6 intended to discredit their belief, as though to say: True that there are giants among men, or otherwise distinguished individuals, but they have not come into being from the union of heavenly hosts with the daughters of men. Some pre-natal psychological factors were at work to call forth their existence. Moreover, in contradistinction to the doctrine of the idol-worshippers, they were not immortals, but destined to die as any other human being. This is the burden of: *Let my spirit not abide in man forever, for he is but flesh* (v. 3) . . .

The *nephilim* (v. 4) were allegedly a product of these mixed unions. In respect to this race, too, the Torah stresses that they were mere *gibborim* ("heroes") and by no means denizens of the celestial realm. Nephilim (Nefilim) is derived from *nafal* ("to fall"); they were the heroes who had fallen by the sword and whose story is told at length in Ezek. 32, where *nafal* is used five times in connection with these *gibborim.* Further, while they are represented in Gen. 6:4 as a still flourishing race, they are described in Ezek. 32 as the inmates of the Netherworld (*she'ol*). This shows that they were already extinct in the days of Ezekiel.

Umberto Cassuto,
Me-Adam ad Noah

NOTES TO THE COMMENTARY

Chapter I

1. R. Nehemiah in Gen. R., T.S. 1, 205; R. Saadiah Gaon; RaDaK; R. Bahya.
2. R. Judah in Gen R., T.S. 1, 205; Rashi; Ibn Ezra; RaLBaG.
3. RaMBaM; RaMBaN; Sforno; GRE.
4. Idem.; cf. Appendix, *The Concept of Time.* Dillman translates *B'reshith* as "In the very beginning." Delitzsch has for it: "In the very first beginning, the commencement of the world, when time itself began."
5. (on e) R. Azariah dei Rossi, *Imre Binah,* ch. 25.
6. Yefe Toar on Gen. R. 3, 1.
7. J. H. Hertz.
8. Philo, ed. H. Lewy, p. 27.
9. Abrabanel.
10. Commentators.
11. Ibn Ezra.
12. Rashi.
13. RaNHaW.
14. T.S. 1, 325. See Appendix: *Creation and the Atom.*
15. Commentators.
16. See T.S. 1, 294.
17. Ibn Caspi.
18. Rashi.
19. Ibn Caspi.
20. Onkelos.
21. Maimonides.
22. SHaDaL.
23. Targum Jerushalmi. Rashi. T.S. 1, 323. 341.
24. Rashi. Ibn Ezra.
25. Hertz, J. H.
26. Cassuto.
27. RaSaG.
28. Ibn Caspi.
29. RaMBaN. T.S. 1, 27. 344. 358.
30. Ibn Ezra.
31. RaMBaN.
32. T.S. 1, 384. 389. See also Kasher, *Shabbath B'reshith v'Shabbath Sinai,* in *Talpioth,* 5704.
33. Idem.
34. Idem.
35. Idem.
36. Idem.
37. Idem.
38. Botser Ol'loth.
39. Ibn Caspi.
40. Hertz, J. H.
41. Commentators.
42. Idem.
43. Idem.
44. Ibn Ezra.
45. Hertz, J. H.
46. Rashi. T.S. 1, 411.
47. Hertz, J. H.
48. Ibn Ezra.
49. RaMBaN.
50. Idem.
51. Benamozegh. T.S. 1, 146. 448. See also Appendix: *Concept of Time.*
52. Hertz, J. H.
53. Ibn Ezra. ShaDaL.
54. Rashi. RaMBaN.
55. Rashi.
56. T.S. 1, 501.
57. Abrabanel.
58. Ibn Ezra. RaMBaN.
59. T.S. 1, 509.
60. RaMBaN.
61. Hertz, J. H.
62. Idem.
63. Ibn Ezra.
64. Rashi. RaMBaN.
65. T.S. 1, 513.
66. Hertz, J. H.
67. Idem.
68. Ibn Ezra. RaMBaN.
69. Commentators.
70. Idem.
71. Ibn Ezra. Rashi.
72. Sforno.
73. RaMBaN. RaDaK.
74. Rashi. RaMBaN.
75. GRE.
76. Septuagint. Vulgate.
77. Rashi.
78. Commentors. T.S. 1, 564.
79. RaDaK.
80. ShaDaL.
81. Hertz, J. H.
82. Rashi (on verse 7).
83. RaMBaN.
84. Ibn Ezra.
85. Hertz, J. H.
86. Sforno.
87. Rashi. ShaDaL.
88. Hertz, J. H.
89. Rashi.
90. Idem.
91. Hertz, J. H.
92. Ibn Ezra.
93. Rashi. RaMBaN.
94. Hertz, J. H.
95. Ibn Ezra.
96. RaMBaN and others.
97. Hertz, J. H.
98. Onkelos.
99. ShaDaL. Heidenheim.
100. Hertz, J. H.
101. ShaDaL.
102. Rashi.
103. Onkelos. RaMBaN.
104. RaMBaN. Abrabanel.
105. Rashi and Sifthe Hakamim.
106. Hertz, J. H.
107. Ancient Commentators. Ibn Ezra. T.S. 1, 679 .706. 709.
108. ShaDaL.
109. R. Jacob Emden.
110. ShaDaL.
111. Rashi
112. Cassuto.
113. ShaDaL.
114. Sforno.
115. Hertz, J. H.
116. Benamozegh.
117. Rashi.
118. Hertz, J. H.
119. Commentators.
120. Rashi.
121. RaMBaN.
122. Idem.
123. Rashi.
124. Idem.
125. Ibn Ezra.
126. Idem.
127. Rashi.
128. Ibn Ezra.
129. RaMBaN.
130. Commentators.
131. Rashi.
132. Sforno.
133. RaMBaN.
134. Rashi. Ibn Ezra. Sforno.
135. Botser Ol'loth. T.S. 1, 739.
136. RaDaK.

137. Minhah B'lulah.
138. RaSaG. T.S. 1, 759.
139. RaSaG. ShaDaL.
140. Hertz, J. H.
141. Idem.
142. Rashi.
143. ShaDaL.
144. Sforno. RaNHaW.
145. Rashi.
146. Idem.
147. RaMBaM.
148. Ibn Ezra.
149. RaMBaN.
150. Sforno.
151. Hertz, J. H.
152. Philo, ed. H. Lewy, pp. 55f.
153. T.S. 1, 750.
154. ShaDaL.
155. RaMBaN.
156. ShaDaL.
157. Rashi.
158. Idem.
159. Biur.
160. Hertz, J. H.
161. Hirsch, S. R.
162. Hertz, J. H.
163. ShaDaL. T.S. 1, 793.
164. Hertz, J. H.
165. ShaDaL.
166. Hertz, J. H.
167. ShaDaL.
168. Rashi. Ibn Ezra.
169. RaMBaN. Sforno.
170. Hertz, J. H.
171. Botser Ol'loth.
172. T.S. 1, 808. 811.
173. Hertz, J. H.
174. Sforno.
175. Hirsch, S. R.
176. Idem.
177. Idem.
178. Botser Ol'loth.

CHAPTER II

1. Hertz, J. H.
2. ShaDaL.
3. RaMBaN.
4. Hertz, J. H.
5. Hirsch, S. R.
6. Rashi. Sforno.
7. Rashi.
8. Ibn Ezra. RaDaK.
9. Hertz, J. H.
10. Hirsch, S. R.
11. Rashi.
12. RaMBaN.
13. RaSaG.
14. ShaDaL.
15. Hertz, J. H.
16. Rashi.
17. Ibn Ezra.
18. RaMBaN.
19. Hertz, J. H.
20. Idem.
21. Rashi.
22. RaDaK.
23. ShaDaL.
24. R. Wolf Heidenheim.
25. RaMBaN.
26. Hertz, J. H.
27. Rashi.
28. Sforno.
29. Rashi.
30. Biur.
31. RaMBaM.
32. Most commentators.
33. Hertz, J. H.
34. Idem.
35. Onkelos.
36. Rashi.
37. RaMBaN.
38. Idem.
39. GRE.
40. RaLaSh. ShaDaL.
41. Hertz, J. H.
42. R. Meir Hefetz.
43. Hertz, J. H.
44. ShaDaL.
45. RaLaSh.
46. Sforno.
47. Hertz, J. H.
48. RaSaG.
49. Hertz, J. H.
50. RaSaG.
51. Rashi.
52. Hertz, J. H.
53. Idem.
54. ShaDaL.
55. Idem.
56. Ibn Ezra. RaMBaN.
57. Sforno.
58. Ibn Ezra. RaMBaN.
59. Sforno.
60. Rashi.
61. Sforno.
62. Ibn Ezra.
63. Hertz, J. H.
64. Idem.
65. Rashi.
66. Onkelos.
67. Rashi, RaDaK.
68. Ibn Ezra.
69. Sforno.
70. Idem.
71. Hertz, J. H.
72. Rashi.
73. Commentators; T.S. 2, 177.
74. Onkelos.
75. Abrabanel.
76. RaMBaN.
77. Sforno.
78. Hertz, J. H.
79. Sforno.
80. Rashi.
81. Hertz, J. H.
82. RaMBaN.
83. Botser Ol'loth.
84. Rashi.
85. Hertz, J. H.
86. Rashi.
87. Hertz, J. H.
88. Rashi.
89. T.S. 2, 213.
90. ShaDaL.
91. RaNHaW.
92. Rashi.
93. Hertz, J. H.
94. Ibn Ezra.
95. Sforno.
96. Hertz, J. H.
97. Ibn Ezra.
98. Idem.
99. Hertz, J. H.
100. Early Comms. T.S. 2, 243.
101. RaMBaN.
102. Hertz, J. H.
103. Idem.
104. Rashi.
105. RaMBaN.
106. Hertz, J. H.
107. Idem.
108. Rashi.
109. RaMBaN.
110. Hertz, J. H.
111. Rashi.
112. Sforno.
113. Idem.
114. Hertz, J. H.
115. Rashi.
116. RaLaSh. Benamozegh.
117. RaMBaN.
118. Idem. RaLaSh.
119. Hertz, J. H.
120. Rashi.
121. Hertz, J. H.
122. Rashi. Ibn Ezra.
123. Hertz, J. H.
124. Sforno.
125. ShaDaL. RaLaSh.
126. Sforno.
127. Hertz, J. H.
128. Sforno.
129. Hertz, J. H.
130. ShaDaL.

131. Idem.
132. Hertz, J. H.
133. ShaDaL.
134. Sforno.
135. Ibn Ezra.
136. Rashi.
137. Sforno.
138. Hertz, J. H.

Chapter III

1. Rashi.
2. Sforno. Philo.
3. Ibn Ezra.
4. Hertz, J. H.
5. Commentaries. T.S. 3, 9.
6. RaSaG.
7. RaMBaM.
8. Rashi.
9. Sforno.
10. Minhah B'lulah.
11. T.S. 3, 7.
12. Hertz, J. H.
13. Rashi.
14. ShaDaL.
15. Sforno.
16. Abrabanel.
17. Hertz, J. H.
18. Onkelos. Cf. Anthol. 3, 9.
19. Ibn Ezra.
20. Rashi.
21. Sforno.
22. Hertz, J. H.
23. Rashi.
24. RaMBaN. Sforno.
25. Hertz, J. H.
26. Rashi.
27. Idem.
28. RaMBaN.
29. Rashi.
30. Botser Ol'loth.
31. ShaDaL.
32. Hertz, J. H.
33. Rashi. RaMBaN.
34. Sforno.
35. Hertz, J. H.
36. Rashi.
37. Idem.
38. Sforno.
39. Hertz, J. H.
40. ShaDaL.
41. Rashi.
42. Hertz, J. H.
43. Rashi. RaMBaN. Ibn Ezra.
44. RaMBaN.
45. Rashi. ShaDaL.
46. Ibn Ezra.
47. Rashi.
48. RaMBaN. RaLaSh.
49. Sforno.
50. Hirsch, S. R.
51. Sforno.
52. Hertz, J. H.
53. Botser Ol'loth.
54. Rashi. Ibn Ezra.
55. RaLaSh.
56. Hertz, J. H.
57. Idem.
58. Rashi. Sforno.
59. Rashi.
60. RaMBaN. Hizkuni.
61. Commentaries. T.S. 3, 73.
62. Sforno.
63. Hertz, J. H.
64. ShaDaL. RaLaSh.
65. Hertz, J. H.
66. Rashi.
67. Idem.
68. Idem.
69. Jacob, B.
70. Sforno.
71. Idem.
72. Hertz, J. H.
73. Idem.
74. Rashi.
75. Midrash Haggadol, *ad. loc.*
76. Sforno.
77. Idem.
78. Rashi.
79. Kahana.
80. Jacob, B.
81. Rashi.
82. Ibn Ezra.
83. Sforno.
84. Rashi.
85. Idem.
86. RaMBaN.
87. Hertz, J. H.
88. Sforno.
89. Rashi.
90. Ibn Ezra.
91. Hertz, J. H.
92. Rashi. T.S. 3, 148. 151.
93. Rashi.
94. Hertz, J. H.
95. Idem.
96. Hertz, J. H.
97. Rashi.
98. Idem. Ibn Ezra.
99. Onkelos. Ibn Ezra.
100. Hertz, J. H.
101. Hertz, J. H.
102. Idem.
103. T.S. 2, 126.
104. Anthology ch. 3, par. 86.
105. Hirsch, S. R.
106. Onkelos. Rashi. RaMBaN. See Anthology ch. 3, 92.
107. Hertz, J. H.
108. Idem.
109. Rashi.
110. RaMBaN.
111. Sforno.
112. RaLaSh.
113. Sforno.
114. Ibn Ezra.
115. Sforno.
116. Hertz.
117. Idem.
118. Rashi.
119. RaDaK.
120. Hertz, J. H.
121. RaDaK.
122. Philo. ed. Lewy, pp. 21. 25.
123. Hirsch. S. R.

Chapter IV

1. Rashi.
2. Hertz, J. H.
3. Abrabanel.
4. Gen. R.
5. Rashi.
6. RaMBaN.
7. Onkelos.
8. RaMBaN.
9. Hertz, J. H.
10. T.S. 4, 28.
11. Ibn Ezra.
12. Abrabanel. Malbim.
13. Hertz, J. H.
14. Idem.
15. Onkelos.
16. ShaDaL.
17. J. Megillah 1:11.
18. RaMBaN. Ibn Ezra.
19. Rashi.
20. Hertz, J. H.
21. Rashi. T.S. 4, 38.
22. Abrabanel.
23. Hirsch, S. R.
24. Sforno.
25. RaMBaN. Sforno.
26. RaLaSh.
27. Sforno.
28. Idem.
29. Commentators.
30. Ibn Ezra.
31. RaMBaN. RaLaSh.
32. Sforno.
33. Onkelos. Rashi. RaDaK.
34. RaMBaN. Sforno. ShaDaL.
35. Rashi.
36. Idem. Commentators.

37. Ibn Ezra.
38. RaLaSh.
39. Rashi.
40. RaMBaN.
41. Rashi.
42. Ibn Ezra. ShaDaL. RaLaSh.
43. Daath Z'kenim.
44. Hertz, J. H.
45. Sforno.
46. Rashi.
47. Kerem Hemed, 1, p. 80.
48. Hertz, J. H.
49. Idem.
50. Ibn Ezra.
51. RaLaSh.
52. Rashi.
53. Hertz, J. H.
54. Rashi.
55. Ibn Ezra. RaMBaN. RaDaK. Hizkuni.
56. Botser Ol'loth.
57. RaMBaN. Sforno.
58. Idem.
59. Hertz, J. H.
60. RaLaSh.
61. Rashi.
62. RaMBaN. Sforno.
63. Ibn Ezra. RaDaK.
64. Abrabanel.
65. RaMBaN.
66. Onkelos.
67. RaMBaN.
68. RaDaK.
69. Hertz, J. H.
70. Idem.
71. RaMBaN.
72. Idem. Sforno.
73. Rashi.
74. Onkelos.
75. Hizkuni.
76. Ibn Ezra.
77. RaMBaN.
78. Botser Ol'loth.
79. Rashi.
80. ShaDaL. Botser Ol'loth.
81. RaMBaN.
82. Rashi. Ibn Ezra.
83. RaMBaN.
84. Hirsch, S. R.
85. Hertz, J. H.
86. Rashi.
87. Malbim.
88. Anthology, ch. 4, par. 72.
89. Commentators.
90. Hertz, J. H.
91. Rashi.
92. Idem.
93. Onkelos. RaMBaN.
94. ShaDaL. Botser Ol'loth.
95. Hertz, J. H.
96. Idem.
97. Tanhuma.
98. Onkelos.
99. Commentators.
100. Ibn Ezra.
101. Botser Ol'loth.
102. R. Joseph Kimhi.
103. ShaDaL.
104. RaDaK.
105. Ibn Caspi.
106. Hertz, J. H.
107. Anthology 4, 78.
108. T.S. 5, 39.
109. Hertz, J. H.
110. Philo, op. cit., p. 89.
111. Hirsch. S. R.
112. Ibn Ezra. Sforno. RaShBaM.
113. Rashi.
114. RaLaSh.
115. Hoffman.
116. Rashi.

Chapter V

1. Hertz, J. H.
2. ShaDaL.
3. Sforno.
4. RaMBaN.
5. Hertz, J. H.
6. Hirsch, S. R.
7. Hertz, J. H.
8. Ibn Ezra.
9. Sforno.
10. Hertz, J. H.
11. RaMBaN.
12. Idem.
13. Rashi.
14. T.S. 5, 33.
15. ShaDaL.
16. Idem.
17. Ibn Ezra.
18. RaMBaN.
19. Idem.
20. Rashi. Ibn Ezra.
21. Sforno.
22. Rashi.
23. RaLaSh.
24. Rashi.
25. Ibn Ezra.
26. Hertz, J. H.
27. Rashi.
28. Idem.
29. Sforno.
30. ShaDaL.
31. Rashi.
32. Idem.

Chapter VI

1. RaMBaN.
2. ShaDaL.
3. Onkelos. Rashi.
4. Ibn Ezra.
5. Hertz, J. H.
6. ShaDaL.
7. RaMBaN.
8. RaDaK.
9. Onkelos. Septuagint. Vulgate. RaSaG. Ibn Ezra.
10. Ibn Ezra. R. Bahya.
11. Minhah B'lulah.
12. Fuerst.
13. Rashi. RaShBaM. ShaDaL.
14. Sforno.
15. Hertz, J. H.
16. ShaDaL.
17. Rashi.
18. Hertz, J. H.
19. Septuagint. RaSaG. Rashi.
20. Abrabanel. RaNHaW. Hertz.
21. Rashi and Sifthe Hakamim.
22. Rashi.
23. Ibn Ezra.
24. Hertz, J. H.
25. Rashi.
26. Sforno.
27. Rashi.
28. Ibn Ezra. ShaDaL.
29. RaMBaN.
30. Rashi.
31. Idem.
32. Idem.
33. Hertz, J. H.
34. RaMBaN.
35. Hertz, J. H.
36. Sforno.
37. Idem.
38. Hirsch, S. R.
39. Hertz, J. H.
40. Rashi.
41. Idem.
42. Ibn Ezra. RaMBaN.
43. Idem.
44. Sforno.
45. RaMBaN.
46. Hertz, J. H.
47. Ibn Ezra.
48. RaMBaN.
49. Hertz, J. H.
50. Rashi.
51. Hertz, J. H.
52. Ibn Ezra.
53. RaMBaN.
54. Philo, ed. Lewy, pp. 77-8.

SOURCES OF THE COMMENTARY[1]

ABRABANEL: R. Isaac b. Judah Abrabanel, Bible exegete and religious philosopher, 1437-1508. Used and paraphrased many other commentaries in his work on Scriptures.

AKEDAH: *Akedath Yits'hak,* a homiletical biblical commentary by R. Isaac Arama, c. 1420-1494.

R. BAHYA: R. Bahya b. Asher b. Halawa, Spanish biblical exegete and Cabbalist, c. 1255-1340.

BENAMOZEGH: R. Elijah Benamozegh, rabbi, theologian and apologist; author of *Em L'mikrah,* Livorno 1862; 1823-1900.

BIUR: Commentary on the Pentateuch by Moses b. Nahman Mendelssohn (philosopher and translator, 1729-1786) and others.

BOTSER OL'LOTH: Commentary on Scripture by R. Simeon b. Meir Santo, Fürth 1824.

CASSUTO: Prof. Umberto Cassuto, hebraist and historian, author of *Me-Adam ad Noah,* Jerusalem, 1944, b. 1883.

DAATH Z'KENIM: A commentary ascribed traditionally to the *Tosafists,* 12-14th century French Talmudists.

EMDEN, R. JACOB: R. Jacob b. Zvi Ashkenazi Emden, Talmudist and author, 1697-1776.

FUERST: Julius Fürst, bibliographer and lexicographer, 1805-1873.

GORDON: Samuel Loeb Gordon, translator; author of a modern commentary on Scripture, Warsaw and Tel-Aviv, 1900-1930; b. 1867.

GRE: Rabbi Elijah of Vilna (called the Vilna Gaon) renowned Lithuanian Talmudist, 1720-1797.

HEIDENHEIM, R. WOLF: Grammarian and exegete, logical commentary on the Pentateuch by R. Jakob Zebi Meklenburg, 4th ed., Frankfurt a. M., 1880 (1st ed., Leipzig, 1839).

HEIDENHEIM, R. WOLF: Grammarian and exegete, 1757-1832.

HERTZ, J. H.: Joseph Herman Hertz, British chief rabbi, author of *The Pentateuch and Haftorahs with Commentary;* 1872-1946.[2]

HIRSCH, S. R.: Commentary in German on the Pentateuch by R. Samson Raphael Hirsch, late nineteenth-century leader of Orthodox Jewry in Germany.

HIZKUNI: Commentary on Scripture by R. Hezekiah b. Manoah (French exegete of the 13th century), Venice, 1524. It is based upon about 20 other commentaries, principally Rashi.

HOFFMANN: R. David Zvi Hoffmann, Talmudist and biblical exegete, 1843-1921.

IBN CASPI: R. Joseph b. Caspi, philosophical commentator on Scripture, 1297-1340.

IBN EZRA: Rabbi Abraham b. Meir Ibn Ezra, Hebrew poet and biblical commentator, 1093-1167.

IBN JANAH: Jonah ibn Janah, greatest Hebrew philologist of the Middle Ages, c. 985-c. 1050.

JACOB, BENNO: German-Jewish biblical commentator, b. 1862.

JOSEPHUS: Josephus Flavius, military leader, historian and apologist, 37-105.

KAHANA, ABRAHAM: Edited a critical Hebrew commentary on the Bible, of which he wrote several volumes; 1874-1946.

MALBIM: Rabbi Meir Loeb b. Jehiel Mikael Malbim, Russian rabbi and Hebraist, author of *Hatorah v'Hamitsvah,* commentary on the Bible, 1809-1879.

MINHA B'LULAH: Commentary on the Pentateuch by R. Menahem Abraham b. Jacob Ha-cohen Rapa (d. 1596), Cremona, 1582.

MIZRAHI: Elijah b. Abraham Mizrahi, rabbi and Talmudist, author of a commentary on Rashi to Pentateuch, 1455-1526.

OR HA-HAYYIM: Rabbi Hayyim ibn Attar, Talmudist and Cabbalist, author of Or Ha-Hayyim, commentary on Scripture, 1696-1743.

PHILO: Greek-Jewish philosopher and author of voluminous allegorical commentaries on Scripture; 30 B.C.E.-40 C.E. Extracts of an edition of his selected writings (ed. Lewy, East and West Library) have been included.

[1] The following lists but a part of the many works consulted in the preparation of the Commentary—i.e., those directly quoted. It should also be noted that many more explanations on the Biblical verses than are given in the Commentary are to be found in the Talmudic-Midrashic passages cited in the Anthology.

[2] Rev. Dr. J. H. Hertz cites most of the modern commentators on the Bible in his Pentateuch. We have drawn on his work for all their important and significant interpretations.

RaDaK: Rabbi David Kimhi, Hebrew grammarian and exegete, 1160-1235.

RaLBaG: R. Levi b. Gershon (Gersonides), philosopher, exegete, mathematician and astronomer, 1288-1344.

RaMBaM: R. Moshe b. Maimon (Maimonides), famous theologian, metaphysician, commentator and codifier; 1135-1204.

RaMBaN: Rabbi Moshe b. Nahman (Nahmanides), rabbi, Talmudist and Cabbalist, 1194-1270.

RaShBaM: R. Samuel b. Meir, grandson of Rashi, biblical exegete, 1085-1174.

Rashi: R. Solomon b. Isaac, author of the most popular commentaries to Scripture and Talmud, 1040-1105.

Sforno: R. Obadiah Sforno, exegete, philosopher and physician, c. 1475-1550.

RaLaSh: Rabbi Levi Shapiro (Frankfurt), author of *Ha-R'kassim L'bik'ah*, a commentary "to clarify and illuminate the apparently unintelligible verses of Scripture." Altona 1815.

RaNHaW: Naphtali Herz Wessely, Hebrew poet and educationist, 1725-1805.

RaSaG: R. Saadyah (b. Joseph) Gaon, celebrated Jewish scholar, 882-942.

ShaDaL: Samuel David Luzzatto, scholar and philologian, 1800-1865.

TRANSLATIONS

Onkelos: Aramaic translation by Onkelos the *Ger* (proselyte), 1st century C.E.

Peshitta: Ancient Syriac translation of the Bible.

Samaritan Pentateuch: An Aramaic version of Scripture produced by Samaritan Jewry, which contains many of their traditional interpretations.

Septuagint: A Greek translation, widespread among Egyptian Jewry since the 3rd century C.E. Traditionally it was written by 72 Sages to the order of one of the Ptolemey's.

Targum Jerushalmi: An abridged version of *Targum Jonathan, q.v.*, called Targum Jerushalmi II.

Targum Jonathan: A free, expanded translation into Aramaic of Scripture, ascribed to R. Jonathan b. Uziel, called also Targum Jerushalmi I.

Vulgate: Latin translation by Jerome, made c. 383 C.E.; used as the authorized version by the Roman Catholics.

T.S.: *Torah Shelemah,* the Hebrew encyclopedia of Biblical interpretation by Rabbi Menahem M. Kasher, on which this work is based.

SUBJECT INDEX

Genesis I-VI

First figures indicate pages; second figures, after a dash —, indicate paragraph numbers. Thus, 141-2—98-103 means pages 141 to 142, paragraphs 98 to 103.

SUBJECT INDEX

NOTE: A full index to this volume will be printed at the end of the Book of Genesis.